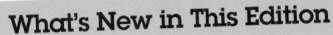

What's New in This Edition

In this seventh edition of **Essentials of Human Communication**, we remain committed to providing a concise yet thorough text that engages students while challenging them to think critically and develop fundamental skills of interpersonal, small group, and public communication. This new edition further highlights the application of skills to the real world and to the workplace, with new Communication Choice Points exercises and updated coverage of technology, an increasingly pervasive element of communication for students. At the same time, the new edition offers a back-to-basics approach, with structural and content changes that emphasize more than ever the essentials of communication. Revisions include:

1. **a new three-part organization** that better aligns with the course's key areas of coverage: the foundations of human communication, interpersonal and group communication, and public speaking. Part One, "Foundations of Human Communication," includes five chapters that cover the communication process, the self and perception, listening, verbal messages, and nonverbal messages. Part Two, "Interpersonal and Small Group Communication," also includes five chapters. Chapters 6, 7, and 8 cover the concepts and skills of interpersonal communication and conversation, interpersonal relationships, and managing interpersonal conflict. Chapters 9 and 10 focus on small group interaction, the types of small groups, and the principles of effective group membership and leadership. Part Three, "Public Speaking," explains the nature of public speaking and the principles for preparing and presenting effective informative and persuasive speeches.

2. **more extensive coverage of interpersonal communication**, with separate chapters on interpersonal communication and conversation (Chapter 6) and interpersonal relationships (Chapter 7). Chapter 6 now includes major discussions of everyday conversations, including small talk, introductions, making excuses and apologies, giving and receiving compliments, and giving and receiving advice.

3. **Communication Choice Points** marginal items in each chapter that highlight situational dilemmas, giving students an opportunity to think critically to assess communication options and apply principles and skills to develop appropriate responses.

4. **increased coverage of technology and communication**, including more on social networking sites (Chapter 1), virtual groups and teams (Chapter 9), and evaluating Internet sources (Chapter 11).

5. **a new focus on politeness**, such as politeness strategies in impression management (Chapter 2), polite and impolite listening, online politeness, politeness and the cell phone, and politeness in social networking (Chapter 4), politeness as a characteristic of verbal messages, gender differences (Chapter 5), and face-attacking and face-enhancing strategies in conflict management (Chapter 8).

6. **exercises and boxes that have been updated** with fresh topics throughout the book, including new ethics boxes on lying, gossip, and leaders' ethical responsibilities.

SEVENTH EDITION

Essentials of Human Communication

Joseph A. DeVito

*Hunter College of the
City University of New York*

Allyn & Bacon

Boston   Columbus   Indianapolis   New York   San Francisco   Upper Saddle River
Amsterdam   Cape Town   Dubai   London   Madrid   Milan   Munich   Paris
Montreal   Toronto   Delhi   Mexico City   Sao Paulo   Sydney   Hong Kong
Seoul   Singapore   Taipei   Tokyo

Editor in Chief, Communication: Karon Bowers
Marketing Manager: Blair Tuckman
Development Manager: David Kear
Development Editor: Kristen Mellitt
Associate Development Editor: Angela Pickard
Media Producer: Megan Higginbotham
Editorial Assistant: Stephanie Chaisson
Managing Editor: Linda Mihatov Behrens
Associate Managing Editor: Bayani Mendoza de Leon
Project Manager: Raegan Keida Heerema
Senior Operations Specialist: Nick Sklitsis
Operations Specialist: Mary Ann Gloriande
Full-Service Project Management/Composition: Nesbitt Graphics, Inc.
Art Director, Cover: Anne Bonanno Nieglos
Designer, Cover: Ilze Lemesis
Cover Photograph: Hill Street Studios/Blend Images/Getty Images, Inc;
Milk Photographie/Corbis; Digital Vision/Getty images, Inc; Jon Feingersh/AGE Fotostock

Library of Congress Cataloging-in-Publication Data

DeVito, Joseph A.
    Essentials of human communication / Joseph A. DeVito. — 7th ed.
      p. cm.
    Includes bibliographical references and index.
    ISBN-13: 978-0-205-68808-1
    ISBN-10: 0-205-68808-X
    1. Communication. I. Title.
    P90.D483 2010
    302.2—dc22
                                          2009038824

Credits appear on page 357, which constitutes a continuation of the copyright page.

1 2 3 4 5 6 7 8 9 10—QWV—13 12 11 10 09

Allyn & Bacon
is an imprint of

www.pearsonhighered.com

ISBN-13: 978-0-205-68808-1
ISBN-10:   0-205-68808-X

Brief Contents

PART ONE

Foundations of Human Communication *1*

PART TWO

Interpersonal and Small Group Communication *119*

PART THREE

Public Speaking *209*

The Interviewing Guidebook

A separate book focusing on informative and employment interviews is available for packaging with this book or for purchase separately.

Contents

PART ONE
Foundations of Human Communication   1

3 Listening in Human Communication 53

4 Verbal Messages 71

5 Nonverbal Messages 92

PART TWO
Interpersonal and Small Group Communication   119

7 Interpersonal Relationships   140

The Interviewing Guidebook

This separate book focuses on informative and employment interviews and is available to be packaged with the text or purchased separately.

The Interviewing GUIDEBOOK

Joseph A. DeVito
Second Edition

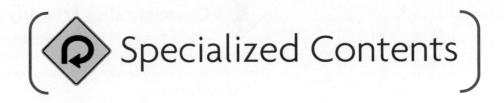

Specialized Contents

Self Tests

These self-assessment tests will help you bring to awareness, analyze, and improve your communication patterns and strategies.

Listen to This

These boxes provide suggestions for listening more effectively in a wide variety of communication situations. At the same time these discussions will remind you that communication can never occur without listening.

Communicating Ethically

These sections examine ethical issues and dilemmas to illustrate the close connection between ethics and communication, to encourage you to think about the ethical implications of your messages, and to stimulate you to formulate your own code of ethical communication.

The Public Speaking Sample Assistant

These sample speeches and outlines, along with their annotations, will assist you in preparing and outlining your own speeches.

Skill Development Experiences

These exercises are designed to help you work actively with the skills and applications discussed in the text and to help you make these skills a part of your everyday communication behavior.

Welcome to
Essentials of Human Communication

Previous editions of *Essentials of Human Communication* have been well received by students and instructors alike, largely because the book answered the need for a brief, interesting, but serious text that emphasized the *essential* skills of human communication, including interpersonal communication, small group communication, and public speaking. The overriding theme and goal of this textbook is to help you build greater competence in these areas. You should emerge from this course a more effective interpersonal communicator, group member and leader, and public speaker. I continue to try my best to follow Einstein's directive that "things should be made as simple as possible, but not simpler." This new, seventh edition remains true to that central purpose.

What's New in the Seventh Edition?

This updated edition contains a variety of new features and topics, in addition to its expansion, clarification, and improved organization of material covered in the sixth edition.

Structural Changes

This seventh edition of *Essentials of Human Communication* is divided into three parts rather than the previous two. Part One, Foundations of Human Communication, includes five chapters that cover the concepts and principles of human communication: the communication process, the self and perception, listening, verbal messages, and nonverbal messages. Part Two, Interpersonal and Small Group Communication, also includes five chapters. Chapters 6, 7, and 8 cover the concepts and skills of interpersonal communication and conversation, interpersonal relationships, and managing interpersonal conflict. Chapters 9 and 10 focus on small group interaction, the types of small groups, and the principles of effective group membership and leadership. Part Three, Public Speaking, explains the nature of public speaking and the principles for preparing and presenting effective informative and persuasive speeches.

Instead of 13 chapters, this edition contains 14. The discussions formerly in Chapter 6 (which covered interpersonal communication, conversation, and interpersonal relationships) have been expanded and are now discussed in both Chapter 6 (Interpersonal Communication and Conversation) and Chapter 7 (Interpersonal Relationships).

Chapter-by-Chapter Changes

Chapter 1 The Essentials of Human Communication now contains more on social networking sites, gives greater attention to communication competence, and includes a new Skill Development Experience, "Exploring Cultural Attitudes."

Chapter 2 The Self and Perception now covers impression management in detail and focuses the influence of perceptual processes on impression formation. In addition, this chapter contains a new Listen to This box, "Listening to Self-Destructive Beliefs," and a new Skill Development Experience, "Using Impression Management Strategies." A topic introduced in this chapter and reappearing in relevant places throughout the text is politeness; in this chapter politeness is discussed as an impression management strategy used to increase attractiveness.

Chapter 3 Listening in Human Communication includes a new section on listening barriers, a new section on polite and impolite listening (along with a table on politeness and the cell phone), and a new Listen to This box, "Listening in the Classroom."

Chapter 4 Verbal Messages includes new principles of politeness and assertiveness (along with a new Test Yourself self-test, "How Assertive Are Your Messages?" and a new Skill Development Experience, "Practicing Assertiveness"), a new Communicating Ethically box, "Lying," and new tables on distinguishing facts and inferences and on essential message guidelines.

Chapter 5 Nonverbal Messages offers new material on the myths about nonverbal communication, cultural differences in time orientation, and nonverbal communication skills. In addition, there is a new Listen to This box, "Listening with Nonverbal Power," and a new table on nonverbal messages and attraction.

Chapter 6 Interpersonal Communication and Conversation now contains major discussions of everyday conversations (including small talk, introducing people, making excuses and apologies, giving and receiving compliments, and giving and receiving advice), as well as a new Listen to This box, "Listening to Emotions," and new exercises on making excuses and apologies and giving and responding to compliments.

Chapter 7 Interpersonal Relationships now includes discussions of flirting, family and workplace rules, a new Communicating Ethically box, "Relationship Ethics," and a Skill Development Experience, "Interpersonal Relationships and the Media."

Chapter 8 Managing Interpersonal Conflict contains a revised introduction on conflict issues and myths, expanded guidelines for more effective conflict management with each of the strategies, a new discussion of conflict and interdependency, and a new Skill Development Experience, "Managing Conflict Early."

Chapter 9 Small Group Communication contains expanded definitions of both the small group and the team, a new Communicating Ethically box, "The Ethics of Gossip," and expanded coverage of consensus, virtual groups and teams (including social networking sites), and electronic brainstorming.

Chapter 10 Members and Leaders in Group Communication contains a new Test Yourself, "What Kind of Group Member Are You?", additional discussion of member roles, new emphasis on member and leader skills, new suggestions for combating groupthink, a new section on the myths of leadership, and new Communicating Ethically and Listen to This boxes on the leader's ethical responsibilities and listening to empower.

Chapter 11 Public Speaking Preparation, Steps 1–6 contains new suggestions for managing apprehension, a new section on starting the speech early and avoiding procrastination, and a new section on evaluating Internet materials.

Chapter 12 Public Speaking Preparation and Delivery, Steps 7–10 includes a discussion of using index cards when delivering a speech and a reorganization of the guidelines for effective speech criticism.

Chapter 13 The Informative Speech makes more explicit the value of supporting materials and also stresses the importance of selecting materials with cultural sensitivity.

Chapter 14 The Persuasive Speech includes a new section, "Follow a Motivating Sequence," which revisits the steps of the motivated sequence introduced in Chapter 11. In addition, there is new material on the pitfalls of anecdotal evidence.

Glossary The two glossaries of the previous edition (one of concepts and one of skills) have been updated and combined into one; skills appear in italics.

The aim of this textbook is to help you become a more effective, more competent communicator. The competent communicator has mastered a wide variety of communication skills (for interpersonal, small group, and public speaking); thinks critically; is culturally aware and sensitive; is ethical; listens effectively; and can apply this competence to the real world of personal and workplace relationships.

Essentials of Human Communication provides you with the skills you need to communicate successfully in your personal, social, and workplace interactions. These skills, interwoven throughout the text, include self-understanding, perceptual skills, listening effectiveness, verbal and nonverbal message construction and reception, interpersonal communication, small group communication, and public speaking.

Skill Development Experience
Exploring Cultural Attitudes

One of the best ways to appreciate the influence of culture on communication is to consider people's attitudes. In groups of five or six—try for as culturally diverse a group as possible—discuss how you think most of the students at your school feel (not how you feel) about each of the following. Use a five-point scale where **5** = most students strongly agree; **4** = most students agree; **3** = students are relatively neutral; **2** = most students disagree; **1** = most students strongly disagree.

_____ **1.** Most feminists are just too sensitive about sexism.
_____ **2.** Courses on sexism should be required in our schools.
_____ **3.** Gay rights means gay men and lesbians demanding special privileges.
_____ **4.** Homosexuals have made many contributions to their societies.
_____ **5.** Racism isn't going to end overnight so minorities need to be patient.
_____ **6.** White people benefit from racism whether they want to or not.

Source: These statements were taken from the Human Relations Attitude Inventory (Koppelman, 2005). The author notes that this inventory is based on one developed by Flavio Vega.

Attitudes strongly influence communication. Understanding the cultural attitudes of yourself and others is prerequisite to effective intercultural communication.

◀ In addition, this edition contains 29 **Skill Development Experiences** integrated into the text. Many are new to this edition and have been rewritten to emphasize practical communication skills. A summary statement appears at the end of each Skill Development Experience with the implicit suggestion that you develop your own summary of what the experience means to you.

▶ The **Why Read This Chapter?** chapter openers continue to address directly every reader's very reasonable question. For each chapter this is answered in two parts: The first previews what you'll learn in the chapter, that is, specific concepts, theories, and research in human communication. The second outlines what you'll be able to do after studying the chapter; that is, the skill or behavioral objectives you should achieve.

Why read this chapter?

Because you'll learn about:
● what nonverbal communication is
● the many forms of nonverbal communication
● the many gender and cultural differences in nonverbal communication

Because you'll learn to:
● use nonverbal messages to communicate a wide variety of meanings
● use appropriate and effective types of nonverbal communication to express your meanings
● communicate appropriately on the basis of gender and cultural factors

◀ Each chapter-end **Summary of Concepts and Skills** includes both a conceptual summary and a skills summary. The conceptual summary provides a brief paragraph encapsulating the chapter's topic and a list of propositions that captures the essential content of the chapter. The skills summary presents the major skills covered in the chapter in a checklist format to allow you to mark those skills you want to work on most.

Summary of Concepts and Skills

This chapter explored interpersonal communication and conversation.

1. Conversation consists of five general stages: opening, feedforward, business, feedback, and closing.
2. Throughout the speaking–listening process, both speaker and listener exchange cues for *conversational turns;* these cues enable the speaker and listener to communicate *about* the communication in which they're engaged.
3. Speakers regulate the conversation through two major types of cues: turn-maintaining cues and turn-yielding cues. Listeners regulate the conversation by using three types of cues: turn-requesting cues, turn-denying cues, and back-channeling cues and interruptions.
4. Dialogue is conversation in which there is genuine two-way [interac]tion; each p[erson is bo]th speak[er and listener.]

9. A compliment is a message of praise, flattery, or congratulations and often enables you to interact with positiveness and immediacy.
10. Advice can be direct, or it can be advice about advice (meta-advice).

Consider your competence in using the skills of effective relationship communication and place a check mark next to the skills you want to work on most.

_____ 1. I understand that conversation occurs in stages and that each stage serves a different function.
_____ 2. I follow the principles of turn-taking in conversation, giving appropriate speaker and listener cues and responding to the cues of others.
_____ 3. I enga[ge] [dia]logic rather th[an mono]logic conv[ersation.]

A special group of communication skills are those of power and empowerment, and these topics are integrated throughout this text. For example, types of power are discussed in Chapter 1; the ways power can be communicated verbally and nonverbally are discussed in Chapters 4 and 5; and the topic of empowering others is integrated with the functions of leadership in Chapter 10.

Because communication is a practical subject, with applications in all aspects of life, this book makes a special effort to illustrate the uses of communication skills in the real world, particularly in the **workplace**. Among the topics covered here that have special application to the workplace are office romance, small groups in the workplace, interpersonal conflict, and the varied uses of power. In addition, numerous examples of workplace situations that call for the application of communication skills appear throughout the text. As you work through this text and the course, you'll find it useful to ask yourself how you can apply this material to the workplace—how you can use this material to function more effectively on the job and achieve your professional goals.

▶ A 10-item **Key Word Quiz** at the end of each chapter will help you review significant vocabulary terms introduced in the chapter. Additional key terms, boldfaced in the chapter, are defined in the glossary and in online flash cards.

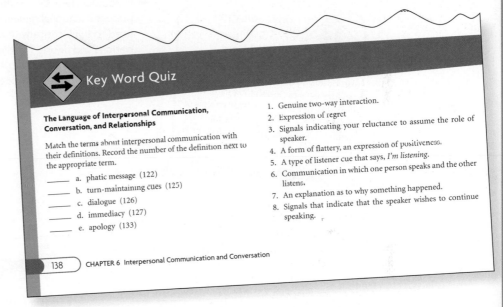

Key Word Quiz

The Language of Interpersonal Communication, Conversation, and Relationships

Match the terms about interpersonal communication with their definitions. Record the number of the definition next to the appropriate term.

_____ a. phatic message (122)
_____ b. turn-maintaining cues (125)
_____ c. dialogue (126)
_____ d. immediacy (127)
_____ e. apology (133)

1. Genuine two-way interaction.
2. Expression of regret
3. Signals indicating your reluctance to assume the role of speaker.
4. A form of flattery, an expression of positiveness.
5. A type of listener cue that says, *I'm listening.*
6. Communication in which one person speaks and the other listens.
7. An explanation as to why something happened.
8. Signals that indicate that the speaker wishes to continue speaking.

138   CHAPTER 6 Interpersonal Communication and Conversation

The Public Speaking Sample Assistant

THE PREPARATION OUTLINE

Here is a relatively detailed preparation outline similar to the outline you might prepare when constructing your speech. The side notes should clarify both the content and the format of a preparation outline.

HAVE YOU EVER BEEN CULTURE SHOCKED?

Thesis: Culture shock can be described in four stages.
Purpose: To inform my audience of the four phases of culture shock.

INTRODUCTION

I. How many of you have experienced culture shock?
  A. Many people experience culture shock, a reaction to being in a culture very different from what they were used to.
  B. By understanding culture shock, you'll be in a better position to deal with it if and when it happens.
II. Culture shock occurs in four stages (Oberg, 1960).
  A. The Honeymoon occurs first.
  B. The Crisis occurs second.
  C. The Recovery occurs third.

Generally, the title, thesis, and purpose of the speech are prefaced to the outline. When the outline is an assignment that is to be handed in, additional information may be required.

Note the general format for the outline; the headings are clearly labeled, and the indenting helps you see the relationship between the items. For example, in introduction II, the outline format helps you to see that A, B, C, and D are explanations for II.

Note that the introduction, body, and conclusion are clearly labeled and separated visually.

Although the speaker assumes that the audience is familiar with culture shock, he or she still includes a brief definition in case some audience members don't know what it is and to refresh the memory of others.

Note that references are integrated throughout the outline, just as they would be in a term paper. In the actual speech, the speaker might say, "Anthropologist Kalervo Oberg, who coined the term culture shock, said in four

◀ In Chapters 11 through 14 of this edition, four sample annotated speeches and three outlines are presented in **Public Speaking Sample Assistant** boxes. These are designed to illustrate further the principles of public speaking and outlining.

Critical thinking enriches all human communication experiences, so this book gives special prominence to this subject. First, the text integrates principles of critical thinking throughout the discussion at points where it is especially relevant. Specifically, distinguishing facts from inferences, avoiding either/or thinking and allness, and discriminating among rather than against others are discussed in the chapter on verbal messages (Chapter 4); the techniques of solving a problem are discussed in the chapter dealing with small group communication (Chapter 9); techniques for listening to new ideas are presented in the context of speech of information (Chapter 13); and guidelines for avoiding the pitfalls in reasoning, from evidence to conclusion, are considered in the discussion of persuasion (Chapter 14).

Communication Choice Point

Leader Guidance

Members of your group are not participating equally. Of the eight members, three monopolize the discussion; the other five say as little as possible. *What are some of the things you might say to get the group into better balance? To whom would you say it? In what context?*

◀ In addition, new **Communication Choice Points** present situational dilemmas, emphasizing the need to think critically to assess communication options and decide what, if anything, to say. These brief marginal items give you opportunities to apply principles and skills to real-world situations.

▶ Fifteen **Test Yourself** features appear in this edition. Some of these self-tests include standard research instruments, such as measures of ethnocentrism, apprehension, love styles, time orientation, verbal aggressiveness, and argumentativeness. Others are designed to involve you in concepts discussed in the chapter. These self-tests focus on your self-esteem, your willingness to self-disclose, and the kind of group member and group leader you are. Each self-test ends with two questions: (1) "How did you do?" gives you instructions for scoring your responses, and (2) "What will you do?" asks you to think about any action you may want to take in light of how you performed.

Test Yourself

How Apprehensive Are You About Public Speaking?

This questionnaire consists of six statements concerning your feelings about public speaking. Indicate the degree to which each statement applies to you by marking whether you (1) strongly agree, (2) agree, (3) are undecided, (4) disagree, or (5) strongly disagree with each statement. There are no right or wrong answers. Don't be concerned that some of the statements are similar to others. Work quickly; just record your first impression.

_____ ❶ I have no fear of giving a speech.

_____ ❷ Certain parts of my body feel very tense and rigid when I am giving a speech.

_____ ❸ I feel relaxed while giving a speech.

_____ ❹ My thoughts become confused and jumbled when I am giving a speech.

_____ ❺ I face the prospect of giving a speech with confidence.

_____ ❻ While giving a speech, I get so nervous that I forget facts I really know.

HOW DID YOU DO? To obtain your public speaking apprehension score, use the following formula: Start with 18 points; add the scores for items 1, 3, and 5; then subtract the scores for items 2, 4, and 6.

A score above 18 shows some degree of apprehension. Most people score above 18, so if you scored relatively high, you're among the vast majority of people. You may find it interesting to compare your apprehension scores from this test and from the test in Chapter 9. Most people would score higher on public speaking apprehension than on apprehension in group discussions.

WHAT WILL YOU DO? As you read the suggestions for reducing apprehension in the text, consider what you can do to incorporate these ideas into your own public speaking experiences. Consider too how these suggestions might be useful in reducing apprehension more generally—for example, in social situations and in small groups and meetings.

So____ ___ from An ___ ___ Rheto___ ___ (9th ___ ___ C. McC___

You're living in a world defined by cultural diversity, where you interact with people differing in affectional orientation, socioeconomic position, race, religion, and nationality. Culture and cultural differences are always influential in communication. For this reason, this text fully integrates culture into every chapter. Topics covered include:

- culture and competence, the relevance of culture, the aim of a cultural perspective, and ethnocentrism, as well as a self-test on cultural beliefs and values and an exercise on cultural attitudes (Chapter 1).

- cultural teachings in self-concept formation, intercultural openness, culture and gender in self-disclosure, and masculine and feminine cultures, as well as the influence of culture on perceptual judgments, personality theory and culture, the role of stereotypes in perception, cultural influences on uncertainty and its avoidance, and cultural sensitivity in perceptual accuracy (Chapter 2).

- the influences of culture and gender on listening (Chapter 3).

- gender and cultural differences in directness and politeness; cultural rules in verbal communication; sexism, heterosexism, racism, and ageism; and cultural identifiers (Chapter 4).

- cultural differences in nonverbal communication, most notably facial expressions, colors, touch, silence, and time orientation (Chapter 5).

- the role of culture and gender in conversation and the cultural differences in such areas as immediacy, greetings, and excuse making (Chapter 6).

- cultural and gender differences in friendship, love, and family (Chapter 7).

- cultural context and conflict, face-enhancing and face-attacking strategies, and the relevance of cultural sensitivity (including differences between high- and low-context cultures) in conflict (Chapter 8).

- the nature and importance of cultural norms in small group communication (Chapter 9).

- cultural differences between individual and collective orientations and high- and low-power distances (Chapter 10).

- guidelines to help public speakers avoid taboo topics when addressing culturally varied audiences as well as guidance for analyzing multicultural audiences (Chapter 11).

- cultural considerations in the language of public speaking, culture shock, and cultural sensitivity in speech criticism (Chapter 12).

- cultural variations in language usage (Chapter 13).

- the impact of cultural differences on the effective use of logical, motivational, and credibility appeals (Chapter 14).

High scores (say, 5s and 4s) indicate a strong commitment to your culture's values and beliefs; low numbers (1s and 2s) indicate a relatively weak commitment.

A different type of cultural identification is ethnocentrism. Before reading about this important concept, examine your own cultural thinking by taking the self-test below.

Test Yourself

How Ethnocentric Are You?

Here are 18 statements representing your beliefs about your culture. For each statement indicate how much you agree or disagree, using the following scale: strongly agree = **5**; agree = **4**; neither agree nor disagree = **3**; disagree = **2**; and strongly disagree = **1**.

____ **1** Most cultures are backward compared to my culture.

____ **2** My culture should be the role model for other cultures.

____ **3** Lifestyles in other cultures are just as valid as those in my culture.

____ **4** Other cultures should try to be like my culture.

____ **5** I'm not interested in the values and customs of other cultures.

____ **6** People in my culture could learn a lot from people in other cultures.

____ **7** Most people from other cultures just don't know what's good for them.

____ **8** I have little respect for the values and customs of other cultures.

____ **9** Most people would be happier if they lived like people in my culture.

____ **10** People in my culture have just about the best lifestyles anywhere.

____ **11** Lifestyles in other cultures are not as valid as those in my culture.

____ **12** I'm very interested in the values and customs of other cultures.

____ **13** I respect the values and customs of other cultures.

Communication Choice Point

Correcting Yourself

Without thinking you make some culturally insensitive remarks and immediately notice lots of nonverbal negative feedback. You want to explain that you're really not the kind of person who normally talks this way. *What options do you have for minimizing the negative effects of your remarks? What specifically would you say?*

► *Essentials of Human Communication* follows in the tradition established by Aristotle, Cicero, and Quintilian—the three great theorists of the ancient world—who viewed ethics as an integral part of communication instruction. This text, too, regards ethics as central. **Communicating Ethically** boxes highlight ethical issues as they relate to concepts and skills presented throughout the book. A list of these Communicating Ethically boxes appears in the Specialized Contents on page xiv.

Communicating Ethically
Plagiarism

Because plagiarism is such an important issue in public speaking, this ethics box is a bit longer than others. It will cover the nature of plagiarism, the reasons plagiarism is unacceptable, and what you can do to avoid plagiarism.

What Is Plagiarism?
Plagiarism is the process of passing off the work (e.g., ideas, words, or illustrations) of others as your own. Plagiarism is *not* the act of using another's ideas—we all do that. Rather, it is using another's ideas without acknowledging that they are the ideas of this other person; it is presenting the ideas as if they were your own. Plagiarism exists on a continuum, ranging from appropriating an entire term paper or speech written by someone else to using a quotation or research finding without citing the author.

Plagiarism also includes situations in which you get help from a friend without acknowledging this assistance. In some cultures—especially collectivist cultures teamwork is strongly encouraged. Students are encouraged to help other students with their work. But in the United States and in many individualist cultures teamwork without acknowledgment is considered plagiarism.

In U.S. institutions of higher education, plagiarism is a serious violation of the rules of academic honesty and is subject to serious penalties, sometimes even expulsion. Further, as with all crimes, ignorance of the law is not an acceptable defense against charges of plagiarism. This last point is especially important, because people often commit plagiarism through ignorance about what does and what does not constitute plagiarism.

Why Plagiarism Is Unacceptable
Here are a few reasons why plagiarism is wrong.

● Plagiarism is a violation of another's intellectual property rights. Much as it would be wrong to take another person's watch without permission, it is wrong to take another person's ideas without giving due credit.

If you're going to play the game properly, you'd better know every rule.

—BARBARA JORDAN
(1936–1996), Texas Congresswoman

Listen to This
Listening to Messages in Conflict

Listening in conflict situations is often extremely difficult; tempers may be running high, and you may be finding yourself under attack. Here are some suggestions for listening more effectively in conflict:

● Act and think as a listener. Turn off the television, stereo, or computer; face the other person. Devote your total attention to the other person.
● Make sure you understand what the person is saying and feeling. Use perception checking (Chapter 2) and active listening techniques (Chapter 3).
● Express your support or empathy: *I can understand how you feel. I can appreciate that my handling the checkbook could create a feeling of inequality.*
● If appropriate, indicate your agreement: *You're right to be disturbed.*
● State your thoughts and feelings as objectively as you can; avoid criticism or blame.
● Get ready to listen to the other person's responses to your statements.

I never take my own side in a quarrel.

—ROBERT FROST
(1874–1963), U.S. poet

deal with a conflict or when winning seems unlikely, the person may cry, and thus silence the other person.

Another silencer is to feign extreme emotionalism—to yell and scream and pretend to be losing control. Still another is to develop some "physical" reaction—headaches and shortness of breath are probably the most popular. One of the major problems with such silencers is that as an opponent you can never be certain that they are mere tactics; they may be real physical reactions that you should pay attention to. Regardless of what you d... conflict remain unexamined an... ...lved.

◄ Effective listening is crucial to all forms of human communication. *Essentials of Human Communication* gives listening a central role in human communication in two ways. First, listening is identified in Chapter 1 as one of the crucial skills of competence. Second, Chapter 3 is devoted entirely to listening: the stages of listening, the styles of effective listening, and the influences of culture and gender on listening. Third, each chapter contains a **Listen to This** box that highlights the role of listening in relationship to the topics discussed in the chapter: for example, "Listening to Self-Destructive Beliefs" (Chapter 2), "Listening to Messages in Conflict" (Chapter 8), and boxes on listening to criticism, new ideas, and fallacies of argument (Chapters 11, 12, and 13). A complete list of Listen to This boxes appears in the Specialized Contents on page xiii.

Resources in Print and Online

Supplement	Format Available	Description
FOR INSTRUCTORS		
Instructor's Manual and Test Bank ISBN: 0205786634	Online Print	Prepared by Nader Chaaban, Montgomery College, this comprehensive instructor resource has both chapter-by-chapter teaching material as well as a fully reviewed Test Bank. The Instructor's Manual portion centers around six Unit Planning resources: Chapter Concepts, Knowledge Objectives, Skills Objectives, Instructional Outline, Questions for Discussion, and Activities for Skill Development. The Test Bank contains more than 600 multiple-choice, true/false, completion, and matching questions organized by chapter. Each question is referenced by page. Available for download at www.pearsonhighered.com/irc (access code required).
MyTest ISBN: 0205715753	Online	This flexible, online test generating software includes all questions found in the Test Bank section of the printed Instructor's Manual and Test Bank. This computerized software allows instructors to create their own personalized exams, to edit any or all of the existing test questions, and to add new questions. Other special features of this program include random generation of test questions, creation of alternate versions of the same test, scrambling of question sequence, and test preview before printing. Available at www.pearsonmytest.com (access code required).
PowerPoint™ Presentation Package ISBN: 0205786626	Online	This text-specific package provides a basis for your lecture with PowerPoint™ slides for each chapter of the book. The transparency masters that were traditionally included in the Instructor's Manual and Test Bank have been adapted for electronic use for this edition. Available for download at www.pearsonhighered.com/irc (access code required).
Pearson Allyn & Bacon Introduction to Communication Video Library	Print	Pearson Allyn & Bacon's Introduction to Communication Video Library contains a range of videos from which adopters can choose. Videos to choose from cover a variety of topics and scenarios for communication foundations, interpersonal communication, small group communication, and public speaking. Please contact your Pearson representative for a complete list of videos and their contents to choose which would be most useful for your class. Some restrictions apply.
Lecture Questions for Clickers for Introduction to Communication ISBN: 0205547230	Online	Prepared by Keri Moe, El Paso Community College, this is an assortment of questions and activities covering culture, listening, interviewing, public speaking, interpersonal conflict and more are presented in PowerPoint™. These slides will help liven up your lectures and can be used along with the Personal Response System to get students more involved in the material. Available for download at www.pearsonhighered.com/irc (access code required).
Allyn & Bacon Digital Media Archive for Communication, Version 3.0 ISBN: 0205437095	Print	The Digital Media Archive CD-ROM contains electronic images of charts, graphs, maps, tables, and figures, along with media elements such as video, audio clips, and related web links. These media assets are fully customizable to use with our pre-formatted PowerPoint™ outlines or to import into instructor's own lectures (Windows and Mac).
The Communication Blog	Online	Maintained by the author, this site offers a forum for people teaching basic courses in interpersonal communication, as well as the hybrid and public speaking courses. Regular posts by the author update the text material and share ideas for teaching. Available at http://tcbdevito.blogspot.com.
A Guide for New Teachers of Introduction to Communication: Interactive Strategies for Teaching Communication, 4th Edition ISBN: 0205750001	Online Print	Prepared by Susanna G. Porter, Kennesaw State University with a new chapter on using MyCommunicationLab by Heather Dillon, Urbana, Illinois, this guide is designed to help new teachers effectively teach the introductory communication course. It is full of first-day-of-class tips, great teaching ideas, outside and Pearson resources, and sample activities and assignments. Available for download at www.pearsonhighered.com/irc (access code required).
FOR STUDENTS		
The Interviewing Guidebook, 2nd Edition ISBN: 0205730515	Print	This 112-page book on interviewing by Joseph DeVito has been totally revised and expanded. The Guidebook discusses both the informative interview and the employment interview, along with the various types of résumés and the letters that are a part of the job interview (available for purchase).

Resources *(continued)*

Supplement	Format Available	Description
FOR STUDENTS		
Preparing Visual Aids for Presentations, Fifth Edition ISBN: 020561115X	Print	Prepared by Dan Cavanaugh, this 32-page visual guide provides a host of ideas for using today's multimedia tools to improve presentations, including suggestions for planning a presentation, guidelines for designing visual aids and storyboarding, and a walkthrough that shows how to prepare a visual display using PowerPoint™ (available for purchase).
Brainstorms ISBN: 0673981363	Print	Joseph A. DeVito's guide to thinking more creatively about communication, or anything else, is a perfect complement to the book's unique emphasis on critical thinking. Students find 19 practical, easy-to-use creative thinking techniques along with insights into the creative thinking process (available for purchase).
Pearson Allyn & Bacon Introduction to Communication Study Site (Open access)	Online	The Pearson Allyn & Bacon Introduction to Communication Study Site features practice tests, learning objectives, and weblinks. The site is organized around the major topics typically covered in the Introduction to Communication course. These topics have also been correlated to the table of contents for your book! Available at www.abintrocommunication.com.
Public Speaking in the Multicultural Environment, Second Edition ISBN: 0205265111	Print	Prepared by Devorah A. Lieberman, Portland State University, this booklet helps students learn to analyze cultural diversity within their audiences and adapt their presentations accordingly (available for purchase).
The Speech Outline: Outlining to Plan, Organize, and Deliver a Speech: Activities and Exercises ISBN: 032108702X	Print	Prepared by Reeze L. Hanson and Sharon Condon of Haskell Indian Nations University, this outlining book includes activities, exercises, and answers to help students develop and master the critical skill of outlining (available for purchase).
Multicultural Activities Workbook ISBN: 0205546528	Print	Prepared by Marlene C. Cohen and Susan L. Richardson of Prince George's Community College, Maryland, this workbook is filled with hands-on activities that help broaden the content of speech classes to reflect diverse cultural backgrounds. The checklists, surveys, and writing assignments all help students succeed in speech communication by offering experiences that address a variety of learning styles (available for purchase).
Speech Preparation Workbook ISBN: 013559569X	Print	Prepared by Jennifer Dreyer and Gregory H. Patton of San Diego State University, this workbook takes students through the stages of speech creation—from audience analysis to writing the speech—and includes guidelines, tips, and easy to fill-in pages (available for purchase).
Study Card for Introduction to Speech Communication ISBN: 0205474381	Print	Colorful, affordable, and packed with useful information, the Pearson Allyn & Bacon Study Cards make studying easier, more efficient, and more enjoyable. Course information is distilled down to the basics, helping you quickly master the fundamentals, review a subject for understanding, or prepare for an exam. Because they're laminated for durability, you can keep these Study Cards for years to come and pull them out whenever you need a quick review (available for purchase).
VideoLab CD-ROM ISBN: 0205561616	Print	This interactive study tool for students can be used independently or in class. It provides digital video of student speeches that can be viewed in conjunction with corresponding outlines, manuscripts, notecards, and instructor critiques. A series of drills to help students analyze content and delivery follows each speech (available for purchase).
FOR INSTRUCTORS AND STUDENTS		
MyCommunicationLab	Online	MyCommunicationLab is a state-of-the-art, interactive, and instructive solution for communication courses. Designed to be used as a supplement to a traditional lecture course, or to completely administer an online course, MyCommunicationLab combines a Pearson eText, multimedia, video clips, activities, research support, tests and quizzes to completely engage students. See next page for more details.

Save time and improve results with **PEARSON mycommunicationlab**

Designed to amplify a traditional course in numerous ways or to administer a course online, **MyCommunicationLab** for Introductory Communication courses combines pedagogy and assessment with an array of multimedia activities—videos, speech preparation tools, assessments, research support, multiple newsfeeds—to make learning more effective for all types of students. Now featuring more resources, including a video upload tool, this new release of **MyCommunicationLab** is visually richer and even more interactive than the previous version—a leap forward in design with more tools and features to enrich learning and aid students in classroom success.

Teaching and Learning Tools

✓ *NEW VERSION!* **Pearson eText:** Identical in content and design to the printed text, the Pearson eText provides students access to their text whenever and wherever they need it. In addition to contextually placed multimedia features in every chapter, our new Pearson eText allows students to take notes and highlight, just like a traditional book.

✓ **Videos and Video Quizzes:** Interactive videos provide students with the opportunity to watch video clips that portray different communication scenarios, interviews with well-known communication scholars, and sample speeches including both professional and student speeches. Many videos are annotated with critical thinking questions or include short, assignable quizzes that report to the instructor's gradebook.

✓ **Self-Assessments:** Online self-assessments including SCAM, PRCA-24, and assessments that test introversion, shyness, and communication competence, as well as pre- and post-tests for every chapter, help students to learn about different communication styles and assess their own. The tests generate a customized study plan for further assessment and focus students on areas in which they need to improve. Instructors can use these tools to show learning over the duration of the course.

✓ *UPDATED!* **MyOutline:** MyOutline offers step-by-step guidance for writing an effective outline, along with tips and explanations to help students better understand the elements of an outline and how all the pieces fit together. Outlines that students create can be downloaded to their computer, e-mailed as attachments, printed, or saved in the tool for future editing. Instructors can either select from several templates based on our texts, or they can create a template with their own outline structure for students to use.

✓ *UPDATED!* **Topic Selector:** This interactive tool helps students get started generating ideas and then narrowing down topics. Our Topic Selector is question based, rather than drill-down, in order to help students really learn the process of selecting topics. Once they have determined their topic, students are directed to credible online sources for guidance with the research process.

✓ *NEW!* **ABC News RSS feed:** MyCommunicationLab provides an online feed from ABC news, updated hourly, to help students choose and research group assignments and speeches.

✓ *NEW!* **MySearchLab:** Pearson's MySearchLab™ is the easiest way for students to start a research assignment or paper. Complete with extensive help on the research process and four databases of credible and reliable source material, MySearchLab™ helps students quickly and efficiently make the most of their research time.

Cutting-Edge Technology

✓ *NEW!* **MediaShare:** With this new video upload tool, students are able to upload group assignments, interpersonal role plays, and speeches for their instructor and classmates to watch (whether face-to-face or online) and provide online feedback and comments. Structured much like a social networking site, MediaShare can help promote a sense of community among students.

✓ *NEW!* **Audio Chapter Summaries:** Every chapter includes an audio chapter summary, formatted as an MP3 file, perfect for students reviewing material before a test or instructors reviewing material before class.

✓ *NEW!* **Quick and Dirty Tips Podcast:** Through an agreement with Quick and Dirty Tips, MyCommunicationLab now features a RSS Feed of *The Public Speaker's Quick and Dirty Tips for Improving Your Communication Skills*, which covers topics such as conflict, negotiation, networking, pronunciation, eye contact, overcoming nervousness, interviewing skills, accent modification, and more!

Online Administration

No matter what course management system you use—or if you do not use one at all, but still wish to easily capture your students' grades and track their performance—Pearson has a MyCommunicationLab option to suit your needs. Contact one of Pearson's Technology Specialists for more information and assistance.

A MyCommunicationLab access code is offered at no additional cost when packaged with selected Pearson Communication texts. To get started, contact your local Pearson Publisher's Representative at www.pearsonhighered.com/replocator.

Acknowledgments

I would like to thank the many reviewers who critically analyzed the previous edition. They gave graciously of their time and expertise and offered a variety of useful and insightful suggestions for this new edition. I thank you all; your comments have resulted in many improvements. Thank you to Jennifer L. Fairchild, Eastern Kentucky University; Christine K. Foster, Bergen Community College; Fernando Ganivet, Miami-Dade College; Douglas B. Hoehn, Bergen Community College; Sarah Nagel-Stout, Kellogg Community College; Anthony Ongyod, Chesapeake College; and Roselyn M. Turner, Estrella Mountain Community College.

I also want to thank the many people from Allyn & Bacon who provided guidance and support throughout the process of this extensive revision. I want to thank Editor-in-Chief Karon Bowers for her always timely and wise counsel; Development Manager David Kear for his consistently sage guidance; Developmental Editor Kristen Mellitt, whose useful comments on just about everything that appears here made the book a lot better; Associate Development Editor Angela Pickard for her effective and creative handling of supplements; and Project Editor Tom Conville who, as always, guided the book from manuscript to finished text with efficiency, expertise, and good humor, making this author's life a lot easier. I also want to thank Sheila Norman for finding the many excellent photos that appear in this edition and Amy Chamberlain for her great copyediting.

Joseph A. DeVito
jadevito@earthlink.net
http://tcbdevito.blogspot.com
www.pearsonhighered.com/devito

CHAPTER

1 The Essentials of Human Communication

Why read this chapter?

Because you'll learn about:

- human communication: its nature and skills
- the essential concepts and principles of human communication
- the role of culture in communication

Because you'll learn to:

- use the essential elements and principles of human communication in your daily interactions
- acknowledge the role of culture in all forms of human communication

*O*f all the knowledge and skills you have, those concerning communication are among your most important and useful. Your communication ability will influence how effectively you live your personal and professional life; it will influence your effectiveness as a friend and lover, as a member and leader of small groups (both social and business), and as a public speaker, communicating information and influencing the attitudes and behaviors of others.

This first section introduces human communication, beginning with the skills and forms of human communication and some of the popular but erroneous beliefs that can get in the way of effective communication.

Foundations of Human Communication

Human communication consists of the sending and receiving of verbal and nonverbal messages between two or more people. This seemingly simple (but in reality quite complex) process is the subject of this book, to which this chapter provides a foundation. Let's begin by looking at the skills you'll learn as you progress through this book and this course.

SKILLS OF HUMAN COMMUNICATION

Among the skills you'll learn through your study of human communication are these:

- *Self-presentation skills* enable you to present yourself as (and just for starters) a confident, likable, approachable, and credible person. It is also largely through your communication skills (or lack of them) that you display negative qualities.
- *Relationship skills* help you build friendships, enter into love relationships, work with colleagues, and interact with family members. These are the skills for initiating, maintaining, repairing, and sometimes dissolving relationships of all kinds.
- *Interviewing skills* enable you to interact to gain information, to successfully present yourself to get the job you want, and to participate effectively in a wide variety of other interview types. (This topic is covered in a separate supplement, *The Interviewing Guidebook*.)
- *Group interaction and leadership skills* help you participate effectively in relationship and task groups—informative, problem-solving, and brainstorming groups, at home or at work—as a member and as a leader.
- *Presentation* or *public speaking skills* will enable you to manage your fear and make it work for you, rather than against you. These skills will enable you to communicate information to small and large audiences and influence their attitudes and behaviors.

You'll learn these skills and reap the benefits as you develop facility in the varied forms of communication, to which we now turn.

FORMS OF HUMAN COMMUNICATION

You'll accomplish these objectives and acquire these skills as you engage in and master a variety of communication forms. **Intrapersonal communication** is the communication you have with yourself. Through intrapersonal communication you talk with, learn about, and judge yourself. You persuade yourself of this or that, reason about possible decisions to make, and rehearse messages that you plan to send to others. In intrapersonal communication you might, for example, wonder how you did in an interview and what you could have done differently. You might conclude you did a pretty good job but tell yourself you need to be more assertive when discussing salary.

Interpersonal communication occurs when you interact with a person with whom you have some kind of relationship; it can take place face-to-face as well as through electronic channels (e-mail or instant messaging, e.g.) or even in traditional

Communication Choice Points

Throughout this text you'll find marginal Communication Choice Point items that identify a situation in which you need to make a decision to say something (or, of course, to remain silent). These items encourage you (1) to identify your potential choices (based on the theory and research discussed here) and (2) to apply the skills discussed in the text.

letter writing. For example, you e-mail your friends or family about your plans for the weekend, ask someone in class for a date, or confront a colleague's racist remarks at the water cooler. Through interpersonal communication you interact with others, learn about them and yourself, and reveal yourself to others. Whether with new acquaintances, old friends, lovers, family members, or colleagues at work, it's through interpersonal communication that you establish, maintain, sometimes destroy, and sometimes repair personal relationships.

Interviewing is communication that proceeds by question and answer. Through interviewing you learn about others and what they know, counsel or get counseling from others, and get or don't get the job you want. Today much interviewing (especially initial interviews) takes place through e-mail and (video) phone conferencing.

Small group or **team communication** is communication among groups of, say five to ten people and may take place face-to-face or in virtual space. Small group communication serves *relationship needs* such as those for companionship, affection, or support and *task needs* such as balancing the family budget, electing a new chairperson, or designing a new ad campaign. Through small group communication you interact with others, solve problems, develop new ideas, and share knowledge and experiences. You live your work and social life largely in groups, from school orientation meetings to executive board meetings, from informal social groups to formal meetings discussing issues of local or international concern. You also may spend a significant amount of time in chat rooms, where you may interact with people from different cultures living thousands of miles away, and on social networking sites (e.g., Facebook and MySpace) in which you learn about and communicate with others.

Public communication is communication between a speaker and an audience. Audiences range in size from several people to hundreds, thousands, and even millions. Through public communication others inform and persuade you. And you, in turn, inform and persuade others—to act, to buy, or to think in a particular way. Much as you can address large audiences face-to-face, you also can address such audiences electronically. Through newsgroups, blogs, or social networks, for example, you can post your "speech" for anyone to read and then read their reactions to your message. And with the help of the more traditional mass media of radio and television, you can address audiences in the hundreds of millions as they sit alone or in small groups all over the world.

Computer-mediated communication is a general term that includes all forms of communication between people that take place through some kind of computer, whether it's on your smart phone or via a standard Internet connection. Examples include e-mail, blogging, instant messaging, or chatting on social network sites such as Facebook, MySpace, or Twitter. Throughout this text, we'll make frequent reference to the similarities and differences between face-to-face and computer-mediated communication.

E-mail is still the most common use of Internet communication. The number of daily e-mails is now in the billions. E-mail communication is **asynchronous**, meaning that it does not take place in real time. You may send your message today, but the receiver may not read it for a week and may take another week to respond. Consequently, much of the spontaneity created by face-to-face, real-time communication is lost. You may, for example, be very enthusiastic about a topic when you send your e-mail but hardly remember it by the time someone responds.

Through instant messaging or IM you interact online in (essentially) real time; the communication messages are **synchronous**—they occur at the same time and are similar to phone communication except that IM is text-based rather than voice-based. Among college students, as you probably know, the major purpose of IM is to maintain "social connectedness" (Kindred & Roper, 2004). And, of course, today most businesses in the United States now use IM as part of their total communications network (Strom, 2006).

In chat groups and especially in social networking groups like Facebook, MySpace, and Twitter you communicate in some cases asynchronously and in some cases synchronously. According to one survey, 75 percent of all online users aged 18–24 and 57 percent aged 25–34 have a profile on one or more social network sites (Lenhart, 2009).

Communication Choice Point

Negative Communication Effects

You post a really negative remark on your friend's Facebook wall. The next day you realize you shouldn't have been so negative. You want to remain friends; you need to say something. *What are your options for communicating your feelings? What would you do?*

Communication Choice Point

Message Overload

Several relatives have developed chain e-mail lists and send you virtually everything they come upon as they surf the Internet. You need to stop this e-mail overload. But, most of all, you don't want to insult your relatives or make them feel guilty. *What are some of the things you might say? What are the advantages and disadvantages of saying nothing?*

Among the main uses of social networking are: to keep up with friends (89 percent of users noted this among their reasons for using such sites), to make plans with friends (57 percent), and to make friends (49 percent). Whereas e-mail and IM are largely text-based systems, social network communication includes voice, photos, and videos. Such sites enable you to communicate with people you would never meet or interact with otherwise. Because many of these groups are international, they provide excellent exposure to other ideas, and ways of communicating, as well as a good introduction to intercultural communication.

Blogs and interactive websites now enable you to communicate your opinions for others to read and react to, and to communicate your reactions to what others say. Increasingly, blogs are being used for more relational purposes, such as maintaining family or group ties and encouraging frequent communication among family or group members.

Mass communication refers to communication from one source to many receivers who may be scattered throughout the world. Newspapers, magazines, radio, television, and film are the major mass media. The coverage of mass communication in the study of human communication presented here is focused on media literacy, helping you to become a wiser, more critical user of the media. A variety of Media Literacy boxes appear on MyCommunicationLab (www.mycommunicationlab.com).

As you can see if you glance through your college catalog, each of these forms of communication is likely to be covered in separate and more detailed courses. For example, most communication departments offer separate courses in interpersonal communication, small group communication, public speaking, and so on. This course and this text introduce the essentials of such communication forms, giving you the knowledge and skills to become a more effective communicator and at the same time the background to move on to more detailed study, whether in additional courses or in your own reading.

This book focuses on all these forms of communication—and on you as both message sender and message receiver. It has two major purposes:

- to explain the *concepts and principles,* the *theory and research* in human communication, so that you'll have a firm understanding of what communication is and how it works.

- to provide you with *skills* in human communication (including the skills of critical thinking) that will help you increase your own communication competence and effectiveness in the real world. A multitude of social interaction and workplace examples throughout the book present useful and practical techniques that you'll take with you when you leave the college classroom.

MYTHS ABOUT HUMAN COMMUNICATION

A good way to begin your study of human communication is to examine just a few of the popular but erroneous beliefs about communication, many of which are contradicted by research and theory. Understanding these myths and why they are false will help eliminate potential barriers and pave the way for more effective and efficient learning about communication.

The more you communicate, the better your communication will be. Although this proposition seems logical—the same idea lies behind the popular belief that practice makes perfect—it actually is at the heart of much faulty learning. Practice may help make perfect if you practice the right habits. But if you practice bad habits, you're likely to grow less, rather than more, effective. Consequently, it's important to learn and practice the principles of effectiveness.

When two people are in a close relationship, neither person should have to communicate needs and wants explicitly; the other person should know what these are. This assumption is at the heart of many interpersonal difficulties. People aren't mind readers, and to expect them to be sets up barriers to open and honest communication.

Interpersonal or group conflict is a reliable sign that the relationship or group is in trouble. Conflict is inevitable in relationships and in groups. As famed author William Ellery Channing put it: "Difficulties are meant to rouse, not discourage. The human spirit is to grow strong by conflict." If the conflict is managed effectively, it may actually benefit the individuals and the relationship.

Like good communicators, leaders are born, not made. Leadership, like communication and listening, is a learned skill. You'll develop leadership abilities as you learn the principles of human communication and those unique to group communication and group leadership.

Fear of speaking in public is detrimental and must be eliminated. Most speakers are nervous—and, to be perfectly honest, you're probably not going to learn from this book or this course to eliminate what is commonly called stage fright or communication apprehension. But you can learn to *manage* your fear, making it work for you rather than against you; you can learn, and this is crucial, to become a more effective speaker regardless of your current level of anxiety.

Communication Models and Concepts

In early **models** (representations) or theories, the communication process was thought to be linear. According to this *linear* view, the speaker spoke and the listener listened. Communication was seen as proceeding in a relatively straight line. Speaking and listening were seen as taking place at different times; when you spoke, you didn't listen, and when you listened, you didn't speak (Figure 1.1).

A more satisfying view, the one held currently, sees communication as a transactional process in which each person serves as both speaker and listener, as simultaneously communicating and receiving messages (Watzlawick, Beavin, & Jackson, 1967; Watzlawick, 1977, 1978; Barnlund, 1970). At the same time that you send messages, you're also receiving messages from your own communications and from the reactions of the other person (Figure 1.2).

The transactional view also sees the elements of communication as interdependent (never independent). This means that each element exists in relation to the others. A change in any one element of the process produces changes in the other elements. For example, if you're having a meeting with a group of your coworkers and your boss enters the room, this change in "audience" will lead to other changes. Perhaps you'll change what you're saying or how you're saying it. Regardless of what change is introduced, other changes will occur as a result.

In communication people act and react on the basis of the present situation as well as on the basis of their histories, past experiences, attitudes, cultural beliefs, and a host of related factors. Because of this, actions and reactions in communication are determined not only by what is said, but also by the way the recipient of the message interprets what is said. Your responses to a movie, for example, don't depend solely on the words and pictures in the film; they also depend on your previous experiences, present emotions, knowledge, physical well-being, and more. For this reason, two people listening to the same message will often derive two very different meanings.

Communication occurs when you send or receive messages and when you assign meaning to another person's signals. All human communication occurs within a context, via one or more channels, is distorted by noise, and has some effect. We can expand the basic transactional model of communication by adding these essential elements, as shown in Figure 1.3.

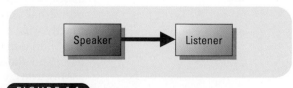

FIGURE 1.1

The Linear View of Human Communication
The speaker speaks and the listener listens.

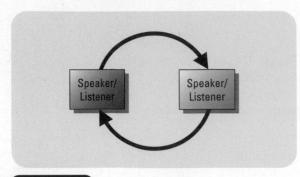

FIGURE 1.2

The Transactional View of Human Communication
Each person serves simultaneously as speaker and listener; at the same time that you send messages, you also receive messages from your own communications as well as from the reactions of the other person(s).

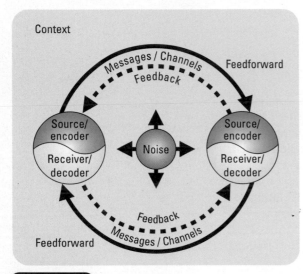

FIGURE 1.3

The Essentials of Human Communication
This is a general model of communication between two people and most accurately depicts interpersonal communication. It puts into visual form the various elements of the communication process. How would you revise this model to depict small group interaction or public speaking?

SOURCES–RECEIVERS

According to the transactional model, each person involved in communication is both a **source** (speaker) and a **receiver** (listener); hence the term *sources–receivers*. You send messages when you speak, write, gesture, or smile. You receive messages in listening, reading, seeing, smelling, and so on. At the same time that you send messages, you're also receiving messages: You're receiving your own messages (you hear yourself, feel your own movements, see many of your own gestures), and, at least in face-to-face communication, you're receiving the messages of the other person—visually, auditorily, or even through touch or smell. As you speak, you look at the person for responses—for approval, understanding, sympathy, agreement, and so on. As you decipher these nonverbal signals, you're performing receiver functions.

When you put your ideas into speech, you're putting them into a code, hence **encoding.** When you translate the sound waves (the speech signals) that impinge on your ears into ideas, you take them out of the code they're in, hence **decoding.** Thus, speakers or writers are referred to as **encoders,** and listeners or readers as **decoders.** The linked term *encoding–decoding* emphasizes the fact that you perform these functions simultaneously.

Usually, you encode an idea into a code that the other person understands—for example, English, Spanish, or Indonesian, depending on the shared knowledge that you and your listener possess. At times, however, you may want to exclude others by speaking in a language that only one of your listeners knows or by using jargon. Adults, when speaking of things they don't want children to understand, may spell out key words—a code that the young children don't yet understand. The use of abbreviations and jargon in text messaging is another example of how people communicate in a code that only certain people will understand.

MESSAGES

Communication **messages** take many forms and are transmitted or received through one sensory organ or a combination of them. You communicate verbally (with words) and nonverbally (without words). Your meanings or intentions are conveyed with words (Chapter 4) and with the clothes you wear, the way you walk, and the way you smile (Chapter 5). Everything about you communicates a message.

Feedforward Messages **Feedforward** is information you provide before sending your primary messages (Richards, 1951). It reveals something about the messages to come and includes, for example, the preface or table of contents of a book, the opening paragraph of a chapter, movie previews, magazine covers, and introductions in public speeches.

Feedforward may be verbal ("Wait until you hear this one") or nonverbal (a prolonged pause or hands motioning for silence to signal that an important message is about to be spoken). Or, as is most often the case, it is some combination of verbal and nonverbal. Feedforward may refer to the content of the message to follow ("I'll tell you exactly what they said to each other") or to the form ("I won't spare you the gory details"). In e-mail, feedforward is given in the header, where the name of the sender, the date, and the subject of the message are identified. Caller ID is also an example of feedforward.

Another type of feedforward is **phatic communication,** or "small talk" that opens the way for "big talk." It includes the "How are you?" and "Nice weather" greetings that are designed to maintain rapport and friendly relationships (Placencia, 2004; Burnard,

2003). Similarly, listeners' short comments that are unrelated to the content of the conversation but indicate interest and attention also may be considered phatic communication (McCarthy, 2003).

Feedback Messages When you send a message—say, in speaking to another person—you also hear yourself. That is, you get **feedback** from your own messages; you hear what you say, you feel the way you move, you see what you write. In addition to this self-feedback, you also get feedback from others. This feedback can take many forms. A frown or a smile, a yea or a nay, a pat on the back or a punch in the mouth are all types of feedback.

Feedback tells the speaker what effect he or she is having on listeners. On the basis of feedback, the speaker may adjust, modify, strengthen, deemphasize, or change the content or form of the messages. For example, if someone laughs at your joke (giving you positive feedback), it may encourage you to tell another one. If the feedback is negative—no laughing, just blank stares—then you may resist relaying another "humorous" story.

Metamessages A **metamessage** is a message that refers to another message; it is communication about communication. For example, remarks such as "This statement is false" or "Do you understand what I am trying to tell you?" refer to communication and are therefore "metacommunicational."

Nonverbal behavior may also be metacommunicational. Obvious examples include crossing your fingers behind your back or winking when telling a lie. On a less obvious level, consider the blind date. As you say, "I had a really nice time," your nonverbal messages—the lack of a smile, failure to maintain eye contact—metacommunicate and contradict the verbal "really nice time," suggesting that you did not enjoy the evening. Nonverbal messages may also metacommunicate about other nonverbal messages. The individual who, on meeting a stranger, both smiles and extends a totally lifeless hand shows how one nonverbal behavior may contradict another.

COMMUNICATION CONTEXT

Communication exists in a context that determines, to a large extent, the meaning of any verbal or nonverbal message. The same words or behaviors may have totally different meanings when they occur in different contexts. For example, the greeting "How are you?" means "Hello" to someone you pass regularly on the street but "Is your health improving?" to a friend in the hospital. A wink to an attractive person on a bus means something completely different from a wink that signifies a put-on or a lie. Divorced from the context, it's impossible to tell what meaning was intended from just examining the signals.

The context will also influence what you say and how you say it. You communicate differently depending on the specific context you're in. Contexts have at least four aspects: physical, cultural, social-psychological, and temporal or time.

- The *physical context* is the tangible or concrete environment, the room, park, or auditorium; you don't talk the same way at a noisy football game as you do at a quiet funeral.
- The *cultural context* involves the lifestyles, beliefs, values, behavior, and communication of a group; it is the rules of a group of people for considering something right or wrong.
- The *social-psychological context* has to do with the status relationships among speakers, the formality of the situation, the norms of a group or organization; you don't talk the same way in the cafeteria as you would at a formal dinner at your boss's house.
- The *temporal context* is a message's position within a sequence of events; you don't talk the same way after someone tells you about the death of a close relative as you do after someone reveals they've won the lottery.

These four contexts interact—each influences and is influenced by the others. For example, arriving late for a date (temporal context) may lead to changes in the degree of friendliness (social–psychological context), which would depend on the cultures of you and your date (cultural context) and may lead to changes in where you go on the date (physical context).

CHANNEL

The communication **channel** is the vehicle or medium through which messages pass. Communication rarely takes place over only one channel. Rather, two, three, or four channels may be used simultaneously. In face-to-face conversations, for example, you speak and listen (vocal channel), but you also gesture and receive signals visually (visual channel). You also emit and smell odors (olfactory channel) and often touch one another; this tactile channel, too, is communication.

Another way to classify channels is by the means of communication. Thus, face-to-face contact, telephones, e-mail, movies, television, smoke signals, and telegraph all are types of channels.

At times one or more channels may be damaged. For example, in individuals who are blind, the visual channel is impaired and adjustments have to be made. Table 1.1

TABLE 1.1	Communication Tips

Between People with and People without Visual Impairments

Louis Braille	Helen Keller	Ray Charles	David Paterson

People vary greatly in their visual abilities; some are totally blind, some are partially sighted, and some have unimpaired vision. Ninety percent of people who are "legally blind" have some vision. All people, however, have the same need for communication and information. Here are some tips for making communication better between those who have visual impairments and those without such difficulties.

If you're the sighted person and are talking with a visually impaired person:

1. Identify yourself. Don't assume the visually impaired person will recognize your voice.

2. Face your listener; you'll be easier to hear. Don't shout. Most people who are visually impaired are not hearing impaired. Speak at your normal volume.

3. Because your gestures, eye movements, and facial expressions cannot be seen by the visually impaired listener, encode into speech all the meanings you wish to communicate.

4. Use audible turn-taking cues. When you pass the role of speaker to a person who is visually impaired, don't rely on nonverbal cues; instead, say something like "Do you agree with that, Joe?"

5. Use normal vocabulary and discuss topics that you would discuss with sighted people. Don't avoid terms like "see" or "look" or even "blind." Don't avoid discussing a television show or the way your new car looks; these are normal topics for all people.

If you are a visually impaired person, interacting with a sighted person:

1. Help the sighted person meet your special communication needs. If you want your surroundings described, ask. If you want the person to read the road signs, ask.

2. Be patient with the sighted person. Many people are nervous talking with people who are visually impaired for fear of offending. Put them at ease in a way that also makes you more comfortable.

Sources: These suggestions were drawn from a variety of sources: www.cincyblind.org, www.abwa.asn.au/, and www.batchelor.edu.au/disability/communication (all accessed April 29, 2008).

gives you an idea of how such adjustments between people with visual impairments and those without such impairments can make communication more effective.

NOISE

Noise is anything that interferes with your receiving a message. At one extreme, noise may prevent a message from getting from source to receiver. A roaring noise or line static can prevent entire messages from getting through to your phone receiver. At the other extreme, with virtually no noise interference, the message of the source and the message received are almost identical. Most often, however, noise distorts some portion of the message a source sends as it travels to a receiver. Just as messages may be auditory or visual, noise comes in both auditory and visual forms. Four types of noise are especially relevant:

- *Physical noise* is interference that is external to both speaker and listener; it interferes with the physical transmission of the signal or message and would include the screeching of passing cars, the hum of a computer, sunglasses, blurred type or fonts that are too small or difficult to read, misspellings and poor grammar, and popup ads.
- *Physiological noise* is created by barriers within the sender or receiver and would include visual impairments, hearing loss, articulation problems, and memory loss.
- *Psychological noise* refers to mental interference in the speaker or listener and includes preconceived ideas, wandering thoughts, biases and prejudices, close-mindedness, and extreme emotionalism. You're likely to run into psychological noise when you talk with someone who is close-minded or who refuses to listen to anything he or she doesn't already believe.
- *Semantic noise* is interference that occurs when the speaker and listener have different meaning systems; it would include language or dialectical differences, the use of jargon or overly complex terms, and ambiguous or overly abstract terms whose meanings can be easily misinterpreted. You see this type of noise regularly in the medical doctor who uses "medicalese" without explanation or in the insurance salesperson who speaks in the jargon of the insurance industry.

As you can see from these examples, noise is anything that distorts your receiving the messages of others or their receiving your messages.

A useful concept in understanding noise and its importance in communication is **signal-to-noise ratio.** In this term the word *signal* refers to information that you'd find useful, and *noise* refers to information that is useless (to you). So, for example, a mailing list or newsgroup that contains lots of useful information is high on signal and low on noise; one that contains lots of useless information is high on noise and low on signal.

All communications contain noise. Noise can't be totally eliminated, but its effects can be reduced. Making your language more precise, sharpening your skills for sending and receiving nonverbal messages, and improving your listening and feedback skills are some ways to combat the influence of noise.

EFFECTS

Communication always has some **effect** on those involved in the communication act. For every communication act, there is some consequence. For example, you may gain knowledge or learn how to analyze, synthesize, or evaluate something. These are intellectual or cognitive effects. You may acquire new feelings, attitudes, or beliefs or change existing ones (affective effects). You may learn new bodily movements, such as how to throw a curve ball, paint a picture, give a compliment, or express surprise (psychomotor effects).

Communication Competence

Communication competence refers to (1) your knowledge and understanding of how communication works and (2) your ability to use communication effectively (Spitzberg & Cupach, 1989, 2002). Your understanding of communication would include a knowledge of the elements involved in communication, how these elements interact, and how each communication situation is both different from and similar to other situations. Your knowledge would also include an understanding of the choices you have for communicating in any given situation.

Using communication effectively would involve your ability to select and implement the best choices for communicating, and to read and adjust to the ongoing feedback that you receive from your own messages and that guide the choices you make in selecting future messages.

The more you know about communication, the more choices you'll have available for your day-to-day interactions. It's like learning vocabulary. The more vocabulary you know, the more choices you have to express yourself. In a similar way, the aim of this book is to increase your communicative competence and thus to give you a broad range of options to use in your own communications.

Let's spell out the nature of communication competence in more detail by discussing the major themes of competence that contemporary research and theory identify and that are highlighted in this text.

THE COMPETENT COMMUNICATOR THINKS CRITICALLY AND MINDFULLY

An essential part of communication skill is the ability to think critically about the communication situations you face and the options for communicating that you have available; this is crucial to your success and effectiveness.

Without critical thinking there can be no competent exchange of ideas. Critical thinking is logical thinking; it's thinking that is well reasoned, unbiased, and clear. It involves thinking intelligently, carefully, and with as much clarity as possible. And, not surprisingly, critical thinking is one of the stepping stones to effective management (Miller, 1997).

A special kind of critical thinking is mindfulness. **Mindfulness** is a state of awareness in which you're conscious of your reasons for thinking or behaving. In its opposite, **mindlessness,** you lack conscious awareness of what or how you're thinking (Langer, 1989). To apply interpersonal skills effectively in conversation, you need to be mindful of the unique communication situation you're in, of your available communication options, and of the reasons why one option is likely to be better than the others (Elmes & Gemmill, 1990; Burgoon, Berger, & Waldron, 2000).

As you progress through your study of human communication, actively increase your own mindfulness (Langer, 1989):

- Create and re-create categories. Group things in different ways; remember that people are constantly changing, so the categories into which you may group them also should change. Learn to see objects, events, and people as belonging to a wide variety of categories. Try to see, for example, your prospective romantic partner in a variety of roles—child, parent, employee, neighbor, friend, financial contributor, and so on.

- Be open to new information and points of view, even when these contradict your most firmly held beliefs. New information forces you to reconsider what might be outmoded ways of thinking and can help you challenge long-held, but now inappropriate, beliefs and attitudes.

- Beware of relying too heavily on first impressions (Chanowitz & Langer, 1981; Langer, 1989). Treat first impressions as tentative, as hypotheses that need further investigation. Be prepared to revise, reject, or accept these initial impressions.

- Think before you act. Especially in delicate situations such as anger or commitment messages, it's wise to pause and think over the situation mindfully (DeVito, 2003b). In this way you'll stand a better chance of acting and reacting appropriately.

"Never say anything on the phone that you wouldn't want your mother to hear at your trial."

—SYDNEY BIDDLE BARROWS

You'll find frequent opportunities to apply mindful, critical thinking throughout your reading of the text but perhaps especially in the Skill Development Experiences, in the Communication Choice Points, and in the Test Yourself quizzes.

THE COMPETENT COMMUNICATOR RECOGNIZES THE ROLE OF POWER

All communication transactions involve **power,** the ability to influence the thoughts and behavior of others. In fact, you can look at the principles and skills of communication covered in this text as skills and principles of power—the power to speak your own mind, the power to influence a friend, the power to lead a group responsibly and efficiently, the power to get your point across to an audience. As motivational speaker Anthony Robbins put it, "Communication is power. Those who have mastered its effective use can change their own experience of the world and the world's experience of them." Because of the central importance of power in all forms of communication, concepts and principles relevant to power are discussed throughout the text and, in fact, considered later in this chapter as one of the essential principles of human communication.

THE COMPETENT COMMUNICATOR IS CULTURALLY SENSITIVE

Communication competence is culture-specific; that is, the principles of effective communication vary from one culture to another, and what proves effective in one culture may prove ineffective in another. For example, in American culture you would call a person you wished to date three or four days in advance. In certain Asian cultures, you might call the person's parents weeks or even months in advance. Thus, discussions of cultural implications accompany all of the major topics considered in this text.

Some examples include the major ways in which cultures differ and the implications these differences have for communication; cultural differences in politeness; cultural and gender differences in nonverbal messages such as facial expressions, colors, touch, silence, and time; cultural differences in approaches to small group communication and leadership; and cultural differences in varied aspects of public speaking such as language usage and approaches to proof and evidence.

THE COMPETENT COMMUNICATOR IS ETHICAL

Human communication also involves questions of ethics, the study of good and bad, of right and wrong, of moral and immoral. Ethics is concerned with actions, with behaviors; it's concerned with distinguishing between behaviors that are moral (ethical, good, right) and those that are immoral (unethical, bad, wrong). Not surprisingly, there's an ethical dimension to any communication act (Neher & Sandin, 2007; Bok, 1978).

In addition to this introductory discussion, ethical dimensions of human communication are presented in each of the remaining chapters in Communicating Ethically boxes. As a kind of preview, here are just a few of the ethical issues raised. As you read these questions, think about your own ethical beliefs and how they would influence the way you answered the questions.

- What are your ethical obligations as a listener? (Chapter 3, p. 58)
- When is it unethical to remain silent? (Chapter 5, p. 109)
- When is gossiping ethical and when is it unethical? (Chapter 9, p. 180)
- At what point in a relationship do you have an obligation to reveal intimate details of your life? (Chapter 7, p. 150)
- Are there ethical and unethical ways to engage in conflict and conflict resolution? (Chapter 8, p. 173)

Woven through these discussions of ethics are two overriding questions that will influence all your ethical decisions: (1) Are ethical principles objective or subjective? (2) Does the end justify the means?

In an **objective view of ethics,** you'd argue that the rightness or wrongness of an act is absolute and exists apart from the values or beliefs of any individual or culture. With this view, you'd hold that there are standards that apply to all people in all situations at all times. If lying, false advertising, using illegally obtained evidence, and revealing secrets you've promised to keep were considered unethical, then they would be unethical regardless of circumstances or of cultural values and beliefs. In an objective view the end can never justify the means; an unethical act is never justified regardless of how good or beneficial its results (or ends) might be.

In a **subjective view of ethics,** you'd argue that absolute statements about right and wrong are too rigid and that the ethics of a message depends on the culture's values and beliefs as well as on the particular circumstances. Thus, a subjective position would claim that lying might be wrong to win votes or sell cigarettes, but that it might be quite ethical if good would result from it—as when we try to make friends feel better by telling them that they look great or that they'll get well soon. In a subjective view a good end would often justify the use of means that would in other situations be considered unethical.

As a preface to these future discussions, consider some of the popular beliefs about ethics, perhaps one or more of which you hold personally. For each of the following statements, place a T (for True) if you feel the statement accurately explains what ethical behavior is, and an F (for False) if you feel the statement does not accurately explain what ethical behavior is.

_____ 1. My behavior is ethical when I feel (in my heart) that I'm doing the right thing.

_____ 2. My behavior is ethical when it is consistent with my religious beliefs.

_____ 3. My behavior is ethical when it is legal.

_____ 4. My behavior is ethical when the majority of reasonable people would consider it ethical.

_____ 5. My behavior is ethical when it benefits more people than it harms.

These statements are based on responses given to the question, "What does ethics mean to you?" (**www.scu.edu/ethics/practicing/decision/whatisethics.html**, accessed March 20, 2009). All five of these statements are (generally) False; none of them state a useful explanation of what is and what is not ethical.

Statement 1 is False simply because people often do unethical things they feel are morally justified. Jack the Ripper killing prostitutes is a good historical example but there are many current ones such as stalking (*I'm so in love I need to be with this person*) or insurance scams (*My family needs the money more than the insurance company*). Even though Jack, the stalker, and the scam artist may feel justified in their own minds, it doesn't make their behavior moral or ethical.

Statement 2 must be False when you realize that different religions advocate very different kinds of behavior, often behaviors that contradict one another. Examples abound in almost every issue of a daily newspaper.

Statement 3 must be false when you realize so much discrimination against certain people is perfectly legal in many parts of the world, and, in many countries, war (even preemptive war) is legal.

Statement 4 is False because the thinking of the majority changes with the times and has often proven to be extremely immoral. The burning of people supposed to be witches or of those who spoke out against majority opinion (as in the Inquisition) are good examples.

Statement 5 comes the closest to being possibly and sometimes true, but it's more generally false. The reason it's more false than true is that the burning of witches, for example, was in the interest of the majority as was slavery and discrimination against gay men and lesbians, certain religions, or different races. But, despite this majority interest, we'd readily recognize these actions as immoral.

THE COMPETENT COMMUNICATOR IS AN EFFECTIVE LISTENER

Often we tend to think of competence in communication as "speaking effectiveness," paying little attention to listening. But listening is an integral part of communication; you cannot be a competent communicator if you're a poor listener.

If you measured importance by the time you spend on an activity, then—according to the research studies available—listening would be your most important communication activity. Studies conducted from 1929 to 1980 show that listening was the most often used form of communication. For example, in a study of college students conducted in 1980 (Barker, Edwards, Gaines, Gladney, & Holley), listening also occupied the most time: 53 percent compared to reading (17 percent), speaking (16 percent), and writing (14 percent). In a more recent survey, the figures for the four communication activities were: listening (40%), talking (35%), reading (16%), and writing (9%) (Watkins, 2007). Again, listening is the most often used of all communication activities.

Because of the importance of listening, it is emphasized in this text in two major ways: (1) Chapter 4 is devoted exclusively to listening and covers the nature and importance of listening, the steps you go through in listening, the role of culture and gender in listening, and ways to increase your listening effectiveness. (2) In each of the remaining chapters, Listen to This boxes are included to illustrate how listening relates to the topic of each chapter and to provide a variety of specific listening skills. Among the topics of these boxes are the importance of listening to yourself, the role of gender differences, and ways to listen during conflict.

Communication Choice Point

Silence

Your partner (who is extremely sensitive to criticism) talks constantly. There is never any silence, which you desperately crave. You're determined to combat this and create periods of occasional silence. yet, you don't want to start an argument. *What are some of the things you might say, or avoid saving? How might you introduce the topic?*

Principles of Communication

Several principles are essential to an understanding of human communication in all its forms. These principles, as you'll see throughout the text, also have numerous practical implications for your own communication effectiveness.

COMMUNICATION IS PURPOSEFUL

You communicate for a purpose; some motivation leads you to communicate. When you speak or write, you're trying to send some message and to accomplish some goal. Although different cultures emphasize different purposes and motives (Rubin, Fernandez-Collado, & Hernandez-Sampieri, 1992), five general purposes seem relatively common to most, if not all, forms of communication:

- to learn: to acquire knowledge of others, the world, and yourself
- to relate: to form relationships with others, to interact with others as individuals
- to help: to assist others by listening, offering solutions
- to influence: to strengthen or change the attitudes or behaviors of others
- to play: to enjoy the experience of the moment

Popular belief and research findings both agree that men and women use communication for different purposes. Generally, men seem to communicate more for information and women more for relationship purposes (Gamble & Gamble, 2003; Stewart, Cooper, & Stewart, 2003; Helgeson, 2009). Gender differences also occur in electronic communication. For example, women chat more for relationship reasons; men chat more to play and to relax (Leung, 2001).

COMMUNICATION IS A PROCESS OF ADJUSTMENT

The principle of **adjustment** states that communication can take place only to the extent that the communicators use the same system of signals (Pittenger, Hockett, & Danehy, 1960). You will be unable to communicate with another person to the extent that your language systems differ. Parents and children, for example, not only have largely different vocabularies, but also may assign different meanings to the terms they do share. Different cultures, even when they use a common language, often have greatly different nonverbal communication systems. In reality, no two individuals use identical signal systems, so this principle is relevant to all forms of communication.

Part of the art of communication is identifying the other person's signals, learning how they're used, and understanding what they mean. Those in close relationships will realize that learning the other person's signals takes a great deal of time and often a great deal of patience. If you want to understand what another person means (by smiling, by saying "I love you," by arguing about trivia) rather than merely acknowledging what the other person says or does, you have to learn that person's system of signals.

An interesting theory revolving largely around adjustment is **communication accommodation theory.** This theory holds that speakers adjust to, or *accommodate* to, the speaking style of their listeners in order to gain, for example, social approval and greater communication efficiency (Giles, Mulac, Bradac, & Johnson, 1987; Giles, 2008). For example, when two people have a similar speech rate, they seem to be attracted more to each other than to those with dissimilar rates (Buller, LePoire, Aune, & Eloy, 1992). Still another study found that roommates who had similar communication attitudes (both roommates were high in communication competence and willingness to communicate, and low in verbal aggressiveness) were highest in roommate liking and satisfaction (Martin & Anderson, 1995). And in interethnic interactions, people who saw themselves as similar in communication styles were attracted to each other more than to those they perceived as having different communication styles (Lee & Gudykunst, 2001).

COMMUNICATION IS AMBIGUOUS

Ambiguity is the condition in which something can be interpreted in more than one way. The first type, *language ambiguity,* is created by words that can be interpreted differently. Informal time terms offer good examples; *soon, right away, in a minute, early, late,* and similar terms can be understood differently by different people. The terms are ambiguous. A more interesting type of ambiguity is grammatical ambiguity. You can get a feel for this type of ambiguity by trying to paraphrase—rephrase in your own words—the following sentences:

- What has the cat in its paws?
- Flying planes can be dangerous.
- They are frying chickens.

Each of these ambiguous sentences can be interpreted and paraphrased in at least two different ways:

- What does the cat have in its paws? What monster has the cat in its paws?
- To fly planes is dangerous. Planes that fly can be dangerous.
- Those people are frying chickens. Those chickens are for frying.

Although these examples are particularly striking—and are the work of linguists who analyze language—some degree of ambiguity exists in all communication. When you express an idea, you never communicate your meaning exactly and totally; rather, you communicate your meaning with some reasonable accuracy—enough to give the other person a reasonably clear idea of what you mean.

The second type of ambiguity is *relationship ambiguity.* All relationships are ambiguous to some extent. Consider your own close relationships and ask yourself the following questions. Answer using a six-point scale on which 1 = completely or almost completely uncertain and 6 = completely or almost completely certain. How certain are you about:

1. what you can or cannot say to each other in this relationship?
2. whether or not you and your partner feel the same way about each other?
3. how you and your partner would describe this relationship?
4. the future of the relationship?

Communication Choice Point

Relationship Ambiguity

You've been dating Jessie on and off for the past six months. Today Jessie asks you to come to dinner and meet the parents. You're not sure what this means, what message Jessie's trying to send. *What options do you have for disambiguating this dinner invitation message? What would you say?*

You probably were not able to respond with 6s for all four questions, and equally likely that your relationship partner would not respond with all 6s to these questions, adapted from a relationship uncertainty scale (Knobloch & Solomon, 1999).

You can look at the skills of human communication presented throughout this text as means for appropriately reducing ambiguity and making your meaning as unambiguous as possible.

COMMUNICATION INVOLVES CONTENT AND RELATIONSHIP DIMENSIONS

Communication exists on at least two levels. A single message can refer to something external to both speaker and listener (e.g., the weather) as well as to the relationship between speaker and listener (e.g., who is in charge). These two aspects are referred to as **content and relationship dimensions** of communication (Watzlawick, Beavin, & Jackson, 1967). In the cartoon below, the father is explicitly teaching his son the difference between content and relationship messages. In real life this distinction is rarely discussed (outside of textbooks and counseling sessions).

Some research shows that women send more **relationship messages** than men; they talk more about relationships in general and about the present relationship in particular. Men engage in more content talk; they talk more about things external to the relationship (Wood, 1994; Pearson, West, & Turner, 1995; Helgeson, 2009).

Problems often result from a failure to distinguish between the content and the relationship levels of communication. Consider a couple, Pat and Chris. Pat made plans to attend a rally with friends during the weekend without first asking Chris, and an argument has ensued. Both would probably have agreed that attending the rally was the right choice to make. Thus, the argument is not centered on the content level. The argument, instead, centers on the relationship level. Chris expected to be consulted about plans for the weekend. Pat, in not doing so, rejected this definition of the relationship.

COMMUNICATION HAS A POWER DIMENSION

Power, as mentioned earlier, has to do with your ability to influence or control the behaviors of another person. Power influences the way you communicate, and the way you communicate influences the power you wield. Research has identified six types of power: legitimate, referent, reward, coercive, expert, and information or persuasion (French & Raven, 1968; Raven, Centers, & Rodrigues, 1975). Let's take a look at each.

You hold **legitimate power** when others believe you have a right—by virtue of your position—to influence or control others' behaviors. For example, as an employer, judge, manager, or police officer, you'd have legitimate power by virtue of your role.

You have **referent power** when others wish to be like you. Referent power holders often are attractive, have considerable prestige, and are well liked and well respected. For example, you may have referent power over a younger brother because he wants to be like you.

You have **reward power** when you control the rewards that others want. Rewards may be material (money, promotion, jewelry) or social (love, friendship, respect). For example, teachers have reward power over students because they control grades, letters of recommendation, and social approval.

You have **coercive power** when you have the ability to administer punishments to or remove rewards from others if they do not do as you wish. Usually, people who have reward power also have coercive power. For example, teachers

"It's not about the story. It's about Daddy taking time out of his busy day to read you the story."

© Peter C. Vey/Condé Nast Publications/www.cartoonbank.com.

may give poor grades or withhold recommendations. But be careful: Coercive power may reduce your other power bases. It can have a negative impact when used, for example, by supervisors on subordinates in business (Richmond et al., 1984).

You have **expert power** when others see you as having expertise or special knowledge. Your expert power increases when you're perceived as being unbiased and as having nothing personally to gain from exerting this power. For example, judges have expert power in legal matters and doctors have expert power in medical matters.

You have **information power**—also called "persuasion power"—when others see you as having the ability to communicate logically and persuasively. For example, researchers and scientists may acquire information power because people perceive them as informed and critical thinkers.

The power you wield is not static; it can be increased or decreased depending on what you do and don't do. For example, you might increase your reward power by gaining wealth and using it to exert influence, or you might increase your persuasive power by mastering the principles of public speaking.

You can also decrease or lose power. Probably the most common way to lose power is by unsuccessfully trying to control another's behavior. For example, if you threaten someone with punishment and then fail to carry out your threat, you'll most likely lose power. Another way to lose power is to allow others to control you or to take unfair advantage of you. When you don't confront these power tactics of others, you lose power.

COMMUNICATION IS PUNCTUATED

Communication events are continuous transactions that have no clear-cut beginning or ending. As a participant in or an observer of communication, you divide this continuous, circular process into causes and effects, or stimuli and responses. The **punctuation of communication** is the segmenting of the continuous stream of communication into smaller pieces (Watzlawick, Beavin, & Jackson, 1967). Some of these pieces you label causes (or stimuli) and others effects (or responses).

Consider this example: The manager of a local supermarket lacks interest in the employees, seldom offering any suggestions for improvement or any praise for jobs well done. The employees are apathetic and morale is low. Each action (the manager's lack of involvement and the employees' low morale) stimulates the other. Each serves as the stimulus for

Communication Choice Point

Establishing Power

As a new teacher, you want to establish your power as soon as possible. *What options do you have for communicating your power? What are some of the things you would say if you were a fourth-grade teacher? If you were a college professor?*

the other but there is no identifiable initial starting point. Each event may be seen as a stimulus or as a response.

To understand what the other person in an interaction means from his or her point of view, try to see the sequence of events as punctuated by the other person. The manager, for example, needs to see the problem from the point of view of the employees and the employees need to see it from the viewpoint of the manager. Further, recognize that neither person's punctuation reflects what exists in reality. Rather, it reflects the subjective and fallible perception of each individual (the other person as well as yourself).

© Sam Gross/Condé Nast Publications/www.cartoonbank.com.

COMMUNICATION IS INEVITABLE, IRREVERSIBLE, AND UNREPEATABLE

Inevitability   Communication is inevitable; that is, in interactional situations it is always taking place, even when a person may not intend or want to communicate. To understand the **inevitability** of communication, think about a student sitting in the back of a classroom with an expressionless face, perhaps staring out the window. Although the student might claim not to be communicating with the instructor, the instructor may derive a variety of messages from this behavior. Perhaps the instructor assumes that the student lacks interest, is bored, or is worried about something. In any event, the teacher is receiving messages even though the student may not intentionally be sending any (Watzlawick, Beavin, & Jackson, 1967; Motley, 1990a, 1990b; Bavelas, 1990). This does not mean that all behavior is communication. For instance, if the student looked out the window and the teacher didn't notice, no communication would have taken place. The two people must be in an interactional situation and the behavior must be perceived for the principle of inevitability to operate.

Notice, too, that when you're in an interactional situation, you cannot *not* respond to the messages of others. For example, if you notice someone winking at you, you must respond in some way. Even if you don't respond actively or openly, your lack of response is itself a response: It communicates.

Irreversibility   Another all-important attribute of communication is its **irreversibility.** Once you say something or click "send" on your e-mail, you cannot uncommunicate the message. You can, of course, try to reduce its effects. You can say, for example, "I really didn't mean what I said." But regardless of how hard you try to negate or reduce the effects of a message, the message itself, once it has been received, cannot be taken back. In a public speaking situation in which the speech is recorded or broadcast, inappropriate messages may have national or even international effects. Here, attempts to reverse what someone has said (e.g., efforts to offer clarification) often have the effect of further publicizing the original statement.

In face-to-face communication, the actual signals (nonverbal messages and sound waves in the air) are evanescent; they fade almost as they are uttered. Some written messages, especially computer-mediated messages such as those sent through e-mail, are unerasable. E-mails among employees in large corporations or even at colleges are often stored on disk or tape and may not be considered private by managers and administrators (Sethna, Barnes, Brust, & Kaye, 1999). Much litigation has involved evidence of racist or sexist e-mails that senders thought had been erased but weren't. E-mails and entire hard drives are finding their way into divorce proceedings. As a result of the permanency of computer-mediated communication, you may wish to be especially cautious in these messages.

In all forms of communication, because of irreversibility (and unerasability), be careful not to say things you may be sorry for later, especially in conflict situations, when tempers run high. Commitment messages—"I love you" messages and their variants— also need to be monitored. Messages that you considered private but that might be

Communication Choice Point

The Irreversibility of Communication

You refer to your best friend's current romantic partner with the name of an ex-partner. From both their expressions you can tell your friend never mentioned the ex. You need to get your friend out of the trouble you just created. *What are some of the things you might say? What would you be sure not to say?*

interpreted as sexist, racist, or homophobic may later be retrieved by others and create all sorts of problems for you and your organization. In group and public communication situations, when the messages are received by many people, it's especially crucial to recognize the irreversibility of communication.

Unrepeatability   Finally, communication is *unrepeatable*. A communication act can never be duplicated. The reason is simple: Everyone and everything is constantly changing. As a result, you can never recapture the exact same situation, frame of mind, or relationship dynamics that defined a previous communication act. For example, you can never repeat meeting someone for the first time, comforting a grieving friend, leading a small group for the first time, or giving a public speech. You can never replace an initial impression; you can only try to counteract this initial (and perhaps negative) impression by making subsequent impressions more positive.

Culture and Human Communication

Culture consists of the beliefs, ways of behaving, and artifacts of a group. By definition, culture is transmitted through communication and learning rather than through genes.

A walk through any large city, many small towns, or just about any college campus will convince you that the United States is a collection of lots of different cultures. These cultures coexist somewhat separately, but all influence one another. This coexistence has led some researchers to refer to these cultures as *cocultures* (Shuter, 1990; Samovar & Porter, 1991; Jandt, 2003).

Gender is considered a cultural variable largely because cultures teach boys and girls different attitudes, beliefs, values, and ways of communicating and relating to one another. This means that you act like a man or a woman in part because of what your culture has taught you about how men and women should act. This is not to deny that biological differences also play a role in the differences between male and female behavior. In fact, research continues to uncover the biological roots of behavior we once thought was entirely learned—acting happy or shy, for example (McCroskey, 1997).

Yet we're living in a time of changing gender roles. Many men, for example, are doing more housekeeping chores and caring for their children. More obvious perhaps is that women are becoming more visible in career fields once occupied exclusively by men—politics, law enforcement, the military, and the clergy are just some examples. And, of course, women are increasingly present in the corporate executive ranks; the glass ceiling may not have disappeared, but it has cracked.

Because your communication is heavily influenced by the culture in which you were raised, culture is highly relevant to communication, and a cultural perspective serves numerous important purposes.

THE IMPORTANCE OF CULTURE

Because of (1) demographic changes, (2) increased sensitivity to cultural differences, (3) economic interdependency, and (4) advances in communication technology, it's impossible to communicate effectively without being aware of how culture influences human communication.

Demographic Changes   Whereas at one time the United States was a country largely populated by Europeans, it's now greatly influenced by the enormous number of new citizens from Latin and South America, Africa, and Asia. This is true on college and university campuses as well. With these changes have come different customs and the need to understand and adapt to new ways of looking at communication. For example, consider health care workers and patients. Each group needs to understand how the other communicates about illness, sees ways to prevent health problems, and views taking medication. Police officers and civilians need to understand each other's views of "disorderly conduct," "the right to assemble," and "free speech."

Sensitivity to Cultural Differences As a people, we've become increasingly sensitive to cultural differences. U.S. society has moved from an *assimilationist perspective* (the idea that people should leave their native culture behind and adapt to their new culture) to a view that values *cultural diversity* (people should retain their native cultural ways). And with some notable exceptions—hate speech, racism, sexism, homophobia, and classism come quickly to mind—we're more concerned with saying the right thing and ultimately with developing a society in which all cultures can coexist and enrich one another. At the same time, the ability to interact effectively with members of other cultures often translates into financial gain and increased employment opportunities and advancement prospects.

"I am not an Athenian or a Greek, but a citizen of the world."

—SOCRATES

Economic Interdependence Today most countries are economically dependent on one another. Our economic lives depend on our ability to communicate effectively across cultures. Similarly, our political well-being depends in great part on that of other cultures. Political unrest in any part of the world—Africa, Eastern Europe, or the Middle East, to take a few examples—affects our own security. Intercultural communication and understanding now seem more crucial than ever.

Communication Technology The rapid spread of communication technology has brought different cultures from around the world right into our homes. News from remote countries is commonplace. Technology has made intercultural communication easy, practical, and inevitable. It's common to have social network friends from a wide geographical areas, from different countries and cultures—something that would have been impossible before the advent of computer-mediated communication. Daily, the media bombard you with evidence of racial tensions, religious disagreements, sexual bias, and, in general, the problems caused when intercultural communication fails. And, of course, the Internet has made intercultural communication as easy as writing a note on your laptop. You can now communicate daily by e-mail or social network sites just as easily with someone in Europe or Asia, for example, as with someone in another city or state.

DIMENSIONS OF CULTURE

Because of its importance in all forms of human communication, culture is given a prominent place in this text. Throughout this text theories and research findings that bear on culture and communication are discussed. Prominent among these discussions are the five major dimensions of culture. By way of a brief preview, these dimensions are:

- *Uncertainty avoidance:* The degree to which a culture values predictability. In high-uncertainty-avoidance cultures, predictability and order are extremely important; in low-uncertainty-avoidance cultures, risk-taking and ambiguity are tolerated more easily.

- *Masculinity–femininity:* The extent to which cultures embrace traditionally masculine characteristics such as ambition and assertiveness or embrace traditionally feminine characteristics such as caring and nurturing others.

- *Power distance:* The way power is distributed throughout the society. In high-power-distance cultures, there is a great power difference between those in authority and others. In low-power-distance cultures, power is distributed more evenly.

- *Individualism–collectivism:* A culture's emphasis on the importance of the individual or of the group. Individualist cultures value such qualities as self-reliance, independence, and individual achievement; collectivist cultures emphasize social bonds, the primacy of the group, and conformity to the larger social group.

- *High and low context:* The extent to which information is seen as embedded in the

"From the moment of his birth, the customs into which he is born shape his experience and behavior. By the time he can talk, he is the little creature of his culture."

—RUTH BENEDICT

context or tacitly known among members. In high-context cultures information is part of the context and does not have to be verbalized explicitly. In low-context cultures information is made explicit and little is taken for granted.

THE AIM OF A CULTURAL PERSPECTIVE

Because culture permeates all forms of communication, and because what messages are effective in one culture may prove totally ineffective in another culture, it's necessary to understand its influences if you're to understand how communication works and master its skills. As illustrated throughout this text, culture influences communications of all types (Moon, 1996). It influences what you say to yourself and how you talk with friends, lovers, and family in everyday conversation. It influences how you interact in groups and how much importance you place on the group versus the individual. It influences the topics you talk about and the strategies you use in communicating information or in persuading.

Cultural differences exist across the communication spectrum—from the way you use eye contact to the way you develop or dissolve a relationship (Chang & Holt, 1996). But these differences should not blind you to the great number of similarities among even the most widely separated cultures. Close interpersonal relationships, for example, are common in all cultures, although they may be entered into for very different reasons by members of different cultures. Further, when reading about cultural differences, remember that they are usually matters of degree. For example, most cultures value honesty, but not all value it to the same extent. The advances in media and technology and the widespread use of the Internet, among other factors, are influencing cultures and cultural change and are perhaps homogenizing cultures, lessening intercultural differences, and increasing similarities. They're also Americanizing various cultures—because the dominant values and customs evidenced in the media and on the Internet are in large part American.

This book's emphasis on cultural understanding does not imply that you should accept all cultural practices or that all cultural practices must be evaluated as equally good (Hatfield & Rapson, 1996). For example, cockfighting, foxhunting, and bullfighting are parts of the cultures of some Latin American countries, England, and Spain, respectively; but you need not find these activities acceptable or equal to cultural practices in which animals are treated kindly. Similarly, you can reject your own culture's values and beliefs; its religion or political system; or its attitudes toward the homeless, the disabled, or the culturally different. Of course, going against your culture's traditions and values is often very difficult. Still, it's important to realize that culture *influences* but does not *determine* your values or behavior. Often, for example, personality factors (your degree of assertiveness, extroversion, or optimism, e.g.) will prove more influential than culture (Hatfield & Rapson, 1996).

ETHNIC IDENTITY AND ETHNOCENTRISM

As you learn your culture's ways, you develop an **ethnic identity,** a commitment to the beliefs and philosophy of your culture (Chung & Ting-Toomey, 1999). The degree to which you identify with your cultural group can be measured by your responses to measures such as the list below (from Ting-Toomey, 1981). Using a five-point scale from 1 = strongly disagree to 5 = strongly agree, indicate how true the following statements are about you:

_____ I am increasing my involvement in activities with my ethnic group.

_____ I involve myself in causes that will help members of my ethnic group.

_____ It feels natural being part of my ethnic group.

_____ I have spent time trying to find out more about my own ethnic group.

_____ I am happy to be a member of my ethnic group.

_____ I have a strong sense of belonging to my ethnic group.

_____ I often talk to other members of my group to learn more about my ethnic culture.

Skill Development Experience

Exploring Cultural Attitudes

One of the best ways to appreciate the influence of culture on communication is to consider people's attitudes. In groups of five or six—try for as culturally diverse a group as possible—discuss how you think most of the students at your school feel (not how you feel) about each of the following. Use a five-point scale where **5** = most students strongly agree; **4** = most students agree; **3** = students are relatively neutral; **2** = most students disagree; **1** = most students strongly disagree.

_____ 1. Most feminists are just too sensitive about sexism.

_____ 2. Courses on sexism should be required in our schools.

_____ 3. Gay rights means gay men and lesbians demanding special privileges.

_____ 4. Homosexuals have made many contributions to their societies.

_____ 5. Racism isn't going to end overnight so minorities need to be patient.

_____ 6. White people benefit from racism whether they want to or not.

Source: These statements were taken from the Human Relations Attitude Inventory (Koppelman, 2005). The author notes that this inventory is based on one developed by Flavio Vega.

Understanding the cultural attitudes of yourself and others is prerequisite to effective intercultural communication.

High scores (say, 5s and 4s) indicate a strong commitment to your culture's values and beliefs; low numbers (1s and 2s) indicate a relatively weak commitment.

A different type of cultural identification is ethnocentrism. Before reading about this important concept, examine your own cultural thinking by taking the self-test below.

Communication Choice Point
Correcting Yourself

Without thinking you make some culturally insensitive remarks and immediately notice lots of nonverbal negative feedback. You want to explain that you're really not the kind of person who normally talks this way. *What options do you have for minimizing the negative effects of your remarks? What specifically would you say?*

Test Yourself

How Ethnocentric Are You?

Here are 18 statements representing your beliefs about your culture. For each statement indicate how much you agree or disagree, using the following scale: strongly agree = **5**; agree = **4**; neither agree nor disagree = **3**; disagree = **2**; and strongly disagree = **1**.

_____ **1** Most cultures are backward compared to my culture.

_____ **2** My culture should be the role model for other cultures.

_____ **3** Lifestyles in other cultures are just as valid as those in my culture.

_____ **4** Other cultures should try to be like my culture.

_____ **5** I'm not interested in the values and customs of other cultures.

_____ **6** People in my culture could learn a lot from people in other cultures.

_____ **7** Most people from other cultures just don't know what's good for them.

_____ **8** I have little respect for the values and customs of other cultures.

_____ **9** Most people would be happier if they lived like people in my culture.

_____ **10** People in my culture have just about the best lifestyles anywhere.

_____ **11** Lifestyles in other cultures are not as valid as those in my culture.

_____ **12** I'm very interested in the values and customs of other cultures.

_____ **13** I respect the values and customs of other cultures.

_____ ⑭ I do not cooperate with people who are different.

_____ ⑮ I do not trust people who are different.

_____ ⑯ I dislike interacting with people from different cultures.

_____ ⑰ Other cultures are smart to look up to my culture.

_____ ⑱ People from other cultures act strange and unusual when they come into my culture.

HOW DID YOU DO? This test gave you the opportunity to examine some of your own cultural beliefs—particularly those cultural beliefs that contribute to ethnocentrism. The person low in ethnocentrism would have high scores (4s and 5s) for items 3, 6, 12, and 13 and low scores (1s and 2s) for all the others. The person high in ethnocentrism would have low scores for items 3, 6, 12, and 13 and high scores for all the others.

WHAT WILL YOU DO? Use this test to bring your own cultural beliefs to consciousness so you can examine them logically and objectively. Ask yourself if your beliefs are productive and will help you achieve your professional and social goals, or if they're counterproductive and will actually hinder your achieving your goals.

Source: This test is taken from Wrench, McCroskey, & Richmond (2008, pp. 394–395) and was originally published in Neuliep, Chaudoir, & McCroskey (2001).

As you've probably gathered from taking this test, **ethnocentrism** is the tendency to see others and their behaviors through your own cultural filters, often as distortions of your own behaviors. It's the tendency to evaluate the values, beliefs, and behaviors of your own culture as superior and as more positive, logical, and natural than those of other cultures. Although ethnocentrism may give you pride in your own culture and its achievements

---

TABLE 1.2	**The Ethnocentrism Continuum**

This table summarizes some of the interconnections between ethnocentrism and communication. Five degrees of ethnocentrism are identified; in reality, there are as many degrees as there are people. The "communication distances" are general terms that highlight the attitude which dominates that level of ethnocentrism. Under "communications" are some of the major ways people might interact given their particular degree of ethnocentrism. Can you identify your own ethnocentrism in this table? For example, are there groups to which you have low ethnocentrism? Middle? High? What accounts for these differences? This table draws on the work of several intercultural researchers (Lukens, 1978; Gudykunst & Kim, 1992; Gudykunst, 1991).

Degree of Ethnocentrism	Communication Distance	Communications
Low ↑	Equality	You treat others as equals; you view different customs and ways of behaving as equal to your own.
	Sensitivity	You want to decrease the distance between yourself and others.
	Indifference	You lack concern for others; you prefer to interact in a world of similar others.
	Avoidance	You avoid and limit interactions, especially intimate communication with interculturally different others.
High ↓	Disparagement	You engage in hostile behavior and belittle others; you view different cultures and ways of behaving as inferior to your own.

and encourage you to sacrifice for the culture, it also may lead you to see other cultures as inferior and may make you unwilling to profit from the contributions of other cultures. For example, recent research shows a "substantial relationship" between ethnocentrism and homophobia (Wrench & McCroskey, 2003).

Ethnocentrism exists on a continuum (Table 1.2). People are not either ethnocentric or nonethnocentric; most are somewhere between these polar opposites. And, of course, your degree of ethnocentrism often varies depending on the group on which you focus. For example, if you're Greek American, you may have a low degree of ethnocentrism when dealing with Italian Americans but a high degree when dealing with Turkish Americans or Japanese Americans. Your degree of ethnocentrism will influence your communication in all its forms, as we'll see throughout this text.

 # Summary of Concepts and Skills

This chapter considered the nature of human communication, its major elements and principles, communication competence, and the role of culture in human communication.

1. Communication is the act, by one or more persons, of sending and receiving messages that are distorted by noise, occur within a context, have some effect (and some ethical dimension), and provide some opportunity for feedback.
2. Communication is transactional. It is a process of interrelated parts in which a change in one element produces changes in other elements.
3. The essentials of communication—the elements present in every communication act—are sources–receivers; messages (feedforward, feedback, and metamessages); context (physical, cultural, social–psychological, and temporal); channel; noise (physical, physiological, psychological, and semantic); and effects.
4. Communication competence refers to your knowledge of how communication works and your ability to use communication effectively.
5. Communication is purposeful. Through communication, you learn, relate, help, influence, and play.
6. Communication is a process of adjustment in which each person must adjust his or her signals to the understanding of the other if meaning is to be transmitted.
7. Communication and relationships are always—in part— ambiguous.
8. Communication involves both content and relationship dimensions.
9. Communication and relationships invariably involve issues of power.
10. Communication sequences are punctuated for processing. Individuals divide the communication sequence into stimuli and responses in different ways.
11. In any interactional situation, communication is inevitable (you cannot not communicate, nor can you not respond to communication), irreversible (you cannot take back messages), and unrepeatable (you cannot exactly repeat messages).

12. Culture permeates all forms of communication, and intercultural communication is becoming more and more frequent as the United States becomes home to a variety of cultures and does business around the world.
13. Significant dimensions along which cultures may differ are uncertainty avoidance, masculinity–femininity, power distance, individualism–collectivism, and high and low context.
14. Ethnocentrism, existing on a continuum, is the tendency to evaluate the beliefs, attitudes, and values of our own culture positively and those of other cultures negatively.

Several important communication skills emphasized in this chapter are presented here in summary form (as they are in every chapter). These skill checklists don't include all the skills covered in the chapter but rather are representative of the most important skills. Place a check mark next to those skills that you feel you need to work on most.

_____ 1. I'm sensitive to contexts of communication. I recognize that changes in physical, cultural, social–psychological, and temporal contexts will alter meaning.

_____ 2. I assess my channel options and evaluate whether my message will be more effective if delivered face-to-face, through e-mail, or by some third party, for example.

_____ 3. I look for meaning not only in words, but also in nonverbal behaviors.

_____ 4. I am sensitive to the feedback and feedforward that I give to others and that others give to me.

_____ 5. I combat the effects of the various types of physical, psychological, and semantic noise that distort messages.

_____ 6. I listen not only to the more obvious content messages but also to the relational messages that I (and others) send, and I respond to the relational messages of others to increase meaningful interaction.

_____ 7. Instead of looking only at the punctuation patterns, I also look at the patterns that others might be using in order to understand better the meanings communicated.

_____ 8. Because communication is transactional, I recognize that all elements influence every other element in the communication process and that each person communicating is simultaneously a speaker/listener.

_____ 9. Because communication is purposeful, I look carefully at both the speaker's and the listener's purposes.

_____ 10. Because communication is inevitable, irreversible, and unrepeatable, I look carefully for hidden meanings, am cautious in communicating messages that I may later wish to withdraw, and am aware that any communication act occurs but once.

_____ 11. I am sensitive to cultural variation and differences, and I see my own culture's teachings and those of other cultures without undue bias.

 # Key Word Quiz

The Essentials of Human Communication

Match the terms about human communication with their definitions. Record the number of the definition next to the appropriate term.

_____ a. intrapersonal communication (2)

_____ b. metamessages (7)

_____ c. encoding (6)

_____ d. communication competence (10)

_____ e. computer-mediated communication (17)

_____ f. feedback (7)

_____ g. power (11)

_____ h. transactional view of communication (5)

_____ i. ethnocentrism (22)

_____ j. ethnic identity (20)

1. Communication between two or more people through some electronic means
2. Knowledge of communication and the ability to apply that knowledge for effective communication
3. The view of communication that sees each person as taking both speaker and listener roles simultaneously
4. Communication with yourself
5. Commitment to the beliefs and values of your culture
6. The process of putting ideas into a code; for example, thinking of an idea and then describing it in words
7. The tendency to see others and their behaviors through your own cultural filters
8. The messages you get back from your own messages and from the responses of others to what you communicate
9. Messages that refer to other messages
10. The ability to influence the behaviors of others

These ten terms and additional terms used in this chapter can be found in the glossary and on flashcards on MyCommunicationLab (**www.mycommunicationlab.com**).

Answers: a. 4; b. 9; c. 6; d. 2; e. 1; f. 8; g. 10; h. 3; i. 7; j. 5

MyCommunicationLab

Visit MyCommunicationLab (**www.mycommunicationlab.com**) for a wealth of additional information on the essentials of human communication. Flash cards, videos, skill building exercises, sample test questions, and additional examples and discussions will help you continue your study of human communication.

2 The Self and Perception

Why read this chapter?

Because you'll learn about:

- self-concept, self-awareness, and self-esteem
- the process of self-disclosure
- the nature and workings of perception
- impression formation and impression management

Because you'll learn to:

- communicate with a better understanding of who you are
- regulate self-disclosures and respond appropriately to the disclosures of others
- increase your own accuracy in perceiving other people and their messages
- manage the impressions you communicate to others

This chapter looks at the self—perhaps the most important element in any form of communication—and especially at the ways in which you and others perceive yourself. With this as a background, we will examine the ways in which we perceive others and the ways they perceive us.

The Self in Human Communication

Who you are and how you see yourself influence not only the way you communicate but also how you respond to the communications of others. This first section explores the self: the self-concept and how it develops; self-awareness and ways to increase it; self-esteem and ways to enhance it; and self-disclosure, or communication that reveals who you are.

SELF-CONCEPT

Your **self-concept** is your image of who you are. It's how you perceive yourself: your feelings and thoughts about your strengths and weaknesses, your abilities and limitations. Self-concept develops from the image that others have of you, comparisons between yourself and others, your cultural experiences, and your evaluation of your own thoughts and behaviors (Figure 2.1).

Others' Images of You   If you wished to see how your hair looked, you'd probably look in a mirror. But what if you wanted to see how friendly or how assertive you are? According to the concept of the **looking-glass self** (Cooley, 1922), you'd look at the image of yourself that others reveal to you through the way they communicate with you.

Of course, you would not look to just anyone. Rather, you would look to those who are most significant in your life, such as your friends, family members, and romantic partners. If these significant persons think highly of you, you will see a positive self-image reflected in their behaviors; if they think little of you, you will see a more negative image.

Comparisons with Others   Another way you develop self-concept is by comparing yourself with others, most often with your peers (Festinger, 1954). For example, after an exam, you probably want to know how you performed relative to the other students in your class. This gives you a clearer idea of how effectively you performed. If you play on a baseball team, it's important to know your batting average in comparison to those of your teammates. You gain a different perspective when you see yourself in comparison to your peers.

Cultural Teachings   Your culture instills in you a variety of beliefs, values, and attitudes about such things as success (how you define it and how you should achieve it); the relevance of religion, race, or nationality; and the ethical principles you should follow in business and in your personal life. These teachings provide benchmarks against which you can measure yourself. Your ability, for example, to achieve what your culture defines as success contributes to a positive self-concept; your failure to achieve what your culture values contributes to a negative self-concept.

Especially important in self-concept are cultural teachings about gender roles—how a man or woman should act. A popular classification of cultures is in

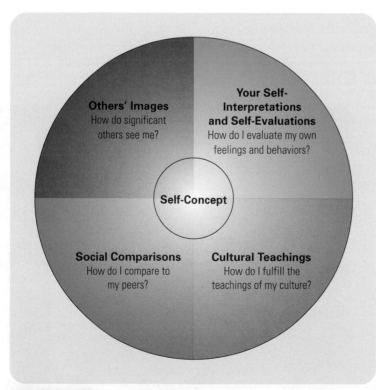

FIGURE 2.1   The Sources of Self-Concept

The four contributors to how you see yourself. As you read about self-concept, consider the influence of each factor throughout your life. Which factor influenced you most as a preteen? Which influences you most now? Which will influence you most in 25 or 30 years?

terms of their masculinity and femininity (Hofstede, 1997). [Some intercultural theorists note that equivalent terms would be cultures based on "achievement" and "nurturance," but because ressearch is conducted under the terms *masculine* and *feminine* and these are the terms you'd use to search electronic databases, we use them here (Lustig & Koester, 2006).] Masculine cultures socialize people to be assertive, ambitious, and competitive. For example, members of masculine cultures are more likely to confront conflicts directly and to fight out any differences; they're more likely to emphasize win–lose conflict strategies. Feminine cultures socialize people to be modest and to value close interpersonal relationships. They, for example, are more likely to emphasize compromise and negotiation in resolving conflicts, win–win solutions.

When you display the traits prized by your culture—whether they be masculine or feminine—you're likely to be rewarded and complimented, and this feedback contributes to a positive self-concept. Displaying contrary traits is likely to result in criticism, which, in turn, will contribute to a more negative self-concept.

Self-Interpretations and Self-Evaluations

Your self-interpretations (your reconstruction of your behavior in a given event and your understanding of it) and self-evaluations (the value—good or bad—that you place on that behavior) also contribute to your self-concept. For example, let's say you believe that lying is wrong. If you then lie and view what you said as a lie (rather than as, say, a polite way of avoiding an issue), you will probably evaluate this behavior in terms of your internalized beliefs about lying and will react negatively to your own behavior. You may, for example, experience guilt about violating your own beliefs. On the other hand, let's say that you pull someone out of a burning building at great personal risk. You will probably evaluate this behavior positively; you'll feel good about your behavior and, as a result, about yourself.

SELF-AWARENESS

Self-awareness is basic to all communication and is achieved when you examine several aspects of yourself as they might appear to others as well as to you. One commonly used tool for this examination is the Johari window, a metaphoric division of the self into four areas (Figure 2.2).

Your Four Selves Divided into four areas or "panes," the Johari window shows different aspects or versions of the self. The four versions are the open self, blind self, hidden self, and unknown self. These areas are not separate from one another but interdependent. As one dominates, the others recede to a greater or lesser degree; or, to stay with our metaphor, as one windowpane becomes larger, one or more others become smaller.

- The *open self* represents all the information, behaviors, attitudes, and feelings about yourself that you, and also others, know. This could include your name, skin color, sex, age, religion, and political beliefs. The size of the open self varies according to your personality and the people to whom you're relating. You may be more open with some people than you are with others. For example, you may have a large open self about your romantic life with your friends (you tell them everything) but a very small open self about the same issues with, say, your parents.

- The *blind self* represents knowledge about you that others have but you don't. This might include your habit of finishing other people's sentences or your

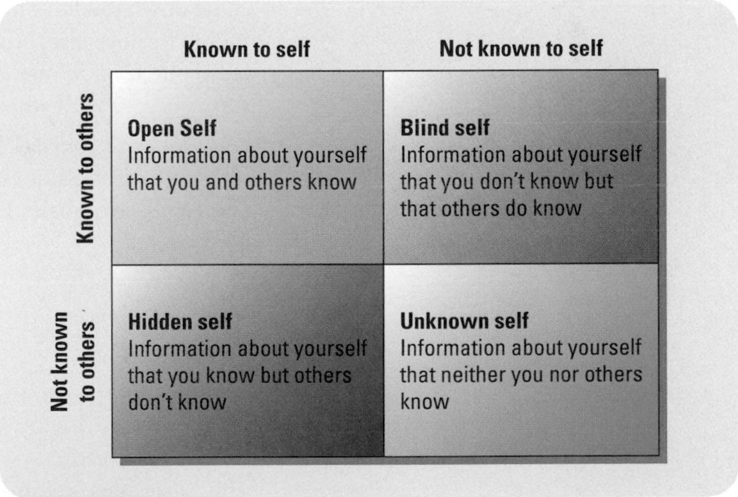

	Known to self	**Not known to self**
Known to others	**Open Self** Information about yourself that you and others know	**Blind self** Information about yourself that you don't know but that others do know
Not known to others	**Hidden self** Information about yourself that you know but others don't know	**Unknown self** Information about yourself that neither you nor others know

FIGURE 2.2 **The Johari Window**

A commonly used tool for examining what we know and don't know about ourselves. It can also help explain the nature of self-disclosure, covered later in this chapter. The window gets its name from its originators, *Joseph* Luft and *Harry* Ingham.

Source: Joseph Luft, *Group Process: An Introduction to Group Dynamics*, 3rd ed. Copyright © 1984. New York: McGraw-Hill. Reprinted by permission.

Communication Choice Point

Increasing Self-Awareness

You've asked several different people at school for a date, but so far all you've received are rejections. Something's wrong; you're not that bad. *What are some things you can do to increase your self-awareness of your dating techniques? To whom would you be most likely to speak? What would you say?*

way of rubbing your nose when you become anxious. A large blind self indicates low self-awareness and interferes with accurate communication. It's important to reduce your blind self and learn what others know about you. You can do this by following the suggestions offered below, in "Growing in Self-Awareness."

- The *unknown self* represents those parts of yourself that neither you nor others know. This is information buried in your subconscious. You may, for example, learn of your obsession with money, your fear of criticism, or the kind of lover you are through hypnosis, dreams, psychological tests, or psychotherapy.

- The *hidden self* represents all the knowledge you have of yourself but keep secret from others. This windowpane includes all your successfully kept secrets, such as your fantasies, embarrassing experiences, and any attitudes or beliefs of which you may be ashamed. You probably keep secrets from some people and not from others; for example, you might not tell your parents you're dating someone of another race or religion, but you may reveal this to a close friend.

Growing in Self-Awareness Because self-awareness is so important in communication, try to increase awareness of your own needs, desires, habits, beliefs, and attitudes. You can do this in various ways.

- *Listen to others.* Conveniently, others are constantly giving you the very feedback you need to increase self-awareness. In every interaction, people comment on you in some way—on what you do, what you say, how you look. Sometimes these comments are explicit: "Loosen up" or "Don't take things so hard." Often they're "hidden" in the way others look at you or in what they talk about. Pay close attention to this kind of information.

- *Increase your open self.* Revealing yourself to others will help increase your self-awareness. As you talk about yourself, you may see connections that you had previously missed. With feedback from others, you may gain still more insight. Also, by increasing your open self, you increase the chances that others will reveal what they know about you.

- *Seek information about yourself.* Encourage people to reveal what they know about you. Use situations that arise every day to gain self-information: "Do you think I came down too hard on the kids today?" "Do you think I was assertive enough when asking for the raise?" But seek this self-awareness in moderation. If you do it too often, your friends may soon perceive you as insecure or self-centered and look for someone else with whom to talk.

- *Dialogue with yourself.* No one knows you better than you know yourself. Ask yourself self-awareness questions: What motivates me to act as I do? What are my short- and long-term goals? How do I plan to achieve them? What are my strengths and weaknesses?

SELF-ESTEEM

Self-esteem is a measure of how valuable you think you are. People with high self-esteem think very highly of themselves, whereas people with low self-esteem view themselves negatively.

The basic idea behind self-esteem is that when you feel good about yourself—about who you are and what you're capable of doing—you will perform better. When you get up to give a speech and you visualize yourself as successful and effective, you're more likely to give a good speech. If, on the other hand, you think you're going to forget your speech, mispronounce words, or mix up your presentation aids, you are less likely to be successful. Increasing self-esteem will, therefore, help you to function more effectively in school, in interpersonal relationships, and in careers. Here are five suggestions for increasing self-esteem.

Listening to Self-Destructive Beliefs

Here are four beliefs that when taken to extremes are unrealistic and ultimately self-destructive. (Butler, 1981; Ellis, 1988; Beck, 1988):

● Perfect: Do you hear yourself telling you to perform at unrealistically high levels at work, school, and home, acting as if anything short of perfection is unacceptable?

● Strong: Do you believe that weakness and any of the more vulnerable emotions such as sadness, compassion, or loneliness are wrong?

● Pleasing: Do you constantly seek approval from others and assume that only if you gain it, will you be a worthy and deserving person?

● Fast and complete. Do you do things quickly and try to take on more responsibilities than any one person might be expected to handle?

The thing that is really hard, and really amazing, is giving up on being perfect and beginning the work of becoming yourself.
—ANNA QUINDLEN (1953–), U.S. author and journalist

Do recognize that it's the extreme form of these beliefs that creates problems. Certainly, trying hard and being strong are not unhealthy when they're realistic. It's only when they become absolute—when you try to be everything to everyone—that they become impossible to achieve and create problems.

Listening to these self-destructive beliefs is a first step toward eliminating them. A second step involves recognizing that these beliefs are unrealistic and self-defeating and replacing them with more realistic ones. Following psychotherapist Albert Ellis (Ellis & Dryden, 2007), for example, you might try replacing the unrealistic desire to please everyone in everything you do with a more realistic attitude: *Although it would be nice if I pleased others, it certainly isn't essential.*

Attack Self-Destructive Beliefs   Challenge any beliefs you have about yourself that are unproductive or that make it more difficult for you to achieve your goals—for example, the belief that you have to succeed in everything you do, the belief that you have to be loved by everyone, the belief that you must be strong at all times, and/or the belief that you must please others (Butler, 1981; Einhorn, 2006). Replace these self-destructive beliefs with more productive ideas, such as "It would be nice to be loved by everyone, but it isn't necessary to my happiness."

Seek Out Nourishing People   Psychologist Carl Rogers (1970) drew a distinction between *noxious* and *nourishing* people. Noxious people criticize and find fault with just about everything. Nourishing people, on the other hand, are positive and optimistic, and make us feel good about ourselves. To enhance your self-esteem, seek out nourishing people and avoid noxious people. At the same time, seek to become more nourishing yourself so that you can build others' self-esteem while improving your own.

Work on Projects That Will Result in Success   Some people want to fail, or so it seems. Often they select projects that will result in failure simply because they are impossible to complete. Avoid this trap and choose projects that will result in success. Each success will help build self-esteem and make the next success a little easier. If a project does fail, recognize that this does not mean you're a failure. Everyone fails somewhere along the line. Failure is something that happens to you; it's not something you've created, and it's not something inside you. Further, your failing once does not mean that you will fail the next time. Remember to keep failure in perspective.

Remind Yourself of Your Successes   Some people have a tendency to focus, sometimes too much, on their failures, their missed opportunities, their social mistakes. If your objective is to correct what you did wrong or to identify the skills that you need to correct these failures, then focusing on failures can have some positive value. But if you merely focus on failure without any plans for correction, then you're likely to

"Let others confide in you. It may not help you, but it will surely help them."
—ROGER G. IMHOFF

make life more difficult for yourself and to limit your self-esteem. To counteract the tendency to recall failures, remind yourself of your successes. Recall these successes both intellectually and emotionally. Realize why they were successes, and relive the emotional experience when you sank the winning basket or helped your friend overcome personal problems. And while you're at it, recall your positive qualities. For a start, read down the list of the essential interpersonal skills on the inside covers of this book and check off those you'd consider among your assets. To this list add any other qualities you number among your positive attributes.

Secure Affirmation   It's frequently recommended that you remind yourself of your successes with affirmations—that you focus on your good deeds; on your positive qualities, strengths, and virtues; and on your productive and meaningful relationships with friends, loved ones, and relatives (Aronson, Cohen, & Nail, 1998; Aronson, Wilson, & Akert, 2007).

The idea behind this advice is that the way you talk to yourself will influence what you think of yourself. If you *affirm* yourself—if you tell yourself that you're a success, that others like you, that you will succeed on the next test, and that you will be welcomed when asking for a date—you will soon come to feel more positive about yourself. Self-affirmations include statements like: "I'm a worthy person," "I'm responsible and can be depended upon," "I'm capable of loving and being loved," and "I can accept my past but also let it go."

Some researchers argue, however, that such affirmations—although extremely popular in self-help books—may not be very helpful. These critics contend that if you have low self-esteem, you're not going to believe your self-affirmations, because you don't have a high opinion of yourself to begin with (Paul, 2001). They propose that the alternative to self-affirmation is affirmation secured from others. You'd obtain this, for example, by becoming more competent in communication and interacting with more positive people. In this way you'd get more positive feedback from others—which, these researchers argue, is more helpful than self-talk in raising self-esteem.

Seeing a connection, a relationship, with people similar to yourself also seems to increase self-esteem. For example, deaf people who identified with the larger deaf community had greater self-esteem than those who didn't so identify (Jambor & Elliott, 2005). Similarly, identification with a cultural group also seems to encourage positive self-esteem (McDonald, McCabe, Yeh, Lau, Garland, & Hough, 2005).

Self-Disclosure

Self-disclosure is a type of communication in which you reveal information about yourself (Jourard, 1968, 1971a, 1971b). You can look at self-disclosure as taking information from the hidden self and moving it to the open self. Overt statements about the self (e.g., "I'm getting fat"), slips of the tongue (e.g., using the name of your ex instead of your present lover's name), unconscious nonverbal movements (e.g., self-touching movements or eye avoidance), and public confessions (e.g., "Well, Jerry, it's like this . . ."), all can be considered forms of self-disclosure. A new and popular variation on self-disclosure is Twitter; when you send a tweet responding to the question, "What are you doing?" you're disclosing something about yourself, most often something you'd readily reveal to others. Usually, however, the term *self-disclosure* refers to the conscious revealing of information that you don't reveal to everyone, as in the statements "I'm afraid to compete; I guess I'm afraid I'll lose" or "I love you."

Self-disclosure is "information"—something previously unknown by the receiver. This information may vary from the relatively commonplace ("I'm really afraid of that French exam") to the extremely significant ("I'm depressed; I feel like committing suicide"). For self-disclosure to occur, the communication must involve at least two people. You cannot self-disclose to yourself—the information must be received and understood by at least one individual.

Communication Choice Point

Self-Esteem

Your best friend has hit a new low in self-esteem—a long-term relationship failed, an expected promotion never materialized, a large investment went sour. You want to help your friend regain self-esteem. *What are your options? What's the first thing you would do or say?*

An interesting variation on self-disclosure occurs when someone else takes information from your hidden self and makes it public. Although third-party disclosure can concern any aspect of a person's hidden self—for example, an athlete's prison record or drug habit, a movie star's alcoholism, or a politician's financial dealings—the media have made a special case out of revealing a person's affectional orientation; the process is called *outing* (Gross, 1991; Signorile, 1993; Johansson & Percy, 1994). Those against outing argue that people have a right to privacy and no one else should take that right from them. Because outing can have severe consequences—for example, loss of job, expulsion from the military, or social and physical harassment—no one but the individual him- or herself has the right to reveal such information. Those in favor of outing argue that it's an expedient political and social weapon to silence those gay men and lesbians who—perhaps in an effort to keep their own affectional orientation secret—support or refuse to protest homophobic policies.

The following self-test focuses on the influences of self-disclosure to be discussed next and will help you to personalize the discussion to follow.

Test Yourself

How Willing to Self-Disclose Are You?

Respond to each of the following statements by indicating the likelihood that you would disclose such items of information to, say, other members of this class in a one-on-one *interpersonal* situation, in a public speaking situation, and in online communication (for instance, an e-mail or blog). Use the following scale to fill in all three columns: 1 = would definitely self-disclose; 2 = would probably self-disclose; 3 = don't know; 4 = would probably not self-disclose; and 5 = would definitely not self-disclose.

Information	Interpersonal Communication	Public Communication	Online Communication
1 My attitudes toward other religions, nationalities, and races	_____	_____	_____
2 My financial status: how much money I earn, how much I owe, how much I have saved	_____	_____	_____
3 My feelings about my parents	_____	_____	_____
4 My sexual fantasies	_____	_____	_____
5 My physical and mental health	_____	_____	_____
6 My ideal romantic partner	_____	_____	_____
7 My drinking and/or drug behavior	_____	_____	_____
8 My most embarrassing moment	_____	_____	_____
9 My unfulfilled desires	_____	_____	_____
10 My self-concept	_____	_____	_____

HOW DID YOU DO? There are, of course, no right or wrong answers to this self-test. The higher your scores, the more apt to disclose you are in this channel. Generally, people will self-disclose most in interpersonal communication situations, least in public communication situations, and somewhere in between in online communication.

WHAT WILL YOU DO? Taking this test, and ideally discussing it with others who also complete it, should get you started thinking about your own self-disclosing behavior and especially the factors that influence it. How does your personality influence your self-disclosure behavior? Are there certain topics on which you are less willing to disclose than others? Are you more likely to disclose positive secrets than negative ones? Are there topics about which you wish you had the opportunity to self-disclose but somehow can't find the right situation?

FACTORS INFLUENCING SELF-DISCLOSURE

Many factors influence whether or not you disclose, what you disclose, and to whom you disclose. Among the most important factors are who you are, your culture, your gender, who your listeners are, and your topic and channel.

Who You Are Highly sociable and extroverted people self-disclose more than those who are less sociable and more introverted. People who are comfortable communicating also self-disclose more than those who are apprehensive about talking in general. Competent people engage in self-disclosure more than less competent people. Perhaps competent people have greater self-confidence and more positive things to reveal. Similarly, their self-confidence may make them more willing to risk possible negative reactions (McCroskey & Wheeless, 1976).

Your Culture Different cultures view self-disclosure differently. Some cultures (especially those high in masculinity) view disclosing inner feelings as weakness. Among some groups, for example, it would be considered "out of place" for a man to cry at a happy occasion such as a wedding, whereas in some Latin cultures that same display of emotion would go unnoticed. Similarly, it's considered undesirable in Japan for workplace colleagues to reveal personal information, whereas in much of the United States it's expected (Barnlund, 1989; Hall & Hall, 1987). Indians are reluctant to self-disclose for fear that what they say will reflect negatively on their reputation and family (Hastings, 2000). And in a study of Muslim, Druze, and Jewish adolescents in Israel, Muslim students disclosed most and Druze students least (Shechtman, Hiradin, & Zina, 2003).

There is some indication that the political climate at a given time will influence the cross-cultural self-disclosure patterns of all people. Significant self-disclosures between Christian Americans and Muslim Americans, for example, are likely to be more guarded than before September 11, 2001, and the Iraq War, as are self-disclosures between recent immigrants and other Americans (Barry, 2003).

Important similarities also exist across cultures. For example, people from Great Britain, Germany, the United States, and Puerto Rico are all more apt to disclose personal information—hobbies, interests, attitudes, and opinions on politics and religion—than information on finances, sex, personality, or interpersonal relationships (Jourard, 1971a). Similarly, one study showed self-disclosure patterns between American males to be virtually identical to those between Korean males (Won-Doornink, 1991).

Your Gender The popular stereotype of gender differences in self-disclosure emphasizes males' reluctance to speak about themselves. For the most part, research supports this view; women do disclose more than men (Helgeson, 2009). There are exceptions, however. For example, men and women make negative disclosures about equally (Naifeh & Smith, 1984), and boys are more likely than girls to disclose family information on the Internet (www.CNN.com, accessed May 17, 2000). Another notable exception occurs in initial encounters. Here, men will disclose more intimate information than women, perhaps "in order to control the relationship's development" (Derlega,

Winstead, Wong, & Hunter, 1985). Still another exception may be found in a study of Americans and Argentineans; here males indicated a significantly greater willingness to self-disclose than females (Horenstein & Downey, 2003).

Women disclose more than men about their previous romantic relationships, their feelings for close same-sex friends, their greatest fears, and what they don't like about their partners (Sprecher, 1987). Women also increase the depth of their disclosures as a relationship becomes more intimate, whereas men seem not to change their self-disclosure levels. In addition, for women, there are fewer taboo topics (Goodwin & Lee, 1994). Finally, women self-disclose more to members of their extended families than men (Komarovsky, 1964; Argyle & Henderson, 1985; Moghaddam, Taylor, & Wright, 1993).

Your Listeners Self-disclosure occurs more readily in small groups than in large groups. **Dyads**, or groups of two people, are the most hospitable setting for self-disclosure. With one listener you can monitor your disclosures, continuing if there's support from your listener and stopping if not. With more than one listener, such monitoring becomes difficult, because the listeners' responses are sure to vary.

Research shows that you disclose most to people you like (Derlega, Winstead, Wong, & Greenspan, 1987) and to people you trust (Wheeless & Grotz, 1977). You also come to like those to whom you disclose (Berg & Archer, 1983). At times, self-disclosure occurs more in temporary than in permanent relationships—for example, between strangers on a train or plane, in a kind of "in-flight intimacy" (McGill, 1985). In this situation two people establish an intimate, self-disclosing relationship during a brief period of travel, but they don't pursue the connection beyond that point.

You are more likely to disclose when the person you are with discloses. This **dyadic effect** (what one person does, the other person also does) probably leads you to feel more secure and reinforces your own self-disclosing behavior. Disclosures are also more intimate when they're made in response to the disclosures of others (Berg & Archer, 1983). This dyadic effect, however, is not universal across all cultures. For example, although Americans are likely to follow the dyadic effect and reciprocate with explicit, verbal self-disclosure, Koreans aren't (Won-Doornink, 1985). As you can appreciate, this easily results in intercultural differences; for example, an American may be insulted if his or her Korean counterpart doesn't reciprocate with self-disclosures that are similar in depth.

Your Topic and Channel You also are more likely to disclose about some topics than others. For example, you're more likely to self-disclose information about your job or hobbies than about your sex life or financial situation (Jourard, 1968, 1971a). Further, you're more likely to disclose favorable rather than unfavorable information. Generally, the more personal and negative the topic, the less likely you are to self-disclose.

In recent years research has addressed differences in self-disclosure depending on the channel—on whether communication is face-to-face or computer-mediated. Some researchers have pointed to a *disinhibition effect* that occurs in online communication; people seem less inhibited communicating by e-mail or in chat groups, for example, than in face-to-face situations. One reason may be that in online communication there is a certain degree of anonymity and invisibility (Suler, 2004). Research also finds that reciprocal self-disclosure occurs more quickly and at higher levels of intimacy online than it does in face-to-face interactions (Levine, 2000; Joinson, 2001).

THE REWARDS AND DANGERS OF SELF-DISCLOSURE

Self-disclosure often brings rewards, but it can also create problems. Whether or not you self-disclose will depend on your assessment of the possible rewards and dangers.

Self-Disclosure Rewards Among the rewards of self-disclosure are:

- *Self-knowledge.* Self-disclosure helps you gain a new perspective on yourself and a deeper understanding of your own behavior. As you talk about yourself and listen to the reactions of others, you're likely to learn a great deal about yourself.

"In order to have a conversation with someone, you must reveal yourself."

—JAMES BALDWIN

- *Improved coping abilities.* Self-disclosure helps you deal with problems, especially guilt. Because you feel that past mistakes, for example, are a basis for rejection, you may develop guilt. By self-disclosing negative feelings and receiving support rather than rejection, you may be better able to deal with guilt, perhaps reducing or even eliminating it.

- *Communication enhancement.* Self-disclosure often improves communication. You understand the messages of others largely to the extent that you understand the individuals. You can tell what certain nuances mean, whether a person is serious or joking, and whether the person is being sarcastic out of fear or resentment.

- *More meaningful relationships.* By self-disclosing you tell others that you trust, respect, and care enough about them and your relationship to reveal yourself. This, in turn, leads the other individual to self-disclose and forms at least the start of a relationship that is honest and open and allows for more complete communication. Within a sexual relationship, self-disclosure increases sexual rewards and general relationship satisfaction. These two benefits, in turn, increase sexual satisfaction (Byers & Demmons, 1999).

Self-Disclosure Dangers   Among the dangers of self-disclosure are:

- *Personal risks.* The more you reveal about yourself to others, the more areas of your life you expose to possible attack. Especially in the competitive context of work (or even romance), the more that others know about you, the more they'll be able to use against you.

- *Relationship risks.* Even in close and long-lasting relationships, self-disclosure can cause problems. Parents, normally the most supportive people in most individuals' lives, frequently reject children who self-disclose their homosexuality, their plans to marry someone of a different race, or their belief in another faith. Your best friends—your closest intimates—may reject you for similar self-disclosures.

- *Professional risks.* Sometimes self-disclosure may result in professional or material losses. Politicians who disclose that they have been in therapy may lose the support of their own political party and find that voters are unwilling to vote for them. Teachers who disclose disagreement with school administrators may find themselves being denied tenure, teaching undesirable schedules, and becoming victims of "budget cuts." In the business world self-disclosures of alcoholism or drug addiction often result in dismissal, demotion, or social exclusion.

Remember that self-disclosure, like any other communication, is irreversible (see Chapter 1). You cannot self-disclose and then take it back. Nor can you erase the conclusions and inferences listeners make on the basis of your disclosures. Remember, too, to examine the rewards and dangers of self-disclosure in light of cultural rules. As with all cultural rules, following rules about self-disclosure brings approval, and violating them brings disapproval.

GUIDELINES FOR SELF-DISCLOSURE

Because self-disclosure is so important and so delicate a matter, here are some guidelines for (1) deciding whether and how to self-disclose, (2) responding to the disclosures of others, and (3) resisting the pressure to self-disclose.

Guidelines for Making Self-Disclosures   In addition to weighing the potential rewards and dangers of self-disclosure, consider the following factors. These hints will help you raise the right questions before you make what must be your own decision.

Communication Choice Point

Corrective Self-Disclosure

When you met your current partner—with whom you want to spend the rest of your life—you minimized the extent of your romantic history. You now want to come clean and disclose your "sordid" past and need to preface this in some way. *What kinds of feedforward might you use? Through what channels? What would you say?*

- *Consider the motivation for the self-disclosure.* Self-disclosure should be motivated by a concern for the relationship, for the others involved, and for yourself. Self-disclosure should serve a useful and productive function for all persons involved. Self-disclosing past indiscretions because you want to clear the air and be honest may be worthwhile; disclosing the same indiscretions to hurt your partner, however, is likely to damage the relationship.

- *Consider the appropriateness of the self-disclosure.* Self-disclosure should be appropriate to the context and to the relationship between you and your listener. Before making any significant self-disclosure, ask whether this is the right time (Do you both have the time to discuss this at the length it requires?) and place (Is the place free of distractions? Is it private?). Ask, too, whether this self-disclosure is appropriate to the relationship. Generally, the more intimate the disclosure, the closer the relationship should be. It's probably best to resist making intimate disclosures (especially negative ones) with non-intimates or with casual acquaintances, or in the early stages of a relationship.

- *Consider the disclosures of the other person.* During your disclosures, give the other person a chance to reciprocate with his or her own disclosures. If the other person does not reciprocate, reassess your own self-disclosures. It may be that for this person at this time and in this context, your disclosures are not welcome or appropriate. For example, if you reveal your romantic mistakes to a friend and your friend says nothing or reveals only the most minor details, it may be a cue to stop disclosing. Generally, it's best to disclose gradually and in small increments so you can monitor your listener's responses and retreat if they're not positive enough.

- *Consider the possible burdens self-disclosure might entail.* Carefully weigh the potential problems that you may incur as a result of your disclosure. Can you afford to lose your job if you disclose your prison record? Are you willing to risk relational difficulties if you disclose your infidelities? Are you willing to post on Facebook those images of you partying that a graduate school admissions officer or a prospective employer might see? Also, ask yourself whether you're making unreasonable demands on the listener. For example, consider the person who swears his or her mother-in-law to secrecy and then discloses having an affair with a neighbor. This disclosure places an unfair burden on the mother-in-law, who is now torn between breaking her promise of secrecy and allowing her child to believe a lie.

Guidelines for Facilitating and Responding to Others' Disclosures When someone discloses to you, it's usually a sign of trust and affection. In carrying out this most important receiver function, keep the following guidelines in mind:

- *Support and reinforce the discloser.* Express support for the person during and after the disclosures. Try to refrain from judgment. Concentrate on understanding and empathizing with the discloser. Make your supportiveness clear through your verbal and nonverbal responses: Maintain eye contact, lean toward the speaker, ask relevant questions, and echo the speaker's thoughts and feelings. Men are generally more reluctant to show emotional support, at least to the degree that women do; the reason, according to recent research, is that men don't want their behavior to be regarded as feminine (Burleson, Holmstrom, & Gilstrap, 2005).

- *Be willing to reciprocate.* When you make relevant and appropriate disclosures of your own in response to another's disclosures, you're demonstrating your understanding of that person's meanings and at the same time your willingness to communicate on a meaningful level. If your colleague at work discloses an embarrassing dating situation and you reveal one of your own, you're indicating understanding on a deeper level than you would if you responded only with "That's funny" or "I know what you mean."

- *Keep the disclosures confidential.* When someone discloses to you, it's because the person wants you to know about his or her feelings and thoughts. If you reveal these disclosures to others, negative effects are inevitable. But most important, betraying a

Communication Choice Point

Regulating Self-Disclosure

You're currently engaged to Kerry, but over the past few months you've been seeing someone else and have fallen in love. Now you want to break off your engagement and disclose this new relationship. But you don't want to hurt Kerry. *What are some of your choices? What would you say? Through what channel?*

Communication
Choice Point

**Disclosure
Encouragement**

You're dating a wonderful
person who is, unfortunately, extremely secretive. You wish to encourage greater disclosure
but don't want to seem pushy or nosy. *What
are some of the things you might say to encourage your dating partner to disclose?*

confidence is unfair; it debases what could be and should be a meaningful interpersonal experience. It's interesting to note that one of the netiquette rules of e-mail is
that you shouldn't forward a message to third parties without the writer's permission. Generally, this rule is useful for self-disclosure: Maintain confidentiality; don't
pass on disclosures made to you to others without permission.

- *Don't use the disclosures against the person.* Many self-disclosures expose some kind
  of vulnerability. If you later turn around and use a disclosure against someone, you
  betray the confidence and trust invested in you. Regardless of how angry you may
  get, resist the temptation to use the disclosures of others as weapons. If a friend confides a fear of cats and you later use this to ridicule or tease that person, you're likely
  to create relationship problems.

Guidelines for Resisting Pressure to Self-Disclose   You may, on occasion,
find yourself in a position in which a friend, colleague, or romantic partner pressures
you to self-disclose. In such situations, you may wish to weigh the pros and cons of self-disclosure and make your own decision as to whether and what you'll disclose. If your
decision is not to disclose and you're still being pressured, then you need to say something. **Don't be pushed.** Although there may be specific legal or ethical reasons for disclosing certain information under certain circumstances, generally you don't have to
disclose if you don't want to. Recognize that you're in control of what you reveal and of
when and to whom you reveal it. Self-disclosure has significant consequences. If you're
not sure you want to reveal something, then don't, at least not until you've had additional time to think about it.

Should you decide to not disclose, here are two suggestions:

- *Be indirect and move to another topic.* Avoid the question that asks you to disclose and
  change the subject. If someone presses you to disclose your past financial problems,
  move the conversation to financial problems in general or nationally, or change the
  topic altogether. This is a polite way of saying, "I'm not talking about this," and may
  be the preferred choice in certain situations and with certain people. Most often people will get the hint.

- *Be assertive in your refusal to disclose.* If necessary, say very directly, "I'd rather not
  talk about that now" or "Now is not the time for this type of discussion."

With an understanding of the self in human communication, we can explore perception—the processes by which you come to understand yourself and others and, of
course, the processes by which others come to understand you.

Perception

Communication
Choice Point

Disclosure Pressure

You're dating this wonderful
person who self-discloses easily and fully
and who is now putting pressure on you to
reveal more about yourself. You just aren't
ready. *What are some of the things you can
say to satisfy your partner's need for you to
disclose and your own need to not reveal
more about yourself right now?*

Perception is your way of understanding the world; it helps you make sense of what psychologist William James called the "booming buzzing confusion." More technically, perception is the process by which you become aware of objects, events, and especially
people through your senses of sight, smell, taste, touch, and hearing. Your perceptions
result both from what exists in the outside world *and* from your own experiences, desires, needs and wants, loves and hatreds. Perception is important in communication because it influences your communication choices. The messages you send and listen to will
depend on how you see the world, how you see yourself, how you size up a specific situation, or what you think of the people with whom you interact.

Perception is a continuous series of processes that blend into one another. For
convenience of discussion we can separate these processes into five stages (which may
occur in a split second): (1) You sense or pick up some kind of stimulation; (2) you
organize the stimuli in some way; (3) you interpret and evaluate what you perceive;
(4) you store your perception in memory; and (5) you retrieve it when needed
(Figure 2.3).

STIMULATION (STAGE ONE)

At the first stage of perception, your sense organs are *stimulated*—you hear a new CD, you see a friend, you smell someone's perfume, you taste an orange, you feel another's sweaty palm. Naturally, you don't perceive everything; rather, you engage in **selective perception,** which includes selective attention and selective exposure.

In **selective attention** you attend to those things that you anticipate will fulfill your needs or will prove enjoyable. For instance, when daydreaming in class, you don't hear what the instructor is saying until he or she calls your name. Your selective attention mechanism focuses your senses on the sound of your name.

In **selective exposure** you tend to expose yourself to information that will confirm your existing beliefs, will contribute to your objectives, or will prove satisfying in some way. For example, after you buy a car, you're more apt to read and listen to advertisements for the car you just bought, because these messages tell you that you made the right decision. At the same time, you will tend to avoid advertisements for the cars that you considered but eventually rejected, because these messages would tell you that you made the wrong decision.

You're also more likely to perceive stimuli that are greater in intensity than surrounding stimuli. For example, television commercials normally play at a greater intensity than regular programming to ensure that you take special notice. And you're more likely to perceive stimuli that have novelty value; for example, you're more likely to notice the coworker who dresses in a unique way than the one who dresses like everyone else.

ORGANIZATION (STAGE TWO)

At the second stage of perception, you organize the information your senses pick up. You do so in three ways: (1) by rules, (2) by schemata, and (3) by scripts.

Organization by Rules One frequently used rule is that of **proximity**, or physical closeness. The rule says that things physically close together constitute a unit. Thus, using this rule, you will tend to perceive people who are often together, or messages spoken one right after the other, as units, as belonging together.

Another rule is **similarity**: the idea that things that are physically similar or look alike belong together and form a unit. This principle leads you to see people who dress alike as belonging together. Similarly, you might assume that people who work at the same jobs, who are of the same religion, who live in the same building, or who talk with the same accent belong together.

You use the rule of **contrast** when you conclude that some items (people or messages, e.g.) don't belong together because they're too different from each other to be part of the same unit. So, for example, in a conversation or a public speech, you'll focus your attention on changes in intensity or rate because these contrast with the rest of the message.

Organization by Schemata Another way you organize material is by creating **schemata**, mental templates or structures that help you organize the millions of items of information you come into contact with every day as well as those you already have in memory. Schemata may thus be viewed as general ideas about people (Pat and Chris, Japanese, Baptists, New Yorkers); about yourself (your qualities, abilities, and even liabilities); or about social roles (the attributes of police officers, profes-

FIGURE 2.3   **The Stages of Perception**

Perception occurs in five stages: stimulation, organization, interpretation–evaluation, memory, and recall. An understanding of how perception works will help make your own perceptions (of yourself and of others) more accurate.

Stage One — Stimulation
Stage Two — Organization
Stage Three — Interpretation Evaluation
Stage Four — Memory
Stage Five — Recall

"He didn't actually threaten me, but I perceived him as a threat."

© Lee Lorenz/Condé Nast Publications/www.cartoonbank.com.

sors, or multimillionaires). The word *schemata,* by the way, is the plural of *schema* and is preferred to the alternative plural *schemas.*

You develop schemata from your own experience—actual experience as well as vicarious experience from television, reading, and hearsay. For example, you may have a schema that portrays college athletes as strong, ambitious, academically weak, and egocentric. You've probably developed schemata for different religious, racial, and national groups; for men and women; and for people of different affectional orientations. Each group that you have some familiarity with will be represented in your mind in some kind of schema. Schemata help you organize your perceptions by allowing you to classify millions of people into a manageable number of categories or classes. As you'll soon see, however, schemata can also create problems—they can influence you to see what is not there or to miss seeing what does exist.

Organization by Scripts A **script** is a type of schema that focuses on an action, event, or procedure. It's a general idea of how some event should unfold; it's the rules governing events and their sequence. For example, you probably have a script for eating in a restaurant, with the actions organized into a pattern something like this: Enter, take a seat, review the menu, order, eat your food, ask for the bill, pay the bill, leave a tip, exit the restaurant. Similarly, you probably have scripts for how you do laundry, how you behave in an interview, the stages you go through in introducing a friend to someone else, and the way you ask for a date.

Everyone relies on shortcuts—rules, schemata, and scripts are all useful shortcuts to simplify understanding, remembering, and recalling information about people and events. If you didn't have such shortcuts, you'd have to treat each person, role, or action differently. This would make every experience totally new, totally unrelated to anything you already know. You'd be unable to generalize, draw connections, or otherwise profit from previously acquired knowledge.

Shortcuts, however, may mislead you; they may contribute to your remembering things that are consistent with your schemata (even if they didn't occur) and distorting or forgetting information that is inconsistent.

Because you form schemata and scripts on the basis of your own cultural beliefs and experiences, you might inappropriately apply these to members of other cultures. For this reason, judgments about members of other cultures are often ethnocentric. It's easy to infer that when members of other cultures do things that conform to your scripts, they're right, and when they do things that contradict your scripts, they're wrong—a classic example of ethnocentric thinking. As you can appreciate, this tendency may contribute to intercultural misunderstandings.

INTERPRETATION–EVALUATION (STAGE THREE)

The interpretation–evaluation step (a linked term because the two processes cannot be separated) is inevitably subjective and is greatly influenced by your experiences, needs, wants, values, expectations, physical and emotional state, gender, and beliefs about the way things are or should be—your rules, schemata, and scripts.

For example, when you meet a new person who is introduced to you as a college football player, you will tend to apply your schema to this person and view him as strong, ambitious, academically weak, and egocentric. You will, in other words, see this person through the filter of your schema for college athletes and evaluate him accordingly. Similarly, when viewing someone asking for a date, you will apply your script to this event and view it through the script. You will interpret the actions of the suitor as appropriate or inappropriate depending on your script for date-requesting behavior and on the ways in which the suitor performs the sequence of actions.

MEMORY (STAGE FOUR)

You store in memory the stimulation from your senses, your organization of these stimuli, and your interpretation and evaluation of them. So, for example, you have in memory your schema for college athletes, and you know that Ben Williams is a football player. Ben Williams is then stored in memory with "cognitive tags" that tell you he's strong, ambitious, academically weak, and egocentric. That is, despite the fact that you've not witnessed Ben's strength or ambitions and have no idea of his academic record or psychological profile, you still may store your memory of Ben along with the qualities that make up your script schema for "college athletes."

Now, let's say that at different times you hear that Ben failed Spanish I (normally an A or B course at your school), that Ben got an A in chemistry (normally a tough course), and that Ben is transferring to Harvard as a theoretical physics major. Because schemata act as filters or gatekeepers, they allow certain information to be stored in relatively objective form, much as you heard or read it, but may distort or prevent other information from being stored. As a result, these three items of information about Ben may get stored very differently in your memory along with your schema for college athletes.

For example, you may readily store the information that Ben failed Spanish, because it's consistent with your schema; it fits neatly into the template that you have of college athletes (Aronson, Wilson, & Akert, 2002). Depending on the strength of your schema, you may also store in memory (even though you didn't hear it) the "information" that Ben did poorly in other courses as well. The information that Ben got an A in chemistry, because it contradicts your schema (it just doesn't seem accurate), may easily be distorted or lost. The information that Ben is transferring to Harvard, however, is a bit different. This information also is inconsistent with your schema, but it is so drastically inconsistent that you may begin to look at it mindfully. Perhaps you'll begin to question your schema for athletes, or perhaps you'll view Ben as an exception to the general rule. In either case, you're likely to etch Ben's transferring to Harvard very clearly in your mind.

So what you remember about a person or an event isn't an objective recollection but more likely heavily influenced by your preconceptions or your schemata about what belongs and what doesn't belong. Your reconstruction of an event or person may contain a lot of information that was not in your original experience and may omit a lot that was part of this experience.

RECALL (STAGE FIVE)

At some later date, you may want to recall or access information you have stored in memory. Let's say you want to retrieve your information about Ben because he's the topic of discussion among you and a few friends. As you'll see in the discussion of listening in the next chapter, memory isn't reproductive; you don't simply reproduce what you've heard or seen. Rather, you reconstruct what you've heard or seen into a whole that is meaningful to you—depending in great part on your schemata and scripts—and it's this reconstruction that is stored in your memory. Now, when you want to retrieve this information from memory, you may recall it with a variety of inaccuracies. For example, you're likely to:

- recall information that is consistent with your schema. In fact, you may not even recall the specific information you're looking for (say, about Ben) but actually just your schema (which contains the information about college athletes and therefore about Ben).
- fail to recall information that is inconsistent with your schema. You have no place to put that information, so you easily lose or forget it.
- recall information that drastically contradicts your schema, because it forces you to think about (and perhaps rethink) your schema and its accuracy; it may even force you to revise your schema.

Examine each of the following situations and indicate how each of the persons identified might conceivably view the situation:

1. A single mother, Leslie, has two small children (ages 7 and 12) who often lack some of the important possessions children their age should have—such as school supplies, sneakers, and toys—because she can't afford to buy them. Yet Leslie smokes two packs of cigarettes a day.

   The mother sees . . .
   The 12-year-old daughter sees . . .
   The children's teacher sees . . .

2. Dakota has extremely high standards and feels that getting all As in college is an absolute necessity. In fear of receiving that first B (after three and a half years of nothing but As), Dakota cheats on an examination and gets caught by the instructor.

   Dakota sees . . .
   The instructor sees . . .
   The average B student sees . . .

Each person perceives the world differently. We increase our own effectiveness when we understand the perceptions of others.

3. Juan is a supervisor in an automobile factory; he has been ordered to increase production or be fired. In desperation Juan delivers a really tough message to the workers—many of whom are greatly insulted and, as a result, slow down rather than increase their efforts.

   Juan sees . . .
   The average worker sees. . . .
   Juan's supervisor sees . . .

Impression Formation

With an understanding of the self and how perception works, we can look at the ways they are intimately connected: first in **impression formation** and then in impression management—academic terms for what you do everyday.

Impression formation (sometimes referred to as **person perception**) refers to the processes you go through in forming an impression of another person. Here, we look at a variety of impression management processes, each of which has pitfalls and potential dangers, and then some of the ways we can increase accuracy in impression formation.

IMPRESSION FORMATION PROCESSES

How you perceive another person and ultimately come to some kind of evaluation or interpretation of him or her is influenced by a variety of processes. Here, we consider some of the more significant: the self-fulfilling prophecy, personality theory, primacy–recency, stereotyping, consistency, and attribution.

Self-Fulfilling Prophecy A **self-fulfilling prophecy** is a prediction that comes true because you act on it as if it were true. Put differently, a self-fulfilling prophecy occurs when you act on your schema as if it were true and, in doing so, make it true. Self-fulfilling prophecies occur in such widely different situations as parent–child relationships, educational settings, and business (Merton, 1957; Rosenthal, 2002; Madon, Guyll, & Spoth, 2004; Tierney & Farmer, 2004). There are four basic steps in the self-fulfilling prophecy:

1. You make a prediction or formulate a belief about a person or a situation. For example, you predict that Pat is friendly in social situations.

2. You act toward that person or situation as if such a prediction or belief were true. For example, you act as if Pat were a friendly person.

3. Because you act as if the belief were true, it becomes true. For example, because of the way you act toward Pat, he or she becomes comfortable and friendly.

4. You observe your effect on the person or the resulting situation, and what you see strengthens your beliefs. For example, you observe Pat's friendliness, and this reinforces your belief that Pat is, in fact, friendly.

The self-fulfilling prophecy also can be seen when you make predictions about yourself and fulfill them. For example, suppose you enter a group situation convinced that the other members will dislike you. Almost invariably you'll be proved right; to you, the other members will appear to dislike you. What you may be doing is acting in a way that encourages the group to respond to you negatively. In this way, you fulfill your prophecies about yourself.

Personality Theory   Each person has a theory of personality (usually subconscious or implicit) that suggests which characteristics of an individual go with other characteristics. Consider, for example, the following brief statements. Note the word in parentheses that you think best completes each sentence.

Carlo is energetic, eager, and (intelligent, stupid).

Kim is bold, defiant, and (extroverted, introverted).

Joe is bright, lively, and (thin, heavy).

Eve is attractive, intelligent, and (likable, unlikable).

Susan is cheerful, positive, and (outgoing, shy).

Angel is handsome, tall, and (friendly, unfriendly).

What makes some of these choices seem right and others wrong is your implicit personality theory, the system of rules that tells you which characteristics go with which other characteristics. Your theory, for example, may have told you that a person who is energetic and eager is also intelligent, not stupid—although there is no logical reason why a stupid person could not be energetic and eager.

The widely documented **halo effect** is a good example of how this personality theory works. If you believe a person has some positive qualities, you're likely to infer that she or he also possesses other positive qualities. There is also a reverse halo (or "horns") effect: If you know a person possesses several negative qualities, you're more likely to infer that he or she also has other negative qualities. For example, you're more likely to perceive physically attractive people as more generous, sensitive, trustworthy, and interesting than those who are less attractive. And the *horns effect* or *reverse halo effect* will lead you to perceive those who are unattractive as mean, dishonest, antisocial, and sneaky (Katz, 2003).

In using personality theories, apply them carefully and critically so as to avoid perceiving qualities in an individual that your theory tells you should be present but aren't, or seeing qualities that are not there (Plaks, Grant, & Dweck, 2005).

Primacy–Recency   Assume for a moment that you're enrolled in a course in which half the classes are extremely dull and half extremely exciting. At the end of the semester, you evaluate the course and the instructor. Would your evaluation be more favorable if the dull classes occurred in the first half of the semester and the exciting classes in the second? Or would it be more favorable if the order were reversed? If what comes first exerts the most influence, you have a **primacy effect.** If what comes last (or most recently) exerts the most influence, you have a **recency effect.**

In the classic study on the effects of primacy–recency in perception, college students perceived a person who was described as "intelligent, industrious, impulsive, critical, stubborn, and envious" more positively than a person described as "envious, stubborn, critical, impulsive, industrious, and intelligent" (Asch, 1946). Notice that the descriptions are identical; only the order was changed. Clearly, there's a tendency to use early information to get a general idea about a person and later information to make this impression more specific. The initial information helps you form a schema for the person. Once that schema is formed, you're likely to resist information that contradicts it.

One interesting practical implication of primacy–recency is that the first impression you make is likely to be the most important—and is likely to be made very quickly (Sunnafrank & Ramirez, 2004; Willis & Todorov, 2006). The reason for this is that the schema that others form of you functions as a filter to admit or block additional information about you. If the initial impression or schema is positive, others are likely (1) to readily remember additional positive information, because it confirms this original positive image or schema; (2) to easily forget or distort negative information, because it contradicts this original positive schema; and (3) to interpret ambiguous information as positive. You win in all three ways—if the initial impression is positive.

The tendency to give greater weight to early information and to interpret later information in light of early impressions can lead you to formulate a total picture of an individual on the basis of initial impressions that may not be typical or accurate. For example, if you judge a job applicant as generally nervous when he or she may simply be showing normal nervousness in an interview for a much-needed job, you will have misperceived this individual. Similarly, this tendency can lead you to distort subsequent perceptions so as not to upset your original schema. For example, you may fail to see signs of deceit in someone you like because of your early impressions that this person is a good and honest individual.

Stereotyping   One of the most common shortcuts in perception is stereotyping. A **stereotype** is a fixed impression of a group of people; it's a type of schema. We all have attitudinal stereotypes—of national, religious, sexual, or racial groups, or perhaps of criminals, prostitutes, teachers, or plumbers. If you have these fixed impressions, you will, on meeting a member of a particular group, often see that person primarily as a member of that group and apply to him or her all the characteristics you assign to the group. If you meet someone who is a prostitute, for example, there are a host of characteristics for prostitutes that you may apply to this one person. To complicate matters further, you will often "see" in this person's behavior the manifestation of characteristics that you would not "see" if you didn't know what the person did for a living. Stereotypes can easily distort accurate perception and prevent you from seeing an individual purely as an individual. Stereotypes can be especially prevalent in online communication; because there are few visual and auditory cues, it's not surprising that people often rely heavily on stereotypes in forming impressions of online partners (Jacobson, 1999).

The tendency to group people and to respond to individuals primarily as members of groups can lead you to perceive an individual as possessing those qualities (usually negative) that you believe characterize his or her group (e.g., "All Mexicans are . . ."). As a result, you may fail to appreciate the multifaceted nature of all individuals and groups. Stereotyping also can lead you to ignore each person's unique characteristics so that you fail to benefit from the special contributions each individual might bring to an encounter.

Consistency   The tendency to maintain balance among perceptions or attitudes is called **consistency** (McBroom & Reed, 1992). You expect certain things to go together and other things to not. On a purely intuitive basis, for example, respond to the following sentences by noting your expected response:

1. I expect a person I like to (like, dislike) me.
2. I expect a person I dislike to (like, dislike) me.
3. I expect my friend to (like, dislike) my friend.
4. I expect my friend to (like, dislike) my enemy.
5. I expect my enemy to (like, dislike) my friend.
6. I expect my enemy to (like, dislike) my enemy.

According to most consistency theories, your expectations would be as follows: You would expect a person you liked to like you (1) and a person you disliked to dislike you (2). You would expect a friend to like a friend (3) and to dislike an enemy (4). You would expect your enemy to dislike your friend (5) and to like your other enemy (6). All these expectations are intuitively satisfying.

Further, you would expect someone you liked to possess characteristics you like or admire, and your enemies to not have those same traits. Conversely, you would expect people you liked to lack unpleasant characteristics and those you disliked to possess them. The downside here is that you might be wrong: Your friend may possess negative qualities (which your friendship may lead you to miss) and your enemy may possess positive qualities (which your emnity may lead you to miss).

Attribution of Control   Another way in which you form impressions is through the **attribution** of control, a process by which you focus on explaining why someone behaved as he or she did. For example, suppose you invite your friend Desmond to dinner at 7 p.m. and he arrives at 9. Consider how you would respond to each of these reasons:

> Reason 1: "I just couldn't tear myself away from the beach. I really wanted to get a great tan."
>
> Reason 2: "I was driving here when I saw some guys mugging an old couple. I broke it up and took the couple home. They were so frightened that I had to stay with them until their children arrived. The storm knocked out all the cell towers and electricity, so I had no way of calling to tell you I'd be late."
>
> Reason 3: "I got in a car accident and was taken to the hospital."

Depending on the reason, you would probably attribute very different motives to Desmond's behavior. With reasons 1 and 2, you'd conclude that Desmond was in control of his behavior; with reason 3, that he was not. Further, you would probably respond negatively to reason 1 (Desmond was selfish and inconsiderate) and positively to reason 2 (Desmond was a good samaritan). Because Desmond was not in control of his behavior in reason 3, you would probably not attribute either positive or negative motivation to it. Instead, you would probably feel sorry that he got into an accident.

In perceiving and especially in evaluating other people's behavior, you frequently ask if they were in control of their behavior. Generally, research shows that if you feel a person was in control of negative behaviors, you'll come to dislike him or her. If you believe the person was not in control of negative behaviors, you'll come to feel sorry for, and not blame, him or her.

In your attribution of controllability—or in attributing motives on the basis of any other reasons (e.g., hearsay or observations of the person's behavior) beware of several potential errors: (1) the self-serving bias, (2) overattribution, and (3) the fundamental attribution error.

- You commit the **self-serving bias** when you take credit for the positive and deny responsibility for the negative. For example, you're more likely to attribute your positive outcomes (say, you get an A on an exam) to internal and controllable factors—to your personality, intelligence, or hard work. And you're more likely to attribute your negative outcomes (say, you get a D) to external and uncontrollable factors—to the exam's being exceptionally difficult or to your roommate's party the night before (Bernstein, Stephan, & Davis, 1979; Duval & Silva, 2002).
- **Overattribution** is the tendency to single out one or two obvious characteristics of a person and attribute everything that person does to this one or these two characteristics. For example, if a person is blind or was born into great wealth, there's often a tendency to attribute everything that person does to such factors. So you might say, "Alex overeats because he's blind," or "Lillian is irresponsible because she never has had to work for her money." To prevent overattribution, recognize that most behav-

Communication Choice Point

Overattribution

Your friends overattribute your behavior, attitudes, values, and just about everything you do to your racial origins. *What communication choices do you have for explaining the illogical nature of this overattribution without insulting your friends? What would you say?*

iors and personality characteristics result from lots of factors. You almost always make a mistake when you select one factor and attribute everything to it.

- The **fundamental attribution error** occurs when you overvalue the contribution of internal factors (e.g., a person's personality) and undervalue the influence of external factors (e.g., the context or situation the person is in). The fundamental attribution error leads you to conclude that people do what they do because that's the kind of people they are, not because of the situation they're in. When Pat is late for an appointment, you're more likely to conclude that Pat is inconsiderate or irresponsible than to attribute the lateness to a possible bus breakdown or traffic accident.

INCREASING ACCURACY IN IMPRESSION FORMATION

Successful communication depends largely on the accuracy of the impressions you form of others. We've already identified the potential barriers that can arise with each of the perceptual processes, for example, the self-serving bias or overattribution. In addition to avoiding these barriers, here are other ways to increase your accuracy in impression formation.

Analyze Impressions Subject your perceptions to logical analysis, to critical thinking. Here are three suggestions.

- **Recognize your own role in perception.** Your emotional and physiological state will influence the meaning you give to your perceptions. A movie may seem hysterically funny when you're in a good mood but just plain stupid when you're in a bad mood. Understand your own biases. For example, do you tend to perceive only the positive in people you like and only the negative in people you don't like?
- **Avoid early conclusions.** On the basis of your observations of behaviors, formulate hypotheses to test against additional information and evidence; avoid drawing conclusions that you then look to confirm. Look for a variety of cues pointing in the same direction. The more cues point to the same conclusion, the more likely your conclusion will be correct. Be especially alert to contradictory cues that seem to refute your initial hypotheses. At the same time, seek validation from others. Do others see things the same way you do? If not, ask yourself if your perceptions may be distorted in some way.
- **Beware of the just world hypothesis.** Many people believe that the world is just: Good things happen to good people and bad things happen to bad people (Aronson, Wilson, & Akert, 2006; Hunt, 2000). Put differently, you get what you deserve! Even when you mindfully dismiss this assumption, you may use it mindlessly when perceiving and evaluating other people. Consider a particularly vivid example: If a woman is raped in certain cultures (e.g., in Bangladesh or Yemen), she is considered by many in that culture (certainly not all) to have disgraced her family and to be deserving of severe punishment—in some cases, death. And although you may claim that this is unfair (and it surely is), much research shows that even in the United States many people do blame the rape victim, especially if the victim is male (Adams-Price, Dalton, & Sumrall, 2004; Anderson, 2004). The belief that the world is just creates perceptual distortions by leading you to overemphasize the influence of internal factors (this happened because this person is good or bad) and to de-emphasize the influence of situational factors (the external circumstances) in your attempts to explain the behaviors of other people or even yourself.

Check Perceptions **Perception checking** is another way to reduce uncertainty and to make your perceptions more accurate. The goal of perception checking is to further explore the thoughts and feelings of the other person, not to prove that your initial perception is correct. With this simple technique, you lessen your chances of misinterpreting another's feelings. At the same time, you give the other person an opportunity to elaborate on his or her thoughts and feelings. In its most basic form, perception checking consists of two steps:

1. Describe what you see or hear, recognizing that descriptions are not really objective but are heavily influenced by who you are, your emotional state, and so on. At the same time, you may wish to describe what you think is happening. Try to do this as descriptively (not evaluatively) as you can. Sometimes you may wish to offer several possibilities, for example, "You've not talked with me all week. You say that my work is fine but you don't seem to want to give me the same responsibilities as the other editorial assistants."

2. Seek confirmation: Ask the other person if your description is accurate. Avoid mind reading. Don't try to read the thoughts and feelings of another person just from observing their behaviors. Regardless of how many behaviors you observe and how carefully you examine them, you can only guess what is going on in someone's mind. A person's motives are not open to outside inspection; you can only make assumptions based on overt behaviors. So be careful that your request for confirmation does not sound as though you already know the answer. Avoid phrasing your questions defensively, for example, "You really don't want to go out, do you? I knew you didn't when you turned on the television." Instead, ask for confirmation in as supportive a way as possible, such as, "Would you rather watch TV?" or "Are you displeased with my work? Is there anything I can do to improve my job performance?"

Reduce Uncertainty   In every communication situation, there is some degree of ambiguity. A variety of strategies can help reduce uncertainty about another person (Berger & Bradac, 1982; Gudykunst, 1993; Brashers, 2007).

- Observing another person while he or she is engaged in an active task, preferably interacting with others in an informal social situation, will often reveal a great deal about the person, as people are less apt to monitor their behaviors and more likely to reveal their true selves in informal situations.

- You can sometimes manipulate situations so as to observe the person in more specific and revealing contexts. Employment interviews, theatrical auditions, and student teaching are good examples of situations arranged to give you an accurate view of the person in action.

- When you log on to an Internet group and lurk, reading the exchanges between the other group members before saying anything yourself, you're learning about the people in the group and about the group itself, thus reducing uncertainty. When uncertainty is reduced, you're more likely to make contributions that will be appropriate to the group and less likely to violate the group's norms.

- Learn about a person through asking others. You might inquire of a colleague if a third person finds you interesting and might like to have dinner with you.

- Interact with the individual. For example, you can ask questions: "Do you enjoy sports?" "What would you do if you got fired?" You also gain knowledge of another by disclosing information about yourself. These disclosures help to create an environment that encourages disclosures from the person about whom you wish to learn more.

Increase Cultural Sensitivity   Recognizing and being sensitive to cultural differences will help increase your accuracy in perception. For example, Russian or Chinese artists such as ballet dancers will often applaud their audience by clapping. Americans seeing this may easily interpret it as egotistical. Similarly, a German man will enter a restaurant before a woman in order to see if the place is respectable enough for the woman to enter. This simple custom can easily be interpreted as rude by people from cultures in which it's considered courteous for the woman to enter first (Axtell, 2007).

Cultural sensitivity will help counteract the difficulty most people have in understanding the nonverbal messages of people from other cultures. For example, it's easier to interpret the facial expressions of members of your own culture than those of an-

Communication Choice Point
Relationship Uncertainty

You've been dating someone casually over the past six months. You want to move to a more exclusive relationship in which you only date each other, but you've been getting mixed signals. *In what ways might you go about discovering how your partner feels?*

Communication Choice Point

First Impression Correction

You made a bad impression at work—you drank too much at an office party and played the clown. This is an impression you want to change fast. Although you can't erase such an impression, you need to counteract it in some way. *What might you say and do to help lessen the negative effects?*

other culture (Weathers, Frank, & Spell, 2002). This "in-group advantage" will assist your perceptional accuracy for members of your own culture but will often hinder your accuracy for members of other cultures (Elfenbein & Ambady, 2002).

Within every cultural group there are wide and important differences. As all Americans are not alike, neither are all Indonesians, Greeks, or Mexicans. When you make assumptions that all people of a certain culture are alike, you're thinking in stereotypes. Recognizing differences between another culture and your own, and among members of the same culture, will help you perceive people and situations more accurately.

Impression Management: Goals and Strategies

Impression management (some writers use the term *self-presentation* or *identity management*) refers to the processes you go through to communicate the impression you want other people to have of you.

Impression management is largely the result of the messages communicated. In the same way that you form impressions of others largely on the basis of how they communicate, verbally and nonverbally, they also form impressions of you based on what you say (your verbal messages) and how you act and dress (your nonverbal messages). Communication messages, however, are not the only means for impression formation and management. For example, you also communicate your self-image and judge others by the people with whom they associate; if you associate with VIPs, then surely you must be a VIP yourself, the conventional wisdom goes. Or you might form an impression of someone on the basis of that person's age or gender or ethnic origin. Or you might rely on what others have said about the person and form impressions that are consistent with these comments. And, of course, they might well do the same in forming impressions of you.

Part of the art and skill of communication is to understand and be able to manage the impressions you give to others. Mastering the art of impression management will enable you to present yourself as you want others to see you, at least to some extent.

The strategies you use to achieve this desired impression will depend on your specific goal. Below is a classification based on seven major communication goals and strategies. Note that although they may help you communicate the impression you want to convey, each of these strategies may also backfire and communicate exactly the opposite of your intended purpose.

TO BE LIKED: AFFINITY-SEEKING AND POLITENESS STRATEGIES

If you're new at school or on the job and you want to be well liked, included in the activities of others, and thought of highly, you'd likely use **affinity-seeking strategies** and **politeness strategies.** Another set of strategies often used to increase likability is immediacy strategies (these are discussed in Chapter 6, pp. 127–129).

Affinity-Seeking Strategies   Using the affinity-seeking strategies outlined here will probably increase your chances of being liked (Bell & Daly, 1984). Such strategies are especially important in initial interactions, and their use by teachers has even been found to increase student motivation (Martin & Rubin, 1998; Myers & Zhong, 2004; Wrench, McCroskey, & Richmond, 2008).

- Present yourself as comfortable and relaxed.
- Follow the cultural rules for polite, cooperative, respectful conversation.
- Appear active, enthusiastic, and dynamic.
- Stimulate and encourage the other person to talk about him- or herself; reinforce his or her disclosures and contributions. Self-disclose yourself.
- Communicate interest in the other person and include him or her in your social activities and groupings.

- Appear optimistic and positive rather than pessimistic and negative.
- Appear honest, reliable, and interesting.
- Arrange circumstances so that you and the other person come into frequent contact.
- Communicate warmth, supportiveness, and empathy.
- Demonstrate that you share significant attitudes and values with the other person.

Not surprisingly, plain old flattery also goes a long way toward improving your likability. Flattery can increase your chances for success in a job interview, the tip a customer is likely to leave, and even your credibility (Varma, Toh, & Pichler, 2006; Seiter, 2007; Vonk, 2002).

There is also, however, a potential negative effect that can result from affinity-seeking strategies. Using them too often or in ways that might appear insincere may lead people to see you as attempting to ingratiate yourself for your own advantage and not really meaning "to be nice."

Politeness Strategies   Another set of strategies people often use to appear likable, politeness strategies may be viewed in terms of negative and positive types (Goffman, 1967; Brown & Levinson, 1987; Holmes 1995; Goldsmith, 2007). Both are responsive to two needs that each individual has:

1. **positive face**—the desire to be viewed positively by others, to be thought of favorably, and
2. **negative face**—the desire to be autonomous, to have the right to do as you wish.

Politeness in interpersonal communication, then, refers to behavior that allows others to maintain both positive and negative face and impoliteness refers to behaviors that attack either positive face (e.g., you criticize someone) or negative face (e.g., you make demands on someone).

To help another person maintain *positive face*, you speak respectfully to and about that person, you give him or her your full attention, you say "excuse me" when appropriate. In short you treat the person as you would want to be treated. In this way you allow the person to maintain positive face through what is called *positive politeness*. You *attack* the person's positive face when you speak disrespectfully about that individual, ignore the person or his or her comments, and fail to use the appropriate expressions of politeness such as *thank you* and *please*.

To help another person maintain *negative face,* you respect the person's right to be autonomous and so you request rather than demand that he or she do something; you say, "Would you mind opening a window" rather than "Open that window, damn it!" You might also give the person an "out" when making a request, allowing the person to reject your request if that is not what he or she wants. So you say, "If this is a bad time, please tell me, but I'm really strapped and could use a loan of $100" rather than "Loan me a $100" or "You have to lend me $100." If you want a recommendation, you might ask, "Would it be possible for you to write me a recommendation for graduate school?" rather than say, "You have to write me a recommendation for graduate school." In this way you enable the person to maintain negative face through what is called *negative politeness.*

Of course, we do this almost automatically and asking for a favor without any consideration for a person's negative face needs would seem totally insensitive. In most situations, however, this type of attack on negative face often appears in more subtle forms. For example, your mother saying "Are you going to wear that?"—to use Deborah Tannen's (2006) example—attacks negative face by criticizing or challenging your autonomy. This comment also attacks positive face by questioning your ability to dress properly.

As with all the strategies discussed here, politeness, too, may have negative consequences. Overpoliteness, for example, is likely to be seen as phony and be resented. Overpoliteness will also be resented if it's seen as a persuasive strategy.

Communication Choice Point

Online Dating

You've decided to join an online dating service. *How might you present yourself as likable? What types of information would you want to include and exclude, in your profile?*

Impression management strategies may also be used unethically and for less than noble purposes. For example, people may use affinity-seeking strategies to get you to like them so that they can then extract favors from you. Politicians frequently portray themselves as credible in order to win votes. The same could be said of the stereotypical used-car salesperson or insurance agent trying to make a sale. Some people use self-handicapping or self-deprecating strategies to get you to see their behavior from a perspective that benefits them rather than you. Self-monitoring strategies are often deceptive, designed to present a more polished image than what might surface without self-monitoring. And, of course, influencing strategies have been used throughout history in deception as well as in truth. Even image-confirming strategies can be used to deceive, as when people exaggerate their positive qualities (or make them up) and hide their negative ones.

As you review these seven strategies, try to identify at least one specific example of when each would be ethical and one specific example of when each strategy would be unethical. From this analysis, try to derive a general principle that could be used to distinguish between ethical and unethical impression management strategies.

Be content to seem what you really are.

—MARCUS AURELIUS
(121–180), Roman
emperor and philosopher

TO BE BELIEVED: CREDIBILITY STRATEGIES

If you were a politician and wanted people to vote for you, at least part of your strategy would involve attempts to establish your **credibility** (which consists of your competence, your character, and your charisma). For example, to establish your competence, you might mention your great educational background or the courses you took that qualify you as an expert. To establish that you're of good character, you might mention how fair and honest you are, your commitment to enduring values, or your concern for those less fortunate. And to establish your charisma—your take-charge, positive personality—you might demonstrate enthusiasm, be emphatic, or focus on the positive while minimizing the negative.

If you stress your competence, character, and charisma too much, however, you risk being seen as someone who lacks the very qualities that you seem too eager to present to others. Generally, people who are truly competent need say little directly about their own competence; their actions and their success will reveal it.

TO EXCUSE FAILURE: SELF-HANDICAPPING STRATEGIES

If you were about to tackle a difficult task and were concerned that you might fail, you might use what are called **self-handicapping strategies.** In the more extreme form of this strategy, you actually set up barriers or obstacles to make the task impossible. That way, when you fail, you won't be blamed or thought ineffective—after all, the task was impossible. Let's say you aren't prepared for your human communication exam and you believe you're going to fail. Using this self-handicapping strategy, you might stay out late at a party the night before so that when you do poorly in the exam, you can blame it on the party rather than on your intelligence or knowledge. In a less extreme form, you might manufacture excuses for failure and have them ready if you do fail. For example, you might prepare to blame a poorly cooked dinner on your defective stove.

On the negative side, using self-handicapping strategies too often may lead people to see you as generally incompetent or foolish. After all, a person who parties the night before an exam for which he or she is already unprepared is clearly demonstrating poor judgment.

Skill Development Experience

Using Impression Management Strategies

Try formulating impression management strategies for each of the following situations. In your responses focus on one or two things you would say or do to achieve the stated goals.

- **To Be Liked:** You're new at work and want your colleagues to like you.
- **To Be Believed:** You're giving a speech on something you feel deeply about; you want others to believe you.
- **To Excuse Failure:** You know you're going to fail that mid-term and you need a good excuse.
- **To Secure Help:** You need help doing something on your computer that would take you hours to do on your own; you can't bear doing it alone.
- **To Hide Faults:** You don't have as many computer skills as your résumé might suggest and you need to appear to know a great deal.
- **To Be Followed:** You want members of the group to see you as the leader and, in fact, to elect you group leader.
- **To Confirm Self-Image:** You want your colleagues to see you as a fun (but dedicated) worker.

Practicing with these strategies will help you understand the ways in which people (including yourself) manage the impressions they give to others.

TO SECURE HELP: SELF-DEPRECATING STRATEGIES

If you want to be taken care of and protected, or if you simply want someone to come to your aid, you might use **self-deprecating strategies.** Confessions of incompetence and inability often bring assistance from others. And so you might say, "I just can't fix that drain and it drives me crazy; I just don't know anything about plumbing" with the hope that another person will offer to help.

But be careful: Your self-deprecating strategies may convince people that you are, in fact, just as incompetent as you say you are. Or people may see you as someone who doesn't want to do something and so pretends to be incompetent to get others to do it. This strategy is not likely to benefit you in the long run.

TO HIDE FAULTS: SELF-MONITORING STRATEGIES

Much impression management is devoted not merely to presenting a positive image, but to suppressing the negative, to **self-monitoring strategies.** Here, you carefully monitor (self-censor) what you say or do. You avoid your normal slang to make your colleagues think more highly of you; you avoid chewing gum so you don't look juvenile or unprofessional. While you readily disclose favorable parts of your experience, you actively hide the unfavorable parts.

But if you self-monitor too often or too obviously, you risk being seen as someone unwilling to reveal him- or herself, and perhaps not trusting enough of others. In more extreme cases, you may be viewed as dishonest, as hiding your true self or trying to fool other people.

TO BE FOLLOWED: INFLUENCING STRATEGIES

In many instances you'll want to get people to see you as a leader. Here, you can use a variety of **influencing strategies.** One set of such strategies are those normally grouped under power—your knowledge (information power), your expertise (expert power), your right to lead by virtue of your position as, say, a doctor, judge, or accountant (legitimate power). Or using leadership strategies, you might stress your prior experience, broad knowledge, or previous successes.

Communication Choice Point

Impressions

You've just joined a social networking site. *How might you write your profile and use the many features of the site to make youself appear credible and a perfect future employee? What would you be sure not to do?*

Influencing strategies can also backfire. If you try to influence someone and fail, you'll be perceived as having less power than before your unsuccessful attempt. And, of course, if you're seen as someone who is influencing others for self-gain, your attempts to influence might be resented or rejected.

TO CONFIRM SELF-IMAGE: IMAGE-CONFIRMING STRATEGIES

You may sometimes use **image-confirming strategies** to reinforce your positive perceptions about yourself. If you see yourself as the life of the party, you'll tell jokes and try to amuse people. This behavior confirms your own self-image and also lets others know that this is who you are and how you want to be seen. At the same time that you reveal aspects of yourself that confirm your desired image, you actively suppress other aspects of yourself that would disconfirm this image.

If you use image-confirming strategies too frequently, you risk being seen as too perfect to be genuine. If you try to project an exclusively positive image, it's likely to turn others off—people want to see their friends and associates as real with some faults and imperfections. Also recognize that image-confirming strategies invariably involve your focusing on yourself, and with that comes the risk of appearing self-absorbed.

A knowledge of these impression management strategies and the ways in which they are effective and ineffective will give you a greater number of choices for achieving such widely diverse goals as being liked, being believed, excusing failure, securing help, hiding faults, being followed, and confirming your self image.

 ## Summary of Concepts and Skills

This chapter explored the self, the ways you perceive yourself, and perception, the way you perceive others and others perceive you.

1. Self-concept, the image that you have of yourself, is composed of feelings and thoughts about both your abilities and your limitations. Self-concept develops from the image that others have of you, the comparisons you make between yourself and others, the teachings of your culture, and your own interpretations and evaluations of your thoughts and behaviors.

2. The Johari window model of the self is one way to view self-awareness. In this model there are four major areas: the open self, the blind self, the hidden self, and the unknown self. To increase self-awareness, analyze yourself, listen to others to see yourself as they do, actively seek information from others about yourself, see yourself from different perspectives, and increase your open self.

3. Self-esteem is the value you place on yourself and may be enhanced by attacking self-destructive beliefs, seeking out nourishing others, working on projects that will result in success, and securing affirmation.

4. Self-disclosure is a form of communication in which information about the self that is normally kept hidden is communicated to one or more others.

5. Self-disclosure is more likely to occur when the potential discloser (1) feels competent, is sociable and extroverted, and is not apprehensive about communication; (2) comes from a culture that encourages self-disclosure; (3) is a woman; (4) is talking to supportive listeners who also disclose; and (5) talks about impersonal rather than personal topics and reveals positive rather than negative information.

6. The rewards of self-disclosure include increased self-knowledge, the ability to cope with difficult situations and guilt, communication efficiency, and chances for more meaningful relationships. The dangers of self-disclosure include personal and social rejection and material loss.

7. Before self-disclosing, consider the motivation for the self-disclosure, the possible burdens you might impose on your listener or yourself, the appropriateness of the self-disclosure, and the disclosures of the other person.

8. When listening to others' disclosures, try to understand what the discloser is feeling, support the discloser, be willing to reciprocate, keep the disclosures confidential, and don't use the disclosures against the person.

9. When you don't want to disclose, try being firm, being indirect and changing the topic, or assertively stating your unwillingness to disclose.

10. Perception is the process by which you become aware of the many stimuli impinging on your senses. It occurs in five stages: Sensory stimulation occurs, is organized, is interpreted–evaluated, is held in memory, and is recalled.

11. Six important processes influence the way you form impressions: Self-fulfilling prophecies, personality theory, primacy–recency, stereotyping, the tendency to expect consistency, and attributions of controllability.

12. To increase your accuracy in impression formation, analyze your impressions and recognize your role in perception; check your impressions; reduce uncertainty; and become culturally sensitive by recognizing the differences between you and others and also the differences among people from other cultures.

13. Among the goals and strategies of impression management are these: to be liked (affinity-seeking and politeness strategies); to be believed (credibility strategies that establish your competence, character, and charisma); to excuse failure (self-handicapping strategies); to secure help (self-deprecating strategies); to hide faults (self-monitoring strategies); to be followed (influencing strategies); and to confirm one's self-image (image-confirming strategies).

14. Each of these impression management strategies can backfire and give others negative impressions. And each of these strategies may be used to reveal your true self or to present a false self and deceive others in the process.

Throughout this discussion of the self and perception, a variety of skills were identified. Place a check mark next to those skills that you feel you need to work on most.

_____ 1. I seek to understand my self-concept and to be realistic about my strengths and weaknesses.

_____ 2. I actively seek to increase self-awareness by talking with myself, listening to others, reducing my blind self, seeing myself from different perspectives, and increasing my open self.

_____ 3. I seek to enhance my self-esteem by attacking self-destructive beliefs, seeking out nourishing others, working on projects that will result in success, and securing affirmation.

_____ 4. I regulate my disclosures on the basis of the unique communication situation.

_____ 5. In deciding whether or not to self-disclose, I take into consideration my motivation, the possible burdens on my listener and on me, the disclosure's appropriateness to the other person and its context, and the other person's disclosures.

_____ 6. I respond to the disclosures of others by trying to feel what the other person is feeling, using effective and active listening skills, expressing supportiveness, refraining from criticism and evaluation, and keeping the disclosures confidential.

_____ 7. I resist disclosing when I don't want to by being firm, by trying indirectness and changing the topic, and/or by stating assertively my refusal to disclose.

_____ 8. I think mindfully when I use perceptual shortcuts so that they don't mislead me and result in inaccurate perceptions.

_____ 9. I guard against ethnocentric thinking by regarding the behavior and customs of others from a multicultural viewpoint rather than from just my cultural perspective.

_____ 10. I bring to consciousness my implicit personality theories.

_____ 11. To guard against the self-fulfilling prophecy, I take a second look at my perceptions when they conform too closely to my expectations.

_____ 12. Recognizing how primacy–recency works, I actively guard against first impressions that might prevent accurate perceptions of future events; I formulate hypotheses rather than conclusions.

_____ 13. I recognize stereotyping in the messages of others and avoid it in my own.

_____ 14. I am aware of and careful to avoid the self-serving bias, overattribution, and the fundamental attribution error when trying to account for another person's behavior.

_____ 15. I think critically about perception, analyzing my perceptions, checking my perceptions for accuracy, using uncertainty reduction strategies, and acting with cultural sensitivity.

_____ 16. I can use the strategies of impression management (to be liked, to be believed, to excuse failure, to secure help, to hide faults, to be followed, and to confirm my self-image) effectively and ethically.

The Language of the Self and Perception

Match the terms about the self and perception with their definitions. Record the number of the definition next to the appropriate term.

_____ a. stereotype (42)

_____ b. attribution (43)

_____ c. self-fulfilling prophecy (40)

_____ d. credibility strategies (48)

_____ e. social comparison (26)

_____ f. personality theory (41)

_____ g. self-concept (26)

_____ h. self-esteem (28)

_____ i. self-disclosure (30)

_____ j. self-serving bias (43)

1. Techniques to make yourself seem competent, of high character, and charismatic

2. Concluding that a person has certain positive qualities because you know that he or she has other positive qualities

3. The process by which you compare yourself to others, most often your peers

4. Your image of who you are

5. A measure of how valuable you think you are

6. The process of talking to others about yourself, of revealing things that you normally keep hidden

7. The tendency to take credit for positive outcomes and to deny responsibility for negative outcomes

8. The process by which we try to explain the motivation for a person's behavior

9. The process of making a prediction that comes true because you made the prediction and acted as if it were true

10. A fixed impression of a group of people

These ten terms and additional terms used in this chapter can be found in the glossary and on flashcards on MyCommunicationLab (www.mycommunicationlab.com).

Answers: a. 10 b. 8 c. 9 d. 1 e. 3 f. 2 g. 4 h. 5 i. 6 j. 7

MyCommunicationLab

PEARSON
mycommunicationlab

www.mycommunicationlab.com

Visit MyCommunicationLab (www.mycommunicationlab.com) for a wealth of additional information on the self and perception in human communication. Flash cards, videos, skill building exercises, sample text questions, and additional examples and discussions will help you continue your study of these fundamental communication concepts.

3 Listening in Human Communication

Why read this chapter?

Because you'll learn about:
- the ways in which you listen
- the styles of listening you can use
- the role of culture and gender in listening

Because you'll learn to:
- listen more effectively during each of the five listening stages
- adjust your listening according to your specific situation
- listen with an awareness of cultural and gender differences

This chapter examines **listening**, which, according to the International Listening Association, is "the process of receiving, constructing meaning from, and responding to spoken and/or nonverbal messages" (Emmert, 1994, cited in Brownell, 2006). Here we look at the importance of listening, the nature of the listening process, the major barriers to listening effectiveness, varied styles of listening for different situations, and some cultural and gender differences in listening.

The Importance of Listening: Professional and Relationship Benefits

The skills of listening will prove crucial to you in both your professional and personal lives (Brownell, 2006). In today's workplace listening is regarded as a crucial skill. One study concluded that employees' communication skills are especially significant in this era of technological transformation; workers' advancement will depend on their ability to speak and write effectively, to display proper etiquette, and *to listen attentively*. In a survey of 40 CEOs of Asian and Western multinational companies, respondents cited a lack of listening skills as *the major shortcoming* of top executives (Witcher, 1999).

There can be little doubt that listening skills play a crucial role in developing and maintaining a variety of interpersonal relationships (Brownell, 2006). When asked what they want in a partner, women overwhelmingly reply, "a partner who listens." And most men would agree that they too want a partner who listens. Among friends, listening skills rank consistently high; in fact, it would be hard to think of a person as a friend if that person were not a good listener.

The effective listener is more likely to emerge as group leader, an effective salesperson, an attentive and effective healthcare worker, and an effective manager (Johnson & Bechler, 1998; Lauer, 2003; Stein & Bowen, 2003; Levine, 2004; Pelham & Kravitz, 2008; Brownell, 2008). Recently medical educators, claiming that doctors are not trained to listen to their patients, have introduced what they call "narrative medicine" to teach doctors how to listen to their patients and to recognize how their perceptions of their patients are influenced by their own emotions (Smith, 2003).

Another important professional benefit of listening is to establish and communicate power. In much the same way that you communicate power with your words or gestures, you also communicate your power through listening. When you listen appropriately and effectively you are able also to empower other people, such as your relationship partner or colleague.

"There is only one cardinal rule: one must always listen to the patient."

—OLIVER SACKS

Stages of Listening

Listening is a collection of skills involving attention and concentration *(receiving)*, learning *(understanding)*, **memory** *(remembering)*, critical thinking *(evaluation)*, and feedback *(responding)*. Listening can go wrong at any stage; however, you can enhance your listening ability by strengthening these skills, which are needed during each step of the process (Figure 3.1).

Note that the process of listening is circular: The response of person A stimulates a response from person B, which stimulates a response from person A, and so on. All five stages overlap. When you listen, you're performing all five processes at essentially the same time. For example, when listening in conversation, you're not only paying attention to what other people are saying but also critically evaluating what they just said and perhaps giving feedback. Let's take a look at each stage separately.

RECEIVING

Hearing (which is not the same as *listening*), begins and ends with the first stage of the listening process, receiving. Hearing happens when you get within range of some auditory stimulus. Listening, on the other hand, only just begins when the messages the speaker sends are received, or heard.

At the *receiving* stage, you note not only what is said (verbally and nonverbally) but also what is omitted. For example, you receive not only the politician's summary of accomplishments in education but also his or her omission of failures in health care or pollution control. This receiving stage of listening can be made more effective if you

- focus attention on the speaker's verbal and nonverbal messages, on what is said and what is not said and not on what you'll say next;
- avoid distractions in the environment;
- maintain your role as listener by not interrupting the speaker; and
- confront **mixed messages**—messages that communicate different and contradictory meanings.

At times, speakers may ask hearers to cut them some slack and to receive their messages without prejudice, a process referred to as **disclaiming**. Some of the more popular *disclaimers* are these (Hewitt & Stokes, 1975):

- *Hedging* asks that you (the listener) separate the message from the speaker—that if you reject the message, you shouldn't also reject the speaker ("I didn't read the whole book, so I may not be entirely accurate, but . . .").
- *Credentialling* asks you not to disqualify the speaker for saying something that may be taken negatively ("You know, I'm not sexist, but it seems to me that . . .").
- *Sin licenses* ask you for permission to deviate in some way from what is considered normal operating procedure ("This is probably not the place to say this, but . . .").
- *Cognitive disclaimers* ask you to see the speaker as being in full possession of his or her faculties ("I know I drank a bit, but I'm as clear on this as ever . . .").
- *Appeals for the suspension of judgment* ask you to delay your judgment until you hear the speaker out ("This may sound weird at first, but just listen to this . . .").

In this brief discussion of receiving, and in fact throughout this chapter on listening, the unstated assumption is that both individuals can receive auditory signals without difficulty. But for many people who have hearing impairments, listening presents a variety of problems. Table 3.1 provides tips for communication between deaf and hearing people.

UNDERSTANDING

Understanding occurs when you decode the speaker's signals, when you learn what the speaker means. *Understanding* means grasping both the thoughts that are expressed and the emotional tone that accompanies them—for example, the urgency, joy, or sorrow

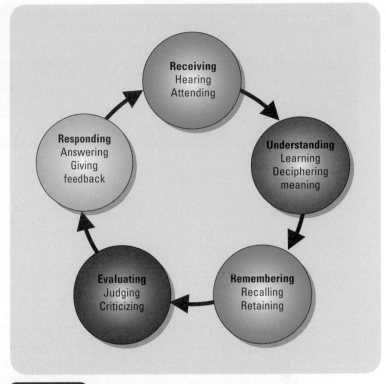

FIGURE 3.1 **A Five-Stage Model of the Listening Process**

This model depicts the various stages involved in listening. Note that receiving, or hearing, is not the same thing as listening, but is in fact only the first step in a five-step process. This model draws on a variety of previous models that listening researchers have developed (e.g., Alessandra, 1986; Barker, 1990; Brownell, 1987; Steil, Barker, & Watson, 1983). In what other ways might you visualize the listening process?

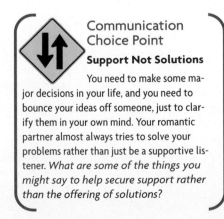

Communication Choice Point

Support Not Solutions

You need to make some major decisions in your life, and you need to bounce your ideas off someone, just to clarify them in your own mind. Your romantic partner almost always tries to solve your problems rather than just be a supportive listener. *What are some of the things you might say to help secure support rather than the offering of solutions?*

TABLE 3.1　Communication Tips

Between People with and without Hearing Difficulties

| Ludwig van Beethoven | Thomas Edison | Pete Townshend | Marlee Matlin |

People with hearing loss differ greatly in their hearing ability: Some are totally deaf and can hear nothing, others have some hearing loss and can hear some sounds, and still others have impaired hearing but can hear most speech. Although people with profound hearing loss can speak, their speech may appear labored and may be less clear than the speech of those with unimpaired hearing. Here are some suggestions for more effective communication between people who hear well and those who have hearing problems.

If you have unimpaired hearing:

1. Set up a comfortable context. Reduce the distance between yourself and the person with a hearing impairment. Reduce background noise: Turn off the television and even the air conditioner.

2. Avoid interference. Make sure the visual cues from your speech are clearly observable; for example, face the person squarely and avoid smoking, chewing gum, or holding your hand over your mouth. Make sure the lighting is adequate.

3. Speak at an adequate volume. But avoid shouting, which can distort your speech and may insult the person. Be careful to avoid reducing volume at the ends of your sentences.

4. Phrase ideas in different ways. Because some words are easier to lip-read than others, it often helps if you can rephrase your ideas in different words.

5. Avoid overlapping speech. In group situations only one person should speak at a time. Similarly, direct your comments to the person with hearing loss himself or herself; don't talk to the person through a third party. Elementary school teachers, for example, have been found to direct fewer comments to deaf children than to hearing students (Cawthon, 2001).

6. Ask for additional information. Ask the person if there is anything you can do to make it easier for him or her to understand you.

7. Don't avoid common terms. Use terms like *hear*, *listen*, *music*, or *deaf* when they're relevant to the conversation. Trying to avoid these common terms will make your speech sound artificial.

8. Use nonverbal cues. Nonverbals can help communicate your meaning; guestures indicating size or location and facial expressions indicating emotions and feelings are often helpful.

If you have impaired hearing:

1. Do your best to eliminate background noise.

2. Move closer to the speaker if this helps you hear better. Alert the speaker that this closer distance will help you hear better.

3. Ask for adjustments. If you feel the speaker can make adjustments to ease your comprehension, ask. For example, ask the speaker to repeat a message, to speak more slowly or more distinctly, or to increase his or her volume.

4. Position yourself for best reception. If you hear better in one ear than another, position yourself accordingly and, if necessary, clue the speaker in to this fact.

5. Ask for additional cues. If necessary, ask the speaker to write down certain information, such as phone numbers or website addresses. Carrying a pad and pencil will prove helpful for this and in the event that you wish to write something down for others.

Sources: These suggestions were drawn from a variety of sources: Tips for Communicating with Deaf People (Rochester Institute of Technology, National Technical Institute for the Deaf, Division of Public Affairs), **http://www.his.com/~lola/deaf.html**, **http://www.zak. co.il/deaf-info/old/comm_strategies.html**, **http://www.agbell.org/**, **http://www.dol.gov/odep/pubs/fact/comucate.htm**, and **http://spot.pcc.edu/~rjacobs/career/communication_tips.htm** (all websites accessed May 7, 2008).

expressed in the message. The understanding phase of listening can be made more effective if you

- relate the speaker's new information to what you already know (e.g., in what way a new proposal will change your present health care);
- see the speaker's messages from the speaker's point of view, in part by not judging the message until it's fully understood as the speaker intended it; and
- rephrase (paraphrase) the speaker's ideas, a simple process that's especially important when listening to complicated instructions.

REMEMBERING

Messages that you receive and understand need to be retained for some period of time. In some small group and public speaking situations, you can augment your memory by taking notes or by taping the messages. In most interpersonal communication situations, however, such note taking would be considered inappropriate, except to write down a phone number or directions, for example.

What you remember is not what was actually said but what you think (or remember) was said. You don't simply *reproduce* in your memory what the speaker said; rather, you *reconstruct* the messages you hear into a system that makes sense to you—a concept noted in the discussion of perception in Chapter 2.

You can make this *remembering* phase of listening more effective if you

- identify the central ideas and the major support advanced;
- summarize the message in an easier-to-retain form, not ignoring crucial details or qualifications; and
- repeat names and key concepts to yourself or, if appropriate, aloud.

EVALUATING

Evaluating consists of judging the messages you hear. At times you may try to evaluate the speaker's underlying intent, often without much conscious awareness. For example, Elaine tells you she is up for a promotion and is really excited about it. You may then try to judge her intention. Does she want you to use your influence with the company president? Is she preoccupied with the possible promotion and therefore telling everyone? Is she looking for a pat on the back? Generally, if you know a person well, you will be able to identify his or her intention and respond appropriately.

In other situations, your evaluation may be more like critical analysis. For example, in a business meeting on upgrading office equipment, you would evaluate the office manager's proposals while listening to them. As you listened, you'd be asking yourself, "Are the proposals practical? Will they increase productivity? What is the evidence? Are there more practical alternatives?" This evaluation stage of listening can be made more effective if you

- resist evaluating until you fully understand the speaker's point of view;
- assume that the speaker is a person of goodwill and give the speaker the benefit of any doubt by asking for clarification on issues you object to (e.g., are there any other reasons for accepting this new proposal?); and
- distinguish facts from inferences (see Chapter 4), opinions, personal interpretations, or biases by the speaker.

RESPONDING

Responding occurs in two forms: (1) responses you make while the speaker is talking and (2) responses you make after the speaker has stopped talking. Responses made while the speaker is talking should be supportive and should acknowledge that you're listening. These responses are **backchanneling cues:** messages (words and gestures) that let the speaker know you're paying attention, as when you nod in agreement or say, "I see" or "Uh-huh."

As a listener you have at least two ethical obligations. As you read this, consider whether there are other obligations that a listener might have.

First, you owe it to the speaker to give his or her message an honest hearing and to avoid pre-judgment: Try to put aside prejudices and preconceptions so you can evaluate the message fairly. At the same time, try to empathize with the speaker. You don't have to agree, but try to understand emotionally as well as intellectually what the speaker means. Then accept or reject the speaker's ideas on the basis of the information offered.

Second, you owe the speaker honest responses. Just as you should be honest with the listener when speaking, you should be honest with the speaker when listening. This means reflecting on what the speaker says and giving open and sincere feedback. Just as the listener has a right to expect an active speaker, the speaker has the right to expect an active listener.

Listening is not merely not talking, though even that is beyond most of our powers; it means taking a vigorous, human interest in what is being told us.

—ALICE DUER MILLER
   (1874–1941), U.S. poet
   and mathematician

Responses after the speaker has stopped talking are generally more elaborate and might include empathy ("I know how you must feel"); requests for clarification ("Do you mean this new health plan will replace the old plan, or will it only be a supplement?"); challenges ("I think your evidence is weak"); and/or agreement ("You're absolutely right, and I'll support your proposal when it comes up for a vote"). You can improve this responding phase of listening if you

- express support for the speaker throughout the talk by using varied backchanneling cues (however, using only one—such as saying, "Uh-huh" repeatedly—will make it appear that you're not listening but "on auto pilot");
- express support for the speaker in your final responses; and
- take ownership of your responses by stating your thoughts and feelings as your own, using **I-messages** (e.g., "I think the new proposal will entail greater expense than you outlined" rather than "Everyone will object to the plan's cost").

Table 3.2 presents some problematic listening responses and some suggestions for correcting them.

Listening Barriers

In addition to practicing the various skills for each stage of listening, consider some of the common barriers to listening. Here are four such barriers and some suggestions for dealing with them as both listener and speaker, because both speaker and listener are responsible for effective listening.

DISTRACTIONS: PHYSICAL AND MENTAL

Physical barriers might include hearing impairment, a noisy environment, or loud music. Multi-tasking (e.g., watching TV and listening to someone) with the aim of being supportive, for example, simply doesn't work. As both listener and speaker, try to remove whatever physical barriers can be removed; for those that you can't remove, adjust your listening and speaking to lessen the effects as much as possible. As a listener, focus on the speaker; you can attend to the room and the other people later.

Mental distractions too get in the way of focused listening. These barriers may take the form of thinking about your upcoming Saturday night date or becoming too emotional to think (and listen) clearly. When listening, recognize that you can think

Communication Choice Point
Listening Avoidance
Your best friend's latest relationship has just broken up, and your friend comes to you in the hope that you'll listen to all the details. This seems to happen about once a week. You're fed up; you're determined not to spend the next three hours listening to this tale of woe. *What are some of the things you can say to get you out of listening to this boring recital but at the same time not alienate your friend?*

TABLE 3.2 Problem-Causing Listening Responses and How to Correct Them

Here are only a few examples of listening responses that can present effective and satisfying communication.

Problem-Causing Responses	Correctives
The static listener gives no feedback, remains relatively motionless, reveals no expression.	Give feedback as appropriate: smile, nod, and otherwise appropriately respond to the content and feeling of the message.
The monotonous feedback giver seems responsive, but the responses never vary; regardless of what is said, the response is the same.	Give varied feedback that is relevant to the conversation.
The overly expressive listener reacts to just about everything with extreme responses.	React in a tone consistent with the speaker's message.
The eye avoider looks all around the room and at others but never at you.	Look at the speaker; don't stare but make the speaker your eyes' main focus
The preoccupied listener listens to other things at the same time, often with headphones turned up so loud that it interferes with the speaker's thinking.	Show the speaker that he or she is your primary focus; shut down the iPhone and the television; turn away from the computer screen.
The waiting listener listens for a cue to take over the speaking turn.	Hear the speaker out and then speak; refrain from giving cues that you want to speak while the speaker is in the middle of saying something.
The thought-completing listener listens a little and then finishes the speaker's thought.	Express respect by allowing the speaker to complete his or her thoughts. Completing someone's thoughts often communicates the message that nothing important is going to be said (*I already know it*).
The critical listener evaluates everything you say, often negatively.	Avoid criticism, unless the situation calls for it, and always stress the positive.
The advising listener gives advice at the first mention of a problem or decision.	Avoid giving advice unless specifically asked and resist what is supposedly the male tendency to solve problems.
The never-ending listener wants the speaker to keep talking, often long after the speaker has said what he or she wants to say.	Learn to exchange speaking and listening roles; they are each best when relatively short. Allow conversations to end naturally instead of unnecessarily prolonging them.

about your date or other distracting thoughts later. In speaking, make what you say compelling and relevant to the listener.

BIASES AND PREJUDICES

Biases and prejudices against groups or individuals will invariably distort listening. For example, a gender bias assumes that only a member of a certain sex can be knowledgeable about a given topic. This bias will distort incoming messages that contradict this assumption. Be willing to subject your biases and prejudices to contradictory information; after all, if they're worth having, they should stand up to differences of opinion. When as a speaker you feel your listener may have certain prejudices, ask for a suspension of bias: "I know you don't think women are knowledgeable about sports, but just hear me out about why I think the team's offense isn't working . . ."

LACK OF APPROPRIATE FOCUS

Focusing on what a person is saying is necessary for effective listening. And yet, there are many influences that can lead you astray. For example, listeners often get lost because they focus on irrelevancies, such as an especially vivid example that conjures up old memories. Try not to get detoured from the main idea. Try to repeat the idea to yourself and see

Listen to This

Listening in the Classroom

Right now, a large part of your listening takes place in the classroom: listening to the instructor and to other students. In addition to following the general guidelines for listening, here are a few additional suggestions for making your classroom listening more effective. After all, if you're going to spend the time, you might as well spend it efficiently.

1. Prepare yourself to listen. Sit up front where you can see your instructor and any visual aids clearly and comfortably. You listen with your eyes as well as your ears.
2. Avoid distractions caused by mental daydreaming as well as physical distractions like your laptop, iPhone, or newspaper.
3. Pay special attention to the introduction; this will often contain a preview and will help you outline the lecture. Listen also for key words and phrases (often written on the board or on PowerPoint slides)) and for orienting remarks such as "another reason," "three major causes," and "first." Use these cues to help you outline the lecture.
4. Assume what is said is relevant. It may eventually prove irrelevant, but if you listen with the assumption of irrelevancy, you'll miss everything.
5. Listen for understanding; avoid taking issue with what is said until you understand fully and then, of course, take issue if you wish. For example don't rehearse in your own mind your arguments against a particular position. When you do this, you run the risk of missing additional explanations or qualifications.

> *It is the privilege of wisdom to listen.*
> —OLIVER WENDELL HOLMES (1809–1894), U.S. professor and poet

the details in relation to this main concept. As a speaker, try to avoid language or examples that may divert attention from your main idea.

Another misplaced focus is often on the responses a listener is going to make while the speaker is still speaking. Anticipating how you're going to respond or what you're going to say (and even interrupting the speaker) prevents you from hearing the message in full. Instead, make a mental note of something and then get back to listening. As a speaker, when you feel someone is preparing to argue with you, ask him or her to hear you out: "I know you disagree with this, but let me finish and we'll get back to that."

PREMATURE JUDGMENT

Perhaps the most obvious form of premature judgment is assuming you know what the speaker is going to say and that there's no need to really listen. Let the speaker say what he or she is going to say before you decide that you already know it. As a speaker, it's often wise to assume that listeners will do exactly this, so make clear that what you're saying will be unexpected.

A common listener reaction is to draw conclusions or judgments on incomplete evidence. Sometimes, listeners will stop listening after hearing, for example, an attitude they disagree with or some sexist or culturally insensitive remark. Instead, this is a situation that calls for especially concentrated listening so that you don't rush to judgment. Wait for the evidence or argument; avoid making judgments before you gather all the information. Listen first, judge second. As a speaker, be aware of this tendency and, when you feel this is happening, ask for a suspension of judgment. A simple "Hear me out" is often sufficient.

Styles of Effective Listening

Before reading about the principles of effective listening, examine your own listening habits and tendencies by taking the following self-test, "How do you listen?"

Test Yourself

How Do You Listen?

Respond to each question using the following scale:

1 = always; 2 = frequently; 3 = sometimes; 4 = seldom; and 5 = never

_____ ❶ I listen to what the speaker is saying and feeling; I try to feel what the speaker feels.

_____ ❷ I listen objectively; I focus on the logic of the ideas rather than on the emotional meaning of the message.

_____ ❸ I listen without judging the speaker.

_____ ❹ I listen critically; I rarely suspend my critical, evaluative faculties.

_____ ❺ I listen to the literal meaning, to what the speaker says, rather than playing psychiatrist and focusing on the hidden or deeper meanings.

_____ ❻ I listen for the speaker's hidden meanings, to what the speaker means but isn't verbalizing.

HOW DID YOU DO?   These statements focus on the ways of listening discussed in this next section. All of these ways are appropriate at some times but not at others, so the only responses that are really inappropriate are "always" and "never." Effective listening is listening that is tailored to the specific communication situation.

WHAT WILL YOU DO?   Consider how you might use your responses on this self-test to begin to improve your listening effectiveness. A good way to begin is to review the statements and try to identify situations in which each statement would be appropriate and those in which each would be inappropriate.

As stressed throughout this chapter, listening is **situational:** The type of listening that is appropriate will vary with the situation, each set of circumstances calling for a different combination of listening styles. The art of effective listening is in making appropriate choices along the following five dimensions: (1) empathic and objective listening, (2) nonjudgmental and critical listening, (3) surface and depth listening, (4) polite and impolite listening, and (5) active and inactive listening. We'll take a look at each of these dimensions.

EMPATHIC AND OBJECTIVE LISTENING

To understand what a person means and what a person is feeling, you need to listen with some degree of **empathy** (Rogers, 1970; Rogers & Farson, 1981). To empathize with others is to feel with them: to see the world as they see it and to feel what they feel. **Empathic listening** will also help you enhance your relationships (Barrett & Godfrey, 1988; Snyder, 1992).

To express empathy, it's often helpful to do so in two ways, corresponding to the two parts of true empathy: thinking empathy and feeling empathy (Bellafiore, 2005). In _thinking empathy_ you express an understanding of what the person means. For example, when you paraphrase someone's comment, showing that you understand the meaning the person is trying to communicate, you're demonstrating thinking empathy. The second part of empathy is _feeling empathy_; here you express your ability to feel what the other person is feeling. For example, if a friend tells you of problems at home, you might respond by saying, "Your problems at home do seem to be getting worse. I can imagine how you feel so angry at times."

"Listening, not imitation, may be the sincerest form of flattery."

—JOYCE BROTHERS

Although for most communication situations empathic listening is the preferred mode of responding, there are times when you need to go beyond it and to measure the speaker's meanings and feelings against some objective reality. It's important to listen as Peter tells you how the entire world hates him and to understand how he feels and why he feels this way. But then you need to look a bit more objectively at the situation and perhaps see Peter's paranoia or self-hatred. Sometimes you have to put your empathic responses aside and listen with objectivity and detachment. In adjusting your empathic and objective listening focus, keep the following recommendations in mind:

- Punctuate from the speaker's point of view (Chapter 1). That is, see the sequence of events as the speaker does and try to figure out how this perspective can influence what the speaker says and does.

- Engage in equal, two-way conversation. To encourage openness and empathy, try to eliminate any physical or psychological barriers to equality; for example, step from behind the large desk separating you from your employees. Avoid interrupting the speaker—a sure sign that you think what you have to say is more important.

- Seek to understand both thoughts and feelings. Don't consider your listening task finished until you've understood what the speaker is feeling as well as thinking.

- Avoid "offensive listening"—the tendency to listen to bits and pieces of information that will enable you to attack the speaker or find fault with something the speaker has said.

- Strive especially to be objective when listening to friends and foes alike. Guard against "expectancy hearing," in which you fail to hear what the speaker is really saying and instead hear what you expect.

NONJUDGMENTAL AND CRITICAL LISTENING

Effective listening includes both nonjudgmental and critical responses. You need to listen nonjudgmentally—with an open mind and with a view toward understanding. But you also need to listen critically—with a view toward making some kind of evaluation or judgment. Clearly, it's important to listen first for understanding while suspending judgment. Only after you've fully understood the relevant messages should you evaluate or judge.

Supplement open-minded listening with critical listening. Listening with an open mind will help you understand the messages better; listening with a critical mind will help you analyze and evaluate the messages. In adjusting your nonjudgmental and critical listening, focus on the following guidelines:

- Avoid filtering out or oversimplifying difficult or complex messages. Similarly, avoid filtering out undesirable messages. Clearly, you don't want to hear that something you believe is untrue or that ideals you hold are self-destructive. Yet it's important that you reexamine your beliefs by listening to these messages.

- Recognize your own biases. These may interfere with accurate listening and cause you to distort message reception through a process of **assimilation**—the tendency to integrate and adapt what you hear or think you hear to your own biases, prejudices, and expectations.

- Recognize and combat the normal tendency to *sharpen*—to highlight, emphasize, and perhaps embellish one or two aspects of a message. See the message as a whole.

Table 3.3 presents a few fallacies of language that you need to identify in thinking critically about what you hear.

SURFACE AND DEPTH LISTENING

In most messages there's an obvious meaning that you can derive from a literal reading of the words and sentences. But in reality, most messages have more than one level of meaning. Sometimes the other level is the opposite of the literal meaning; at other

Communication Choice Point

Empathic Listening

Your neighbors, who've avoided work all their lives and lived off unfairly obtained government disability payments, have just won the lottery for $36 million. They want you to share their joy and invite you over for a champagne toast. *What are some of the things you can do to strengthen your ability to empathize with these people? What might you say to show empathic listening?*

TABLE 3.3 Listening to Fallacies of Language

Here are four language fallacies that often get in the way of meaningful communication and need to be identified in critical listening. Often they're used to fool you; these are ways in which language can be used to serve less-than-noble purposes, to convince or persuade you without giving you valid reasons. After reviewing these fallacies, take a look at some of the commercial websites for clothing, books, music, or any product you're interested in, and try to find examples of these fallacies.

Fallacy	Example	Notes
Weasel words are those whose meanings are slippery and difficult to pin down (Pei, 1956; Hayakawa & Hayakawa, 1990).	A commercial claiming that medicine M works "better than Brand X" but doesn't specify how much better or in what respect Medicine M performs better. It's quite possible that it performs better in one respect but less effectively according to nine other measures.	Other weasel words are "help," "virtually," "as much as," "like" (as in "it will make you feel like new"), and "more economical." Ask yourself, "Exactly what is being claimed?" For example, "What does 'may reduce cholesterol' mean?"
Euphemisms make the negative and unpleasant appear positive and appealing.	An executive calls the firing of 200 workers "downsizing" or "reallocation of resources." Justin Timberlake's reference to the highly publicized act with Janet Jackson during the 2004 Super Bowl as a "wardrobe malfunction."	Often euphemisms take the form of inflated language designed to make the mundane seem extraordinary, the common seem exotic ("the vacation of a lifetime," "unsurpassed vistas"). Don't let words get in the way of accurate first-hand perception.
Jargon is the specialized language of a professional class.	For example, the language of the computer hacker, the psychologist, and the advertiser.	When used to intimidate or impress, as with people who aren't members of the profession, it prevents meaningful communication. Don't be intimidated by jargon; ask questions when you don't understand.
Gobbledygook is overly complex language that overwhelms the listener instead of communicating meaning.	Extra-long sentences, complex grammatical constructions, and rare or unfamiliar words.	Some people normally speak in complex language. But, others use complexity to confuse and mislead. Ask for simplification when appropriate.

times it seems totally unrelated. Consider some frequently heard types of messages. Carol asks you how you like her new haircut. On one level, the meaning is clear: Do you like the haircut? But there's also another and perhaps more important level: Carol is asking you to say something positive about her appearance. In the same way, the parent who complains about working hard at the office or in the home may, on a deeper level, be asking for an expression of appreciation.

To recognize these other meanings, you need to engage in depth listening. If you respond only to the surface-level communication (i.e., the literal meaning), you miss the opportunity to make meaningful contact with the other person's feelings and needs. If you say to the parent, "You're always complaining. I bet you really love working so hard," you fail to respond to this call for understanding and appreciation. In regulating your surface and depth listening, consider the following guidelines:

- **Focus on both verbal and nonverbal messages.** Recognize both consistent and inconsistent "packages" of messages and use these as guides for drawing inferences about the speaker's meaning. Ask questions when in doubt. Listen also to what is omitted: Speakers communicate by what they leave out as well as by what they include.

- **Listen for both content and relational messages.** The student who constantly challenges the teacher is, on one level, communicating disagreement over content. However, on another level—the relationship level—the student may be voicing objections to the instructor's authority or authoritarianism. The instructor needs to listen and respond to both types of messages.

"I was distracted for a moment. Go on."

© Peter Mueller/Condé Nast Publications/www.cartoonbank.com.

- **Make special note of statements that refer back to the speaker.** Remember that people inevitably talk about themselves. Whatever a person says is, in part, a function of who that person is. Attend carefully to those personal, self-referential messages.

- **Don't disregard the literal meaning of messages.** Balance your listening between surface and underlying meanings. Respond to the different levels of meaning in the messages of others as you would like others to respond to yours—sensitively but not obsessively, readily but not overambitiously.

POLITE AND IMPOLITE LISTENING

Politeness is often thought of as the exclusive function of the speaker, as solely an encoding or sending function. But, politeness (or impoliteness) may also be signaled through listening (Fukushima, 2004).

Of course, there are times when you would not want to listen politely (e.g., to someone being verbally abusive or condescending or using racist or sexist language). In these cases you might want to show your disapproval by showing that you're not listening. But most often you'll want to listen politely, and you'll want to express this politeness through your listening behavior. Here are a few suggestions for demonstrating that you are in fact listening politely; these are strategies designed to be supportive of the speaker's positive and negative face needs:

- *Avoid interrupting the speaker.* Avoid trying to take over the speaker's turn. Avoid changing the topic. If you must respond and can't wait until the speaker finishes, then say it as briefly as possible and pass the turn back to the speaker.

- *Give supportive listening cues.* These might include nodding your head, giving minimal verbal responses such as "I see" or "yes, it's true" or moving closer to the speaker. Listen in a way that demonstrates that what the speaker is saying is important. In some cultures, polite listening cues must be cues of agreement (Japanese culture is often used as an example); in other cultures, polite listening cues are attentiveness and support rather than cues of agreement (as in much of United States, for example).

- *Show empathy with the speaker.* Demonstrate that you understand and feel the speaker's thoughts and feelings by giving responses that show this level of understanding—smiling or cringing or otherwise echoing the feelings of the speaker. If you echo the speaker's nonverbal expressions, your behavior is likely to be seen as empathic.

- *Maintain eye contact.* In much of the United States this is perhaps the single most important rule. If you don't maintain eye contact when someone is talking to you, then you'll appear not to be listening, and definitely not listening politely. This rule, however, does not hold in all cultures. In some Latin and Asian cultures, polite listening would consist of looking down and avoiding direct eye contact when, for example, listening to a superior or much older person.

- *Give positive feedback.* Throughout the listening encounter, perhaps especially after the speaker's turn (when you continue the conversation as you respond to what the speaker has said), positive feedback will be seen as polite and negative feedback as impolite. If you must give negative feedback, then do so in a way that does not attack the person's negative face: For example, first mention areas of agreement and what you liked about what the person said and stress your good intentions. Then, when you give negative feedback, it is important to do it in private. Public criticism feels especially threatening, and the original speaker will surely see it as a personal attack.

A somewhat different slant on politeness and listening can be seen in "forcing" people to listen when they don't want to. Generally, the polite advice is to notice when the other person wants to leave and to allow the person to discontinue listening. Closely related to this is the "forced" listening that many cell phone users impose on others, a topic addressed in Table 3.4

ACTIVE AND INACTIVE LISTENING

One of the most important communication skills you can learn is that of **active listening**. Consider the following interaction: You're disappointed that you have to redo your entire budget report, and you say, "I can't believe I have to redo this entire report. I really worked hard on this project, and now I have to do it all over again." To this you get three different responses:

ANNETTE: That's not so bad; most people find they have to redo their first reports. That's the norm here.
CAROLINE: You should be pleased that all you have to do is a simple rewrite. Peggy and Michael both had to completely redo their entire projects.
BARBARA: You have to rewrite that report you've worked on for the last three weeks? You sound really angry and frustrated.

All three listeners are probably trying to make you feel better. But they go about it in very different ways and, it appears, with very different results. Annette tries to lessen the significance of the rewrite. This type of well-intended and extremely common response does little to promote meaningful communication and understanding. Caroline tries to give the situation a positive spin. In their responses, however, both Annette and Caroline also suggest that you should not feel the way you do; they imply that your feelings are not legitimate and should be replaced with more logical feelings.

Barbara's response, however, is different from the others. Barbara uses active listening. Active listening owes its development to Thomas Gordon (1975), who made it a cornerstone of his P-E-T (Parent Effectiveness Training) technique; it is a process of sending back to the speaker what you as a listener think the speaker meant—both in content and in feelings. Active listening, then, is not merely repeating the speaker's exact words but, rather, putting together into some meaningful whole your understanding of the speaker's total message.

Active listening helps you check your understanding of what the speaker said and, more important, what he or she meant. Reflecting back perceived meanings to the speaker

"Listen long enough and the person will generally come up with a solution."
—MARY KAY ASH

TABLE 3.4	Politeness and the Cell Phone

The ubiquity of the cell phone has led to enormous increases in telephone communication, but it has also created problems, many of which are problems of politeness. Because much cell phone use occurs in public spaces, people often are forced to listen to conversations that don't involve them.

General Rule	Specifics	Adjustments
Avoid using cell phones where inappropriate.	Especially avoid calling in restaurants, hospitals, theaters, museums, commuter buses or trains, and in the classroom.	If you must make or take a call when in these various situations, try to move to a less public area.
Silence your cell.	Put your phone on vibrate mode, or let your voicemail answer and take a message when your call might interfere with others.	When you can't avoid taking a call, speak as quietly as possible and as briefly as possible.
Avoid unwanted photo-taking	Don't take pictures of people who aren't posing for you, and erase photos if the person you photographed requests it.	Of course, if there's an accident or a robbery, you may want to photograph the events.
Avoid extended talking when your reception is weak.	Talking on your cell on a crowded street will probably result in poor reception, which is annoying to the other person.	In an emergency, caution trumps politeness.
Consider the other person.	It's easy to assume that when you have nothing better to do, the person you're calling also has nothing better to do.	As with any phone call, it's wise to ask if this is a good time to call—a strategy that helps maintain the autonomy (negative face) of the person you're calling.

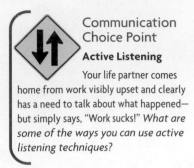

Communication Choice Point

Active Listening

Your life partner comes home from work visibly upset and clearly has a need to talk about what happened—but simply says, "Work sucks!" *What are some of the ways you can use active listening techniques?*

gives the speaker an opportunity to offer clarification and correct any misunderstandings. Active listening also lets the speaker know that you acknowledge and accept his or her feelings. In this example, Barbara listened actively and reflected back what she thought you meant while accepting what you were feeling. Note too that she also explicitly identified your emotions ("You sound angry and frustrated"), allowing you the opportunity to correct her interpretation. Still another function of active listening is that it stimulates the speaker to explore feelings and thoughts. Barbara's response encourages you to elaborate on your feelings and perhaps to better understand them as you talk them through. When combined with empathic listening, active listening proves the most effective approach for successful sales transactions (Comer & Drollinger, 1999).

Three simple techniques may help you succeed in active listening: paraphrase the speaker's meaning, express understanding, and ask questions.

- *Paraphrase the speaker's meaning.* Stating in your own words what you think the speaker means and feels helps ensure understanding and demonstrates your interest. **Paraphrasing** gives the speaker a chance to extend what was originally said. However, remember to be objective; be especially careful not to lead the speaker in the direction you think he or she should go. And, don't overdo it; paraphrase when you feel there's a chance for misunderstanding or when you want to keep the conversation going.

- *Ask questions.* Asking questions strengthens your own understanding of the speaker's thoughts and feelings and elicits additional information ("How did you feel when you read your job appraisal report?"). Ask questions to provide only enough stimulation and support so the speaker will feel he or she can elaborate on these thoughts and feelings.

- *Express understanding of the speaker's feelings.* In addition to paraphrasing the content, echo the feelings the speaker expressed or implied ("You must have felt horrible"). This expression of feelings will help you further check your perception of the speaker's feelings. It also will allow the speaker to see his or her feelings more objectively—especially helpful when they're feelings of anger, hurt, or depression—and to elaborate on these feelings.

In communicating your understanding back to the speaker, be especially careful to avoid sending what are called "solution messages" (Gordon, 1975)—messages that tell the person how he or she *should* feel or what he or she *should* do. Four types of messages send solutions, and you'll want to avoid them in your active listening:

- *ordering messages:* "Do this." "Don't touch that."

- *warning and threatening messages:* "If you don't do this, you'll . . ." "If you do that, you'll . . ."

- *preaching and moralizing messages:* "People should all . . ." "You have responsibilities . . ."

- *advising messages:* "Why don't you . . ." "I think you should . . ."

Listening Differences: Culture and Gender

Listening is difficult in part because of the inevitable differences in the communication systems between speakers and listeners. Because each person has had a unique set of experiences, each person's communication and meaning system is going to be unique. When speaker and listener come from different cultures or are of different genders, the differences and their effects are, naturally, much greater.

CULTURE AND LISTENING

In today's multicultural world, where people from very different cultures live and work together, it's especially important to understand the ways in which cultural differences can influence listening. Three of these cultural influences on listening are (1) language and speech, (2) nonverbal behaviors, and (3) feedback.

Language and Speech   Even when a speaker and a listener speak the same language, they speak it with different meanings and different accents. Speakers of the same

Here are three situations that might require active listening. For each situation compose an active listening response in which you (a) paraphrase the speaker's meaning, (b) express understanding of the speaker's meaning, and (c) ask questions to clarify any potential misunderstandings.

1. Your friend has just broken up a love affair and is telling you about it: *I can't seem to get Chris out of my head. All I do is think about what we used to do and all the fun we used to have.*

2. A young nephew tells you that he cannot talk with his parents. No matter how hard he tries, they just don't listen. *I tried to tell them that I can't play baseball and I don't want to play baseball. But they ignore me and tell me that all I need is practice.*

3. Your mother has been having a difficult time at work. She was recently passed up for a promotion and received one of the lowest merit raises given in the company. *I'm not sure what I did wrong. I do my work, mind my own business, don't take my sick days like everyone else. How could they give that promotion to Helen who's only been with the company for two years? Maybe I should just quit.*

Active listening allows you to connect with another person by demonstrating your understanding and support.

language will, at the very least, have different meanings for the same terms because they have had different experiences. For example, the word "parents" to someone brought up in a series of foster homes will be drastically different from someone who grew up in a "traditional" family.

Speakers and listeners who have different native languages and who may have learned English as a second language will have even greater differences in meaning. If you learned your meaning for *house* in a culture in which everyone lives in his or her own house with lots of land around it, then communicating with someone whose meaning of house was learned in a neighborhood of high-rise tenements is going to be difficult. Although each of you will hear the word *house*, the meanings you'll develop will be drastically different. In adjusting your listening—especially in an intercultural setting—understand that the speaker's meanings may be very different from yours even though you're speaking the same language.

In many classrooms throughout the United States, there will be a wide range of accents. Those whose native language is tonal, such as Chinese (in which differences in pitch signal important meaning differences), may speak English with variations in pitch that may be puzzling to others. Those whose native language is Japanese may have trouble distinguishing *l* from *r*, because Japanese does not include this distinction. The native language acts as a filter and influences the accent given to the second language.

In low-context cultures (e.g., the United States, Germany, Scandinavia) listening involves "hearing" what is explicitly stated in the spoken message. In high-context cultures (e.g., China, Japan, Korea) listening involves "hearing" the message through a knowledge of the history of the person speaking, gleaning what is implied or only hinted at.

Nonverbal Behaviors Speakers from different cultures have different *display rules*, cultural rules that govern which nonverbal behaviors are appropriate and which are inappropriate in a public setting. As you listen to other people, you also "listen" to their nonverbals. If nonverbal signals are drastically different from what you would expect on the basis of the verbal message, you may see them as a kind of noise or interference or even as a contradictory message. If a colleague at work, for example, consistently averts her eyes when talking with you, you may interpret this as an indication of shyness or dishonesty (which are often associated with averted eyes), but it may be merely a sign that your colleague's culture discourages direct eye contact. (Some, often collectivist, cultures consider direct eye contact overly forward, impolite, or inappropriate [Axtell, 2007].

Communication Choice Point
Hate Speech

Your work colleagues in neighboring cubicles regularly use derogatory racial terms. You really don't want to listen to this and want to protest this kind of talk. At the same time, however, you don't want to alienate people you're going to have to work with for some time. *What are some of the things you can say to register your protest (cooperatively)?*

W hat listening styles would you probably use in each of these situations (i.e., empathic and objective, nonjudgmental and critical, surface and depth, or active and inactive)? What listening styles obviously would be inappropriate in each situation?

Regulate your listening on the basis of the specific situation in which you find yourself.

1. Your steady dating partner for the last five years tells you that spells of depression are becoming more frequent and more long lasting.
2. Your five-year-old daughter says she wants to become a nurse.
3. Your brother tells you he's been accepted into Harvard's MBA program.
4. Your supervisor explains the new computerized mail system.

Other, often individualist, cultures consider direct eye contact a sign of honesty and forthrightness.) To complicate matters further, different cultures often have very different meanings for the same nonverbal gesture. For example, the thumb and forefinger forming a circle means "OK" in most of the United States, but it means "money" in Japan, "zero" in some Mediterranean countries, and "I'll kill you" in Tunisia.

Feedback   Members of some cultures give very direct and very honest feedback. Speakers from these largely individualist cultures—the United States is a good example—expect feedback to be an honest reflection of what their listeners are feeling. In other largely collectivist cultures—Japan and Korea are good examples—it's more important to be positive (and to respect the other person's need for positive face) than to be truthful. As a result, people may respond with positive feedback (say, in commenting on a business colleague's proposal) even if it doesn't reflect their true opinion. Listen to feedback, as you would to all messages, with a full recognition that various cultures view feedback very differently.

GENDER AND LISTENING

Men and women learn different styles of listening, just as they learn different styles for using verbal and nonverbal messages. Not surprisingly, these different styles can create difficulties in opposite-sex communication.

Rapport and Report Talk   According to Deborah Tannen (1990) in her best-selling *You Just Don't Understand: Women and Men in Conversation*, women seek to share feelings, build rapport, and establish closer relationships, and use listening to achieve these ends. Men, on the other hand, play up their expertise, emphasize it, and use it to dominate the interaction. Their focus is on reporting information. Tannen argues that in conversation a woman seeks to be liked, so she expresses agreement. The goal of a man, on the other hand, is to be given respect, so he seeks to show his knowledge and expertise.

Listening Cues   Men and women give different types of listening cues and, consequently, show that they're listening in different ways. In conversation, a woman is more apt to give lots of listening cues—interjecting "Yeah" or "Uh-huh," nodding in agreement, and smiling. A man is more likely to listen quietly, without giving lots of listening cues as feedback. Women also make more eye contact when listening than do men, who are more apt to look around and often away from the speaker (Brownell, 2006). As a result of these differences, women seem to be more engaged in listening than do men.

Communication Choice Point
Listening Cues
Friends have told you that people don't address comments directly to you because you don't give listening cues to let the other person know that you're listening and interested. *What are some of the things you can do to help change this perception?*

Amount and Purposes of Listening Tannen argues that men listen less to women than women listen to men. The reason, says Tannen, is that listening places the person in an inferior position, but speaking places the person in a superior position. Men may seem to assume a more confrontational posture while listening and to ask questions that are argumentative or seek to puncture holes in the speaker's position as a way to play up their own expertise. Women are more likely than men to ask supportive questions and offer constructive criticism. Men and women act this way both to members of the same and of the opposite sex; their usual ways of speaking and listening don't seem to change depending on whether the person they're communicating with is male or female.

It's important to note that not all researchers agree that there is sufficient evidence to support the claims of Tannen and others about gender differences (Goldsmith & Fulfs, 1999).

Gender differences are changing drastically and quickly; it's best to take generalizations about gender as starting points for investigation and not as airtight conclusions (Gamble & Gamble, 2003). Further, be mindful that, as you no doubt have observed from your own experiences, gender differences—although significant—are far outnumbered by similarities.

 # Summary of Concepts and Skills

This chapter has discussed the ways you listen and how you can listen more effectively.

1. Listening is crucial to success in a wide range of professions and in personal relationships.
2. Listening may be defined as "the process of receiving, constructing meaning from, and responding to spoken and/or nonverbal messages."
3. Listening serves a variety of purposes: You listen to learn; to relate to others; to influence the attitudes, beliefs, and behaviors of others; to play; and to help. Listening is a five-step process consisting of receiving, understanding, remembering, evaluating, and responding.
4. Both listener and speaker share in the responsibility for effective listening.
5. Among the obstacles to effective listening are physical and mental distractions, biases and prejudices, lack of appropriate focus, and premature judgment.
6. Effective listening involves a process of making adjustments—depending on the situation—along dimensions such as empathic and objective listening, nonjudgmental and critical listening, surface and depth listening, polite and impolite listening, and active and inactive listening.
7. Culture influences listening in a variety of ways. Contributing to listening difficulties are cultural differences in language and speech, nonverbal behaviors, and feedback.
8. Men and women listen differently and perhaps for different reasons. For example, women give more messages that say, "I'm listening" than men. According to some theorists, women use listening to show empathy and to build rapport, and men minimize listening because it puts them in a subordinate position.

Throughout this discussion of listening, a variety of skills were identified. Place a check mark next to those skills that you feel you need to work on most.

_____ 1. I recognize that listening serves a variety of purposes, and I adjust my listening on the basis of my purposes: for example, to learn, relate, influence, play, or help.

_____ 2. I realize that listening is a multistage process, and I regulate my listening behavior as appropriate in receiving, understanding, remembering, evaluating, and responding.

_____ 3. In receiving messages I seek to increase my chances of effective listening by, for example, paying attention to the speaker's verbal and nonverbal messages; avoiding distractions; and focusing on what the speaker is saying, not on what I'm going to say next.

_____ 4. I facilitate understanding in listening by relating new information to what I already know and trying to see the messages from the speaker's point of view.

_____ 5. In remembering the speaker's messages, I try to identify the central ideas and the major supporting materials, summarize the main ideas, and repeat important concepts to etch them more firmly in my mind.

_____ 6. In evaluating messages, I first make sure I understand the speaker's point of view and seek to identify any sources of bias or self-interest.

_____ 7. In responding, I am supportive of the speaker and own my own thoughts and feelings.

_____ 8. I am mindful of the common listening obstacles (i.e., distractions, biases, lack of focus, and premature judgment) and try to reduce their effects.

_____ 9. I am especially careful to adjust my listening on the basis of the immediate situation between empathic and objective, nonjudgmental and critical, surface and depth, polite and impolite, and active and inactive listening.

_____ 10. I practice active listening when appropriate by paraphrasing the speaker's meaning, expressing my understanding of the speaker's feelings, and asking questions.

_____ 11. I recognize the influence of culture on listening and cultural differences in listening and take these into consideration when listening in intercultural situations.

_____ 12. I recognize gender differences in listening and take these into consideration when communicating with members of the opposite sex.

 ## Key Word Quiz

The Language of Listening

Match the terms about listening with their definitions. Record the number of the definition next to the appropriate term.

_____ a. active listening (65)

_____ b. paraphrasing (66)

_____ c. situational listening (61)

_____ d. disclaiming (55)

_____ e. listening (54)

_____ f. assimilation (62)

_____ g. backchanneling cues (57)

_____ h. memory (54)

_____ i. I-messages (58)

_____ j. empathic listening (61)

1. The process of asking the listener to receive your message without prejudice, to give you a fair hearing.

2. A reconstructive rather than a reproductive process.

3. The tendency to integrate and interpret what you hear or think you hear in terms of your own expectations and biases.

4. A process of sending back to the speaker what you think the speaker meant.

5. Restating what another says but in your own words.

6. An approach to listening in which effective listening style depends on the specifics of the communication.

7. A five-step process consisting of receiving, understanding, remembering, evaluating, and responding.

8. Listening responses that let the speaker know that you're paying attention.

9. Listening to what a person is feeling as well as to what the person is thinking.

10. Messages in which you take responsibility for your thoughts and actions rather than attributing these to others.

These ten terms and additional terms used in this chapter can be found in the glossary and on flashcards on MyCommunicationLab (www.mycommunicationlab.com).

Answers: a. 4; b. 5; c. 6; d. 1; e. 7; f. 3; g. 8; h. 2; i. 10; j. 9

MyCommunicationLab

PEARSON mycommunicationlab

www.mycommunicationlab.com

Visit MyCommunicationLab (www.mycommunicationlab.com) for additional information on listening in human communication. Flash cards, videos, skill building exercises, sample text questions, and additional examples and discussions will help you continue your study of the skills of effective listening.

4 Verbal Messages

Why read this chapter?

Because you'll learn about:
- the nature of verbal messages
- the principles governing verbal messages

Because you'll learn to:
- use verbal messages more effectively in all your communication experiences
- avoid language that might be considered sexist, heterosexist, racist, or ageist
- avoid common pitfalls of language usage that can also distort your thinking

*y*our messages normally occur in "packages" consisting of both verbal and nonverbal signals (Pittenger, Hockett, & Danehy, 1960). Usually, verbal and nonverbal behaviors reinforce, or support, each other. For example, you don't usually express fear with words while the rest of your body relaxes. You don't normally express anger with your face while your words are warm and cheerful. Your entire being works as a whole—verbally and nonverbally—to express your thoughts and feelings. When you communicate, you use two major signal systems—verbal and nonverbal.

This chapter focuses on the verbal message system: the system's key principles, the concepts of confirmation and disconfirmation, and the ways you can use verbal messages most effectively. The next chapter will examine the nonverbal message system.

Principles of Verbal Messages

Your verbal messages, of course, rely on the rules of grammar; you can't just make up sounds or words or string words together at random and expect to be understood. But following the rules of grammar is not enough to achieve effective communication. Instead, you need to understand the principles of verbal messages. Here we look at six principles.

MESSAGE MEANINGS ARE IN PEOPLE

To discover the meaning a person is trying to communicate, it's necessary to look into the people as well as the words. The word *cancer*, for example, will mean something very different to a mother whose child has just been diagnosed with cancer and to an oncologist.

Also recognize that, as you change, you also change the meanings you created out of past messages; although the message sent may not have changed, the meanings you created from it yesterday and the meanings you create today may be quite different. Yesterday, when a special someone said, "I love you," you created certain meanings. But today, when you learn that the same "I love you" was said to three other people, you drastically change the meaning you derive from those three words.

MESSAGES ARE DENOTATIVE AND CONNOTATIVE

You speak both denotatively and connotatively. **Denotation** has to do with the objective meaning of a term, the meaning you would find in a dictionary. It's the meaning that people who share a common language assign to a word. **Connotation** is the subjective or emotional meaning that specific speakers or listeners give to a word. Take as an example the word *migrants* (used to designate Mexicans coming into the United States to better their economic condition) with the word *settlers* (meaning Europeans who came to the United States for the same reason) (Koppelman, 2005). Though both terms describe essentially the same activity (and are essentially the same denotatively), they differ widely in their connotations, with the former often negatively evaluated and the latter often positively valued.

Semanticist S. I. Hayakawa (Hayakawa & Hayakawa, 1990) coined the terms **snarl words** and **purr words** to clarify further the distinction between denotation and connotation. Snarl words are highly negative: "She's an idiot," "He's a pig," "They're a bunch of losers." Purr words are highly positive: "She's a real sweetheart," "He's a dream," "They're the greatest." Snarl and purr words, although they may sometimes seem to have denotative meaning and to refer to the "real world," are actually connotative in meaning. These terms do not describe objective realities but rather express the speaker's feelings about people or events.

"I'd like you to head up the new team of the recently let go."

MESSAGES VARY IN ABSTRACTION

Consider the following list of terms:

entertainment

film

American film

classic American film

Casablanca

At the top is an **abstraction**, or general concept—the word *entertainment*. Note that *entertainment* includes all the other items on the list plus various other items—*television, novels, drama, comics,* and so on. *Film* is more specific and concrete. It includes all of the items below it as well as various other items such as *Indian film* or *Russian film*. It excludes, however, all entertainment that is not film. *American film* is again more specific than *film* and excludes all films that are not American. *Classic American film* further limits *American film* to those considered to be timeless. *Casablanca* specifies concretely the one item to which reference is made.

As this example illustrates, verbal messages vary from general and abstract to specific and concrete. Effective verbal messages include words from a wide range of abstractions. At times, a general term may suit your needs best. Generally, however, the specific term will prove the better choice. As you get more specific—less abstract—you more effectively guide the images that come to your listeners' minds.

MESSAGE MEANINGS VARY IN POLITENESS

It will come as no surprise that messages vary greatly in politeness. Polite messages (1) reflect positively on the other person (as with compliments or pats on the back) and allow the person to maintain positive face and (2) respect the other person's right to be independent and autonomous (as does asking permission, or acknowledging the person's right to refuse) and allow the person to maintain negative face. Impolite messages attack our needs to be seen positively (as with criticism or negative facial expressions) and to be autonomous (as does making demands or forcing another to do something).

Politeness and Directness
Directness is usually less polite than indirectness and may infringe on a person's need to maintain negative face: "Write me a recommendation," "Lend me $100." Indirectness—"Do you think you could write a recommendation for me?" "Would it be possible to lend me $100?"—is often more polite because it allows the person to maintain autonomy and provides an acceptable way for the person to refuse your request (thus helping to maintain the person's negative face needs).

Indirect messages allow you to express a desire without insulting or offending anyone; they allow you to observe the rules of polite interaction. So instead of saying, "I'm bored with this group," you say, "It's getting late and I have to get up early tomorrow." Instead of saying, "This food tastes like cardboard," you say, "I just started my diet." In each instance you're stating a preference but are saying it indirectly so as to avoid offending someone.

The differences between direct and indirect messages may easily create misunderstandings. For example, a person who uses an indirect style of speech may be doing so to be polite and may have been taught this style by his or her culture. If you assume, instead, that the person is using indirectness to be manipulative, because your culture regards it so, then miscommunication is inevitable.

Politeness and Gender
There are considerable gender differences in politeness (Tannen, 1994b, Holmes, 1995; Kapoor, Hughes, Baldwin, & Blue, 2003; Dindia & Canary, 2006). Among the research findings are, for example, that women are more polite and more indirect in giving orders than are men; they are more likely to say, for example, "it would be great if these letters could go out today" than "Have these letters out by three."

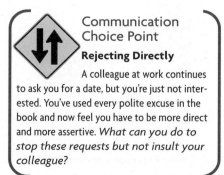

Communication Choice Point

Rejecting Directly

A colleague at work continues to ask you for a date, but you're just not interested. You've used every polite excuse in the book and now feel you have to be more direct and more assertive. *What can you do to stop these requests but not insult your colleague?*

Men are more likely to be indirect when they express weakness, reveal a problem, or admit an error. Generally, men will speak indirectly when expressing meanings that violate the masculine stereotype (e.g., messages of weakness or doubt or incompetence). Women's greater politeness is also seen in the finding that women express empathy, sympathy, and supportiveness more than men. Women also apologize more than men, and both women and men make most of their apologies to women.

Politeness Online Internet communication has very specific rules for politeness, called **netiquette** (Kallos, 2005). Much as the rules of etiquette provide guidance in communicating in social situations, the rules of netiquette provide guidance in communicating over the Net and concern everyone using computer-mediated communication (CMC) (Berry, 2004; Fuller, 2004). These rules are helpful for making Internet communication more pleasant and easier and also for achieving greater personal efficiency. Here are several netiquette guidelines:

- *Familiarize yourself with the chatroom or listserv before contributing.* Before asking questions about the system, read the Frequently Asked Questions (FAQs). "Lurk" before speaking. Lurking (which, in CMC, is good) will help you learn the rules of the particular group and will help you to avoid saying things you'd like to take back.

- *Be brief.* Communicate only the information that is needed clearly, briefly, and in an organized way.

- *Don't shout.* WRITING IN CAPS IS PERCEIVED AS SHOUTING. It's okay to use capital letters occasionally to achieve emphasis. If you wish to give emphasis, highlight like _this_ or *this*.

- *Don't spam or "flame."* Don't send unsolicited mail, repeatedly send the same mail, or post the same message (or irrelevant messages) to lots of people or groups. As in face-to-face conflicts, don't make personal attacks on other users.

- *Avoid offensive language.* Refrain from expressions that would be considered offensive to others, such as sexist or racist terms.

A special case of online politeness concerns the ever popular social networking sites, which have developed their own rules of netiquette, some of which are noted in Table 4.1.

MESSAGES VARY IN ASSERTIVENESS

Assertiveness refers to a willingness to stand up for your rights but with respect for the rights of others. Assertive people operate with an "I win, you win" philosophy; they assume that both parties can gain something from an interaction, even from a confrontation. Assertive people are more positive and score lower on measures of hopelessness than do nonassertive people (Velting, 1999). Assertive people are willing to assert their own rights, but unlike their aggressive counterparts, they don't hurt others in the process. Assertive people speak their minds and welcome others' doing likewise.

Realize that, as with many other aspects of communication, there will be wide cultural differences when it comes to assertiveness. For example, the values of assertiveness are more likely to be extolled in individualist cultures than in collectivist cultures. Assertiveness will be valued more by those cultures that stress competition, individual success, and independence. It will be valued much less by those cultures that stress cooperation, group success, and interdependence of all members. U.S. students, for example, are found to be significantly more assertive than Japanese and Korean students (Thompson, Klopf, & Ishii, 1991; Thompson & Klopf, 1991). Thus, for a given situation, assertiveness may be an effective strategy in one culture but would create problems in

Communication Choice Point

Politeness

You meet a friend who's with someone you've never met before. You begin badmouthing your college experience—using even more obscene and profane language than normal—until your friend breaks in and introduces you to Professor Reynolds, your new major advisor. *What are some of the things you can say to lessen the negative effect you've just created?*

TABLE 4.1	Social Networking Politeness

The social networking sites such as Facebook and MySpace have developed their own rules of politeness. Here are several:

1. Refuse a request for friendship gently or ignore it. There's no need to go into great detail about why you don't want to be friends with this person. And if you're refused, don't ask for reasons. Social networkers consider it impolite to ask for reasons why your request is refused.

2. Engage in social networking foreplay before asking someone to be your friend. For example, send a personal message to the person complimenting the person's post.

3. Avoid writing anything negative on a person's wall or posting unflattering photos of another person or messages that will embarrass another person or generate conflict.

4. Don't use social networking information outside the network. It's considered inappropriate and impolite to relay information on Facebook, for example, to those who are not themselves friends.

5. Avoid asking to be friends with someone who you suspect may have reason for not wanting to admit you. For example, your work associate may not want you to see her or his profile; if you ask, you put your colleague in an awkward position. You might use indirect messages; for example, you might say that you want to expand your networking to work colleagues and see how your colleague responds.

another. Assertiveness with an elder in many Asian and Hispanic cultures may be seen as insulting and disrespectful.

Most people are nonassertive in particular situations. If you're one of these people, and if you wish to modify your behavior, here are some suggestions for communicating assertiveness (Windy & Constantinou, 2005; Bower & Bower, 2005). (If you are always nonassertive and are unhappy about this, then you may need to work with a therapist to change your behavior.)

- Describe the problem; don't evaluate or judge it. *We're all working on this advertising project together. You're missing half our meetings and you still haven't produced your first report.* Be sure to use I-messages and to avoid messages that accuse or blame the other person.

- State how this problem affects you; tell the person how you feel. *My job depends on the success of this project, and I don't think it's fair that I have to do extra work to make up for what you're not doing.*

- Propose solutions that are workable and that allow the person to save face. Describe or visualize the situation if your solution were put into effect. *If you can get your report to the group by Tuesday, we'll still be able to meet our deadline. I could give you a call on Monday to remind you.*

- Confirm understanding. *It's clear that we can't produce this project if you're not going to pull your own weight. Will you have the report to us by Tuesday?*

Keep in mind that assertiveness is not always the most desirable response. Effectively assertive people are assertive when they want to be, but they can back down if the situation calls for it, such as when they risk emotionally hurting another person. Let's say that an older relative wishes you to do something for her or him. You could assert your rights and say no, but because this would probably hurt this person's feelings, it might be better simply to do as asked.

A note of caution should be added to this discussion. It's easy to visualize a situation in which, for example, people are talking behind you in a movie, and with your newfound enthusiasm for assertiveness, you tell them to be quiet. It's also easy to see yourself getting smashed in the teeth as a result. In applying the principles of assertive communication, be careful that you don't go beyond what you can handle effectively.

Skill Development Experience

Practicing Assertiveness

For any one of the following situations, compose (a) an aggressive, (b) a nonassertive, and (c) an assertive response. Then, in one sentence, explain why your message of assertiveness will be more effective than the aggressive or nonassertive message.

Assertiveness is the most direct and honest response in situations such as these. Usually it's also the most effective.

1. You've just redecorated your apartment, making it exactly as you want it. A good friend of yours brings you a house gift—the ugliest poster you've ever seen—and insists that you hang it over your fireplace, the focal point of your living room.

2. Your friend borrows $30 and promises to pay you back tomorrow. But tomorrow passes, as do 20 subsequent tomorrows. You know that your friend has not forgotten about the debt, and you also know that your friend has more than enough money to pay you back.

3. Your next-door neighbor repeatedly asks you to take care of her four-year-old while she runs some errand or another. You don't mind helping out in an emergency, but this occurs almost every day.

MESSAGES ARE INFLUENCED BY CULTURE AND GENDER

Your verbal messages are influenced in large part by your culture and gender. Let's look first at some of the cultural influences.

Cultural Influences Your culture teaches you that certain ways of using verbal messages are acceptable and certain ways are not. When you follow these **cultural rules**, or cultural principles, in communicating, you're seen as a properly functioning member of the culture. When you violate the principles, you risk being seen as deviant or perhaps as offensive. Here are a variety of such principles:

- *The principle of cooperation.* The principle of **cooperation** holds that, in any communication interaction, both parties will make an effort to help each other to understand each other. That is, we assume cooperation. This general principle has four subprinciples, or **conversational maxims**. As you read down the list, ask yourself how you follow these maxims in your everyday conversation:

  ~ The maxim of *quality:* Say what you know or assume to be true, and do not say what you know to be false.
  ~ The maxim of *relation:* Talk about what is relevant to the conversation.
  ~ The maxim of *manner:* Be clear, avoid ambiguities (as much as possible), be relatively brief, and organize your thoughts into a meaningful pattern.
  ~ The maxim of *quantity:* Be as informative as necessary to communicate the information.

- *The principle of peaceful relations.* This principle holds that when you communicate your primary goal is to maintain peaceful relationships. This means that you would never insult anyone; in fact, when communicating according to this principle, you may even express agreement with someone when you really disagree, which violates the principle of cooperation and the maxim of quality (Midooka, 1990).

- *The principle of self-denigration.* This principle advises you to avoid taking credit for accomplishments and to minimize your abilities or talents in conversation (Gu, 1997). At the same time, through self-denigration you raise the image of the people with whom you're talking.

Lying occurs when you try to make others believe something is true that you believe is untrue (Ekman, 2009; Knapp, 2007; Burgoon & Hoobler, 2002). You can lie by commission (i.e., by making explicitly false statements) or by omission (i.e., by omitting relevant information, thus allowing others to draw incorrect inferences). Similarly, you can lie verbally (e.g., in speech or writing) or nonverbally (e.g., wearing an innocent facial expression instead of acknowledging the commission of some wrong, or nodding knowingly instead of expressing honest ignorance) (O'Hair, Cody, & McLaughlin, 1981). Lies range from "white lies" and truth stretching to lies that form the basis of relationship infidelity, libel, and perjury. Not surprisingly, lies have ethical implications.

Some lies may be considered *ethical lies*, lies that are commonly accepted by society as harmless, right, and even as having some good effects (e.g., lying to a child to protect a fantasy belief in Santa Claus or the tooth fairy, or publicly agreeing with someone to enable the person to save face). Some ethical lies may even be considered to be required (e.g., lying to protect someone from harm or telling the proud parents that their child is beautiful). Other lies are clearly *unethical*, for example, lying to defraud investors, to falsely accuse someone of a crime, or to slander someone.

Many other lies, however, are more difficult to classify. Here are a few such examples to get you started thinking about the ethics of deception:

- Is it ethical to lie to get what you deserve but couldn't get any other way? For example, is it ethical to lie to get a well-earned promotion or a raise?
- Is it ethical to lie to your relationship partner to avoid a conflict and, perhaps, splitting up? Would it make a difference if the issue was a minor one (e.g., you were late for an appointment because you wanted to see the end of the football game) or a major one (e.g., continued infidelity)?
- Is it ethical to lie to get yourself out of an unpleasant situation? For example, would it be ethical to lie to get out of an unpleasant date, an extra office chore, or a boring conversation?

> *Always tell the truth. That way, you don't have to remember what you said.*
>
> —MARK TWAIN
> (1835–1910), U.S.
> humorist

- *The principle of directness.* As explained earlier, directness and indirectness communicate different impressions. Levels of directness also vary greatly from culture to culture and between men and women. In most of the United States, directness is the preferred style. "Be up front" and "Tell it like it is" are commonly heard communication guidelines. Contrast these with the following two principles of indirectness found in the Japanese language (Tannen, 1994a):

  ~ *Omoiyari,* close in meaning to *empathy*, says that listeners need to understand the speaker without the speaker's being specific or direct. This style places a much greater demand on the listener than would a direct speaking style.

  ~ *Sassuru* advises listeners to anticipate a speaker's meanings and to use subtle cues from the speaker to infer his or her total meaning.

Cultural differences often can create misunderstandings. For example, a person from a culture that values an indirect style of speech may be speaking indirectly to be polite. If, however, you're from a culture that values a more direct style of speech, you may assume that the person is using indirectness to be manipulative, which may be how your culture regards indirectness.

Gender Influences   Verbal messages reflect considerable gender influences also. For example, take politeness. Generally, studies from various different cultures show that women's speech is more polite than men's speech, even on the telephone (Brown, 1980; Wetzel, 1988; Holmes, 1995; Smoreda & Licoppe, 2000). Women seek areas of agreement in conversation and in conflict situations more often than men do. Similarly, young girls are more apt to try to modify expressions of disagreement, whereas young boys are

Communication Choice Point

Cultural Maxims

In introducing yourself to your class, you tell of your high grades, success in sports, and plans to transfer to Harvard. The students following you, however, all appear very modest. You quickly realize that you misunderstood the culture of this classroom. *What are some things you can say to counteract the snob image you inadvertently communicated?*

apt to express more "bald disagreements" (Holmes, 1995). Women also use more polite speech when seeking to gain another person's compliance than men do (Baxter, 1984).

Disconfirmation and Confirmation

The terms *confirmation* and *disconfirmation* refer to the extent to which you acknowledge another person. Consider this situation. You've been living with someone for the last six months and you arrive home late one night. Your partner, let's say Pat, is angry and complains about your being so late. Which of the following is most likely to be your response?

1. Stop screaming. I'm not interested in what you're babbling about. I'll do what I want, when I want. I'm going to bed.

2. What are you so angry about? Didn't you get in three hours late last Thursday when you went to that office party? So knock it off.

3. You have a right to be angry. I should have called to tell you I was going to be late, but I got involved in an argument at work, and I couldn't leave until it was resolved.

In response 1, you dismiss Pat's anger and even indicate dismissal of Pat as a person. In response 2, you reject the validity of Pat's reasons for being angry but do not dismiss either Pat's feelings of anger or Pat as a person. In response 3, you acknowledge Pat's anger and the reasons for it. In addition, you provide some kind of explanation and, in doing so, show that both Pat's feelings and Pat as a person are important and that Pat has the right to know what happened. The first response is an example of disconfirmation, the second of rejection, and the third of confirmation.

Psychologist William James once observed that "no more fiendish punishment could be devised, even were such a thing physically possible, than that one should be turned loose in society and remain absolutely unnoticed by all the members thereof." In this often-quoted observation, James identifies the essence of disconfirmation (Watzlawick, Beavin, & Jackson, 1967; Veenendall & Feinstein, 1995). **Disconfirmation** is a communication pattern in which we ignore someone's presence as well as that person's communications. We say, in effect, that this person and what this person has to say are not worth serious attention or effort. The Amish community practices an extreme form of disconfirmation called "shunning," in which the community members totally ignore a person who has violated one or more of their rules. The specific aim of shunning is to get the person to repent and to reenter the community of the faithful. All cultures practice some form of exclusion for those who violate important cultural rules.

Note that **rejection** is not the same as disconfirmation. In rejection, you disagree with the person; you indicate your unwillingness to accept something the other person says or does. However, you do not deny that person's significance.

Confirmation is the opposite of disconfirmation. In confirmation you not only acknowledge the presence of the other person but also indicate your acceptance of this person, of this person's self-definition, and of your relationship as defined or viewed by this other person. Disconfirmation and confirmation may be communicated in a wide variety of ways. Table 4.2 shows a few examples.

You can gain insight into a wide variety of offensive language practices by viewing them as types of disconfirmation—as language that alienates and separates. Four obvious disconfirming practices are racism, heterosexism, ageism, and sexism; we'll look at these practices next.

Another "-ism" is **ableism**—discrimination against people with disabilities. This particular practice is handled throughout this text in a series of tables offering tips for communicating with people with and without a variety of disabilities:

- between people with and without visual problems (Chapter 1)
- between people with and without physical disabilities (Chapter 2)
- between people with and without hearing problems (Chapter 3)
- between people with and without speech and language disorders (Chapter 6)

Communication Choice Point

Discouraging Disconfirmation

For the last several months you've noticed how disconfirming your neighbors are toward their preteen children; it seems the children can never do anything to the parents' satisfaction. *What are some of the things you might say (if you do decide to get involved) to make your neighbors more aware of their communication patterns and the possible negative effects these patterns might have?*

TABLE 4.2   Confirmation and Disconfirmation

As you review this table (based largely on Galvin, Bylund, & Brommel, 2007), try to imagine a specific illustration of each of the ways of communicating disconfirmation and confirmation.

Confirmation	Disconfirmation
1. Acknowledge the presence and the contributions of the other by either supporting or taking issue with what the other says.	1. Ignore the presence and the messages of the other person; ignore or express (nonverbally and verbally) indifference to anything the other says.
2. Make nonverbal contact by maintaining direct eye contact, touching, hugging, kissing, or otherwise demonstrating acknowledgment of the other; engage in *dialogue*—communication in which both persons are speakers and listeners, both are involved, and both are concerned with each other.	2. Make no nonverbal contact; avoid direct eye contact; avoid touching the other person; engage in *monologue*—communication in which one person speaks and one person listens, there is no real interaction, and there is no real concern or respect for each other.
3. Demonstrate understanding of what the other says and means and reflect these feelings to demonstrate your understanding.	3. Jump to interpretation or evaluation rather than working at understanding what the other means; express your own feelings, ignore the feelings of the other, or give abstract, intellectualized responses.
4. Ask questions of the other concerning both thoughts and feelings and acknowledge the questions of the other; return phone calls and answer e-mails and letters.	4. Make statements about yourself; ignore any lack of clarity in the other's remarks; ignore the other's requests; and fail to answer questions, return phone calls, or answer e-mails and letters.
5. Encourage the other to express thoughts and feelings, and respond directly and exclusively to what the other says.	5. Interrupt or otherwise make it difficult for the other to express him- or herself; respond only tangentially or by shifting the focus in another direction.

RACIST SPEECH

According to Andrea Rich (1974), "any language that, through a conscious or unconscious attempt by the user, places a particular racial or ethnic group in an inferior position is racist." **Racist speech** is speech that puts down, minimizes, and marginalizes a person or group because of their race. Not only does racist speech express racist attitudes, it also contributes to the development of racist attitudes in those who use or hear the language. Even when racism is subtle, unintentional, or even unconscious, its effects are systematically damaging (Dovidio, Gaertner, Kawakami, & Hodson, 2002).

Racism exists on both individual and institutional levels (Koppelman, 2005). *Individual racism* takes the form of negative attitudes and beliefs held about specific races. Assumptions that certain races are intellectually inferior to others or incapable of particular types of achievements are clear examples of individual racism. Prejudices against American Indians, African Americans, Hispanics, and Arabs in particular have been with us throughout U.S. history and are still a part of many people's lives today. Such racism can be seen, for example, in the negative terminology that some people use to refer to members of other races and to disparage their customs and accomplishments.

Institutional racism takes forms such as communities' de facto school segregation, companies' reluctance to hire members of minority groups, and banks' unwillingness to extend loans to members of some ethnic groups or readiness to charge these groups higher interest rates. Here are some "obvious" suggestions for avoiding racist speech:

- avoid using derogatory terms for members of a particular race
- avoid basing your interactions with members of other races on stereotypes perpetuated by the media

"For me, words are a form of action, capable of influencing change."

—INGRID BENGIS

- avoid mentioning race when it's irrelevant, as in references to "the African American surgeon" or "the Asian athlete"
- avoid attributing individuals' economic or social problems to the race of the individuals rather than to their actual sources: for example, institutionalized racism or general economic problems that affect everyone

HETEROSEXIST SPEECH

Heterosexist speech also exists on both individual and institutional levels. *Individual heterosexism* refers to attitudes, behaviors, and language that disparage gay men and lesbians and includes the belief that all sexual behavior that is not heterosexual is unnatural and deserving of criticism and condemnation. Such beliefs are at the heart of antigay violence and "gay bashing." Individual heterosexism also includes the idea that homosexuals are more likely than heterosexuals to commit crimes (actually, they are neither more nor less likely) or to molest children (actually, child molesters are overwhelmingly heterosexual married men) (Abel & Harlow, 2001; Koppelman, 2005). It also includes the belief that homosexuals cannot maintain stable relationships or effectively raise children, a belief that contradicts research evidence (Fitzpatrick, Jandt, Myrick, & Edgar, 1994; Johnson & O'Connor, 2002).

Institutional heterosexism is easy to identify. The ban on gay marriage in many states and the fact that at this time only a handful of states allow gay marriage is a good example of institutional heterosexism. Other examples include the Catholic Church's ban on homosexual priests, the U.S. military's prohibition against service by openly gay people, and the many laws prohibiting adoption of children by gay people. In some cultures (e.g., in India, Malaysia, Pakistan, and Singapore) homosexual relations are illegal; penalties range from the punishment for a "misdemeanor" in Liberia to life in jail in Singapore and death in Pakistan.

Heterosexist speech includes derogatory terms used for lesbians and gay men. For example, surveys in the military showed that 80 percent of those surveyed had heard "offensive speech, derogatory names, jokes or remarks about gays" and that 85 percent believed that such derogatory speech was "tolerated" (*New York Times*, March 25, 2000, p. A12). You also see heterosexism in more subtle forms of language usage; for example, someone who qualifies a person's profession with "gay" or "lesbian"—as in "gay athlete" or "lesbian doctor"—says in effect that athletes and doctors are not normally gay or lesbian.

Still another instance of heterosexism is the presumption of heterosexuality. Usually, people assume the person they're talking to or about is heterosexual. And usually they're correct, because most people are heterosexual. At the same time, however, this presumption denies the legitimacy of a lesbian or gay identity. This practice is very similar to the social presumptions of whiteness and maleness that we have taken significant steps toward eliminating. Here are a few additional suggestions for avoiding heterosexist (or what some call *homophobic*) speech:

- Avoid offensive nonverbal mannerisms that parody stereotypes when talking about gay men and lesbians. Avoid the "startle eyeblink" with which some people react to gay couples (Mahaffey, Bryan, & Hutchison, 2005).
- Avoid "complimenting" gay men and lesbians by saying that they "don't look it." This is not a compliment.
- Avoid making the assumption that every gay or lesbian knows what every other gay or lesbian is thinking. It's very similar to asking a Japanese person why Sony is investing heavily in the United States or, as one comic put it, asking an African American, "What do you think Jesse Jackson meant by that last speech?"
- Avoid denying individual differences. Comments such as "Lesbians are so loyal" or "Gay men are so open with their feelings" ignore the reality of wide differences within any group and are potentially insulting to all groups.

Communication Choice Point

Homophobia

You're bringing your college roommate home for the holidays. She's an outspoken lesbian, but your family is rather homophobic. You want to prepare your family and your roommate for their holiday get-together. *What are some things you might say to prepare your roommate and your family for what probably will be a bumpy weekend?*

Skill Development Experience

Confirming, Rejecting, and Disconfirming

For each situation (a) write three potential responses, one of each type indicated, and (b) indicate what effects each type of response is likely to generate.

1. Angel receives this semester's grades in the mail; they're a lot better than previous semesters' grades but are still not great. After opening the letter, Angel says: *I really tried hard to get my grades up this semester.* Angel's parents respond:

   With disconfirmation: _____
   With rejection: _____
   With confirmation: _____

2. Carrie's boyfriend of seven years left her and married another woman. Carrie confides this to Samantha, who responds:

   With disconfirmation: _____
   With rejection: _____
   With confirmation: _____

Although each type of response serves a different purpose, confirming responses seem most likely to promote communication satisfaction.

- Avoid overattribution—the tendency to attribute almost everything a person does, says, and believes to the fact that the person is gay or lesbian. This tendency helps to activate and perpetuate stereotypes.

- Remember that relationship milestones are important to all people. Ignoring anniversaries or, say, the birthday of a relative's partner is bound to cause resentment.

AGEIST SPEECH

Although used mainly to refer to prejudice against older people, the term **ageism** can refer to prejudice against people of other age groups also. For example, if you describe all teenagers as selfish and undependable, you're discriminating against a group purely because of their age and thus are ageist in your statements. In some cultures—some Asian and African cultures, for example—the old are revered and respected. Younger people seek out elders for advice on economic, ethical, and relationship issues.

Individual ageism can be seen, for example, in the general disrespect many people exhibit toward for older people and in negative age-based stereotypes. *Institutional ageism* can be seen in mandatory retirement laws and age restrictions in certain occupations (rather than restrictions based on demonstrated competence). In less obvious forms ageism emerges in the media's portrayal of old people as incompetent, complaining, and, as evidenced perhaps most clearly in both television and films, lacking romantic feelings. Rarely, for example, do television shows or films show older people working productively, being cooperative and pleasant, and engaging in romantic and sexual relationships.

Popular language is replete with examples of linguistic ageism; expressions such as "little old lady," "old hag," "old-timer," "over the hill," "old coot," and "old fogy" are some examples. As with sexism, qualifying a description of someone in terms of his or her age demonstrates ageism. For example, if you refer to "a quick-witted 75-year-old" or "an agile 65-year-old" or "a responsible teenager," you're implying that these qualities are unusual in people of these ages and thus need special mention. One of the problems with this kind of stereotyping is that it's simply wrong. There are, for example, many 75-year-olds who are extremely quick-witted (and, for that matter, many 30-year-olds who aren't).

© Peter Steiner/Condé Nast Publications/www.cartoonbank.com.

You also communicate ageism when you speak to older people in overly simple words or explain things that don't need explaining. Nonverbally, you demonstrate ageist communication when, for example, you avoid touching an older person but touch others, when you avoid making direct eye contact with the older person but readily do so with others, or when you speak at an overly high volume (suggesting that all older people have hearing difficulties).

One useful way to avoid ageism is to recognize and avoid the illogical stereotypes that ageist language is based on:

- Avoid talking down to a person because he or she is older. Most older people are not mentally slow but remain mentally alert.

- Refrain from refreshing an older person's memory each time you see the person. Older people can and do remember things.

- Avoid implying that relationships are no longer important. Older people continue to be interested in relationships.

- Speak at a normal volume and maintain a normal physical distance. Being older does not necessarily mean being hard of hearing or being unable to see.

- Engage older people in conversation as you would wish to be engaged. Older people are interested in the world around them.

SEXIST SPEECH

Sexist speech also exists on both an individual and an institutional level. *Individual sexism* involves prejudicial attitudes about men or women based on rigid beliefs about gender roles. These beliefs may include, for example, the notion that all women should be caretakers, should be sensitive at all times, and should acquiesce to men's decisions concerning political or financial matters. Also sexist are the beliefs that all men are insensitive, interested only in sex, and incapable of communicating feelings.

Institutional sexism involved customs and practices that discriminate against people because of their gender. Clear examples come from the world of business: the widespread practice of paying women less than men for the same job and the frequent discrimination against women in the upper levels of management. Another clear example of institutionalized sexism is the divorce courts' practice of automatically, or almost automatically, granting child custody to the mother rather than the father.

Of particular interest here is **sexist language**: language that disparages someone because of his or her gender (but usually language derogatory toward women). The National Council of Teachers of English (NCTE) has proposed guidelines for nonsexist (gender-free, gender-neutral, or sex-fair) language. These guidelines concern the use of the generic word *man*, the use of generic *he* and *his*, and sex role stereotyping (Penfield, 1987):

- Avoid using *man* generically. Using the term to refer to both men and women emphasizes maleness at the expense of femaleness. Gender-neutral terms can easily be substituted. Instead of "mankind," say "humanity," "people," or "human beings." Similarly, the use of terms such as *policeman* or *fireman* and other terms that presume maleness as the norm—and femaleness as a deviation from this norm—are clear and common examples of sexist language.

- Avoid using *he* and *his* as generic. Instead, you can alternate pronouns or restructure your sentences to eliminate any reference to gender. For example, the NCTE guidelines (Penfield, 1987) suggest that instead of saying, "The average student is worried about his grades," you say, "The average student is worried about grades."

- Avoid sex role stereotyping. When you make the hypothetical elementary school teacher female and the college professor male or refer to doctors as male and nurses as female, you're sex role stereotyping, as you are when you mention the sex of a professional in terms such as "female doctor" or "male nurse."

Communication Choice Point

Objecting to Disconfirmation

A supervisor at work persists in using sexist, heterosexist, and racist language. You want to object to this type of talk. *What options do you have for voicing your objections? To whom would you address these objections? What would you say?*

CULTURAL IDENTIFIERS

One way to develop nonracist, nonheterosexist, nonageist, and nonsexist speech is to examine the preferred cultural identifiers to use in talking to and about members of different groups. Keep in mind, however, that preferred terms frequently change over time, so keep in touch with the most current preferences (Schwartz & Task Force, 1995; Faigley, 2009).

One general guideline is to *include* rather than *exclude*; excluding is a form of talk in which you use the terms of your own cultural group as universal, as applying to everyone. For example, *church* refers to the place of worship for some religions, not all religions. Similarly, *Bible* refers to the Christian religious scriptures and is not a general term for religious scriptures. Nor does the *Judeo-Christian tradition* include the religious traditions of everyone. Similarly, the terms *marriage*, *husband*, and *wife* refer to some heterosexual relationships and exclude others; in most of the world they also exclude gay and lesbian relationships.

Consider the vast array of alternative terms that are inclusive rather than exclusive. For example, the Association of American University Presses (Schwartz & Task Force, 1995) recommends using *place of worship* instead of *church* when you wish to include the religious houses of worship of all people. Similarly, *committed relationship* is more inclusive than *marriage*, *couples therapy* is more inclusive than *marriage counseling*, and *life partner* is more inclusive than *husband* or *wife*. *Religious scriptures* is more inclusive than *Bible*. Of course, if you're referring to, say, a specific Baptist church or married heterosexual couples, then the terms *church* and *marriage* are perfectly appropriate.

Race and Nationality   Generally, the term *African American* is preferred over *black* in referring to Americans of African descent (Hecht, Jackson, & Ribeau, 199?). However, a recent Gallop poll (**www.gallup.com/poll/28816/Black-African-American.aspx?**, accessed July 1, 2008) concluded: "The fundamental conclusion from these data underscores what has been found previously: A majority of blacks in America today do not have a preference for the use of the term black or African American. Black is often used with white, as well as in a variety of other contexts (for example, Department of Black and Puerto Rican Studies, the Journal of Black History, and Black History Month)." The American Psychological Association recommends that both terms be capitalized, but the Chicago Manual of Style (the manual used by most newspapers and publishing houses) recommends using lowercase. The terms *Negro* and *colored*, although used in the names of some organizations (e.g., the United Negro College Fund and the National Association for the Advancement of Colored People), are not used outside these contexts.

White is generally used to refer to those whose roots are in European cultures and usually does not include Hispanics. Analogous to *African American* (which itself is based on a long tradition of terms such as *Irish American* and *Italian American*) is the phrase *European American*. Few European Americans, however, call themselves that; most prefer to emphasize their national origins, as in, for example, *German American* or *Greek American*. This preference may well change as Europe moves toward becoming a more cohesive and united entity. *People of color*—a more literary-sounding term appropriate perhaps to public speaking but awkward in most conversations—is preferred to *nonwhite*, which implies that whiteness is the norm and nonwhiteness is a deviation from that norm. The same is true of the term *non-Christian*: It implies that people who have other beliefs deviate from the norm.

Generally, the *Hispanic* refers to anyone who identifies himself or herself as belonging to a Spanish-speaking culture. *Latina* (female) and *Latino* (male) refer to persons whose roots are in one of the Latin American countries, such as Haiti or Guatemala. *Hispanic American* refers to U. S. residents whose ancestry is in a Spanish culture; the term includes Mexican, Caribbean, and Central and South Americans. In emphasizing Spanish heritage, however, the term is really inaccurate; it leaves out the large numbers of people in the Caribbean and in South America whose origins are African, Native American, French, or Portuguese. *Chicana* (female) and *Chicano* (male) refer to persons with roots in Mexico, although it often connotes a nationalist attitude (Jandt, 2004) and is considered offensive by many Mexican Americans. *Mexican American* is generally preferred.

Communication Choice Point

Misusing Cultural Identifiers

During a conversation a group of classmates all use negative self-reference terms. Trying to be one of the group, you too use these terms—but almost immediately realize that the linguistic privilege allowing insiders to use self-derogatory names does not apply to outsiders (i.e., you). You don't want anyone to think that you normally talk this way. *How can you try to reverse their impressions or at least minimize their negativity?*

Inuk (plural, *Inuit*), also spelled with two *n*'s (*Innuk* and *Innuit*), is preferred to *Eskimo* (a term the U.S. Census Bureau uses), a term applied to the indigenous peoples of Alaska and Canada by Europeans and that literally means "raw meat eaters."

The word *Indian* technically refers only to someone from India, not to members of other Asian countries or to the indigenous peoples of North America. *American Indian* or *Native American* is preferred, even though many Native Americans do refer to themselves as Indians and Indian people. The word *squaw*, used to refer to a Native American woman and still used in some U.S. place names and textbooks, is clearly a term to be avoided; its usage is almost always negative and insulting (Koppelman 2005).

In Canada indigenous people are called *first people* or *first nations*. The term *native American* (with a lowercase *n*) is most often used to refer to persons born in the United States. Although technically the term could refer to anyone born in North or South America, people outside the United States generally prefer more specific designations such as *Argentinean, Cuban,* or *Canadian*. The term *native* describes an indigenous inhabitant; it is not used to indicate "someone having a less developed culture."

Muslim (rather than the older *Moslem*) is the preferred form to refer to a person who adheres to the religious teachings of Islam. *Quran* (rather than *Koran*) is the preferred term for the scriptures of Islam. *Jewish people* is often preferred to *Jews*, and *Jewess* (a Jewish female) is considered derogatory.

When English-language history books were being written exclusively from a European perspective, Europe was taken as the focal point and the rest of the world was defined in terms of its location relative to that continent. Thus, Asia became "the East" or "the Orient," and Asians became "Orientals"—a term that is today considered inappropriate or "Eurocentric." It is preferable simply to refer to people from Asia as *Asians,* just as people from Africa are *Africans* and people from Europe are *Europeans*.

Affectional Orientation   Generally, *gay* is the preferred term to refer to a man who has an affectional preference for other men, and *lesbian* is the preferred term for a woman who has an affectional preference for other women (Lever, 1995). (*Lesbian* means "homosexual woman," so the term *lesbian woman* is redundant.) *Homosexual* refers to both gays and lesbians, but more often to a sexual orientation to members of one's own sex. *Gay* and *lesbian* refer to a lifestyle and not only to sexual orientation. *Gay* as a noun, although widely used, may prove offensive in some contexts, as in "We have two gays on the team." Because most scientific thinking holds that sexuality is not a matter of choice, the terms *sexual orientation* and **affectional orientation** are preferred to *sexual preference* or *sexual status* (which also is vague).

Age   Older person is generally preferred to *elder, elderly, senior,* or *senior citizen* (which technically refers to someone older than 65). Terms designating age are rarely necessary. There are times, of course, when you need to refer to a person's age group, but most of the time you don't—in much the same way that gender, race, and affectional orientation terms are usually irrelevant.

Sex   Generally, the term *girl* should be used only to refer to very young females and is equivalent to boy. Neither term should be used for people older than 13 or 14. *Girl* is never used to refer to a grown woman, nor is *boy* used to refer to people in blue-collar positions, as it once was. *Lady* is negatively evaluated by many because it connotes the stereotype of the prim and proper woman. *Woman* or *young woman* is preferred.

Principles for Using Verbal Messages Effectively

The principles governing the verbal messages system suggest a variety of practices for using language more effectively. Here are six additional guidelines for making your verbal messages more effective and a more accurate reflection of the world in which

we live: (1) extensionalize—avoid intensional orientation, (2) see the individual—avoid allness, (3) distinguish between facts and inferences—avoid fact–inference confusion, (4) discriminate among—avoid indiscrimination, (5) talk about the middle—avoid polarization, and (6) update messages—avoid static evaluation.

EXTENSIONALIZE: AVOID INTENSIONAL ORIENTATION

Intensional orientation refers to the tendency to view people, objects, and events in terms of how they're talked about or labeled rather than in terms of how they actually exist. **Extensional orientation** is the opposite: the tendency to look first at the actual people, objects, and events and then at the labels—to be guided by what you see happening rather than by the way something or someone is talked about.

Intensional orientation occurs when you act as if the words and labels were more important than the things they represent—as if the map were more important than the territory. In its extreme form, intensional orientation is seen in the person who is afraid of dogs and who begins to sweat when shown a picture of a dog or when hearing people talk about dogs. Here the person is responding to a label as if it were the actual thing. In its more common form, intensional orientation occurs when you see people through your schemata instead of on the basis of their specific behaviors. For example, it occurs when you think of a professor as an unworldly egghead before getting to know the specific professor.

The corrective to intensional orientation is to focus first on the specific object, person, or event and then on the way in which the object, person, or event is talked about. Labels are certainly helpful guides, but don't allow them to obscure what they're meant to symbolize.

SEE THE INDIVIDUAL: AVOID ALLNESS

The world is infinitely complex, and because of this you can never say all there is to say about anything—at least not logically. This is particularly true when you are dealing with people. You may think you know all there is to know about certain individuals or about why they do, what they do, but you don't know everything.

You may, for example, go on a first date with someone who, at least during the first hour or so, turns out to be less interesting than you would have liked. Because of this initial impression you may infer that this person is generally dull. Yet, it could be that this person is simply ill-at-ease or shy during first meetings. The problem is that you run the risk of judging a person on the basis of a very short acquaintanceship. Further, if you then define this person as dull, you're likely to treat the person as dull and create a self-fulfilling prophecy.

Famed British prime minister Benjamin Disraeli once said that "to be conscious that you are ignorant is a great step toward knowledge." This observation is an excellent example of a non-**allness** attitude. If you recognize that there is always more to learn, you leave yourself open to this additional information and are better prepared to assimilate it.

A useful extensional device that can help you avoid allness is to end each statement, sometimes verbally but always mentally, with an *et cetera* (etc.)—a reminder that there is more to learn, know, and say; that every statement is inevitably incomplete. To be sure, some people overuse "et cetera." They use it as a substitute for being specific, which defeats its purpose. Instead, it should be used to mentally remind yourself that there is more to know and more to say.

DISTINGUISH BETWEEN FACTS AND INFERENCES: AVOID FACT—INFERENCE CONFUSION

Language enables you to form statements of facts and inferences without making any linguistic distinction between the two. Similarly, when you listen to such statements you often don't make a clear distinction between statements of facts and statements of inference. Yet there are great differences between the two. Barriers to clear thinking can result when inferences are treated as facts, a tendency called **fact–inference** confusion.

For example, you can make statements about things that you observe, and you can make statements about things that you have not observed. In form or structure these statements are similar; they cannot be distinguished from each other by any grammatical analysis. You can say, "She is wearing a blue jacket" as well as "She is harboring an illogical hatred." If you were to diagram these sentences, they would yield identical structures, and yet you know that they're different types of statements. In the first sentence, you can observe the jacket and the blue color; the sentence constitutes a factual statement. But how do you observe "illogical hatred"? This is an inferential rather than a descriptive statement, made not on the basis solely of what you observe but on the basis this plus your own conclusions.

Making inferential statements is necessary if you're to talk about much that is meaningful. However, a problem arises when you act as though those inferential statements are factual statements. You may wish to test your ability to distinguish facts from inferences by taking the accompanying self-test "Can You Distinguish Facts from Inferences?"

Test Yourself

Can You Distinguish Facts from Inferences?

Carefully read the following report and the observations based on it. Indicate whether you think the observations are true, false, or doubtful on the basis of the information presented in the report. Write T if the observation is definitely true, F if the observation is definitely false, and ? if the observation may be either true or false. Judge each observation in order. Do not reread the observations after you have indicated your judgment, and do not change any of your answers.

A well-liked college teacher had just completed making up the final examinations and had turned off the lights in the office. Just then a tall, broad figure with dark glasses appeared and demanded the examination. The professor opened the drawer. Everything in the drawer was picked up and the individual ran down the corridor. The dean was notified immediately.

_____ ❶ The thief was tall, broad, and wore dark glasses.

_____ ❷ The professor turned off the lights.

_____ ❸ A tall figure demanded the examination.

_____ ❹ The examination was picked up by someone.

_____ ❺ The examination was picked up by the professor.

_____ ❻ A tall, broad figure appeared after the professor turned off the lights in the office.

_____ ❼ The man who opened the drawer was the professor.

_____ ❽ The professor ran down the corridor.

_____ ❾ The drawer was never actually opened.

_____ ❿ Three persons are referred to in this report.

HOW DID YOU DO? After you respond to all the statements, form small groups of five or six and discuss the answers. Look at each statement from each member's point of view. For each statement, ask yourself, "How can you be absolutely certain that the statement is true or false?" You should find that only one statement can be clearly identified as true and only one as false; eight should be marked "?".

WHAT WILL YOU DO? Think about this exercise and try to formulate specific guidelines that will help you distinguish facts from inferences.

> **Communication Choice Point**
>
> **Confronting a Lie**
>
> You ask about the previous night's whereabouts of your romantic partner of two years and are told something you're almost certain is false. You don't want to break up the relationship over this, but you do want the truth and an opportunity to resolve the problems that contributed to this situation. *What are some of the things you might say? What are some things you'd definitely avoid saying?*

Some of the essential differences between factual and inferential statements are summarized in Table 4.3. Distinguishing between these two types of statements does not imply that one type is better than the other. Both types of statements are useful and important. The problem arises when you treat an inferential statement as if it were fact. Phrase your inferential statements as tentative. Recognize that such statements may be wrong. Leave open the possibility of other alternatives.

TABLE 4.3 **Differences between Factual and Inferential Statements**

These differences highlight the important distinctions between factual and inferential statements and are based on the discussions of Haney (1973) and Weinberg (1959). As you go through this table, consider how you would classify such statements as: "God exists," "Democracy is the best form of government," "This paper is white," "The Internet will grow in size and importance over the next 10 years," and "This table is based on Haney and Weinberg."

Factual Statements	Inferential Statements
May be made only after observation	May be made at any time
Are limited to what has been observed	Go beyond what has been observed
May be made only by the observer	May be made by anyone
May be about only the past or the present	May be about any time—past, present, or future
Approach certainty	Involve varying degrees of probability
Are subject to verifiable standards	Are not subject to verifiable standards

DISCRIMINATE AMONG: AVOID INDISCRIMINATION

Nature seems to abhor sameness at least as much as vacuums, for nowhere in the universe can you find identical entities. Everything is unique. Language, however, provides common nouns, such as teacher, student, friend, enemy, war, politician, liberal, and the like, that may lead you to focus on similarities within the group rather than individuals' differences.

Indiscrimination, a form of stereotyping, can be seen in such statements as these:

- He's just like the rest of them: lazy, stupid, a real slob.
- I really don't want another ethnic on the board of directors. One is enough for me.
- Read a romance novel? I read one when I was 16. That was enough to convince me.

A useful antidote to indiscrimination is the extensional device called the index, a spoken or mental subscript that identifies each individual in a group as an individual even though all members of the group may be covered by the same label. For example, when you think and talk of an individual politician as only a "politician," you may fail to see the uniqueness in this politician and the differences between this particular politician and other politicians. However, when you think with the index—when you think not of politician but of politician$_1$ or politician$_2$ or politician$_3$—you're less likely to fall into the trap of indiscrimination and more likely to focus on the differences among politicians. The same is true with members of cultural, national, or religious groups; when you think and even talk of Iraqi$_1$ and Iraqi$_2$, you'll be reminded that not all Iraqis are the same. The more you discriminate among individuals covered by the same label, the less likely you are to discriminate against any group.

TALK ABOUT THE MIDDLE: AVOID POLARIZATION

Polarization, often referred to as the fallacy of "either/or," is the tendency to look at the world and to describe it in terms of extremes—good or bad, positive or negative, healthy or sick, brilliant or stupid, rich or poor, and so on. Polarized statements come in many forms: for example,

- After listening to the evidence, I'm still not clear who the good guys are and who the bad guys are.
- Well, are you for us or against us?
- College had better get me a good job. Otherwise, this has been a big waste of time.

Most people and situations exist somewhere between the extremes of good and bad, healthy and sick, brilliant and stupid, rich and poor. Yet there seems to be a strong tendency to view only the extremes and to categorize people, objects, and events in terms of these polar opposites (Gamson, 1998).

You can easily demonstrate this tendency by filling in the opposites for each of the following words:

		Opposite
tall	___:___:___:___:___:___	_____
heavy	___:___:___:___:___:___	_____
strong	___:___:___:___:___:___	_____
happy	___:___:___:___:___:___	_____
legal	___:___:___:___:___:___	_____

Filling in the opposites should have been relatively easy and quick. The words should also have been fairly short. Further, even if various people were to supply their own opposites, there would be a high degree of agreement among them.

Now try to fill in the middle positions with words meaning, for example, "midway between tall and short," "midway between heavy and light," and so on. Do this before reading any farther.

These midway responses (compared to the opposites) were probably more difficult to think of and took you more time. The responses should also have been long words or phrases of several words. Further, different people would probably agree less on these midway responses than on the opposites.

This exercise illustrates the ease with which you can think and talk in opposites and the difficulty you have in thinking and talking about the middle. But recognize that the vast majority of cases exist between extremes. Don't allow the ready availability of extreme terms to obscure the reality of what lies in between (Read, 2004).

In some cases, of course, it's legitimate to talk in terms of two values. For example, either this thing you're holding is a book or it isn't. Clearly, the classes "book" and "not-book" include all possibilities. There is no problem with this kind of statement. Similarly, you may say that a student either will pass this course or will not, as these two categories include all the possibilities.

You create problems when you use this either/or form in situations in which it's inappropriate: for example, "The supervisor is either for us or against us." The two choices simply don't include all possibilities: The supervisor may be for us in some things and against us in others, or he or she may be neutral. Right now there is a tendency to group people into categories of pro- and antiwar; similarly, you see examples of polarization in opinions about the Middle East, with some people entirely and totally supportive of one side and others entirely and totally supportive of the other side. However, polarizing categories are created for almost every important political or social issue: "pro" and "anti" positions on abortion and taxes, for example. These extremes do not include all possibilities and prevent us from entertaining the vast middle ground that exists on all such issues and in most people's minds.

UPDATE MESSAGES: AVOID STATIC EVALUATION

Language changes very slowly, especially when compared to the rapid pace at which people and things change. When you retain a judgment of a person, despite the inevitable changes in the person, you're engaging in **static evaluation**.

Although you would probably agree that everything is in a constant state of flux, the relevant question is whether you *act* as if you know this. Do you treat your little sister as if she were 10 years old, or do you treat her like the 20-year-old woman she has become? Your evaluations of yourself and others need to keep pace with the rapidly changing real world. Otherwise you'll be left with attitudes and beliefs—static evaluations—about a world that no longer exists.

To guard against static evaluation, use a device called the **date**, a mental subscript that enables you to look at your statement in the context of time. Dating your statement is especially important when your statements are evaluative. Remember that Gerry Smith$_{2002}$ is not Gerry Smith$_{2010}$, that academic abilities$_{2006}$ are not academic abilities$_{2010}$.

These six guidelines will not solve all problems in verbal communication, but they will help you to more accurately align your language with reality. At the same time, recognize that each of these six guidelines can be used to deceive you. For example, when people treat individuals as they're labeled or influence you to respond to people in terms of their labels (often racist, sexist, or homophobic), they are using intensional orientation unethically. Similarly, when people present themselves as knowing everything about something (gossip is often a good example), they are exploiting the natural tendency for people to think in allness terms to achieve their own ends. When people present inferences as if they are facts (again, gossip provides a good example) to secure your belief or

"What we know of other people is only our memory of the moments during which we knew them. And they have changed since then . . . at every meeting we are meeting a stranger."

—T. S. ELIOT

when they stereotype, they are relying on your tendency to confuse facts and inferences and to fail to discriminate. And, when people talk in terms of opposites (polarize) or as if things and people don't change (static evaluation) in order to influence you, they are again assuming you won't talk about the middle ground or ask for updated information.

 # Summary of Concepts and Skills

Focusing on verbal messages, this chapter first looked at the nature of language and identified several major ways in which language works. The next section examined confirmation and disconfirmation and the related topics of racist, heterosexist, ageist, and sexist language. The final section presented ways to make verbal communication more accurate and effective.

1. Communication is a package of verbal and nonverbal signals.
2. Language is both denotative (i.e., objective and generally easily agreed on) and connotative (i.e., subjective and generally highly individual in meaning).
3. Language varies in abstraction; it can range from extremely general to extremely specific.
4. Language varies in directness; it can state exactly what you mean, or it can hedge and state your meaning very indirectly.
5. Language meanings are in people, not simply in words.
6. Language is influenced by culture and gender.
7. Disconfirmation is the process of ignoring the presence and the communications of others. Confirmation means accepting, supporting, and acknowledging the importance of other people.
8. Racist, heterosexist, ageist, and sexist language disconfirms, puts down, and negatively evaluates various groups.
9. To make verbal messages more effective, realize that language symbolizes reality and is not the reality itself; that language can express both facts and inferences but doesn't indicate this grammatically; that language can obscure distinctions, as when it provides lots of extreme terms but few terms to describe the middle ground; and that language tends to be static, whereas people and events are forever changing.

The study of verbal messages and of how meaning is communicated from one person to another has important implications for the skills of effective communication. Place a check mark next to those skills that you feel you need to work on most.

_____ 1. Because communication is a package of signals, I ensure my verbal and nonverbal messages reinforce rather than contradict each other.

_____ 2. I try to understand not only objective, denotative meanings but also the speaker's subjective, connotative meanings.

_____ 3. I recognize that snarl and purr words describe the speaker's feelings and not objective reality.

_____ 4. I use terms varying in abstraction to best communicate my meanings.

_____ 5. I vary my directness depending on the situation and my communication goal.

_____ 6. I take special care to make spoken messages clear and unambiguous, especially when using terms for which people will have very different connotative meanings.

_____ 7. I recognize cultural and gender differences in the use of verbal messages and avoid assuming that my principles are followed by members of other cultures.

_____ 8. I focus attention not only on words but also on the person communicating, recognizing that meanings are largely in the person.

_____ 9. I avoid disconfirmation and instead use messages that confirm the other person.

_____ 10. I avoid racist, heterosexist, ageist, and sexist language and, in general, language that puts down other groups.

_____ 11. I use the cultural identifiers that facilitate communication and avoid those that set up barriers to effective interaction.

_____ 12. I avoid responding intensionally to labels as if they are objects; instead, I respond extensionally and look first at the reality and secondarily at the words.

_____ 13. To avoid allness, I end my statements with an implicit "et cetera" in recognition that there is always more to be known or said.

_____ 14. I distinguish facts from inferences and respond to inferences with tentativeness.

_____ 15. I avoid indiscrimination by viewing the uniqueness in each person and situation.

_____ 16. I avoid polarization by using "middle ground" terms and qualifiers in describing the world, especially people.

_____ 17. I mentally date my statements and thus avoid static evaluation.

Key Word Quiz

The Language of Verbal Messages

Match the terms about verbal messages with their definitions. Record the number of the definition next to the appropriate term.

_____ a. static evaluation (89)

_____ b. confirmation (78)

_____ c. intensional orientation (85)

_____ d. direct messages (73)

_____ e. ableism (78)

_____ f. denotation (72)

_____ g. disconfirmation (78)

_____ h. polarization (88)

_____ i. connotation (72)

_____ j. the maxim of quality (76)

1. The objective meaning of a term; the meaning you'd find in a dictionary.
2. Messages that are often considered impolite.
3. The principle that speakers follow in saying what they know or assume to be true.
4. A communication pattern in which you ignore someone's presence as well as that person's communication.
5. The failure to recognize the influence of change.
6. The subjective or emotional meaning that specific speakers give a word.
7. A communication pattern in which you indicate your acceptance of the other person's self-definition.
8. The tendency to view people, objects, and events in the way they're talked about or labeled.
9. The tendency to talk and think in terms of extremes or opposites.
10. Discrimination against people with disabilities.

These ten terms and additional terms used in this chapter can be found in the glossary and on flashcards on MyCommunicationLab (**www.mycommunicationlab.com**).

Answers: a. 5 b. 7 c. 8 d. 2 e. 10 f. 1 g. 4 h. 9 i. 6 j. 3

MyCommunicationLab

PEARSON mycommunicationlab

www.mycommunicationlab.com

Visit MyCommunicationLab (**www.mycommunicationlab.com**) for a wealth of additional information on verbal messages. Flash cards, videos, skill building exercises, sample test questions, and additional examples and discussions will help you continue your study of verbal messages and the corresponding skills for effective communication.

TABLE 5.2   **Five Body Movements**

What other examples can you think of for these five movements?

	Name and Function	Examples
	EMBLEMS directly translate words or phrases; they are especially culture specific.	"OK" sign, "come here" wave, hitchhiker's sign
	ILLUSTRATORS accompany and literally "illustrate" verbal messages.	Circular hand movements when talking of a circle; hands far apart when talking of something large
	AFFECT DISPLAYS communicate emotional meaning.	Expressions of happiness, surprise, fear, anger, sadness, disgust/contempt
	REGULATORS monitor, maintain, or control the speech of another.	Facial expressions and hand gestures indicating "keep going," "slow down," or "what else happened?"
	ADAPTORS satisfy some need.	Scratching your head

Your general **attractiveness**, which includes both visual appeal and pleasantness of personality, is also a part of body communication. Attractive people have the advantage in just about every activity you can name. They get better grades in school, are more valued as friends and lovers, and are preferred as coworkers (Burgoon, Buller, & Woodall, 1996). Although we normally think that attractiveness is culturally determined—and to some degree it is—some research shows that definitions of attractiveness are becoming universal (*New York Times*, March 21, 1994, p. A14). A person rated as attractive in one culture is likely to be rated as attractive in other cultures—even in cultures in which people are quite different in appearance.

FACIAL AND EYE COMMUNICATION

The facial area, including the eyes, is probably the single most important source of nonverbal messages.

Facial Communication   Throughout your interpersonal interactions, your face communicates many things, especially your emotions. In fact, facial movements alone seem to communicate the degree of pleasantness, agreement, and sympathy felt; the rest of the body doesn't provide any additional information in those realms. But for other aspects—for example, the intensity with which an emotion is felt—both facial and bodily cues enter in (Graham, Bitti, & Argyle, 1975; Graham & Argyle, 1975). These cues are so important in communicating your full meaning that graphic representations are now commonly used in electronic communication. On the Internet, emoticon buttons to help you encode your emotions graphically are now common. Table 5.3 identifies some of the more common emoticons.

Some nonverbal research claims that facial movements may communicate at least the following eight emotions: happiness, surprise, fear, anger, sadness, disgust, contempt, and interest (Ekman, Friesen, & Ellsworth, 1972). Try to communicate surprise using only facial movements. Do this in front of a mirror and try to describe in as much detail as possible the specific movements of the face that make up a look of surprise. If you signal surprise like most people, you probably use raised and curved eyebrows, horizontal forehead wrinkles, wide-open eyes, a dropped-open mouth, and lips parted with no tension.

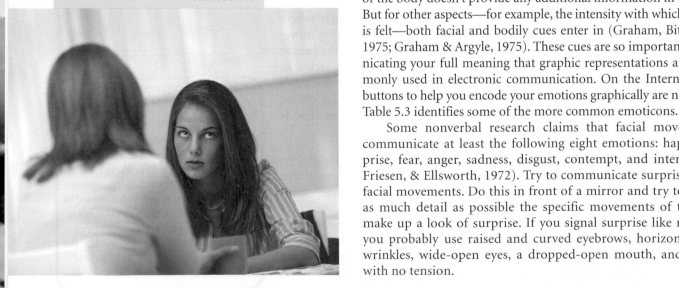

"The body says what words cannot."

—MARTHA GRAHAM

These are some of the emoticons used in computer communication. The first six are widely used in the United States; the last three are popular in Japan and illustrate how culture influences such symbols. Because Japanese culture considers it impolite for women to show their teeth when smiling, the emoticon for a woman's smile shows a dot signifying a closed mouth. Additional emoticons, acronyms, and abbreviations can be found at www.cafeshops.com/netlingo.

Emoticon	Meaning	Emoticon	Meaning
:-)	Smile: I'm kidding	{*****}	Hugs and kisses
:-(	Frown: I'm feeling down	^.^	Woman's smile
;-)	Wink	^_^	Man's smile
*	Kiss	^0^	Happy
{ }	Hug		

Facial Management.   As you grew up, you learned your culture's system of nonverbal communication. You also learned certain **facial management techniques** that enable you to express feelings while achieving certain desired effects—for example, to hide certain emotions and to emphasize others. Consider your own use of such facial management techniques. As you do so, think about the types of situations in which you would use facial management techniques for each of the following purposes (Malandro, Barker, & Barker, 1989; Metts & Planalp, 2002):

- to intensify—for example, to exaggerate your astonishment at a surprise party to make your friends feel better.
- to deintensify—for example, to cover up your own joy about good news in the presence of a friend who didn't receive any such news.
- to neutralize—for example, to cover up your sadness so as not to depress others.
- to mask—for example, to express happiness in order to cover up your disappointment at not receiving a gift you expected.
- to simulate—to express an emotion you don't feel.

Facial management techniques help you display emotions in socially acceptable ways. For example, if someone gets bad news in which you secretly take pleasure, the social display rule dictates that you frown and otherwise nonverbally signal sorrow. If you place first in a race and your best friend barely finishes, the display rule requires that you minimize your expression of happiness—and certainly avoid any signs of gloating. If you violate these display rules, you'll appear insensitive. So, although facial management techniques may be deceptive, they're expected and even required by the rules for polite interaction.

Facial Feedback.   According to the **facial feedback hypothesis**, your facial expression influences your level of physiological arousal. People who exaggerate their facial expressions show higher physiological arousal than those who suppress these expressions. In research studies, those who neither exaggerated nor suppressed their expressions had arousal levels between these two extremes (Lanzetta, Cartwright-Smith, & Kleck, 1976; Zuckerman, Klorman, Larrance, & Spiegel, 1981). In one interesting study, subjects held a pen in their teeth in such a way as to simulate a sad expression. They were then asked to rate photographs. Results showed that mimicking sad expressions actually increased the degree of sadness the subjects reported feeling when viewing the photographs (Larsen, Kasimatis, & Frey, 1992). So, not only does your facial expression influence the judgments and impressions others have of you, it also influences your own level of emotional arousal (Cappella, 1993).

"Look at me. Do I look worried?"

© Bernard Schoenbaum/Condé Nast Publications/www.cartoonbank.com.

Eye Communication The messages communicated by the eyes vary depending on the duration, direction, and quality of the eye behavior. For example, every culture has rather strict, though unstated, rules for the proper duration of eye contact. In one study conducted in England, the average length of gaze was found to be 2.95 seconds. The average length of mutual gaze (i.e., two persons gazing at each other) is 1.18 seconds (Argyle & Ingham, 1972; Argyle, 1988). When eye contact falls short of this amount, members of some cultures may think the person is uninterested, shy, or preoccupied. When the appropriate amount of time is exceeded, they may perceive the person as showing unusually high interest or even hostility.

The direction of the gaze also communicates. In the United States it is considered appropriate to glance alternately at the other person's face, then away, then again at the face, and so on. The rule for public speakers is to scan the entire audience, not focusing for too long on or ignoring any one area of the audience. When you break these directional rules, you communicate different meanings—abnormally high or low interest, self-consciousness, nervousness over the interaction, and so on. How wide or narrow your eyes get during an interaction also communicates meaning, especially interest level and emotions such as surprise, fear, and disgust.

You use eye contact to serve several important functions (Knapp & Hall, 2006; Malandro, Barker, & Barker, 1989; Richmond, McCroskey, & Hickson, 2008).

- *To monitor feedback.* For example, when you talk with others, you try to understand their reactions to what you're saying; you try to read their feedback and, on this basis, adjust what you say.

- *To secure attention.* When you speak with two or three other people, you maintain eye contact to secure the attention and interest of your listeners.

- *To regulate the conversation.* Eye contact helps you regulate, manage, and control the conversation: for example, nodding at a person to signal that you'd like the person to respond.

- *To signal the nature of the relationship.* Eye communication can also serve as a tie-sign and helps to signal the nature of the relationship between two people: for example, it can indicate your affection for or dislike of another person.

- *To signal status.* Eye contact is often used to signal status and aggression. Among many younger people, prolonged eye contact from a stranger is taken to signify aggressiveness and may even prompt physical violence.

- *To compensate for physical distance.* By making eye contact you overcome psychologically the physical distance between yourself and another person. When you catch someone's eye at a party, for example, you become psychologically closer even though you may be separated by considerable physical distance.

When you avoid eye contact or avert your glance, you also communicate meanings. One function of eye avoidance is to help others maintain their privacy. For example, you might engage in what is called **civil inattention**. When you see a couple arguing in public, for example, you might turn your eyes away (although your eyes may be wide open) as if to say, "I don't mean to intrude; I respect your privacy" (Goffman, 1967).

Eye avoidance also can signal lack of interest—in another person, a conversation, or some visual stimulus. At times you may hide your eyes to block off unpleasant stimuli, or you may close your eyes to block out visual stimuli and thus heighten other senses. For example, you may listen to music with your eyes closed. Lovers often close their eyes while kissing, and many prefer to make love in a dark or dimly lit room.

"What we learn through the ears makes less impression upon our minds than what is presented to the trustworthy eye."

—HORACE

SPATIAL COMMUNICATION

Space is an especially important factor in nonverbal interpersonal communication, although we seldom think about it. Edward T. Hall (1959, 1963, 1966), who pioneered the study of spatial communication, called this study **proxemics**. We can sample this broad area by looking at proxemic distances and territoriality.

Proxemic Distances   Hall (1959, 1966) distinguishes four distances that define types of relationships between people; each distance communicates specific kinds of messages.

At an **intimate distance**, ranging from touching to 18 inches apart, the presence of the other individual is unmistakable. Each person experiences the sound, smell, and feel of the other's breath. You use intimate distance for lovemaking and wrestling, for comforting and protecting. This distance is so short that most people do not consider it proper in public.

Personal distance constitutes the protective "bubble" that defines your personal space, which measures from 18 inches to 4 feet. This imaginary bubble keeps you protected and untouched by others. You can still hold or grasp another person at this distance—but only by extending your arms—allowing you to take certain individuals such as loved ones into your protective bubble. At the outer limit of personal distance, you can touch another person only if both of you extend your arms.

At a **social distance**, ranging from 4 to 12 feet, you lose the visual detail you have at personal distance. You conduct impersonal business and interact at a social gathering at this social distance. The more distance you maintain in your interactions, the more formal they appear. Many people in executive and management positions place their desks so that they are assured of at least this distance from employees.

Public distance, measuring from 12 to 25 feet or more, protects you. At this distance you could take defensive action if threatened. On a public bus or train, for example, you might keep at least this distance from a drunk. Although you lose fine details of the face and eyes at this distance, you are still close enough to see what is happening. These four distances are summarized in Table 5.4.

Territoriality   Another type of communication having to do with space is **territoriality**, a possessive reaction to an area or to particular objects. You interact basically in three types of territory (Altman, 1975):

- **Primary territories** are areas that you might call your own; these areas are your exclusive preserve. Primary territories might include your room, your desk, or your office.

TABLE 5.4	Relationships and Proxemic Distances

Note that the four proxemic distances can be further divided into close and far phases and that the far phase of one level (say, the personal level) blends into the close phase of the next level (social). Do your relationships also blend into one another or are your personal relationships totally separate from your social relationships?

Relationship	Distance		Relationship	Distance	
Intimate Relationship	Intimate Distance 0 _____ 18 inches Close phase / Far phase		Social Relationship	Social Distance 4 _____ 12 feet Close phase / Far phase	
Personal Relationship	Personal Distance 1½ _____ 4 feet Close phase / Far phase		*Public Relationship*	Public Distance 12 _____ 25+ feet *Close phase* / *Far phase*	

Communication Choice Point

Proxemics

Like the close-talker in an episode of *Seinfeld*, one of your team members at work maintains an extremely close distance when talking. In addition, he's a heavy smoker and reeks of smoke. You need to say something. *What are some of the things you might say? In what context would you say it?*

- **Secondary territories** are areas that don't belong to you but that you have occupied and with which you're associated. They might include your usual table in the cafeteria, your regular seat in the classroom, or your neighborhood turf.

- **Public territories** are areas that are open to all people; they may be owned by some person or organization, but they are used by everyone. They are places such as movie theaters, restaurants, and shopping malls.

When you operate in your own primary territory, you have an interpersonal advantage, often called the **home field advantage**. In their own home or office, people take on a kind of leadership role: They initiate conversations, fill in silences, assume relaxed and comfortable postures, and maintain their positions with greater conviction. Because the territorial owner is dominant, you stand a better chance of getting your raise approved, your point accepted, or a contract resolved in your favor if you're in your own territory (e.g., your office or your home) rather than in someone else's (e.g., your supervisor's office) (Marsh, 1988).

Like many animals, humans mark both their primary and secondary territories to signal ownership. Humans use three types of **markers:** central, boundary, and earmarkers (Goffman, 1971). **Central markers** are items you place in a territory to reserve it for you—for example, a drink at the bar, books on your desk, or a sweater over a library chair. Some people, perhaps because they can't own territories, might use markers to indicate a kind of pseudo-ownership or to appropriate someone else's turf or a public territory for their own use (Childress, 2004). Examples include graffiti and the markings of gang boundaries.

Boundary markers serve to divide your territory from that of others. In the supermarket checkout line, the bar placed between your groceries and those of the person behind you is a boundary marker, as are fences, armrests that separate your seat from those on either side, and the contours of the molded plastic seats on a bus.

Earmarkers—a term taken from the practice of branding animals on their ears— are identifying marks that indicate your possession of a territory or object. Trademarks, nameplates, and initials on a shirt or attaché case are all examples of ear markers.

Markers are also important in giving you a feeling of belonging. For example, one study found that students who marked their college dorm rooms by displaying personal

Skill Development Experience

Sitting at the Company Meeting

Nonverbal choices influence your communication effectiveness and your image as a communicator.

The accompanying graphic represents a table with 12 chairs, one of which is occupied by the "boss." For each of the following messages, indicate (a) where you would sit to communicate each message and (b) any other possible messages that your choice of seat will probably communicate.

1. You want to ingratiate yourself with your boss.

2. You aren't prepared and want to be ignored.

3. You want to challenge the boss's proposal that is scheduled to come up for a vote.

4. You want to get to know better the person at seat number 7.

items stayed in school longer than did those who didn't personalize their spaces (Marsh, 1988).

Again, like animals, humans use territory to signal their status. For example, the size and location of your territory (your home or office, say) indicates something about your status. Status is also signaled by the unwritten law governing the right of invasion. Higher-status individuals have a "right" to invade the territory of lower-status persons, but the reverse is not true. The boss of a large company, for example, can barge into the office of a junior executive, but the reverse would be unthinkable. Similarly, a teacher may invade a student's personal space by looking over her or his shoulder as the student writes, but the student cannot do the same to the teacher.

ARTIFACTUAL COMMUNICATION

Artifactual messages are messages conveyed through objects or arrangements made by human hands. The colors you prefer, the clothing or jewelry you wear, the way you decorate your space, and even bodily scents communicate a wide variety of meanings.

Color Communication

There is some evidence that the colors with which people surround themselves affect them physiologically. For example, respiration rates increase in the presence of red light and decrease in the presence of blue light. Similarly, eye blinks increase in frequency when eyes are exposed to red light and decrease when exposed to blue. These findings seem consistent with our intuitive feelings that blue is more soothing and red more provocative. After the administration at one school changed the classroom walls from orange and white to blue, the students' blood pressure levels decreased and their academic performance improved (Ketcham, 1958; Malandro, Barker, & Barker, 1989).

Colors influence our perceptions and behaviors (Kanner, 1989). People's acceptance of a product, for example, is strongly influenced by its packaging. In one experiment consumers in the United States described the very same coffee taken from a yellow can as weak, from a dark brown can as too strong, from a red can as rich, and from a blue can as mild. Even our acceptance of a person may depend on the colors that person wears. Consider, for example, the comments of one color expert (Kanner, 1989, p. 23): "If you have to pick the wardrobe for your defense lawyer heading into court and choose anything but blue, you deserve to lose the case. . . ." Black is so powerful that it can work against the lawyer with the jury. Brown lacks sufficient authority. Green will probably elicit a negative response; it's likely to be seen as too different from the expected and acceptable norm for lawyers.

Clothing and Body Adornment

People make inferences about who you are partly on the basis of how you dress. Whether accurate or not, these inferences will affect what people think of you and how they react to you. Your social class, your seriousness, your attitudes your concern for convention, your sense of style, and perhaps even your creativity will all be judged—in part at least—by the way you dress. In the business world, what you wear may communicate your position within the hierarchy and your willingness and desire to conform to the clothing norms of the organization. It also may communicate your level of professionalism, which seems to be the reason some organizations favor dress codes (Smith, 2003).

Your jewelry also communicates messages about you. Wedding and engagement rings are obvious examples. If you wear a Rolex watch or large precious stones, others are likely to infer that you are rich. Men who wear earrings will be judged differently from men who don't.

The way you wear your hair says something about who you are—from a concern about being up to date to a desire to shock to, perhaps, a lack of interest in appearances. Men with long hair, to take only one example, will generally be judged as less conservative than those with shorter hair. And in a study of male baldness, participants rated a man

Communication Choice Point

Clothing Communication

One of your friends has been passed over for promotion several times. You think you know the reason—your friend dresses inappropriately. *What are some things you might say to help, knowing that you friend is extremely sensitive to criticism?*

with a full head of hair as younger and more dominant, masculine, and dynamic than the same man without hair (Butler, Pryor, & Grieder, 1998).

Body piercings and tattoos communicate too. Although people wearing, for example, nose rings or belly button jewelry may wish to communicate positive meanings, those interpreting the messages of body piercings seem to infer that wearers are communicating an unwillingness to conform to social norms and a willingness to take greater risks than those without such piercings (Forbes, 2001). In a study of employers' perceptions, employers rated and ranked job applicants with eyebrow piercings significantly lower than those without such piercings (Acor, 2001). Nose-pierced job candidates received lower scores on measures of credibility such as ratings of character and trustworthiness, as well as on sociability and hirability (Seiter & Sandry, 2003).

Tattoos—whether temporary or permanent—likewise communicate a variety of messages, often the name of a loved one or some symbol of allegiance or affiliation. Tattoos also communicate to the wearers themselves. For example, tattooed students see themselves (and perhaps others do as well) as more adventurous, creative, individualistic, and risk prone than those without tattoos (Drews, Allison, & Probst, 2000). Tattoos and piercings on health care professionals have been found to communicate such undesirable traits as impulsiveness, unpredictability, and a tendency toward being reckless or violent (Rapsa & Cusack, 1990; Smith, 2003).

Space Decoration

The decoration of your workplace tells a lot about you. The office with the mahogany desk and bookcase and oriental rugs communicates importance and status within an organization, just as a metal desk and bare floor indicate an entry-level employee much farther down in the company hierarchy.

Similarly, people will make inferences about you based on the way you decorate your home. The expensiveness of the furnishings may communicate your status and wealth; their coordination, your sense of style. The magazines on your coffee table may reflect your interests, and the arrangement of chairs around a television set may reveal how important watching television is to you. The contents of bookcases lining the walls reveal the importance of reading in your life. In fact, there is probably little in your home that does not send messages from which others will make inferences about you. At the same time, the lack of certain items will communicate something about you. Consider what messages you would get from a home where no television, phone, or books could be seen.

People also will make judgments about your personality on the basis of room decorations, e.g., your openness to new experiences (distinctive decorating usually communicates openness, as would travel souvenirs), conscientiousness, emotional stability, degree of extroversion, and agreeableness.

Smell Communication

Smell communication, or olfactory communication, is extremely important in a wide variety of situations; indeed, the study known as **olfactics** is now "big business" (Kleinfeld, 1992). Although we often think of women as the primary users of perfumes and scents, increasingly men are using them as well—not only the cologne and aftershave lotions they have long used but more recently body sprays, for which the market has been estimated at $180 million (Dell, 2005). Different scents have different effects. For example, there is some evidence (although not conclusive) that the smell of lemon contributes to a perception of health. The smells of lavender and eucalyptus seem to increase alertness, and the smell of rose oil seems to reduce blood pressure. Research also finds that smells can influence your body's chemistry, which in turn influences your emotional state. For example, the smell of chocolate results in the reduction of theta brain waves, thus bringing a sense of relaxation and a reduced level of attention (Martin, 1998). Findings such as these have contributed to the growth of aromatherapy (Furlow, 1996). Because humans possess "denser skin concentrations of scent glands than almost any other mammal," it has been argued that we need only to discover how we use scent to communicate a wide variety of messages (Furlow, 1996, p. 41). Two particularly important messages scent communicates are those of attraction and identification.

Communication Choice Point

Artifactual Communication

One problem with a group of interns you're mentoring is that they've done questionable things on various social networking sites—posted inappropriate pictures, used biased language, and in general portrayed themselves as not serious enough. You need to get them to become aware of how damaging this could be, at least at XYZ Company. *What might you say? What channel would you use to communicate your thoughts? Would you communicate to them individually or as a group?*

Attraction Messages.　People use perfumes, colognes, aftershave lotions, powders, and the like in an effort to enhance attractiveness. You also use scents to make yourself feel better. When you smell pleasant, you feel better about yourself; when you smell unpleasant, you feel less good about yourself—and probably shower and perhaps put on some cologne.

Identification Messages.　Smell is often used to create an image or an identity for a product. Advertisers and manufacturers spend millions of dollars each year creating scents for cleaning products and toothpastes, for example, which have nothing to do with products' cleaning power; instead, they function solely to create an image for the products. There is also evidence that we can identify specific significant others by smell. For example, young children were able to identify the T-shirts of their brothers and sisters solely by smell (Porter & Moore, 1981).

TOUCH COMMUNICATION

Touch communication, or tactile communication, is perhaps the most primitive form of nonverbal communication (Montagu, 1971). Touch develops before the other senses; a child is stimulated by touch even in the womb. Soon after birth, the child is fondled, caressed, patted, and stroked. In turn, the child explores its world through touch and quickly learns to communicate a variety of meanings through touch.

Touching varies greatly from one culture to another. For example, African Americans touch each other more than European Americans, and touching declines from kindergarten to the sixth grade for European Americans but not for African American children (Burgoon, Buller, & Woodall, 1996). Japanese people touch each other much less than Anglo-Saxons, who in turn touch much less than southern Europeans (Morris, 1977; Burgoon, Buller, & Woodall, 1996).

Not surprisingly, touch also varies with your relationship stage. In the early stages of acquaintance, you touch little; in intermediate stages of relationship development (i.e., involvement and intimacy), you touch a great deal; and at stable or deteriorating stages of a relationship, you again touch little (Guerrero & Andersen, 1991).

The Meanings of Touch　Researchers in the field of **haptics**, or the study of touch communication, have identified the major meanings of touch (Jones, 2005; Jones & Yarbrough, 1985). Here are five of the most important.

- Touch may communicate *positive emotions* such as support, appreciation, inclusion, sexual interest or intent, and affection.
- Touch often communicates *playfulness,* either affectionately or aggressively.
- Touch may also *control* or direct the behaviors, attitudes, or feelings of another person. To get attention, for example, you may touch a person as if to say, "Look at me" or "Look over here."
- *Ritual* touching centers on greetings and departures, as in shaking hands to say hello or good-bye or hugging, kissing, or putting your arm around another's shoulder when greeting or saying farewell.
- *Task-related* touching occurs while you are performing some function—for example, removing a speck of dust from another person's face or helping someone out of a car.

As you can imagine, touching may also get you into trouble. For example, touching that is too positive (or too intimate) too early in a relationship may send the wrong signals. Similarly playing that is too rough or holding someone's arm to control their movements may be resented. Using ritualistic touching incorrectly or in ways that may be culturally insensitive may likewise get you into difficulty.

Touch Avoidance　Much as we have a tendency to touch and be touched, we also have a tendency to avoid touch from certain people or in certain circumstances. Researchers in nonverbal communication have found some interesting relationships between **touch avoidance** and other significant communication variables (Andersen & Leibowitz, 1978).

Communication Choice Point

Smell

Your colleague in the next cubicle wears extremely strong cologne that you find horrendous. You can't continue smelling this horrible scent any longer. *What choices do you have to changing this colleague's use of cologne? What might you say? What channel would you use?*

Communication Choice Point

Touch Boundaries

A colleague at work continually touches you in passing—your arm, your shoulder, your waist. These touches are becoming more frequent and more intimate. You want this touching to stop. *What are some of your options for stopping this behavior? To whom would you speak/write? What would you say?*

Touch avoidance is positively related to communication apprehension: Those who fear oral communication also score high on touch avoidance. Touch avoidance is also high in those who self-disclose little. Both touch and self-disclosure are intimate forms of communication; people who are reluctant to get close to another person by self-disclosing also seem reluctant to get close by touching.

Touch avoidance is also affected by age and gender (Guerrero & Andersen, 1994; Crawford, 1994). Older people have higher touch-avoidance scores for opposite-sex persons than do younger people. Males score higher on same-sex touch avoidance than do females, which matches our stereotypes (Martin & Anderson, 1993). That is, men avoid touching other men, but women may and do touch other women. On the other hand, women have higher touch-avoidance scores for opposite-sex touching than do men (Andersen, Andersen, & Lustig, 1987).

PARALANGUAGE AND SILENCE

Paralanguage is the vocal but nonverbal dimension of speech. It has to do with *how* you say something rather than what you say. As we'll see, silence is the absence of sound but not of communication.

Paralanguage   An old exercise teachers used to increase students' ability to express different emotions, feelings, and attitudes was to have the students repeat a sentence while accenting or stressing different words each time. Placing the stress on different words easily communicates significant differences in meaning. Consider the following variations of the sentence "Is this the face that launched a thousand ships?"

1. *Is* this the face that launched a thousand ships?
2. Is *this* the face that launched a thousand ships?
3. Is this the *face* that launched a thousand ships?
4. Is this the face that *launched* a thousand ships?
5. Is this the face that launched *a thousand ships?*

Each sentence communicates something different—in fact, each asks a different question, even though the words are the same. All that varies among the sentences is which words are stressed, one aspect of paralanguage.

In addition to stress, paralanguage includes such vocal characteristics as rate, volume, and rhythm. It also includes the vocalizations you make when crying, whispering, moaning, belching, yawning, and yelling (Trager, 1958, 1961; Argyle, 1988). A variation in any of these vocal features communicates. When you speak quickly, for example, you communicate something different from when you speak slowly. Even though the words are the same, if the speed (or volume, rhythm, or pitch) differs, the meanings people receive also differ.

Judgments about People.   Many people make judgments about people's personalities on the basis of their paralinguistic cues. For example, they might conclude that your colleague who speaks softly when presenting ideas at a meeting isn't sure of the ideas' usefulness and believes that no one really wants to listen to them. Or they might assume that people who speak loudly have overinflated egos or those who speak in a monotone are uninterested in what they are saying and perhaps in life in general. All such judgments are based on little evidence, yet they persist in much popular talk.

Research has found that people can accurately judge the socioeconomic status (whether high, middle, or low) of speakers from 60-second voice samples (Davitz, 1964). Participants also rated people whom they judged to be of high status as more credible than speakers judged to be of middle and low status.

Listeners also can accurately judge the emotional states of speakers from vocal expression alone. In these studies, speakers recite the alphabet or numbers while expressing emotions. Some emotions are easier to identify than others; it is easy to distinguish between hate and sympathy but more difficult to distinguish between fear and anxiety (Scherer, 1986).

Earlier in this chapter we saw that impression management is one of the major functions of nonverbal communication. Now that you've read about the types of nonverbal messages, consider how you would manage yourself nonverbally in the following situations. For each of these situations, indicate (1) the impressions you'd want to create (e.g., an image as a hardworking self-starter); (2) the nonverbal cues you'd use to create these impressions; and (3) the nonverbal cues you'd be especially careful to avoid.

Interpersonal messages are a combination of verbal and nonverbal signals; even subtle variations in, say, eye movements or intonation can drastically change the impression communicated.

1. You want a job at a conservative, prestigious law firm and are meeting for your first face-to-face interview.
2. You want a part in a movie in which you'd play a homeless drug addict.
3. You're single and you're applying to adopt a child.
4. You want to ask another student to go out with you.
5. You want to convince your romantic partner that you did not see your ex last night; you were working.

Judgments about Communication Effectiveness. Speech rate is an important component of paralanguage. In one-way communication (when one person is doing all or most of the speaking and the other person is doing all or most of the listening), those who talk fast (about 50 percent faster than normal) are more persuasive. That is, people agree more with a fast speaker than with a slow speaker and find the fast speaker more intelligent and objective (MacLachlan, 1979).

Although, generally, research finds that a faster-than-normal speech rate lowers listener comprehension, a rapid rate may still have the advantage in communicating information (MacLachlan, 1979; Jones, Berry, & Stevens, 2007). For example, when speaking rate increases by 50 percent, comprehension level drops by only 5 percent. When the rate doubles, the comprehension level drops only 10 percent. If, however, the speeds are more than twice that of normal speech, comprehension level falls dramatically.

Exercise caution in applying this research to all forms of communication (MacLachlan, 1979). While the speaker is speaking, the listener is generating, or framing, a reply. If the speaker talks too rapidly, the listener may not have enough time to compose a reply and may become resentful. Furthermore, the increased rate may seem so unnatural that the listener may focus on the speed rather than on the message being communicated.

Silence

Just as words and gestures communicate meaning, so does silence. (see Jaworski, 1993). Here we look at some functions of silence and at a theory of silence that has important implications for society as a whole.

Functions of Silence. Silence allows the speaker and the listener *time to think*, time to formulate and organize the meaning of the message. For example, a lawyer may have many sophisticated points to make during closing arguments to the jury. A skilled lawyer will use silence, not only to give herself or himself time to present these issues in an organized way, but also to give the jury time to digest the information presented.

Silence may also signal *the importance of the message*. Before and after messages of intense conflict or those confessing undying love, there is often silence. The pre-message silence seems to prepare the receiver for the importance of these messages while the post-message silence allows the time needed to digest the message.

Some people use silence as a *weapon* to hurt others. We often speak of giving someone "the silent treatment." After a conflict, for example, one or both individuals may remain silent as a kind of punishment. Silence used to hurt others may also take the form of refusal to acknowledge the presence of another person, as in disconfirmation (see Chapter 4); in this case, silence is a dramatic demonstration of the total indifference one person feels toward the other.

People sometimes use silence because of *personal anxiety* or shyness, or in response to threats. You may feel anxious or shy among new people and prefer to remain silent. By remaining silent you preclude the chance of rejection. Only when you break your silence and attempt to communicate with another person do you risk rejection.

Like the eyes, face, or hands, silence can also *communicates emotional responses* (Ehrenhaus, 1988). Sometimes silence communicates a determination to be uncooperative or defiant: By refusing to engage in verbal communication, you defy the authority or the legitimacy of the other person's position. Silence often communicates annoyance; in this case, it is usually accompanied by a pouting expression, arms crossed in front of the chest, and flared nostrils. Silence also may express affection or love, especially when coupled with longing gazes into another's eyes.

Of course, you also may use silence when you simply have *nothing to say*, when nothing occurs to you or you do not want to say anything. James Russell Lowell expressed this well: "Blessed are they who have nothing to say and who cannot be persuaded to say it."

The Spiral of Silence.   The "spiral of silence" theory offers a somewhat different perspective on silence. This theory, originally developed to explain the media's influence on opinion, argues that you're more likely to voice agreement than disagreement (Noelle-Neumann, 1973, 1980, 1991; Severin & Tankard, 2001; Scheufele & Moy, 2000). The theory claims that when a controversial issue arises, you estimate the opinions of others and figure out which views are popular and which are not. You also estimate the rewards and the punishments you'd probably get from expressing popular or unpopular positions. You then use these estimates to determine which opinions you'll express and which you won't.

Generally, you're more likely to voice your opinions when you agree with the majority than when you disagree. You may do this to avoid being isolated from the majority or for fear of being proved wrong or being disliked. Or you may simply assume that the majority, because they're a majority, must be right.

As people with minority views remain silent, the majority position gets stronger (because those who agree with it are the only ones speaking); so, as the majority position becomes stronger and the minority position becomes weaker, the silence becomes an ever-widening spiral. The Internet (blogs and social network sites, especially) may in some ways act as a counteragent to the spiral of silence, because it provides so many opportunities to express minority viewpoints (anonymously if you wish) and to quickly find like-minded others (McDevitt, Kiousis, & Wahl Jorgenen, 2003).

TIME COMMUNICATION

The study of **temporal communication**, known technically as **chronemics**, concerns the use of time—how you organize it, react to it, and communicate messages through it (Bruneau, 1985, 1990).

An especially important aspect of temporal communication is **psychological time:** the relative importance people place on the past, present, or future. With a *past* orientation, you have a particular reverence for the past. You relive old times and regard the old methods as the best. You see events as circular and recurring and find that the wisdom of yesterday is applicable also to today and tomorrow. With a *present* orientation, you live in the present—for now—without planning for tomorrow. With a *future* orientation, you look toward to and live for the future; we save today, work hard in college, and deny yourself luxuries because you are preparing for the future. Before reading about some of the consequences of the ways people view time, take the following self-test, "What time do you have?" to assess your own psychological time orientation.

Communication Choice Point

Remaining Silent

Your college roommate is selling term papers and uses your jointly owned computer to store them. You're becoming increasingly uncomfortable about the situation and want to distance yourself from this unethical behavior. *How might you distance yourself or sever yourself entirely from this operation, without creating too much trouble in the same dorm room you'll have to continue sharing for the rest of the year? What would you say? How would you say it?*

Communicating Ethically
Communication Silence

In the U.S. legal system, although people have the right to remain silent so as not to incriminate themselves, they are obliged to reveal information about, for example, the criminal activities of others that they may have witnessed. However, rightly or wrongly (and this in itself is an ethical issue), psychiatrists, lawyers, and some clergy are often exempt from this general rule. Similarly, a wife can't be forced to testify against her husband, nor a husband against his wife.

Unlike the legal system, however, most day-by-day communication situations lack written rules, so it's not always clear whether or when silence is ethical. For example, most people (though not all) would agree that you have the right to withhold information that has no bearing on the matter at hand. Consider, for example, in what situations would it be ethical to remain silent about your previous relationship history, affectional orientation, or religion and in what situations silence would be unethical.

The power of choosing good and evil is within the reach of all.

—ORIGEN
(185–254), Greek theologian

Test Yourself

What Time Do You Have?

For each statement, indicate whether the statement is true (T) or untrue (F) of your general attitude and behavior. A few statements are repeated; this is to facilitate interpreting your score.

_____ ❶ Meeting tomorrow's deadlines and doing other necessary work come before tonight's partying.

_____ ❷ I meet my obligations to friends and authorities on time.

_____ ❸ I complete projects on time by making steady progress.

_____ ❹ I am able to resist temptations when I know there is work to be done.

_____ ❺ I keep working at a difficult, uninteresting task if it will help me get ahead.

_____ ❻ If things don't get done on time, I don't worry about it.

_____ ❼ I think that it's useless to plan too far ahead because things hardly ever come out the way you planned anyway.

_____ ❽ I try to live one day at a time.

_____ ❾ I live to make better what is rather than to be concerned about what will be.

_____ ❿ It seems to me that it doesn't make sense to worry about the future, because fate determines that whatever will be, will be.

_____ ⑪ I believe that getting together with friends to party is one of life's important pleasures.

_____ ⑫ I do things impulsively, making decisions on the spur of the moment.

_____ ⑬ I take risks to put excitement in my life.

_____ ⑭ I get drunk at parties.

_____ ⑮ It's fun to gamble.

_____ ⑯ Thinking about the future is pleasant to me.

_____ ⑰ When I want to achieve something, I set subgoals and consider specific means for reaching those goals.

_____ ⑱ It seems to me that my career path is pretty well laid out.

_____ ⑲ It upsets me to be late for appointments.

_____ ⑳ I meet my obligations to friends and authorities on time.

_____ ㉑ I get irritated at people who keep me waiting when we've agreed to meet at a given time.

_____ ㉒ It makes sense to invest a substantial part of my income in insurance premiums.

_____ ㉓ I believe that "A stitch in time saves nine."

_____ ㉔ I believe that "A bird in the hand is worth two in the bush."

_____ ㉕ I believe it is important to save for a rainy day.

_____ ㉖ I believe a person's day should be planned each morning.

_____ ㉗ I make lists of things I must do.

_____ ㉘ When I want to achieve something, I set subgoals and consider specific means for reaching those goals.

_____ ㉙ I believe that "A stitch in time saves nine."

HOW DID YOU DO? This time test measures seven different factors. If you selected true (T) for all or most of the questions within any given factor, you are probably high on that factor. If you selected untrue (F) for all or most of the questions within any given factor, you are probably low on that factor.

The first factor, measured by questions 1 through 5, is a future, work-motivated, perseverance orientation. People high in this factor have a strong work ethic and are committed to completing tasks despite difficulties and temptations. The second factor (6 through 10) is a present, fatalistic, worry-free orientation. High scorers on this factor live one day at a time, not necessarily to enjoy the day but to avoid planning for the next day or anxiety about the future. The third factor (11 through 15) is a present, pleasure-seeking, partying orientation. People high in this factor enjoy the present, take risks, and engage in a variety of impulsive actions. The fourth factor (16 through 18) is a future, goal-seeking, and planning orientation. High scorers on this factor derive special pleasure from planning and achieving a variety of goals.

The fifth factor (19 through 21) is a time-sensitivity orientation. People who score high are especially sensitive to time and its role in social obligations. The sixth factor (22 through 25) is a future, practical-action orientation. People high in this factor do what they have to do—take practical actions—to achieve the future they want. The seventh factor (26 through 29) is a future, somewhat obsessive daily-planning orientation. High scorers on this factor make daily "to do" lists and devote great attention to specific details.

WHAT WILL YOU DO? Now that you have some idea of how you treat the different types of time, consider how these attitudes and behaviors work for you. For example, will your time orientations help you achieve your social and professional goals? If not, what might you do about changing these attitudes and behaviors?

Source: Adapted from "Time in Perspective" by Alexander Gonzalez and Philip G. Zimbardo. Reprinted with permission from _Psychology Today_ magazine. Copyright © 1985 Sussex Publishers, Inc.

Consider some of the findings on these time orientations (Gonzalez & Zimbardo, 1985). Future income is positively related to future orientation; the more future oriented you arc, thc greater your income is likely to be. Present orientation is strongest among lowest-income males and also among those with high emotional distress and hopelessness (Zaleski, Cycon, & Kurc, 2001).

The time orientation you develop depends largely on your socioeconomic class and your personal experiences (Gonzalez & Zimbardo, 1985). For example, parents in unskilled and semiskilled occupations are likely to teach their children a present-oriented fatalism and a belief that enjoying yourself is more important than planning for the future. Parents who are teachers or managers, for example, teach their children the importance of planning and preparing for the future along with strategies for success.

Different time perspectives also account for much intercultural misunderstanding, because different cultures often teach their members drastically different time orientations. For example, members of some Latin cultures would rather be late for an appointment than end a conversation abruptly. The Latin person sees the lateness as politeness toward the person with whom he or she is conversing, but people of another culture may see it as impolite to the person with whom he or she had the appointment (Hall & Hall, 1987).

Culture, Gender, and Nonverbal Communication

This chapter has already noted a few cultural and gender-related differences in nonverbal communication. The roles of culture and gender in certain areas of nonverbal communication, however, have become the focus of sustained research. Here we consider only a sampling of research on communication via gestures, the face and eyes, color, silence, touch, and time.

In general, research shows that women are better senders and receivers of nonverbal messages than are men (Hall, 1998; Burgoon & Hoobler, 2002). For example, in a review of 21 research studies, 71 percent found women to be superior senders of nonverbal signals. And in a review of 61 studies on decoding, 84 percent found women to be superior receivers (Hall, 1998).

GESTURES

As shown in Figure 5.1, there is much variation in gestures and their meanings among different cultures (Axtell, 1993). Consider a few common gestures that you might use without thinking but that could get you into trouble if you were to use them in another culture:

- Folding your arms over your chest would be considered disrespectful in Fiji.
- Waving your hand would be insulting in Nigeria and Greece.
- Gesturing the "thumbs up" would be rude in Australia.
- Tapping your two index fingers together would be considered an invitation to sleep together in Egypt.
- Pointing with your index finger would be impolite in many Middle Eastern countries.
- Bowing to a lesser degree than your host would be considered a statement of your superiority in Japan.
- Inserting your thumb between your index and middle finger in a clenched fist would be viewed in certain African countries as a wish that evil befall someone.
- Resting your feet on a table or chair would be insulting in some Middle Eastern cultures.

FACIAL EXPRESSION AND EYE MOVEMENTS

The wide variations in facial communication that we observe in different cultures seem to have to do more with which reactions are publicly permissible than with differences in the ways people show their emotions. For example, in one study Japanese and U.S. students watched a film of an operation (Ekman, 1985). The experimenters videotaped the students both in an interview about the film and alone while watching the film. When alone, the students showed very similar reactions. In the interview, however, the U.S. students displayed facial expressions indicating displeasure, but the Japanese students did not show any great emotion. Similarly, it's considered "forward" or inappropriate for Japanese women to reveal broad smiles, so women in Japan will hide their smiles, sometimes with their hands (Ma, 1996). Women in the United States, on the other hand, have no such restrictions and are more likely to smile openly. Thus, many differences may reflect not the way different cultures express emotions but rather the cultural rules for displaying emotions in public (Matsumoto, 1991).

Not surprisingly, eye messages vary with both culture and gender. Individualist cultures generally consider direct eye contact to be an expression of honesty and forthrightness, but the Japanese, for example, often view this as a lack of respect. The Japanese and collectivist cultures generally will glance at the other person's face rarely, and then only for very short periods (Axtell, 1990). Interpreting another's eye contact messages with your own cultural rules is a risky undertaking: Eye movements that you may interpret as insulting may have been intended to show respect.

Women make eye contact more and maintain it longer (both in speaking and in listening) than men. This holds true whether women are interacting with other women or with men. This difference in eye behavior may result from women's greater tendency to display their emotions (Wood, 1994). When women interact with other women, they generally display affiliative and supportive eye contact, but when men interact with other men, they tend to avert their gaze (Gamble & Gamble, 2003).

COLORS

Colors vary greatly in their meanings from one culture to another. To illustrate this cultural variation, here are some of the many meanings that popular colors communicate in a variety of different cultures (Dreyfuss, 1971; Hoft, 1995; Dresser, 1996; Singh &

Pereira, 2005). As you read this section, you may want to consider your own meanings for these colors and where your meanings came from.

- *Red.* In China red signifies prosperity and rebirth and is used for festive and joyous occasions; in France and the United Kingdom it indicates masculinity; in many African countries, blasphemy or death; and in Japan, anger and danger. Red ink, especially among Korean Buddhists, is used only to write a person's name at the time of death or on the anniversary of the person's death; this can create problems when U.S. teachers use red ink to mark homework.
- *Green.* In the United States green signifies capitalism, go ahead, and envy; in Ireland, patriotism; among some Native American cultures, femininity; to the Egyptians, fertility and strength; and to the Japanese, youth and energy.
- *Black.* In Thailand black signifies old age; in parts of Malaysia, courage; and in much of Europe, death.
- *White.* In Thailand white signifies purity; in many Muslim and Hindu cultures, purity and peace; and in Japan and other Asian countries, death and mourning.
- *Blue.* In Iran blue signifies something negative; in Ghana, joy; among the Cherokee it signifies defeat; for the Egyptian, virtue and truth; and for the Greek, national pride.
- *Yellow.* In China yellow signifies wealth and authority; in the United States, caution and cowardice; in Egypt, happiness and prosperity; and in many countries throughout the world, femininity.
- *Purple.* In Latin America purple signifies death; in Europe, royalty; in Egypt, virtue and faith; in Japan, grace and nobility; in China, barbarism; and in the United States, nobility and bravery.

"Culture is communication, and communication is culture."

—EDWARD T. HALL

TOUCH

The functions and examples of touching discussed earlier were based on studies in North America; in other cultures these functions are not served in the same way. In some cultures, for example, some task-related touching is viewed negatively and is to be avoided. Among Koreans it is considered disrespectful for a store owner to touch a customer in, say, handing back change; doing so is considered too intimate a gesture. Members of other cultures who are used to such touching may consider the Koreans' behavior cold and aloof. Muslim children in many countries are socialized to refrain from touching members of the opposite sex, a practice that can easily be interpreted as unfriendly by American children, who are used to touching one another (Dresser, 1996).

Students from the United States reported being touched twice as much as did the Japanese students. In Japan there is a strong taboo against strangers' touching, and the Japanese are therefore especially careful to maintain sufficient distance (Barnlund, 1975).

Some cultures, such as those of southern Europe and the Middle East, are contact cultures. Others, such as those of northern Europe and Japan, are noncontact cultures. Members of contact cultures maintain close distances, touch each other in conversation, face each other more directly, and maintain longer and more focused eye contact. Members of noncontact cultures maintain greater distance in their interactions, touch each other rarely if at all, avoid facing each other directly, and maintain much less direct eye contact. As a result, northern Europeans and Japanese may be perceived as cold, distant, and uninvolved by southern Europeans—who may in turn be perceived as pushy, aggressive, and inappropriately intimate.

PARALANGUAGE AND SILENCE

Cultural differences need to be taken into consideration also in evaluating the results of studies on speech rate. In one study, for example, Korean male speakers who spoke rapidly were given unfavorable credibility ratings, in contrast to the positive ratings received by Americans who spoke rapidly (Lee & Boster, 1992). Researchers have suggested that in individualistic societies a rapid-rate speaker is seen as more competent than a slow-rate speaker, but in collectivist cultures a speaker who uses a slower rate is judged more competent.

Similarly, not all cultures view silence in the same way (Vainiomaki, 2004). In the United States, for example, silence is often interpreted negatively. At a business meeting or even in informal social groups, the silent member may be seen as not listening or as having nothing interesting to add, not understanding the issues, being insensitive, or being too self-absorbed to focus on the messages of others. Other cultures, however, view silence more positively. In many situations in Japan, for example, silence is a response that is considered more appropriate than speech (Haga, 1988).

The traditional Apache, to take another example, regard silence very differently than do European Americans (Basso, 1972). Among the Apache, mutual friends do not feel the need to introduce strangers who may be working in the same area or on the same project. The strangers may remain silent for several days. This period enables them to observe and evaluate each other. Once this assessment is made, the individuals talk. When courting, especially during the initial stages, the Apache remain silent for hours; if they do talk, they generally talk very little. Only after a couple has been dating for several months will they have lengthy conversations. These periods of silence are often erroneously attributed to shyness or self-consciousness. But the use of silence is explicitly taught to Apache women, who are especially discouraged from engaging in long discussions with their dates. Silence during courtship is a sign of modesty to many Apache.

TIME

Culture influences time communication in a variety of ways. Here we look at three: time orientation, monochronism and polychronism, and the social clock.

Time Orientation

Not surprisingly, time orientation is heavily influenced by culture. Some cultures—individualistic cultures in particular—seem to emphasize a future orientation; members work hard today for a better future and without much regard for the past, for example. Collectivist cultures, on the other hand, have greater respect for the past; the past is often looked to for guidance for the present. According to some intercultural researchers, many Asian cultures (e.g., Japanese and Chinese) place great value on the past; Latinos and Native Americans place more emphasis on the present; and European Americans emphasize the future (Lustig & Koester, 2006).

Attitudes toward the importance of time vary from one culture to another. For example, one study measured the accuracy of clocks in six cultures—Japan, Indonesia, Italy, England, Taiwan, and the United States. Japan had the most accurate and Indonesia the least accurate clocks. The researchers also measured the speed at which people in these six cultures walked; results showed that the Japanese walked the fastest, the Indonesians the slowest (LeVine & Bartlett, 1984).

Monochronism and Polychronism

Another important cultural distinction exists between **monochronic** and **polychronic time orientations** (Hall, 1959, 1976; Hall & Hall, 1987). Monochronic peoples or cultures, such as those of the United States, Germany, Scandinavia, and Switzerland, schedule one thing at a time. These cultures compartmentalize time and set sequential times for different activities. Polychronic peoples or cultures, such as those of Latin America, the Mediterranean, and the Arab world, on the other hand, schedule multiple things at the same time. Eating, conducting business with several different people, and taking care of family matters may all go on at once. No culture is entirely monochronic or polychronic; rather, these are general or

TABLE 5.5   Monochronic and Polychronic Time

As you read down this table based on Hall (1983) and Hall & Hall (1987), note the potential for miscommunication that might develop when M-time and P-time people interact. Have any of these differences ever created interpersonal misunderstandings for you?

The Monochronic-Time Person	The Polychronic-Time Person
Does one thing at a time	Does several things at once
Treats time schedules and plans very seriously; feels they may be broken only for the most serious of reasons	Treats time schedules and plans as useful (not sacred); feels they may be broken for a variety of purposes
Considers the job the most important part of a person's life, ahead of even family	Considers the family and interpersonal relationships more important than the job
Considers privacy extremely important; seldom borrows or lends to others; works independently	Is actively involved with others; works in the presence of and with lots of people at the same time

preponderant tendencies. Some cultures combine both time orientations; in Japan and in parts of American culture, for example, both orientations can be found. Table 5.5 identifies some of the distinctions between these two time orientations.

Social Clocks   Your culture maintains a social clock—a time schedule for the right time to do various important things, such as starting to date, finishing college, buying your own home, or having a child. The social clock tells you whether you're keeping pace with your peers, are ahead of them, or are falling behind (Neugarten, 1979; Greene, 2003). On the basis of this social clock, which you learned as you grew up, you evaluate your own social and professional development. If you're keeping pace with the rest of your peers (e.g., you started dating at the "appropriate" age or you're finishing college at the "appropriate" age), you'll feel well adjusted, competent, and a part of the group. If you're late, you'll probably experience feelings of dissatisfaction. Although today the social clock is becoming more flexible and more tolerant of deviations from the acceptable time table, it still exerts pressure on each of us to keep pace with our peers (Peterson, 1996).

Nonverbal Communication Skills

As you have read this chapter, you've probably already deduced a number of suggestions for improving your own nonverbal communication. Here, we bring together some suggestions for both receiving and sending nonverbal messages.

Perhaps the most general skill that applies to both receiving and sending is to become mindful of nonverbal messages—those of others as well as your own. Observe those whose nonverbal behavior you find particularly effective and those whose behavior you find ineffective and try to identify exactly what makes some practices successful and others unsuccessful. Consider this chapter as a brief introduction to a lifelong study.

In addition to mindfulness, general suggestions about nonverbal messages can be offered under two headings: decoding (or interpreting) and encoding (or sending).

DECODING NONVERBAL MESSAGES

When you make judgements or draw conclusions about another person on the basis of her or his nonverbal messages, consider these suggestions:

- Be tentative. Resist the temptation to draw conclusions from nonverbal behaviors. Instead, develop hypotheses (i.e., educated guesses) about what is going on, and test the validity of your hypotheses on the basis of other evidence.

- When making judgments, mindfully seek alternative judgments. Your first judgment may be in error; one good way to test it is to consider alternative judgments. When your romantic partner creates a greater-than-normal distance between you, it may signal an annoyance with you but it can also signal that your partner needs more space.

- Notice that messages come from lots of different channels and that reasonably accurate judgments can be made only when multiple channels are taken into consideration. Although textbooks (like this one) must present the areas of nonverbal communication separately, the various elements all work together in actual communication situations.

- Even after you've explored the different channels, consider the possibility that you are incorrect. This is especially true when you make a judgment that another person is lying based on, say, eye avoidance or long pauses. These nonverbal signals may mean lots of things (as well as the possibility of lying).

- Interpret your judgments and conclusions in a cultural context: For example, if you interpret someone's "overly close" distance as intrusive or pushy because that's your culture's interpetation, you may miss the possibility that this distance is simply standard in the other person's culture or is a way of signalling closeness and friendliness.

Consider the multitude of factors that can influence the way a person behaves nonverbally: For example, a person's physical condition or personality or particular situation may all influence a person's nonverbal communication. A sour stomach may be more responsible for a person's unpleasant facial expressions than any interpersonal factor.

ENCODING NONVERBAL MESSAGES

In using nonverbal messages to express your meanings, consider these suggestions:

- Keep your nonverbal messages consistent with your verbal messages; that is, avoid saying one thing and sending nonverbal messages that say something else—at least when you want to be believed.

- Monitor your own nonverbal messages with the same care that you monitor your verbal messages. If it's not appropriate to say, "this meal is terrible," then it's not appropriate to have a negative expression when you're asked if you want seconds.

- Avoid extremes and monotony. Too little nonverbal communication or too much are likely to be responded to negatively. Similarly, always giving the same nonverbal message—say, continually smiling and nodding your head when listening to a friend's long story—is likely to be seen as insincere.

- Take the situation into consideration. Effective nonverbal communication is situational; to be effective you must adapt your nonverbal messages accordingly. Nonverbal behavior appropriate to one situation may be totally inappropriate in another.

 Summary of Concepts and Skills

This chapter explored nonverbal communication—communication without words—and looked at the functions nonverbal messages serve, the channels of nonverbal communication, and some of the cultural and gender-related influences on and differences in nonverbal communication.

1. Nonverbal messages may be integrated with verbal messages to accent or emphasize a part of the verbal message; to complement or add nuances of meaning; to contradict verbal messages; to regulate, control, or indicate a desire to control the flow of verbal messages; to repeat or restate a verbal message; or to substitute or take the place of verbal messages.

2. Important relationship functions of nonverbal communication include forming and managing impressions, forming and defining relationships, structuring conversation and social interaction, influencing and deceiving, and expressing emotion.

3. The body communicates a variety of meanings with different types of nonverbal behaviors: emblems (which rather directly translate words or phrases); illustrators (which accompany and literally "illustrate" the verbal messages); affect displays (which communicate emotional meaning); regulators (which coordinate, monitor, maintain, or control the speech of another individual); and adaptors (which occur without conscious awareness and usually serve some kind of physical need, as in scratching an itch).

4. Facial movements may communicate a wide variety of emotions. The most frequently studied are happiness, surprise, fear, anger, sadness, and disgust/contempt. Through facial management techniques you can control your facial expression of emotions. The facial feedback hypothesis claims that facial display of an emotion can lead to physiological and psychological changes.

5. Eye movements may be used to seek feedback, cue others to speak, signal the nature of a relationship, or compensate for increased physical distance.

6. Proxemics is the study of the communicative function of space and spatial relationships. Four major proxemic distances are intimate distance, ranging from actual touching to 18 inches; personal distance, ranging from 18 inches to 4 feet; social distance, ranging from 4 to 12 feet; and public distance, ranging from 12 to over 25 feet.

7. Your treatment of space is influenced by such factors as status, culture, context, subject matter, gender, age, and positive or negative evaluation of the other person.

8. Territoriality is a possessive reaction to an area of space or to particular objects. Markers are devices that identify a person's territory; these include central, boundary, and ear markers.

9. Artifactual communication involves messages conveyed by human-made objects or arrangements; it includes communication through color choice, clothing and body adornment, space decoration, and smell.

10. Haptics is the study of touch communication. Touch may communicate a variety of meanings, the most important being positive affect, playfulness, control, ritual, and task-relatedness. Touch avoidance is the desire to avoid touching and being touched by others.

11. Paralanguage consists of the vocal but nonverbal dimension of speech. It includes stress, rate, pitch, volume, and rhythm as well as pauses and hesitations. On the basis of paralanguage people make judgments about conversational turns and about each other—the speaker's believability, for example. Silence also serves important communication functions.

12. Chronemics, or the study of time communication, examines the messages communicated by our treatment of time. Psychological time has to do with people's orientations toward the past, present, or future.

13. Among important cultural and gender-related differences in nonverbal communication are variations in gestures, facial expressions and displays, the meanings of color, the appropriateness and uses of touch, the uses of paralanguage and silence, and the treatment of time.

This chapter has covered a wide variety of nonverbal communication skills. Place a check mark next to those skills that you feel you want to work on most.

_____ 1. I recognize the varied functions that nonverbal messages (my own and those of others) serve: for example, to form and manage impressions, to define relationships, and to structure conversations.

_____ 2. I use body and gesture messages to help communicate my desired meanings, and I recognize these messages in others.

_____ 3. I use my eyes to seek feedback, to inform others to speak, to signal the nature of my relationship with others, and to compensate for physical distance.

_____ 4. I give others the space they need: for example, I give extra space to those who are angry or disturbed.

_____ 5. I am sensitive to the markers (i.e., central, boundary, and ear) of others and use these markers to define my own territories.

_____ 6. I use artifacts thoughtfully to communicate desired messages.

_____ 7. I am sensitive to the touching behaviors of others and distinguish among touches that communicate positive emotion, playfulness, control, and ritual or task-related messages.

_____ 8. I recognize and respect each person's touch-avoidance tendency. I am especially sensitive to cultural and gender differences in touching preferences and in touch-avoidance tendencies.

_____ 9. I vary paralinguistic features (e.g., rate, emphasis, pauses, tempo, volume) to communicate my intended meanings.

_____ 10. I use silence to communicate varied meanings (e.g., for example, disappointment or the need for time to think), and I examine the silence of others for meanings just as I would eye movements or body gestures.

_____ 11. I interpret time cues with an awareness of the cultural perspective of the person with whom I am interacting.

_____ 12. I balance my time orientation and don't ignore the past, present, or future.

_____ 13. In decoding nonverbal messages, I draw conclusions tentatively, consider alternative judgments, take into consideration the varied nonverbal channels, consider the possibility of being incorrect, interpret the judgments in a cultural context, and consider also influences from other factors.

_____ 14. In encoding my own nonverbal messages, I aim for consistency between verbal and nonverbal messages, monitor my nonverbal messages, avoid extremes, and take the situation into consideration.

Key Word Quiz

The Language of Nonverbal Messages

Match the terms about nonverbal messages with their definitions. Record the number of the definition next to the appropriate term.

_____ a. facial feedback hypothesis (99)

_____ b. artifactual communication (103)

_____ c. civil inattention (100)

_____ d. secondary territory (102)

_____ e. adaptors (97)

_____ f. paralanguage (106)

_____ g. facial management techniques (99)

_____ h. haptics (105)

_____ i. central markers (102)

_____ j. emblems (96)

1. Body gestures that directly translate into words or phrases.
2. Gestures that satisfy some personal need, such as scratching.
3. Strategies that enable you to express feelings nonverbally so as to achieve your desired purpose.
4. Eye movements that respect another's privacy and avoid looking at something that might cause another embarrassment.
5. The assumption that your facial expressions influence the way you feel.
6. Items you place in a territory to reserve it for yourself or someone else.
7. The study of touch communication.
8. The vocal but nonverbal dimension of speech; includes, for example, vocal volume and stress.
9. Messages that are communicated through objects and their arrangements.
10. An area that doesn't belong to you but that you have occupied and with which you're associated.

These ten terms and additional terms used in this chapter can be found in the glossary and on flashcards on MyCommunicationLab (www.mycommunicationlab.com).

Answers: a. 5 b. 9 c. 4 d. 10 e. 2 f. 8 g. 3 h. 7 i. 6 j. 1

MyCommunicationLab

PEARSON
mycommunicationlab

www.mycommunicationlab.com

Visit MyCommunicationLab (www.mycommunicationlab.com) for a wealth of additional information on nonverbal communication. Flash cards, videos, skill building exercises, sample text questions, and additional examples and discussions will help you continue your study of nonverbal communication.

CHAPTER

6 Interpersonal Communication and Conversation

Why read this chapter?

Because you'll learn about:

- interpersonal communication and conversation
- the principles of conversation
- some of the ways in which conversation works in everyday life

Because you'll learn to:

- open, maintain, and close conversations more effectively
- engage in more satisfying conversations
- use a variety of techniques (e.g., excusing, apologizing, complimenting) to make conversations more effective

Interpersonal communication is communication that occurs between two people who have a relationship and who are thus influenced by each other's communication messages. It includes what takes place between a server and a customer, a son and his father, two people in an interview, and so on. This definition makes it almost impossible for communication between two people not to be considered interpersonal—inevitably, some relationship exists. Even a stranger asking directions from a local resident has established a clearly defined relationship as soon as the first message is sent. Sometimes this relational, or "dyadic," definition of interpersonal communication is extended to include small groups of people, such as family members, groups of three or four friends, or work colleagues.

Another way to look at interpersonal communication is along a continuum ranging from relatively impersonal to highly personal (Miller, 1978, 1990). At the impersonal end of the spectrum there is simple conversation between people who really don't know each other: the server and the customer, for example. At the highly personal end is the communication that takes place between people who are intimately interconnected, such as a father and son (see Figure 6.1).

A few characteristics distinguish these two extremes. First, in the impersonal example, the individuals are likely to respond to each other according to the roles they are currently playing: The server treats the customer not as a unique individual but as one of many customers, and the customer, in turn, acts toward the server not as if he or she were a unique individual but as he or she would act toward any server. The father and the son, however, react to each other as unique individuals.

Notice too that the server and the customer interact according to the rules of society governing the server–customer interaction. The father and the son, on the other hand, interact on the basis of personally established rules. The way they address each other, their touching behavior, and their degree of physical closeness, for example, are unique to them and are established by them rather than by society.

Still another difference is that the messages that the server and customer exchange are themselves impersonal; there is little self-disclosure and little emotional content, for example. In the father–son example, the messages may run the entire range and may at times be highly personal with lots of disclosure and emotion.

There are, of course, many gradations between these extremes. Some friendships, for example, are casual; others are highly intimate. Romantic pairs vary in their levels of intimacy, and so do families.

This chapter introduces interpersonal communication, explains the process of conversation and some of its essential principles, and tackles some everyday conversation situations.

FIGURE 6.1 **An Interpersonal Continuum**

Here is one possible interpersonal continuum. Other people would position the relationships differently. You may want to try constructing an interpersonal continuum of your own relationships.

Conversation

Conversation, whether face-to-face or online, takes place in five steps: opening, feed-forward, business, feedback, and closing. Of course, there are variations in the process, depending on, for example, whether your interaction is face-to-face or computer-mediated. When reading about the process of conversation, therefore, keep in mind the wide range of forms in which conversation can take place—face-to-face, over the phone, as well as via the Internet—and the similarities and differences among them.

Similarly, realize that not everyone speaks with the fluency and ease that textbooks often assume. Speech and language disorders, for example, can seriously disrupt the conversation process if some elementary guidelines aren't followed. Table 6.1 offers suggestions for making such conversations run more smoothly.

OPENING

The first step in conversation is the opening, which usually involves some kind of greeting: "Hi." "How are you?" "Hello, this is Joe." In face-to-face conversation, greet-ings can be verbal or nonverbal but are usually both (Krivonos & Knapp, 1975; Knapp, 1984). In e-mail (and in most computer communication), the greetings are verbal

TABLE 6.1	Communication Tips

Between People with and without Speech and Language Disorders

Demosthenes   Lewis Carroll   Winston Churchill   Mel Tillis

Speech and language disorders vary widely—from fluency problems such as stuttering, to indistinct articulation, to difficulty in finding the right word, or aphasia. Following a few simple guidelines can facilitate communication between people with and without speech and language disorders.

If you're the person without a speech or language disorder:

1. Avoid finishing another's sentences. Although you may think you're helping the person who stutters or has word-finding difficulty, finishing the person's sentences may communicate the idea that you're impatient and don't want to spend the extra time necessary to interact effectively.

2. Avoid giving directions to the person with a speech disorder. Saying "slow down" or "relax" will often seem insulting and will make further communication more difficult.

3. Maintain eye contact. Show interest and at the same time avoid showing any signs of impatience or embarrassment.

4. Ask for clarification as needed. If you don't understand what the person said, ask him or her to repeat it. Don't pretend that you understand when you don't.

5. Don't treat people who have language problems like children. A person with aphasia, say, who has difficulty with names or nouns generally, is in no way childlike.

If you're the person with a speech or language disorder:

1. Let the other person know what your special needs are. For example, if you stutter, you might tell others that you have difficulty with certain sounds and so they need to be patient.

2. Demonstrate your own comfort. Show that you have a positive attitude toward the interpersonal situation. If you appear comfortable and positive, others will also.

Sources: These suggestions were drawn from a variety of sources: www.nsastutter.org/material/indep.php?matid=189, www.aphasia.org/, http://spot.pcc.edu/~rjacobs/career/communication_tips.htm, and www.dol.gov/odep/pubs/fact/comucate.htm (all accessed May 20, 2008).

with perhaps an emoticon or two thrown in. As video and sound capabilities become more wide-spread on the Internet, this difference from face-to-face conversation will diminish. Verbal greetings include, for example, verbal salutes ("Hi," "Hello"), initiation of the topic ("The reason I called . . ."), references to the other ("Hey, Joe, what's up?"), and personal inquiries ("What's new?" "How are you doing?"). Nonverbal greetings include waving, smiling, shaking hands, and winking (and their emoticon equivalents).

FEEDFORWARD

In the second step of conversation, you usually give some kind of **feedforward**, by which you may seek to accomplish a variety of functions. One function is to open the channels of communication, usually with some *phatic message* (see Chapter 1)—a message that signals that communication will take place rather than communicating any significant denotative information. An example would be "Haven't we met before?"

Communication Choice Point

Opening a Conversation

On the first day of class, you and another student are the first to come into the classroom and are sitting in the room alone. *What are some options you have for opening a conversation?*

or "Nice day, isn't it?" Another function of feedforward is to preview future messages, as in, "I'm afraid I have bad news for you" or "Listen to this before you make a move." In office memos and e-mail, the feedforward function is served—in part—by the header that indicates the subject of your message, the recipient, and who receives courtesy copies.

Here are a few suggestions for giving effective feedforward.

- Use feedforward to estimate the receptivity of the person to what you're going to say. For example, before asking a friend for a loan, you'd probably feedforward your needy condition and say something like, "I'm really strapped for cash and need to get my hands on $200 to pay my car loan," and wait for the other person to say (you hope), "Can I help?"

- Use feedforward that's consistent with your subsequent messages. If your main message is one of bad news, then your feedforward needs to be serious and help prepare the other person for this bad news. You might, for example, say something like, "I need to tell you something you're not going to want to hear. Let's sit down."

- The more important or complex the message, the more important and more extensive your feedforward needs to be. For example, in public speaking in which the message is relatively long, the speaker is advised to give fairly extensive feedforward, or what is called an orientation or preview. At the start of a business meeting, the leader may give feedforward in the form of an agenda or meeting schedule.

Communication Choice Point

Feedforward

You want to break up your relationship with someone you've been dating rather steadily over the last eight months. You want to remain friends but end the romance, something your partner has no idea about. *What might you say as a preface (as feedforward) to your breakup speech?*

BUSINESS

The third step is the business, or the substance and focus, of the conversation. Business is a good term for this stage, because it emphasizes that most conversations are directed at achieving some goal. You converse to fulfill one or several of the general purposes of interpersonal communication: to learn, relate, influence, play, or help, as Chapter 1 described. In conversation you conduct this business through an exchange of speaker and listener roles—you talk about the new supervisor, what happened in class, or your vacation plans.

FEEDBACK

The fourth step of conversation, **feedback**, is the reverse of the second. In feedback you reflect back on the conversation. You normally do this immediately in face-to-face conversation and in your response to a previous e-mail. You say, for example, "So, you may want to send Jack a get-well card," or "Wasn't that the dullest meeting you ever went to?"

Because each situation is unique, it's difficult to offer specific suggestions for making your feedback more effective. But, with some adjustments for the specifics of the situation, the following guides might prove helpful:

- Focus on the behavior or the message rather than the motives behind the message or behavior. Say, for example, "This letter has too many errors and must be redone," rather than, "You're not concentrating or you don't care enough about these letters to do them correctly."

- If your feedback is largely negative, try to begin with something positive. There are always positives if you look hard enough. The negatives will be much easier to take after hearing some positives.

- Select an appropriate time and place. When feedback is negative, be especially careful to do this in private and when there is sufficient time to discuss the problems in full.

- Ask for feedback on your feedback: For example, say, "Does this make sense?" "Do you understand what I'm asking?"

<table>
</table>

Communication Choice Point

Closing a Conversation

After a long meeting, you walk out with a colleague who doesn't seem to know how to end the conversation and just continues to go over what has already been said. You have to get back to your desk. *What are some options you have for ending this conversation without insulting your colleague?*

The other half of the feedback equation is the person receiving the feedback (Robbins & Hunsaker, 2006). When you are the recipient, be sure to show your interest in the feedback. This is vital information meant to help you improve. Encourage the feedback giver. Don't argue; don't be defensive.

CLOSING

The fifth and last step of the conversation process, the opposite of the first step, is the closing, the good-bye (Knapp, Hart, Friedrich, & Shulman, 1973; Knapp & Vangelisti, 2009). Like the opening, the closing may be verbal or nonverbal but usually is a combination of both. Just as the opening signals access, the closing signals the intention to end access. The closing usually also signals some degree of supportiveness, such as expressing your pleasure in the interaction ("Well, it was good talking with you"). The closing may also summarize the interaction to offer more of a conclusion to the conversation.

Not all conversations divide neatly into these five steps, of course. Often the opening and the feedforward are combined, as when you see someone on campus and say, "Hey, listen to this," or when someone in a work situation says, "Well, folks, let's get the meeting going." In a similar way, the feedback and the closing may be combined: "Look, I've got to think more about this commitment, okay?"

Different cultures have different rules and customs in conversation as in all aspects of communication. In some cultures, for example, the openings are especially short; in others they are elaborate, lengthy, and in some cases highly ritualized. And what is appropriate at a given step in one culture may not be appropriate in another culture. As you can see, it's easy to violate another culture's conversational rules in intercultural communication situations. Such violations may have significant consequences: If you are not aware of cultural differences, you may mistakenly interpret someone's "violations" as aggressiveness, stuffiness, or pushiness and take an immediate dislike to the person, putting a negative cast on future communications. Of course, knowing the other's cultural rules would clarify things for you. But in the absence of specific knowledge, it's probably wise to assume that, when someone of another culture exhibits conversational behaviors that seem strange to you, the behaviors are cultural in origin and no offense is intended.

Principles of Conversation

Three important principles will provide further perspective on conversation: (1) turn-taking, (2) dialogue, and (3) immediacy.

THE PRINCIPLE OF TURN-TAKING

Throughout the speaking–listening process, both speaker and listener exchange cues for what are called **conversational turns** (Burgoon, Buller, & Woodall, 1996; Duncan, 1972; Pearson & Spitzberg, 1990). These cues enable the speaker and listener to communicate about the communication in which they're currently engaged; that is, a form of **metacommunication** takes place through the exchange of these often subtle cues. The use of turn-taking cues—like almost every aspect of human communication—will naturally vary from one culture to another. The description that follows here is valid largely for the United States and many Western cultures (Iizuka, 1993; Lee, 1984; Grossin, 1987; Ng, Loong, He, Liu, & Weatherall, 2000). As you read the following discussion, take a look at Figure 6.2; it provides a visual guide to the various turn signals.

Conversational Wants

	To speak	To listen
Speaker	1 Turn-maintaining cues	2 Turn-yielding cues
Listener	3 Turn-requesting cues	4 Turn-denying cues

FIGURE 6.2 **Turn-Taking and Conversational Wants**

Quadrant 1 represents the speaker who wants to speak (continue to speak) and uses turn-maintaining cues; quadrant 2, the speaker who wants to listen and uses turn-yielding cues; quadrant 3, the listener who wants to speak and uses turn-requesting cues; and quadrant 4, the listener who wants to listen (i.e., continue listening) and uses turn-denying cues. Back-channeling cues would appear in quadrant 4, because they are cues that listeners use while they continue to listen.

Speaker Cues   Speakers regulate the conversation through two major types of cues: turn-maintaining cues and turn-yielding cues. Using these cues effectively not only ensures communication efficiency but also increases likeability (Place & Becker, 1991; Heap, 1992).

Turn-Maintaining Cues.   Through **turn-maintaining cues** you can communicate your wish to maintain the role of speaker in a variety of ways:

"It is alright to hold a conversation, but you should let go of it now and then."

—RICHARD ARMOUR

- audibly inhaling breath to show that you have more to say
- continuing a gesture or series of gestures to show that you've not yet completed your thought
- avoiding eye contact with the listener so as not to indicate your passing along your speaking turn
- vocalizing pauses ("er," "umm") to prevent the listener from speaking and to show that you're still talking

In most conversations we expect the speaker to maintain relatively brief speaking turns and to turn over the speaking role to the listener willingly (when so signaled by the listener). People who don't follow those unwritten rules are likely to be evaluated negatively.

Turn-Yielding Cues.   *Turn-yielding cues* tell the listener that the speaker is finished and wishes to exchange the role of speaker for the role of listener. They tell the listener (if in a group, such cues may be addressed to a specific listener or to just any listener) to take over the role of speaker. For example, at the end of a statement you may add some cue such as "okay?" or "right?" to ask one of the listeners to assume the role of speaker. You also can indicate that you've finished speaking by dropping your intonation or pausing at length (Wennerstrom & Siegel, 2003), by making direct eye contact with a listener, by asking a question, or by nodding in the direction of a particular listener.

Listener Cues   As a listener you can regulate the conversation by using three types of cues: turn-requesting cues, turn-denying cues, and back-channeling cues and interruptions.

Turn-Requesting Cues.   *Turn-requesting cues* let the speaker know that you would like to say something and take a turn as speaker. Sometimes you can do this simply by saying, "I'd like to say something," but often it's done more subtly through some vocalized "er" or "um" that tells the speaker that you would like to speak. The request to speak is also often made with facial and mouth gestures. Frequently a listener will indicate a desire to speak by opening his or her eyes and mouth wide as if to say something, by beginning to gesture with a hand, or by leaning forward.

Turn-Denying Cues.   You can use **turn-denying cues** to indicate your reluctance to assume the role of speaker: for example, by intoning a slurred "I don't know" or by giving some brief grunt that signals you have nothing to say. Often people accomplish turn denying by avoiding eye contact with the speaker (who wishes them now to take on the role of speaker) or by engaging in some behavior that is incompatible with speaking such as coughing or blowing their nose.

Back-Channeling Cues and Interruptions.   **Back-channeling cues** are used to communicate various types of information back to the speaker without assuming the role of speaker. Some researchers call brief utterances—such as "mm-hm," "uh-huh," and "yeah"—that tell the speaker you're listening *acknowledgment tokens* (Schegloff, 1982; Drummond & Hopper, 1993). Other researchers call them *overlaps* to distinguish them from those interruptions that are aimed at taking over the speaker's turn (Tannen, 1994). Back-channeling cues are generally supportive and confirming and show that you're listening and are involved in the interaction (Kennedy & Camden, 1988), but you can communicate a variety of messages with these back-channeling cues (Burgoon, Buller, & Woodall, 1996; Pearson & Spitzberg, 1990):

- *To indicate agreement or disagreement.* A smile, nod of approval, brief comments such as "Right" and "Of course," or a vocalization like "uh-huh" signals agreement. Frowning, shaking your head, or making comments such as "No" and "Never" signal disagreement.

- *To indicate degree of involvement.* An attentive posture, forward leaning, and focused eye contact tell the speaker that you're involved in the conversation. An inattentive posture, backward leaning, and avoidance of eye contact communicate a lack of involvement.

- *To pace the speaker.* Ask the speaker to slow down by raising your hand near your ear and leaning forward or to speed up by continued nodding of your head. Cue the speaker verbally by asking the speaker to slow down or to speed up.

- *To ask for clarification.* Puzzled facial expressions, perhaps coupled with a forward lean or direct interjection of "Who?" "When?" or "Where?" signal your need for clarification.

Interruptions, in contrast to back-channeling cues, are attempts to take over the role of the speaker. These are not supportive and are often disconfirming. Interruptions are often interpreted as attempts to change the topic to one that the person knows more about or to emphasize one's authority. Interruptions are often seen as attempts to assert power and to maintain control. Not surprisingly, research finds that superiors (bosses and supervisors) and those in positions of authority (police officers and interviewers) interrupt those in inferior positions more than the other way around (Carroll, 1994; Ashcraft, 1998).

Numerous studies have focused on gender differences in interruption behavior. Research finds that the popular belief that men interrupt more than women is basically accurate. Men interrupt other men and women more than women interrupt. For example, one analysis of 43 published studies on interruptions and gender differences showed that men interrupted significantly more than women (Anderson, 1998). In addition, the more malelike the person's gender identity—regardless of the person's biological sex—the more likely the person will interrupt (Drass, 1986). Fathers interrupt their children more than mothers do (Greif, 1980). Some research, however, finds no differences (Stratford, 1998; Crown & Cummins, 1998; Smith-Lovin & Brody, 1989; Donaldson, 1992).

Whatever gender differences do exist, however, seem small. More important than gender in determining who interrupts whom is the specific type of situation; some situations such as task-oriented situations, may call for many interruptions, and others, such as relationship discussions, may call for lots of back-channeling cues (Anderson, 1998).

THE PRINCIPLE OF DIALOGUE

Often the term *dialogue* is used as a synonym for *conversation*. But dialogue is more than simple conversation; it's conversation in which there is genuine two-way interaction (Buber, 1958; Yau-fair Ho, Chan, Peng, & Ng, 2001; McNamee & Gergen, 1999). It's useful to distinguish the ideal dialogic communicator from his or her opposite, the totally monologic communicator. Of course, no one totally and always engages in dialogue, and no one is totally monologic. These types are extremes, intended to clarify the differences between these types of communication.

In **dialogue** each person is both speaker and listener, sender and receiver. It's conversation in which there is deep concern for the other person and for the relationship between the two. The objective of dialogue is mutual understanding and empathy. There is respect for the other person, not because of what this person can do or give but

Communication Choice Point

Dealing with Interruptions

One of your friends repeatedly interrupts you and others and takes the conversation off onto a totally different topic. *What are some of the things you might say or do to stop this annoying behavior but not insult your friend? What would be the ideal situation in which to bring this up? What channel of communication would you use?*

simply because this person is a human being and therefore deserves to be treated honestly and sincerely.

In a dialogic interaction you respect the other person enough to allow that person the right to make his or her own choices without coercion, without the threat of punishment, without fear or social pressure. A dialogic communicator believes that other people can make decisions that are right for them and implicitly or explicitly lets them know that, whatever choices they make, they will still be respected.

The dialogic communicator avoids negative criticism and negative personal judgments and instead practices using positive criticism ("I liked those first two explanations best; they were really well reasoned"). This person avoids dysfunctional communication patterns and keeps the channels of communication open by displaying a willingness to listen. While listening this person lets you know it by giving you cues (e.g., nonverbal nods, brief verbal expressions of agreement, paraphrasing) that tell you he or she is paying attention. When in doubt the dialogic communicator asks for clarification—asks for your point of view, your perspective—and thus signals a real interest in you and in what you have to say. This person does not manipulate the conversation so as to get positive comments.

Monologic communication is the opposite: In **monologue** one person speaks and the other listens—there's no real interaction between participants. The monologic communicator is focused only on his or her own goals and has no real concern for the listener's feelings or attitudes; this speaker is interested in the other person only insofar as that person can serve his or her purposes.

The monologic communicator frequently uses negative criticism ("I didn't like that explanation") and negative judgments ("You're not a very good listener, are you?"). This communicator also often uses dysfunctional communication patterns such as expressing an unwillingness to talk or to listen to what the other person has to say. The monologic communicator rarely demonstrates that he or she understands you; this person gives no cues that he or she is listening (cues such as paraphrasing or expressing agreement with what you say). Nor would this person request clarification of your ideas, because he or she is less interested in you than in representing him- or herself. Still another characteristic of this person is a tendency to request that you say positive things about him or her ("How did you like the way I handled that?").

THE PRINCIPLE OF IMMEDIACY

Of all the characteristics of effective communication, immediacy most clearly defines effective conversation. **Immediacy** is the creation of closeness, a sense of togetherness, of oneness, between speaker and listener. When you communicate immediacy you convey a sense of interest and attention, a liking for and an attraction to the other person. And, as noted in our discussion of impression management strategies (pp. 46–50), immediacy strategies are often used to make someone like us.

Not surprisingly, people respond to communication that is immediate more favorably than to communication that is not. You can increase your interpersonal attractiveness, the degree to which others like you and respond positively toward you, by using immediacy behaviors. In addition there is considerable evidence to show that immediacy behaviors are effective in teaching and in health care (Richmond, Smith, Heisel, & McCroskey, 2001; Richmond, McCroskey, & Hickson, 2008).

You can communicate immediacy with both verbal and nonverbal messages (Mottet & Richmond, 1998; Richmond, McCroskey, & Hickson, 2008):

- Self-disclose: reveal something significant about yourself.
- Refer to the other person's good qualities, say, dependability, intelligence, character: for example, "You're always so reliable."
- Express your positive view of the other person and of your relationship: for example, "I'm sure glad you're my roommate; you know everyone."

Communication Choice Point

Turning Monologue into Dialogue

You're dating a wonderful person, your ideal in every way except one, which is that your conversations together are a series of monologues; there is little dialogue. *What are some of the things you might do to change this situation and to encourage more dialogue?*

"Two monologues do not make a dialogue."
—JEFF DALY

Listening to the emotions of others is a difficult but essential part of conversation. Here are a few guidelines for making it a little easier and a lot more effective.

1. Confirm the other person and his or her emotions. A simple "You must be worried about finding another position" confirms the feelings of a person who has just lost a job.

2. Show interest by encouraging the person to explore his or her feelings. Use simple encouragers like "I see" or "I understand." Or ask questions to let the speaker know that you're listening and that you're interested.

3. Give the person permission to express feelings. Let the person know that it's acceptable and okay with you if she and he expresses feelings in the ways that feel most comfortable—for example, by crying or talking about old times.

4. Don't try to force the person to talk about experiences or feelings she or he may not be willing to share.

5. Be especially sensitive to leave-taking cues. Don't overstay your welcome.

6. Empathize. See the situation from the point of view of the speaker. Avoid comments such as "Don't cry; it wasn't worth it," which can easily be interpreted as a rejection of the person's feelings.

7. Focus on the other person; don't refocus the conversation on yourself.

8. Don't try to solve their problems. Instead, provide a supportive atmosphere that encourages the person to express her or his feelings.

9. Avoid trying to focus on the bright side. Avoid expressions such as "You're lucky you have some vision left" or "It was better this way; Pat was suffering so much."

10. Avoid interrupting, even when the other person's pauses are overly long. Emotional expression frequently involves extra-long pauses.

Anger is a signal, and one worth listening to.

—HARRIET LERNER
(1944–), U.S. psychologist
and author

- Talk about commonalities, things you and the other person have done together or share.
- Demonstrate your responsiveness by giving feedback cues that indicate you want to listen more and that you're interested: for example, "And what else happened?"
- Express psychological closeness and openness by, for example, maintaining physical closeness and arranging your body to exclude third parties.
- Maintain appropriate eye contact and limit looking around at others.
- Smile and express your interest in the other person.
- Focus on the other person's remarks. Make the speaker know that you heard and understood what was said, and give the speaker appropriate verbal and nonverbal feedback.

At the same time that you'll want to demonstrate these immediacy messages, try also to avoid nonimmediacy messages such as interrupting the other person, avoiding small talk, making potentially offensive or condescending comments, closing off the channels of communication ("I don't have the time to chat"), or talking about things for which the other person has no reference or experience. Nonverbally, avoid speaking in a monotone, looking away from the person you're talking to, frowning while talking, having a tense body posture, and avoiding gestures (Richmond, McCroskey, & Hickson, 2008).

Not all cultures or all people respond in the same way to immediacy messages. For example, in the United States (and in individualist and low-power-distance cultures generally) immediacy behaviors are seen as friendly and appropriate. In other cultures (e.g., many collectivist and high-power-distance cultures), however, the same immediacy

Communication Choice Point

Immediacy

You've become interested in one of the other students in your class and would really like to date her or him. You want to appear friendly and interested but not overly pushy. *How might you use immediacy to make yourself appear likeable, friendly, and interesting? In what context would you attempt this? Through what channel?*

behaviors may be viewed as overly familiar—as presuming that a relationship is close when it is only an acquaintanceship (Axtell, 1994, 2007).

Also, recognize that some people may take your immediacy behaviors as indicating a desire for increased intimacy in the relationship. So, while you're trying to signal a friendly closeness, the other person may perceive a romantic invitation. Recognize too that because immediacy behaviors prolong and encourage in-depth communication, they may not be responded to favorably by persons who are fearful about communication and who want to get the interaction over with as soon as possible (Richmond, McCroskey, & Hickson, 2008).

Everyday Conversations

Having covered the basic principles of conversation, we can now explore a variety of everyday conversation situations: making small talk, introducing other people or ourselves, excusing and apologizing, complimenting, and offering advice.

SMALL TALK

Before reading about small talk, examine your own small talk behavior by taking the accompanying self-test:

Test Yourself

How Do You Small Talk?

Examine your small talk communication by responding to the following questions.

_____ ❶ On an elevator with three or four strangers, I'd be most likely to
   a. try to avoid interacting
   b. respond to another but not initiate interaction
   c. be the first to talk

_____ ❷ When I'm talking with someone and I meet a friend who doesn't know the person, I'm with, I'd be most apt to
   a. avoid introducing them
   b. wait until they introduce each other
   c. introduce them to each other

_____ ❸ At a party with people I've never met before, I'd be most likely to
   a. wait for someone to talk to me
   b. nonverbally indicate that I'm receptive to someone interacting with me
   c. initiate interaction with others nonverbally and verbally

_____ ❹ When confronted with someone who doesn't want to end the conversation I'd be most apt to
   a. just stick it out and listen
   b. tune out the person and hope time goes by quickly
   c. end it firmly myself

_____ ❺ When the other person monologues, I'd be most apt to
   a. listen politely
   b. try to change the focus
   c. exit as quickly as possible

HOW DID YOU DO? Lots of *a* responses would indicate some level of dissatisfaction and discomfort with the experience of small talk. If you had lots of *b* responses then you probably experience both satisfaction and dissatisfaction with small talk. Lots of *c* responses would indicate comfort and satisfaction with small talk. Put in terms of assertiveness, discussed in Chapter 4 (pp. 74–75), the *a* responses are unassertive, the *b* responses are indirect (not totally unassertive but not assertive either), and the *c* responses are direct and assertive.

WHAT WILL YOU DO? If your small talk experiences are not satisfying to you, read on. You will learn about the value of small talk, as well as guidelines for more successfully engaging in small talk.

All of us engage in small talk. Sometimes, we use it as a preface to big talk. For example, before a conference with your boss or even a job interview, you're likely to engage in some preliminary small talk. "How are you doing?" "I'm pleased this weather has finally cleared up." The purpose here is to ease into the major topic, or the "big talk."

Sometimes, small talk is a politeness strategy and a more extensive way of saying hello as you pass someone in the hallway or meet a neighbor at the post office. You might say, "Good seeing you, Jack. You're looking ready for the big meeting," or "See you in Geology at 1."

Sometimes, your relationship with another person revolves totally around small talk, perhaps with your barber or hair dresser, a colleague at work, your next door neighbor, or a fellow student you sit next to in class. In these relationships, neither person makes an effort to deepen the relationship, and it remains on a small talk level.

Despite its name, small talk serves important purposes. One is simply to pass the time more pleasantly than you might in silence. Small talk also demonstrates that the normal rules of politeness are operating. In the United States, for example, you would be expected to smile and at least say hello to people in an elevator in your apartment building, and perhaps at your place of work. Furthermore, small talk confirms to others that all is well with you. Should you scowl and avoid eye contact with someone in your apartment building elevator, you'd signal that something is wrong.

The Topics and Contexts of Small Talk Small talk topics must be noncontroversial in the sense that they are something about which you and the other person are unlikely to disagree. If a topic is likely to arouse deep emotions or different points of view, then it is probably not a suitable topic for small talk.

Small talk is also relatively short in duration. The context in which small talk occurs allows for only a brief interaction. Waiting in line to get into a movie, riding in an elevator, or stopping briefly in the hallway of a school on the way to class are the kinds of occasions that create small talk opportunities. The cocktail party, at which guests are meant to mingle and exchange pleasantries, is perhaps the classic example.

Another popular occasion, which is an exception to this short duration characteristic, is sitting next to someone on a long plane flight. Here, the small talk—assuming you keep it to small talk—can last for hours. Sometimes, as explained in the discussion of self-disclosure in Chapter 2 (pp. 30–36), this situation produces a kind of "in-flight intimacy" in which you engage in significant self-disclosure, revealing secrets you normally keep hidden, largely because you know you'll never see this person again.

Guidelines for Effective Small Talk Although "small," this talk still requires the application of the communication skills for "big" talk. As already noted, remember that the best topics are non-controversial and that most small talk is relatively brief. Here are a few additional guidelines for more effective small talk.

"It's definitely true. Inane conversation is better with masks."

© Steve Duenes/Condé Nast Publications/www.cartoonbank.com.

- Be positive. No one likes a negative doomsayer. So, comment on the weather when it's nice; move to another topic when it isn't.

- Be sensitive to leave taking cues. Small talk is necessarily brief, but at times one person may want it to be a preliminary to big talk and another person may see it as the sum of the interaction.

- Stress similarities rather than differences; this is a good way to ensure that the small talk stays noncontroversial.

- Answer questions with enough elaboration to give the other person information to use to interact with you. The more elaborate answer also signals your willingness to engage in small talk, whereas the simple "yes" response can be interpreted as indicating you don't want to interact.

- Avoid monologuing. Listen and be responsive to the other person. Even small talk is two-way and requires each person to talk and each person to listen. Remember the principles of turn-taking and dialogue.

- In selecting the topics of your small talk, remember that you will be associated with the topics you frequently talk about. If all your small talk concerns Britney Spears, Paris Hilton, and Brangelina, then you might become defined as someone who is only interested in shallow celebrity gossip.

Communication Choice Point

Making Small Talk

You're on an elevator with three other people from your office building. The elevator gets stuck without any indication of when power will go back on. You figure now is the time for small talk. *What are some things you might say to make the situation more comfortable?*

INTRODUCING PEOPLE

One of the interpersonal communication situations that often creates difficulties is the introduction of one person to another. Let's say you're with Jack and bump into Jill, who stops to talk. Because they don't know each other, it's your job to introduce them. Generally, it's best to do this simply but with enough detail to provide a context for further interaction. It might go something like this:

Jill Williams, this is Jack Smith, who works with me at XYZ as marketing manager. I went to college with Jill, and if I'm not mistaken, she has just returned from Hawaii.

With this introduction Jack and Jill can say something to each other based on the information provided in this brief (32-word) introduction. They can talk about working at XYZ, what it's like being a marketing manager, what Jill majored in, what Hawaii is like, what Jill did in Hawaii, and so on. If you simply said, "Jill this is Jack," there would be virtually nothing for Jack and Jill to talk about.

Also, if you know that the two people have something in common, you might mention this—for example, that Jack is also a native New Yorker or Jill is also a marathon runner. This will help to ease the communication between Jack and Jill and is likely to make the interaction more meaningful and satisfying. If you're unsure whether to reveal a particular fact in your introduction, it's best to leave it out. For example, introducing Jack as "soon to be single" may reveal more than Jack would like. The safest policy is to include only obviously public information.

Some situations make a normally easy introduction somewhat difficult:

1. If you forget the person's name, the best thing to do is to admit it and say something like "I don't know why I keep thinking your name is Joe; I know it's not. I'm blocking." You're not the only one who forgets names, and few people take great offense when this happens.

2. You don't have to reveal what your relationship is with the person you're with if you don't want to. You can simply say, "This is Jack," and then hope that the other person won't ask. Of course, if you want to reveal your relationship, then do so: "This is Jack, my_____ (lover, boyfriend, girlfriend, significant other, life partner, parole officer, or whatever term you want to use to define your relationship)."

3. In deciding whether to introduce people by their full names or first names only, it's best to be consistent with the norms operating in your specific culture. Also, be consistent with the two people you introduce. If you don't know both last names,

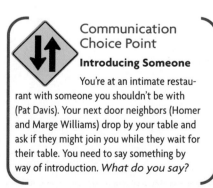

Communication Choice Point

Introducing Someone

You're at an intimate restaurant with someone you shouldn't be with (Pat Davis). Your next door neighbors (Homer and Marge Williams) drop by your table and ask if they might join you while they wait for their table. You need to say something by way of introduction. *What do you say?*

TABLE 6.2	Six Steps to an Effective Handshake

Dos	Don'ts
Make eye contact at the beginning and maintain it throughout the handshake.	Look away from the person or down at the floor or at your shaking hand.
Smile and otherwise signal positiveness.	Appear static or negative.
Extend your entire right hand.	Extend only your fingers or your left hand.
Grasp the other person's hand firmly but without so much pressure that it would be uncomfortable.	Grasp the other person's fingers as if you really don't want to shake hands but you're making a gesture to be polite.
Pump 3 times; a handshake in the United States lasts about 3 to 4 seconds. In other cultures, it might be shorter or, more often, longer.	Give the person a "dead fish": Be careful that the other person's pumping doesn't lead you to withdraw your own pumping. Pumping much more than 3 times.
Release your grasp while still maintaining eye contact.	Hold your grasp for an overly long time or release too early.

use just first names for both parties. Likewise, if you introduce one person by his or her full name, do the same for the other person.

4. If the two people are of obviously different ranks, then the person of lower rank is introduced to the person of higher rank. Thus, you'd introduce the child to the adult, the private to the general, the junior executive to the senior executive, the student to the professor: For example, "Professor Smith, I'd like to introduce my roommate Jack." Another commonly practiced rule of the introduction is to introduce the man to the woman: "Marie, I'd like to introduce Stephen."

In the United States the handshake is the most essential gesture of the introduction and generally follows rather specific rules (see Table 6.2). In other cultures, different rules operate. For example, in Muslim cultures people will hug people of the same sex but not of the opposite sex. In Latin America, South America, and the Mediterranean, people are more likely to hug (and perhaps kiss on the cheek) than are Northern Europeans, Asians, and many from the United States. Given the great Hispanic influence on the United States today, it's probable that the hug-kiss will grow in general popularity. Asians are more reluctant to extend their hands and more often bow, with a lower bow required when a person of lower status meets someone of higher status.

As you can imagine, cultural differences may create intercultural difficulties and misunderstandings. For example, if you shake hands in a culture that hugs and kisses, you may appear standoffish. If you hug and kiss in a culture that is used to shaking hands, you may seem presumptuous and overly friendly. The best advice is to watch what the people of the culture you're in do and try to do likewise. At the same time, don't get upset if members of other cultures unknowingly "violate" your own culture's rituals. After all, one ritual is no more inherently logical or correct than any other.

EXCUSES AND APOLOGIES

If you engage in conversation for any length of time, it's likely that at some point you'll say the wrong thing. Then, because you can't erase the message (recall from Chapter 1 that communication is irreversible), you may try to offer an explanation to account for what happened. The most common methods for doing so are the excuse and the apology, two closely related types of what might be called *conversational correctives*.

Excuses are "explanations or actions that lessen the negative implications of an actor's performance, thereby maintaining a positive image for oneself and others" (Snyder, 1984; Snyder, Higgins, & Stucky, 1983). Apologies are expressions of regret or sorrow for having done what you did or for what happened. Often the two are blended—*I didn't realize how fast I was driving* (the excuse); *I'm really sorry* (the apology). Let's separate them and look first at the excuse.

The Excuse **Excuses** are especially appropriate when you say or are accused of saying something that runs counter to what is expected, sanctioned, or considered "right" by the people with whom you're in conversation. Ideally, you hope, the excuse will lessen the negative impact of your message.

The major motive for excuse making seems to be to maintain your self-esteem, to project a positive image of yourself to others. Excuses also represent an effort to reduce stress: You may feel that if you can offer an excuse—especially a good one that is accepted by those around you—it will reduce the negative reaction and the subsequent stress that accompanies a poor performance.

Excuses also may enable you to maintain effective interpersonal relationships after some negative behavior. For example, after criticizing a friend's behavior and observing his or her negative reaction to your criticism, you might offer an excuse such as, "I'm really exhausted. I'm just not thinking straight." Excuses enable you to place your messages—even your possible failures—in a more favorable light.

Good and Bad Excuses. The most important question for most people is what makes a good excuse and what makes a bad excuse (Snyder, 1984; Slade, 1995). Good excuse makers use excuses in moderation; bad excuse makers rely on excuses too often. Good excuse makers accept responsibility for their failures and avoid blaming others, but bad excuse makers won't acknowledge their mistakes and are quick to pass the blame. Not surprisingly, excuse makers who accept responsibility will be perceived as more credible, competent, and likable than those who deny responsibility (Dunn & Cody, 2000).

What makes one excuse effective and another ineffective will vary from one culture to another and will depend on factors already discussed, such as the culture's individualism–collectivism, its power distance, the values it places on assertiveness, and various other cultural tendencies (Tata, 2000). But, at least in the United States, researchers seem to agree that the best excuses in interpersonal communication contain four elements (Slade, 1995; Coleman, 2002).

1. You demonstrate that you understand the problem and that your partner's feelings are legitimate and justified. Avoid minimizing the issue or your partner's feelings ("It was only $100; you're overreacting," "I was only two hours late," "It was only one time").

2. You acknowledge your responsibility. If you did something wrong, avoid qualifying your responsibility ("I'm sorry if I did anything wrong") or expressing a lack of sincerity ("Okay, I'm sorry; it's obviously my fault—again"). On the other hand, if you can demonstrate that you had no control over what happened and therefore cannot be held responsible, your excuse is likely to be highly persuasive (Heath, Stone, Darley, & Grannemann, 2003).

3. You acknowledge your own displeasure at what you did; you make it clear that you're not happy with yourself for your actions.

4. You make it clear that your misdeed will never happen again.

Some researchers include a fifth step, which is actually an apology. Here you would express regret and perhaps ask forgiveness for what you did. Let's look at the apology more specifically.

The Apology In its most basic form, an **apology** is an expression of regret for something you did. The most basic of all apologies is simply, *I'm sorry*. In popular usage, the apology includes some admission of wrongdoing on the part of the person making the apology. Sometimes the wrongdoing is acknowledged explicitly (*I'm sorry I lied*) and sometimes only by implication (*I'm sorry you're so upset*). In many cases the apology also includes a request

"And oftentimes excusing of a fault doth make the fault the worse by the excuse."

—WILLIAM SHAKESPEARE

for forgiveness and some assurance that the behavior won't be repeated *(Please forgive my lateness; it won't happen again).*

According to the Harvard Business School Working Knowledge website (http://hbswk.hbs.edu/archive/3481.html, accessed May 20, 2008) apologies are useful for two main reasons. Apologies (1) help repair relationships and (2) repair the reputation of the wrongdoer. If you do something wrong in your relationship, for example, an apology will help you repair the relationship with your partner and perhaps reduce the level of conflict. At the same time, however, realize that other people know about your behavior and an apology will help improve their image of you.

An effective apology, like an effective excuse, must be crafted for the specific situation. Effective apologies to a long-time lover, to a parent, or to a new supervisor are likely to be very different because the individuals and the relationships are different. Therefore, the first rule of an effective apology is to take into consideration the uniqueness of the situation—the people, the context, the cultural rules, the relationship, the specific wrongdoing—for which you want to apologize. Although each situation will call for a somewhat different message of apology, you can follow some general guidelines.

Some Dos for Effective Apologies.

- Admit wrongdoing if indeed wrongdoing occurred. Accept responsibility. Own your own actions; don't try to pass them off as the work of someone else. Instead of *"Smith drives so slow, it's a wonder I'm only 30 minutes late,"* say *"I should have taken traffic into consideration."*
- Be apologetic. Say (and mean) the words *I'm sorry* or *What I did was wrong.*
- State in specific rather than general terms what you've done. Instead of "I'm sorry for what I did" say, "I'm sorry for getting drunk at the party and flirting with everyone."
- Express understanding of how the other person feels and acknowledge the legitimacy of these feelings, for example, "You have every right to be angry; I should have called."
- Express your regret that this has created a problem for the other person: "I'm sorry I made you miss your appointment."
- Offer to correct the problem (whenever this is possible): "I'm sorry I didn't clean up the mess I made; I'll do it now."
- Give assurance that this will not happen again. Say, quite simply, "It won't happen again," or better and more specifically, "I won't be late again."

Some Don'ts for Effective Apologies.
At the same time that you follow the suggestions for crafting an effective apology, try to avoid these common "dont's":

- Apologize when it isn't necessary.
- Justify your behavior by mentioning that everyone does it or that others have done worse.
- Accuse the other person of contributing to the problem: "I should have known you're overly anxious about receiving the figures exactly at 9 a.m."
- Minimize the hurt that this may have caused. Avoid comments such as, "So the figures arrived a little late. What's the big deal?"
- Include excuses with the apology. Avoid such combinations as "I'm sorry the figures are late but I had so much other work to do." An excuse often negates the apology by saying, in effect, *I'm really not sorry because there was good reason for what I've done.*
- Take the easy way out and apologize through e-mail. Generally, it's preferable to use a more personal mode of communication—face-to-face or phone, for example. It's more difficult, but it's more effective.

Skill Development Experience

Formulating Excuses and Apologies

Excuses and apologies are often helpful in lessening the possible negative effects of a mishap. Here are several situations in which you might want to offer an excuse and/or an apology. For each of the following situations, formulate one excuse or apology that you think will prove effective.

1. Your boss confronts you with your office telephone log. The log shows that you've been making lots of long-distance personal phone calls, a practice that is explicitly forbidden.

2. In talking with your supervisor, you tell a joke that puts down lesbians and gay men. Your supervisor tells you she finds the joke homophobic and offensive; she adds that she has a gay son and is proud of it. This supervisor's approval is essential to your retention.

3. You're caught in a lie. You told your romantic partner that you were going to visit your parents but were discovered to have visited a former lover. You don't want to break up your relationship over this.

Excuses and apologies will not reverse your errors, but they may help repair—at least to some extent—conversational or relationship damage.

COMPLIMENTING

A **compliment** is a message of praise, flattery, or congratulations. The compliment functions like a kind of interpersonal glue; it's a way of relating to another person with positiveness and immediacy. It's also a conversation starter: "I like your watch; may I ask where you got it?" Another purpose the compliment serves is to encourage the other person to compliment you—even if not immediately (which often seems inappropriate).

Compliments can be unqualified or qualified. The unqualified compliment is a message that is purely positive. "Your paper was just great, an A." The qualified message is not entirely positive: "Your paper was great, an A; if not for a few problems, it would have been an A+." You might also give a qualified compliment by qualifying your own competence: for example, "That song you wrote sounded great, but I really don't know anything about music."

A "backhanded compliment" is really not a compliment at all; it's usually an insult masquerading as a compliment. For example, you might be giving a backhanded compliment if you were to say, "That sweater takes away from your pale complexion; it makes you look less washed out" (it compliments the color of the sweater but criticizes the person's complexion).

Compliments are sometimes difficult to give and even more difficult to respond to without discomfort or embarrassment. Fortunately, there are easy-to-follow guidelines.

Giving a Compliment   Here are a few suggestions for giving a compliment.

- Be real and honest. Say what you mean and refrain from giving compliments you don't believe in. They'll probably sound insincere.

- Compliment in moderation. A compliment that is too extreme (for example, "That's the best decorated apartment I've ever seen in my life") may be viewed as dishonest. Similarly, don't compliment at every possible occasion; if you do, your compliments will seem too easy to win and not really meaningful.

- Be totally complimentary; avoid qualifying your compliments. If you hear yourself giving a compliment and then adding *but* or *however*, stop and rethink what you are going to say. Many people will remember the qualification rather than the compliment, and it will instead feel like a criticism.

- Be specific. Direct your compliment at something specific rather than something general. Instead of saying, "I liked your story," you might say, "I liked your story—it made me realize something I had forgotten. . . ."

Skill Development Experience

Giving and Responding to Compliments

Complimenting and responding to compliments gracefully is an acquired skill.

This exercise is in two parts.

1. Formulate a compliment in which you say something favorable and positive (no backhanded compliments allowed) about another person's reliability, intelligence, sense of style, fair mindedness, independence, perceptiveness, warmth, sense of humor, or any other quality that might normally be commented upon favorably.

2. Assume that the compliment you just formulated was addressed to you. How would you feel? What would you say in response to such a compliment?

- Be personal in your own feelings—"Your song really moved me; it made me recall so many good times"—but not personal about the other person—"Your hair looks so natural; is that a weave or a toupee?"

- Some interpersonal watchers recommend that you compliment people for their accomplishments rather than for who they are or for things over which they have no control. So, for example, compliment people for their clear reports, their poetry, their problem solving, their tact, and so on, but not for being attractive or having beautiful green eyes.

Receiving a Compliment In receiving a compliment, people generally take either one of two options: denial or acceptance.

Many people deny the compliment ("It's nice of you to say, but I know I was terrible"), minimize it ("It isn't like I wrote the great American novel; it was just an article that no one will read"), change the subject ("So, where should we go for dinner?"), or say nothing. Each of these responses denies the legitimacy of the compliment. Accepting the compliment is a much better alternative. An acceptance might consist simply of (1) a smile with eye contact—avoid looking at the floor or (2) a simple "thank you" and, if appropriate, (3) a personal reflection in which you explain (very briefly) the meaning of the compliment and why it's important to you (e.g., "I really appreciate your comments; I worked really hard on the project and it's great to hear it was effective").

ADVICE

Most people like to give advice. Advising someone else about what they should do might make you feel competent and authoritative. Giving advice may even be part of your job description. For example, if you're a teacher, lawyer, health care provider, religious leader, or psychiatrist, you are in the advice-giving business.

Advice is best viewed as the process of giving another person a suggestion for thinking or behaving, usually to effect a change. In many cases it will take the form of a suggestion for solving a problem. For example, you might advise a friend to change his or her way of looking at something—a broken love affair, a financial situation, or a career path—or you might advise someone to do something, such as to start dating again, to invest in certain stocks, or to go back to school to complete a degree. Sometimes, advice serves to encourage a person to stick with what she or he is currently thinking or doing.

One of the most important types of advice is what could be called *meta-advice*, advice about advice. At least three types of meta-advice can be identified.

- *To explore options and choices.* This type of meta-advice would focus on helping the person explore the available options. For example, if a friend were to ask what he or she should do about never having a date, you might help your friend explore the available options (such as dating websites, speed dating, and singles groups) and the advantages and disadvantages of each.

- *To seek expert advice.* If confronted with a request for advice about a subject you know little about, the best advice is often a referral to someone who is an expert in the field. When a friend asks what to do about a persistent cough, the best advice seems to be the meta-advice to "talk to your doctor."

- *To delay decision.* If asked for advice about a decision that doesn't have to be made immediately, one form of meta-advice would be to delay the decision and collect additional information. If, for example, your advice-seeker has two weeks to decide on whether or not to take a job with XYZ Company, your meta-advice might be to delay the decision while researching the company more thoroughly.

Meta-advice is one of the safest types of advice to give. When you meta-advise someone to explore options more thoroughly, you're not so much giving advice as you are helping the advice-seeker to collect the information needed to make his or her own decision.

Giving Advice   Here are some suggestions for giving advice effectively:

- *Listen.* This is the first rule for advice giving. Listen to the person's thoughts and feelings to discern what he or she really wants. The person who says, for example, "I just don't know what to do" may be requesting support and active listening rather than advice. The person may simply want to ventilate in the presence of a friend. If you're in doubt as to what the person is seeking, ask.

- *Empathize.* Try to feel what the other person is feeling. Perhaps you might recall similar situations you were in or similar emotions you experienced. Think about the importance of the issue to the person and, in general, try to put yourself in his or her position.

- *Be tentative.* If you give advice, give it with the qualifications it requires. The advice seeker has a right to know how sure (or unsure) you are of the advice or what evidence (or lack of evidence) you have that the advice will work.

- *Offer options.* When appropriate, offer several options and give the pros and cons of each: *If you do X, then A and B are likely to follow.* Even better, allow the advice seeker to identify the possible consequences of each option.

- *Ensure understanding.* Often people seeking advice are emotionally upset and may not remember everything in the conversation. Seek feedback after giving advice by saying, for example, "Do you think my suggestion is workable?"

- *Keep the interaction confidential.* People often seek advice about very personal matters. It's best to keep such conversations confidential, even if you're not explicitly asked to do so.

- *Avoid* should *statements.* People seeking advice still ultimately have to make their own decisions. It's better to say, "You *might* do X" or "You *could* do Y" rather than "You *should* do Z." Avoid demanding—or even implying—that the person has to follow your advice. This attacks the person's negative face, his or her need for autonomy.

Responding to Advice   Here are a few suggestions for receiving advice.

- If you asked for advice, then accept what the person says. You owe it to the advice-giver to listen to and consider the advice, even if you decide not to follow it.

- Resist the temptation to retaliate or criticize the advice-giver, even if you didn't ask for advice. Instead of responding with "Well, your hair doesn't look that great either," consider if the advice has any merit. If you decide to reject the advice, ask yourself why someone would think you were in need of such advice in the first place.

- Interact with the advice. Talk about it with the advice-giver. A process of asking and answering questions is likely to produce added insight into the problem.

- Express your appreciation for the advice. It's often difficult to give advice. Showing the advice-giver some gratitude in return is a good idea.

Summary of Concepts and Skills

This chapter explored interpersonal communication and conversation.

1. Conversation consists of five general stages: opening, feedforward, business, feedback, and closing.
2. Throughout the speaking–listening process, both speaker and listener exchange cues for *conversational turns;* these cues enable the speaker and listener to communicate *about* the communication in which they're engaged.
3. Speakers regulate the conversation through two major types of cues: turn-maintaining cues and turn-yielding cues. Listeners regulate the conversation by using three types of cues: turn-requesting cues, turn-denying cues, and back-channeling cues and interruptions.
4. Dialogue is conversation in which there is genuine two-way interaction; each person is both speaker and listener, sender and receiver. Monologue communication is the opposite: One person speaks and the other listens—there's no real interaction between participants.
5. Immediacy is the creation of closeness, a sense of togetherness, between speaker and listener.
6. Small talk is pervasive, noncontroversial, and often serves as a polite way of introducing one's self or a topic.
7. Introducing one person to another or yourself to others will vary with the culture.
8. Excuses are explanations designed to lessen any negative implications of a message (Snyder, 1984; Snyder, Higgins, & Stucky, 1983). Apologies are expressions of regret or sorrow for having done what you did or for what happened.
9. A compliment is a message of praise, flattery, or congratulations and often enables you to interact with positiveness and immediacy.
10. Advice can be direct, or it can be advice about advice (meta-advice).

Consider your competence in using the skills of effective relationship communication and place a check mark next to the skills you want to work on most.

_____ 1. I understand that conversation occurs in stages and that each stage serves a different function.

_____ 2. I follow the principles of turn-taking in conversation, giving appropriate speaker and listener cues and responding to the cues of others.

_____ 3. I engage in dialogic rather than monologic conversation.

_____ 4. I adjust my immediacy cues as appropriate to the conversation and the relationship.

_____ 5. I can engage in small talk in a variety of situations with comfort and ease.

_____ 6. I can comfortably introduce people to each other and myself to others.

_____ 7. I can formulate effective excuses and apologies and can use them appropriately in interpersonal interactions.

_____ 8. I can extend and receive a compliment graciously.

_____ 9. I can effectively offer meta-advice and follow the general rules for giving and receiving advice.

Key Word Quiz

The Language of Interpersonal Communication, Conversation, and Relationships

Match the terms about interpersonal communication with their definitions. Record the number of the definition next to the appropriate term.

_____ a. phatic message (122)

_____ b. turn-maintaining cues (125)

_____ c. dialogue (126)

_____ d. immediacy (127)

_____ e. apology (133)

1. Genuine two-way interaction.
2. Expression of regret
3. Signals indicating your reluctance to assume the role of speaker.
4. A form of flattery, an expression of positiveness.
5. A type of listener cue that says, *I'm listening.*
6. Communication in which one person speaks and the other listens.
7. An explanation as to why something happened.
8. Signals that indicate that the speaker wishes to continue speaking.

_____ f. turn-denying cues (125)

_____ g. monologue (127)

_____ h. compliment (135)

_____ i. excuse (133)

_____ j. back-channeling cues (125)

9. The quality of togetherness, of oneness, that joins speaker and listener.

10. Communication that opens the channels of communication.

These ten terms and additional terms used in this chapter can be found in the glossary and on flashcards on MyCommunicationLab (**www.mycommunicationlab.com**).

Answers: a. 10 b. 3 c. 1 d. 9 e. 2 f. 8 g. 6 h. 4 i. 7 j. 5

MyCommunicationLab

PEARSON
mycommunicationlab
www.mycommunicationlab.com

Visit MyCommunicationLab (**www.mycommunicationlab.com**) for a wealth of additional information on conversation. Flash cards, videos, skill building exercises, sample text questions, and additional examples and discussions will help you continue your study of interpersonal communication and especially conversation.

7 Interpersonal Relationships

Why read this chapter?

Because you'll learn about:
- the major types and theories of interpersonal relationships
- the influence of culture and technology on your relationships

Because you'll learn to:
- communicate in relationships (friendship, romance, family, and work) more effectively
- assess and manage your own relationships in light of research and theory
- communicate more effectively in different cultural and technological contexts

$\mathcal{T}$his chapter will look at the stages of relationships, the varied types of relationships, theories that explain why you enter and exit relationships, and the influence of culture, technology, and work on our relationships.

The Stages of Interpersonal Relationships

You and another person don't become intimate friends immediately on meeting. Rather, you build an intimate relationship gradually, through a series of steps or stages. The same is true of most relationships.

The six-stage model in Figure 7.1 describes the main stages in most relationships: contact, involvement, intimacy, deterioration, repair, and dissolution, each of which has an early and a late phase. These stages describe relationships as they are; they don't evaluate or prescribe how relationships should be. For a particular relationship, you might wish to modify the basic model, but as a general description the stages seem fairly

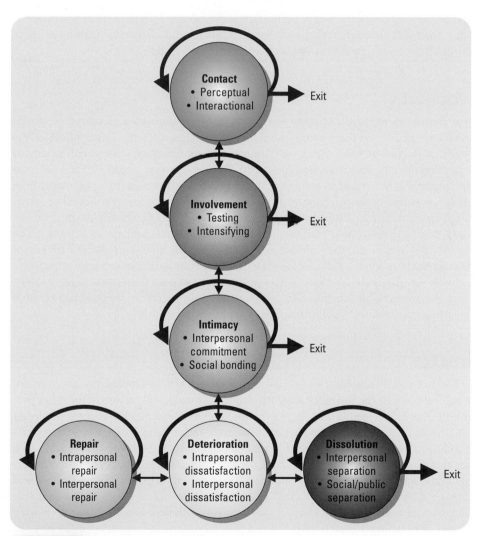

FIGURE 7.1 **The Six Stages of Relationships**

Because relationships differ so widely, it's best to think of this or any relationship model as a tool for talking about relationships rather than as a specific map that indicates how you move from one relationship position to another. Can you identify other steps or stages that would further explain what goes on in relationship development? What happens when the two people in a relationship experience the stages differently? Can you provide an example from literature or from your own experience?

standard. They are also applicable generally to face-to-face as well as to online relationships. As you read about these stages, keep in mind that both partners may not perceive their relationship in the same way; one person, for example, may see the relationship as having reached the intimate stage and the other may not.

CONTACT

At the initial phase of the **contact** stage, there is some kind of *perceptual contact*—you see, hear, and perhaps smell the person. From this you get a physical picture: gender, approximate age, height, and so on. After this perception there is usually *interactional contact*, which is superficial and relatively impersonal. This is the stage at which you exchange basic information that is preliminary to any more intense involvement ("Hello, my name is Joe"); you initiate interaction ("May I join you?") and engage in invitational communication ("May I buy you a drink?"). According to some researchers, it's at this stage—within the first four minutes of initial interaction—that you decide whether you want to pursue the relationship (Zunin & Zunin, 1972). At the contact stage, physical appearance is especially important, because it's the characteristic most readily seen. Yet, through verbal and nonverbal behaviors, personal qualities such as friendliness, warmth, openness, and dynamism are also revealed.

INVOLVEMENT

At the **involvement** stage a sense of mutuality, of being connected, develops. Here you experiment and try to learn more about the other person. At the initial phase of involvement, a kind of *testing* goes on. You want to see whether your initial judgment proves reasonable. You may ask questions: "Where do you work?" "What are you majoring in?" If you want to get to know the person even better, you might continue your involvement by intensifying your interaction and by beginning to reveal yourself, though in a preliminary way. In a dating relationship, you might, for example, use a variety of strategies to help you move to the next stage and perhaps to intimacy. For example, you might increase contact with your partner; give your partner tokens of affection such as gifts, cards, or flowers; write affectionate messages on a person's Facebook wall, increase your own personal attractiveness; do things that suggest intensifying the relationship, such as flirting or making your partner jealous; and become more physically intimate (Tolhuizen, 1989).

INTIMACY

The contact and involvement stages make up **relationship development**—a movement toward intimacy. At the **intimacy** stage you commit yourself still further to the other person and establish a relationship in which this individual becomes your best or closest friend, lover, or companion. You also come to share each other's social networks, a practice followed by members of widely different cultures (Gao & Gudykunst, 1995) and seen most clearly on social network sites. Both the quantity and the quality of your interpersonal exchanges increase (Emmers-Sommer, 2004), and of course you also talk more and in greater detail about the relationship (Knobloch, Haunani, & Theiss, 2006). Not surprisingly, your relationship satisfaction also increases with the move to this stage (Siavelis & Lamke, 1992). One research study defined intimacy as the feeling that you can be honest and open when talking about yourself, sharing thoughts and feelings that you don't reveal in other relationships (Mackey, Diemer, & O'Brien, 2000).

The intimacy stage usually divides itself into two phases. In the *interpersonal commitment* phase, the two people commit themselves to each other in a private way. In the *social bonding* phase, the commitment is made public—perhaps to family and friends, perhaps to the public at large. Here you and your partner become a unit, an identifiable pair.

Communication Choice Point

Relationship Résumé

Although you've been mostly honest in your two-month Internet relationship, you have padded your relationship résumé—lopped off a few years and pounds and made your temporary job seem like the executive fast track. You now want to come clean. *What might you do in preface to this revelation? What would you say? What channel would you use?*

Skill Development Experience

Practicing Cherishing Messages

Cherishing behaviors are an especially insightful way to affirm another person and to increase favor exchange, a concept that comes from the work of William Lederer (1984). **Cherishing behaviors** are those small gestures you enjoy receiving from your partner (e.g., a smile, a wink, a squeeze, a kiss, a phone call, an "I love you").

Prepare a list of ten cherishing behaviors that you would like to receive from your real or imagined relationship partner. Identify cherishing behaviors that are

a. specific and positive—nothing overly general or negative

b. focused on the present and future rather than on issues about which you've argued in the past

c. capable of being performed daily

d. easily executed—nothing that you have to go out of your way to accomplish

If you have a relationship partner, ask him or her also to prepare a list, and exchange lists, and begin exchanging cherishing behaviors. Ideally, you and your partner will begin to perform these cherishing behaviors for one another. In time these behaviors should become a normal part of your interaction, which is exactly what you'd hope to achieve.

Lists of cherishing behaviors will also give you insight into your own relationship needs and the kind of communicating partner you want.

DETERIORATION

The relationship **deterioration** stage is characterized by a weakening of the bonds between the friends or lovers. The first phase of deterioration is usually *intrapersonal dissatisfaction:* You begin to experience personal dissatisfaction with everyday interactions and begin to view the future with your partner more negatively. If this dissatisfaction grows, you pass to the second phase, *interpersonal deterioration.* You withdraw and grow further and further apart. You share less of your free time. You exchange fewer messages. When you're together, there are awkward silences, fewer disclosures, less physical contact, and a lack of psychological closeness. Conflicts become more common and their resolution more difficult.

Relationship deterioration involves unique communication patterns. These patterns are in part a response to the deterioration; you communicate the way you do because you feel that your relationship is in trouble. However, these patterns are also causative: The communication patterns you use largely determine the fate of your relationship. Here are a few communication patterns that characterize relationship deterioration and are often the cause of it.

- *Withdrawal.* Nonverbally, withdrawal is seen in the greater space the partners need and in the speed with which tempers flare when that space is invaded. Other nonverbal signs of withdrawal include a decrease in eye contact and touching; less similarity in clothing; and fewer displays of items associated with the other person, such as bracelets, photographs, and rings (Miller & Parks, 1982; Knapp & Vangelisti, 2000). Verbally, withdrawal involves a decreased desire to talk and especially to listen. At times partners may use small talk not as a preliminary to serious conversation but as an alternative, perhaps to avoid confronting serious issues.

- *Decline in self-disclosure.* Self-disclosing communications decline significantly. If the relationship is dying, you may think self-disclosure isn't worth the effort. Or you may limit your self-disclosures because you feel that the other person may not accept them or can no longer be trusted to be supportive and empathic.

- *Deception.* Deception increases as relationships break down. Sometimes this takes the form of clear-cut lies that people may use to avoid arguments over such things as staying out all night, not calling, or being seen in the wrong place with the wrong

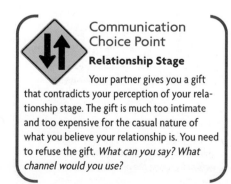

Communication
Choice Point
Relationship Stage
Your partner gives you a gift that contradicts your perception of your relationship stage. The gift is much too intimate and too expensive for the casual nature of what you believe your relationship is. You need to refuse the gift. *What can you say? What channel would you use?*

"We swam. We made sand castles. I'm sorry, Michael—I thought you understood that this was just a summer thing."

© Chris Weyant/Condé Nast Publications/www.cartoonbank.com.

person. At other times, lies may be used because of a feeling of shame; you may not want the other person to think less of you. One of the problems with deception is that it has a way of escalating, eventually creating a climate of distrust and disbelief.

- *Negative versus positive messages.* During deterioration, negative messages increase and positive messages decrease. Once you praised the other's behaviors, but now you criticize them. Often the behaviors have not changed significantly; what has changed is your way of looking at them. What was once a cute habit now becomes annoying; what was once "different" now becomes inconsiderate. When a relationship is deteriorating, there is a decline in requests for pleasurable behaviors (e.g., "Will you fix me my favorite dessert?") and a rise in requests to stop unpleasant or negative behaviors (e.g., "Will you stop monopolizing the phone?") (Lederer, 1984). Even the social niceties get lost as requests deteriorate from "Would you please make me a cup of coffee, honey?" to "Get me some coffee, will you?" to "Where's my coffee?"

REPAIR

At the relationship **repair** stage, some partners may pause during deterioration and try to repair their relationship. Others, however, may progress without stopping to dissolution.

At the first repair phase, *intrapersonal repair*, you analyze what went wrong and consider ways of solving your relational difficulties. You might at this stage consider changing your behaviors or perhaps changing your expectations of your partner. You might also evaluate the rewards of your relationship as it is now and the rewards to be gained if your relationship ended.

Should you decide that you want to repair your relationship, you might move to the *interpersonal repair* phase—you might discuss with your partner the problems in the relationship, the changes you want to see, and perhaps what you'd be willing to do and what you'd want your partner to do. This is the stage of negotiating new agreements and new behaviors. You and your partner might try to repair your relationship by yourselves, or you might seek the advice of friends, family, or relationship therapists.

DISSOLUTION

The **dissolution** stage, the last stage in the relationship model, involves cutting the bonds that tie you together. In the beginning it usually takes the form of *interpersonal separation*: You might move into your own apartments and begin to lead separate lives. If the separation works better than the original relationship, you enter the phase of *social* or *public separation*. Avoidance of each other and a return to a "single" status are among the primary characteristics of the dissolution of a relationship.

Given both the inevitability that some relationships will break up and the significant effects such breakups will have on you, here are some steps you can take to ease the pain during this difficult time. These suggestions apply to the termination of any type of relationship—whether a friendship or a romantic relationship, and whether through death, separation, or breakup.

- *Break the Loneliness–Depression Cycle.* The two most common feelings following the end of a relationship are loneliness and depression. In most cases, fortunately, loneliness and depression are temporary. When depression lasts, is especially deep, or disturbs your normal functioning, it's time to seek professional help.
- *Take Time Out.* Resist the temptation to jump into a new relationship while you still have strong feelings about the old one and before a new one can be assessed with some objectivity.
- *Bolster Self-Esteem.* If your relationship fails, you may experience a decline in self-esteem (Collins & Clark, 1989). Your task now is to regain the positive self-image you need in order to function effectively.

Communication Choice Point

Relationship Dissolution

You realize that your six-month relationship is going nowhere, and you want to break it off. It's just not exciting and not taking you where you want to go. You want to avoid making a scene. *What would you say? Where would you say it? What kinds of feedforward would you use before breaking the news?*

- *Seek Support*. Seeking the support of others is one of the best antidotes to the unhappiness caused when a relationship ends. Tell your friends and family of your situation—in only general terms, if you prefer—and make it clear that you want support. Seek out people who are positive and nurturing, and avoid those who will paint the world in even darker tones or blame you for what happened.

Interpersonal Relationship Types

Each relationship, whether friendship or love, a primary relationship or a work relationship, is unique. Yet there are general types that research has identified—and these categories will offer considerable insight into your own interpersonal relationships.

FRIENDSHIP

One theory of **friendship** identifies three major types: friendships of reciprocity, receptivity, and association (Reisman, 1979, 1981). The friendship of **reciprocity**, the ideal type, is characterized by loyalty, self-sacrifice, mutual affection, and generosity. A friendship of reciprocity is based on equality. Each individual shares equally in giving and receiving the benefits and rewards of the relationship.

In the *friendship of receptivity*, in contrast, there is an imbalance in giving and receiving; one person is the primary giver and the other the primary receiver. This is a positive imbalance, however, because each person gains something from the relationship. The different needs of both the person who receives affection and the person who gives it are satisfied. This is the friendship that may develop between a teacher and a student or between a doctor and a patient. In fact, a difference in status is essential for the friendship of receptivity to develop.

The *friendship of association* is transitory; it might be described as a friendly relationship rather than a true friendship. Associative friendships are the kind you have with classmates, neighbors, or coworkers. There is no great loyalty, no great trust, no great giving or receiving. The association is cordial but not intense.

"Laughter is not at all a bad beginning for a friendship."

—OSCAR WILDE

LOVE

Like friendships, romantic partnerships come in different styles as well. Before reading about these styles, take the following self-test to identify your own love style.

Test Yourself

What Kind of Lover Are You?

Respond to each of the following statements with T for "true" (if you believe the statement to be a generally accurate representation of your attitudes about love) or F for "false" (if you believe the statement does not adequately represent your attitudes about love).

_____ **1** My lover and I have the right physical "chemistry" between us.

_____ **2** I feel that my lover and I were meant for each other.

_____ **3** My lover and I really understand each other.

_____ **4** I believe that what my lover doesn't know about me won't hurt him/her.

_____ **5** My lover would get upset if he/she knew of some of the things I've done with other people.

_____ **6** When my lover gets too dependent on me, I want to back off a little.

_____ **7** I expect to always be friends with my lover.

_____ **8** Our love is really a deep friendship, not a mysterious, mystical emotion.

_____ **9** Our love relationship is the most satisfying because it developed from a good friendship.

_____ **10** In choosing my lover, I believed it was best to love someone with a similar background.

_____ **11** An important factor in choosing a partner is whether or not he/she would be a good parent.

_____ **12** One consideration in choosing my lover was how he/she would reflect on my career.

_____ **13** Sometimes I get so excited about being in love with my lover that I can't sleep.

_____ **14** When my lover doesn't pay attention to me, I feel sick all over.

_____ **15** I cannot relax if I suspect that my lover is with someone else.

_____ **16** I would rather suffer myself than let my lover suffer.

_____ **17** When my lover gets angry with me, I still love him/her fully and unconditionally.

_____ **18** I would endure all things for the sake of my lover.

HOW DID YOU DO? This scale, from Hendrick and Hendrick (1990), is based on the work of Lee (1976), as is the discussion of the six types of love that follows. This scale is designed to enable you to identify your own beliefs about love. The statements relate to the six types of love described in the following discussion: eros, ludus, storge, pragma, mania, and agape. Statements 1 through 3 are characteristic of the eros lover. If you answered "true" to these statements, you have a strong eros component to your love style. If you answered "false," you have a weak eros component. Statements 4 to 6 refer to ludus love; 7 to 9, to storge love; 10 to 12, to pragma love; 13 to 15, to manic love, and 16 to 18, to agapic love.

WHAT WILL YOU DO? What can you do to become more aware of the different love styles and become a more well-rounded lover? Incorporating the qualities of effective interpersonal communication—for example, being more flexible, more polite, and more other-oriented—will go a long way toward making you a more responsive love partner.

Source: From "A Relationship-Specific Version of the Love Attitudes Scale" by C. Hendrick and S. Hendrick, 1990, *Journal of Social Behavior and Personality, 5,* 239–254. Used by permission of Select Press.

Communication Choice Point

Refusing a Date

A fellow student in one of your classes asks you for a date. You're really very excited and have been waiting for this all semester. *What are your options for communicating a clear yes, but without appearing overly eager?*

Eros love seeks beauty and sensuality and focuses on physical attractiveness, sometimes to the exclusion of qualities others might consider more important and more lasting. The erotic lover has an idealized image of beauty that is unattainable in reality. Consequently, the erotic lover often feels unfulfilled.

Ludic love seeks entertainment and excitement and sees love as fun, a game. To the ludic lover, love is not to be taken too seriously; emotions are to be held in check lest they get out of hand and make trouble. The ludic lover retains a partner only so long as the partner is interesting and amusing. When the partner is no longer interesting enough, it's time to change.

Storge love is a peaceful and tranquil love. Like ludus, storge lacks passion and intensity. Storgic lovers set out not to find a lover but to establish a companionable relationship with someone they know and with whom they can share interests and activities. Storgic love is a gradual process of unfolding thoughts and feelings and is sometimes difficult to distinguish from friendship.

Pragma love is practical and traditional and seeks compatibility and a relationship in which important needs and desires will be satisfied. The pragma lover is concerned with the social qualifications of a potential mate even more than with personal qualities; family and background are extremely important to the pragma lover, who relies not so much on feelings as on logic.

Manic love is an obsessive love that needs to give and receive constant attention and affection. When attention and affection are not constant, or when an expression of increased commitment is not returned, reactions such as depression, jealousy, and self-doubt can lead to extreme lows.

Agapic love is compassionate and selfless. The agapic lover loves both the stranger on the road and the annoying neighbor. Jesus, Buddha, and Gandhi practiced and preached this unqualified spiritual love—a love that is offered without concern for personal reward or gain and without any expectation that the love will be reciprocated.

PRIMARY RELATIONSHIPS AND FAMILIES

Primary relationships are central to family life. It should be noted, however, that the U.S. **family** comes in many configurations and has undergone profound changes in recent decades. Table 7.1 provides a few statistics on the U.S. family in 1970 and in 2002. One obvious change is the rise in the percentage of one-parent families. There are now almost 12 million single-parent households in the United States. In 1998 about 28 percent of children under 18 lived with only one parent (about 23 percent with their mother and about 4 percent with their father), according to the 2009 *World Almanac and Book of Facts.*

Another change is the increasing number of people living together in an exclusive relationship who are not married. For the most part these cohabitants live as if they were married: There is an exclusive sexual commitment; there may be children; there are shared financial responsibilities, shared time, and shared space. These relationships mirror traditional marriages, except that in marriage the union is recognized by a religious body, the state, or both, whereas in a relationship of cohabitants it is not.

"We love because it's the only true adventure."

—NIKKI GIOVANNI

TABLE 7.1　The Changing Face of Family

Here are a few statistics on the nature of the U.S. family for 1970 and 2002, as reported by the *New York Times Almanac 2009* and *The World Almanac and Book of Facts 2009*, along with some possible trends these figures indicate. What other trends do you see occurring in the family?

Family Characteristic	1970	2002	Trends
Number of members in average family	3.58	3.21	Reflects the tendency toward smaller families
Families without children	44.1%	52%	Reflects the growing number of families opting to not have children
Families headed by married couples	86.8%	76.3%	Reflects growing trends for heterosexual couples to live as a family without marriage, for singles to have children, and for gay men and lesbians to form families
Females as heads of households	10.7%	17.7%	Reflects the growing number of women having children without marriage and the increase in divorce and separation
Single-parent families	13%	27.8%	Reflects the growing trend for women (especially) to maintain families without a partner
Households headed by never-married women with children	248,000	4.3 million	Reflects the growing trend for women to have children and maintain a family without marriage
Children living with only one parent	12%	23%	Reflects the growing divorce rate and the increased number of children born to unwed mothers
Children between 25 and 34 living at home with parents	8% (11.9 million)	9.3% (19.2 million)	Reflects the increased economic difficulties of establishing one's own home and perhaps the increased divorce rate and later dates for marriage (especially among men)

Some families are headed by gay male or lesbian couples who live together as domestic partners or, in some cases, spouses. Many of these couples have children from previous heterosexual unions, through artificial insemination, or by adoption. Although accurate statistics are difficult to secure, primary relationships among gay men and lesbians seem more common than the popular media might lead us to believe. Although homosexuality and gay marriage remain controversial to some, recent research shows that same-sex couples are as committed and satisfied in their relationships as are heterosexual couples (Roisman, Clausell, Holland, Fortuna, & Elieff, 2008; Balsam, Beauchaine, Rothblum, & Solomon, 2008).

The communication principles that apply to the traditional nuclear family (i.e., the mother-father-child family) also apply to these relationships. In the following discussion, the term *primary relationship* denotes the relationship between two principal parties—husband and wife, lovers, or domestic partners, for example—and the term *family* may denote a broader constellation that includes children, relatives, and assorted significant others.

A **primary relationship** is a relationship between two people that the partners see as their most important interpersonal relationship. An interesting typology of primary relationships (based on more than 1,000 couples' responses to questions concerning their degree of sharing, their space needs, their conflicts, and the time they spend together) identifies three basic types: traditionals, independents, and separates (Fitzpatrick, 1983, 1988, 1991; Noller & Fitzpatrick, 1993).

Traditional couples share a basic belief system and philosophy of life. They see themselves as a blending of two persons into a single couple rather than as two separate individuals. They're interdependent and believe that each individual's independence must be sacrificed for the good of the relationship. Traditionals believe in mutual sharing and do little separately. This couple adheres to traditional sex roles, and there are seldom any power struggles or role conflicts. In their communications traditionals are highly responsive to each other. They lean toward each other, smile, talk a lot, interrupt each other, and finish each other's sentences.

Independents stress their individuality. The relationship is important, but never more important than each person's individual identity. Although independents spend a great deal of time together, they don't ritualize it, for example, with schedules. Each individual spends time with outside friends. Independents see themselves as relatively androgynous—as individuals who combine traditionally feminine and traditionally masculine roles and qualities. The communication between independents is responsive. They engage in conflict openly and without fear. Their disclosures are quite extensive and include high-risk and negative disclosures that are typically absent among traditionals.

Separates live together, but they view their relationship more as a matter of convenience than a result of their mutual love or closeness. They seem to have little desire to be together and, in fact, usually are together only at ritual occasions such as mealtime or holiday get-togethers. It's important to these separates that each has his or her own physical as well as psychological space. Separates share little; each seems to prefer to go his or her own way. Separates hold relatively traditional values and beliefs about sex roles, and each person tries to follow the behaviors normally assigned to each role. The most significant characteristic of this type is that each person sees him- or herself as a separate individual and not as a part of a "we."

Theories of Interpersonal Communication and Relationships

Several theories offer insight into why and how people develop and dissolve relationships. Here we'll examine five such theories: attraction, relationship rules, social penetration, social exchange, and equity.

ATTRACTION

Attraction theory holds that people form relationships on the basis of **attraction**. You are no doubt drawn, or attracted, to some people and not attracted to others. In a similar way, some people are attracted to you and some are not. If you're like most people, you're attracted to others on the basis of four major factors:

- *Physical attractiveness and personality.* It's easily appreciated that people like physically attractive people more than they like physically unattractive people. What isn't so obvious is that we also feel a greater sense of familiarity with more attractive people than with less attractive people; that is, we're more likely to think we've met a person before if that person is attractive (Mohin, 2003). Additionally, you probably tend to like people who have a pleasant rather than an unpleasant personality, although people differ on what is an attractive personality to them and what isn't. The fact that different people find different personality characteristics attractive, that there does seem to be someone for everyone, may be a comforting thought.

- *Similarity.* According to the **similarity** principle, if you could construct your mate, it's likely that your mate would look, act, and think very much like you (Burleson, Samter, & Luccetti, 1992; Burleson, Kunkel, & Birch, 1994). Generally, people like those who are similar to them in nationality, race, abilities, physical characteristics, intelligence, and attitudes (Pornpitakpan, 2003). Sometimes people are attracted to their opposites, in a pattern called **complementarity**: For example, a dominant person might be attracted to someone who is more submissive. Generally, however, people prefer those who are similar.

- *Proximity.* If you look around at people you find attractive, you will probably find that they are the people who live or work close to you. People who become friends are the people who have had the greatest opportunity to interact with each other.

Communicating Ethically
Relationship Ethics

A starting place for considering the ethical issues and guidelines that operate within a friendship or romantic, family, or workplace relationship can be identified with the acronym ETHICS: empathy (Cheney & Tompkins, 1987), talk (rather than force), honesty (Krebs, 1989), interaction management, confidentiality, and supportiveness (Johannesen, 2001).

- Empathy: People in relationships have an ethical obligation to empathize with their relationship partners.
- Talk: Decisions in a relationship should be arrived at by talk rather than by force—by persuasion, not coercion.
- Honesty: Relationship communication should be honest and truthful.
- Interaction management: Relationship communication should be satisfying and comfortable and is the responsibility of all individuals.
- Confidentiality: People have a right to expect that what they say in close relationships will not be revealed to others.
- Supportiveness: A supportive and cooperative climate should characterize the interpersonal interactions of people in relationships.

As you reflect on these suggestions consider what other qualities you'd consider to be a part of relationship ethics. Put differently, what other ethical qualities would you want in a close relationship partner?

The first step in the evolution of ethics is a sense of solidarity with other human beings.

—ALBERT SCHWEITZER (1875–1965), German philosopher and physician

- *Reinforcement.* You're attracted to people who give rewards or reinforcements, which can range from a simple compliment to an expensive cruise. You're also attracted to people you reward (Jecker & Landy, 1969; Aronson, Wilson, & Akert, 2007). That is, you come to like people for whom you do favors.

RELATIONSHIP RULES

You can gain an interesting perspective on interpersonal relationships by looking at them in terms of the rules that govern them (Shimanoff, 1980). The general assumption of **rules theory** is that relationships—friendship, love, family, and work—are held together by adherence to certain rules. When those rules are broken, the relationship may deteriorate and even dissolve.

Relationship rules theory helps to clarify several aspects of relationships. First, these rules help you identify successful versus destructive relationship behavior. By looking at the rules of a relationship, you can better identify the reasons a relationship is in trouble (i.e., what rules were broken) and how it may be repaired (i.e., what rules need to be reinforced and honored). Further, if you know what the rules are, you will be better able to master the social skills involved in developing and maintaining relationships. Because these rules vary from one culture to another, it is important to understand when your partner may be operating with rules different from your own. Gender rules for initiating a date or sex are good examples, and you can easily appreciate the culture clash that can result when one of these rules is broken.

Friendship Rules   Friendship rules include such behaviors as standing up for your friend in his or her absence, sharing information and feelings about successes, demonstrating emotional support for your friend, trusting and offering to help your friend when in need, and trying to make your friend happy when you're together

(Argyle & Henderson, 1984; Argyle, 1986). When these and other rules are followed, the friendship is strong and mutually satisfying. When the rules are broken, the friendship suffers and may die. For example, the friendship would be in trouble when one or both friends are intolerant of the other's friends, discuss confidences with third parties, fail to demonstrate positive support, nag, and/or fail to trust or confide in the other.

According to friendship rules theory, then, maintaining a friendship depends on your knowing the rules and having the ability to apply the appropriate interpersonal skills friendships require (Trower, 1981; Blieszner & Adams, 1992).

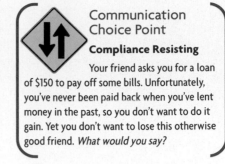

Communication Choice Point

Compliance Resisting

Your friend asks you for a loan of $150 to pay off some bills. Unfortunately, you've never been paid back when you've lent money in the past, so you don't want to do it gain. Yet you don't want to lose this otherwise good friend. *What would you say?*

Romantic Rules Romantic relationships may also be viewed from a rules perspective. For example, one research study identified eight rules that romantic relationships establish and follow (Baxter, 1986). These rules keep the relationship together—or, when broken, lead to deterioration and eventually dissolution. The general form for each rule is: "If parties are in a close relationship, they should . . ."

1. acknowledge each other's individual identities and lives beyond the relationship.
2. express similar attitudes, beliefs, values, and interests.
3. enhance each other's self-worth and self-esteem.
4. be open, genuine, and authentic with each other.
5. remain loyal and faithful to each other.
6. have substantial shared time together.
7. reap rewards commensurate with their investments relative to the other party.
8. experience a mysterious and inexplicable "magic" in each other's presence.

Family Rules Family communication research points to the importance of rules in defining and maintaining the family (Galvin, Bylund, & Brommel, 2007). Family rules encompass three main interpersonal communication issues (Satir, 1983):

- What can you talk about? Can you talk about the family finances? grandpa's drinking? your sister's lifestyle?
- How can you talk about something? Can you joke about your brother's disability? Can you address directly questions of family history and family skeletons?
- To whom can you talk? Can you talk openly to extended family members such as cousins and aunts and uncles? Can you talk to close neighbors about family health issues?

Like the rules of friends and lovers, family rules tell you which behaviors will be rewarded (and therefore what you should do) and which will be punished (what you should not do). Rules also provide a kind of structure that defines the family as a cohesive unit and that distinguishes it from other similar families. Not surprisingly, the rules a family develops are greatly influenced by culture. Although there are many similarities among families throughout the world, there are also differences (Georgas, et al., 2001). For example, members of collectivist cultures are more likely to restrict family information from outsiders as a way of protecting the family than are members of individualist cultures. This tendency to protect the family can create serious problems: in cases of wife abuse, for example. Many women will not report spousal abuse because of this desire to protect the family image, not letting on that things aren't perfect at home (Dresser, 1996, 2005).

Workplace Rules Rules also govern your workplace relationships. These rules are usually a part of the corporate culture that an employee would learn from observing other employees (especially those who move up the hierarchy) as well as from official memos on dress, sexual harassment, and the like. Of course, each organization will have different rules, so it's important to see what rules are operating in any given situation. Among the rules that you might find are:

- Work very hard.
- Be cooperative in teams; the good of the company comes first.
- Don't reveal company policies and plans to workers at competing firms.
- Don't form romantic relationships with other workers.
- Avoid even the hint of sexual harassment.

SOCIAL PENETRATION

Social penetration theory is a theory not of why relationships develop but of what happens when they do develop; it describes relationships in terms of the number of topics that people talk about and their degree of "personalness" (Altman & Taylor, 1973). The **breadth** of a relationship has to do with the number of topics you and your partner talk about. The **depth** of a relationship involves the degree to which you penetrate the inner personality—the core—of the other individual. The individual can be represented as a circle divided into various parts (see Figure 7.2). These parts represent topics or areas of interpersonal communication, or communication breadth. Further, the circle and its parts consist of concentric inner circles, rather like an onion. These represent the different levels of communication, or its depth.

When a relationship begins to deteriorate, the breadth and depth will, in many ways, reverse themselves, in a process called **depenetration**. For example, while ending a relationship, you might cut out certain topics from your interpersonal communications. At the same time you might discuss the remaining topics in less depth. In some instances of relational deterioration, however, both the breadth and the depth of interaction increase. For example, when a couple breaks up and each is finally free from an oppressive relationship, they may—after some time—begin to discuss problems and feelings they would never have discussed when they were together. In fact, they may become extremely close friends and grow to like each other more than when they were together (Baxter, 1983).

SOCIAL EXCHANGE AND EQUITY

Social exchange theory claims that you develop relationships that will enable you to maximize your profits (Thibaut & Kelley, 1986; Stafford, 2008)—a theory based on an economic model of profits and losses. The theory begins with the following equation: Profits = Rewards – Costs. Rewards are anything that you would incur costs to obtain. Research has identified six types of rewards in a relationship: money, status, love, information, goods, and services (Baron, Branscombe, & Byrne, 2009). For example, to get the reward of money, you might have to work rather than play. To earn (the status of)

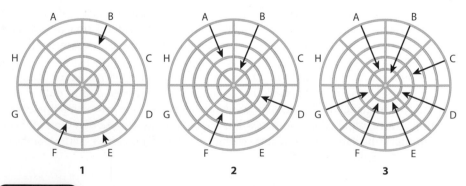

FIGURE 7.2   **Models of Social Penetration**

How accurately do the concepts of breadth and depth express your communication in relationships of different intensities? Can you identify other aspects of messages that change as you go from only talking to an acquaintance, to being a casual friend, to intimate?

an A in an interpersonal communication course, you might have to write a term paper or study more than you want to.

Costs are things that you normally try to avoid, that you consider unpleasant or difficult. Examples might include working overtime, washing dishes and ironing clothes, watching your partner's favorite television show that you find boring, or doing favors for those you dislike.

Equity theory uses the ideas of social exchange but goes a step farther and claims that you develop and maintain relationships in which the ratio of your rewards relative to your costs is approximately equal to your partner's (Walster, Walster, & Berscheid, 1978; Messick & Cook, 1983; Stafford, 2008). For example, if you and a friend start a business and you put up two-thirds of the money and your friend puts up one-third, equity would demand that you get two-thirds of the profits and your friend get one-third. An equitable relationship, then, is simply one in which each party derives rewards that are proportional to their costs. If you contribute more to the relationship than your partner, then equity requires that you should get greater rewards. If you both work equally hard, then equity demands that you should get approximately equal rewards.

Equity theory puts into clear focus the sources of relational dissatisfaction seen every day. For example, in a relationship both partners may have full-time jobs, but one partner may also be expected to do the major share of the household chores. Thus, although both may be deriving equal rewards—they have equally good cars, they live in the same three-bedroom house, and so on—one partner is paying more of the costs. According to equity theory, this partner will be dissatisfied.

Equity theory claims that you will develop, maintain, and be satisfied with relationships that are equitable. You will not develop, will be dissatisfied with, and will eventually terminate relationships that are inequitable. The greater the inequity, the greater the dissatisfaction and the greater the likelihood that the relationship will end.

Culture, Technology, Work, and Relationships

Interpersonal relationships vary widely depending on culture, both the larger culture and the cultures of the individuals, on the technological channels used, and on

Communication Choice Point

Negotiating Equity

You feel your romantic relationship of the last three months has become inequitable—you seem to do more of the work but get few benefits, while your partner does less work but gets more benefits. You want to correct this imbalance before the relationship goes any further. *What are some options you have for negotiating greater equity? What are some of the things you might say?*

"We can only learn to love by loving."

—IRIS MURDOCH

whether the relationships occur inside or outside the workplace. For a more complete understanding of interpersonal relationships today, it is necessary to look at these three factors.

CULTURE AND GENDER

Cultural contexts and gender distinctions vary greatly around the world. This text's discussion of relationships up to this point has assumed, for example, that you voluntarily choose your relationship partners—that you consciously choose to pursue certain relationships and not others. In some cultures, however, your parents choose your romantic partner for you. In some cases your husband or wife is chosen to unite two families or to bring some financial advantage to your family or village. An arrangement such as this may have been made by your parents when you were an infant or even before you were born. In most cultures, of course, even when arranged marriages are not the norm, there's pressure to marry "the right" person and to be friends with certain people and not others.

In the United States, researchers study and textbook authors write about dissolving relationships and how to survive relationship breakups. It's generally assumed that you have the right to exit an undesirable relationship. However, in some cultures you simply cannot dissolve a relationship once it's formed or once there are children. In the practice of Roman Catholicism, once people are validly married, they're always married and cannot dissolve that relationship. More important to such cultures may be issues such as how to maintain a relationship that has problems, what to do to survive in an unpleasant relationship, and how to repair a troubled relationship (Moghaddam, Taylor, & Wright, 1993).

Your culture influences the difficulties that you go through when relationships break up. For example, married persons whose religion forbids divorce and remarriage will experience religious disapproval and condemnation as well as the same economic and social difficulties and emotional pain everyone else goes through. In the United States child custody almost invariably goes to the woman, and this presents emotional burdens for the man. In Iran child custody goes to the man, which presents added emotional burdens for the woman. In India women experience greater difficulty than men in divorce because of their economic dependence on men, cultural beliefs about women, and the patriarchal order of the family (Amato, 1994).

There are also significant gender differences in interpersonal relationships. Perhaps the best-documented finding—already noted in the discussion of self-disclosure in Chapter 2—is that women self-disclose more than men. This difference holds throughout male and female friendships. Male friends self-disclose less often and with less intimate details than female friends do, and men generally do not view self-disclosure as a necessary aspect of their friendships (Hart, 1990). Women engage in significantly more affectional behaviors with their friends than do males, which may account for the greater difficulty men experience in initiating and maintaining close friendships (Hays, 1989). *Relational* communication, in all its forms and functions, seems a much more important dimension of women's friendships.

Men's friendships often are built around shared activities: attending a ball game, playing cards, or working on a project at the office. Women's friendships, on the other hand, are built more around a sharing of feelings, support, and "personalism."

There are gender similarities and differences also in love. Women and men seem to experience love to a similar degree (Rubin, 1973). However, women indicate greater love than men do for their same-sex friends. This may reflect a real difference between the sexes, or it may be a function of the greater social restrictions on men. A man is not supposed to admit his love for another man, but women are permitted to communicate their love for other women.

Men and women differ in the types of love they prefer (Hendrick, Hendrick, Foote, & Slapion-Foote, 1984). For example, on a love self-test similar to the "What kind of lover are you?" test presented earlier, men scored higher on erotic and ludic love, whereas women scored higher on manic, pragmatic, and storgic love. No difference was found for agapic love.

Another gender difference frequently noted is that of romanticism. Research generally confirms that, contrary to popular depictions in the media, men are more romantic than women. For example, researchers have found that "men are more likely than women to believe in love at first sight, in love as the basis for marriage and for overcoming obstacles, and to believe that their partner and relationship will be perfect" (Sprecher & Metts, 1989). This difference seems to increase as the romantic relationship develops: Men become more romantic and women less romantic (Fengler, 1974).

In their reactions to broken romantic affairs, women and men exhibit both similarities and differences. For example, the tendency to recall only pleasant memories and to revisit places with past associations was about equal among women and men. However, men engage in more dreaming about the lost partner and in more daydreaming as a reaction to the breakup than women do.

TECHNOLOGY

Also significant is the influence of technology on romantic relationships. In face-to-face relationships, you perceive the other person through nonverbal cues—you see the person's eyes, face, body—and you perceive this immediately. In online relationships of only a few years ago, physical attractiveness was signaled exclusively through words and self-descriptions (Levine, 2000). Here, as you can appreciate, although a face-to-face encounter strongly favors those who were physically attractive, the online encounter favored those who were verbally adept at self-presentation and did not disadvantage less attractive individuals. Now, with photos, videos, and audio being a part of many online dating and social networking sites, this advantage is fading, but probably won't be entirely erased. Certainly, a face-to-face encounter still provides more nonverbal cues about the person than any computer interaction does.

There are advantages to establishing relationships online. For example, strictly online relationships are safe in terms of avoiding physical violence and sexually transmitted diseases. Most of the social networking sites, such Facebook and MySpace, have built-in protections that enable you to control the kinds of information about yourself that you reveal. Unlike relationships established in face-to-face encounters, in which physical appearance tends to outweigh personality, Internet communication reveals your inner qualities first. Rapport and mutual self-disclosure become more important than physical attractiveness in promoting intimacy (Cooper & Sportolari, 1997). And, contrary to a popular opinion, online relationships rely just as heavily on the ideals of trust, honesty, and commitment as do face-to-face relationships (Whitty & Gavin, 2001). Friendship and romantic interaction on the Internet are a natural boon to shut-ins and extremely shy people, for whom traditional ways of meeting someone are often difficult.

Of course, there are also disadvantages. For one thing, depending on the program you're using, you may not be able to see the person. Even if photos are exchanged, how certain can you be that the photos are of the person or that they were taken recently? In addition, you may not be able to hear the person's voice, and this too hinders you as you seek to develop a total picture of the other person.

Online, people can present a false self with little chance of detection; minors may present themselves as adults, and adults may present themselves as children in order to conduct illicit and illegal sexual communications and, perhaps, initiate meetings. Similarly, people can present themselves as poor when they're rich, as mature when they're immature, as serious and committed when they're just enjoying the online experience. Although people can also misrepresent themselves in face-to-face relationships, the fact that it's easier to do so online probably accounts for greater frequency of misrepresentation in computer relationships (Cornwell & Lundgren, 2001).

WORK

Workplace relationships, especially workplace romances, provide a unique perspective on the advantages and disadvantages of relationships. Real life is quite different from television depictions of workers, who are always best friends and who move in and out of interoffice romances with no difficulty—at least no difficulty that can't be resolved in 24 minutes.

Opinions vary widely concerning workplace romances. On the positive side, the work environment seems a perfect place to meet a potential romantic partner. After all, by virtue of the fact that you're working in the same office, you're probably both interested in the same field, have similar training and ambitions, and spend considerable time together—all factors that foster the development of a successful interpersonal relationship.

Another advantage is that office romances can lead to greater work satisfaction. If you're romantically attracted to another worker, it can make going to work, working together, and even working added hours more enjoyable and more satisfying. If their relationship is good and mutually satisfying, the individuals are likely to develop empathy for each other and to act in ways that are supportive, cooperative, and friendly—all characteristics of effective workplace communication.

Among the disadvantages is the discomfort this may cause other workers. Seeing the loving couple every day may generate destructive office gossip. Others may see the lovers as a team that must be confronted as a pair; they may feel that they can't criticize one without incurring the wrath of the other.

Office relationships may cause problems for management when, for example, a promotion is to be made or relocation decisions are necessary. Can you legitimately ask one lover to move to Boston and the other to move to San Francisco? Will it be difficult for management to promote one lover to a position in which he or she will become the supervisor of the other?

When an office romance goes bad or when it's one-sided, it can be especially difficult. One obvious problem is that it can be stressful for the former partners to see each other regularly and to continue to work together. Other workers may feel they have to take sides, being supportive of one partner and critical of the other, which can cause friction throughout the organization. Another, perhaps more serious, issue is the potential for charges of sexual harassment, especially if the romance was between a supervisor and a worker.

The generally negative attitude of management toward workplace relationships and the problems inherent in dealing with the normal stresses of both work and romance seem to outweigh the positive benefits that may be derived from such relationships. Therefore, workers are generally advised not to romance their colleagues. Friendship seems the much safer course.

Summary of Concepts and Skills

This chapter explored interpersonal relationships—their stages and types; the reasons they be formed; and the influence of culture, technology, and work on relationships.

1. Relationships may be viewed in terms of six stages: contact, involvement, intimacy, deterioration, repair, and dissolution. Each of these stages can be further broken down into an early and a late phase.

2. Among the major causes of relationship deterioration are a lessening of the reasons for establishing the relationship, changes in the people involved, sexual difficulties, and work and financial problems.

3. Friendships may be classified as those of reciprocity, receptivity, and association.

4. Six primary love styles have been identified: eros, ludus, storge, mania, pragma, and agape.

5. Primary relationships and families may be classified into traditionals, independents, and separates.

6. Attraction depends on such factors as physical and personality attractiveness, similarity (especially attitudinal), reinforcement, and proximity.

7. The relationship rules theory views relationships as held together through adherence to an agreed on set of rules.

8. Social penetration theory describes relationships in terms of breadth (i.e., the number of topics you talk about) and depth (i.e., the degree of personalness with which you pursue the topics).

9. Social exchange theory holds that you develop relationships that yield the greatest profits. You seek relationships in which the rewards exceed the costs and are likely to dissolve relationships when the costs exceed the rewards.

10. Equity theory claims that you develop and maintain relationships in which the rewards are distributed in proportion to costs. When your share of the rewards is less than would be demanded by equity, you are likely to experience dissatisfaction and exit the relationship.

11. Relationships of all kinds and in all their aspects are heavily influenced by culture, as are the theories that explain relationships and the topics relationship research focuses on.

12. Gender differences in both friendship and love are often considerable and influence the ways in which these relationships are viewed and the communication that takes place within them.

13. All aspects of relationships—from development through maintenance and, sometimes, to dissolution—are greatly influenced by advances in technology and the opportunities it affords for communication.

14. Romantic relationships in the workplace present both opportunities and dangers.

Throughout this discussion of interpersonal relationships, a variety of relationship skills were discussed. Place a check mark next to those skills that you feel you want to work on most.

_____ 1. I adjust my communication patterns on the basis of the relationship's intimacy.

_____ 2. I can identify changes in communication patterns that may signal deterioration.

_____ 3. I can use the accepted repair strategies to heal an ailing relationship: for example, reversing negative communication patterns, using cherishing behaviors, and adopting a positive action program.

_____ 4. I can deal with relationship dissolution and apply such skills as breaking the loneliness-depression cycle, bolstering self-esteem, and seeking support.

_____ 5. I understand the different types of friendships and can identify the goals that each type serves.

_____ 6. I understand the different types of love and can appreciate the varied ways in which people can love.

_____ 7. I understand the varied types of primary relationships and families and can see the similarities and differences among them.

_____ 8. I can effectively manage physical proximity, reinforcement, and emphasizing similarities as ways to increase interpersonal attractiveness.

_____ 9. I can apply the rules of friendship, romantic, family, and work relationships as appropriate.

_____ 10. I can identify, and to some extent control, the rewards and costs of my relationships.

_____ 11. I can appreciate the other person's perception of relationship equity and can modify my own behavior to make the relationship more productive and satisfying.

_____ 12. I understand that relationships are influenced by both culture and gender, and I take these differences into consideration when trying to understand interpersonal relationships.

_____ 13. I understand the differences between face-to-face and online relationships and can modify my behavior accordingly.

_____ 14. I take into consideration the advantages and the disadvantages of workplace romantic relationships.

Key Word Quiz

The Language of Interpersonal Communication, Conversation, and Relationships

Match the terms about interpersonal communication with their definitions. Record the number of the definition next to the appropriate term.

_____ a. cherishing behaviors (143)

_____ b. deterioration (143)

_____ c. reciprocity (145)

_____ d. family types (147)

_____ e. agapic love (147)

_____ f. social exchange theory (152)

_____ g. equity theory (153)

_____ h. depenetration (152)

_____ i. storge love (147)

_____ j. involvement (142)

1. A friendship of loyalty and mutual affection.
2. An important stage between contact and intimacy.
3. A theory claiming that you experience relational satisfaction when there is an equal distribution of rewards and costs between the two persons in the relationship.
4. The process by which a deteriorating relationship decreases in breadth and depth.
5. A love that is peaceful and tranquil.
6. Small gestures people enjoy receiving.
7. A love that is compassionate and selfless.
8. The stage at which the bonds between people are weakened.
9. Characterized by three types: traditional, independents, and separates.
10. A theory based on the expectation of fairness.

These ten terms and additional terms used in this chapter can be found in the glossary and on flashcards on MyCommunicationLab (www.mycommunicationlab.com).

Answers: a. 6 b. 8 c. 1 d. 9 e. 7 f. 10 g. 3 h. 4 i. 5 j. 2

MyCommunicationLab

PEARSON
mycommunicationlab

www.mycommunicationlab.com

Visit MyCommunicationLab (www.mycommunicationlab.com) for additional materials on interpersonal relationships. Flash cards, videos, skill building exercises, sample text questions, and additional examples and discussions will help you continue your study of interpersonal relationships.

8 Managing Interpersonal Conflict

Why read this chapter?

Because you'll learn about:

- the nature and principles of interpersonal conflict
- the strategies that people use in conflict situations

Because you'll learn to:

- engage in interpersonal conflicts so that they result in strengthening, not weakening, your relationship
- manage conflicts so that both parties emerge from the conflict reasonably satisfied

*O*f all your interpersonal interactions, those involving conflict are among your most important. Interpersonal conflict often creates ill will, anxiety, and problems for relationships. But, as you'll soon see, conflict also can create opportunities for improving and strengthening relationships.

Preliminaries to Interpersonal Conflict

Before considering the stages and strategies of conflict management, it is necessary to define exactly what is meant by *interpersonal conflict*, the issues around which interpersonal conflict often centers, and some of the myths surrounding conflict.

DEFINITION OF INTERPERSONAL CONFLICT

You want to go to the movies with your partner. Your partner wants to stay home. Your insisting on going to the movies interferes with your partner's staying home, and your partner's determination to stay home interferes with your going to the movies. You can't both achieve your goals, so there will be conflict.

As this example illustrates, **interpersonal conflict** is disagreement between or among connected individuals (e.g., close friends, lovers, family members) who perceive their goals as incompatible (Hocker & Wilmot, 2007; Folger, Poole, & Stutman, 2005; Cahn & Abigail, 2007). More specifically, conflict occurs when people:

- are interdependent (they're connected in some significant way); what one person does has an impact or an effect on the other person.

- are mutually aware that their goals are incompatible; if one person's goal is achieved, then the other person's goal cannot be achieved. For example, if one person wants to buy a new car and the other person wants to pay down the mortgage, and there is not enough money to do both, there is conflict.

- perceive each other as interfering with the attainment of their own goals. For example, you may want to study but your roommate may want to party; the attainment of either goal would interfere with the attainment of the other goal.

An important implication of this concept of interdependency is that, the greater the interdependency, the greater (1) the number of issues around which conflict can center and (2) the impact of the conflict and the conflict management interaction on the individuals and on the relationship (see Figure 8.1). Looked at in this way, it's easy to appreciate the importance to your relationships of understanding interpersonal conflict and learning strategies for effective conflict management.

INTERPERSONAL CONFLICT ISSUES

Interpersonal conflicts cover a wide range of issues and have been categorized differently by different researchers. One system, for example, classifies conflicts into four categories (Canary, 2003): (1) goals to be pursued (e.g., disagreement between parent and child on what college to attend or what romantic partner to get involved with); (2) the allocation of resources such as money or time (e.g., partners' differing on how to spend their money); (3) decisions to be made (e.g., whether to save or splurge the recent bonus); and (4) behaviors that are considered appropriate or desirable by one person but inappropriate or undesirable by the other (e.g., disagreement over one person's flirting or drinking or not working as hard on the relationship).

FIGURE 8.1 **Conflict and Interdependency**

This figure illustrates that, as interdependency increases, so do the potential for and the importance of conflict. In this figure, the relationship "classmates" is positioned in the middle. Fill in the figure with relationships that are less interdependent and relationships that are more interdependent and test the effectiveness of this simple relationship. Does it effectively depict the likelihood and the significance of your own interpersonal conflicts?

Another approach, based on surveys of gay, lesbian, and heterosexual couples, found six major issues that virtually all couples share (Kurdek, 1994). These issues are arranged here in order, with the first being the most commonly cited. As you read this list, ask yourself how many of these issues you argue about.

- intimacy issues such as affection and sex
- power issues where one person makes excessive demands on the other or makes decisions unilaterally concerning mutual friends or how you'll spend your leisure time
- personal flaws involving, for example, drinking or smoking, personal grooming, and driving style
- personal distance issues such as frequent absence and heavy school or job commitments
- social issues such as politics and social policies, parents, and personal values
- distrust involving, for example, previous lovers and lying

"The ultimate test of a relationship is to disagree, but to hold hands."

—ALEXANDRIA PENNEY

MYTHS ABOUT INTERPERSONAL CONFLICT

Many people have problems dealing with conflict because they hold false assumptions about what conflict is and what it means. Think about your own assumptions about interpersonal and small group conflict, which were probably shaped by the communications you witnessed in your family and in your social interactions. For example, do you think the following are true or false?

Conflict is best avoided. Time will solve the problem; it will all blow over.

If two people experience relationship conflict, it means their relationship is in trouble.

Conflict damages an interpersonal relationship.

Conflict is destructive because it reveals our negative selves—our pettiness, our need to be in control, our unreasonable expectations.

In any conflict, there has to be a winner and a loser. Because goals are incompatible, someone has to win and someone has to lose.

These are myths and, as we'll see in this chapter, they can interfere with your ability to deal with conflict effectively.

Principles of Interpersonal Conflict

You can further your understanding of interpersonal conflict by looking at some general principles: (1) conflict can center on content or relationship issues, (2) conflict can be positive or negative, (3) conflict is influenced by culture and gender, and (4) conflict styles have consequences.

CONTENT AND RELATIONSHIP CONFLICT

Using concepts developed in Chapter 1, you can distinguish between content conflict and relationship conflict. **Content conflict** centers on objects, events, and persons that are usually, though not always, external to the parties involved in the conflict. Content conflicts have to do with the millions of issues that people argue and fight about every day: the merit of a particular movie, what to watch on television, the fairness of the last examination or job promotion, the way to spend our savings.

Relationship conflicts are equally numerous and are those that center on the nature and meaning of your relationship. Examples include clashes that arise when a

Communication Choice Point

Escalating to Relationship Conflict

Your own interpersonal conflicts often start out as content conflicts but quickly degenerate into relationship conflicts, and that's when things get ugly. *What types of things might you say or do to keep conflicts and their resolution focused on content and not on the relationship?*

younger brother refuses to obey his older brother, two partners both want their say in making vacation plans, or a mother and daughter each want to have the final word concerning the daughter's lifestyle. Here the conflicts are concerned not so much with external objects as with the relationships between the individuals—with issues such as who is in charge, whether there is equal say in decision making, and who has the right to set down rules of behavior.

Of course, content and relationship dimensions are always easier to separate in a textbook than they are in real life, in which many conflicts contain elements of both. For example, you can probably imagine both content and relationship dimensions in each of the "content" issues mentioned. Yet certain issues seem oriented more toward one dimension than the other. For example, disagreements on political and social issues are largely content focused, whereas intimacy and power issues are largely relational.

CONFLICT CAN BE NEGATIVE OR POSITIVE

Although interpersonal conflict is always stressful, it's important to recognize that it has both negative and positive aspects.

Negative Aspects Conflict often leads to increased negative regard for the opponent. One reason for this is that many conflicts involve unfair fighting methods (which we'll examine shortly) and are focused largely on hurting the other person. When one person hurts the other, increased negative feelings are inevitable; even the strongest relationship has limits.

At times, conflict may lead you to close yourself off from the other person. When you hide your true self from an intimate, you prevent meaningful communication from taking place. Because the need for intimacy is so strong, one or both parties may then seek intimacy elsewhere. This often leads to further conflict, mutual hurt, and resentment—qualities that add heavily to the costs carried by the relationship. Meanwhile, rewards may become difficult to exchange. In this situation, the overall costs increase and the rewards decrease, which often leads to relationship deterioration and eventual dissolution.

Positive Aspects The major value of interpersonal conflict is that it forces you to examine a problem and work toward a potential solution. If both you and your opponent use productive conflict strategies (which will be described in this chapter), the relationship may well emerge from the encounter stronger, healthier, and more satisfying than before. And you may emerge stronger, more confident, and better able to stand up for yourself (Bedford, 1996).

Through conflict and its resolution, you also can stop resentment from increasing and let your needs be known. For example, suppose your partner needs lots of attention when she/he comes home from work, but you need to review and get closure on the day's work. If you both can appreciate the legitimacy of these needs, then you can find solutions. Perhaps you can make your important phone call after your partner's attention needs are met, or perhaps your partner can delay the need for attention until you get closure about work. Or perhaps together you can find a way for your closure needs and your partner's attention needs to be met simultaneously through, for example, talking while cuddling at the end of the day. This situation would be considered a *win–win*.

Consider, too, that when you try to resolve conflict within an interpersonal relationship, you're saying in effect that the relationship is worth the effort. Usually, confronting a conflict indicates commitment and a desire to preserve the relationship.

"I can't remember what we're arguing about, either. Let's keep yelling, and maybe it will come back to us."

© David Sipress/Condé Nast Publications/www.cartoonbank.com.

CONFLICT IS INFLUENCED BY CULTURE AND GENDER

As in other areas of interpersonal communication, it helps to consider conflict in light of the influences of culture and gender. Both exert powerful influences on how people view and resolve conflicts.

Conflict and Culture Culture influences both the issues that people fight about and the ways of dealing with conflict that people consider appropriate and inappropriate. Researchers have found, for example, that cohabiting 18-year-olds are more likely to experience conflict with their parents about their living style if they live in the United States than if they live in Sweden, where cohabitation is much more accepted. Similarly, male infidelity is more likely to cause conflict between U.S. spouses than in southern European couples. Students from the United States are more likely to engage in conflict with another U.S. student than with someone from another culture; Chinese students, on the other hand, are more likely to engage in a conflict with a non-Chinese student than with another Chinese (Leung, 1988).

The types of interpersonal conflicts that tend to arise depend on the cultural orientation of the individuals involved. For example, in **collectivist cultures**, such as those of Ecuador, Indonesia, and Korea, conflicts most often involve violations of larger group norms and values, such as failing in your role, for example, as family provider or overstepping your social status by publicly disagreeing with a superior. Conversely, in **individualistic cultures**, such as those of the United States, Canada, and Western Europe, conflicts are more likely to occur when people violate expected norms for example, not defending a position in the face of disagreement (Ting-Toomey, 1985).

U.S. and Japanese people differ in their view of the purpose and outcome of conflict. The Japanese (a collectivist culture) see conflicts and conflict resolution in terms of compromise; people from the United States (an individualist culture), on the other hand, see conflict in terms of winning (Gelfand, Nishii, Holcombe, Dyer, Ohbuchi, & Fukuno, 2001). Also, different cultures teach their members different views of conflict strategies (Tardiff, 2001). For example, in Japan it's especially important that you not embarrass the person with whom you are in conflict, especially if the disagreement occurs in public. This face-saving principle prohibits the use of such strategies as personal rejection or verbal aggressiveness. Many Middle Eastern and Pacific Rim cultures discourage women from direct and forceful expressions; rather, these societies expect more agreeable and submissive postures. In general, members of collectivist cultures tend to avoid overt conflict more than members of individualist cultures (Dsilva & Whyte, 1998; Haar & Krabe, 1999; Cai & Fink, 2002).

Conflict and Gender Do men and women engage in interpersonal conflict differently? One of the few stereotypes that are supported by research is that of the withdrawing and sometimes aggressive male. Men are more apt to withdraw from a conflict situation than are women. It has been argued that this may happen because men become more psychologically and physiologically aroused during conflict (and retain this heightened level of arousal much longer than do women) and so may try to distance themselves and withdraw from the conflict to prevent further arousal. Another explanation for the male tendency to withdraw is that the culture has taught men to avoid conflict. Still another explanation is that withdrawal is an expression of power (Gottman & Carrere, 1994; Canary, Cupach, & Messman, 1995; Goleman, 1995a; Noller, 1993).

Women, on the other hand, want to get closer to the conflict; they want to talk about it and resolve it. Even adolescents reveal these differences; in a study of boys and girls aged 11 to 17, boys withdrew more than girls, but were more aggressive when they didn't withdraw (Lindeman, Harakka, & Keltikangas-Jarvinen, 1997). Similarly, a study of offensive language found that girls were more easily offended by language than boys, but boys were more apt to fight when they were offended by the words used (Heasley, Babbitt, & Burbach, 1995a, 1995b). Another study

"I was thinking about what we should do this weekend, and I have a few ideas for you to reject."

Communication Choice Point

Resolving Differences

You've just moved into a new apartment. Unfortunately, your next-door neighbors play their stereo too loudly and long into the night. You need to say something but just aren't sure how to go about it. *What options do you have for dealing with this situation? To whom might you speak? Through what channel? What would you say?*

showed that young girls used more prosocial strategies (i.e., behaviors designed to help others rather than oneself) than boys (Rose & Asher, 1999).

Other research has found that women tend to be more emotional and men more logical when they argue (Schaap, Buunk, & Kerkstra, 1988; Canary, Cupach, & Messman, 1995). Women have been defined as conflict "feelers" and men as conflict "thinkers" (Sorenson, Hawkins, & Sorenson, 1995). Furthermore, women are more apt to reveal their negative feelings than are men (Schaap, Buunk, & Kerkstra, 1988; Canary, Cupach, & Messman, 1995).

It should be mentioned that some research fails to support these gender differences in conflict style—the differences that cartoons, situation comedies, and films portray so readily and so clearly. For example, several studies dealing with both college students and men and women in business found no significant differences in the ways men and women engage in conflict (Wilkins & Andersen, 1991; Canary & Hause, 1993; Gottman & Levenson, 1999).

CONFLICT STYLES HAVE CONSEQUENCES

The way in which you engage in conflict has consequences for the resolution of the conflict and for the relationship involved. Figure 8.2 identifies five basic styles of engaging in conflict and is especially relevant to understanding interpersonal conflicts (Blake & Mouton, 1984). Descriptions of the five styles, plotted among the dimensions of concern for self and concern for the other person, provide insight into the ways people engage in conflict and highlight some of the advantages and disadvantages of each style. As you read through these styles, try to identify your own conflict style as well as the styles of those with whom you have close relationships.

Competing: I Win, You Lose   The competitive style involves great concern for your own needs and desires and little for those of others. As long as your needs are met, you think the conflict has been dealt with successfully. In conflict motivated by competitiveness, you'd be likely to be verbally aggressive and to blame the other person.

This style represents an "I win, you lose" philosophy. This is the conflict style of a person who simply imposes his or her will on the other: "I make the money, and we'll vacation at the beach or not at all." But this philosophy often leads to resentment on the part of the person who loses, which can cause additional conflicts. Further, the fact that you win and the other person loses probably means that the conflict hasn't really been resolved but has only concluded (for now).

Avoiding: I Lose, You Lose   Conflict avoiders are relatively unconcerned with their own or with their opponents' needs or desires. They avoid any real communication about the problem, change topics when the problem is brought up, and generally withdraw both psychologically and physically.

As you can appreciate, the avoiding style does little to resolve any conflicts and may be viewed as an "I lose, you lose" philosophy. If a couple can't agree about where to spend their vacation, but each person refuses to negotiate a resolution to the disagreement, the pair may not take any vacation at all; both sides lose. Interpersonal problems rarely go away of their own accord; rather, if they exist, they need to be faced and dealt with effectively. Avoidance merely allows the conflict to fester and probably grow, only to resurface in another guise.

Accommodating: I Lose, You Win   In accommodating you sacrifice your own needs for the needs of the other person(s). Your primary goal is to maintain harmony and peace in the relationship or group. This style may help maintain peace and may satisfy the opposition, but it does little to meet your own needs, which are unlikely to go away.

FIGURE 8.2   **Five Conflict Styles**

This figure is adapted from Blake and Mouton's (1984) approach to managerial leadership and conflict. Try to locate your usual conflict style on this grid. How well does this style work for you?

Accommodation represents an "I lose, you win" philosophy. If your partner wants to vacation in the mountains and you want to vacation at the beach, and you, instead of negotiating an agreement acceptable to both, give in and accommodate, then you lose and your partner wins. Although this style may make your partner happy (at least on this occasion), it's not likely to provide a lasting resolution to an interpersonal conflict. You'll eventually sense unfairness and inequality and may easily come to resent your partner, and perhaps even yourself.

Collaborating: I Win, You Win

In **collaborating** you address both your own and the other person's needs. This style, often considered the ideal, takes time and a willingness to communicate—especially to listen to the perspectives and needs of the other person.

"She asked for a divorce, but I outsmarted her and ran into the next room."

© Peter C. Vey/Condé Nast Publications/www.cartoonbank.com.

Collaboration enables each person's needs to be met, an "I win, you win" situation. For example, you might both agree to split the vacation— one week in the mountains and one week at the beach. Or you might agree to spend this year's vacation at one resort and next year's at the other. This is obviously the style that, in an ideal world, most people would choose for interpersonal conflict.

Compromising: I Win and Lose, You Win and Lose

Compromise is the kind of strategy you might refer to as "meeting each other halfway," "horse trading," or "give and take." There's some concern for your own needs and some concern for the other's needs. This strategy is likely to result in maintaining peace, but there will be a residue of dissatisfaction over the inevitable losses that each side has to endure.

Compromise represents an "I win and lose, you win and lose" philosophy. So, if you and your partner can't vacation at both the beach and the mountains, then you might settle for weekend trips or use the money to have a hot tub installed instead. These may not be your first choices, but they're not bad and may satisfy (to some degree at least) each of your vacation wants.

Conflict Management Strategies

In managing conflict you can choose from a variety of productive or unproductive strategies, which we'll investigate here. Realize that the strategies you choose will be influenced by numerous factors, among them (1) the goals to be achieved, (2) your emotional state, (3) your cognitive assessment of the situation, (4) your personality and communication competence, and (5) your family history (Koerner & Fitzpatrick, 2002). Understanding these factors may help you select more appropriate and more effective conflict strategies.

- *The goals (short-term and long-term) you wish to achieve.* If you only want to salvage today's date, you may want to simply "give in" and ignore the difficulty. If you want to build a long-term relationship, on the other hand, you may want to fully analyze the cause of the problem and look for strategies that will enable both parties to win.

- *Your emotional state.* You're unlikely to select the same strategies when you're sad as when you're angry. You will tend to use different strategies if you're seeking to apologize than if you're looking for revenge.

- *Your cognitive assessment of the situation.* For example, your attitudes and beliefs about what is fair and equitable will influence your readiness to acknowledge the fairness in the other person's position. Your own assessment of who (if anyone) is the cause of the problem will also influence your conflict style. You may also assess the likely effects of various possible strategies. For example, do you risk alienating your teenager if you use force?

- *Your personality and communication competence.* For example, if you're shy and unassertive, you may tend to avoid conflict rather than fight actively. If you're extroverted and have a strong desire to state your position, then you may be more likely to fight actively and to argue forcefully.

Communication Choice Point

Avoiding Conflict

Your work team members all seem to have the same conflict style: avoidance. When there is disagreement, they refuse to argue for one alternative or the other or even to participate in the discussion. You need spirited discussion and honest debate if your team is going to come up with appropriate solutions. *What options do you have for dealing with this problem? What would you say?*

Skill Development Experience

Generating Win–Win Solutions

For any one of the situations listed, (a) generate as many win–lose solutions as you can—solutions in which one person wins and the other loses; (b) generate as many possible win–win solutions as you feel the individuals involved in the conflict could reasonably accept; and (c) explain in one sentence the difference between win–lose and win–win solutions

Win–win solutions exist for most interpersonal conflict situations if the people involved are willing to put in a little effort to find them.

1. Jessie and Johnnie have decided to get a pet. Jessie wants a cat; Johnnie wants a dog.
2. Casey, who has been in a 12-year relationship with Devon, recently received a $10,000 bonus and has already used the whole amount for a down payment on a new car. Devon was expecting to share the bonus.
3. Pat smokes and stinks up the apartment. Chris hates this, and they argue about it almost daily.

- *Your family history.* If, for example, your parents argued aggressively about religious differences, you might tend to be aggressive when your partner expresses different religious beliefs. If you haven't *un*learned family conflict patterns, you're likely to repeat them.

AVOIDANCE AND FIGHTING ACTIVELY

Conflict **avoidance** may involve actual physical flight. You may leave the scene of the conflict (e.g., walk out of the apartment or go to another part of the office), fall asleep, or blast the stereo to drown out all conversation. Avoidance also may take the form of emotional or intellectual avoidance, in which you may leave the conflict psychologically by not dealing with any of the arguments or problems raised.

Sometimes avoidance is a response to demands—a conflict pattern known as *demand-withdrawal.* Here one person makes demands (e.g., *You* will *go out again tonight*) and the other person, unwilling to accede to the demands, withdraws from the interaction (Canary, Cupach, & Messman, 1995; Sagrestano, Heavey, & Christensen, 2006; Guerrero, Andersen, Afifi, 2007). This pattern is obviously unproductive, but it can be easily broken by either individual—either by not making demands or by not withdrawing and instead participating actively in the conflict management.

Nonnegotiation is a special type of avoidance. Here you refuse to discuss the conflict or to listen to the other person's argument. At times nonnegotiation takes the form of hammering away at your own point of view until the other person gives in—a technique called "steamrolling."

Instead of avoiding the issues, take an active role in your interpersonal conflicts:

- Involve yourself on both sides of the communication exchange. Be an active participant; voice your own feelings and listen carefully to your opponent's feelings. This is not to say that periodic moratoriums are not helpful; sometimes they are. But in general, be willing to communicate.

- Another part of active fighting involves owning your thoughts and feelings. For example, when you disagree with your partner or find fault with her or his behavior, take responsibility for these feelings. Say, for example, "I disagree with . . ." or "I don't like it when you. . . ." Avoid statements that deny your responsibility: for example, "Everybody thinks you're wrong about . . ." or "Chris thinks you shouldn't. . . ."

- Focus on the present, on the here and now, rather than on issues that occurred two months ago. Similarly, focus your conflict on the person with whom you're fighting, not on the person's parents, child, or friends.

FORCE AND TALK

When confronted with conflict, many people prefer not to deal with the issues but rather to force their position on the other person. **Force** may be emotional or physical. In either case, however, the issues are avoided and the "winner" is the combatant who exerts the most force. This is the technique of warring nations, quarreling children, and even some normally sensible and mature adults.

"*What's amazing to me is that this late in the game we still have to settle our differences with rocks.*"

© Jack Ziegler/Condé Nast Publications/www.cartoonbank.com.

In one study more than 50 percent of both single people and married couples reported that they had experienced physical violence in their relationships. If symbolic violence was included (e.g., threatening to hit the other person or throwing something), the percentages rose above 60 percent for singles and above 70 percent for married couples (Marshall & Rose, 1987). In another study, 47 percent of a sample of 410 college students reported some experience with violence in a dating relationship. In most cases the violence was reciprocal—each person in the relationship used violence. In cases in which only one person was violent, the research results are conflicting. For example, some surveys (e.g., Deal & Wampler, 1986; Cate, Henton, Koval, Christopher, & Lloyd, 1982) have found that in such cases the aggressor was significantly more often the female partner. Other research, however, has tended to confirm the widespread view that men are more likely to use force than women (DeTurck, 1987).

Instead of resorting to force, consider the value of talking and listening:

- Explain what you think the problem is about and listen to what the other person says about the problem.
- Talk about what you want and listen to what the other person wants.
- Talk over possible solutions and listen to the proposed solutions of the other person.
- Talk the conflict through a logical sequence from understanding the problem through evaluating a solution (take a look at the problem-solving sequence discussed in the next chapter, pp. 186–188).

DEFENSIVENESS AND SUPPORTIVENESS

Although talking is preferred to using force, not all talk is equally productive in conflict resolution. One of the best ways to look at destructive versus productive talk is to look at how the style of your communications can create unproductive **defensiveness** or a productive sense of **supportiveness**, a system developed by Jack Gibb (1961). The type of talk that generally proves destructive and sets up defensive reactions in the listener is talk that is evaluative, controlling, strategic, indifferent or neutral, superior, and certain.

Evaluation When you evaluate or judge another person or what that person has done, that person is likely to become resentful and defensive and perhaps at the same time to become equally evaluative and judgmental. In contrast, when you describe what happened or what you want, it creates no such defensiveness and is generally seen as supportive. The distinction between evaluation and description can be seen in the differences between **you-messages** and **I-messages**.

Evaluative You-Messages	Descriptive I-Messages
You never reveal your feelings.	I sure would like hearing how you feel about this.
You just don't plan ahead.	I need to know what our schedule for the next few days will be.
You never call me.	I'd enjoy hearing from you more often.

If you put yourself in the role of the listener hearing these statements, you probably can feel the resentment or defensiveness that the evaluative messages (you-messages) would create and the supportiveness from the descriptive messages (I-messages).

Control When you try to control the behavior of the other person, when you order the other person to do this or that, or when you make decisions without mutual discussion and agreement, defensiveness is a likely response. Control messages deny the legitimacy of the person's contributions and in fact deny his or her importance. When, on the other hand, you focus on the problem at hand—not on controlling the situation or getting your own way—defensiveness is much less likely. This problem orientation invites mutual participation and recognizes the significance of each person's contributions.

Strategy When you use strategy and try to get around other people or situations through **manipulation**—especially when you conceal your true purposes—others are likely to resent it and to respond defensively. But when you act openly and with **spontaneity**, you're more likely to create an atmosphere that is equal and honest.

Neutrality When you demonstrate **neutrality**—in the sense of indifference or a lack of caring for the other person—it's likely to create defensiveness. Neutrality seems to show a lack of empathy or interest in the thoughts and feelings of the other person; it is especially damaging when intimates are in conflict. This kind of talk says, in effect, "You're not important or deserving of attention and caring." When, on the other hand, you demonstrate empathy, defensiveness is unlikely to occur. Although it can be especially difficult in conflict situations, try to show that you can understand what the other person is going through and that you accept these feelings.

Superiority When you present yourself as superior to the other person, you put the other person in an inferior position, and this is likely to be resented. Such superiority messages say in effect that the other person is inadequate or somehow second class. A superior attitude is a violation of the implicit equality contract that people in a close relationship have. The other person may then begin to attack your superiority; the conflict can quickly degenerate into a conflict over who's the boss, with personal attacks being the mode of interaction.

"It is seldom the fault of one when two argue."

—SWEDISH PROVERB

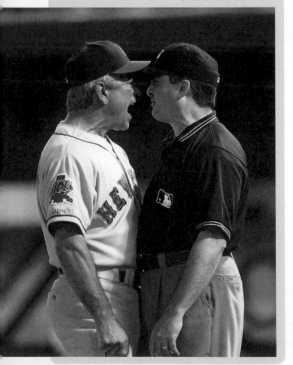

Certainty The person who appears to know it all is likely to be resented, so **certainty** often sets up a defensive climate. After all, there is little room for negotiation or mutual problem solving when one person already has the answer. An attitude of **provisionalism**—"Let's explore this issue together and try to find a solution"—is likely to be much more productive than **closed-mindedness**.

To summarize, the following are suggestions for fostering supportiveness rather than defensiveness:

- Talk descriptively rather than evaluatively.
- Focus on the problem rather than on personalities.
- Act and react honestly and spontaneously, rather than strategically.
- Empathize with the other person.
- Approach the conflict resolution process as an equal and treat the other person as an equal.
- Be provisional; suggest rather than demand.

FACE-ATTACKING AND FACE-ENHANCING STRATEGIES

In the discussion of politeness, the concepts of face and face-threatening acts were introduced (Chapter 2, p. 47). These concepts have special relevance to interpersonal conflict. **Face-attacking** conflict strategies are those that attack a person's positive face (e.g., making comments that criticize the person's contribution to a relationship or the person's ability) or a person's negative face (e.g., making demands on a person's time or resources that attack the person's autonomy). Face-enhancing strategies, on the other hand, are those that support and confirm a person's positive face (e.g.,

praise, a pat on the back, a sincere smile) or negative face (e.g., giving the person space and asking rather than demanding).

One popular but destructive face-attacking strategy is **beltlining** (Bach & Wyden, 1968). Much like fighters in a ring, each of us has an emotional "beltline." When you hit below it, you can inflict serious injury. When you hit above the belt, however, the person is able to absorb the blow. With most interpersonal relationships, especially those of long standing, you know where the beltline is. You know, for example, that to hit Pat with the inability to have children is to hit below the belt. You know that to hit Chris with the failure to get a permanent job is to hit below the belt. This type of face-attacking strategy doesn't help move a conflict toward resolution, and often has the opposite effect of intensifying it. Keep blows to areas your opponent can absorb and handle.

Another such face-attacking strategy is **blame**. Instead of focusing on a solution to a problem, some members try to affix blame to the other person. Whether true or not, blaming is generally unproductive for at least two reasons. First, it diverts attention away from the problem and from its potential solution. Second, it creates resentment that is likely to be responded to with resentment. The conflict then spirals into personal attacks, leaving the individuals and the relationship worse off than before the conflict was ever addressed.

Strategies that enhance positive face involve helping the other person to maintain a positive image, an image as competent and trustworthy, able and good. Even when you get what you want, say by bargaining, it's wise to help the other person retain positive face; this makes it less likely that future conflicts will arise and increases the likelihood that the relationship can be repaired (Donahue, 1992).

Instead of using face-attacking strategies, consider face-saving strategies:

- Confirm the other person's self-image.
- Listen supportively and actively.
- Use I-messages that avoid blaming the other person.
- Use excuses and apologies as appropriate (see Chapter 6, pp. 132–135).
- Respect the other's negative face needs by making few (if any) demands, respecting the other's time, giving the other person space, especially in times of stress, and expressing respect for the other's point of view.

SILENCERS AND FACILITATING OPEN EXPRESSION

Silencers are a wide variety of unproductive fighting techniques that literally silence the other individual. One frequently used silencer is crying. When a person is unable to

deal with a conflict or when winning seems unlikely, the person may cry, and thus silence the other person.

Another silencer is to feign extreme emotionalism—to yell and scream and pretend to be losing control. Still another is to develop some "physical" reaction—headaches and shortness of breath are probably the most popular. One of the major problems with such silencers is that as an opponent you can never be certain that they are mere tactics; they may be real physical reactions that you should pay attention to. Regardless of what you do, the conflict remains unexamined and unresolved.

In addition to avoiding silencers, avoid power tactics (e.g., raising your voice or threatening physical force) that suppress or inhibit freedom of expression. Such tactics are designed to put the other person down and to subvert real interpersonal equality.

Instead of using silencers, try to facilitate open expression:

- Listen actively and give appropriate and positive feedback.
- Verbalize your appreciation for how the other person sees the conflict (say, by punctuating the conflict episode differently).
- Create or increase **immediacy** (discussed in Chapter 6).
- Give the other person permission to express him- or herself openly and honestly.

GUNNYSACKING AND PRESENT FOCUS

The word **gunnysacking** refers to the unproductive process of storing up grievances—as if in a gunnysack—and then unloading them when an argument arises (Bach & Wyden, 1968). The immediate occasion for unloading stored-up grievances may be relatively simple (or so it may seem at first); for example, say you come home late one night without calling. Instead of arguing about this, the gunnysacker pours out a mass of unrelated past grievances. As you probably know from experience, gunnysacking does nothing to help resolve conflict and often begets further gunnysacking. Frequently, the trigger problem never gets addressed. Instead, resentment and hostility escalate.

Instead of gunnysacking, focus on the present:

- Concentrate on the here and now, rather than on issues that occurred two months ago.
- Focus your conflict on the person with whom you're fighting, not on the person's mother, child, or friends.

VERBAL AGGRESSIVENESS AND ARGUMENTATIVENESS

An especially interesting perspective on conflict has emerged from work on verbal aggressiveness and argumentativeness, concepts that were isolated by communication researchers but quickly interested people in other disciplines such as psychology, education, and management, among others (Infante, 1988; Rancer, 1998; Wigley, 1998; Rancer & Avtgis, 2006). Understanding these two concepts will help you understand some of the reasons why things go wrong and some of the ways in which you can use conflict to improve rather than damage your relationships.

Verbal Aggressiveness **Verbal aggressiveness** is a method of winning an argument by inflicting psychological pain, by attacking the other person's self-concept. The technique is a type of disconfirmation in that it seeks to discredit the individual's view of self. To explore this tendency further, take the following self-test of verbal aggressiveness.

"Difficulties are meant to rouse, not discourage. The human spirit is to grow strong by conflict."

—WILLIAM ELLERY CHANNING

Test Yourself

How Verbally Aggressive Are You?

This scale measures how people try to obtain compliance from others. For each statement, indicate the extent to which you feel it's true of you in your attempts to influence others. Use the following scale:

5 = strongly agree; **4** = agree; **3** = undecided; **2** = disagree; and **1** = strongly disagree.

_____ **1** If individuals I am trying to influence really deserve it, I attack their character.

_____ **2** When individuals are very stubborn, I use insults to soften their stubborness.

_____ **3** When people behave in ways that are in very poor taste, I insult them in order to shock them into proper behavior.

_____ **4** When people simply will not budge on a matter of importance, I lose my temper and say rather strong things to them.

_____ **5** When individuals insult me, I get a lot of pleasure out of really telling them off.

_____ **6** I like poking fun at people who do things that are stupid in order to stimulate their intelligence.

_____ **7** When people do things that are mean or cruel, I attack their character in order to help correct their behavior.

_____ **8** When nothing seems to work in trying to influence others, I yell and scream in order to get some movement from them.

_____ **9** When I am unable to refute others' positions, I try to make them feel defensive in order to weaken their positions.

_____ **10** When people refuse to do a task I know is important without good reason, I tell them they are unreasonable.

HOW DID YOU DO? In order to compute your verbal aggressiveness score, simply add up your responses. A total score of 30 would indicate the neutral point, not especially aggressive but not especially confirming of the other either. If you scored about 35, you would be considered moderately aggressive; and if you scored 40 or more, you'd be considered very aggressive. If you scored below the neutral point, you'd be considered

> "The aim of an argument or discussion should not be victory, but progress."
>
> —JOSEPH JOUBERT

less verbally aggressive and more confirming when interacting with others. In looking over your responses, make special note of the characteristics identified in the 10 statements that relate to the tendency to act verbally aggressive. Note those inappropriate behaviors that you're especially prone to commit.

WHAT WILL YOU DO? Because verbal aggressiveness is likely to seriously reduce communication effectiveness, you probably want to reduce your tendencies to respond aggressively. Review the times when you acted verbally aggressive. What effect did such actions have on your subsequent interactions? What effect did they have on your relationship with the other person? What alternative ways of getting your point across might you have used? Might these have proved more effective? Perhaps the most general suggestion for reducing verbal aggressiveness is to increase your argumentativeness.

Source: From a 20-item scale developed by Infante and Wigley (1986) and factor analyzed by Beatty, Rudd, and Valencic (1999). See "Verbal Aggressiveness" by D. Infante and C. J. Wigley, 1986, *Communication Monographs*, 53; and "A Re-evaluation of the Verbal Aggressiveness Scale: One Factor or Two?" by M. J. Beatty, J. E. Rudd, & K. M. Valencic, 1999, *Communication Research Reports*, 16, pp. 10–17. Copyright © 1986 by the National Communication Association. Reprinted by permission of the publisher and authors.

Argumentativeness Contrary to popular belief, argumentativeness is a quality to be cultivated rather than avoided. The term **argumentativeness** refers to your willingness to argue for a point of view, your tendency to speak your mind on significant issues. It's the mode of dealing with disagreements that is the preferable alternative to verbal aggressiveness (Infante & Rancer, 1995).

Test Yourself

How Argumentative Are You?

This questionnaire contains statements about your approach to controversial issues. Indicate how often each statement is true for you personally according to the following scale:

1 = almost never true; **2** = rarely true; **3** = occasionally true; **4** = often true; and **5** = almost always true.

_____ **1** While in an argument, I worry that the person I am arguing with will form a negative impression of me.

_____ **2** Arguing over controversial issues improves my intelligence.

_____ **3** I enjoy avoiding arguments.

_____ **4** I am energetic and enthusiastic when I argue.

_____ **5** Once I finish an argument, I promise myself that I will not get into another.

_____ **6** Arguing with a person creates more problems for me than it solves.

_____ **7** I have a pleasant, good feeling when I win a point in an argument.

_____ **8** When I finish arguing with someone, I feel nervous and upset.

_____ **9** I enjoy a good argument over a controversial issue.

_____ **10** I get an unpleasant feeling when I realize I am about to get into an argument.

_____ **11** I enjoy defending my point of view on an issue.

_____ **12** I am happy when I keep an argument from happening.

Communication Choice Point

Verbal Aggressiveness

Your partner persists in being verbally aggressive whenever you have an argument. Regardless of what the conflict is about, your self-concept is attacked. *What are some of the things you might say or do to stop these attacks? What channel(s) would you use?*

_____ ⑬ I do not like to miss the opportunity to argue a controversial issue.

_____ ⑭ I prefer being with people who rarely disagree with me.

_____ ⑮ I consider an argument an exciting intellectual challenge.

_____ ⑯ I find myself unable to think of effective points during an argument.

_____ ⑰ I feel refreshed and satisfied after an argument on a controversial issue.

_____ ⑱ I have the ability to do well in an argument.

_____ ⑲ I try to avoid getting into arguments.

_____ ⑳ I feel excitement when I expect that a conversation I am in is leading to an argument.

HOW DID YOU DO? To compute your argumentativeness score follow these steps:

1. Add up your scores on items 2, 4, 7, 9, 11, 13, 15, 17, 18, and 20.
2. Add 60 to the sum obtained in step 1.
3. Separately, add up your scores on items 1, 3, 5, 6, 8, 10, 12, 14, 16, and 19.

To compute your argumentativeness score, subtract the total obtained in step 3 from the total obtained in step 2. The following guidelines will help you interpret your score: Scores between 73 and 100 indicate high argumentativeness; scores between 56 and 72 indicate moderate argumentativeness; and scores between 20 and 55 indicate low argumentativeness.

WHAT WILL YOU DO? The researchers who developed this test note that both high and low "argumentatives" may experience communication difficulties. The high argumentative, for example, may argue needlessly, too often, and too forcefully. The low argumentative, on the other hand, may avoid taking a stand even when it is appropriate to do so. Persons scoring somewhere in the middle are probably the most interpersonally skilled and adaptable, arguing when it is necessary but avoiding arguments that are needless and repetitive. Does your experience support this observation? What specific actions might you take to improve your argumentativeness?

Source: From "A Conceptualization and Measure of Argumentativeness," by D. Infante and A. Rancer, 1982, _Journal of Personality Assessment, 46,_ pp. 72–80. Copyright © 1982 Lawrence Erlbaum Associates, Inc. Reprinted by permission of Lawrence Erlbaum Associates, Inc., and the authors.

Communicating Ethically

Ethical Fighting

Communication strategies also have an ethical dimension, and it's important to look at the ethical implications of conflict management strategies. Here are a few questions to consider as you reflect on the conflict strategies discussed in this chapter:

- Does conflict avoidance have an ethical dimension? For example, is it unethical for one relationship partner to refuse to discuss disagreements or to walk out of an argument?
- Can the use of physical force to influence another person ever be ethical? Can you identify a situation in which it would be appropriate for someone with greater physical strength to overpower another person to compel that person to accept his or her point of view?
- Are face-attacking strategies inherently unethical, or might it be appropriate to use them in certain situations? Can you identify such situations?
- Is verbal aggressiveness necessarily unethical?

Honest disagreement is often a good sign of progress.

—GANDHI (1869–1948),
Indian spiritual and
political leader

Communication Choice Point

Conflict Management

Your dorm mate is very popular and has an open-door policy. Throughout the day and evening, friends drop by to chat, borrow a book, check their e-mail, and do a range of things—all of which prevents you from studying. You need to resolve this problem. *What can you say to your roommate to begin to resolve this conflict? What channel would you use?*

As you can appreciate from these two self-tests, argumentativeness differs greatly from verbal aggressiveness (Rancer & Avtgis, 2006). Argumentativeness is constructive in a variety of communication situations and leads to relationship satisfaction. In organizations, it enhances relationships between subordinates and supervisors. Verbal aggressiveness is destructive and leads to relationship dissatisfaction. In organizations, it demoralizes workers.

Argumentative individuals are generally seen as having greater credibility; they're seen as more trustworthy, committed, and dynamic than their argumentative counterparts. In addition, argumentativeness is likely to increase your power of persuasion and will also increase the likelihood that you'll be seen as a leader. Aggressiveness tactics, on the other hand, decrease your power and your likelihood of being seen as a leader.

Instead of being verbally aggressive, try to practice argumentativeness (Infante, 1988; Rancer & Avtgis, 2006):

- Treat disagreements as objectively as possible; avoid assuming that, because someone takes issue with your position or your interpretation, they're attacking you as a person.

- Center your arguments on issues rather than personalities. Avoid attacking a person (rather than a person's arguments), even if this would give you a tactical advantage—it will probably backfire at some later time and make your relationship or group participation more difficult.

- Reaffirm the other person's sense of competence; compliment the other person as appropriate.

- Allow the other person to state her or his position fully before you respond; avoid interrupting.

- Stress equality, and stress the similarities that you have with the other person or persons; stress your areas of agreement before attacking with disagreements.

- Express interest in the other person's position, attitude, and point of view.

- Avoid getting overemotional; using an overly loud voice or interjecting vulgar expressions will prove offensive and eventually ineffective.

- Allow people to save face; never humiliate another person.

Summary of Concepts and Skills

This chapter looked at the nature of interpersonal conflict and at how best to manage conflict.

1. Interpersonal conflict (in face-to-face situations and in cyberspace) is a disagreement between or among connected individuals whose positions are to some degree both interrelated and incompatible.
2. Conflict can be content or relationship oriented but is usually a combination of both.
3. Conflict can have both negative and positive effects.
4. Conflict is heavily influenced by both culture and gender, and any effective management of conflict needs to consider these influences.
5. Conflict management strategies are influenced by the goals you seek, your emotional state, your cognitive assessment of the situation, your personality and communication competence, and your family history.

6. Conflict management strategies include making decisions between win–win and win–lose strategies, between active fighting and avoidance, talk and force, supportiveness and defensiveness, face-enhancing and face-attacking, empathy and blame, open expression and silence, present orientation and gunnysacking, and argumentativeness and verbal aggressiveness.

The skills covered in this chapter are vital to managing interpersonal conflict. Place a check mark next to those skills you want to work on most.

_____ 1. I seek to derive positive benefits from interpersonal conflict and to avoid conflict's possible negative outcomes.

_____ 2. I engage in conflict with an understanding of the cultural and gender influences present.

_____ 3. I understand the consequences of different conflict styles and adjust my style of conflict depending on the specific circumstances.

_____ 4. I look for win–win strategies rather than win–lose strategies.

_____ 5. I engage in conflict actively rather than avoid the problem.

_____ 6. I talk conflict differences through rather than try to force my way of thinking on the other person.

_____ 7. I express support rather than encourage defensiveness.

_____ 8. I use I-messages (rather than you-messages) and assume responsibility for my thoughts and feelings.

_____ 9. I use face-enhancing rather than face-attacking tactics.

_____ 10. I express empathy rather than try to blame the other person.

_____ 11. I facilitate open expression rather than try to silence the other.

_____ 12. I focus on the present rather than gunnysack.

_____ 13. I use the skills of argumentativeness rather than verbal aggressiveness.

 # Key Word Quiz

The Language of Conflict Management

Match the terms about interpersonal conflict management with their definitions. Record the number of the definition next to the appropriate term.

_____ a. interpersonal conflict (160)

_____ b. accommodating style (165)

_____ c. face-attacking strategies (168)

_____ d. gunnysacking (170)

_____ e. beltlining (169)

_____ f. collaborating style (165)

_____ g. verbal aggressiveness (171)

_____ h. neutrality (168)

_____ i. content conflict (161)

_____ j. argumentativeness (172)

1. An "I win, you win" approach to conflict management.
2. The willingness to argue for a point of view and to speak your mind without attacking the other person.
3. A kind of indifference that is likely to create defensiveness.
4. Disagreement between connected individuals.
5. Conflict strategies that attack the other person's self-image.
6. A conflict strategy in which stored-up prior grievances are introduced into the present conflict.
7. A conflict strategy in which one person attacks the other with criticisms that are difficult to absorb.
8. Disagreement that addresses issues external to the relationship and that does not challenge the agreed-on interpersonal relationship between the conflicting parties.
9. A method of trying to win an argument by inflicting psychological pain or distress.
10. An approach to conflict in which you sacrifice your own needs for the needs of the other person.

These ten terms and additional terms used in this chapter can be found in the glossary and on flashcards at MyCommunicationLab (www.mycommunicationlab.com).

Answers: a. 4; b. 10; c. 5; d. 6; e. 7; f. 1; g. 9; h. 3; i. 8; j. 2

MyCommunicationLab

Visit MyCommunicationLab (www.mycommunicationlab.com) for a wealth of additional information on the interpersonal conflict management. Flash cards, videos, skill building exercises, sample text questions, and additional examples and discussions will help you continue your study and understanding of interpersonal conflict and especially its effective management.

9 Small Group Communication

Why read this chapter?

Because you'll learn about:

- the nature of small group communication, whether face-to-face or online
- the types of small groups and the influence of culture on them
- the formats that different types of groups follow

Because you'll learn to:

- communicate in groups with an understanding of the unique nature of the small group
- communicate in brainstorming groups more creatively and more effectively
- share information (i.e., learn and teach) in groups more effectively
- solve or manage problems in groups more efficiently and more effectively

*C*onsider the number of groups to which you belong. Your family is the most obvious example, but you might also be a member of a team, a class, a club, an organization, a sorority or fraternity, a collection of friends on Facebook or MySpace, a work group at your job, or perhaps a band or theater group. Some of your most important and satisfying communications probably take place in small groups and teams like these.

Mastering the skills of small group communication and leadership will enable you to function more productively and creatively in groups, enjoy group interaction more, and lead groups more comfortably and effectively. Your ability to function in a group—as a member and as a leader—is an essential job skill in today's workplace (Morreale & Pearson, 2008).

In this introduction to small group communication, the chapter will first cover the essential concepts and principles of the small group, look at culture and the group, and then focus on the various types of groups.

Essentials of Small Groups and Teams

Let's begin with some basic definitions.

THE SMALL GROUP

A **small group** is (1) a collection of individuals who (2) are connected to one another by some common purpose, (3) are interdependent, (4) have some degree of organization among them, and (5) see themselves as a group.

Collection of Individuals   Generally, a small group consists of approximately 3 to 12 people. The collection of individuals must be few enough in number that all members may communicate with relative ease as both senders and receivers. If the group gets much larger than 12, this becomes difficult. On Facebook and similar social networking sites, the number of individuals in a group often numbers in the hundreds of friends. These would not be a small groups—communicating via these sites is more akin to public speaking—but the subgroups that form would likely fall into the small group category.

Common Purpose   The members of a group must be connected to one another through some common purpose. People on a bus normally do not constitute a group, because they're not working toward a common goal. However, if the bus were to get stuck in a ditch, the riders may quickly become a group and work together to get the bus back on the road. This does not mean that all members of a group must have exactly the same purpose, but generally there must be some similarity in the individuals' reasons for interacting.

Interdependence   In a small group, members are interdependent, meaning that the behavior of one member is significant to and has an impact on all other members. When one member attacks or supports the ideas of another member, that behavior influences the other members and the group as a whole. When one member proposes a great idea, that behavior has an effect on all group members.

Organizing Rules   Members of small groups must be connected by some organizing rules, or structure. At times the structure is rigid, as in groups operating under parliamentary procedure, in which each comment must follow prescribed rules. At other times, as in a social gathering, the structure is very loose; however, there's some organization and some structure: Two people don't speak at the same time, comments or questions by one member are responded to by others rather than ignored, and so on.

"Never doubt that a small group of thoughtful, committed citizens can change the world. Indeed, it is the only thing that ever has."

—MARGARET MEAD

Self-Perception as a Group   Last, members of small groups feel they are, in fact, members of this larger whole. This doesn't mean that individuality is ignored or that members do not see themselves as individuals; it simply means that each member thinks, feels, and acts as a part of the group. The more members see themselves as part of the group, the greater the group cohesion (or sense of "groupness"); the more they see themselves as individuals, separate from the group, the less the group cohesion. Members in highly cohesive groups are usually more satisfied and more productive than members of low-cohesiveness groups.

THE TEAM

A *team* is a particular kind of small group. As such it possesses all of the characteristics of the small group, as well as some additional qualities. Drawing on a number of small group researchers in communication and organizational theory, the team can be defined as a small group (1) constructed for a specific task, (2) whose members have clearly defined roles and (3) are committed to achieving the same goal, and (4) which is content focused (Beebe & Masterson, 2009; Kelly, 2006; Hofstrand, 2006 (**www.extension.iastate.edu**, accessed May 3, 2008).

Specific Purpose   A team is often constructed for a specific task. After it is completed the members of the **task group** may be assigned to other teams or go their separate ways. Players on a baseball team, for example, come together for practice and for the actual game but after the game, they each go their separate ways. After the book is published, members of the book team may go on to work on different books with different team members.

Clearly Defined Roles   In a team, member's roles are rather clearly defined. A sports team is a good example. Each player has a unique function: the short stop's functions are very different from the pitcher's or the catcher's, for example. In business, for example, the team that is responsible for publishing a book, say, would also consist of people with clearly defined roles, including the editor, the designer, the marketing manager, the sales manager, the photo researcher, the author, and so on. Each brings a unique perspective to the task and each is an authority in a specific area.

Goal Directed   In a team all members are committed to achieving the same, clearly identified goal. Again, a sports team is a good example: All members are committed to winning the game. In the publishing business example, all members of the team are committed to producing a successful book.

Content Focused   Teams are generally content focused. In terms of the distinction between content and relationship messages introduced in Chapter 1 (pp. 15–16), teams communicate largely through the exchange of content messages—on winning the game or creating the book—and much less through messages about the interpersonal relationships of its members.

VIRTUAL GROUPS AND TEAMS

Small groups and teams use a wide variety of channels. Often, interactions take place face-to-face; this is the channel that probably comes to mind when you think of groups. Nowadays much small group and team interaction also takes place online, among geographically separated members who communicate as a group via computer or phone connections. These *virtual*

"Honey, please don't talk to Daddy when he's in a chat room."

groups and teams serve both relationship and social purposes on the one hand (these are best thought of as small groups) and business and professional purposes on the other (these are best thought of as teams).

Perhaps the best example of virtual groups serving relationship purposes are social networking sites, where friends interact in groups but may be separated by classrooms or by oceans. And, increasingly, these social networking sites are being used to perform business tasks as well, for finding jobs, conducting business, solving organizational problems, and conducting just about any kind of function that a face-to-face group would serve.

Business and professional purposes often are served by virtual teams. Some of these team members may be working at home, but increasingly, virtual teams consist of people who are in different work spaces, perhaps in different parts of an office building, perhaps in different countries.

The same principles of effective group communication apply to all kinds of groups and teams, whether social or business, face-to-face or virtual (we'll use the most inclusive term "small group" to refer to all types of groups). Whether you're working on a team project with colleagues in different countries, communicating with new friends on MySpace, or interacting face-to-face with your extended family, the principles discussed here will prove useful.

SMALL GROUP STAGES

With knowledge of the various kinds of small groups, we can now look at how groups interact in the real world. Small group interaction develops in much the same way as a conversation. As in conversation (see Chapter 6), there are five stages: opening, feedforward, business, feedback, and closing. The *opening* period is usually a getting-acquainted time during which members introduce themselves and engage in small talk (e.g., "How was your weekend?" "Does anyone want coffee?"). Your objective here is to get comfortable with the group members. After this preliminary get-together, there is usually some *feedforward*—some attempt to identify what needs to be done, who will do it, and so on. In a more formal group, the agenda (which is a perfect example of feedforward) may be reviewed and the tasks of the group identified. This is much like making a "to do" list. The *business* portion is the actual discussion of the tasks—the problem solving, the sharing of information, or whatever else the group needs to achieve. At the *feedback* stage, the group may reflect on what it has done and perhaps on what remains to be done. Some groups may even evaluate their performance at this stage: for example, *We need to focus more on the financial aspects* or *We need to consider additional alternatives*. At the *closing* stage, the group members return to their focus on individuals and will perhaps exchange closing comments ("Good seeing you again," "See you next time").

Note that the group focus shifts from members to task and then back again to members. A typical pattern would look like Figure 9.1. Different groups will naturally follow different patterns. For example, a work group that has gathered to solve a problem is likely to spend a great deal more time focused on the task than on each other, whereas an informal social group, say two or three couples who get together for dinner, will spend most of their time focused on the concerns of individuals. Similarly, the amount of time spent on the opening or closing, for example, will vary with the type and purpose of the group.

SMALL GROUP FORMATS

Small groups serve their functions in a variety of formats. Among the most popular small group formats for relatively formal functions are the round table, the panel, the symposium, and the symposium–forum (Figure 9.2).

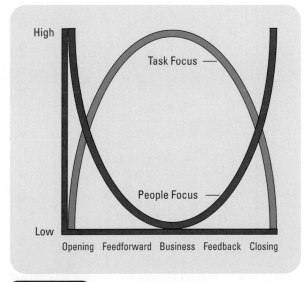

FIGURE 9.1 **Small Group Stages and the Focus on Task and People**

Do the groups to which you belong follow these five stages when interacting? How do these groups divide their focus between people and task?

Gossip is social talk that involves making evaluations about persons who are not present during the conversation, and it can occur between only two people or in a small group, as in office gossip at the cafeteria, for example (Eder & Enke, 1991; Wert & Salovey, 2004). One study estimates that approximately two-thirds of people's conversation time is devoted to social topics, and that most of these topics can be considered gossip (Dunbar, 2004). Gossip bonds people together and solidifies their relationship; it creates a sense of camaraderie (Greengard, 2001; Hafen, 2004). At the same time, of course, it helps to create an in-group (i.e., those doing the gossiping) and an out-group (i.e., those being gossiped about).

As you might expect, in many instances gossip would be considered unethical. Some instances generally identified as unethical include the following (Bok, 1983):

- when gossip is used to unfairly hurt another person, for example, spreading gossip about an office romance or an instructor's past indiscretions
- when you know that what you're saying is not true, for example, lying to make another person look bad or spreading false rumors
- when no one has the right to such personal information, for example, revealing the income of neighbors to others or revealing another student's poor grades to your friends
- when you've promised secrecy, for example, revealing something that you promised not to repeat to others

As you reflect on these, try to identify specific situations in which these principles were followed or violated.

> *Good people do not need laws to tell them to act responsibly, while bad people will find a way around the laws.*
>
> —PLATO (428–348 BC),
> Greek philosopher

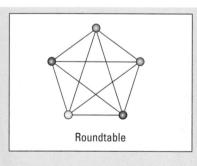

Roundtable

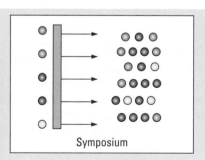

Symposium

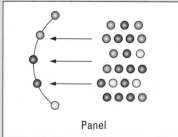

Panel

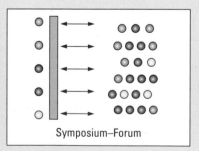

Symposium–Forum

FIGURE 9.2 **Small Group Formats**

With how many of these group formats have you had experience?

- In the round table format, group members arrange themselves physically (usually in chairs) in a circular or semicircular pattern. They share information or solve a problem without any set pattern of who speaks when. Group interaction is informal, and members contribute as they see fit. A leader or moderator may be present; he or she may, for example, try to keep the discussion on the topic or encourage more reticent members to speak up.

- In the panel, group members are "experts" but participate informally and without any set pattern of who speaks when, as in a round table. The difference is that they are sitting, often side-by-side, in front of an audience, whose members may interject comments or ask questions. Many talk shows, such as *Late Night with Jimmy Fallon* and *The Oprah Winfrey Show*, use this format.

- In the **symposium**, each member delivers a prepared presentation much like a public speech. All speeches address different aspects of a single topic. A symposium leader introduces the speakers, provides transitions from one speaker to another, and may provide periodic summaries.
- The symposium–forum consists of two parts: a symposium with prepared speeches and a forum, with questions from the audience and responses by the speakers. The leader introduces the speakers and moderates the question-and-answer session.

These four formats are *general* patterns that describe a wide variety of groups. Within each type, there will naturally be variation. For example, in the symposium–forum, there is no set pattern for how much time will be spent on the symposium part and how much on the forum part. Combinations may also be used. Thus, for example, group members may each present a position paper (basically a symposium) and then participate in a round table discussion.

Communication Choice Point

Group Pressure

All of your colleagues at your new job pad their expense accounts. You don't want to go along with this, but if you don't, everyone else will be found out. You don't want to make waves, yet you don't want to do something unethical. *What are some of the options you have for dealing with this issue? What might you say? To whom? Through what channel?*

SMALL GROUP APPREHENSION

Just as you may have apprehension about public speaking (this will be discussed in Chapter 11), you probably experience apprehension to some degree in group discussions. Because small groups vary so widely, you're likely to experience different degrees of apprehension depending on the nature of the specific group. Work groups, for example, may cause greater apprehension than groups of friends. And interacting with superiors is likely to generate greater anxiety than meeting with peers or subordinates. Similarly, the degree of familiarity you have with the group members and the extent to which you see yourself as a part of the group (as opposed to an outsider) also will influence your level of apprehension. You may wish at this point to take the following self-test, "How apprehensive are you in group discussions?"

Test Yourself

How Apprehensive Are You in Group Discussions?

This brief test is designed to measure your apprehension in small group communication situations. The questionnaire consists of six statements concerning your feelings about participating in group discussions. Indicate the degree to which each statement applies to you by marking whether you (1) strongly agree, (2) agree, (3) are undecided, (4) disagree, or (5) strongly disagree. (Each of these answers then becomes the "score" for each item.) There are no right or wrong answers. Do not be concerned that some of the statements are similar. Work quickly; just record your first impression.

_____ ❶ I dislike participating in group discussions.

_____ ❷ Generally, I am comfortable while participating in group discussions.

_____ ❸ I am tense and nervous while participating in group discussions.

_____ ❹ I like to get involved in group discussions.

_____ ❺ Engaging in a group discussion with new people makes me tense and nervous.

_____ ❻ I am calm and relaxed while participating in group discussions.

HOW DID YOU DO? To obtain your score, use the following formula:

Start with 18; add the scores for items 2, 4, and 6; then subtract the scores for items 1, 3, and 5.

A score of over 18 shows some degree of apprehension.

WHAT WILL YOU DO? Think about the kinds of groups that generate the most anxiety for you. Can you identify the major characteristics of these high-apprehension groups? How do these differ from groups generating little apprehension? What other factors might influence your small group apprehension? When you read the suggestions for reducing public speaking anxiety given in Chapter 10, consider how you might use them in the various types of groups in which you participate.

Source: From *An Introduction to Rhetorical Communication* (7th ed.), by James C. McCroskey, 1997, Englewood Cliffs, NJ: Prentice-Hall. Copyright © 1997 by Allyn and Bacon. Reprinted by permission.

SMALL GROUP CULTURE

Many groups—especially those of long standing—develop cultural norms and are greatly influenced by their own high- or low-context orientation. Each of these cultural dimensions influences the group, its members, and its communication.

Group Norms

Group norms are rules or standards identifying which behaviors are considered appropriate (such as being willing to take on added tasks or directing conflict toward issues rather than toward people) and which are considered inappropriate (such as arriving late or failing to contribute actively). These rules for appropriate behavior are sometimes explicitly stated in a company contract or policy: *All members must attend department meetings.* Sometimes they are unstated: *Group members should be well groomed.* Regardless of whether norms are spelled out, they are powerful regulators of members' behaviors.

Norms may apply to individual members as well as to the group as a whole and, of course, will differ from one cultural group to another (Axtell, 1990, 1993). For example, although someone from the United States might prefer to get right down to business, a Japanese person might prefer rather elaborate socializing before addressing the business at hand. In the United States, men and women in business are expected to interact when making business decisions as well as when socializing. In Muslim and Buddhist societies, however, religious restrictions prevent mixing between the sexes. In some cultures (e.g., those of the United States, Bangladesh, Australia, Germany, Finland, and Hong Kong), punctuality for business meetings is very important. But in others (e.g., those of Morocco, Italy, Brazil, Zambia, Ireland, and Panama), punctuality is less important; being late is no great insult and in some situations is even expected. In the United States and in much of Asia and Europe, meetings are held between two parties. In many Persian Gulf states, however, a business executive is likely to conduct meetings with several different groups—sometimes dealing with totally different issues—at the same time. In the United States very little interpersonal touching goes on during business meetings, but in Arab countries touching such as hand holding is common and is a gesture of friendship.

You're more likely to accept the norms of your group's culture under certain conditions:

You feel your group membership is important and you want to continue your membership in the group. For example, you want to continue working at XYZ Corp or you want to be invited to the group members' social events.

Your group is cohesive: You and the other members are closely connected, are attracted to one another, and depend on one another. Two clear examples of this kind of cohesive group are the family and the gang. In each case, members are closely connected, like one another, and depend on one another financially and socially.

You would be punished by negative reactions or exclusion from the group for violating its norms (Napier & Gershenfeld, 1989). These reactions and punishments can vary tremendously in strength—from mild

"A group is best defined as a dynamic whole based on interdependence, rather than on similarity."

—KURT LEWIN

displeasure that will soon be forgotten to total ostracism from the group. In some Mennonite and Amish groups a member will be shunned (i.e., totally ignored) by all other members for doing something that the group considers sinful. Among Jehovah's Witnesses, a member may be "disfellowshipped" for violating the group's norms and will be ignored by most other members of the group.

High- and Low-Context Cultures

A cultural distinction that has special relevance to small group communication (and to public speaking, as we'll see in Chapter 11) is that between high- and low-context cultures. A **high-context culture** is a culture in which much of the information conveyed is communicated by the context, or in the person, rather than in explicitly coded in verbal messages. In a high-context culture, people have lots of information in common, and this shared knowledge does not have to be made explicit. A **low-context culture**, on the other hand, is a culture in which most of the information is communicated in explicitly stated verbal messages. In a low-context culture, people do not assume that they share certain information and so must make all crucial details explicit.

According to Edward T. Hall (1976), who first identified this dimension, and Singh and Pereira (2005), who applied this dimension to electronic communication, high-context cultures include those of countries in Asia, Africa, and South America (such as Japan, China, Korea, Malaysia, and Indonesia), whereas low-context cultures are those of many countries in northern Europe (e.g., Denmark, Germany, Switzerland), North America (e.g., the United States, Canada), and Australia and New Zealand.

Members of high-context cultures spend a lot of time getting to know each other before engaging in any important transactions. Because of this prior personal knowledge, a great deal of information is shared and therefore does not have to be explicitly stated. High-context societies, for example, rely on nonverbal cues for reducing uncertainty (Sanders, Wiseman, & Matz, 1991). Members of low-context cultures spend less time getting to know each other and therefore do not have that shared knowledge. As a result everything has to be stated explicitly. When this simple difference is not taken into account, misunderstandings can result. For example, the directness and explicitness characteristic of the low-context culture may prove insulting, insensitive, or unnecessary to members of a high-context culture. Conversely, to members of a low-context culture, someone from a high-context culture may appear vague, underhanded, and even dishonest in his or her reluctance to be explicit or to engage in what a low-context culture would consider to be open and direct communication.

Members of high-context cultures also tend to be reluctant to question the judgments of their superiors. For example, if a product were being manufactured with a defect, workers might hesitate to communicate this to management (Gross, Turner, & Cederholm, 1987). Similarly, workers might detect problems in procedures proposed by management but never communicate these concerns to management. In an intercultural organization, knowledge of this tendency would alert a low-context management to look more deeply into the absence of communication.

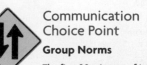

Communication Choice Point

Group Norms

The first 20 minutes of just about every meeting at work invariably revolves around personal talk. You really don't enjoy this interaction; you want to participate in the work part of the meeting but not in the interpersonal part. *What are some of your options in this situation? Which option do you think will most likely advance your career? What do you say?*

Communication Choice Point

Group Culture

You're new to an organization and want to learn, as quickly as possible, its operating cultural rules, which you don't want to violate. *What choices do you have for seeking out this information? What would you say? To whom? Through what channel?*

Brainstorming Groups

Many small groups exist solely to generate ideas. **Brainstorming** is a process often used in such groups; it's a technique for analyzing a problem by generating as many ideas as possible (Osborn, 1957; Beebe & Masterson, 2009). Although brainstorming also can be useful when you're trying to come up with ideas by yourself—ideas for speeches or term papers, ideas for a fun vacation, or ways to make money—it is more typical in small group settings. Organizations have come to embrace brainstorming, because it lessens group members' inhibitions and encourages all participants to exercise their creativity. It also fosters cooperative teamwork; members soon learn that their own ideas and creativity are sparked by the contributions of others. The technique builds member pride and ownership in the final solution (or product or service), because all members contribute to it.

"The best way to have a good idea is to have a lot of ideas."

—LINUS PAULING

Brainstorming occurs in two phases. The first is the brainstorming period itself; the second is the evaluation period. The procedures are simple. First, a problem is selected. The "problem" may be almost anything that is amenable to many possible solutions or ideas—for example, how to recruit new members to the organization or how to market a new product. Before the actual session, group members are informed of the problem so they can think about the topic. When the group meets, each person contributes as many ideas as he or she can think of. Companies often use chalkboards, whiteboards, or easels to record all the ideas. A brainstorming group may appoint one person to be the scribe; that person keys the group's notes into a laptop for instant circulation via e-mail to other group members after the group has concluded its business. During the initial idea-generating session, members follow four rules:

Rule 1. No evaluation is permitted at this stage. All ideas are recorded for the group to see (or hear later). Prohibiting both verbal and nonverbal evaluation encourages group members to participate freely.

This first rule is perhaps the most difficult for members to follow, so you might want to practice responding to what are called "idea killers." For example, what might you say if someone were to criticize an idea with the following comments?

- We tried it before and it didn't work.
- No one would vote for it.
- It's too complex.
- It's too simple.
- It would take too long.

- It'll cost too much.
- We don't have the facilities.
- What we have is good enough.
- It just doesn't fit us.
- It's not possible.

Rule 2. Quantity of ideas is the goal. The more ideas generated, the more likely it is that a useful solution will be found.

Rule 3. Combinations and extensions of ideas are encouraged. Although members may not criticize a particular idea, they may extend or combine it. The value of a particular idea may lie in the way it stimulates another idea.

Rule 4. Freewheeling (i.e., developing as wild an idea as possible) is desirable. A wild idea can be tempered easily, but it's not so easy to elaborate on a simple or conservative idea.

After all the ideas are generated—a period that lasts about 15 or 20 minutes—the group evaluates the entire list. Unworkable ideas are crossed off the list; those showing promise are retained and evaluated. During this phase, criticism is allowed.

Skill Development Experience

Brainstorming

Together with a small group or with the class as a whole, sit in a circle and brainstorm on one of the topics identified in Skill Development Experience, "Solving Problems in Groups" on page 189. Be sure to appoint someone to write down all the contributions, or record the discussion. After this brainstorming session, consider these questions:

1. Did any members give negative criticism (even nonverbally)?
2. Did any members hesitate to contribute really wild ideas? Why?
3. Was it necessary to re-stimulate the group members at any point? Did this help?
4. Did possible solutions emerge that would not have been thought of without the group stimulation?

Brainstorming is useful even if you do it by yourself. Follow the same rules.

Information-Sharing Groups

The purpose of information-sharing groups is to acquire new information or skills by sharing knowledge. In most information-sharing groups, all members have something to teach and something to learn; a good example is a group of students sharing information to prepare for an exam. In others, the group interaction takes place because some members have information and some do not. An example is a discussion between a patient and a health care professional.

EDUCATIONAL OR LEARNING GROUPS

Members of educational or learning groups may follow a variety of discussion patterns. For example, a historical topic such as the development of free speech or equal rights might be explored chronologically, with the discussion progressing from the past into the present and, perhaps, into predictions of the future. Issues in developmental psychology, such as a child's language development or physical maturity, might also be discussed chronologically. Other topics lend themselves to spatial development. For example, the development of the United States might take a spatial pattern—from east to west—or a chronological pattern—from 1776 to the present. Other suitable patterns, depending on the topic and the group's needs, might be cause and effect, problem and solution, or structure and function.

Perhaps the most popular discussion pattern is the topical pattern. A group might discuss the legal profession by itemizing and discussing each of the profession's major functions. Another might consider a corporation's structure in terms of its major divisions. Groups could further systematize each of these topics by, say, listing the legal profession's functions in order of importance or complexity or ordering the corporation's major structures in terms of decision-making power.

FOCUS GROUPS

A different type of learning group is the **focus group**, a small group that is assembled and subjected to a kind of in-depth interview, often for market research. The aim of conducting a focus group is to discover through a sample of people what it is that

---

Listen to This

Listening to Others' Perceptions

I make progress by having people around me who are smarter than I am and listening to them.

—HENRY J. KAISER (1882–1967), U.S. industrialist and shipbuilder

"Galileo and the Ghosts" is a technique for seeing how a particular group of people perceives a problem, person, or situation (DeVito, 1996). As you read about this technique, try setting up your own ghost team. It involves two steps:

Set up a mental "ghost-thinking team," much as corporations and research institutes maintain think-tanks. Select a team of four to eight people (or "people") you admire, for example, historical figures such as Aristotle or Galileo, fictional figures such as Wonder Woman or Sherlock Holmes, public figures such as Hillary Clinton or Ralph Nader, or persons from other cultures or of a different sex or affectional orientation.

Pose a question or problem and then listen to how this team of ghosts perceives your problem. Of course, you're really listening to yourself, but you are putting your perspectives aside and attempting to think like these other people. The technique forces you to step outside your normal role and to consider the perceptions of someone totally different from you.

Communication Choice Point

Stimulating Contributions

You're in charge of a focus group in which members will discuss what they like and dislike about the websites they visit. The problem you anticipate, based on past experience, is that a few members will do all the talking and the rest will hardly talk at all. *What are some of the ways you can confront this problem? What might you say?*

people in general think about an issue or product; for example, what do men between 18 and 25 think of a particular brand of aftershave lotion and its packaging? In the focus group, a leader/interviewer tries to discover the members' beliefs, attitudes, thoughts, and feelings to use as a guide for decisions on, for example, changing the scent or redesigning the packaging. It is the leader's task to prod members to analyze their thoughts and feelings on a deeper level and to use the thoughts of one member to stimulate the thoughts of others.

Generally, a focus group leader, who is usually a professional facilitator rather than a member of the hosting organization itself, assembles approximately 12 people who represent the general population. The leader explains the process, the time limits, and the general goal of the group—let's say, for example, to discover why these 12 individuals requested information on the XYZ health plan but purchased a plan from another company. The leader then asks a variety of questions. In our example the questions might be, "How did you hear about the XYZ health plan? What other health plans did you consider before making your actual purchase? What influenced you to buy the plan you eventually bought? Were any other people influential in helping you make your decision?" Through the exploration of these and similar questions, the facilitator and the relevant organizational members (who may be seated behind a one-way mirror, watching the discussion) may put together a more effective health plan or more effective advertising strategies.

Problem-Solving Groups

A **problem-solving group** meets to solve a particular problem or to reach a decision on some issue. In a sense, this is the most demanding kind of group. It requires not only a knowledge of small group communication techniques but also a thorough knowledge of the particular problem on the part of all group members. Also, for the most successful outcome, it usually demands faithful adherence to a set of procedural rules.

THE PROBLEM-SOLVING SEQUENCE

The **problem-solving sequence** identifies six steps and owes its formulation to philosopher John Dewey's insights into how people think (see Figure 9.3). These steps are designed to make problem solving more efficient and effective.

Define and Analyze the Problem
In many instances the nature of the problem is clearly specified. For example, a work team might discuss how to package new CD-ROMs for Valentine's Day. In other instances, however, the problem may be vague, and it may be up to the group to define it. For example, the general problem may be poor campus communications, but such a vague and general topic is difficult to tackle in a problem-solving discussion. Limit the problem to a manageable area for discussion. Focus on one subdivision of the issue, such as the student newspaper, student–faculty relationships, registration, examination scheduling, student advisory services, or the college website.

Define the problem as an open-ended question ("How can we improve the college website?") rather than as a statement ("The website needs to be improved") or as a yes/no question ("Does the website need improvement?"). The open-ended question allows greater freedom of exploration.

Establish Criteria for Evaluating Solutions
Decide how you'll evaluate the solutions before proposing any of them. Identify the standards or criteria you'll use in evaluating solutions or in preferring one solution over another. Generally, problem-solving groups consider two types of criteria: practical and value criteria. As an example of practical criteria, you might decide that the solutions must not increase the budget or that a solution must lead to a 10 percent increase in website visits.

The value criteria are more difficult to identify. For example, value criteria might state that the website information must not violate anyone's right to privacy or must provide a forum for all members of the college community.

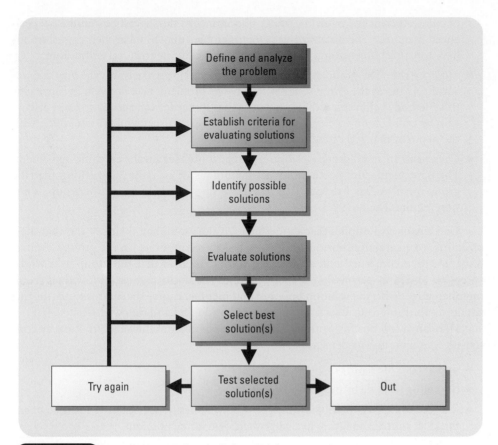

FIGURE 9.3   **The Problem-Solving Sequence**

Although most small group theorists would advise you to follow the problem-solving pattern as presented here, others would alter it somewhat. For example, some would advise you to reverse steps 2 and 3: to identify possible solutions first and then consider the criteria for evaluating them (Brilhart & Galanes, 1992). The advantage of this approach is that you're likely to generate more creative solutions, because you will not be restricted by standards of evaluation. The disadvantage is that you may spend a great deal of time generating impractical solutions that will never meet the standards you will eventually propose.

Identify Possible Solutions   Identify as many solutions as possible. Focus on quantity rather than quality. Brainstorming may be particularly useful at this point. Solutions to the website improvement problem might include incorporating reviews of faculty publications, student evaluations of specific courses, reviews of restaurants in the campus area, outlines for new courses, and employment information.

Evaluate Solutions   After all solutions have been proposed, evaluate each. For example, does incorporating reviews of area restaurants meet the criteria? Would it increase the budget, for example? Would posting grades violate students' rights to privacy? Each potential solution should be matched against the evaluating criteria.

Select the Best Solution(s)   Select the best solution and put it into operation. Let's assume that reviews of faculty publications and outlines for new courses best meet the evaluating criteria for solutions. The group might then incorporate these two new items into the website.

Groups use different decision-making methods when deciding, for example, which solution to accept. The method to be used should, naturally, be stated at the outset of the group discussion. The three main decision-making methods are:

- *Decision by authority:* Group members voice their feelings and opinions, but the leader, boss, or chief executive makes the final decision. This method has the advantages of being efficient and of giving greater importance to the suggestions of more experienced members. The disadvantage is that members may feel that their contributions have too little influence and therefore may not participate with real enthusiasm.

- *Majority rule:* The group agrees to abide by the majority decision and may vote on various issues as the group searches to solve its problem. Like decision by authority, this method is efficient. A disadvantage is that it may lead the group to limit discussion by calling for a vote once a majority has agreed. Also, members not voting with the majority may feel disenfranchised and left out.

- *Consensus:* In small group decision making, consensus means reaching agreement. The agreement does not have to be unanimous; it is, rather, something that the group members can live with; they agree that they can do whatever the group's solution requires (Kelly, 1994).

Consensus also implies that all members of the group had their say and that their opinions were carefully considered. The best of these opinions (in the group's estimation) are then combined and synthesized into a solution that the group as a whole agrees on and gives permission to follow. It does not imply that each individual group member agrees with the solution but only that members agree that at this time (for this situation, for this group) this solution should be adopted and followed.

Here are a few tips for working in a group designed to achieve its solution by consensus. Members and leader should:

- understand the nature of consensus, what it is and what it isn't.

- be willing to abide by the group's decisions.

- feel free to express their opinions, openly and honestly, and listeners must be open-minded, with a willingness to change their own initial opinions.

- make an honest attempt to incorporate as many of the members' needs, thoughts, and proposals into the final solution as reasonable and possible.

- be willing to put the group's needs ahead of their individual needs.

Consensus is the most time-consuming of the decision-making methods. However, it is also the method that best secures the cooperation and participation of all members in implementing the group's decisions. If you want members of the group to be satisfied with and committed to the decision, consensus seems to be the best way to arrive at a solution (Beebe & Masterson, 2009).

Test Selected Solutions
After putting solutions into operation, test their effectiveness. The group might, for example, poll the students or college employees about the new website. Or the group might analyze the number of visits to the website to see if the number of visits increases by the desired 10 percent. If the selected solutions prove ineffective, the group will need to return to a previous stage and repeat that part of the process. This often involves selecting other solutions to test. But it also may mean going even farther back in the process—to a reanalysis of the problem, an identification of other solutions, or a restatement of criteria, for example.

PROBLEM SOLVING AT WORK

The problem-solving sequence discussed here is used widely in work settings in a variety of different types of groups. Two group interaction types that rely largely on the problem-solving sequence are popular in business: the nominal group technique and quality circles.

The Nominal Group Technique
The **nominal group** technique is a method of problem solving that uses limited discussion and confidential

"A problem well stated is a problem half solved."

—CHARLES F. KETTERING

Together with four, five, or six others, problem-solve one of the following questions: (a) *What should we do about the homeless?* (b) *What should we do to improve the college's website?* (c) *What should we do to better prepare ourselves for the job market?* (d) *How can social networking sites be used more effectively?* or (e) *How can we improve student–faculty communication?* Before beginning discussion of the topic, prepare a discussion outline, answering the following questions:

Following patterns like this helps you move a discussion along without unnecessary detours and ensures you'll cover all essential steps.

1. What is the problem? What causes it? What are its effects?
2. What criteria should a solution have to satisfy?
3. What are some possible solutions?
4. What are the advantages and disadvantages of each of these solutions?
5. What solution seems best (in light of the advantages and disadvantages)?
6. How might we test this solution?

voting to obtain a group decision. It is extremely useful for increasing the number of ideas generated by group members (Roth, Schleifer, & Switzer, 1995). A nominal group is especially helpful when some members are reluctant to voice their opinions in a regular problem-solving group or when the issue is controversial or sensitive—for example, "sexism, racism, or homophobia in the workplace," "office romantic relationships," or "ways to downsize." With this technique each member contributes equally and each contribution is treated equally. Another advantage of this technique is that it can be accomplished in a relatively short period of time. The nominal group procedure can be divided into seven steps (Kelly, 1994):

1. The problem is defined and clarified for all members.

2. Each member writes down (without discussion or consultation with others) his or her ideas on or possible solutions to the problem.

3. Each member—in sequence—states one idea from his or her list, which is recorded on a board or flip chart so everyone can see it. This process is repeated until all suggestions are stated and recorded. Duplicates are then eliminated. Group agreement is secured before ideas are combined.

4. Each suggestion is clarified (without debate). Ideally, each suggestion should be given equal time.

5. Each member rank-orders the suggestions.

6. The rankings of each suggestion are combined to get a group ranking, which is then written on the board.

7. Clarification, discussion, and possible reordering may follow.

The highest-ranking solution might then be selected to be tested, or several high-ranking solutions may be put into operation.

Quality Circles Quality circles are groups of workers (usually 6 to 12) whose task it is to investigate and make recommendations for improving the quality of some organizational function. The members are drawn from the workers whose area of the business is being studied. Thus, for example, if the problem is how to improve advertising on the Internet, the quality circle membership would consist of people from the advertising and information technology departments. Generally, the motivation for establishing quality circles is economic; the company's aim is to improve quality and profitability.

10 Members and Leaders in Small Group Communication

Why read this chapter?

Because you'll learn about:

- small group members, their roles, and ways of participating
- approaches to and functions of leadership
- the role of culture in members' and leaders' behaviors

Because you'll learn to:

- participate more effectively as a member of a small group
- lead a variety of small groups more effectively
- participate in and lead groups in light of significant cultural differences

As you saw in Chapter 9, you're a part of many different groups, and you serve a wide variety of roles and functions in these groups. This chapter focuses on both membership and leadership in small groups. By gaining insight into these roles and functions, you'll increase your own effectiveness as a group member and leader.

Members in Small Group Communication

Each of us serves many **roles**, patterns of behaviors that we customarily perform and that we're expected by others to perform. Javier, for example, is a part-time college student, father, bookkeeper, bowling team captain, and sometime poet. That is, he acts as a student—attends class, reads textbooks, takes exams, and does the things we expect of college students. He also performs those behaviors associated with fathers, bookkeepers, and so on. In a similar way, you develop relevant ways of behaving when participating in small groups.

MEMBER ROLES

Group member roles fall into three general classes—group task roles, group building and maintenance roles, and individual roles—a classification introduced in early research (Benne & Sheats, 1948) and still widely used today (Lumsden & Lumsden, 1996; Beebe & Masterson, 2009). These roles are frequently served by leaders as well.

Group Task Roles   *Group task roles* help the group focus on achieving its goals. Effective group members serve several roles. Some people lock into a few specific roles, but this single focus is usually counterproductive—it's better for the roles to be spread more evenly among the members and for the roles to be alternated frequently. Here are some examples of group task roles.

- *The information seeker or giver* or *the opinion seeker or giver* asks for or gives facts or opinions, seeks clarification of issues being discussed, and presents facts or opinions to group members: "Sales for May were up 10 percent. Do we have the sales figures for June?"

- *The initiator-contributor* presents new ideas or new perspectives on old ideas, suggests new goals, or proposes new procedures or organizational strategies. "We need to also look at the amount of time visitors spend on our new site."

- *The elaborator* gives examples and tries to work out possible solutions, trying to build on what others have said. "That three-part division worked at ABC and should work here as well."

- *The evaluator–critic* evaluates the group's decisions, questions the logic or practicality of the suggestions, and provides the group with both positive and negative feedback: "That's a great idea, but it sounds expensive."

- *The procedural technician* or *recorder* takes care of various mechanical duties, such as distributing group materials and arranging the seating; writing down the group's activities, suggestions, and decisions; and/or serving as the group's memory: "We have another meeting scheduled to discuss just this issue, so perhaps we can skip it for today."

Group Building and Maintenance Roles   No group can be task oriented at all times. Group members have varied interpersonal relationships, and these need to be nourished if the group is to function effectively. Group members need to be satisfied if they are to be productive. Group building and maintenance roles serve these relationship needs. Here are some examples of these roles.

"Remember, in this negotiation you're the 'Paula Abdul.'"

© Leo Cullum/Condé Nast Publications/www.cartoonbank.com.

- *The encourager* or *harmonizer* provides members with positive reinforcement through social approval or praise for their ideas and mediates the various differences between group members: "Pat, another great idea."
- *The compromiser* tries to resolve conflict between his or her ideas and those of others and offers compromises: "This looks like it could work if each department cut back at least 10 percent."
- *The gatekeeper-expediter* keeps the channels of communication open by reinforcing the efforts of others. "Those were really good ideas; we're on a roll."
- *The standard setter* proposes standards for the functions of the group or for its solutions. "We need to be able to increase the number of visits by several thousand a day."
- *The follower* goes along with members, passively accepts the ideas of others, and functions more as an audience than as an active member: "If you all agree, that's fine with me."

Individual Roles   Whereas group task and group building and maintenance roles are productive and help the group achieve its goal, individual roles are counterproductive. They hinder the group from achieving its goal and are individual rather than group oriented. Such roles, often termed dysfunctional, hinder the group's effectiveness in terms of both productivity and personal satisfaction. Here are some examples of **individual roles**.

- *The aggressor* expresses negative evaluation of members and attacks the group: "That's a terrible idea. It doesn't make any sense."
- *The recognition seekers* and *self-confessors* tries to focus attention on themselves, boast about their accomplishments rather than the task at hand, and express their own feelings rather than focus on the group: "The system I devised at B&B was a great success; everyone loved it. We should just go with that."
- *The blocker* provides negative feedback, is disagreeable, and opposes other members or suggestions regardless of their merit. "You're dreaming if you think that will work."
- *The special interest pleader* disregards the goals of the group and pleads the case of some special group. "This solution isn't adequate; it doesn't address the needs of XYZ."
- *The dominator* tries to run the group or members by pulling rank, flattering members, or acting the role of boss: "I've been here the longest; I know what works and what doesn't work."

A popular individual role born on the Internet is *trolling*, the practice of posting messages that you know are false or outrageous just so you can watch the group members correct you or get emotionally upset by your message. As in any group, behavior such as trolling or flaming wastes time and energy and diverts the group from its primary objective.

MEMBER PARTICIPATION AND SKILLS

Here are several guidelines to help make your participation in small group communication more effective and enjoyable.

Be Group Oriented   When participating in a small group, you serve as a member of a team. You share common goals with the other group members, and your participation is valuable to the extent that it advances this shared goal. In a team situation, you need to pool your talents, knowledge, and insights to promote the best possible solution for the group. Although a group orientation calls for the participation and cooperation of all group members, this guideline does not suggest that you abandon your individuality, personal values, or beliefs for the group's sake. Individuality *with* a group orientation is most effective. And because the most effective and the most creative solutions often emerge from a combination of ideas, approach small group situations with flexibility;

For each of the five individual roles, compose a response or two that you as a leader might make in order to deal with this dysfunctional role playing. Be careful that your responses don't alienate the individual or the group.

One major value of small group interaction is that everyone profits from the insights of everyone else; individual roles can get in the way.

Individual, Dysfunctional Roles	Responding to Individual Roles
The aggressor:	
The recognition seeker or self-confessor:	
The blocker:	
The special interest pleader:	
The dominator:	

come to the group with ideas and information but without firmly formulated conclusions. The importance of a group orientation is also seen in one of the rules of netiquette, which holds that you should not protest the subject of, say, a mailing list or a chat group. If you don't wish to be group oriented and discuss what the group is discussing, you're expected to unsubscribe from the mailing list or withdraw from the group.

Center Conflict on Issues   Conflict in small group situations is inevitable; it's a natural part of the give and take of ideas and often promotes a better outcome. To manage conflict effectively, however, center it on issues rather than on personalities. When you disagree, make it clear that your disagreement is with the ideas expressed, not with the person who expressed them. For example, if you think that a colleague's ideas to raise funds for your social service agency are impractical and shortsighted, concentrate your criticisms on your colleague's proposed plan and suggest ways that the plan could be improved rather than attacking your colleague personally. Similarly, when someone disagrees with you, try not to take it personally or react emotionally. Rather, view the disagreement as an opportunity to discuss issues from an alternative point of view. In the language of the Internet, don't flame— don't attack the person. And don't contribute to flame wars by flame baiting, or saying things that will further incite the personal attacks.

"Do not wait for leaders; do it alone, person to person."

—MOTHER TERESA

Be Critically Open-Minded   When members join a group with their minds already made up, the small group process degenerates into a series of debates in which each person argues for his or her position—a clear example of members' taking on individual and dysfunctional roles. Group goals are neglected and the group process breaks down.

Let's say you have spent several hours developing what you think is the best, most effective advertising campaign to combat your company's low sales numbers. At the group meeting, however, members' reactions are extremely critical. Instead of becoming defensive, listen to their criticisms and try to think of ways that your plan could be modified to be as effective as possible for the company. To avoid this situation in the future, try to come to the group with ideas rather than conclusions; with suggestions rather than final decisions; and, of course, with information that will contribute to the discussion and the group goal. Be willing to accept other

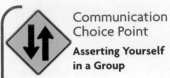

Communication Choice Point

Asserting Yourself in a Group

In your meetings at work, the supervisor consistently ignores your cues that you want to say something—and when you do manage to say something, no one reacts. You're determined to change this situation. *What do you say? To whom? Through what channel?*

people's suggestions as well as to revise your own in light of the discussion. Listen openly but critically to comments of all members (including your own).

Ensure Understanding Make sure all participants understand your ideas and information. If something is worth saying, it's worth making clear. When in doubt, ask: "Is that clear?" "Did I explain that clearly?" Make sure, too, that you fully understand other members' contributions, especially before you disagree with them. In fact, it's often wise to preface any expression of disagreement with some kind of paraphrase to ensure you really are in disagreement. For example, you might say, "If I understand you correctly, you feel that marketing should bear sole responsibility for updating the product database." After waiting for the response, you would state your thoughts.

Beware of Groupthink In groupthink agreement among members becomes so important that it shuts out realistic and logical analysis of a problem and of possible alternatives (Janis, 1983; Mullen, Tara, Salas, & Driskell, 1994). The term *groupthink* is meant to signal the "deterioration of mental efficiency, reality testing, and moral judgment that results from in-group pressures" (Janis, 1983, p. 9).

Some specific behaviors of group members that can lead to groupthink include limiting the discussion to only a few alternative solutions, not reexamining decisions despite indications of possible dangers, and spending little time discussing why certain initial alternatives were rejected. For example, if the group rejects an alternative because it is too costly, members engaged in groupthink will devote little time, if any, to exploring ways of reducing the cost.

In groupthink, members are extremely selective about the information they consider. Members tend to ignore facts and opinions contrary to the group's position, and they readily and uncritically accept those that support the group's position. The following symptoms should help you recognize groupthink in groups you observe or participate in (Janis, 1983; Schafer & Crichlow, 1996; Richmond, McCroskey, & McCroskey, 2005):

- **Illusion of invulnerability.** Group members think the group and its members are invulnerable, that they are virtually beyond being harmed.
- **Avoidance.** Members create rationalizations to avoid dealing with warnings or threats.
- **Assumption of morality.** Members believe their group is moral and, often, that any opposition is immoral.
- **Intolerance of differences of opinion.** Those opposed to the group are perceived in simplistic, stereotyped ways, and group pressure is applied to any member who expresses doubts or questions the group's arguments or proposals.
- **Self-censorship.** Members censor their own doubts.
- **Assumption of unanimity.** Group members believe that all members are in unanimous agreement, whether this is stated or not. This belief is encouraged, of course, by members' censoring their own doubts and not allowing differences of opinion to be discussed.
- **Gatekeeping.** Group members emerge whose function it is to guard the information that gets to other members, especially when it may create diversity of opinion.
- **Peer pressure.** Groupthinkers pressure others to go along with the group and not to express any disagreement.

Once you recognize the symptoms, you can attempt to combat groupthinking in the following ways:

- When too-simple solutions are offered to problems, try to illustrate (with specific examples, if possible) for the group members (with specific examples, if possible) how the complexity of the problem is not going to yield to the solutions offered.
- When you feel that members are not expressing their doubts about the group or its decisions, encourage members to voice disagreement. Ask members to play devil's

advocate, to test the adequacy of the solution. Or, if members resist, do it yourself. Similarly, if you feel there is unexpressed disagreement, ask specifically if anyone disagrees. If you still get no response, it may be helpful to ask everyone to write his or her comments anonymously and then read them aloud to the group.

- To combat the group pressure toward agreement, reward members who do voice disagreement or doubt. Say, for example, "That's a good argument; we need to hear more about the potential problems of this proposal. Does anyone else see any problems?"

Communication Choice Point

Groupthink

Your work group is displaying all the symptoms of groupthink you've read about. You want to get the group's members to reevaluate their decision-making processes. *What do you say? To whom? Through what channel?*

Leaders in Small Group Communication

Leadership is defined in two very different ways in research and theory:

- Leadership is the process of influencing the thoughts, feelings, and behaviors of group members and establishing the direction that others follow; leadership and influence are parts of the same skill.

- Leadership is the process of empowering others; the leader is the person who helps others to maximize their potential and to take control of their lives.

These two definitions are not mutually exclusive; in fact, most effective leaders do both; they influence and they empower. As you read about leadership, keep these two definitions in mind and see leadership as embodying both power and empowerment.

In many small groups one person serves as leader. In other groups leadership may be shared by several persons. In some cases a person may be appointed the leader or may serve as leader because of her or his position within the company or hierarchy. In other cases the leader may emerge as the group proceeds in fulfilling its functions or instead may be elected by the group members. Two significant factors exert considerable influence on who emerges as group leader. One is the extent of active participation: The person who talks the most is more likely to emerge as leader (Mullen, Salas, & Driskell, 1989; Shaw & Gouran, 1990). The second factor is effective listening: Members who listen effectively will emerge as leaders more often than those who don't (Johnson & Bechler, 1998; Bechler & Johnson, 1995).

The **emergent leader** performs the duties of leadership without being asked or expected to and gradually becomes recognized by the members as the group's leader. Because this person already has proved her- or himself to be an effective leader, it's not surprising that this emergent leader often becomes the designated leader for future groups.

The role of the leader or leaders is vital to the well-being and effectiveness of the group. Even in leaderless groups in which all members are equal, leadership functions must still be served.

MYTHS ABOUT LEADERSHIP

Many common beliefs about leadership are erroneous. The following are three examples of myths about leadership paraphrased from small group theorists (Bennis & Nanus, 2003):

- *Myth: The skills of leadership are rare.* Actually, all of us have the potential for leadership. There are millions of people throughout the world who are serving leadership functions in government, business, education, and countless other fields.

- *Myth: Leaders are born.* Actually, the major leadership skills can be learned by just about everyone. No specific genetic endowment is necessary. We all can improve our leadership abilities.

- *Myth: Leaders are all charismatic.* Actually, only some leaders are. According to one survey of leaders (Bennis & Nanus, 2003, p. 208): "Our leaders were all 'too human'; they were short and tall, articulate and inarticulate, dressed for success and dressed for failure, and there was virtually nothing in terms of physical appearance, personality, or style that set them apart from their followers."

"Reason and judgment are the qualities of a leader."

—TACITUS

APPROACHES TO LEADERSHIP

Not surprisingly, **leadership** has been the focus of considerable research attention. Researchers have identified several views of leadership, called *approaches*. Looking at a few of these approaches will give you a better idea of the varied ways in which leadership may be viewed and a better grasp of what leadership is and how it may be achieved.

The Traits Approach   The *traits approach* views the leader as the one who possesses those characteristics or skills that contribute to leadership. This approach is valuable for stressing the characteristics that often (but not always) distinguish leaders from nonleaders. For example, some of the world's leading corporations seek technology project managers and leaders by looking for people who have "the right mix of technological savvy, teambuilding skills, communication know-how, and interpersonal management skills" (Crowley, 1999, p. 76). Research has found that the traits most frequently associated with leadership include intelligence, self-confidence, determination, integrity, and sociability (Northouse, 1997).

A shortcoming of the traits approach is that these qualities often vary with situation in which the leader functions, such as the group type, the personalities and roles of the other members, and the group's cultural context. Thus, for some groups (e.g., a new computer game company), a youthful, energetic, humorous leader might be most effective; for other groups (e.g., a medical diagnosis team), an older, more experienced and serious leader might be most effective.

The Functional Approach   The *functional approach* to leadership focuses on what the leader should do in a given situation. We've already encountered some of these functions in the discussion of group roles. Other functions associated with leadership are setting group goals, giving the group members direction, and summarizing the group's progress (Schultz, 1996). Additional functions are identified in the section entitled "Leadership Skills" later in this chapter.

The Transformational Approach   The *transformational approach* describes a "transformational" (also called visionary or charismatic) leader who elevates the group's members, enabling them not only to accomplish the group task but also to emerge as more empowered individuals (Hersey, Blanchard, & Johnson, 2001). At the center of the transformational approach is the concept of charisma, that quality of an individual that makes us believe or want to follow him or her. Gandhi, Martin Luther King Jr., and John F. Kennedy are often cited as examples of transformational leaders. These leaders were role models, were seen as extremely competent and able, and articulated moral goals (Northouse, 1997). We'll return to this concept of charisma and its these qualities when we examine credibility in Chapter 14.

The Situational Approach   The *situational approach* holds that the effective leader shifts his or her emphasis between task accomplishment (i.e., identifying and focusing on the specific problem that the group must solve) and member satisfaction (i.e., providing for the psychological and interpersonal needs of the group members) on the basis of the specific group situation. This twofold function, you'll notice, rests on essentially the same distinction between relationship and task groups that we considered in Chapter 9. Some groups call for a high focus on task issues and need little people encouragement; this might be the case, for example, with a group of experienced scientists researching a cure for AIDS. In contrast, a group of recovering alcoholics might require leadership that stresses the members' emotional needs. The general idea of situational leadership is that there is no one style of leadership that fits all situations; each situation will call for a different ratio of emphasis on task and on member satisfaction (Fielder, 1967).

An interesting extension of this basic approach views leadership as consisting of four basic styles, illustrated in Figure 10.1 (Hersey, Blanchard, & Johnson, 2001). The situational approach claims that groups differ in their ability to accomplish a task (i.e., their know-how or "task maturity") and their willingness and commitment to accomplishing it (i.e., their "relationship maturity"). In a group with task maturity, the members are knowledgeable about and experienced with the topic, task, and group process. Because of this maturity, the members are able to set realistic and attainable goals and are willing to take responsibility for their decisions. A group with low task maturity lacks knowledge necessary to complete the task and so needs task guidance from the leader. In a group with high relationship maturity, the members are motivated to accomplish the task and are confident in their abilities to do so. In a group with low relationship maturity, the members lack sufficient motivation and so need encouragement from the leader.

Effective leadership, according to this theory, depends on the leader's assessment of the group's ability to do the task and their willingness and commitment to do it. To complicate matters a bit, the group's ability and willingness will change as the group develops—so the particular style of leadership will have to change in response. This theory identifies four leadership styles:

- The *telling style* leader provides high levels of task guidance; this leader *tells* the group members what to do, when and where to do it, and how to do it. This style is most appropriate for a group that lacks knowledge of the issues involved and needs direct guidance on how to complete the task. The telling style gives little relationship assistance, little social support. Other words used to describe this style would be *directing*, *structuring*, or *guiding*.

- The *selling style* leader gives the group high levels of both task guidance and relationship support. This leader not only tells people what to do but also tells them why they should do it; the leader wants to get the members' psychological support (i.e., to get them to "buy into" the task at hand). It's a persuasive strategy; it is high on both task guidance and relationship support. Other terms that define this style of leadership include *explaining*, *clarifying*, and *persuading*.

- The *participating style* leader gives the group high levels of relationship support but little in the way of task direction. This leadership style is appropriate for a group that knows what to do (hence little task direction is needed) but that seems to have lost the motivation or willingness to accomplish the task. Other terms useful to describe this leadership style include *facilitating*, *encouraging*, *committing*, and *collaborating*.

- The *delegating style* leader gives little task direction and little emotional support. This leadership style is most appropriate for a group that knows what to do and how to do it and also has the confidence, commitment, and motivation to accomplish the task. The leader merely needs to delegate tasks for the group's goals to be accomplished. Other words describing this style of leadership include *observing* and *mentoring*.

At this point you should find it interesting to analyze your own leadership qualities by taking the following self-test, "What Kind of Leader Are You?" It will help personalize the preceding discussion on the four approaches to leadership.

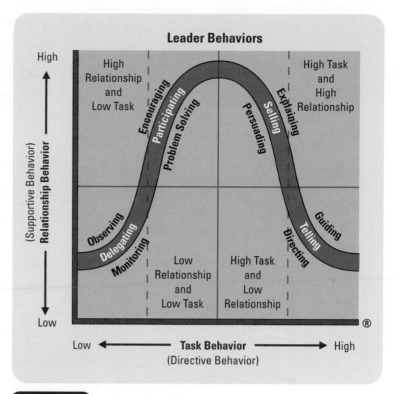

FIGURE 10.1 **A Model of Situational Leadership**

This figure depicts four different styles of leadership that differ in the degree to which they are supportive or directive. Are there any leadership styles with which you're uncomfortable? What skills can you acquire to help you feel more comfortable and competent with these styles?

Source: Hersey, P., Blanchard, K. H., & Johnson, D. E. (2001). *Management of organizational behavior: Leading human resources* (8th ed., p. 271). Upper Saddle River, NJ: Prentice-Hall. Copyright © 2001 by Center for Leadership Studies. Copyrighted material. Reprinted with permission.

Communication Choice Point

Situational Leadership

You're a member of an introductory Internet Design team whose leader uses a delegating style that isn't working. Group members are all new to this business and need more direction and guidance. The group members have elected you to clue the leader into appropriate and inappropriate styles. *What are some options for dealing with this problem? What preliminary information might you want to collect before saying anything? What might you say? Where would you say it?*

What Kind of Leader Are You?

This self-test will help you think about yourself in the role of leader. Respond to each of the following statements with T if you feel the statement is often or always true of your leadership behavior or F if you feel the statement often or always does not apply to your leadership behavior.

_____ **1** Popular with group members

_____ **2** Knowledgeable about the topics discussed

_____ **3** Dependable

_____ **4** Effective in establishing group goals

_____ **5** Competent in giving directions

_____ **6** Capable of energizing group members

_____ **7** Charismatic (i.e., dynamic, engaging, powerful)

_____ **8** Empowering of group members

_____ **9** Moral and honest

_____ **10** Skilled in satisfying both task and relationship needs

_____ **11** Flexible in adjusting leadership style on the basis of the situation

_____ **12** Able to delegate responsibility

HOW DID YOU DO? This test was designed to encourage you to look at yourself in terms of the four approaches to leadership discussed in this chapter. Perceptions 1–3 refer to the _traits approach_ to leadership, which defines a leader as someone who possesses certain qualities. If you answered T for these statements, you have the qualities normally associated with the trait theory of leadership. F responses would indicate that you don't see yourself possessing these traits. Perceptions 4–6 refer to the _functional approach_, which defines a leader as someone who performs certain functions. T responses indicate that you serve the functions normally viewed as the province of a leader. Perceptions 7–9 refer to the _transformational approach_, which defines a leader as someone who enables the group members to become the best they can be. T responses indicate your leadership is transformational. Perceptions 10–12 refer to the _situational approach_, which defines a leader as someone who can adjust his or her style to balance the needs of the specific situation. T responses indicate your flexibility to adjust to changing circumstances.

WHAT WILL YOU DO? As you read the remainder of this chapter, try to identify specific skills and competencies you might learn that would enable you to respond with T to all 12 statements.

GENERAL STYLES OF LEADERSHIP

In addition to the styles identified in the situational approach to leadership (see Figure 10.1), small group theorists also distinguish among laissez-faire, democratic, and authoritarian leaders (Bennis & Nanus, 1985; Hackman & Johnson, 1991). As you'll see, these three styles represent a different way of looking at leadership and leadership style.

The **laissez-faire leader** takes no initiative in directing or suggesting alternative courses of action. Rather, this leader allows the group to develop and progress on its own, even allowing it to make its own mistakes. The laissez-faire leader answers questions and provides information only when specifically asked. During the interaction, this

In addition to mastering the skills of effective and efficient leadership, as a leader you also need to consider the ethical issues involved in leading a group. Because the leader is often called a "chair," CHAIR seems an appropriate acronym to help identify at least some of the characteristics of the ethical leader. As you reflect on these qualities, you'll probably think of other ethical qualities that a leader should possess.

- **C**oncern for the welfare of group members. Leaders who are more concerned with their own personal interests, rather than with the group task or the interpersonal needs of the members, are acting unethically.
- **H**onesty. Leaders should be honest with the group members by, for example, revealing any hidden agendas and presenting information fairly.
- **A**ccountability. Leaders should take responsibility for their actions and decisions, admit making mistakes, and take corrective action when necessary.
- **I**ntegrity. Leaders have integrity; they take the high road. They don't lie or deceive. And they avoid actions that would violate the rights of others.
- **R**esponsiveness. The leader must be responsive to all members of the group.

> *You cannot make yourself feel something you do not feel, but you can make yourself do right in spite of your feelings.*
> —PEARL S. BUCK
> (1892–1973), U.S. writer

leader neither compliments nor criticizes group members or the group's progress. Generally, this type of leadership results in a satisfied but inefficient group.

The **democratic leader** provides direction but allows the group to develop and progress the way its members wish; this form of leadership is similar to the "participating style" in the situational approach. The democratic leader encourages group members to determine their own goals and procedures and aims to stimulate self-direction and self-actualization of the group members. Unlike the laissez-faire leader, the democratic leader contributes suggestions and comments on member and group performance. Generally, this form of leadership results in both satisfaction and efficiency.

The **authoritarian leader** is the opposite of the laissez-faire leader. As in the "telling style" of leadership in the situational approach, this leader determines group policies and makes decisions without consulting or securing agreement from the members. The authoritarian leader discourages member-to-member communication and encourages communication from member to leader. This person is concerned with getting the group to accept his or her decisions rather than making its own. If the authoritarian leader is a competent individual, the group may be highly efficient, but its members are unlikely to be personally satisfied.

LEADERSHIP SKILLS

Keeping the various views of leadership in mind, especially the situational theory with its concern for both task and people, we can look at some of the major functions leaders serve and their corresponding skills, the skills of leadership. These functions/skills are not exclusively the leader's; they are often shared or served wholly by group members. But when there's a specific leader, she or he is expected to perform these functions and exhibit the skills for accomplishing these goals.

Prepare Members and Start Interaction Groups form gradually and often need to be eased into meaningful discussion. As the leader, you need to prepare members for the small group interaction as well as for the discussion of a specific issue or problem. Don't expect diverse members to work together cohesively to solve a problem

Communication Choice Point
Leadership Styles
The leader of your work group (and the group members' supervisor) is extremely authoritarian, and the entire group has asked you to confront the leader to change to a more democratic style. *What are some options you have for communicating this to the leader? What would you say? What communication context would you choose?*

Communication Choice Point

Leader Guidance

Members of your group are not participating equally. Of the eight members, three monopolize the discussion; the other five say as little as possible. *What are some of the things you might say to get the group into better balance? To whom would you say it? In what context?*

without first becoming familiar with one another. Similarly, if members are to discuss a specific problem, a proper briefing may be necessary. If materials need to be distributed before the actual discussion, consider e-mailing them to members. Or perhaps members need to view a particular film or television show. Whatever the preparations, you need to organize and coordinate them. Once the group is assembled, you may need to stimulate the members to interact.

Build Group Cohesiveness   Groups vary greatly in **cohesiveness**—the members' closeness to and liking for each other. Generally cohesiveness is positive and cohesive groups seem to be more effective. For example, the members enjoy the interaction more and consequently come to meetings on time and stay until the end. Cohesive group members are more likely to be satisfied with the time spent in the group and to develop a "we-ness," seeing the group as a unit. Because members are comfortable with one another, they will be more willing to offer suggestions and ideas that may at first seem impossible, which may help the group eventually find a workable solution.

In a group that is excessively cohesive, however, members may be less apt to disagree with one another, which may hinder the group's critical analysis of any proposed idea. This can be a first step to groupthink. And, not surprisingly, overly cohesive groups may suffer from spending too much time on socializing within the group and not enough time on business.

Still, a cohesive group is more likely to be successful. In building cohesiveness, the leader should stress the positives, reward members frequently, and make the entire group experience as pleasant and personally rewarding as possible. Simple compliments and expressions of fondness will help build a cohesive group. Accomplishments also build cohesiveness. Therefore, setting attainable goals (perhaps even a series of intermediate goals rather than only one long-range goal) will help a group become more cohesive.

Maintain Effective Interaction   Even after the group has begun to interact, you'll need to monitor the members' effective interaction. When the discussion begins to drag, you may need to step in and motivate the group: "Do we have any additional comments on the proposal to eliminate required courses?" "What do you, as members of the college curriculum committee, think about the proposal?" You'll also want to ensure that all members have an opportunity to express themselves.

"Leadership appears to be the art of getting others to want to do something you are convinced should be done."

—VANCE PACKARD

Guide Members through the Agreed-on Agenda   As the leader, you need to keep the discussion on track by asking relevant questions, summarizing the group discussions periodically, or by offering a transition from one issue to the next. This involves following the list of tasks to be accomplished by the group as outlined in the meeting agenda and efficiently managing the amount of time allotted for each event.

Ensure Member Satisfaction   Members have different psychological needs and wants, and many people enter groups because of them. Even though a group may, for example, deal with political issues, members may have come together for psychological as well as for political reasons. If a group is to be effective, it must achieve the group goal (in this case, a political one) without denying the psychological purposes or goals that motivate many of the members to come together. One way to meet these needs is for you as leader to allow digressions and personal comments, assuming they are not too frequent or overly long. Another way is to be supportive and reinforcing.

Empower Group Members An important function of a leader (though not limited to leadership) is to empower others—to help group members gain increased power over themselves and their environment. For example, both as a leader and in your daily life, try to:

- Raise other's self-esteem. Compliment, reinforce. Resist fault finding; it doesn't benefit anyone and in fact disempowers everyone.

- Share skills and decision-making power and authority.

- Be constructively critical. Be willing to offer your perspective—to lend an ear to a first-try singing effort or to listen to a new poem. Be willing to react honestly to suggestions from all group members, not only those in high positions.

- Encourage growth in all forms (academic, relational, and professional). The empowerment of others enhances your own growth and power.

Encourage Ongoing Evaluation and Improvement All groups encounter obstacles as they try to solve a problem, reach a decision, or generate ideas. No group is totally effective. All groups have room for improvement. To improve, the group must focus on itself. Along with trying to solve some external problem, it must try to solve its own internal problems: for example, personal conflicts, failure of members to meet on time, or members who come unprepared. When you notice some serious group failing, address it, perhaps posing that very issue (say, member tardiness) as a problem to be solved.

Manage Conflict As in interpersonal relationships, conflict is a part of small group interaction. And it's a leader's responsibility to deal with it effectively. The conflict management techniques that are useful in small groups are the same techniques discussed in the context of interpersonal communication (see Chapter 8). You may wish to review these now and think of them as small group conflict management strategies.

Mentor Another function of leadership that is especially applicable to the small group but extends beyond it is that of mentoring. A **mentoring** relationship occurs when an experienced individual helps to train a less experienced person or people.

For each situation, indicate what you might say to help empower the other person, using such strategies as (a) raising the other person's self-esteem; (b) listening actively and supportively; (c) being open, positive, and empathic; and (d) avoiding verbal aggressiveness or any unfair conflict strategies.

1. A team member is having lots of difficulties: He recently lost his job, received poor grades in a night class, and is gaining a lot of weight. At the same time, you're doing extremely well. You want to give your team member back his confidence.

2. You're managing four college interns, three men and one woman, who are working on re-designing your company's website. The men are extremely supportive of one another and regularly contribute ideas. Although equally competent, the woman doesn't contribute; she seems to lack confidence. Because the objective of this redesign is to increase the number of female visitors, you really need the woman intern's input and want to empower her.

3. You're a third-grade teacher. Most of the students are from the same ethnic–religious group; three, however, are from a different group. The problem is that these three have not been included in the social groupings of the students; they're treated as outsiders. As a result, these children stumble when they have to read in front of the class and make a lot of mistakes at the chalkboard (though they consistently do well in private). You want to empower these students.

Power is not a zero-sum game; empowering others often adds to, rather than subtracts from, your own power.

An accomplished teacher, for example, might mentor younger teachers who are newly arrived or who have never taught before. A group leader might be the group members' supervisor and may mentor those supervised. The mentor guides new people through the ropes, teaches strategies and techniques for success, and otherwise communicates his or her accumulated knowledge and experience to the "mentee."

The mentoring relationship provides a supportive and trusting learning environment. There's a mutual and open sharing of information and thoughts about the task or job to be done. The relationship enables the novice to try out new skills under the guidance of an expert, to ask questions, and to obtain the feedback necessary for learning complex skills. Mentoring is perhaps best characterized as a relationship in which the experienced and powerful mentor empowers the novice, giving the novice the tools and techniques needed for gaining the same power the mentor already holds.

One study found the mentoring relationship to be one of the three primary paths for career achievement among African American men and women (Bridges, 1996). Another study (of middle-level managers) demonstrated that those who had mentors and participated in mentoring relationships got more promotions and higher salaries than those who didn't have mentors (Scandura, 1992).

At the same time, the mentor benefits from clarifying his or her thoughts, from seeing the job from the perspective of a newcomer, and from considering and formulating answers to a variety of questions. Just as a member learns from the leader, the leader learns from the members.

Membership, Leadership, and Culture

Most of the research (and also the resulting theory) concerning small group communication, membership, and leadership has been conducted in universities in the United States and reflects U.S. culture. So it's important that we look at both membership and leadership from the point of view of different cultures.

Each culture maintains its own belief system, which influences group members' behavior. Members of many Asian cultures, influenced by Confucian principles, believe that "the protruding nail gets pounded down" and are therefore not likely to voice disagreement with the majority of the group. Members of U.S. culture, on the other hand, influenced by the axiom that "the squeaky wheel gets the grease," are likely to voice disagreement or to act in ways different from other group members in order to get what they want (Hofstede, 1997).

Also, each culture has its own rules of preferred and expected leadership style. In the United States, the general and expected style for a group leader is democratic. Our political leaders are elected by a democratic process; similarly, company directors are elected by the shareholders of their corporations. In other situations, of course, leaders are chosen by those in authority. The president of a company will normally decide who will supervise and who will be supervised. Even in this situation, however, the supervisor is expected to behave democratically: to listen to the ideas of the employees; to take their views into consideration when decisions are to be made; to keep them informed of corporate developments; and not to discriminate on the basis of sex, race, or affectional orientation. In the United States people expect that organizational and other group leaders will be changed fairly regularly, much as we change political leaders on a regular basis. In some other cultures, leaders get their positions by right of birth. They are not elected, nor are they expected to behave democratically. Similarly, their tenure as leaders is usually extremely long and may in fact last their entire lives. Their leadership roles are then passed on to their children. In other cases leaders may be chosen by a military dictator.

"Leadership is action, not position."

—DONALD H. MCGANNON

INDIVIDUAL AND COLLECTIVE ORIENTATIONS

Small group cultures and cultures in general differ in the extent to which they promote individualistic values (e.g., power, achievement, hedonism, and stimulation) versus collectivist values (e.g., benevolence, tradition, and conformity).

One of the major differences between an **individual orientation** and a **collective orientation** is in the extent to which an individual's goals or the group's goals are given precedence. Individual and collective tendencies are, of course, not mutually exclusive; this is not an all-or-none orientation, but rather one of emphasis. You probably have both tendencies. Thus, you may, for example, compete with other members of your basketball team to make the most baskets but in a game, you'd likely act in a way that will benefit the entire team (and thus emphasize group goals). In practice, both individual and collective tendencies will help both you and your team achieve your goals. Still, most people and most cultures have a dominant orientation: They're individually oriented (i.e., they see themselves as independent) or collectively oriented (i.e., they see themselves as interdependent) in most situations, most of the time (Singelis, 1994).

In an *individualist culture*, as discussed in Chapter 8, you're responsible to your own conscience; responsibility is largely an individual matter. Examples of individualist cultures include those of the United States, Australia, United Kingdom, Netherlands, Canada, New Zealand, Italy, Belgium, Denmark, and Sweden (Hofstede, 1997; Singh & Pereira, 2005). In a *collectivist culture* you're responsible to the rules of the social group; all members share responsibility for accomplishments as well as for failures. Examples include the cultures of Guatemala, Ecuador, Panama, Venezuela, Colombia, Indonesia, Pakistan, China, Costa Rica, and Peru (Hofstede, 1997; Singh & Pereira, 2004). Individualistic cultures foster competition, whereas collectivist cultures promote cooperation.

One obvious consequence of this difference in orientation can be seen in how individualistic and collectivist groups treat members who commit serious errors.

A group governed by individualistic norms is likely to single out, reprimand, and perhaps fire an errant member. Further, the leader or supervisor is likely to distance him- or herself from this member for fear that the error will reflect negatively on his or her leadership. In a more collectivist culture, the error is more likely to be seen as a group mistake. The group is unlikely to single out the member—especially not in public—and the leader is likely to bear part of the blame. The same is true when one member comes up with a great idea. In individualist cultures that person is likely to be singled out for praise and rewards, even though the effort was to benefit the group. In collectivist cultures the group is recognized and rewarded for the idea.

HIGH AND LOW POWER DISTANCES

In some cultures power is concentrated in the hands of a few, and there is a great difference between the power held by these people and the power held by the ordinary citizen. These are called **high-power-distance cultures.** Examples are the cultures of Malaysia, Panama, Guatemala, Philippines, Venezuela, Mexico, China, the Arab world, Indonesia, and Ecuador (Hofstede, 1997; Singh & Pereira, 2004). In **low-power-distance cultures,** power is more evenly distributed throughout the citizenry; examples include Austria, Israel, Denmark, New Zealand, Ireland, Norway, Sweden, Finland, Switzerland, and Costa Rica (Hofstede, 1997; Singh & Pereira, 2004).

The power distance between groups will influence the group of friends you develop, as well as whom you might date (Andersen, 1991). For example, in India (i.e., high power distance) your group of friends is expected to be chosen from those within your cultural class (as are your dating partners). In Sweden (i.e., low power distance), on the other hand, a person is expected to form friendships (and romances) on the basis not of class or culture but of individual factors such as personality, appearance, and the like.

In low-power-distance cultures, there is a general feeling of equality, which is consistent with acting assertively, so you're expected to confront a friend, partner, or supervisor assertively (Borden, 1991). In high-power-distance cultures, direct confrontation and assertiveness may be viewed negatively, especially if directed at a superior.

In high-power-distance cultures, you're taught to have great respect for authority; people in these cultures see authority as desirable and beneficial and generally do not welcome challenges to authority (Westwood, Tang, & Kirkbride, 1992; Bochner & Hesketh, 1994). In low-power-distance cultures, there's a certain distrust of authority; it's seen as a kind of necessary evil that should be limited as much as possible. This difference in attitudes toward authority can be seen in the classroom. In high-power-distance cultures, there's a great power distance between students and teachers; students are expected to be modest, polite, and totally respectful. In low-power-distance cultures, students are expected to demonstrate their knowledge and command of the subject matter, participate in discussions with the teacher, and even challenge the teacher—something many members of high-power-distance cultures wouldn't think of doing.

High-power-distance cultures rely on symbols of power. For example, titles (e.g., Dr., Professor, Chef, Inspector) are more important in high-power-distance cultures. Failure to include these honorifics in forms of address is a serious breach of etiquette. Low-power-distance cultures rely less on symbols of power, so there is less of a problem if you fail to use a respectful title (Victor, 1992). Regardless, you still may create problems if, for example, you address a medical doctor, police captain, military officer, or professor with "Ms." or "Mr."

The groups in which you'll participate as a member or a leader will vary in power distance; some will be high-power-distance groups and others will be low. You need to recognize which is which, to follow the cultural rules generally, and to break the rules only after you've thought through the consequences.

Summary of Concepts and Skills

This chapter looked at membership and leadership in the small group. It examined the roles of members—some productive and some counterproductive—and considered leadership theories, leadership styles, leadership functions, and cultural factors in small groups.

1. A popular classification of small group member roles divides them into three types: group task roles, group building and maintenance roles, and individual roles.

2. Among the group task roles are those of information seeker or giver, opinion seeker or giver, evaluator–critic, and procedural technician or recorder. Among the group building and maintenance roles are encourager/harmonizer, compromiser, and follower. Among the individual (dysfunctional) roles are aggressor/blocker, recognition seeker/self-confessor, and dominator.

3. Group members should be group oriented, center conflict on issues, be critically open-minded, and ensure understanding.

4. Groupthink is an excessive concern with securing agreement that discourages critical thinking and the exploration of alternative ways of doing things.

5. Three theories of leadership help to clarify aspects of leadership. The traits approach identifies characteristics, such as intelligence and self-confidence, which contribute to leadership. The transformational approach focuses on leaders as people who raise the performance of group members and empower them. The situational approach views leadership as varying its focus between accomplishing the task and serving the members' social and emotional needs, depending on the specific group and the unique situation.

6. An extension of the situational approach to leadership identifies four leadership styles: the telling, selling, participating, and delegating styles. The appropriate style to use depends on the group's level of task and relationship maturity.

7. Three general leadership styles are laissez-faire, democratic, and authoritarian.

8. Among the leader's functions and requisite skills are to prepare members for and start the group interaction, maintain effective interaction, guide members through the agreed-on agenda, ensure member satisfaction, empower members, encourage ongoing evaluation and improvement, and manage conflict.

9. *Mentoring* refers to a relationship in which an experienced and knowledgeable individual helps guide and train a less-experienced person.

10. Group membership and leadership attitudes and behaviors are likely to be heavily influenced by culture, especially by the individual–collective and power-distance orientations.

The skills identified in this discussion center on increasing your ability to function more effectively as a small group member and leader. Place a check mark next to those skills you feel you should work on most.

_____ 1. I avoid playing the popular but dysfunctional individual roles in a small group—those of aggressor, blocker, recognition seeker, self-confessor, and dominator.

_____ 2. When participating in a small group, I am group rather than individual oriented, center the conflict on issues rather than on personalities, am critically open-minded, and make sure that my meanings and the meanings of others are clearly understood.

_____ 3. I recognize the symptoms of groupthink and actively counter my own groupthink tendencies as well as those evidenced in the group.

_____ 4. I adjust my leadership style according to the task at hand and the needs of group members.

_____ 5. As a small group leader, I start group interaction, maintain effective interaction throughout the discussion, keep members on track, ensure member satisfaction, encourage ongoing evaluation and improvement, and prepare members for the discussion as necessary.

_____ 6. I recognize and appreciate the cultural differences that people have toward group membership and leadership.

Key Word Quiz

The Language of Small Group Membership and Leadership

Match the terms about group membership and leadership with their definitions. Record the number of the definition next to the appropriate term.

_____ a. groupthink (196)

_____ b. collective orientation (205)

_____ c. individual roles (194)

_____ d. laissez-faire leader (200)

_____ e. transformational approach (198)

_____ f. group task roles (193)

_____ g. mentoring (204)

_____ h. group building and maintenance roles (193)

_____ i. low-power-distance culture (206)

_____ j. cohesiveness (202)

1. The process or relationship in which a more experienced member helps train a less experienced member.

2. Member roles that help the group focus on achieving its goals.

3. The tendency of a group to overvalue agreement and ignore differences.

4. A cultural view that holds that the group is more important than the individual.

5. Group roles of which encouraging, compromising, and following are examples.

6. A leader who takes no initiative in directing or suggesting alternative courses of action.

7. The closeness and liking for each other of group members.

8. A leadership style that elevates and empowers group members.

9. Group roles of which expressing aggressiveness, dominating, and seeking self-recognition are examples.

10. A culture in which there is a feeling of equality and in which there is little difference in power among members.

These ten terms and additional terms used in this chapter can be found in the glossary and on flashcards on MyCommunicationLab (**www.mycommunicationlab.com**).

Answers: a. 3 b. 4 c. 9 d. 6 e. 8 f. 2 g. 1 h. 5 i. 10 j. 7

MyCommunicationLab

PEARSON
mycommunicationlab
www.mycommunicationlab.com

Visit MyCommunicationLab (**www.mycommunicationlab.com**) for additional information on small group membership and leadership. Flash cards, videos, skill building exercises, sample text questions, and additional examples and discussions will help you continue your study of small group communication members and leaders.

CHAPTER

11 Public Speaking Preparation (Steps 1–6)

Why read this chapter?

Because you'll learn about:
- the nature and importance of public speaking
- audience analysis, research, and organization

Because you'll learn to:
- manage your apprehension
- select and narrow your topic and purpose
- analyze your audience and adapt your speech to them
- research your topic
- organize your speech

*B*efore getting to the steps for preparing and presenting a public speech, let's define public speaking and consider the benefits that will reward your public speaking efforts. In addition, we'll address what is probably your number one problem: the fear that so often accompanies giving speeches. As a preface to this chapter and the remaining discussions of public speaking in Chapters 12 through 14, become familiar with Pearson's public speaking website (www.abpublicspeaking.com).

The Nature of Public Speaking

Public speaking is a form of communication in which a speaker addresses a relatively large audience with a relatively continuous discourse, usually in a face-to-face situation. A student delivering a report to a political science class, a teacher lecturing on the structure of DNA, a minister preaching a sermon, and a politician delivering a campaign speech are all examples of public speaking. Also, delivering a speech to a television camera to be broadcast to an entire nation or over the radio to be heard by a few thousand or a few million people is similar in many ways to what is traditionally thought of as public speaking. It differs in that these mediated messages are not face-to-face, so the audience cannot respond immediately to the message, and the speaker cannot make adjustments on the basis of this feedback. Even given these differences, the principles of public speaking discussed in this and the remaining chapters apply to mediated as well as to face-to-face communication.

In addition to the speeches that you will give in this class and during your college career, you will also be called on to make formal and informal speeches throughout your life. For example, you may make a presentation about a new product at a sales meeting, present your company's rules and regulations to a group of new employees, explain the benefits of a new playground to members of your local PTA, or give a speech about your family genealogy at a family reunion. Regardless of the circumstances under which you give a speech, you will find the 10 steps to public speaking preparation discussed in this chapter and the next extremely practical.

The principles of public speaking, as you'll see, will prove useful in a wide variety of communication situations, whether face-to-face or online, in constructing messages in email, communicating on Facebook, or in the increasingly popular webinars and teleseminars.

BENEFITS AND SKILLS OF PUBLIC SPEAKING

Public speaking draws together a wide variety of social, academic, and career skills. Although these skills are central to public speaking, they also enrich other competencies. Among these are your ability to present yourself to others with confidence and self-assurance and your ability to conduct research efficiently and effectively. Public speaking skills will further help you to understand human motivation, to analyze and evaluate the validity of persuasive appeals, and to use persuasion effectively.

Public speaking will also develop and refine your general communication abilities by helping you:

- explain complex concepts clearly.
- organize a variety of messages for clarity and persuasiveness.
- develop logical, emotional, and ethical appeals to support an argument.
- communicate credibility.
- improve your listening and delivery skills.

It's important to remember, however, that effective public speakers aren't born; they're made. Through instruction, exposure to different speeches, feedback, and individual learning experiences, you can become an effective speaker. Regardless of your present level of competence, you can improve your public speaking skills through proper training.

MANAGING YOUR COMMUNICATION APPREHENSION: 10 SUGGESTIONS

Now that you have a good idea of what public speaking is and what benefits you'll derive from studying it, consider what is probably your major concern: **communication apprehension**, or, in this case, stage fright. People experience apprehension in all types of communication (as illustrated throughout this text), but it is in the public speaking situation that apprehension is most common and most severe (Richmond & McCroskey, 1998; Wrench, McCroskey, & Richmond, 2008). To measure your own fear of speaking in public, take the apprehension self-test that follows.

Test Yourself

How Apprehensive Are You about Public Speaking?

This questionnaire consists of six statements concerning your feelings about public speaking. Indicate the degree to which each statement applies to you by marking whether you (1) strongly agree, (2) agree, (3) are undecided, (4) disagree, or (5) strongly disagree with each statement. There are no right or wrong answers. Don't be concerned that some of the statements are similar to others. Work quickly; just record your first impression.

_____ ❶ I have no fear of giving a speech.

_____ ❷ Certain parts of my body feel very tense and rigid when I am giving a speech.

_____ ❸ I feel relaxed while giving a speech.

_____ ❹ My thoughts become confused and jumbled when I am giving a speech.

_____ ❺ I face the prospect of giving a speech with confidence.

_____ ❻ While giving a speech, I get so nervous that I forget facts I really know.

HOW DID YOU DO? To obtain your public speaking apprehension score, use the following formula: Start with 18 points; add the scores for items 1, 3, and 5; then subtract the scores for items 2, 4, and 6.

A score above 18 shows some degree of apprehension. Most people score above 18, so if you scored relatively high, you're among the vast majority of people. You may find it interesting to compare your apprehension scores from this test and from the test in Chapter 9. Most people would score higher on public speaking apprehension than on apprehension in group discussions.

WHAT WILL YOU DO? As you read the suggestions for reducing apprehension in the text, consider what you can do to incorporate these ideas into your own public speaking experiences. Consider too how these suggestions might be useful in reducing apprehension more generally—for example, in social situations and in small groups and meetings.

Source: Adapted from _An Introduction to Rhetorical Communication_, (9th ed.), by James C. McCroskey, 2006. Englewood Cliffs, NJ: Allyn and Bacon. Copyright © 2006 by Allyn and Bacon. Reprinted by permission.

The following 10 suggestions will help you reduce your public speaking apprehension, as well as any communication apprehension you might have in small group and interpersonal communication situations (Beatty, 1988; Wrench, McCroskey, & Richmond, 2008).

1. _Gain experience._ New situations such as public speaking are likely to make you anxious, so try to reduce their newness. The best way to do this is to get as much public speaking experience as you can. With experience, your initial fears and anxieties will

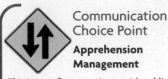

Communication Choice Point

Apprehension Management

This is your first experience with public speaking, and you're very nervous; you're afraid you'll forget your speech and stumble. So you're wondering if it would be a good idea to alert your audience to your nervousness. *If you decide to say something, what would you say? What good reasons can you give for saying nothing?*

give way to feelings of control, comfort, and pleasure. Experience will show you that the feelings of accomplishment in public speaking are rewarding and will outweigh any initial anxiety.

2. *Think positively.* When you see yourself as inferior—when, for example, you feel that others are better speakers or that they know more than you do—anxiety increases. To gain greater confidence, think positive thoughts and be especially thorough in your preparation. Visualize success; dismiss thoughts of failure.

3. *Be realistic in your expectations.* Unrealistically high expectations are likely to create anxiety and make you more fearful of the public speaking situation (Ayres, 1986). You do not have to be perfect; you do not have to give the best speech in the class. View your goal as giving a speech that represents the best you can do.

4. *See public speaking as conversation.* When you're the center of attention, as you are in public speaking, you feel especially conspicuous; this often increases anxiety. It may help, therefore, to think of public speaking as another type of conversation (some theorists call it "enlarged conversation").

5. *Focus on your listeners.* When you focus on your listeners, you'll be less fixated on your own performance and less apprehensive. Focus on informing them about your topic or persuading them to think differently or do something. The more attention you place on your audience, the less you'll have for worrying about your performance.

6. *Stress similarity.* When you feel similar to (rather than different from) your audience, your anxiety should lessen. With all audiences, but especially with multicultural gatherings, stress similarities in experiences, attitudes, and values; it will make you feel more at one with your listeners.

7. *Project confidence.* Stand tall, and maintain direct eye contact with your listeners. Behaving confidently is likely to feed back and lead you to feel confident. Acting confidently is also likely to increase the positive reactions from the audience, which will further help to put you at ease.

8. *Prepare and practice thoroughly.* Much of the fear you experience is a fear of failure. Adequate and even extra preparation will lessen the possibility of failure and the accompanying apprehension. Because apprehension is greatest during the beginning of the speech, try memorizing the first few sentences of your talk. If there are complicated facts or figures, be sure to write these out and plan to read them; this will remove from your mind any worry about forgetting them.

9. *Move about and breathe deeply.* Physical activity—gross bodily movements as well as the small movements of the hands, face, and head—lessens apprehension. Using a visual aid, for example, will temporarily divert attention from you and will allow you to get rid of your excess energy. If you breathe deeply a few times before getting up to speak, you'll sense your body relax. This will help you overcome your initial fear of walking to the front of the room.

10. *Avoid chemicals as tension relievers.* Unless prescribed by a physician, avoid any chemical means for reducing apprehension. Alcohol does not lessen public speaking anxiety (Himle, Abelson, & Haghightgou, 1999), and tranquilizers, marijuana, and artificial stimulants are likely to create problems rather than reduce them. They're likely to impair your ability to remember the parts of your speech, to accurately read audience feedback, and to regulate the timing of your speech.

CULTURE AND PUBLIC SPEAKING

As with all forms of communication, public speaking needs also to be seen within a cultural context. Your audiences are likely to be multicultural, and understanding the sometimes vastly different cultural perspectives of your listeners will help you construct a more culturally sensitive and thus more effective speech.

Listen to This

Listening to Help Reduce Apprehension

As a listener, you can help speakers with their apprehension.

> *The human brain starts working the moment you're born and never stops until you stand up to speak in public.*
>
> —GEORGE JESSEL
> (1898–1981), comedian
> and actor

- *Positively reinforce the speaker.* A nod, a smile, an attentive appearance (especially maintaining eye contact) will help put the speaker at ease. Resist the temptation to check your IMs or talk with a friend.
- *Ask questions in a supportive manner.* If there's a question period, ask information-seeking questions rather than firing off critical challenges. And ask questions in a way that won't encourage defensiveness. Instead of saying, "Your criticism of heavy metal music is absurd," say, "Why do you find the lyrics of heavy metal harmful?"
- *Don't focus on errors.* If the speaker fumbles, don't put your head down, cover your eyes, or otherwise communicate your awareness of the fumble. Instead, continue listening to the content of the speech; let the speaker know that you're focused on what is being said.

Of particular relevance to public speaking is the distinction between low and high context, which was introduced in Chapter 9 (p. 183). You'll recall that people in low-context cultures want explicit information, whereas members of high-context cultures are more apt to rely on the context and what is known from previous interactions. Because members of low-context cultures generally expect information to be communicated explicitly, audiences from such cultures will probably wish to hear a direct statement of your position and an explicit statement of what you want the audience to learn or do. In contrast, people in high-context cultures prefer a less explicit statement and prefer to be led indirectly to your conclusion. An explicit statement ("Vote for Smith" or "Buy Viterall") may be interpreted as too direct and even insulting.

Another frequent difference and source of misunderstanding between high- and low-context cultures has to do with **face-saving** (Hall & Hall, 1987), as discussed in Chapter 2. People in high-context cultures such as that of Japan place great emphasis on face-saving. For example, they may tend to avoid argument for fear of causing others to lose face, whereas people in low-context cultures (with their individualistic orientation) are more likely to use argument to win a point. Similarly, in high-context cultures criticism should take place only in private, to enable the person being criticized to save face; low-context cultures may not make this public/private distinction. Again, in high-context cultures speakers who attack the character of others may be accused of using unethical face-detracting strategies, which may damage their credibility.

Members of high-context cultures are reluctant to express disagreement, especially in a public setting. Audiences from high-context cultures are likely to give you positive feedback even if they dislike, disagree, or don't understand your speech; it is up to you to look deeper for signs of disagreement or comprehension problems, such as inconsistency between verbal and nonverbal cues including quizzical looks.

STARTING EARLY

A common problem in public speaking is the tendency to delay the preparation of the speech. You'll need to substitute this unproductive tendency to procrastinate with a start-early ethic.

Communication Choice Point

Applying Listening Skills

You notice that the speaker approaching the front of the room to give a speech is visibly nervous. What are some of the things you can do as a listener to help the speaker manager this apprehension and get through the speech?

There are many benefits to starting early. At the most obvious level, starting early provides you with the time needed to process the information you're going to talk about and to get used to the idea of preparing for the presentation of your speech.

Starting early also provides you with the time to overcome the inevitable unanticipated roadblocks: a website that you thought would be helpful is now dead, the person you wanted to interview isn't available, or your roommate's parties make the weekends useless for working on your speech. You will also have the time to rehearse your speech to ensure that your delivery will be effective and to help reduce any fear of public speaking you might have. Interesting enough, starting early may enable you to avoid health problems often associated with procrastination: College students who procrastinate experience more colds and flu, more gastrointestinal problems, and more insomnia (Marano, 2003).

Here are several suggestions for overcoming this tendency to delay certain tasks. Supplement these with the excellent advice given on college websites such as that of the University of Buffalo at **http://ub-counseling.buffalo.edu/stress** and of California Polytechnic State University at **http://sas.calpoly.edu/asc/ssl.html**.

1. Be mindful of the fact that delaying your preparation will only make it harder and is likely to increase your anxiety. Make a commitment to starting early. Create a computer file for your speech, collect information, and file it for easy retrieval.

2. Don't lie to yourself about the value of procrastination (Marano, 2003). You don't do better under pressure, for example.

3. Beware of your tendency to seek out distractions—you don't have to rearrange and organize your CDs or redo your Facebook profile, for example. When you get the urge to do something else, become mindful of what you're really doing—making an excuse to delay the task at hand.

4. Work in small units. Fortunately, as already mentioned, this aid to overcoming procrastination is built into the 10-step public speaking system used here; each step is already a relatively small unit. Set aside 20 or 30 minutes (it's often best to start with small units of time) and see what you can do with step 1. Then, when you're farther along in the process, increase the time you spend on each step. Fortunately, it often helps if you reward yourself at the end of the completion of each step: Buy that CD you've been wanting or watch an episode of _Desperate Housewives_.

The rest of the chapter looks at the first 6 of the 10 essential steps for preparing an effective public speech, as summarized in Figure 11.1. The final 4 steps will be covered in the next chapter.

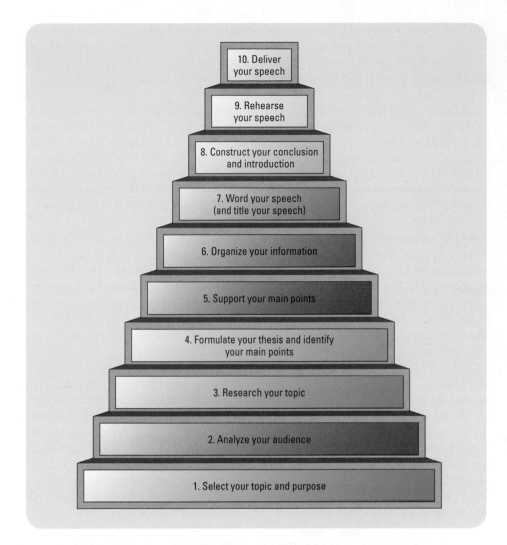

FIGURE 11.1

The Steps in Public Speaking Preparation and Delivery

Speakers differ in the order in which they follow these steps. Some speakers, for example, prefer to begin with audience analysis, asking themselves what the audience is interested in and then selecting the topic and purpose. Some speakers prefer to identify their main points before conducting extensive research; others prefer to allow the propositions to emerge from the research. The order presented here will prove useful to most speakers for most situations; however, vary the order when it serves your purposes. As long as you cover all the steps, you should be in good shape.

Step 1: Select Your Topic and Purpose

The first step in preparing an effective public speech is to select the topic on which you'll speak and the general and specific purposes you hope to achieve.

YOUR TOPIC

Select a worthwhile topic that will be interesting to the audience. If your first speech is to be informative, select a topic about which your audience probably knows little but will be curious to learn more. If your first speech is persuasive, you might select a topic about which you and the audience agree, and aim to strengthen their attitudes. Or you might select a topic on which you and the audience disagree; your aim would be to persuade them to change their attitudes.

Not surprisingly, the appropriateness of a speech topic will vary with the culture of the audience. For example, each culture has its own topics that tend to cause conflict. Generally these subjects should be avoided, especially by visitors from other cultures. Although the topics that are **taboo** vary from one culture to another and from one time to another, generally it is best to avoid criticizing any deeply held belief, whether about religion or politics or child-rearing practices. If you're going to address an audience with members from cultures other than your own, find out what these taboo topics are and avoid them, or at least present them in a way that will not cause audience members to tune you out.

"My summer vacation: How I made money in a bear market."

© Christopher Weyant/Condé Nast Publications/www.cartoonbank.com.

Finding Your Topic   Public speaking topics are all around you. Select a topic that you're interested in and know something about. And, of course, select a topic that your audience will find interesting and worthwhile. You can find topics by examining lists of suitable topics, surveys, and news items or by brainstorming.

Topic Lists.   Most public speaking textbooks contain suggestions for topics suitable for public speeches, as do books for writers (e.g., Lamm & Lamm, 1999). This text's companion website (**www.mycommunicationlab.com**) contains a list of hundreds of topics. Another source of topics is the list of best-selling nonfiction books printed in most newspaper book reviews or found in well-stocked bookstores. Or visit one of the online bookstores (**www.amazon.com, www.bn.com,** or **www.borders.com**) and search the lists of their most popular books. The popularity of these books tells you that people are interested in these topics.

Surveys.   An excellent way to determine what is worthwhile to your audience is to look at some of the national and regional polls concerning what issues people feel are most significant. Search for polling sites with your favorite search engine or start with one of the most widely used, the Gallup poll, at **www.gallup.com**. Surveys of people's major concerns appear regularly in newspapers and magazines and offer perhaps the most timely topics. Some search engines and websites list the topics that users ask for or visit most often; these, too, are useful for helping you discover what people are interested in and what they want to hear more about.

News Items.   Still another useful starting point is a good daily newspaper. Here you'll find the important international, domestic, financial, and social issues all conveniently covered in one place. The editorial page and letters to the editor are also useful for learning what topics are on people's minds. News magazines such as *Time* and *Newsweek* and business-oriented magazines such as *Forbes, Money, Business Week,* and *Fortune* will provide a wealth of suggestions. News shows such as *20/20* and *60 Minutes* and the numerous talk shows often discuss the very issues that concern us all. You can also surf websites, blogs, and newsgroups and discover a host of topics that command people's attention in health, education, politics, religion, science, technology, or just about any other area in which you're interested.

Limiting Your Topic   Plan to cover a limited topic in depth, rather than a broad topic superficially. The limiting process is simple: Repeatedly divide the topic into its significant parts. First, divide your general topic into its component parts, then divide one of these parts into its component parts. Continue until you arrive at a topic that seems manageable—a topic that you can reasonably cover in some depth in the allotted time.

For example, take television programs as a general topic area. Television programs, without some limitation, would take a lifetime to cover adequately. But you could divide this general subject into subtopics such as comedy, children's programs, educational programs, news, movies, soap operas, game shows, and sports. You might then take one of these topics, say comedy, and divide it into subtopics. You might consider comedy on a time basis and divide television comedy into its significant time periods: pre-1960, 1961–1999, and 2000 to the present. Or you might focus on situation comedies. Here you might examine a topic such as "Women in Television Comedy," "Race Relations in Situation Comedy," or "Families in Television Comedies." At this stage the topic is beginning to look manageable. Figure 11.2 presents a tree diagram to further illustrate this process. The diagram begins with a topic even broader than television programs—mass communication. Notice how from the general "Mass Communication" you can get to the relatively specific "Same-Sex or Opposite-Sex Business Relationships in Television Soaps."

YOUR PURPOSE

In some cases you'll select your topic and purpose almost simultaneously. At other times you'll select your topic and later formulate your purpose. In preparing public speeches, you'll need to formulate both a general and a specific purpose.

Communication Choice Point

Topic Appropriateness

Stephen, a 20-year-old student, gave a speech in class on flower arranging—a topic so unexpected that members of the audience giggled and avoided eye contact with Stephen throughout his speech. The instructor asks you to offer a critique of the speech. It's essential that you address the giggling in your critique but you don't want to blame anyone. *What are some ways for dealing with this? What might you say?*

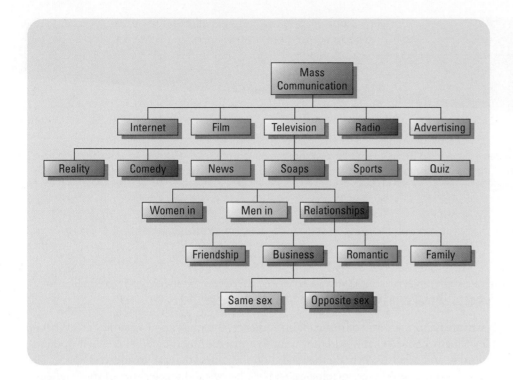

FIGURE 11.2

Tree Diagram for Limiting Speech Topics

Here is a tree diagram illustrating how a topic can be divided until it becomes manageable for a short speech. If you draw your tree diagram freehand, it's likely to look a lot messier than this, with cross-outs and false starts indicated. If you do the diagram on the computer—even with the Table function—then it's likely to look more like the example in this figure. Construct a different tree diagram by selecting Internet, film, radio, or advertising as a topic and subdividing it until you reach a level that would be appropriate for a 5- to 10-minute informative or persuasive speech.

Your General Purpose The two major kinds of public speeches are informative speeches and persuasive speeches. The **informative speech** creates understanding; it clarifies, enlightens, corrects misunderstandings, demonstrates how something works, or explains how something is structured (see Chapter 13). The **persuasive speech**, on the other hand, influences attitudes or behaviors. It may strengthen existing attitudes or change the audience's beliefs. Or it may move the audience to act in a particular way (see Chapter 14).

Your Specific Purpose Your **specific purpose** identifies the information you want to communicate (in an informative speech) or the attitude or behavior you want to change (in a persuasive speech). For example, your specific purpose in an informative speech might be

- to inform my audience of three ways to save time using the Internet for research;
- to inform my audience about how the new interoffice e-mail system works; or
- to inform my audience of the benefits of integrated work teams.

Your specific purpose in a persuasive speech might be

- to persuade my audience that all cigarette advertising should be abolished;
- to persuade my audience that the college should establish courses on the prevention of AIDS and other STDs; or
- to persuade my audience to contribute time to working with students with disabilities.

Whether you intend to inform or to persuade, limit your specific purpose so you'll be able to go into it in some depth. Your audience will benefit more from a speech that covers a small area in depth than one that covers a broad topic superficially.

Avoid the common pitfall of trying to accomplish too much in too short a time. For example, "to inform my audience about the nature of LinkedIn and Plaxo, how they differ from Facebook and MySpace, and why it's necessary to belong to both types of social networking sites" includes several purposes (the last of which is persuasive) Select one of them and build your speech around it.

A limited topic makes your speech easier to construct and easier to understand and remember.

Here are a few overly general topics. Using one of the methods discussed in this chapter (or any other method you're familiar with), limit one of these topics to a subject that would be reasonable for a 5- to 10-minute speech: (1) sports, (2) male–female relationships, (3) parole, (4) surveillance on the Internet, (5) children, (6) student problems, (7) morality, (8) fitness, (9) political corruption, or (10) violence.

Step 2: Analyze Your Audience

If you are going to inform or persuade an audience, you must know who they are. What do they already know? What would they want to know more about? What are their opinions, attitudes, and beliefs? Where do they stand on the issues you wish to address? Specifically, you will want to look at the sociological and psychological characteristics of your audience.

ANALYZE THE SOCIOLOGY OF THE AUDIENCE

In analyzing an audience, be careful not to assume that people covered by the same label are necessarily all alike. As soon as you begin to use a sociological characteristic with an expressed or implied "all," consider the possibility that you may be stereotyping. Don't assume that all women or all older people or all highly educated people think or believe the same things. They don't.

Nevertheless, there are characteristics that seem to be more common among one group than another, and it is these characteristics that you want to explore in analyzing your audience. Four of the most important factors are (1) cultural factors, (2) age, (3) gender, and (4) religion and religiousness.

Cultural Factors   Cultural factors such as nationality, ethnicity, and cultural identity are crucial in audience analysis. Largely because of different training and experiences, the interests, values, and goals of various cultural groups also will differ. Further, cultural factors will influence each of the remaining factors; for example, attitudes toward age and gender will differ greatly from one culture to another.

Perhaps the primary question to ask is, *Are the cultural beliefs and values of the audience relevant to my topic and purpose*? In other words, might the cultural memberships of your audience members influence the way they see the topic? If so, find out what these beliefs and values are and take these into consideration as you build your speech.

Age   Different age groups have different attitudes and beliefs, largely because they have had different experiences in different contexts. Take these differences into consideration in preparing your speeches. For example, let's say that you're an investment counselor and you want to persuade your listeners to invest their money to increase their income. Your speech would have to be very different if you were addressing an audience of retired people (e.g., people in their 60s) than if the audience consisted of young executives (e.g., people in their 30s).

In considering the age of your audience, ask yourself whether age groups differ in the goals, interests, and day-to-day concerns that may be related to your topic and purpose. Graduating from college, achieving corporate success, raising a family, and saving for retirement are concerns that differ greatly from one age group to another.

Gender   The rapid social changes taking place today make it difficult to pin down the effects of gender. As you analyze your audience in terms of gender, ask yourself whether men and women differ in the values that they consider important and that are related to your topic and purpose. Traditionally, men have been found to place greater importance on theoretical, economic, and political values. Traditionally, women have been found to place greater importance on aesthetic, social, and religious values. In framing appeals and in selecting examples, use the values your audience members consider most important.

Ask too whether one gender will find your topic more interesting than the other. Will men and women have different attitudes toward the topic? Men and women do not, for example, respond in the same way to such topics as abortion, rape, and equal pay for equal work. Select your topics and supporting materials in light of the gender of your audience members. When your audience is mixed, make a special effort to give men ways to connect to "women's" topics and women ways to connect to "men's" topics.

Religion and Religiousness   The religion and religiousness of your listeners will often influence the audience's responses to your speech. Religion permeates all topics and all issues. It is obvious that attitudes on such issues as birth control, abortion, and divorce are closely connected to religion. Similarly, views about premarital sex, marriage, child rearing, money, cohabitation, responsibilities toward parents, and thousands of other issues clearly are influenced by religion.

Ask yourself if your topic or purpose might be seen as an attack on the religious beliefs of any segment of your audience. If so, then you might want to make adjustments—not necessarily to abandon your purpose, but to rephrase your arguments or incorporate different evidence. When dealing with any religious beliefs, and particularly when disagreeing with them, recognize that you're going to meet stiff opposition. Proceed slowly and inductively. That is, present your evidence and argument before expressing your disagreement.

ANALYZE THE PSYCHOLOGY OF THE AUDIENCE

Focus your psychological analysis of the audience on three questions: How willing is your audience? How knowledgeable is your audience? And how favorable is your audience?

How Willing Is Your Audience?   If you face an audience that is willing (even eager) to hear your speech, you'll have an easy time relating your speech to them. If, however, your audience is listening unwillingly, consider the following suggestions:

- Secure their attention as early in your speech as possible—and maintain their interest throughout—with supporting materials that will speak to their motives, interests, and concerns.
- Relate your topic and supporting materials directly to your audience's needs and wants; show them how what you are saying will help them achieve what they want.
- Show the audience why they should listen to your speech by connecting your purpose to their purposes, their motives.
- Involve the audience directly in your speech by showing them that you understand their perspective, asking rhetorical questions, and referring to their experiences and interests.
- Focus on a few very strong issues or even a single strong issue.

How Knowledgeable Is Your Audience?   Listeners differ greatly in the knowledge they have of your topic. If your audience knows little about your topic, consider these suggestions:

- Don't talk down to audience members.
- Don't confuse a lack of knowledge with a lack of intelligence.

If your audience knows a great deal about your topic, consider these suggestions:

- Let the audience know that you are aware of their knowledge and expertise and that your speech will not simply repeat what they already know but will go beyond it.
- Emphasize your credibility, especially your competence in this general subject area (see Chapter 14).

How Favorable Is Your Audience?

If you face an audience that has unfavorable attitudes toward your topic or your purpose, or even toward you, consider these suggestions:

- Build on commonalities; emphasize not the differences but the similarities between you and the audience.
- Build your speech from areas of agreement, through areas of slight disagreement, up to the major differences.
- Strive for small gains.
- Ask for a fair hearing.

In the following example, from a speech about research on the biological differences between men and women, a topic that many listeners might have preconceived ideas about, Stephanie Cagniart, a student at the University of Texas at Austin, simply explained that despite much opposition this topic is too important to ignore:

> But because the May 2005 *Scientific American* notes that this research may hold the key to gender equality, as well as lead to far more effective treatments for mental disorders and transform our educational system, we can't ignore this debate.

ANALYSIS AND ADAPTATION DURING THE SPEECH

In your classroom speeches, you'll face a known audience, an audience you've already analyzed and for which you've made appropriate adaptations. At other times, however, you may face an audience that you've not been able to analyze beforehand or that differs greatly from what you expected. In these cases you'll have to analyze and adapt as you speak. Here are a few suggestions.

Focus on Listeners as Message Senders

As you're speaking, look at your listeners. Remember that just as you're sending messages to your audience, they're also sending messages to you. Pay attention to these messages, and make necessary adjustments on the basis of what they tell you.

You can make a wide variety of adjustments to each type of audience response. For example, if your audience show signs of boredom, increase your volume, move closer to them, or tell them that what you're going to say will be of value to them. If your audience show signs of disagreement or hostility, stress a similarity you have with them. If your audience look puzzled or confused, pause a moment and rephrase your ideas, provide necessary definitions, or insert an internal summary. If your audience seem impatient, say, for example, "my last argument" instead of your originally planned "my third argument."

Ask "What If" Questions

The more preparation you put into your speech, the better able you'll be to make on-the-spot adjustments and adaptations. For example, let's say you have been instructed to explain the opportunities available to the nontraditional student at your college. You've been told that your audience will consist mainly of working women in their 30s and 40s who are just beginning college. As you prepare your speech with this audience in mind, ask yourself "what if" questions: What if the audience has a large number of men? What if the audience consists of women much older than 40? What if the audience members come with their relationship partners or their children? Keeping such questions in mind will force you to consider alternatives as you prepare your speech. This way, you'll have adaptations readily available if you face a new or different audience.

Address Audience Responses Directly   Another way of dealing with audience responses is to confront them directly. To those who are giving disagreement feedback, for example, you might say:

> *You may disagree with this position, but all I ask is that you hear me out and see if this new way of doing things will not simplify your accounting procedures.*

Or, to those who seem impatient, you might respond:

> *I know this has been a long day, but give me just a few more minutes and you'll be able to save hours recording your accounts.*

By responding to your listeners' reactions and feedback, you acknowledge your audience's needs. You let them know that you hear them, that you're with them, and that you're responding to their very real needs.

Step 3: Research Your Topic

Throughout the process of preparing your public speeches, you'll conduct research to find examples, illustrations, and definitions to help you inform your listeners; testimony, statistics, and arguments to support your major ideas; and personal anecdotes, quotations, and stories to help you bring your topics to life.

GENERAL RESEARCH PRINCIPLES

Here are a few principles to help you research your speeches more effectively and more efficiently.

- Begin your search by examining what you already know. Write down, for example, what relevant books, articles, or websites you're familiar with or people who might know something about the topic.

- Continue your search by getting an authoritative but general overview of the topic. An encyclopedia article, book chapter, or magazine article will serve this purpose well. This general overview will help you see the topic as a whole and how its various parts fit together.

- Follow up the general overview using increasingly more detailed and specialized sources. Fortunately, many of the general articles contain references or links to direct this next stage of your search for more specific information.

- Distinguish between primary and secondary sources as you research. A **primary source** is original information about a topic or event. An original research study in an academic journal, a corporation's annual report, and an eyewitness report of an accident are all examples of primary sources. By contrast, **secondary sources** relate or discuss information originally presented somewhere else. A summary of research, appearing in a popular magazine; a television news story on a corporation's earnings; and a report by someone who talked with an eyewitness to an accident are examples of secondary sources. Keep in mind that secondary sources are less reliable than primary sources, because they are a step removed from the actual facts or events. The writer of secondary material may have left out important parts, may be biased and have slanted the reporting to reflect his or her attitudes, or may have distorted the material because he or she misunderstood the data. If possible, check the primary source itself to see if anything was left out or if the conclusions are warranted. On the other hand, a secondary source may be more accessible to a layperson. A science reporter summarizing research for a popular magazine may express complicated scientific data in simple language, making it easier for a nonscientist to understand than the original report.

> "The ultimate goal of all research is not objectivity, but truth."
>
> —HELENE DEUTSCH

LIBRARIES

Libraries are the major storehouses of information and have added to their concentration on print sources a major focus on computerized **databases**. Often, you can go to a library to access other libraries or databases maintained by local and national governments, cultural institutions, and various corporations and organizations. You also can go to a brick-and-mortar library to access materials that are not on the Net or that you want in print. Because each library functions somewhat differently, your best bet in learning about a specific library, such as your own college's, is to talk with your librarian about what the library has available and how materials are most easily accessed. Here are a few online libraries that you'll find especially helpful.

- The largest library in the United States is the Library of Congress, which houses millions of books, maps, multimedia resources, and manuscripts. Time spent at this library (begin with www.loc.gov) will be well invested. The home page will guide you to a wealth of information.

- The Virtual Library is a collection of links to 14 subject areas: for example, agriculture, business and economics, computing, communication and media, and education. Visit this at www.vlib.org.

- If you're not satisfied with your own college library, visit the online library catalogs of some of the large universities, such as the University of Pennsylvania (www.library.upenn.edu) or the University of Illinois (http://gateway.library.uiuc.edu).

- The Internet Public Library (www.ipl.org) is actually not a library; it's a collection of links to a wide variety of materials. But it will function much like the reference desk at any of the world's best libraries.

NEWS SOURCES

Often, you'll want to read political speeches, obituaries, financial news, or reports on natural disasters, congressional actions, international developments, United Nations actions, or any of a host of other topics. Or you may wish to locate the time of a particular event and learn something about what else was going on in the world at that particular time. For this type of information, you may want to consult a reliable newspaper. Especially relevant are newspaper indexes, newspaper databases, newspaper and magazine websites, news wire services, and news networks online.

- *Electronic newspaper databases.* Many newspapers can be accessed online. The *New York Times* database, for example, contains complete editorial content of the paper, one of the world's most comprehensive newspapers. All aspects of news and sports, editorials, columns, obituaries, New York and regional news, and the *New York Times Book Review* and *Magazine* are included. The *New York Times* and the *Financial Times* are both available through Research Navigator (www.mycommunicationlab.com).

- *Newspaper and newsmagazine websites.* Most newspapers now maintain their own websites, from which you can access current and past issues. Here are a few to get you started: www.latimes.com (*Los Angeles Times*), www.usatoday.com (*USA Today*), http://online.wsj.com/home-page (*Wall Street Journal*), www.nytimes.com (*The New York Times*) and the *Washington Post* (www.washingtonpost.com). Two particularly useful websites are www.newslink.org/menu.html, which provides access to a variety of online newspapers and magazines, and Hotlinks to Newspapers Online, which provides links to more than 1,000 daily, 400 weekly, and 100 international newspapers (www.newspaperlinks.com).

- *News wire services.* Three wire services should prove helpful. The Associated Press can be accessed at www.ap.org, Reuters at www.reuters.com, and PR Newswire at www.prnewswire.com. The advantage of getting your information from a news wire service is that it's more complete than you'd find in a newspaper, which has to cut copy to fit space requirements—and which, in some cases, may put a politically or socially influenced spin on the news.

- *News networks online.* All of the television news stations maintain extremely useful websites. Here are some of the most useful: CNN at www.cnn.com, ESPN at espn.com, ABC News at www.abcnews.com, CBS News at www.cbsnews.com, and MSNBC News at www.msnbc.com/news.

BIOGRAPHICAL MATERIAL

As a speaker you'll often need information about particular individuals. For example, you may want to look up authors of books or articles to find out something about their education, training, or their writings. Or you may want to find out if there have been critical evaluations of their work in, say, book reviews or articles about them. Knowing something about your sources helps you to evaluate their competence, present their credibility to the audience, and answer audience questions about them.

Perhaps the easiest way to access biographical information is using your favorite search engine: Search for the person's name, placing it in quotation marks. Depending on the person you're looking up, you're likely to get a lot more references than you can reasonably examine, and you'll need to add operators to limit your search. For example, let's say you're interested in getting information on the educational background of Treasury Secretary Timothy Geithner. If you search for *"Timothy F. Geithner"*, Google will return something around 567,000 sites, a lot more than you can reasonably examine. To reduce this number and get a more focused search, you might search for *"Timothy F. Geithner"* + *educational background.* Now the number of sites is just over 400. You can easily scan the first 10 or 20 items, and you're likely to find exactly what you want.

If you're looking for information on a scientist, researcher, or scholar, do a search of the person's name using Google Scholar (www.scholar.google.com).

ACADEMIC RESEARCH ARTICLES

Academic research forms the core of what we know about people and the world; it is the most valid and the most reliable you're likely to find. Research articles report on studies conducted by academicians around the world. For the most part, these articles are conducted by unbiased researchers using the best research methods available. Further, before publication this research is subjected to careful critical review by experts in the specific field of the research. You're likely to find relevant articles by searching any of the online research sources your college library subscribes to or with Research Navigator (www.mycommunicationlab.com).

BOOK SOURCES

Each library catalogs its books, journals, and government documents in a slightly different way, depending on its size and the needs of its users. All college libraries, however, make use of some form of computerized catalog. These are uniformly easy and efficient to use. The catalog is the best place to find out what books are in your college library or in libraries that make their books available through interlibrary loans, for example.

Browsing through any large brick-and-mortar bookstore is almost sure to give you insights into your topic. If you're talking about something that people are interested in today, there are likely to be books dealing with it on the shelves of most bookstores. Visit too some of the online bookstores, such as Amazon.com (www.amazon.com), Barnes & Noble (www.bn.com), or Borders (www.borders.com).

USING AND EVALUATING INTERNET MATERIALS

In doing research on the Internet you've no doubt already noticed that the vast amount of information available often makes finding specific information difficult. Two general guides will help you at the start. First, learn which databases contain the

Communication Choice Point

Asking a Favor

You're preparing a speech on the architectural ideas for rebuilding Ground Zero, and you want to ask some of the famous architects a few questions so you can integrate their most recent thoughts (and interject a more personalized note) into your speech. *What are some of your options for accomplishing this? What would you do?*

"There is no such thing as an uninteresting subject; there are only uninteresting people."

—G. K. CHESTERTON

information you want to find. A *database* is simply organized information on a topic that is contained in one place and can be accessed with relative ease. A dictionary, an encyclopedia, an index to magazines, and a collection of abstracts from hundreds of journals are all examples of databases. Because each library subscribes to a different set of databases, find out which databases are available at your college library as well as at other libraries to which you have access. Review the available databases, single out those that will be especially helpful to you, and learn as much as you can about them. For example, if you're researching a medical topic, then the MEDLINE database will prove especially useful and can be searched for free at the National Library of Medicine's website, www.nlm.nih.gov. If you're looking for sociological statistics, then the U.S. census figures will be essential; you'll want to become familiar with the Census Bureau's website, www.census.gov.

Second, learn about the search engines and directories that will help you find the information you need, and learn how to use them efficiently. Some search engines are *metasearch engines*; these search the databases of a variety of search engines at the same time. These programs are especially useful if you want a broad search and you have the time to sift through lots of websites. Some of the more popular search engines include Ask at www.ask.com, Google at www.google.com, Yahoo! at www.yahoo.com, Vivisimo at www.vivisimo.com, and Bing at www.bing.com.

In using search engines, it's often helpful to limit your search with "operators"—words and symbols that define relationships among the terms for which you're searching. Perhaps the most common are AND, OR, and NOT. Searching for *drugs AND violence* will limit your search to only those documents that contain both words, in any order. Searching for *drugs OR violence* will expand your search to all documents containing either word, and searching for "*drugs and violence*" will yield only documents containing that exact phrase. Searching for *violence AND schools NOT elementary* will yield documents containing both *violence* and *schools* except those that contain the word *elementary*. Each search engine uses a somewhat different system for limiting searches, so you'll have to learn the specific systems used by your favorite search engines.

As you collect materials from the web, keep in mind that anyone can "publish" on the Internet, making it essential that you subject everything you find on the Net to critical analysis. An article on the Internet can be written by world-renowned scientists or by elementary school students; by fair and objective reporters or by people who would spin the issues to serve their own political, religious, or social purposes. It's not always easy to tell which is which. Here are five questions to ask concerning the (1) qualifications, (2) currency, (3) fairness, (4) sufficiency, and (5) accuracy of Internet resources (as well as information from print, from interpersonal interaction, or from the popular media).

Qualifications   Does the author have the necessary credentials? For example, does the author have enough of a background in science or medicine to write authoritatively on health issues? Do an Internet search using the biography sites already discussed, or simply enter the author's name in your favorite search engine and check on his or her expertise.

Currency   When was the information published? When were the sources that are cited in the article written? Generally, the more recent the material, the more useful it will be. With some topics—for example, unemployment statistics, developments in AIDS research, tuition costs, and attitudes toward the Iraq war or same-sex marriage— the currency of the information is crucial to its usefulness because these things change so rapidly. Other topics, such as historical or literary topics, may well rely on information that was written hundreds of years ago. Even with these topics, however, new information frequently sheds light on events that happened in the far distant past. To ensure currency check important figures in a recent almanac, in a newspaper, or at a frequently updated Internet source such as Federal Statistics at www.fedstats.gov.

Fairness   Does the author of the material present the information fairly and objectively, or is there a bias favoring one position? Some websites, although objective on the surface, are actually organs of some political, religious, or social organization. It's often useful to go to the home page and look for information on the nature of the organization sponsoring the website. Reviewing a range of research on the subject will help you see how other experts view the issue. It will also enable you to see whether this author's view of the situation takes into consideration all sides of the issue and whether these sides are represented fairly.

Sufficiency   Is the information presented sufficient to establish the claim or conclusion? The opinion of one dietitian is insufficient to support the usefulness of a particular diet; statistics on tuition increases at five elite private colleges are insufficient to illustrate national trends in tuition costs. Generally, the broader your conclusion, the more information you'll need to meet the requirements for sufficiency. For example, if you want to claim the usefulness of a diet for all people, then you're going to need a great deal of information from different populations—men and women, old and young, healthy and sickly, and so on.

Accuracy   Is the information presented accurate? Of course, determining accuracy is not easy; however, the more you learn about your topic, the more able you'll be to judge the accuracy of information about the topic. Is the information primary or secondary? If it's secondary information, you may be able to locate the primary source material (often a hot link in the Internet article or a reference at the end of a printed text). Check to see whether the information is consistent with information found in other sources and whether the recognized authorities in the field accept this information.

Major book, newspaper, and magazine publishers go to enormous effort to ensure the accuracy of what appears in print or on their websites, so the information they provide is generally reliable. Some publishers, however, are arms of special interest groups with specific agendas. If this is the case with one of your sources, try to balance this publisher's perspective with information that represents other views of the issue. If an article appears in a journal sponsored by a major academic organization such as the American Psychological Association or the National Communication Association, you can be pretty sure that experts in the field have carefully reviewed the article before publication. Again, if an article appears in a well-respected major newspaper like the *New York Times*, the *Washington Post*, or the *Wall Street Journal*, or in any of the major newsmagazines or news networks (or online on their websites), you can be pretty sure that the information is accurate. Of course, these claims of accuracy are generalizations; errors do occur in the most respected publications. Both academic journals and newspapers have printed fraudulent articles.

> **Communication Choice Point**
>
> **Correcting Errors**
>
> In your speech you say that more than 70 percent of the students at your school favor banning alcohol on campus. Toward the end of the speech, you realize that you mixed up the figures; only 30 percent actually favor banning alcohol. During the question-and-answer period no one asks about the figures. *What are some of your options for making this correction? Or would you say nothing?*

INTEGRATING RESEARCH INTO YOUR SPEECH

By integrating and acknowledging your sources of information in your speech, you'll give fair credit to those whose ideas and statements you're using; at the same time you'll help establish your own reputation as a responsible researcher.

Be certain to mention your sources in your speech by citing at least author names and, if helpful, the publication titles and the dates. Check out some of the speeches reprinted in this book and note especially how the speakers integrated their source citations into their speeches. In your written outline, you would then give the complete bibliographical reference.

Here is an example of how you might cite your source:

> My discussion of the causes of anorexic nervosa is based on the work of Dr. Peter Rowan of the Priory Hospital in London. In an article titled "Introducing Anorexia Nervosa," which I last accessed on October 5, 2006, Rowan notes that "this is a disorder of many causes that come together." It's these causes that I want to cover in this talk.

You would then, in the reference list following the speech, identify the author, title of the article, URL (i.e., web address), and the date you visited the site. It would look like this:

> Rowan, P. Introducing Anorexia nervosa. **www.priory-hospital.co.uk.htm/anorexia.htm** (accessed October 5, 2006).

Communicating Ethically
Plagiarism

Because plagiarism is such an important issue in public speaking, this ethics box is a bit longer than others. It will cover the nature of plagiarism, the reasons plagiarism is unacceptable, and what you can do to avoid plagiarism.

What Is Plagiarism?

Plagiarism is the process of passing off the work (e.g., ideas, words, or illustrations) of others as your own. Plagiarism is *not* the act of using another's ideas—we all do that. Rather, it is using another's ideas without acknowledging that they are the ideas of this other person; it is presenting the ideas as if they were your own. Plagiarism exists on a continuum, ranging from appropriating an entire term paper or speech written by someone else to using a quotation or research finding without citing the author.

Plagiarism also includes situations in which you get help from a friend without acknowledging this assistance. In some cultures—especially collectivist cultures teamwork is strongly encouraged. Students are encouraged to help other students with their work. But in the United States and in many individualist cultures teamwork without acknowledgment is considered plagiarism.

In U.S. institutions of higher education, plagiarism is a serious violation of the rules of academic honesty and is subject to serious penalties, sometimes even expulsion. Further, as with all crimes, ignorance of the law is not an acceptable defense against charges of plagiarism. This last point is especially important, because people often commit plagiarism through ignorance about what does and what does not constitute plagiarism.

Why Plagiarism Is Unacceptable

Here are a few reasons why plagiarism is wrong.

- Plagiarism is a violation of another's intellectual property rights. Much as it would be wrong to take another person's watch without permission, it is wrong to take another person's ideas without giving due credit.

If you're going to play the game properly, you'd better know every rule.

—BARBARA JORDAN
(1936–1996), Texas
Congresswoman

Although it's possible to overdo the oral citation—giving more information than the listeners really need—it is more risky to leave out potentially useful information. Because your speeches in this course are learning experiences, it will be better to err on the side of more information rather than less.

Avoid useless expressions such as "I have a quote here" or "I want to quote an example." Let the audience know that you're quoting by pausing before the quote, taking a step forward, or referring to your notes to read the extended quotation. If you want to state more directly that this is a quotation, you might do it this way:

Tony Alessandra, in his book *Charisma*, defines this essential quality most clearly. "Charisma," says Alessandra, "is the ability to influence others positively by connecting with them physically, emotionally, and intellectually."

CITING RESEARCH SOURCES

In citing references, first find out what style manual is used in your class or at your school. Generally, it will be one or another of the style manuals developed by the American Psychological Association (APA), the Modern Language Association (MLA), or the University of Chicago (in their *Manual of Style*). Different colleges and different departments within a given college often rely on different formats for citing research, which, quite frankly, makes a tedious process even worse. Fortunately, there are a variety of websites that provide exactly the information you'll need to cite any reference you might have. For example, Purdue University offers an excellent site that covers APA and MLA

Communication Choice Point

Adaptation and Plagiarism

You're really pressed to come up with a persuasive speech on a contemporary social issue, and you just don't have the time to research it. Fortunately, a friend at another school wrote a term paper for her sociology course that you could easily adapt to your required public speaking assignment. *What are some of your options for dealing with this situation? What do you feel is your ethical obligation in this case?*

- You're in college to develop your own ideas and ways of expressing them; plagiarism defeats this fundamental purpose.
- Evaluations (everything from grades in school to promotions in the workplace) assume that what you present as your work is in fact your work.

Avoiding Plagiarism

Let's start with the easy part. In a speech or term paper, for example, you do not have to—and should not—cite sources for information that is readily available and not likely to be disputed. For example, the population of Thailand, the amendments to the U.S. Constitution, the actions of the United Nations, and the way the heart pumps blood are all common knowledge, and you should not cite the almanac or the book from which you got such information. On the other hand, if you were talking about the attitudes of people from Thailand or the reasons the Constitutional amendments were adopted, then you would need to cite your sources, because this information is not common knowledge and may well be disputed.

For information that is not common knowledge, you need to acknowledge your source. Here are a few simple rules that will help you avoid even the suggestion of plagiarism (for more extended discussion see Stern, 2007):

1. *Acknowledge the source of any ideas you present that are not your own.* If you learned of an idea in your history course, cite the history instructor or history textbook. If you read an idea in an article, cite the article.
2. *Acknowledge the words of another.* When you're quoting another person exactly, you need to cite the person you're quoting. You should also cite the person even when you paraphrase her or his words, because you are still using another person's ideas.
3. *Acknowledge help from others.* If your roommate gave you examples or ideas, or helped you style your speech, acknowledge the help.
4. *When in doubt, it's best to err on the side of over-referencing rather than under-referencing.*

Take a look at some of the plagiarism websites established by different universities; these often include exercises and extended examples; see, for example, Indiana University's at www.indiana.edu/ or Purdue University's at http://owl.english.purdue.edu/owl/resource/589/01/.

style formats and provides examples for citing books, articles, newspaper articles, websites, e-mails, online postings, electronic databases, and more (http://owl.english.purdue.edu/handouts/research). Another excellent website is Capital Community College's guide for writing research papers (http://webster.commnet.edu). Guidelines for using the *Chicago Manual of Style* may be found at Ohio State's website (www.lib.ohio-state.edu).

Step 4: Formulate Your Thesis and Identify Your Main Points

In this step, you choose your thesis and then use it to generate your major points or ideas.

CHOOSE YOUR THESIS

The **thesis** is the main idea that you want to convey to the audience. The thesis of Lincoln's Second Inaugural Address was that northerners and southerners should work together for the good of the entire country. The thesis of many science fiction movies is that working together, people—often from very different cultures and different walks of life—can repel any conquering force and achieve just about anything.

Let's say, for example, you're planning to present a persuasive speech in favor of the election of Senator Winters. Your thesis statement might be, *Winters is the best candidate.* This is what you want your audience to believe, what you want your audience to remember even if they forget everything else. In an informative speech, on the other hand, the thesis statement focuses on what you want your audience to learn. For example, for a speech on jealousy, a suitable thesis might be *Two main theories of jealousy exist*.

The thesis and the purpose of a speech are similar in that they both guide you in selecting and organizing your materials. In some ways, however, they are different:

- Thesis and purpose differ in their form of expression. The thesis is phrased as a complete, declarative sentence. The purpose is phrased as an infinitive phrase ("to inform . . .," "to persuade . . .").
- The thesis focuses on the message; the purpose focuses on the audience. The thesis succinctly identifies the central idea of your speech. The purpose identifies the change you hope to bring about in your audience—for example, to impart information, to change attitudes, or to influence people to act in a certain way.

Especially in the early stages of mastering public speaking, formulate both your thesis statement and your purpose. From there, you will be able to construct a more coherent and more understandable speech. Limit your thesis statement to one central idea. A statement such as "We should support Winters and the entire Democratic party" contains not one but two basic ideas.

As already discussed, in low-context cultures (e.g., the United States, Germany, and Sweden) most audiences wish to hear a direct statement of the speaker's position and an explicit statement of what he or she wants the audience to do. In contrast, high-context cultures (e.g., Japan, China, and Arab countries) prefer a less explicit statement and prefer to be led indirectly to the speaker's conclusion.

GENERATE YOUR MAIN POINTS

Use your thesis statement to generate your main points. Once you phrase the thesis statement, the main divisions of your speech will suggest themselves. Here, for example, is how student speaker Stephanie Cagniart expressed her thesis along with giving a clear orientation of the main points she would be covering:

> The commerce clause is being used by the federal government to dictate social issues—from gun control to same-sex marriage—in a way that threatens our individual liberties and undermines states' rights. So let's first examine why the commerce clause has broadened; second, explore this abuse's dangers; and finally, investigate how we can scale back what the October 20, 2005, *Wanderer Magazine* calls "the clause that ate the Constitution."

To take another example, let's say you are giving a speech on the value of a college education to a group of people in their 30s and 40s who are considering returning to college. Your thesis is *A college education is valuable*. You then ask yourself, Why is it valuable? From these answers you generate your major propositions. You might first brainstorm the question and identify as many answers as you can. Your list might look something like this:

A college education is valuable because:

1. It helps you get a job.
2. It increases your potential to earn a good salary.
3. It gives you greater job mobility.
4. It helps you secure more creative work.
5. It helps you appreciate the arts more fully.
6. It helps you understand an increasingly complex world.
7. It helps you understand different cultures.
8. It helps you avoid taking a regular job for a few years.
9. It helps you meet lots of people and make friends.
10. It helps you increase personal effectiveness.

For purposes of illustration, let's stop at this point. You have 10 possible main points—too many to cover in a short speech. Further, not all are equally valuable or relevant to your audience. Look over the list to make it shorter and more relevant. Here are some suggestions:

Eliminate Points That Seem Least Important
You might want to eliminate, say, number 8—it's inconsistent with the positive value of college, the thesis of your speech. Further, your audience is unlikely to be able to stop working to go to college full-time.

Combine Points That Have a Common Focus
Notice, for example, that the first four points center on jobs. You might, therefore, consider grouping them under a general heading:

A college education will help you secure a better job.

This might be one of your major propositions, which you can develop by defining what you mean by "a better job." You might also use some of the ideas you generated in your brainstorming session. This main point and its elaboration might look like this:

"Sorry, Pop, but your message is no longer relevant to the younger audience."

I. A college education will help you secure a better job.

   A. College graduates earn higher salaries.

   B. College graduates enter more creative jobs.

   C. College graduates have greater job mobility.

Note that A, B, and C are all aspects or subdivisions of "a better job."

Select Points That Are Most Relevant
Ask yourself what will interest your audience most. On this basis, you might drop number 5 on the assumption that your audience will be interested in more practical outcomes. You might eliminate number 9 on the assumption that your audience is not looking to college to help them make friends; they probably already have friends and families that occupy most of their time. Further, you might conclude that this audience cares a lot about personal effectiveness, so you might make this your second major proposition:

A college education will help you increase your personal effectiveness.

Much as you developed the subordinate points in your first proposition by defining what you meant by "a good job," you would define what you mean by "personal effectiveness":

II. A college education will help you increase your personal effectiveness.

   A. A college education will help you increase your ability to communicate.

   B. A college education will help you acquire learning skills.

   C. A college education will help you acquire coping skills.

You would then follow the same procedure used to generate these subordinate points (A, B, and C) to develop the subheadings. For example, you might divide A into two major subheads:

   A. A college education will improve your ability to communicate.

      1. A college education teaches writing skills.

      2. A college education teaches speech skills.

Use Two, Three, or Four Main Points
Remember, your aim is not to cover every aspect of a topic but to emphasize selected parts. Further, you want to have enough time to amplify and support the points you present. With too many propositions, this

becomes impossible. Also, you don't want to present too much information, because your audience simply will not be able to remember it.

Phrase Propositions in Parallel Style To make it easier for listeners to follow and remember your speech, use similar structures in wording your major propositions.

NOT THIS:

Mass Media Functions

    I. The media entertain.

   II. The media function to inform their audiences.

  III. Creating ties of union is a major media function.

  IV. The conferral of status is a function of all media.

THIS:

Mass Media Functions

    I. The media entertain.

   II. The media inform.

  III. The media create ties of union.

  IV. The media confer status.

Develop Main Points Separately and Distinctly Don't overlap your main points.

NOT THIS:

    I. Color and style are important in clothing selection.

THIS:

    I. Color is important in clothing selection.

   II. Style is important in clothing selection.

Step 5: Support Your Main Points

Now that you've researched your topic and identified your thesis and your main points, you need to support each point. In the informative speech, your support primarily amplifies the concepts you discuss. Specifically, you might use:

1. *Examples, illustrations,* and the *testimony* of various authorities to breathe life into abstract or vague concepts.

2. *Definitions* to clarify complex terms and to provide different ways of looking at some process or event.

3. *Numerical data* to explain trends in a wide variety of topics.

4. *Presentation aids*—charts, maps, objects, slides, films, tapes, CDs, and so on—to help clarify vague concepts.

These forms of support are covered in detail in Chapter 13.

In a persuasive speech, your support is proof—material that offers evidence, argument, and motivational appeal and that establishes your credibility and reputation. To persuade your audience to adopt the new production guidelines, for example, you might claim that the guidelines will save time. You must then substantiate your claim by giving proof. You might, for example, show that the new system saves an average of 30 minutes per job, that new employees take less time to learn the new system, and that the new system results in fewer errors and thereby less lost time.

You can persuade your audience with several types of support:

1. *Logical support* includes reasoning from specific instances and from general principles, from causes and effects, and from signs.

2. *Motivational support* includes appeals to the audience's emotions and to their desires for status, financial gain, or increased self-esteem: "No one wants to be at the low end of the hierarchy. Our new Management Seminar will help you climb that corporate ladder faster and easier than you ever thought possible."

3. *Credibility appeals* involve establishing your own personal reputation or credibility, especially your competence, high moral character, and charisma.

These forms of support are covered in depth in Chapter 14.

Step 6: Organize Your Information

Organize your materials to help the audience understand and remember what you say. There are six patterns you might use to organize the body of a speech: time, spatial, topical, problem-solution, cause-effect, and the motivated sequence. Additional help on organization may be found on the website for this text (www.mycommunicationlab.com): see Figure 11.3.

TIME PATTERN

When you organize your topic on the basis of a time, or temporal, relationship, you generally divide the speech into two, three, or four major parts. You might begin with the past and work up to the present or future, or begin with the present or future and work back to the past. For example, you might organize a speech on children's development of speech and language according to a temporal pattern.

General Purpose: To inform

Specific Purpose: To inform my audience of the four stages in the child's acquisition of language

Thesis: The child goes through four stages in learning language.

FIGURE 11.3 **My Outline**

This outlining website is one of the many online resources available at MyCommunicationLab (www.mycommunicationlab.com).

I. Babbling occurs first.

II. Lallation occurs second.

III. Echolalia occurs third.

IV. Communication occurs fourth.

Most historical topics lend themselves to organization by a time pattern. Topics such as events leading to the Civil War, how to plant a vegetable garden, and the history of the Internet are all candidates for temporal patterning.

SPATIAL PATTERN

Similar to temporal patterning is organizing the main points of a speech on the basis of space. Discussions of most physical objects fit well into spatial patterns. For example, a presentation on the structure of a hospital, a school, a skyscraper, or even a dinosaur might lend itself to this pattern. Here, a speech on places to visit in Central America uses a spatial pattern.

General Purpose: To inform

Specific Purpose: To inform my audience of a great way to visit Central America

Thesis: You can have a great visit to Central America by visiting four countries.

I. First, visit Guatemala.

II. Second, visit Honduras.

III. Third, visit Nicaragua.

IV. Fourth, visit Costa Rica.

TOPICAL PATTERN

The **topical pattern** divides the speech topic into subtopics or component parts. This pattern is an obvious choice for organizing a speech on a topic such as, say, the branches of government.

General Purpose: To inform

Specific Purpose: To inform my audience of the ways the three branches of government work

Thesis: Three branches govern the United States.

I. The legislative branch is controlled by Congress.

II. The executive branch is controlled by the president.

III. The judicial branch is controlled by the courts.

The world's major religions, great works of literature, and the problems facing the college graduate are other examples of speech topics that lend themselves to a topical organizational pattern.

PROBLEM–SOLUTION PATTERN

As its name indicates, the problem–solution pattern divides the main ideas into two main parts: problems and solutions. Let's say you're trying to persuade an audience that home health aides should be given higher salaries and increased benefits. In the first part of the speech, you might discuss some of the problems confronting home health aides. In the second part, you would consider the possible solutions to these problems The speech, in outline form, might look like this.

General Purpose: To persuade

Specific Purpose: To persuade my audience of the solutions to the three main problems of the home health care industry

Thesis: The home health care industry can be improved with three changes.

    I. Three major problems confront home health care.

      A. Industry lures away the most qualified graduates.

      B. Numerous excellent health aides leave the field after a few years.

      C. Home health care is currently a low-status occupation.

   II. Three major solutions to these problems exist.

      A. Increase salaries for home health aides.

      B. Make benefits for health aides more attractive.

      C. Raise the status of the home health care profession.

CAUSE–EFFECT/EFFECT–CAUSE PATTERN

Similar to the problem–solution pattern of organization is the cause–effect, or effect–cause, pattern. Using this pattern, you divide the speech into two major sections—causes and effects. Highway accidents, illnesses, or low self-esteem, for example, could be explained using a cause–effect pattern. An outline of the causes and effects of low self-esteem might look something like this:

General Purpose: To persuade

Specific Purpose: To persuade my audience of the causes and effects of low self-esteem

Thesis: Low self-esteem is caused by a history of criticism and unrealistic goals, which lead to depression and an unwillingness to socialize.

    I. Low self-esteem often has two main causes.

      A. A history of criticism can contribute to low self-esteem.

      B. Unrealistic goals can contribute to low self-esteem.

   II. Low self-esteem often has two main effects.

      A. Depression is one frequent effect.

      B. An unwillingness to socialize with others is another frequent effect.

THE MOTIVATED SEQUENCE

The **motivated sequence**, useful for organizing both informative and persuasive speeches, is a pattern in which you arrange information to motivate your audience to respond positively to your purpose (McKerrow, Gronbeck, Ehninger, & Monroe, 2000). It consists of five steps: (1) attention, (2) need, (3) satisfaction, (4) visualization, and (5) action.

1. Attention Make the audience give you their undivided attention. If you execute this step effectively, your audience should be eager to hear what you have to say. You can gain audience attention by, for example, asking a rhetorical question, referring to specific audience members, or using a dramatic or humorous story. These and other ways of gaining attention are discussed more fully in Chapter 13.

2. Need Now you prove that a need exists. The audience should feel that they need to learn or do something. You can establish need by:

- stating the need or problem as it exists or will exist.
- illustrating the need with specific examples, illustrations, statistics, testimony, and other forms of support.
- pointing to how this need affects your specific listeners—for example, their financial status, career goals, or individual happiness.

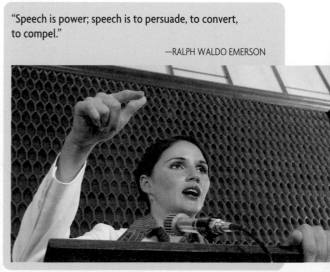

"Speech is power; speech is to persuade, to convert, to compel."

—RALPH WALDO EMERSON

Communication Choice Point

Unpopular Thesis

You've decided to tackle the hypocrisy you see in classmates who publicly support the values of racial equality but privately express racist attitudes. You're afraid, however, that your audience will walk out on you as soon as you state your thesis. *What are some of the things you can do to avoid any knee-jerk reaction from your listeners? What might you say (especially in your introduction) to make them listen to what essentially will be criticism?*

For example, in a speech to convince people in their 60s and 70s to purchase home computers, you might say in this step, "A survey of persons in their 60s and 70s reported that one of their greatest needs was easy and rapid access to medical information. If you are like those in this survey, then the home computer may be your answer."

3. Satisfaction   In the satisfaction step, you present the "solution" that satisfies the need you demonstrated in step 2. This step should convince the audience that what you are informing them about or persuading them to do will satisfy the need. You answer the question, *How will the need be satisfied by what I am asking the audience to learn, believe, or do?* This step usually contains two types of information: (1) a clear statement (with examples and illustrations if necessary) of what you want the audience to learn, believe, or do; and (2) a statement of how or why what you are asking them to learn, believe, or do will lead to satisfying the need identified in step 2

For example, you might say, "With a home computer, you'll be able to get information on thousands of potential drug interactions in seconds." You might then show your listeners, perhaps with an actual demonstration, how this would be done.

4. Visualization   **Visualization** intensifies the audience's feelings or beliefs. It takes the audience beyond the present place and time and helps them imagine what it would be like if the need were satisfied (with the solution suggested in step 3). You can accomplish this by (1) demonstrating the positive benefits to be derived if this advocated proposal were put into operation or (2) demonstrating the negative consequences that will occur if your plan is not followed. You could also combine the two methods and demonstrate both the positive benefits of your plan and the negative effects of the existing situation or of a competing proposal. For example, you might say, "With this simple CD-ROM and these few Web addresses, you'll be able to stay at home and get valuable medical information, instead of fighting traffic and wasting time." You might then demonstrate with a specific example how they would find this information.

5. Action   In the action step, you tell the audience what they should *do* to satisfy the need you have identified. Your goal is to move the audience in a particular direction. Here are a few ways to accomplish this step.

- State exactly what audience members should do.
- Appeal to your listeners' emotions.
- Give the audience guidelines for future action.

For example, you might say, "Read this pamphlet, 'Life on the Computer after 60,' and take a walk to your neighborhood computer store and talk with the salespeople." Or you might suggest that they consider taking an appropriate adult education course at the local community college.

Notice that an informative speech could stop after the satisfaction step. In this example, with the satisfaction step you accomplish the goal of informing the audience about some advantages of home computers for older people. In some cases, though, you may believe it helpful to progress to the action step to emphasize your point.

In a persuasive speech, on the other hand, if you limit your purpose to strengthening or changing attitudes or beliefs, you must go at least as far as visualization. If you aim to get your listeners to behave in a certain way, you'll need to go all the way through the action step.

ADDITIONAL PATTERNS

The six organizational patterns just considered are the most common and are useful for many public speeches. But there are other patterns that also may be appropriate for some presentations.

Structure–Function   The structure–function pattern is useful in informative speeches in which you want to discuss how something is constructed—its structure—and what it does—its function. This pattern might be useful, for example, in a speech about what an organization is and what it does, about the parts of a university and how they operate, or about the sensory systems of the body and their functions. This pattern might also be useful in a discussion about the nature of a living organism: its anatomy (or structure) and its physiology (or function).

Comparison and Contrast   A comparison-and-contrast pattern can work well in informative speeches in which you want to analyze two different theories, proposals, departments, or products in terms of their similarities and differences. In this type of speech, you not only explain each theory or proposal but also explain primarily how they are similar and how they are different.

Pro and Con, Advantages and Disadvantages   The pro-and-con pattern, sometimes called the advantages–disadvantages pattern, is useful in informative speeches in which you want to explain objectively the advantages (the pros) and the disadvantages (the cons) of a plan, method, or product.

Claim and Proof   The claim-and-proof pattern is especially appropriate for a persuasive speech in which you want to prove the truth or usefulness of a particular proposition. It's the pattern frequently used in trials: The prosecution makes a claim that the defendant is guilty and presents proof in the form of varied evidence: for example, evidence that the defendant had a motive, had the opportunity, and had no alibi. The claim-and-proof pattern divides your speech into two major parts. In the first part you explain your claim (e.g., "Tuition must not be raised," "Library hours must be expanded," or "Courses in AIDS education must be instituted"). In the second part you offer your evidence, or proof, of why, for example, tuition must not be raised.

Multiple Definition   The multiple-definition pattern serves well in informative speeches in which you want to explain the nature of a concept (e.g., *What is a born-again Christian? What is a scholar? What is multiculturalism?*). In this pattern each major heading consists of a different type of definition or way of looking at the concept. A variety of definition types are discussed in Chapter 13.

Who, What, Why, Where, When   The "who, what, why, where, when" pattern is the primary pattern in journalism and is useful in informative speeches in which you want to report or explain an event: for example, a robbery, political coup, war, or trial. You divide your speech into five major parts, each answering one of the five "W" questions.

Fiction–Fact   This pattern may be useful when you wish to clarify certain misconceptions that people have about various things. For example, if you were giving a speech on fiction and facts about the flu, you might use this pattern. You could first give the fiction (e.g., that you can get the flu from a flu shot, or antibiotics can help the flu, or older people spread the flu most often) and then follow it by the facts: You can't get the flu from the flu shot; antibiotics are useful only against bacteria, not against viruses; and children, rather than older people, spread the flu most often and most easily.

Because your chosen organizational pattern will serve primarily to help your listeners follow your speech, you may want to tell your listeners (in your introduction or as a transition between the introduction and the body of your speech) what pattern you'll be following. Here are just a few examples:

- "In our discussion of language development, we'll follow the baby from the earliest sign of language through true communication."
- "I'll first explain the problems with raising tuition and then propose a workable solution."
- "First we'll examine the causes of hypertension and then we'll look at its effects."

t this point, you're probably deep into your speech preparation. You've selected and limited your topic. You've analyzed your audience and begun thinking of adaptations you can make based on the nature of your specific audience. You've researched the topic. You've selected your thesis and identified your main points. You've organized the points and selected appropriate supporting materials. This chapter continues explaining the process of preparing a speech and offers suggestions on wording the speech, crafting the conclusion and introduction, rehearsing the speech, and finally delivering the completed public speech.

Step 7: Word Your Speech

When you're reading, you can look up an unfamiliar word or reread difficult portions or sections you didn't catch because of momentary lapses in attention. When you're listening, you don't have this luxury. Because of differences between reading and listening, and because your listeners will hear your speech only once, your talk must be instantly intelligible.

Researchers who have examined a great number of speeches and writings have found several important differences among them (DeVito, 1965, 1981; Akinnaso, 1982). Generally, spoken language consists of shorter, simpler, and more familiar words than does written language. There is more qualification in speech than in writing; for example, when you speak, you generally make greater use of such qualifying expressions as *although*, *however*, and *perhaps*. When you write, you often edit these out. Spoken language also contains a greater number of self-reference terms—*I, me, my*—and more expressions that incorporate the speaker as part of the observation (e.g., "It seems to me that . . ." or "As I see it . . .").

For most speeches, this "oral style" is appropriate. The specific suggestions offered throughout this section will help you to style a speech that will retain the best of the oral style while maximizing comprehension and persuasion.

CLARITY

Clarity in speaking style should be your primary goal. Here are some guidelines to help you make your speech clear:

Be Economical. Don't waste words. Notice the wasted words in expressions such as "at 9 a.m. *in the morning*," "we *first* began the discussion," "I *myself personally*," and "blue *in color*." By withholding the italicized terms, you eliminate unnecessary words and move closer to a more economical and clearer style.

Use Specific Terms and Numbers.   Be specific to create a clearer and more detailed picture. Don't say "dog" when you want your listeners to picture a St. Bernard. Don't say "car" when you want them to picture a limousine. The same is true of numbers. Don't say "earned a good salary" if you mean "earned $90,000 a year." Don't say "taxes will go up" when you mean "taxes will increase 7 percent."

Use Guide Phrases. Use guide phrases to help listeners see that you're moving from one idea to another. Use phrases such as "now that we have seen how . . . , let us consider how . . . ," and "my next argument . . ." Terms such as *first, second, and also, although*, and *however* will help your audience follow your line of thinking.

Use Short, Familiar Terms. Generally, favor the short word over the long word. Favor the familiar over the unfamiliar word. Favor the more commonly used over the rarely used term. Use *harmless* instead of *innocuous, clarify* instead of *elucidate, use* instead of *utilize, find out* instead of *ascertain, cost* or *expense* instead of *expenditure.*

Carefully Assess Idioms. **Idioms** are expressions that are unique to a specific language and whose meaning cannot be deduced from the individual words used. Expressions such as "kick the bucket," and "doesn't have a leg to stand on" are idioms. Either you know the meaning of the expression or you don't; you can't figure it out from knowledge of the individual words only. The positive side of idioms is that they give your speech a casual and informal style; they make your speech sound like a speech and not like a written essay. The negative side is that idioms create problems for audience members who are not native speakers of your language. Many such listeners will simply not understand the meaning of your idioms.

Vary the Levels of Abstraction. Combining high abstraction (i.e., the very general) and low abstraction (i.e., the very concrete) seems to work best. Too many generalizations will be vague and difficult for your audience to comprehend, but too many specifics will leave them wondering what the big picture is.

VIVIDNESS

Select words that make your ideas vivid, that make them come alive in the listeners' minds.

Use Active Verbs. Favor verbs that communicate activity. The verb *to be*, in all its forms—*is, are, was, were,* and *will be*—is relatively inactive. Try replacing such forms with action verbs. Instead of saying, "Management will be here tomorrow," consider "Management descends on us [or jets in] tomorrow."

Use Figures of Speech. A figure of speech is a stylistic device in which words are used beyond their literal meaning. One of the best ways to achieve vividness is to use figures of speech. Table 12.1 presents a few that you may find helpful.

Use Imagery. Inject vividness into your speech by appealing to the audience's senses, especially their visual, auditory, and tactile senses. Using imagery can make your listeners see, hear, and feel what you're talking about. *Visual imagery* enables you to describe people or objects in images the audience can see. When appropriate, describe visual qualities such as height, weight, color, size, shape, length, and contour. Let your audience see the sweat pouring down the faces of coal miners. *Auditory imagery* helps you appeal to the audience's sense of hearing. Let listeners hear the car screeching or roar of angry tenants. *Tactile imagery* enables you to make the audience feel the temperature or texture you're talking about. Let listeners feel the cool water running over their bodies, the fighter's punch, or the sand beneath their feet.

APPROPRIATENESS

Appropriate language is consistent in tone with your topic, your audience, and your own self-image. It's language that does not offend anyone or make anyone feel uncomfortable

Communication Choice Point

Unexpected Feedback

You have just introduced your speech with a story you found extremely humorous; you laughed out loud after you finished it. Unfortunately, the audience just didn't get it—not one smile in the entire audience. *What can you do to avoid making this blank reaction follow you throughout your speech? What might you say? Are there advantages of saying nothing?*

TABLE 12.1	Figures of Speech

These are only a few of the many figures of speech you can use in your speeches. Too many similes or too much hyperbole is likely to make your speech sound unnatural and overly formal, so use these sparingly. On the other hand, a good figure goes a long way toward making your speech memorable. Can you think of additional examples for each of the figures identified here?

Figure	Definition	Examples
Alliteration	Repetition of the same initial consonant sound in two or more words close to one another	Fifty Famous Flavors; March Madness
Hyperbole	Use of extreme exaggeration	I'm so hungry I could eat a horse.
Metaphor	Comparison of two unlike things	She's a lion when she wakes up. He's a real bulldozer.
Personification	Attribution of human characteristics to inanimate objects	This room cries out for activity. My car is tired and wants water.
Simile	Comparison of two unlike objects using the words *like* or *as*	This chairperson takes charge like a bull. The teacher is as gentle as a lamb.
Rhetorical Question	A question used to make a statement or produce some desired effect rather than to secure the answer, which is obvious	Do you want to be popular? Do you want to get promoted? Do you want to get an "A" on the exam?

and seems natural given the situation. Here are some guidelines to help you choose appropriate language.

Speak at the Appropriate Level of Formality. Although public speaking usually takes place in a somewhat formal situation, relatively informal language seems to work best in most situations. One way to achieve a more informal style is to use contractions: *don't* instead of *do not*, *I'll* instead of *I shall*, and *wouldn't* instead of *would not*. Contractions give a public speech the sound and rhythm of conversation—a quality listeners generally like.

Avoid Written-Style Expressions. Avoid expressions that are more familiar in writing, such as "the former" or "the latter" as well as expressions such as "the argument presented above." These make listeners feel you're reading to them rather than talking with them.

Avoid Slang and Vulgar and Offensive Expressions. Be careful not to offend your audience with language that embarrasses them or makes them think you have little respect for them. Although your listeners may use such expressions, they generally resent their use by public speakers. Above all, avoid terms that might be interpreted as sexist, heterosexist, ageist, or racist (see Chapter 4).

PERSONAL STYLE

Audiences favor speakers who use a personal rather than an impersonal style—who speak *with* them rather than *at* them. A personal style makes the audience feel more involved with the speaker and the speech topic.

Use Personal Pronouns. Say "I," "me," "he," "she," and "you." Avoid expressions such as the impersonal *one* (as in, "One is led to believe that . . ."), *this speaker*, and *you, the listeners*. These expressions are overly formal and distance the audience, creating barriers rather than bridges.

Direct Questions to the Audience. Involve the audience by asking them questions. With a small audience, you might even take brief responses. With larger audiences, you might ask the question, pause to allow the audience time to consider their responses, and then move on. When you direct questions to your listeners, you make them feel they are part of the experience. For example, in a speech on abortion, you might ask, "Do you know anyone who had an abortion?" and then pause to consider a few responses from your audience. With a larger audience you might simply say, "I'd like you to think about the people you know who have had abortions. What were their reasons for undergoing abortion?"

Create Immediacy. Create immediacy (a closeness with your audience) by referring directly to your listeners, using *you*; say, "*You'll* enjoy reading . . . " instead of "Everyone will enjoy reading . . . " Refer to commonalities between you and the audience. Say, for example, "We're all children of immigrants," or, "We all want to see this agency run smoother." Refer also to shared experiences and goals: for example, "We all need a more responsive PTA." Finally, recognize and refer to audience feedback. Say, for example, "I can see from your expressions that we're all here for the same reason."

POWER

Public speaking, perhaps even more than interpersonal or small group communication, often requires a powerful style—a style that is certain, definite, and persuasive. Perhaps the first step toward achieving a powerful style of speech is to eliminate the powerless forms that you may use now. The following is a list of the major characteristics of powerless speech (Molloy, 1981; Kleinke, 1986; Johnson, 1987; Dillard & Marshall, 2003; Lakoff, 1975; Timmerman, 2002). As you consider this list, think of your own speech.

- *Hesitations* make you sound unprepared and uncertain: "I, er, want to say that, ah, this one is, er, the best, you know?"

- *Too many intensifiers* make your speech monotonous and don't allow you to stress what you do want to emphasize: "Really, this was the greatest; it was truly awesome, phenomenal."

- *Disqualifiers* signal a lack of competence and a feeling of uncertainty: "I didn't read the entire article, but . . . " "I didn't actually see the accident, but . . . "
- *Self-critical statements* signal a lack of confidence and may make public your own inadequacies: "I'm not very good at this," "This is my first public speech."
- *Slang and vulgar language* signal low social class and hence little power: "No problem!" "@*+#?$!!"

SENTENCE CONSTRUCTION

Effective public speaking style also requires careful attention to the construction of sentences. Here are some guidelines that will help you achieve a clear, vivid, appropriate, and personal speaking style.

Use Short rather than Long Sentences. Short sentences are more forceful and economical. They are easier to understand and to remember. Listeners don't have the time or inclination to unravel long and complex sentences. Help them to listen more efficiently by using short rather than long sentences.

Use Direct rather than Indirect Sentences. Direct sentences are easier to understand. They are also more forceful. Instead of saying, "I want to tell you the three main reasons why we should not adopt the Bennett Proposal," say, "We should not adopt the Bennett Proposal. Let me give you three good reasons."

Use Active rather than Passive Sentences. Active sentences are easier to understand. They also make your speech livelier and more vivid. Instead of saying, "The lower court's original decision was reversed by the Supreme Court," say, "The Supreme Court reversed the lower court's decision." Instead of saying, "The change was favored by management," say, "Management favored the change."

Use Positive rather than Negative Sentences. Positive sentences are easier to comprehend and to remember (DeVito, 1976; Clark, 1974). Notice how sentences A and C are easier to understand than B and D.

A. The committee rejected the proposal.

B. The committee did not accept the proposal.

C. This committee works outside the normal company hierarchy.

D. This committee does not work within the normal company hierarchy.

Vary the Type and Length of Sentences. The advice to use short, direct, active, and positive sentences is valid most of the time. But too many sentences of the same type or length will make your speech boring. Use variety but generally follow the guidelines.

"If you have an important point to make, don't try to be subtle or clever. Use a pile-driver. Hit the point once. Then come back and hit it again. Then hit it a third time—a tremendous whack."

—WINSTON CHURCHHILL

Step 8: Construct Your Conclusion and Introduction

Your conclusion and introduction need special care, because they will determine, in large part, the effectiveness of your speech. Because you've just finished the body of the speech, and the major function of the conclusion is to summarize, it will probably be easier to work first on your conclusion and then on the introduction.

THE CONCLUSION

Devote particular attention to this brief but crucial part of your speech. In your conclusion, summarize your main points and make closing remarks.

Summarize   You may summarize your speech in a variety of ways.

Restate Your Thesis. Restate the essential thrust of your speech—your thesis, or perhaps the purpose you hoped to achieve.

Restate the Importance of Your Thesis. Tell the audience again why your topic or thesis is so important. Here is how Carrie Willis (Schnoor, 2000, p. 15), a student from Tallahassee Community College, restated the importance of the thesis of her speech on "drowsy driving" and summarized her speech's the main points:

> Today, we have gained a better understanding of the problem of falling asleep at the wheel, and why it continues to exist, while finally suggesting several initiatives to help end this epidemic. . . . So next time you're on the road and you find yourself dozing off, pull over and take a nap, because those 30 minutes could save your life.

Restate Your Main Points. Reiterate your two, three, or four main points. For example, in a speech on problems with volunteer fire departments, one student speaker restated his propositions like this: "By examining how volunteer firefighters are jeopardizing our safety, why our communities remain so dependent, and finally prescribing some solutions, we have set the stage for reform" (Schnoor, 1999, p. 46).

Close   The conclusion's second function is to provide closure—to give the speech a crisp and definite end. Don't leave your audience wondering whether you've finished.

Use a Quotation. A quotation that summarizes your thesis or provides an interesting perspective on your point of view often provides effective closure. Make sure that it's clearly and directly related to your speech purpose; otherwise, the audience will spend their time trying to figure out the connection.

Pose a Challenge or Question. You may wish to end your speech with a provocative question or challenge:

- "What do you intend to do about the company's refusal to increase wages?"
- "Go home and clean high-cholesterol foods out of your refrigerator."
- "Sign this petition; it will help put an experienced person in office."

Here's how rock star and social activist Bono posed a challenge to students in his commencement address at the University of Pennsylvania (American Rhetoric Speech Bank at www.americanrhetoric.com, retrieved February 20, 2009):

> That's what this degree of yours is, a blunt instrument. So go forth and build something with it. And remember what John Adams said about Ben Franklin, "He does not hesitate at our boldest Measures but rather seems to think us too irresolute."
>
> Well this is the time for bold measures.
>
> And this is the country.
>
> And you are the generation.

Motivate Your Audience to Do Something.   Remind your audience of what they should do now: For example:

- "The next time you go online, visit one of the websites I mentioned."
- "You can sign up to volunteer at the desk in the Student Union."
- "So, read the article in this handout; it could change your life."

Thank the Audience. Speakers frequently thank their audience. If you do this, do it a bit more elaborately than by saying simply "Thank you." You might relate the thanks to your thesis: "I really appreciate your attention and hope you'll join us in Sunday's protest." Or you might say, "I want to thank you for listening and for your willingness to sign Williams's petition."

THE INTRODUCTION

In your introduction, try to accomplish two goals: First, gain your audience's attention, and second, orient the audience—tell them a little bit about what you'll talk about.

Gain Attention   In your introduction, focus the audience's attention on your topic. Then work to maintain that attention throughout your speech.

Ask a Question. Questions are effective because they are a change from normal statements and involve the audience. They tell the audience that you're talking directly to them and care about their responses. Questions are also useful in setting the stage for what will follow. Here, for example, is how Rev. Reggie Longcrier used a question to frame his speech (**www.pamshouseblend.com/showDiary.do?diaryID=2348**, retrieved February 20, 2009):

> Sen. Edwards has said his opposition to gay marriage has been influenced by his Southern Baptist background. We know religion was once used to justify slavery, segregation and women not being allowed to vote, all of which today are recognized as unconstitutional and socially and morally wrong. So why is it still acceptable to use religion to justify denying gay and lesbian Americans their full and equal rights?

Refer to Specific Audience Members. Involving members directly makes them perk up and pay attention. Depending on the nature of the audience and your knowledge of specific members, you might say something like, "Pat, you defended the NRA, whereas Chris, you argued against it. And Pablo, you argued for a pro-life position on abortion, but Sarah, you argued for a pro-choice position. Even in a small class such as this, there are wide differences in beliefs, values, and attitudes. And that's what I want to talk about today: differences in beliefs and how these can cause conflict in our relationships."

Refer to the Specific Context. Instead of referring to specific people you might note the relevance of the specific context. Here, for example, is how Secretary of State Hillary Clinton referred to the context of her remarks at the U.N. World Conference on Women (**www.americanrhetoric.com**, retrieved February, 20, 2009):

> By gathering in Beijing, we are focusing world attention on issues that matter most in our lives—the lives of women and their families: access to education, health care, jobs and credit, the chance to enjoy basic legal and human rights and to participate fully in the political life of our countries.

Use Illustrations or Dramatic or Humorous Stories. We are all drawn to illustrations and stories about people—they make a speech vivid and concrete. Use them to secure audience attention in the introduction and to maintain it throughout.

Other ways to gain attention include using a visual aid; a short music or video clip; a dramatic, humorous, or interesting quotation; or a startling statistic or series of little-known facts.

Orient the Audience   Previewing what you're going to say will help your listeners follow your thoughts more closely. You can orient the audience in several ways.

Give the Audience a General Idea of Your Subject. One student, for example, in a speech on the problems of Internet education, oriented her audience not only to the topic but also to her problem–solution organizational pattern: "I am going to describe the problem of phony academic institutions on the Internet, focusing primarily on the misleading nature of their names as an advertising strategy. I will then provide some simple solutions to aid the general public in avoiding and exposing these disreputable organizations" (Schnoor, 1999, p. 10).

Give a Detailed Preview of Your Main Points. Identify the propositions you will discuss: for example, "In this brief talk, I will cover four major attractions of New York City: the night life, the theater, restaurants, and museums."

Identify the Goal You Hope to Achieve. A librarian addressing my public speaking class oriented the audience by stating goals in this way: "Pay attention for the next few minutes and you'll be able to locate anything we have in the library by using the new touch-screen computer access system."

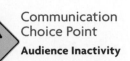

Communication Choice Point

Audience Inactivity

You're giving a speech on the problems of teenage drug abuse, and you notice that the back rows of your audience have totally tuned you out; they're reading, texting, working on their laptops. *What are some options you have to getting their attention? What might you say?*

Communication Choice Point

Introductions

You're scheduled to give a speech on careers in computer technology to high school students who have been forced to attend Career Day on Saturday. If you don't win over this unwilling audience in your introduction, you figure you're finished. *What are some things you can say to get this audience on your side, at least enough so they'll listen fairly to what you have to say?*

"I'll tell you what this election is about. It's about homework, and pitiful allowances, and having to clean your room. It's also about candy, and ice cream, and staying up late."

© Robert Weber/Condé Nast Publications/www.cartoonbank.com.

In this example, President Barack Obama combines some of these purposes in his "Call to Renewal" speech (www.obamaspeeches.com, retrieved February 20, 2009): Today I'd like to talk about the connection between religion and politics and perhaps offer some thoughts about how we can sort through some of the often bitter arguments that we've been seeing over the last several years."

AVOIDING SOME COMMON FAULTS

Here are a few tips for avoiding the mistakes that beginning speakers often make in introducing and concluding their speeches.

Don't Start Your Speech Immediately. Instead, survey your audience; make eye contact and engage their attention. Stand in front of the audience with a sense of control. Pause briefly, then begin speaking.

Don't Display Discomfort or Displeasure. When you walk to the speaker's stand, display enthusiasm and a desire to speak. People much prefer listening to a speaker who shows that she or he enjoys speaking to them.

Don't Apologize. In the United States, avoid expressions such as "I am not an expert on this topic," or "I didn't do as much reading on this topic as I should have." And never start a speech with, "I'm not very good at giving public speeches." Be aware, however, that this rule does not hold in all cultures; in fact, self-deprecating comments are expected in some Asian cultures and in collectivist cultures in general.

Don't Preface Your Introduction. Don't begin with such common but ineffective statement as "Before I begin my talk, I want to say . . ." Statements like this make it difficult for you to open your speech with a strong attention grabber.

Don't Introduce New Material in Your Conclusion. Once you reach your conclusion, it's too late to introduce new material. Instead, reinforce what you have already said, summarize your essential points, or give new expression to ideas already covered.

Don't Race Away from the Speaker's Stand. After your last statement, pause, maintain audience eye contact, and then walk (don't run) to your seat. Show no signs of relief; focus your attention on whatever activity is taking place. If a question period follows your speech and you're in charge of this, pause after completing your conclusion and ask audience members in a direct manner if they have any questions. If there's a chairperson who will ask for questions, pause after your conclusion, then nonverbally signal to the chairperson that you're ready to take questions.

TRANSITIONS AND INTERNAL SUMMARIES

Transitions (sometimes called "connectives") are words, phrases, or sentences that connect the various parts of your speech. Because your audience will hear your speech only once, they may not see the connections you want them to see. By using transitions, you can help your listeners see how one point leads to another or where one argument ends and another begins. Use transitions in at least the following places:

- between the introduction and the body of the speech
- between the body and the conclusion
- between the main points in the body of the speech

Here are the major transitional functions and some stylistic devices that you might use:

1. *To announce the start of a main point or piece of evidence:* "First . . . ," "A second argument . . . ," "A closely related problem . . . ," "If you want further evidence, look at . . . ," "My next point . . . ," or "An even more compelling argument . . ."

2. *To signal that you're drawing a conclusion from previously given evidence and argument:* "Thus . . . ," "Therefore . . . ," "So, as you can see . . . ," or, "It follows, then, that . . ."

3. *To alert the audience that you're introducing a qualification or exception:* "But . . . ," "However, also consider . . . ," or, "On the other hand . . ."

4. *To remind listeners of what you've just said and to stress that it's connected with another issue you now want to consider:* "In contrast to . . . ," "Consider also . . . ," "Not only . . . , but also . . . ," or "In addition to . . . , we also need to look at . . ." One student speaker, Andrew Farmer, did this simply and effectively by saying: "But while the project is astounding *[a point just explained]*, there are also some challenges *[the next point to be made]*. For example, . . ."

5. *To signal the part of your speech that you're approaching:* "By way of introduction . . . ," "In conclusion . . . ," "Now, let's discuss why we are here today . . . ," or, "So, what's the solution? What should we do?"

Closely related to the transition is the **internal summary**, a statement that summarizes what you have already discussed. Usually it summarizes some major subdivision of your speech. Incorporate several internal summaries into your speech—perhaps working them into the transitions connecting, say, the major arguments or issues. An internal summary that is also a transition might look something like this:

The three arguments advanced here were (1) . . . , (2) . . . , (3) . . . Now, what can we do about them? I think we can do two things. First, . . .

Now that you have completed your speech, it's time to put it all together in the form of an outline, something you already did when you identified your main points and amplified them with illustrations and definitions, for example. There are three kinds of speech outlines: the preparation outline, the template outline, and the delivery outline.

THE PREPARATION OUTLINE

A preparation outline like the one in the Public Speaking Sample Assistant box (as well as the template and delivery outlines that are discussed next) will help you not only to organize your thoughts more coherently but also to deliver your speech more effectively.

THE TEMPLATE OUTLINE

Another useful type of outline is the **template**. Much as a template in PowerPoint guides you to fill in certain information in particular places, the template outline serves a similar function; it ensures that you include all the relevant material in reasonable order.

The Public Speaking Sample Assistant

THE PREPARATION OUTLINE

Here is a relatively detailed preparation outline similar to the outline you might prepare when constructing your speech. The side notes should clarify both the content and the format of a preparation outline.

HAVE YOU EVER BEEN CULTURE SHOCKED?

Thesis: Culture shock can be described in four stages.

Purpose: To inform my audience of the four phases of culture shock.

INTRODUCTION

I. How many of you have experienced culture shock?

    A. Many people experience culture shock, a reaction to being in a culture very different from what they were used to.

    B. By understanding culture shock, you'll be in a better position to deal with it if and when it happens.

II. Culture shock occurs in four stages (Oberg, 1960).

    A. The Honeymoon occurs first.

    B. The Crisis occurs second.

    C. The Recovery occurs third.

    D. The Adjustment occurs fourth.

[Let's follow the order in which these four stages occur beginning with the first stage, the honeymoon.]

BODY

I. The Honeymoon occurs first.

    A. The Honeymoon is the period of fascination with the new people and culture.

    B. You enjoy the people and the culture.

        1. You love the people.

            a. For example, the people in Zaire spend their time very differently from the way New Yorkers do.

            b. For example, my first 18 years living on a farm was very different from life in a college dorm.

        2. You love the culture.

            a. The great number of different religions in India fascinated me.

            b. Eating was an especially great experience.

[But like many relationships, contact with a new culture is not all honeymoon; soon there comes a crisis.]

II. The Crisis occurs second.

    A. The Crisis is the period when you begin to experience problems.

        1. One-third of American workers abroad fail because of culture shock (Samovar, Porter, & McDaniel, 2008).

        2. The personal difficulties are also great.

Generally, the title, thesis, and purpose of the speech are prefaced to the outline. When the outline is an assignment that is to be handed in, additional information may be required.

Note the general format for the outline; the headings are clearly labeled, and the indenting helps you see the relationship between the items. For example, in introduction II, the outline format helps you to see that A, B, C, and D are explanations for II.

Note that the introduction, body, and conclusion are clearly labeled and separated visually.

Although the speaker assumes that the audience is familiar with culture shock, he or she still includes a brief definition in case some audience members don't know what it is and to refresh the memory of others.

Note that references are integrated throughout the outline, just as they would be in a term paper. In the actual speech, the speaker might say, "Anthropologist Kalervo Oberg, who coined the term *culture shock*, said it occurs in four stages."

The introduction serves two functions: It gains attention by involving the audience and by stressing the importance of the topic in the audience's desire to gain self-understanding, and it orients the audience to what is to follow. This particular orientation identifies both the number and the names of the stages. If this speech were much longer and more complex, this orientation might also have included brief definitions of each stage.

Another function often served by the introduction is to establish a relationship among yourself as the speaker, the topic, and the audience. In this particular speech, this function might have been served by your telling the audience how you experienced culture shock and how knowing the stages helped you cope with the difficulties. You might then tell the audience that the same would be true for them and thus connect all three major elements of the speech.

The transition at the end of the introduction tells the audience to expect a four-part presentation. Also, the numbers repeated throughout the outline will further aid the audience in keeping track of where you are in the speech. Most important, the transition tells the audience that the speech will follow a temporal thought pattern.

Notice the parallel structure throughout the outline. For example, note that I, II, III, and IV in the body are all phrased in exactly the same way. Although this may seem unnecessarily repetitive, it will help your audience follow your speech more closely and will also help you structure your thoughts logically.

Notice that there are lots of examples in this speech. These examples are identified only briefly in the outline and would naturally be elaborated on in the speech.

When you cite a specific fact, some style manuals require that you include the page number in the source reference.

B. Life becomes difficult in the new culture.

    1. Communication is difficult.

    2. It's easy to offend people without realizing it.

[As you gain control over the various crises, you begin to recover.]

III. The Recovery occurs third.

  A. The Recovery is the period when you learn how to cope.

  B. You begin to learn intercultural competence (Lustig & Koester, 2010).

    1. You learn how to communicate.

      a. Being able to go to the market and make my wants known was a great day for me.

      b. I was able to ask for a date.

    2. You learn the rules of the culture.

      a. The different religious ceremonies each have their own rules.

      b. Eating is a ritual experience in lots of places throughout Africa.

[Your recovery leads naturally into the next and final stage, the adjustment.]

IV. The Adjustment occurs fourth.

  A. The adjustment is the period when you come to enjoy the new culture.

  B. You come to appreciate the people and the culture.

[Let me summarize, then, the stages you go through in experiencing culture shock.]

CONCLUSION

I. Culture shock can be described in four stages.

  A. The Honeymoon is first.

  B. The Crisis is second.

  C. The Recovery is third.

  D. The Adjustment is fourth.

II. By knowing the four stages, you can better understand the culture shock you may now be experiencing on the job, at school, or in your private life.

REFERENCES

Lustig, M. W., & Koester, J. (2010). *Intercultural competence: Interpersonal communication across cultures* (6th ed.). Boston: Allyn & Bacon.

Oberg, K. (1960). Culture shock: Adjustment to new cultural environments. *Practical Anthropology, 7,* 177–182.

Samovar, L. A., Porter, R. E., & McDaniel, E. R. (2008). *Communication between cultures,* 6th ed. Belmont, CA: Cengage.

This reference list includes only those sources that appear in the completed speech.

Notice, too, the internal organization of each major point. Each main assertion in the body contains a definition of the stage (I.A, II.A, III.A, and IV.A) and examples (I.B, II.B, III.B, and IV.B) to illustrate the stage.

Note that each statement in the outline is a complete sentence. You can easily convert this outline into a phrase or key word outline to use in delivery. The full sentences, however, will help you see relationships among items more clearly.

Transitions are inserted between all major parts of the speech. Although they may seem too numerous in this abbreviated outline, they will be appreciated by your audience because the transitions will help them follow your speech.

Notice that these four points correspond to II.A, B, C, and D of the introduction and to I, II, III, and IV of the body. Notice how the similar wording adds clarity.

This step provides closure; it makes it clear that the speech is finished. It also serves to encourage reflection on the part of the audience as to their own experience of culture shock.

At the same time, it also helps you see your speech as a whole—and may reveal gaps that need to be filled or items that are discussed at too great a length. As you become more familiar with the public speaking process, you'll soon be able to develop your speech without any template outline.

The sample template outline in the following Public Speaking Sample Assistant box would be appropriate for a speech using a time, spatial, or topical organization pattern. Note that in this outline there are three main points (I, II, and III in the body). These correspond to items II.A, B, and C in the introduction (where you would orient the audience) and to I.A, B, and C in the conclusion (where you would summarize your major propositions). The transitions are signaled by square brackets. As you review this outline—the watermarked text will remind you of the functions of each outline item—you will see how it can be adapted for use with other organization patterns, such as problem–solution, cause–effect, or the motivated sequence. Additional template outlines for a variety of organizational patterns may be found at MyCommunicationLab.

THE DELIVERY OUTLINE

The **delivery outline** assists you in presenting the speech. Don't use your preparation outline: You may feel inclined to read from it, which is not an effective way to give a speech. Write a brief delivery outline such as that presented in the next Public Speaking Sample Assistant box, which was constructed from the preparation outline on culture shock.

Some public speaking coaches and instructors recommend putting your delivery outline on a 3×5 or 4×6 index card. One advantage is that you will need to condense your delivery outline to only key words and phrases, which will prevent you from reading your speech and help you interact more freely with your audience. When notes are too extensive, speakers have a tendency to read their notes rather than speak to their audience. Another benefit is that the card won't bend as would an $8\frac{1}{2}\times11$ piece of paper. Additional index cards might be used for quotations or statistics that won't fit on the one card. Or you may find it helpful to use three cards, one for each of the three main parts of your speech. If you do use more than one card (probably no more than four), be sure to number and label them clearly; you don't want to have to fumble through the cards looking for a particular quotation or statistic.

If you're using PowerPoint—discussed in detail in the next chapter—then your delivery outline is going to be either the PowerPoint slides themselves or the speaker's notes that you generate along with your PowerPoint presentation (discussed in the "Using Notes" section of this chapter). Here are some guidelines for delivery outlines.

- *Be brief.* Don't allow the outline to stand in the way of direct speaker–audience contact. Use key words to trigger in your mind the ideas you wish to discuss. Notice how brief the sample delivery outline is compared to the preparation outline, yet it's detailed enough to include all essential parts of your speech, even transitions.

- *Be delivery-minded.* Include any delivery guides you might wish to remember while you're speaking—for example, to pause or to show the visual aid.

- *Rehearse your speech with this delivery outline.* Make your rehearsal as close to the real thing as possible.

Step 9: Rehearse Your Speech

This discussion of rehearsal will begin by identifying the general methods of delivery. Then it will offer some suggestions for making your rehearsals efficient and effective.

METHODS OF DELIVERY

Speakers vary widely in delivery methods. Some speak off-the-cuff, with no apparent preparation. Others read their speeches from a manuscript. Others construct a detailed

The Public Speaking Sample Assistant

THE TEMPLATE OUTLINE

Thesis: _____ your main assertion; the core of your speech _____

Specific Purpose: _____ what you hope to achieve from this speech _____

INTRODUCTION

   I. _____ gain attention _____

   II. _____ orient audience _____

     A. _____ first main point; same as I in body _____

     B. _____ second main point; same as II in body _____

     C. _____ third main point; same as III in body _____

[Transition: _____ connect the introduction to the body _____]

BODY

   I. _____ first main point _____

     A. _____ support for I (the first main point) _____

     B. _____ further support for I _____

[Transition: _____ connect the first main point to the second _____]

   II. _____ second main point _____

     A. _____ support for II (the second main point) _____

     B. _____ further support for II _____

[Transition: _____ connect the second main point to the third _____]

   III. _____ third main point _____

     A. _____ support for III _____

     B. _____ further support for III _____

[Transition: _____ connect the third main point (or all main points) to the conclusion _____]

CONCLUSION

   I. _____ summary _____

     A. _____ first main point; same as I in body _____

     B. _____ second main point; same as II in body _____

     C. _____ third main point: same as III in body _____

   II. _____ Closure _____

The Public Speaking Sample Assistant

THE DELIVERY OUTLINE

PAUSE!

LOOK OVER THE AUDIENCE!

    I. Many experience CS

        A. CS: the reaction to being in a culture very different from your own

        B. By understanding CS, you'll be better able to deal with it

PAUSE—SCAN AUDIENCE

    II. CS occurs in 4 stages (WRITE ON BOARD)

        A. Honeymoon

        B. Crisis

        C. Recovery

        D. Adjustment

[Let's examine these stages of CS]

PAUSE/STEP FORWARD

    I. Honeymoon

        A. fascination w/people and culture

        B. enjoyment of people and culture

           1. Zaire example

           2. farm to college dorm

[But, life is not all honeymoon—the crisis]

    II. Crisis

        A. problems arise

           1. 1/3 Am workers fail abroad

           2. personal difficulties

        B. life becomes difficult

           1. communication

           2. offend others

[As you gain control over the crises, you learn how to cope]

PAUSE

    III. Recovery

        A. period of learning to cope

        B. you learn intercultural competence

           1. communication becomes easier

           2. you learn the culture's rules

[As you recover, you adjust]

    IV. Adjustment

        A. learn to enjoy (again) the new culture

        B. appreciate people and culture

[These then are the 4 stages; let me summarize]

PAUSE

CONCLUSION

    I. CS occurs in 4 stages: honeymoon, crisis, recovery, & adjustment

    II. By knowing the 4 stages, you can better understand the culture shock you may now be experiencing on the job, at school, or in your private life.

PAUSE

ASK FOR QUESTIONS

---

outline and compose the speech at the moment of delivery. These represent the three general methods of delivery: impromptu, manuscript, and extemporaneous.

The Impromptu Method An **impromptu speech** involves speaking without preparation. On some occasions, you can't avoid impromptu speaking. In a classroom, you may be asked to comment on the speaker and speech you just heard: In effect, you give an impromptu speech of evaluation. At meetings, people are often asked for impromptu comments on various issues. Or you may have to fill in for someone who has not shown up. You can greatly improve impromptu speaking by cultivating public speaking ability in general. The more proficient you are as a speaker, the better you will be impromptu.

The Manuscript Method   If you give a **manuscript speech**, you write out the speech and read it. This is the safest method when exact timing and wording are required. For example, it could be disastrous if a political leader did not speak from manuscript on sensitive issues. An ambiguous word, phrase, or sentence that may be insulting, belligerent, or conciliatory could cause serious problems. With a manuscript speech, you can control style, content, organization, and all other elements. A variation of the manuscript method is to write out the speech and then memorize it. You then recite the entire speech from memory, much as an actor recites a part in a play. The great disadvantages of the manuscript method are that the speech doesn't sound natural and there is no opportunity to adjust the speech on the basis of audience feedback.

The Extemporaneous Method   The **extemporaneous speech** is useful when exact timing and wording are not required. Good lecturing by college teachers is extemporaneous. They have prepared thoroughly, know what they want to say, and have the lecture's organization clearly in mind. But they are not committed to exact wording. This method allows greater flexibility for feedback. If a point needs clarification, in this style you can elaborate when it will be most effective. It's also easy to be natural, because you're being yourself. And you may move about and interact with the audience.

The major disadvantage of this method is that you may stumble and grope for words. You can address this disadvantage by rehearsing the speech several times. Although you won't give the precise attention to style that you would in the manuscript and memorizing methods, you can memorize certain key phrases.

The extemporaneous method is recommended for most situations, especially classroom speeches, in which the objective is to learn the art of public speaking. Overall it offers the greatest advantages with the fewest disadvantages. However, speaking impromptu and speaking from manuscript are also important skills. Fortunately, the principles of extemporaneous speaking discussed here will help you in these other kinds of speeches as well. Even when you use the extemporaneous method, however, consider the advantages of memorizing certain parts of your speech:

- Memorize your opening and closing lines—perhaps the first and last two or three sentences. This will help you focus your attention on the audience at the two most important moments of your speech.

- Memorize the main points and the order in which you will present them. After all, if you expect your audience to remember these points, they will expect you to remember them as well.

REHEARSING THE SPEECH

Rehearsal should enable you to see how the speech will flow as a whole and to make any necessary changes and improvements. It will also allow you to time your speech so that you stay within the allotted time. The following procedures should help you use your rehearsal time most effectively.

- Rehearse the speech from beginning to end, rather than in parts. Be sure to include all the examples and illustrations (and audiovisual aids if any) in your rehearsal.

- Time the speech during each rehearsal. Adjust your speech—both what you say and your delivery rate—on the basis of this timing.

- Rehearse the speech under conditions as close as possible to those under which you'll deliver it. If possible, rehearse in the room in which you'll present the speech and in front of a few supportive listeners.

- Rehearse the speech in front of a full-length mirror to help you see how you'll appear to the audience. Practice your eye contact, your movements, and your gestures in front of the mirror.

Communication Choice Point

Time Problem

Your speech has run overtime, and you've been given the 30-second stop signal. You wonder if it would be best to ignore the signal and simply continue your speech or if you should wrap it up in 30 seconds. *What options do you have for dealing with this? What are the advantages and disadvantages of each option?*

- Don't interrupt your rehearsal to make notes or changes; do these between rehearsals. If possible, record your speech (ideally, on videotape) so you can hear and see exactly what your listeners will hear and see.

- Rehearse at least three or four times, or as long as your rehearsals continue to result in improvements.

Step 10: Deliver Your Speech

Use your voice and body to complement and reinforce your verbal message.

VOICE

Chapter 5 discussed paralanguage as one of the major nonverbal communication channels (pp. 106–108). In public speaking it's especially important to give attention to such paralanguage dimensions as volume, rate, articulation and pronunciation, and pauses. Using these paralanguage features appropriately will help you complement and reinforce your message.

Volume   The **volume** of your voice is its relative loudness or softness. When your voice is adequately controlled, you adjust its volume according to factors such as the distance between you and your listeners, the competing noise, and the emphasis you want to give an idea. Vary your volume to best reflect your ideas—perhaps increasing volume for key words or phrases, lowering volume when talking about something extremely serious. Be especially careful not to fade away at the ends of sentences.

Rate   Your speech **rate** is the speed at which you speak. About 140 words per minute is average for speaking as well as for reading aloud. If you talk too fast, you deprive your listeners of the time they need to digest what you're saying. If your rate is too slow, your listeners' thoughts will wander. So speak at a pace that engages but doesn't bore and that allows listeners time for reflection.

Articulation and Pronunciation   **Articulation** results from movements of the speech organs as they modify and interrupt the air stream from the lungs. Different movements of the tongue, lips, teeth, palate, and vocal cords produce different sounds. **Pronunciation** is the production of syllables or words according to some accepted standard, such as that of a dictionary. Let's consider some of the most common problems associated with faulty articulation and pronunciation.

Errors of Omission (Articulation).   Omitting sounds or even syllables is a common articulation problem that you can easily overcome with concentration and practice. Here are some examples:

Incorrect	Correct
gov-a-ment	gov-ern-ment
hi-stry	hi-sto-ry
wanna	want to
studyin	studying
a-lum-num	a-lum-i-num
comp-ny	comp-a-ny

Errors of Substitution (Articulation).   Substituting an incorrect sound for the correct one is also easy to fix. Among the most common substitutions are [d] for [t] and [d] for [th]; for example, *wader* for the correct *waiter, dese* for the correct *these, bedder* for the correct *better,* and *ax* for the correct *ask.* Other prevalent substitution errors include

Here are 30 words that are often mispronounced. Consult an online dictionary with audio capabilities and record the correct pronunciations here.

Words Often Mispronounced	Correct Pronunciation	Words Often Mispronounced	Correct Pronunciation
Abdomen		Hierarchy	
Accessory		Jewelry	
Arctic		Library	
Buffet		Miniature	
Candidate		Nausea	
Clothes		Nuclear	
Costume		Probably	
Diagnosis		Prostate	
Especially		Relevant	
Espresso		Repeat	
Et cetera		Salmon	
February		Sandwich	
Federal		Similar	
Forte		Substantive	
Herb		Xenophobia	

Mispronouncing words may significantly lessen your credibility and your own uncertainty about pronunciation may increase your apprehension.

ekcetera for the correct *etcetera*, *congradulations* for the correct *congratulations*, and *lenth* for the correct *length*.

Errors of Addition (Articulation). These errors involve adding sounds where they don't belong. Some examples include:

Incorrect	Correct
acrost	across
athalete	athlete
Americar	America
idear	idea
filim	film
lore	law

Errors of Accent (Pronunciation). Each word has its own accepted **accent**, or stress pattern. Examples of words that are often accented incorrectly include *New Orleáns, ínsurance, compárable,* and *orátor* for the correct *New Órleans, insúrance, cómparable,* and *órator.*

Errors of Adding Sounds (Pronunciation). For some words, many people add sounds that are not part of the standard pronunciation. In the first three examples, the error involves pronouncing letters that are a part of the written word but should remain silent. In the last three examples, sounds are inserted where they don't belong.

Incorrect	Correct
homage	omage
Illinois	Illinoi
evening	evning
airaplane	airplane
burgalar	burglar
mischievious	mischievous

Pauses   **Pauses** are interruptions in the flow of speech. *Filled pauses* are gaps that you fill with vocalizations such as *er, um,* and *ah*. Even expressions such as *well* and *you know,* when used merely to fill up silence, are filled pauses. These pauses are ineffective and detract from the strength of your message. They will make you appear hesitant, unprepared, and unsure.

Unfilled pauses, silences interjected into the stream of speech, can be especially effective if used correctly. Here are a few examples of places where unfilled pauses—silences of a few seconds—can enhance your speech.

- Pause at transitional points. This will signal that you're moving from one part of the speech or from one idea to another. It will help listeners separate the main issues you're discussing.

- Pause at the end of an important assertion. This allows the audience to think about its significance.

- Pause after asking a rhetorical question. This will give the audience time to think about how they would answer.

- Pause before an important idea. This will help signal that what comes next is especially significant.

- Pause before you begin your speech (to scan and assess the audience and gather your thoughts) and after you finish it (to allow your ideas to sink in and to dispel any idea that you're anxious to escape).

BODY ACTION

You speak with your body as well as with your mouth, a point made clear in Chapter 5's discussion of the various nonverbal channels. The four aspects of body action that are especially important in public speaking are eye contact, facial expression, gestures and posture, and movement. As you read about these four channels, be sure to follow the most important and general rule: use consistent packaging; be careful that your verbal and your nonverbal messages do not contradict each other. So, if you say you're happy to be speaking today, your nonverbals (e.g., your facial expression, your general enthusiasm, your posture and eye contact) should echo that sentiment. You don't want to give your audience conflicting cues. Further, consistency among verbal and nonverbal messages will help you communicate assurance, confidence, and conviction.

Eye Contact   The most important single aspect of bodily communication is eye contact. The two major problems with eye contact are not enough eye contact and eye contact that does not cover the audience fairly. Speakers who do not maintain enough eye contact appear distant, unconcerned, and less trustworthy than speakers who look directly at their audience. And, of course, without eye contact, you will not be able to secure that all-important audience feedback. Maintain eye contact with the entire audience. Communicate equally with the audience members on the left and on the right, in

"Within many cultures around the world, it is believed that the eyes are the windows to the soul. In public speaking, since we usually want to arouse both spirit and soul, the eyes become the most important physical equipment of all."

—ROGER E. AXTELL

both the back and the front of the room. Keep in mind, however, that cultures differ widely on the amount and intensity of eye contact they consider appropriate. In some cultures, eye contact that is too intense may be considered offensive.

Facial Expression   Appropriate facial expressions help you express your concern for the public speaking interaction and will help you communicate your comfort and control of the public speaking situation. Nervousness and anxiety, however, can prevent you from relaxing enough for your positive emotions to come through. Time and practice will allow you to relax, and your feelings will reveal themselves appropriately and automatically.

Gestures and Posture   Spontaneous and natural gestures will help illustrate your verbal messages. If you feel relaxed and comfortable with yourself and your audience, you'll generate natural body action without conscious or studied attention. When delivering your speech, stand straight but not stiffly. Try to communicate your command of the situation rather than any nervousness you may feel. Avoid putting your hands in your pockets or leaning on the desk or chalkboard. Avoid self-manipulation (e.g., playing with your hair or touching your face) and backward leaning which can signal an ill-at-ease feeling.

Movement   If you move too little, you may appear fearful or distant. If you move too much, you may lead the audience to concentrate on the movement itself, wondering where you'll wind up next. Use movement to emphasize transitions and to introduce important assertions. For example, when making a transition, you might step forward to signal that something new is coming. Similarly, use movement to signal an important assumption, bit of evidence, or closely reasoned argument. Walk slowly and deliberately (but not too slowly, of course) to and from the podium. Avoid appearing hurried, as if you want to get your speech over with as soon as possible. Walking more slowly will help you convey an air of control.

USING NOTES

Speakers who prepare their speeches around a series of slides made using one of the presentation software packages (such as PowerPoint or Corel Presentations) may use their slides as their notes. In most public speaking classes, your notes will consist of a delivery outline and your audiovisual aids. Effective delivery depends on the smooth use of notes—whether a series of slides or transparencies or an $8\frac{1}{2} \times 11$ inch piece of paper or an index card or two—during the speech. A few simple guidelines may help you avoid common errors (McCroskey, 1997; Kesselman-Turkel & Peterson, 1982).

- Use only your delivery outline when presenting your speech; never use the preparation outline. One $8\frac{1}{2} \times 11$ inch page and no more than four index cards should be sufficient for most speeches. This aid will relieve anxiety over forgetting your speech but not be extensive enough to prevent meaningful speaker–audience interaction.

- Know your notes intimately. Rehearse at least twice with the same notes you will take to the speaker's stand.

- Use your notes with "open subtlety." Don't make your notes more obvious than necessary, but don't try to hide them. Don't gesture with them, but don't turn away from the audience to steal a glance at them, either. Watch the way television talk show personalities use notes; many of these media hosts provide useful models you might want to imitate.

Critically Evaluating Speeches

Part of your function in learning public speaking is learning to evaluate finished, delivered speeches and to express your evaluations in a clear and constructive way. Let's look first at some of the questions you'll want to consider and then at some suggestions for expressing these evaluations.

Although it's a valuable part of public speaking (and of life in general), listening to criticism is difficult. Here are some suggestions for making listening to criticism easier and more effective.

- *Listen with an open mind.* Encourage critics to share their insights by demonstrating your willingness to listen with an open mind. Don't take criticism too personally; view criticism as objectively as you can.

- *Accept the critic's viewpoint.* If the critic says your evidence wasn't convincing, it doesn't help to identify the 12 references that you used in your speech; this critic simply was not convinced. Instead, think about why your evidence was not convincing to this person.

- *Seek clarification.* If you don't understand the criticism, ask for clarification. If you're told that your specific purpose was too broad, but it's unclear to you how you might improve it, ask the critic how you might narrow the specific purpose.

> *I love criticism just as long as it's unqualified praise.*
>
> —NOEL COWARD
> (1899–1973), English
> playwright, actor,
> composer

QUESTIONS TO CONSIDER

The following questions, which come from topics covered in this chapter and Chapter 11, can serve as a beginning guide to speech evaluation. Use them to check your own speeches as well as to evaluate the speeches of others.

The subject and purpose

1. Is the subject worthwhile? relevant? interesting to the audience and speaker?
2. What is the speech's general purpose: to inform, to persuade?
3. Is the topic narrow enough to be covered in some depth?
4. Is the specific purpose clear to the audience?

The audience

5. Has the speaker considered the culture, age, gender, occupation, income, status, and religion of the audience? How does the speaker take these factors into consideration?
6. Has the speaker considered and adapted to the willingness, favorableness, and knowledge of the audience?

The thesis and major propositions

7. Is the speech's thesis clear and limited to one main idea?
8. Are the speech's main points clearly related to the thesis?
9. Are there an appropriate number of main points in the speech (not too many, not too few)?

Research

10. Is the speech adequately researched? Are the sources reliable and up-to-date?
11. Does the speaker seem to understand the subject thoroughly?

Supporting materials

12. Is each major proposition adequately and appropriately supported?

13. Do the supporting materials amplify what they purport to amplify? Do they prove what they purport to prove?

Organization

14. How is the body of the speech organized? What is the organization pattern?

15. Is the organization pattern appropriate to the speech and to the audience?

Wording

16. Is the language clear, vivid, appropriate, personal, and powerful?

17. Are the sentences short, direct, active, positive, and varied?

The conclusion, introduction, and transitions

18. Does the conclusion effectively summarize and close the speech?

19. Does the introduction gain the audience's attention and provide a clear orientation?

20. Are there adequate transitions?

Delivery

21. Does the speaker maintain eye contact with the audience?

22. Are the volume, rate, and pauses appropriate to the audience, occasion, and topic?

23. Are the body actions (i.e., gesture and eye, face, and body movement) appropriate to the speaker, subject, and audience?

"Anyone can be accurate and even profound, but it is damned hard work to make criticism charming."

—H. L. MENCKEN

EXPRESSING YOUR EVALUATION

The major purpose of classroom evaluation is to improve class members' public speaking technique. Through constructive criticism, you, both as a speaker and as a listener–critic, will more effectively learn the principles of public speaking. You will be shown what you do well and what you can improve.

For all the benefits of evaluation, however, many people resist this process. Speakers often perceive evaluations and suggestions for improvement as personal attacks. Before reading the specific suggestions for expressing criticism, take the self-test, "What's wrong with these comments?" Then consider the suggestions that follow the self-test for offering criticism more effectively.

Test Yourself

What's Wrong with These Comments?

Examine each of the following critical comments. For the purposes of this exercise, assume that each comment represents the critic's complete criticism. What's wrong with each?

❶ I loved the speech. It was great. Really great.

❷ The introduction didn't gain my attention.

❸ You weren't interested in your own topic. How do you expect us to be interested?

④ Nobody was able to understand you.

⑤ The speech was weak.

⑥ The speech didn't do anything for me.

⑦ Your position was unfair to those of us on athletic scholarships; we earned those scholarships.

⑧ I found four things wrong with your speech. First, . . .

⑨ You needed better research.

⑩ I liked the speech; we need more police on campus.

HOW DID YOU DO? Before reading the following discussion, try to explain why each of these statements is ineffective.

WHAT WILL YOU DO? To help improve your criticism, try to restate the basic meaning of each of these comments in a more constructive manner.

Communication Choice Point

Ethical Obligations

You and your best friend are taking this course together. Your friend just gave a pretty terrible speech, and unfortunately, the instructor has asked you to offer a critique. The wrinkle here is that the grade the instructor gives will be heavily influenced by what the student critic says. You'd like to give your friend a positive critique so he can earn a good grade—which he badly needs. *What options do you have as an ethical critic? What would you say?*

Say Something Positive Start any criticism with something positive, e.g., "Your visual aids made the cost comparison so easy for me to see and really convinced me to change brands." Also, use positive comments as a preface to any negative ones. Thus, instead of saying—as in the self-test—"The speech didn't do anything for me," tell the speaker what you liked first and then bring up a weakness and suggest how it might be corrected: "Your introduction really made me realize that many colleges have problems with campus violence, but I wasn't convinced early on that we have one here at Andrews. I would have preferred to hear the examples that you gave near the end of the speech—which were excellent, by the way—in the introduction."

Communicating Ethically

Criticizing Ethically

Just as the speaker and the listener have ethical obligations, so does the critic. As you reflect on these few suggestions, consider any additional guidelines that you would like to see critics of public speaking follow (especially in the classroom).

We are here on earth to do good for others. What the others are here for, I don't know.

—W. H. AUDEN
(1907–1973), British American poet

- First, the ethical critic separates personal feelings about the speaker from his or her evaluation of the speech. The ethical critic transcends his or her own biases and looks at the speech as objectively as possible. A liking for the speaker should not lead the critic to give positive evaluations of the speech, nor should disliking the speaker lead to negative evaluations. Similarly, attitudes toward the speaker's thesis should not get in the way of fair and objective evaluation. The ethical critic recognizes the validity of an argument even if it contradicts a deeply held belief and, at the same time, recognizes the fallaciousness of an argument even if it supports a deeply held belief.

- Second, the ethical critic takes responsibility for his or her own thoughts. The best way to express this ownership is to use I-messages rather than you-messages. Instead of saying, "You needed better research," say, "I would have been more persuaded if you had used more recent research."

- Third, the ethical critic rejects any ethnocentric orientation; the ethical critic doesn't negatively evaluate customs and beliefs simply because they differ from her or his own. The ethical critic does not discriminate against or favor speakers simply because they're of a particular gender, race, affectional orientation, nationality, religion, or age group.

The Public Speaking Sample Assistant

A POORLY CONSTRUCTED PERSUASIVE SPEECH

This speech was written to illustrate some really broad as well as some rather subtle errors that a beginning speaker might make in constructing a persuasive speech. First, read the entire speech without reading any of the questions in the right-hand column. Then, after you've read the entire speech, reread each paragraph and respond to the critical thinking questions. What other questions might it be productive to ask?

XXX HAS GOT TO GO

You probably didn't read the papers this weekend, but there's an XXX movie, I mean video, store that moved in on Broad and Fifth streets. My parents, who are retired teachers, are protesting it, and so am I. My parents are organizing a protest for the next weekend.

There must be hundreds of XXX video stores in the country, and they all need to be closed down. I have a lot of reasons.

First, my parents think it should be closed down. My parents are retired teachers and have organized protests over the proposed new homeless shelter and to prevent the city from making that park on Elm Street. So they know what they're doing.

The XXX video place is un-Godly. No people would ever go there. Our religious leader is against it and is joining in the protest.

These stores bring crime into the neighborhood. I have proof of that. Morristown's crime increased after the XXX video store opened. And in Martinsville, where they got rid of the video store, crime did not increase. If we allow the video store in our own town, then we're going to be like Morristown and our crime is going to increase.

These stores make lots of garbage. The plastic wrappings from the videos will add to our already overextended and overutilized landfill. And a lot of them are going to wind up as litter on the streets.

The XXX Video House stays open seven days a week, 24 hours a day. People will be forced to work at all hours and on Sunday, and that's not fair. And the store will increase the noise level at night with the cars pulling up and all.

The XXX Video House—that's its name, by the way—doesn't carry regular videos that most people want. So why do we want them?

The XXX Video House got a lease from an owner who doesn't even live in the community, someone by the name of, well, it's an organization called XYZ Management. And their address is Carlson Place in Jeffersonville. So they don't even live here.

Critical Thinking Questions

What do you think of the title of the speech?

Visualizing yourself as a listener, how would the opening comment make you feel?

Does the speaker gain your attention?

What thesis do you think the speaker will support?

Does mentioning "my parents" help or hurt the speaker's credibility?

What is the speaker's thesis?

What impression are you beginning to get of the speaker?

How do the speaker's parents sound to you? Do they sound like credible leaders with a consistent cause? Chronic protesters (with perhaps a negative agenda)?

What evidence is offered to support the assertion that you should believe the speaker's parents? Is this adequate?

What would you need to know about these people before believing them?

What does this statement assume about the audience?

How would your public speaking class respond to this statement? What are some reasons why the speaker might not have explained how XXX video stores are un-Godly? How will those in the audience who are not religious react to this statement?

What do you think of the reasoning used here? Are there other factors that could have influenced Morristown's crime increase? Is there any evidence that getting rid of the video store resulted in the stable crime rate in Martinsville? What assumption about the audience does the speaker make in using Martinsville and Morristown as analogies?

Do you agree with the argument about the garbage? Is this argument in any way unique to the video store? Is it likely that people will open the wrappers and drop them on the street?

What validity do you give to each of these arguments? Given the 24-hour policy, how might you construct an argument against the video store? Are there advantages of a neighborhood store's 24-hour policy that the audience may be thinking of and thus countering the speaker's argument? If there are, how should the speaker deal with them?

On hearing this, would you be likely to extend this argument and start asking yourself, "Do we now close up all stores that most people don't want?"

Is there a connection between who the owner is and whether the video store should or should not be closed?

Could the speaker have effectively used this information in support of the thesis to close the video store?

A neighboring store owner says he thinks the store is in violation of several fire laws. He says they have no sprinkler system and no metal doors to prevent the spread of a fire. So he thinks they should be closed down, too.

What credibility do you ascribe to the "neighboring store owner"? Do you begin to wonder whether the speaker would be satisfied if the store were brought up to the fire code laws?

Last week on *Oprah,* three women were on and they were in the XXX movie business and they were all on drugs and had been in jail and they said it all started when they went into the porno business. One woman wanted to be a teacher, another wanted to be a nurse, and the other wanted to be a beautician. If there weren't any XXX video stores, then there wouldn't be a porn business and, you know, pornography is part of organized crime and so if you stop pornography you take a bite out of crime.

What is the cause and what is the effect that the speaker is asserting? How likely is it that the proposed cause actually produced the effect? Might there have been causes other than pornography that might have led these women into drugs?

What credibility do you give to people you see on talk shows? Does credibility vary with the specific talk show?

Do you accept the argument that there would be no pornography business without video stores? What would have to be proved to you for you to accept this connection?

How do you respond to the expression "take a bite out of crime"?

One of the reasons I think it should be closed is that the legitimate video stores—the ones that have only a small selection of XXX movies somewhere in the back—will lose business. And if they continue to lose business, they'll leave the neighborhood and we'll have no video stores.

Is the speaker implying that this is the real reason against XXX video stores?

Do you wonder whether the speaker is against XXX videos—as implied in the previous argument—or just against stores that sell these exclusively? What effect does this impression have on your evaluation of the speaker's credibility and thesis?

That's a lot of reasons against XXX movie houses. I have a quote here: Reason is "a portion of the divine spirit set in a human body." Seneca.

How do you feel about the number of "reasons"? Would you have preferred fewer reasons, more fully developed, or more reasons?

What purpose does this quotation serve?

In conclusion and to wrap it up and close my speech, I want to repeat and say again that XXX video stores should all be closed down. They corrupt minors. And they're offensive to men and women and especially women. I hope you'll all protest with the Marshalls—my mother and father—and there will be lots of others there, too.

Might the speaker have introduced the conclusion differently? Now what is the speaker's thesis?

What do you think of the argument that XXX video stores are offensive? What effect does this argument have coming in the conclusion?

Do you think you'd go to the protest? Why?

Be Specific   Criticism is most effective when it's specific. Statements such as "I thought your delivery was bad" or "I thought your examples were good" (or, as in the self-test, "I loved the speech. . . . Really great" and "The speech was weak") are poorly expressed evaluations. These statements don't specify what the speaker might do to improve delivery or to capitalize on the examples used. When commenting, refer to specifics such as the evidence used, the language choices, the delivery style, or whatever else is of consequence, as in "I thought that more recent examples of arson would have made the need for new legislation more convincing" or "Your opening story really got me involved and totally on your side."

Communication Choice Point

Criticizing a Speech

A student has just given a speech on the glory of bullfighting, something you define as animal cruelty. To the speaker, however, bullfighting is an important part of her culture. As you bristle inside, the instructor asks you to critique the speech. *What are your obligations here (to your own beliefs and to the objectivity of ethical criticism)? What might you say?*

Be Culturally Sensitive   There are vast cultural differences in what is considered proper when it comes to criticism. In some cultures, being kind to the person is more important than telling the truth, so members may say things that are complimentary but untrue in a logical sense. In contrast, people in cultures that are highly individualistic and competitive (the United States, Germany, and Sweden are examples) may see public criticism as a normal part of the learning process. Thus, people in these cultures may readily criticize others and are likely to expect the same "courtesy" from other listeners. People from cultures that are more collectivist and that emphasize the group rather than the individual (Japan, Mexico, and Korea are examples) are likely to find giving and receiving public criticism uncomfortable. They may feel that it's more important to be polite and courteous than to help someone learn a skill.

The difficulties are compounded when you interpret unexpected behavior through your own cultural filters. For example, if a speaker who expects comments and criticism gets none, he or she may interpret the silence to mean that the audience didn't care or wasn't listening. But they may have been listening very intently and simply operating according to a different cultural rule, a rule that says it's impolite to criticize or evaluate another person's work, especially in public.

Limit Criticism   Cataloging a speaker's weak points, as in "I found four things wrong with your speech," will overwhelm, not help, the speaker. If you're one of many critics, chances are that others will bring up the same criticisms you noted, so you can feel comfortable limiting your criticism to one or perhaps two points. You might say, for example, "The one thing I would change is your opening quotation; it was interesting but a bit long and somewhat difficult to follow. I think if you had paraphrased the idea, it would have had a greater impact." If you're the sole critic, then you'll want to evaluate the entire speech.

Be Constructive   Give the speaker the insight that you feel will help in future public speaking situations. For example, "The introduction didn't gain my attention" doesn't tell the speaker how he or she might have gained your attention. Instead, you might say, "The example about the computer crash would have more effectively gained my attention in the introduction."

Focus on Behavior   Focus criticism on what the speaker said and did during the actual speech. Try to avoid mind-reading the speaker, assuming that you know *why* the speaker did one thing rather than another. Instead of saying, "You weren't interested in your topic" (a comment that attacks the speaker), say, "I would have liked to see greater variety in your delivery. It would have made me feel you were more interested."

Communication Choice Point

Responding to Criticism

You've just given a speech you thought was pretty good. Yet your audience looked bored, and during the criticism period one person says, "Your speech didn't hold my attention. I was bored. You really should have prepared more." In truth you put a great deal of time into this speech, and you know you incorporated just about every attention-gaining device imaginable. *How do you respond?*

Summary of Concepts and Skills

This chapter looked at the last four steps in the public speaking process: wording the speech, constructing the conclusion and the introduction, rehearsing, and delivering the speech.

1. Compared with written style, oral style contains shorter, simpler, and more familiar words; greater qualification; and more self-referential terms.

2. Effective public speaking style is clear (economical and specific; uses guide phrases and short, familiar, and commonly used terms); vivid (uses active verbs, strong verbs, figures of speech, and imagery); appropriate to your audience (on a suitable level of formality; avoids written-style expressions; avoids slang, vulgar, and offensive terms); personal (uses personal pronouns, asks questions, and creates immediacy); and powerful (avoids hesitations and disqualifiers, for example).

3. Effective sentences for public speeches are generally short, direct, active, positively phrased, and varied in type.

4. Conclusions summarize and close the speech. Introductions gain attention and orient the audience as to what is to follow.

5. Transitions and internal summaries help connect the parts of the speech and help the listeners better remember the speech.

6. Preparation, template, and delivery outlines all serve different functions and will help any speaker, but especially the beginning speaker, in preparing and presenting effective public speeches.

7. There are three basic methods of delivering a public speech. The impromptu method involves speaking without any specific preparation. The manuscript method involves writing out the entire speech and reading it to the audience. The extemporaneous method involves thorough preparation and memorizing the main ideas and their order of appearance, but not a commitment to exact wording.

8. Use rehearsal to time and perfect your speech from beginning to end; rehearse under realistic conditions and with listeners if possible.

9. When you deliver your speech, regulate your voice for greatest effectiveness. For example, adjust your volume on the basis of the distance between you and your audience and

the emphasis you wish to give certain ideas. Adjust your rate on the basis of time constraints, the speech's content, and the listening conditions.

10. Avoid the major problems of articulation and pronunciation; errors of omission, substitution, addition, and accent.

11. Use unfilled pauses to signal a transition between the major parts of the speech, to allow the audience time to think, to allow the audience to ponder a rhetorical question, and to signal the approach of a particularly important idea. Avoid filled pauses; they weaken your message.

12. Effective body action involves maintaining eye contact with your entire audience, allowing your facial expressions to convey your feelings, using your posture to communicate command of the public speaking interaction, gesturing naturally, and moving around a bit.

13. When expressing critical evaluations, try to say something positive, be specific, be objective, limit your criticism, be constructive, focus on behavior, own your own criticism, and be culturally sensitive.

This chapter stressed several significant skills for style and delivery. Place a check mark next to those skills you most want to work on.

_____ 1. I word my speech so it's clear, vivid, appropriate, and personal.

_____ 2. I construct sentences that are short, direct, active, and positive, and I vary the type and length of sentences.

_____ 3. I construct conclusions that summarize the major ideas of the speech and bring the speech to a crisp close.

_____ 4. I construct introductions that gain attention and preview what is to follow.

_____ 5. I use transitions and internal summaries to connect the parts of the speech and to help listeners remember what I say.

_____ 6. In general, I use the extemporaneous method of delivery.

_____ 7. I rehearse my speech often, perfect my delivery, rehearse the speech as a whole, time the speech at each rehearsal, approximate the specific speech situation as much as possible, see and think of myself as a public speaker, and incorporate any delivery notes that may be of value during the actual speech presentation.

_____ 8. I vary my vocal volume and rate to best reflect and reinforce my verbal messages and avoid the common problems with volume and rate.

_____ 9. I avoid the articulation and pronunciation errors of omission, substitution, addition, accent, and pronouncing sounds that should be silent.

_____ 10. I use pauses to signal transitions, to allow listeners time to think, and to signal the approach of a significant idea.

_____ 11. During the speech delivery I maintain eye contact with the entire audience, allow my facial expressions to convey my feelings, gesture naturally, and incorporate purposeful body movements.

_____ 12. When expressing critical evaluations of the speeches of others, I try to say something positive, be specific, be objective, be constructive, be culturally sensitive, and own my own responses.

 Key Word Quiz

The Language of Public Speaking Preparation

Match the terms about public speaking preparation with their definitions. Record the number of the definition next to the appropriate term.

_____ a. impromptu speech (252)

_____ b. powerless forms of language (242)

_____ c. internal summary (247)

_____ d. extemporaneous speech (253)

_____ e. written-style expressions (242)

_____ f. transitions (246)

_____ g. rhetorical question (241)

_____ h. idiom (240)

1. An expression that is unique to specific language and whose meaning cannot be deduced from the individual words.

2. Words, phrases, or sentences that connect the various parts of the speech and guide the listeners to focus on your next argument or idea.

3. A question whose answer is obvious and is used to make a statement.

4. Speech made off-the-cuff, without preparation.

5. The production of words resulting from movements of the speech organs.

6. Faults such as hesitations, disqualifiers, and self-critical statements.

7. A statement that recaps what you've discussed so far.

_____ i. articulation (254)

_____ j. simile (241)

8. A speech that is thoroughly prepared and organized in detail but in which only certain aspects of style are predetermined.

9. A figure of speech that compares two unlike objects, using words such as _like_ or _as_.

10. Expressions such as "the former" and "the above."

These ten terms and additional terms used in this chapter can be found in the glossary and on flashcards on MyCommunicationLab (**www.mycommunicationlab.com**).

MyCommunicationLab

PEARSON mycommunicationlab

www.mycommunicationlab.com

Visit MyCommunicationLab (**www.mycommunicationlab.com**) for additional information on public speaking preparation. Flash cards, videos, skill building exercises, sample text questions, and additional examples and discussions will help you continue your study of public speaking. This site also contains a variety of template outlines for different types of informative and persuasive speeches. Also visit Pearson's public speaking website (**www.abpublicspeaking.com**) for additional guidance in preparing your introductions and conclusions.

13 The Informative Speech

Why read this chapter?

Because you'll learn about:
- the ways in which information is communicated most effectively from speaker to audience
- the varied types of informative speeches

Because you'll learn to:
- apply the principles of communicating information to a variety of informative speeches
- develop a variety of informative speeches
- use presentation software with maximum effectiveness

*T*his chapter covers speeches of information, through which you tell your listeners something they didn't already know, and the next chapter covers speeches of persuasion, through which you change your listeners' attitudes or beliefs or get them to do something. (Chapter-length coverage of a third kind of speech, the "special occasion speech," may be found at MyCommunicationLab [www.mycommunciationlab.com]). Before beginning your journey into these types of speeches—or after giving your next speech—you may want to examine your own satisfaction as a public speaker by taking the self-test "How satisfying is your public speaking?"

Test Yourself

How Satisfying Is Your Public Speaking?

Respond to each of the following statements by recording the number best that represents your feelings after making a recent speech, using this scale:

1 = strongly agree; **2** = moderately agree; **3** = slightly agree; **4** = neutral; **5** = slightly disagree; **6** = moderately disagree; and **7** = strongly disagree

_____ ❶ The audience let me know that I was speaking effectively.

_____ ❷ My speech accomplished nothing.

_____ ❸ I would like to give another speech like this one.

_____ ❹ The audience genuinely wanted to get to know me.

_____ ❺ I was very dissatisfied with my speech.

_____ ❻ I was very satisfied with the speech.

_____ ❼ The audience seemed very interested in what I had to say.

_____ ❽ I did not enjoy the public speaking experience.

_____ ❾ The audience did not seem supportive of what I was saying.

_____ ❿ The speech flowed smoothly.

HOW DID YOU DO? To compute your score, follow these steps:

1. Add the scores for items 1, 3, 4, 6, 7, and 10.
2. Reverse the scores for items 2, 5, 8, and 9 so that 7 becomes 1, 6 becomes 2, 5 becomes 3, 4 remains 4, 3 becomes 5, 2 becomes 6, and 1 becomes 7.
3. Add up the reversed scores for items 2, 5, 8, and 9.
4. Add the totals from steps 1 and 3 to yield your communication satisfaction score.

You may interpret your score along the following scale:

10	20	30	40	50	60	70
Extremely Satisfying	Quite Satisfying	Fairly Satisfying	Average	Fairly Unsatisfying	Quite Unsatisfying	Extremely Unsatisfying

How accurately do you think this scale captures your public speaking satisfaction?

WHAT WILL YOU DO? As you become a more successful and effective public speaker, your satisfaction is likely to increase. What else can you do to increase your satisfaction?

Source: This test was adapted for public speaking on the basis of the conversational satisfaction test developed by Michael Hecht, "The Conceptualization and Measurement of Interpersonal Communication Satisfaction," 1978, *Human Communication Research, 4,* pp. 253–264. Used with permission.

Guidelines for Informative Speaking

To communicate information is to tell your listeners something they don't know, something new. You can inform your audience about a new way of looking at old things or an old way of looking at new things. You may discuss a theory not previously heard of or a familiar concept not fully understood. You may talk about events that the audience may be unaware of or explain happenings they may have misconceptions about. Regardless of what type of informative speech you intend to give, the following guidelines should help.

CENTER INFORMATION ON THE AUDIENCE

The information you communicate in your informative speech should center around and focus on the audience's needs and interests. The audience should want to hear what you have to say. Somewhere early in your speech, answer the audience's unspoken questions: Why should I listen? Why should I care about this information? In your speech, for example, you might stress that what you have to say will save the audience money or time, will help them understand the current financial market, or will enable them to make themselves more attractive. In this way you'll capture and hold your audience's attention by showing them that the information you have is relevant and useful to their goals and interests.

LIMIT THE AMOUNT OF INFORMATION

There's a limit to the amount of information that a listener can take in at one time. Resist the temptation to overload your listeners. Instead of enlarging the breadth of information you communicate, expand its depth. It's better to present two new items of information and explain these in depth, with examples, illustrations, and descriptions, than to present five items without this needed amplification. The speaker who attempts to discuss the physiological, psychological, social, and linguistic differences between men and women, for example, is clearly trying to cover too much and is going to be forced to cover each area only superficially. Instead, select one subdivision of one area—say, language development or differences in language problems—and develop that in depth. Use the techniques for limiting a topic covered in Chapter 11.

ADJUST THE INFORMATION'S LEVEL OF COMPLEXITY

As you know from attending college classes, information can be presented in very simple or very complex form. The level of complexity of the information you communicate should depend on the wide variety of factors considered throughout this book: the level of knowledge your audience has, the time you have available, the purpose you hope to achieve, the topic on which you're speaking, and so on. If you simplify a topic too much, you risk boring or, even worse, insulting your audience; if your talk is too complex, you risk confusing your audience and failing to communicate your message. In your beginning speeches at least, try to keep it simple. Make sure the words you use are familiar to your audience and that you explain clearly any unfamiliar terms.

RELATE NEW INFORMATION TO OLD

Listeners will learn information more easily and retain it longer when you relate it to what they already know. Relate the new to the old, the unfamiliar to the familiar, the unseen to the seen, the untasted to the tasted. Here, for example, Teresa Jacob, a student from Ohio State University (Schnoor, 1997, p. 97), relates the problems of drug interactions (i.e., the new) to the dangers of mixing chemicals in the school lab (i.e., the old or familiar).

> During our high school years, most of us learned in a chemistry class the danger of mixing harmless chemicals in lab. Add one drop of the wrong compound, and suddenly

Communication Choice Point

Unexpected Events

You're going to speak on the new version of Microsoft Windows, which you've used for the past few weeks. Unfortunately, the speaker before you turns out to be a Microsoft program designer and gives a speech on exactly your topic. *If you feel it would be necessary to say something, what are some of your options? What would you say?*

you've created a stink bomb, or worse, an explosion. Millions of Americans run the same risk inside their bodies each day by combining drugs that are supposed to help restore or maintain good health.

MAKE THE INFORMATION EASY TO REMEMBER

The principles of public speaking (of language, delivery, and supporting materials, for example) will all help your listeners remember your speech. Here are a few additional suggestions.

- *Repeat or restate important points.* Help your audience to remember what you want them to remember.

- *Use guide phrases.* Guide your audience's attention to your most important points by saying, for example, "The first point to remember is that . . ."

- *Use internal summary transitions.* These will remind the audience of what you have said and how it relates to what is to follow.

- *Pattern your messages.* If the audience can see the logic of the organization of your speech, they'll be better able to organize (and remember) what you say in their own minds.

- *Focus audience attention.* The best way to focus the listeners' attention is to tell them to focus their attention. Simply say, "I want you to focus on three points that I'll make in this speech. First, . . . " or "What I want you to remember is this: . . . "

Supporting Materials

In constructing your speech you'll want to use a variety of what are called supporting materials—numerical data and illustrations, for example. These supporting materials serve a variety of functions and will help you clarify and explain ideas; make ideas vivid, interesting, and attention getting; and reinforce your ideas so that they are remembered.

In selecting appropriate supporting materials, keep in mind the nature of your audience. Select materials that are appropriate to their educational and age levels and their interests, for example. Also, select materials with cultural sensitivity. Using examples from only one religion (say your own) when a variety of religious beliefs would be more appropriate and relevant is likely to distance your audience rather than draw them to you.

"He or she is greatest who contributes the greatest original practical example."

—WALT WHITMAN

Here we look at some major material types in detail (e.g., examples, illustrations, and narratives; testimony; numerical data; and definitions) and at some additional forms in brief.

EXAMPLES, ILLUSTRATIONS, AND NARRATIVES

Examples, illustrations, and narratives are specific instances that help you explain your ideas. An *example* is a relatively brief specific instance (e.g., "Pat's on the varsity and has a 4.0"). An *illustration* is a longer and more detailed example (e.g., "Pat has always been an athlete but at the same time has always maintained an outstanding academic record, and there are many others on the varsity that have been both athletes and scholars, effectively destroying the stereotype of the dumb jock"). A *narrative* is longer still and presented in the form of an anecdote or short story. The parables in many religious works are good examples of narratives used to illustrate a general principle.

Examples, illustrations, and narratives may be factual or imaginary. Thus, in explaining friendship, you might tell about an actual friend's behavior, or you might formulate a composite, ideal friend and describe how this person would act in a particular situation. In using these forms of support, be sure to include only those details that are needed to help your audience understand the point you're making. Don't clutter up an otherwise pointed example with unnecessary details. Also, because it is the example, illustration, or narrative that listeners will remember most clearly, be sure to connect this very explicitly to the proposition in your speech.

For example, in a speech on unfair sentencing practices, student Jillian Collum provided a particularly dramatic illustration. After stating that a man was sentenced to 55 years in prison under the federal mandatory minimum sentencing laws for selling marijuana, she said:

> The sentencing brief noted that if Angelos had provided weapons to a terrorist organization, hijacked an aircraft, committed second-degree murder, and raped a 10-year-old child he would have received a lower combined sentence than he got for selling about $1,000 worth of marijuana.

TESTIMONY

Testimony may consist of experts' opinions or of witnesses' accounts. Testimony supports your ideas by adding a note of authority. You might, for example, cite an economist's predictions concerning the size of the deficit or the growth rate of the economy. Or you might discuss an art critic's evaluation of a painting or an art movement. You might also consider using an eyewitness's testimony. You might, for example, cite the testimony of an eyewitness to an accident, an inmate who spent two years in a maximum-security prison, or a patient who underwent an operation.

In presenting the testimony, stress the person's credibility. When you cite an authority, make sure the person is in fact an authority. Tell the audience who the authority is, and state the basis for the individual's expertise. The testimony will be much more effective when your audience is convinced that this person is worth listening to.

Here, for example, is how student Ashley Hatcher established the credibility of her testimony:

> As the 2005 book *The Structure of the Innate Mind* states, the answer may lie in Homicide Adaptation Theory, the conclusion of an unprecedented six-year study conducted by leading evolutionary psychologists David Buss and Joshua Duntley from the University of Texas.

Communication Choice Point

Testimony

You want to present the testimony of a retired judge to explain the problems that probation causes. *For your purposes, what would be the ideal qualifications of this judge? How might you weave these qualifications into your speech? What are some of the things you might say?*

If you were presenting someone's testimony on one of these issues, how would you establish the person's qualifications so that your audience would accept what he or she said?

Testimony is likely to be more effective if you establish the person's qualifications to the audience's satisfaction.

- Nutritionist on proper diet
- Real estate agent on the advantages and disadvantages of condos and co-ops
- Psychiatrist on the nature of bipolar disorder
- Biologist on how to feed your pet
- Drama teacher on how to write a play

NUMERICAL DATA

Numerical data are useful for supporting a wide variety of statements. For example, if you want to show that significant numbers of people now get their news from the Internet, you could give the total number of online users for each of the last 10 years and compare that with the numbers of newspaper readers and television news viewers in those same years. These data would then allow you to show that the number of people who get their news from the Internet is increasing while the number of those getting the news from papers and television is declining. Or, you might compare the percentage of a tuition increase at your school to the national average or to the rate of inflation. To illustrate the growth of instant messaging or social networking as a means of communication, you might note the percentage that usage has grown in each of the last five years.

In using numerical data of any kind, consider these suggestions:

- Make sure the numbers are clear, remembering that your audience will hear the figures only once. Round off figures so they're easy to comprehend and retain.

- Make explicit the meaning of the numbers. For example, if you state that the average home health aide makes less than $30,000 a year, you need to compare this figure to the salaries of other workers and to your proposition that salaries need to be increased.

- Reinforce your oral presentation of numerical data with some type of presentation aid—perhaps a slide or a chart. Numbers presented without some kind of visual reinforcement are difficult to grasp and remember.

- Use numbers in moderation. Most listeners' capacity for numerical data presented in a speech is limited, so use figures sparingly.

- Use only reliable and current numerical data and make sure that your audience is aware of their reliability and currency.

DEFINITIONS

Definitions, essentially explanations of terms and concepts that may not be familiar to your listeners, may be useful as a form of support in many types of speeches. Here are several types of definitions you might use.

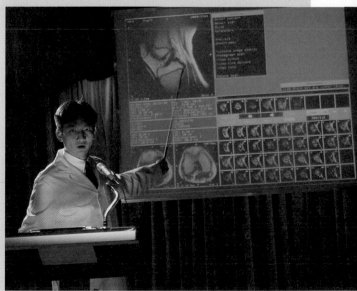

"The beginning of wisdom is the definition of terms."

—SOCRATES

Skill Development Experience

Supporting Statements

Often it's the vivid example or alarming statistic that your listeners will remember most; give your supporting materials concentrated attention.

Select one of these overly broad statements and support it, using at least three different types of supporting material. Because the purpose of this exercise is to provide greater insight into supporting materials, in this case you may invent facts, figures, illustrations, examples, and the like.

1. Immigrants contribute significantly to the U.S. economy.
2. The author of this essay is a real authority.
3. People in their 80s and older have contributed greatly to society.
4. Candidate Williams cares for people.

Define by Etymology   One way to define a term is to trace its historical or linguistic development, or *etymology*. In defining the word *communication*, for example, you might note that it comes from the Latin *communis* meaning "common"; in "communicating" you seek to establish a commonness, a sameness, a similarity with another individual.

Define by Authority   You often can clarify a term by explaining how a particular *authority* views it. For example, you might define "inflation" by citing the definition of a noted economist or define "metal fatigue" in the words of a respected engineer.

Define by Negation   You also might define a term by noting what the term is not, that is, by *negation*, for example, "A teacher isn't someone who teaches you what to learn but rather one who teaches you how to learn."

Define by Direct Symbolization   You also might define a term by direct *symbolization*—by showing the actual thing or a picture or model of it. For example, a speech on magazine layout or types of fabrics might include actual layout pages or fabric samples.

Define by Operations   Definition by *operations* (called an *operational definition*) involves describing how you would construct the object. For example, in defining a chocolate cake, you could tell how to bake a cake.

ADDITIONAL FORMS OF SUPPORT

Other useful forms of support include quotations, comparisons and contrasts, statement of facts, and repetition.

- *Quotations*, verbatim reproductions of what someone else has said, often add spice and wit as well as authority to your speeches. Quotations work best when they're short, easily comprehended, and easily remembered. Most important, connect the quotations directly to the point you're making and do so as smoothly as possible (avoid the too-often-used "I have a quote . . . ").

- *Comparisons and contrasts* clarify the similarities and differences between two ideas, events, or concepts. Focus on major similarities and differences; avoid itemizing all possible ones. Consider using a presentation aid that visualizes the most crucial information.

- *Statements of fact or a series of facts* often help to illustrate and support a statement for position. Make sure you clearly link the facts to your main points. State the connections when introducing the facts and perhaps again after you've finished identifying the list of facts.

One interesting approach to ethics that has particular relevance to public speaking is Karl Wallace's "Ethical Basis of Communication" (1955; see also Johannesen, Valde, & Whedbee, 2007). Wallace suggested four principles or guidelines. As you reflect on these four principles, consider if there are other guidelines about speaking ethics that should be considered.

- The ethical speaker has a thorough knowledge of the topic, an ability to answer relevant questions, and an awareness of the significant facts and opinions bearing on the topic.
- The ethical speaker presents both facts and opinions fairly, without bending or spinning them to personal advantage; the listener makes the final decision.
- The ethical speaker reveals the sources of cited facts and opinions and helps listeners evaluate any biases and prejudices in the sources.
- The ethical speaker acknowledges and respects opposing arguments and evidence and avoids hiding valid opposing arguments from the audience.

> *Never let your sense of morals get in the way of doing what's right.*
>
> —ISAAC ASIMOV
> (1920–1992), Russian American professor and author

- *Repetition* (i.e., repeating ideas in the same words at strategic places during the speech) and *restatement* (i.e., repeating ideas in different words) add clarity and emphasis and will help compensate for the audience's inevitable lapses in attention. Here is an example from President Barak Obama's address to a joint session of Congress as reported in *The New York Times* (February 25, 2009, p. A16):

> If your family earns less than $250,000 a year, you will not see your taxes increased a single dime. I repeat: not one single dime. In fact, the recovery plan provides a tax cut—that's right, a tax cut—for 95 percent of working families.

Presentation Aids

Presentation aids—visual or auditory means for clarifying ideas—are really a form of supporting material. But because they're so important in public speaking today, because they're so numerous and varied, and because technology has provided a wealth of alternatives and some pretty sophisticated techniques, we'll look at presentation aids separately here and will consider them in detail.

As you plan any type of speech, consider using some kind of presentation aid. Ask yourself how you can visually present what you want your audience to remember. For example, if you want your audience to see the growing impact of the sales tax, consider showing them a chart of rising sales taxes over the last 10 years. Of course, you can deliver your entire speech supplemented by projected slides—using PowerPoint, for example.

TYPES OF PRESENTATION AIDS

Among the presentation aids you have available are the object itself or models of the object, graphs, word charts, maps, people, and photographs and illustrations.

The Object Itself   As a general rule (to which there are many exceptions), the best presentation aid is the object itself. Bring it to your speech if you can. Notice that infomercials sell their products not only by talking about them but by showing them to potential buyers. You see the jewelry, the clothing, the new mop from a wide variety of angles and in varied settings.

Models Models—replicas of the actual object—are useful for a variety of purposes. For example, if you wanted to explain complex structures such as the human hearing or vocal mechanisms, the brain, or the structure of DNA, a model would prove useful. Models help to clarify relative size and position, as well as how each part interacts with each other part.

Graphs Graphs are useful for showing differences over time, clarifying how a whole is divided into parts, and comparing different amounts or sizes. Figure 13.1 shows various types of graphs that can be drawn freehand or generated with the graphics capabilities of most word processing or presentation software. Keep your graphs as simple as possible. In a pie chart or bar graph, for example, limit the number of items to five or fewer. As in the graphs in Figure 13.1, be sure you add the legend, the labels, and the numerical values you wish to emphasize.

Word Chart Word charts (which also can contain numbers and graphics) are useful for identifying the key points of one of your propositions or of your entire speech in the order in which you cover them. Figure 13.2 is a good example of a simple word chart that identifies the major topics discussed in the speech. Alternatively, you could use a word chart to clarify relationships among roles in an organization or to identify the steps in a process, such as the stages of language acquisition or of setting up TIVO or steps to take for dealing with sexual harassment (Figures 13.3 and 13.4). Another use of charts is to show information you want your audience to write down, for example, emergency phone numbers, addresses, titles of recommended books, and URLs.

Maps If you want to illustrate the locations of geographic features such as cities, lakes, rivers, or mountain ranges, obviously maps will be useful presentation aids. Maps can be used also for illustrating, for example, population densities, immigration patterns, world literacy rates, varied economic conditions, the spread of diseases, and hundreds of other issues you may wish to examine in your speeches.

People If you want to demonstrate the muscles of the body, different voice patterns, skin complexions, or hairstyles, consider using people as your aids. Aside from the obvious assistance people provide in demonstrating their own personal traits, their presence helps to secure and maintain the attention and interest of the audience.

Photographs and Illustrations Types of trees, styles of art, kinds of exercise machines, and the horrors of war—all can be made more meaningful with photographs and illustrations. The best way to use these images is to convert them to slides so you'll be able to project them in a format large enough for everyone to see clearly. You'll also be able to point to specific parts of the photos as you explain the devastation of war or the fine art of combining colors and textures.

Another way to use photographs and illustrations is to have them printed in a size large enough for the entire audience to see. Try to mount these on cardboard so they'll be easier to handle. Passing pictures around the room is generally a bad idea; listeners will wait for the pictures to circulate to them, wonder what the pictures contain, and miss a great deal of your speech in the interim.

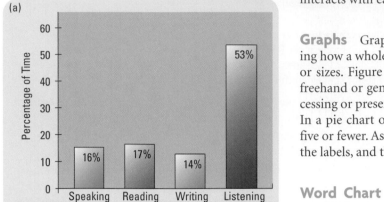

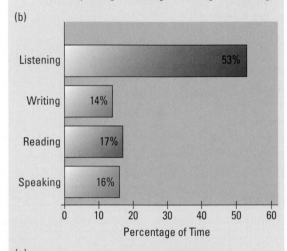

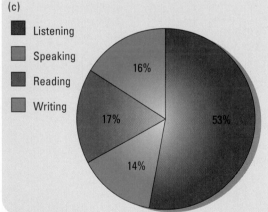

FIGURE 13.1 **Three Graphs**

These three graphs illustrate data from a study on the amount of time people spend on each of the four communication activities (Barker, Edwards, Gaines, Gladney, & Holley, 1980). All three of these graphs are useful for illustrating comparisons. These are only three types of graphs that are easily constructed using the graphics software integrated with most word processing packages or, of course, with the more sophisticated graphics programs.

THE MEDIA OF PRESENTATION AIDS

Once you've decided on the type of presentation aid you'll use, you need to decide on the medium you'll use to present it. Acquire skill in using both low-tech (e.g., the chalkboard or flip chart) and high-tech (e.g., the computerized slide show) resources. In this way you'll be able to select your presentation aids from the wide array available, choosing on the basis of the message you want to communicate and the audience to whom you'll be speaking.

Chalkboards The easiest aid to use, though not necessarily the most effective, is the chalkboard. The chalkboard may be used effectively to record key terms or important numerical data. Don't use it when you can present the same information with a preplanned chart or model. It takes too long to write out anything substantial. If you do write on the board, be careful not to turn your back to the audience, even briefly.

Chartboards Chartboards are useful when you have one or two relatively simple graphs or charts that you want to display during your speech. If you want to display them for several minutes, be sure you have a way of holding them up. For example, bring masking tape if you intend to secure them to the chalkboard, or enlist the aid of an audience member to hold them.

Flip Charts Flip charts—large pads of paper (usually about 24 × 24 inches) mounted on a stand or easel—can be used to record a variety of information that you then reveal by flipping the pages as you deliver your speech. For example, if you were to discuss the various departments in an organization, you might have the key points relating to each department on a separate page of your flip chart, advertising on one page, personnel on another, and so on.

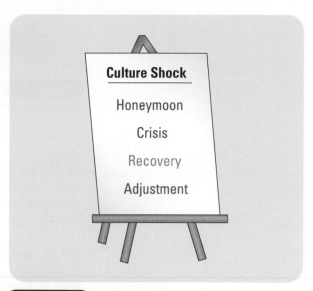

FIGURE 13.2   **Word Chart**

The relative value of this chart and, in fact, of any visual aid depends on the effect it has on the audience.

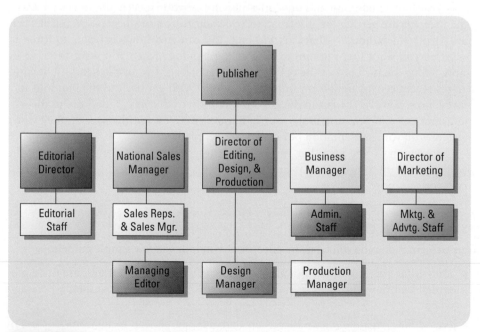

FIGURE 13.3   **An Organizational Chart**

Organizational charts can easily be constructed using the table function on most word processors and then enlarged for an entire audience to see. This figure was constructed in Illustrator.

FIGURE 13.4 **A Flowchart**

This chart identifies the stages a child goes through in learning language. Flowcharts are often useful to guide the audience through the entire speech—each section of the chart might represent a main point of your speech.

Slides and Transparencies   Slides and transparencies are helpful in showing a series of visuals that may be of different types: for example, photographs, illustrations, charts, or tables. The slides can easily be created with many of the popular computer programs (discussed later in the section "Computer-Assisted Presentations," p. 278).

Audio and Videotapes, CDs, and DVDs   Consider the value of using music or recorded speech to support your ideas—and also to add a note of variety that will set your speeches apart from most other speakers' presentations. A speech on advertising jingles, music styles, or dialects would be greatly helped by having actual samples for the audience to hear. Similarly, videos can serve a variety of purposes in public speaking. You might tape a scene relevant to your speech topic from a film or television show and show it at the appropriate time in your speech. Or you might create your own video with a simple camcorder. Videos are best used in small doses; in most instances excerpts of only 20 or 30 seconds will be sufficient to illustrate your point.

Handouts   Handouts—printed materials that you distribute to the audience—are especially helpful when you wish to explain complex material and/or to provide listeners with a permanent record of some aspect of your speech. Handouts encourage listeners to take notes which keeps them actively involved in your presentation. A variety of handouts can be easily prepared with many of the computer presentation packages that we'll consider in the last section of this chapter.

If you distribute your handouts during your speech, you run the risk of your listeners' reading the handout and not concentrating on your speech. On the other hand, if the listeners are getting the information you want to communicate—even if it's primarily from the handout—that isn't too bad. You can encourage listeners to listen to you when you want them to and to look at the handout when you want them to by simply telling them, "Look at the graph on the top of page two of the handout; it summarizes recent census figures on immigration," or "We'll get back to the handout in a minute; now, however, I want to direct your attention to this next slide" (or "to the second argument"). If you distribute your handouts at the end of the speech, they won't interfere with your presentation but may never get read.

Once you have the idea that you want to present with an aid and you know the medium you want to use, direct your attention to preparing and using the aid so it best serves your purpose.

USING PRESENTATION AIDS

Your presentation aids will be more effective if you follow a few simple guidelines.

- *Know your aids intimately.* Be sure you know in what order your aids are to be presented and how you plan to introduce them. Know exactly what goes where and when.

- *Pretest the presentation aids.* Be certain that aids can be seen easily from all parts of the room.

- *Rehearse your speech with the presentation aids.* Do all your rehearsal with your presentation aids so that you'll be able to use them smoothly and effectively.

- *Integrate presentation aids into your speech seamlessly.* Just as a verbal example should flow naturally into the text so should a presentation aid. The aid should appear to be an essential part of the speech.

- *Avoid talking to your aids.* Know your aids so well that you can point to what you want without breaking eye contact with your audience.

- *Use your aids only when they're relevant.* Show each aid when you want the audience to concentrate on it; then remove it. If you don't, the audience's attention may remain focused on the visual when you want them to focus on your next assertion.

COMPUTER-ASSISTED PRESENTATIONS

Computer-assisted presentations possess all of the advantages of aids already noted (e.g., maintaining interest and attention, adding clarity, and reinforcing your message). In addition, however, they have advantages all their own—so many, in fact, that you'll want to seriously consider using this technology in your speeches. They give your speech a professional, up-to-date look, and in the process add to your credibility. They show that you're prepared and that you care about your topic and audience.

Various presentation software packages are available. Figure 13.5 illustrates how a set of slides might look. The slides are built around the "culture shock" speech outline discussed in Chapter 12 and were constructed in PowerPoint. As you review this figure, try to visualize how you'd use a slide show to present your next speech.

Ways of Using Presentation Software Presentation software enables you to produce a variety of aids. For example, you can design your slides on your computer and then print 35 mm slides from a disk. You could do this with your own slide printer, or you could send the files out (via email) to a lab specializing in converting electronic files into 35 mm slides. You may have access to a slide printer at your school, so check there first. Your local office supply store or photocopy shop also may offer these services.

Another option is to create your slides and then show them on your computer screen. If you're speaking to a very small group, it may be possible to have your listeners gather around your computer as you speak. With larger audiences, you'll need a computer projector, or LCD projection panel. Assuming there is a properly equipped computer in the room where you'll be speaking, you can copy your entire presentation to a flash drive or disk and bring it with you the day of your speech.

Computer presentation software also enables you to print out a variety of materials to use as handouts: slides, slides with speaker's notes, slides with room for listener notes, and outlines of your speech. You can print out your complete set of slides to distribute to your listeners, or you can print out a selection of slides from the talk or even slides that you didn't have time to cover in your speech but would like your audience to look at later.

Another useful option is to print out your slides with speaker's notes for your own use. That way you'll have your slides and any notes you may find useful—examples you want to use, numerical data that would be difficult to memorize, quotations that you want to read to your audience, or delivery notes. A sample printout showing a slide plus speaker's notes is provided in Figure 13.6.

Rehearsing with Presentation Programs Presentation packages are especially helpful in enabling you to rehearse your speech and time it precisely. As you rehearse, the computer program records the time you spend on each slide and will display that time under each slide; it will also record the presentation's total time. You can see these times at the bottom of each slide in a variety of views, but they won't appear in the slides the audience sees or in a printed handout such as the one in Figure 13.5. You can use these times to program each slide to run automatically, or you can use the times to see if you're devoting the desired amount of time to each of your ideas. If you find in your rehearsal that your speech is too long, these times can help you see which parts could be shortened.

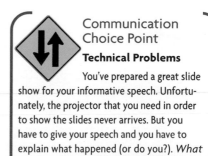

Communication Choice Point

Technical Problems

You've prepared a great slide show for your informative speech. Unfortunately, the projector that you need in order to show the slides never arrives. But you have to give your speech and you have to explain what happened (or do you?). *What are your options for dealing with this unexpected problem? What would you say?*

Slide 1

Speech title

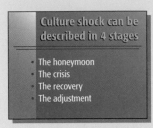

This first slide introduces the topic with the title of the speech. Follow the general rules for titling your speech: Keep it short, provocative, and focused on your audience. If you put a graphic on this page, make sure that it doesn't detract from your title. What other graphics might work well here?

Slide 2

The thesis of the speech

You may or may not want to identify your thesis directly right at the beginning of your speech. Consider the arguments for and against identifying your thesis—both cultural and strategic—and the suggestions for when and how to state the thesis. As a listener, do you prefer it when speakers state their thesis right at the beginning or do you prefer it when the thesis is only implied and left for you to figure out?

Slide 3

Attention-getting device; corresponds to the introduction's "I A–B"

This slide gains attention by relating the topic directly to the audience; it answers the listener's obvious question, "Why should I listen to this speech?"

Slide 4

Orientation; corresponds to the introduction's "II A–D"

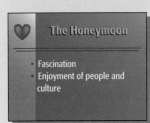

In this slide you give your orientation by identifying your main points. These four bullets will become your four main points.

Slide 5

First main point; corresponds to the body's "I A–B"

This is your first main point. You'd introduce it, perhaps, by saying, "The honeymoon occurs first." If you wanted your audience to keep track of the stage numbers, you could use numbers in your slides; for example, "1. The Honeymoon" or "Stage 1, The Honeymoon." The graphic of the heart is meant to associate culture shock with good times and a romancelike experience. As a listener, would you prefer that the speaker explain this graphic or say nothing about it?

FIGURE 13.5 A Slide Show Speech

Another aspect of rehearsal is checking out the equipment available in the room you'll speak in and its compatibility with the presentation software you're using. If possible, rehearse with the actual equipment you'll have available on the day you're speaking. In this way you can adjust to or remedy any incompatibilities or idiosyncrasies that you come across. You'll discover how long it takes to warm up the slide projector or to load PowerPoint, so you won't have to use up your speaking time for these preparations.

The Actual Presentation During your actual presentation you can control your slides with your mouse, advancing to the next one or going back to a previously shown

Slide 6

Second main point; corresponds to the body's "II A–B"

This is your second point and follows in format the previous slide. Again, a graphic is used. Can you think of a better graphic?

Slide 7

Third main point; corresponds to the body's "III A–B"

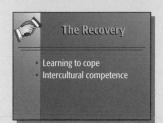

This is your third main point and again follows the format of the previous two slides.

Slide 8

Fourth main point; corresponds to the body's "IV A–B"

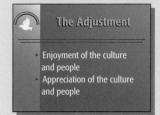

This is your fourth main point; the sound of applause is programmed to come on with this slide, reinforcing the idea that we do adjust to culture shock. Examine the sound effects you have available; what other sound effects would you use in this speech?

Slide 9

Summary; corresponds to the conclusion's "I A–D"

This is your summary of your four points; notice that it's the same as your orientation (Slide 4). This slide violates the general rule to use graphics in moderation. What do you think of the repetition of graphics? Do you think they add reinforcement? Do they detract from the verbal message?

Slide 10

Closure; corresponds to the conclusion's "II"

This slide is intended to wrap up the speech—it contains the title and two graphics that will support the speaker's concluding statement: "By knowing about culture shock you'll be in a better position to deal with it at school and on the job." Notice that the conclusion is tied to the introduction by a similarity in font and text color; it helps signal that this is the last slide and the end of the speech.

FIGURE 13.5　**A Slide Show Speech**　*(continued)*

slide. If you set the package to run automatically, programming each slide to be shown for its own particular amount of time, you won't be tied to the mouse. If you have a remote mouse, you'll have greater flexibility. As when using any presentation aid, make sure that you focus on the audience; don't allow the computer or the slides to get in the way of your immediate contact with the audience.

Now that you have considered the principles of informative speaking, types of supporting materials, and presentation aids, it's time to consider the types of informative speeches: speeches of description, definition, and demonstration.

FIGURE 13.6 Slides and Speaker's Notes

Speeches of Description

In a speech of *description*, you're concerned with explaining an object, person, event, or process. You would describe an object or person in a speech about, for example, the structure of the brain, the contributions of Thomas Edison, the parts of a telephone, the layout of Philadelphia, the hierarchy of a corporation, or the components of a computer system.

You would be describing an event or process in a speech about, for example, the attacks of September 11, 2001; the process of organizing a bodybuilding contest; how a newspaper is printed; how a child acquires language; how people purchase stocks online; or the events leading to the Iraq War.

THESIS AND MAIN POINTS

The thesis of a speech, as explained in Chapter 11, is your single most important concept. The thesis of a speech of description simply states what you'll describe in your speech: for example, "The child acquires language in four stages," or "There are three steps to purchasing stock online," or "Four major events led to the Iraq War."

Select a topic in which you're interested (or consult the Dictionary of Topics at **www.mycommunicationlab.com** for ideas) and then follow the following steps:

1. Formulate a thesis and a specific purpose suitable for an informative speech of approximately 10 minutes.
2. Analyze this class as your potential audience and identify ways in which you can relate this topic to their interests and needs.
3. Generate at least two main points from your thesis.
4. Support these main points with examples, illustrations, definitions, testimony, and so on.
5. Construct a conclusion that summarizes your main ideas and brings the speech to a definite close.
6. Construct an introduction that gains attention and orients your audience.

Discuss these outlines in small groups or with the class as a whole. Try to secure feedback from other members on how you can improve your outline.

Working repeatedly with the process of preparing a speech will ultimately make the process easier, more efficient, and more effective.

The main points of a speech of description are the major subdivisions of the thesis. You derive your main points from your thesis by asking strategic questions: for example, *What are the four stages in child language acquisition? What are the three steps to purchasing stock online? What events led to the Iraq War?*

SUPPORT

Obviously you don't want to simply list your main points; instead, you want to flesh them out and make them memorable, interesting, and most of all, clear. In a speech of description you do this by using a variety of materials that amplify and support your main ideas, including examples, illustrations, testimony, numerical data, and presentation aids.

Because you are giving a speech of description, give extra consideration to the types of description you might use in your supporting materials. Try to describe the object or event with a variety of descriptive categories, from physical to social, psychological, and economic categories.

ORGANIZATION

Consider using a spatial or a topical organization when describing objects and people. For example, if you were to describe the layout of Philadelphia, you might start from the north and work down to the south (using a spatial pattern). If you were to describe the contributions of Thomas Edison, you might select the three or four major contributions and discuss each of these equally (using a topical pattern).

Consider using a temporal pattern when describing events and processes. If you were to describe the events leading up to the Iraq war, for example, you might start with the earliest and work up to the latest. A temporal pattern would also be appropriate for describing how a hurricane develops or how a parade is put together. The "who, what, where, when, and why" pattern of organization can also be useful to describe an event or a process. For example, if you're going to describe how to purchase a house, you might want to consider the people involved (who?), the steps you have to go through (what?), the places you'll have to go (where?), the timing or sequence of the steps (when?), and the advantages and disadvantages of buying the house (why?).

Communication Choice Point

Speech of Description

As you approach the lectern to give a speech of description on how a child acquires language, you notice a woman with a one-year-old child in the audience. *What are your options in this situation? Would you depart from your plans and comment on the woman and child? If you do decide to comment, what are your options? What would you say (if anything)?*

Here is an example of how the bare bones of a descriptive speech might look. Notice that the speaker derives the main points from asking a question about the thesis.

General purpose: _____ To inform

Specific purpose: _____ To describe the way fear works in intercultural communication

Thesis: _____ Fear influences intercultural communication. (How does fear influence intercultural communication?)

    I. _____ We fear disapproval.

    II. _____ We fear embarrassing ourselves.

    III. _____ We fear being harmed.

In delivering such a speech, the speaker might begin by saying:

Three major fears interfere with intercultural communication. First, we fear disapproval—from members of our own group as well as from members of the other person's group. Second, we fear embarrassing ourselves, even making fools of ourselves, by saying the wrong thing or appearing insensitive. And third, we may fear being harmed—our stereotypes of the other group may lead us to see its members as dangerous or potentially harmful to us.

Let's look at each of these fears in more detail. We'll be able to see clearly how they influence our own intercultural communication behavior.

Consider, first, the fear of disapproval. *[The speaker would then amplify and support this fear of disapproval, giving examples of disapproval seen in his or her own experience, the testimony of communication theorists on the importance of such fear, research findings on the effects that such fear might have on intercultural communication, and so on.]*

Speeches of Definition

What is leadership? What is a born-again Christian? What is the difference between sociology and psychology? What is a cultural anthropologist? What is safe sex? These are all topics for informative speeches of definition.

In giving a speech of definition, you may focus on defining a term, defining a system or theory, or pinpointing the similarities and/or differences among terms or systems. For example, a speech in which you define a term might be on such topics as: *What is a smart card? What is machismo? What is creativity? What is affirmative action? What is multiculturalism? What is political correctness?* A speech in which you define a system or theory might address, for example: *What is the classical theory of public speaking? What are the parts of a generative grammar? What are the major beliefs in Confucianism? What is expressionism? What is the "play theory" of mass communication?* Speech topics that would involve your defining similar and dissimilar terms or systems would include *Football and soccer: What's the difference? What do Christians and Muslims have in common?* and *Keyword and directory searches: How do they differ?*

THESIS AND MAIN POINTS

The thesis in a speech of definition is a statement identifying a term or system and stating your intention to define it or to contrast it with other terms: for example, "Christianity and Islam have much in common" or "Text and online dictionaries are similar and different." You derive the main points from asking questions of your thesis: for example, *What do Christianity and Islam have in common? How are text and online dictionaries similar and different?*

SUPPORT

Once you have each of the main points for your speech of definition, support them with examples, testimony, and the like. For example, one of your main points in the

Christianity–Islam example might be that both religions believe in the value of good works. You might then quote from the New Testament and from the Quran to illustrate this belief, you might give examples of noted Christians and Muslims who exemplify this characteristic, or you might cite the testimony of religious leaders who have talked about the importance of good works.

Because this is a speech of definition, you'll want to give special attention to all your definitions, as discussed earlier.

ORGANIZATION

For a speech of definition, an obvious organizational pattern is the pattern of multiple definitions (see Chapter 11). Alternatively, you might consider using a topical order, in which each main idea is treated equally. In either case, however, proceed from the known to the unknown. Start with what your audience knows and work up to what is new or unfamiliar.

Here is an example of how you might go about constructing a speech of definition. In this particular example, the speaker selects three major types of lying for discussion and arranges these in a topical pattern.

Communication Choice Point

Defining

You want to give a speech defining the basic tenets of your religion. Most members of your audience, you suspect, have a negative view of your religion; a few may hold neutral or slightly positive views. You want to acknowledge your understanding of these attitudes. *What are some things you can say to help you get this point across? What would you say?*

General purpose: <u>To inform</u>

Specific purpose: <u>To define lying by explaining the major types of lying</u>

Thesis: <u>There are three major kinds of lying. (What are the three major kinds of lying?)</u>

I. <u>Concealment is the process of hiding the truth</u>
II. <u>Falsification is the process of presenting false information as if it were true.</u>
III. <u>Misdirection is the process of acknowledging a feeling but misidentifying its cause.</u>

In delivering such a speech, the speaker might begin by saying:

> A lie is a lie is a lie. True? Well, not exactly. Actually, there are a number of different ways we can lie. We can lie by concealing the truth. We can lie by falsification, by presenting false information as if it were true. And we can lie by misdirection, by acknowledging a feeling but misidentifying its cause.

Let's look at the first type of lie—the lie of concealment. . . .

Speeches of Demonstration

In using *demonstration*, or in a speech devoted entirely to demonstration, you show the audience how to do something or how something operates. Examples of speeches in which you demonstrate how to do something might include how to give mouth-to-mouth resuscitation, how to drive defensively, how to mix colors, how to ask for a raise, how to burglarproof your house, or how to use PowerPoint in business meetings. Examples of speeches in which you demonstrate how something operates might include how the body maintains homeostasis, how perception works, how divorce laws work, how e-mail works, how a hurricane develops, or how a heart bypass operation is performed.

THESIS AND MAIN POINTS

The thesis for a speech of demonstration identifies what you will show the audience how to do or how something operates: for example, "E-mail works through a series of electronic connections from

"The skill to do comes from doing."
—CICERO

one computer to a server to another computer," or "You can burglarproof your house in three different ways," or "Three guidelines will help you get that raise." You derive the main points by asking a simple *how* or *what question* of your thesis: *How do these electronic connections work? What are the things you can do to burglarproof your house? What are the guidelines for asking for a raise?*

SUPPORT

To support each of the main ideas in a speech of demonstration, you can use a variety of materials. For example, you might show diagrams of houses with different burglarproofing arrangements, demonstrate how various locks work, or show how different security systems work.

Presentation aids are especially helpful in speeches of demonstration. Signs in restaurants demonstrating the Heimlich maneuver, for example, demonstrate the sequence of steps with both words and pictures. The combination of verbal and graphic information makes it easy to understand this important process. In a speech on this topic, however, it would be best to use only the pictures as aids so that written words would not distract your audience from your oral explanation.

ORGANIZATION

In most cases, a temporal pattern will work best in speeches of demonstration. Demonstrate each step in the sequence in which it's to be performed. In this way, you'll avoid one of the major difficulties in demonstrating a process—backtracking. Don't skip steps even if you think they're familiar to the audience; they may not be. Connect each step to the next with appropriate transitions. For example, in explaining the Heimlich maneuver, you might say, "Now that you have your arms around the choking victim's chest, your next step is to . . ." Assist your listeners by labeling the steps clearly: for example, say, "The first step," "The second step," and so on.

Begin with an overview. It's often helpful when demonstrating to give a broad general picture and then present each step in turn. For example, suppose your talk were about how to prepare a wall for painting. You might begin with a general overview to give your listeners a general idea of the process, saying something like this:

> In preparing the wall for painting, you want to make sure that the wall is smoothly sanded, free of dust, and dry. Sanding a wall isn't like sanding a block of wood. So let's look first at the proper way to sand a wall.

Here is an example of the speech of demonstration. In this example, the speaker identifies and demonstrates how to listen actively.

General purpose: _____ To inform _____

Specific purpose: _____ To demonstrate three techniques of active listening _____

Thesis: _____ We can engage in active listening. (How can we engage in active listening?) _____

I. _____ Paraphrase the speaker's meaning _____

II. _____ Express understanding of the speaker's feelings _____

III. _____ Ask questions _____

In delivering the speech, the speaker might begin by saying:

Active listening is a special kind of listening. It's listening with total involvement, with a concern for the speaker. It's probably the most important type of listening you can engage in. Active listening consists of three steps: paraphrasing the speaker's meaning, expressing understanding of the speaker's feelings, and asking questions.

Your first step in active listening is to paraphrase the speaker's meaning. . . .

Communication Choice Point

Demonstrating

You want to demonstrate to your audience how to construct bumper stickers on Facebook. Your audience is probably mixed in terms of their knowledge and use of social networking sites—some know a great deal and others know very little. *What are some things you can do to gain the attention of your entire audience early in your speech? What specifically, might you say?*

The Public Speaking Sample Assistant

AN EXCELLENT INFORMATIVE SPEECH

CONTROLLING THE WEATHER: MOSHE ALAMARO'S PLAN FOR HURRICANE MITIGATION

Jillian Collum*

Unbeknownst to most Americans, in 1984 the United States came under attack from a terrorist group bent on overthrowing our government. Their leader had constructed a machine to create devastating storms. Their goal was clear, and the entire group was committed, well funded and animated. Fortunately, the Cobra Commander's plan failed thanks to some real American heroes—the GI Joes, who used giant mirrors to absorb the machine's solar power. Though the ability to harness natural phenomena has traditionally been restricted to masked cartoon terrorists, one real-life scientist now believes that he too has discovered how to control the weather. But instead of attacking the United States, he wants to protect it. The *Houston Chronicle* of July 12, 2005, reports that Moshe Alamaro, a visiting researcher in MIT's Department of Earth, Atmospheric and Planetary Sciences, has drafted a plan to fight back against hurricanes. Alamaro's "hurricane mitigation" system calls for creating tropical storms to consume all of the warm ocean water that would normally fuel an approaching hurricane. A January 27, 2006, article from the National Oceanic and Atmospheric Administration's website explains that, in 2005, Hurricanes Katrina, Wilma, Rita and Dennis caused over $120 billion in damage, and took the lives of over 1,400 people. Even more alarming, *The New Scientist* of December 24, 2005, notes that the number of strong hurricanes has almost doubled in the last 35 years. And as global warming further increases water temperatures, we could see even more devastating hurricane seasons in the future. So, in order to understand how Moshe Alamaro plans to protect us from the increasing danger of these storms, we must first explore how Alamaro's plan works; next, examine how it will be enacted; and finally, discuss the drawbacks and future implications of this new effort to keep deadly storms at bay.

Cobra Commander's evil plans generally took about thirty minutes to carry out. Moshe Alamaro, however, took a little bit longer when he first presented his ideas at an April 2005 Weather Modification Association conference. To

Did this introduction gain your attention and make you want to continue reading/listening?

Here you start wondering—is this fact or fiction? And in this way the speaker gains your attention. After you complete reading the speech, return to this introduction and try to identify other ways the speaker might have introduced the topic and gained the audience's attention.

When this speech was given (in March 2006), the weather was much in the news, and Hurricane Katrina was referred to almost daily in newspapers' coverage of the rebuilding of New Orleans. The speaker's topic is certainly most timely. Moreover, it addresses something many people have wondered about: Why can't science tell us how to prevent these weather problems from causing so much destruction?

How might you have illustrated how great a sum $120 billion is? How might you have illustrated what the doubling of the yearly number of strong hurricanes over the last 35 years means in terms of their frequency?

Here the speaker explains the importance of the topic briefly. Most people listening to this speech are likely to appreciate the importance of the topic and the need for methods to combat these natural catastrophes.

Here the speaker orients the audience and explains that she'll cover three topics: how the plan works, how it will be enacted, and the future of this effort.

Here the speaker wisely repeats her first point rather than merely assuming that the audience will remember, from the orientation, that the first point concerns how the plan works. And, to further guide the listeners, she explains

*Jillian Collum is a student at the University of Texas at Austin. This speech was delivered at the 2006 American Forensic Association National Individual Events Tournament in Gainsville, Florida, and is reprinted by permission of the speaker.

explore his plan, we'll discuss how hurricanes work, and how Alamaro plans to mitigate them.

Hurricanes are obviously huge, deadly storms, but the *Washington Post* of October 3, 2005, explains that they start out as clusters of regular thunderstorms. These clusters pick up heat and moisture from surface water, which then cools and condenses into clouds and rain, causing the storm to grow larger. This means: The more warm water available to feed the storm, the bigger it will get. According to Canada's *National Post* of August 30, 2005, warm waters have turned recent storms into giants—Katrina was a weak category one hurricane when it passed over southern Florida, but after traveling over the warm waters of the gulf, it grew into a catastrophic category four hurricane almost 400 miles wide.

But Moshe Alamaro plans to neutralize the threat by depriving it of its energy source. His plan is simple: Create man-made tropical storms in the paths of approaching hurricanes. Because tropical storms consume the same fuel as hurricanes—warm water—Alamaro believes that placing tropical storms in front of approaching hurricanes would leave the bigger storms with far less fuel. Without this energy, hurricanes won't be able to grow as large. The *Economist Technology Quarterly* of June 11, 2005, likens this to firefighters' practice of lighting small fires in front of approaching wildfires. The small controlled fires consume fuel, leaving the bigger fire with no energy source when it passes over the area. If this principle is applied to hurricanes, residents in hurricane-prone areas will one day experience more tropical storms, but not so many devastating hurricanes.

While Cobra Commander had a clear plan for defeating the U.S., Moshe Alamaro has a clear plan for taking on hurricanes. We'll explore his ideas further by examining how and where he plans to create tropical storms.

The *Scripps Howard News Service* reported on June 30, 2005, that Alamaro plans to tow a barge equipped with about 20 jet engines into the path of an oncoming hurricane, then ignite the engines with the jets facing upward. The resulting updrafts would siphon heat from the ocean. This heat and moisture would cool and condense into clouds and rain as it rose, creating the manmade tropical storm that would weaken the hurricane. In a February 24, 2006, personal interview, Moshe Alamaro explained that the 20 jet engines would create approximately 100 tons of thrust. Since a barge can carry 1,000 tons, there is no danger of it sinking. Additionally, the previously cited *Economist* reveals that the costs for this project would be relatively low, since jet engines could be retrieved from retired U.S. and Soviet bombers. This would mean that

that she'll explain the plan by first explaining how hurricanes work.

Here is a very simple explanation of how hurricanes grow, which is a necessary step to understanding how Alamaro's plan works.

Here the speaker explains the plan and also helps the audience understand it by relating it to something they're already familiar with—namely, the practice of using small fires to fight large fires.

If you're familiar with Cobra Commander, then these frequent references work well. Would they work in your class?

protecting Central America and the southern U.S. would cost less than $1 billion a year, a small price to pay compared to the $120 billion in hurricane damage in 2005 alone.

In his presentation to the Weather Modification Association, Alamaro suggested two ways to carry out his plan. First, barges carrying the jet engines could be dispatched to intercept advancing hurricanes. However, this plan could be logistically difficult, since hurricanes can quickly switch course. So Alamaro also suggested a second plan, which would call for barges to continuously patrol the shoreline during hurricane season. These barges would then create tropical storms to pre-emptively lower the ocean's temperature in any areas where it may be high. This would mean that when hurricanes did come through an area, they would have less warm water with which to grow. *Popular Science* of October 2005 reveals that we may begin to see this plan take shape within the next five years.

Because Cobra Commander was so diabolical, the Joes always had to be wary of the next obstacle he was planning for them. Moshe Alamaro knows he too will face challenges, in the form of drawbacks and implications.

Like most events in nature, hurricanes serve a purpose. According to the Central Florida Hurricane Center website on November 7, 2005, hurricanes serve to redistribute excess heat from the tropics to the mid-latitudes in order to keep the global climate system balanced. The *Boston Globe* of September 6, 2004, reports that hurricanes have other beneficial purposes—they refresh waterways, revive dry areas, and bulk up barrier islands with redistributed sand. Also, in his report to the Weather Modification Association, Alamaro cautioned that if the man-made tropical storm gets too close to the target hurricane, there is a small possibility the two could merge, forming an even larger hurricane. So, while Alamaro's plan has the potential to prevent hurricane damage, it could disrupt our environment by eliminating the beneficial aspects of these storms, or it could make a dangerous storm even stronger.

Finally, Alamaro's plan may result in the weaponization of hurricanes. According to the April 2005 Weather Modification Association report, it may be possible to design the man-made tropical storms to steer the target hurricane in a particular direction. The *Boston Globe* of July 3, 2005, notes that militaries—both cartoon and real—have long dreamed of controlling the weather to gain an edge over their enemies. In fact, during the Vietnam War, the U.S. military sprayed silver iodide on clouds to create rain over the Ho Chi Minh Trail in order to make it muddy and impassable to foes. So, it isn't hard to imagine how militaries, or even terrorist organizations, may be interested in steering hurricanes toward well-populated areas to wreak

Here the speaker goes into her second point—how the plan will work. This is relatively straightforward and follows clearly from the first point. If you chose to use a transition here, how might you phrase it?

Here the speaker offers a transition from the second point to the third and links this to Cobra Commander. In what other ways might you have phrased a transition?

How would you describe the research presented in this speech?

Here the speaker explains the drawbacks and implications fairly and objectively. We don't feel the speaker is minimizing the dangers of the plan, and perhaps because of this we believe the speaker. In other words, the fairness of these explanations heightens the speaker's credibility.

havoc on their enemies. But while Alamaro's plan does have the potential for harm, it could also be used to save millions of dollars and thousands of lives.

Though Cobra Commander's efforts to create dangerous storms were thwarted, Mother Nature continues to throw deadly disasters our way, meaning that anyone who figures out how to stop them will be a real American hero. After examining how Moshe Alamaro's "hurricane mitigation" plan works, how it will be carried out, and its drawbacks and future implications, we finally know all about this promising new technology. And as the GI Joes taught us, "knowing is half the battle."

The speaker's conclusion serves two major purposes. The speaker summarizes the speech's main points and closes with a quotation relating back to the theme of Cobra Commander.

Summary of Concepts and Skills

This chapter covered the nature of the informative speech and ways you can most effectively communicate information.

1. When preparing informative speeches, observe the guidelines for informative speaking: Limit the amount of information, adjust the level of complexity, stress the information's relevance and usefulness, relate new information to information the audience already knows, and make your speech easy to remember.

2. To make your ideas clear to your audience, use amplifying materials such as examples, illustrations, and narratives; testimony; numerical data; definitions; and presentation aids.

3. Three general types of informative speeches are speeches of description, in which you explain an object, person, event, or process; speeches of definition, in which you define a term, system, theory, or set of principles; and speeches of demonstration, in which you explain how something works or how to do something.

Effective public speakers need to master a variety of informing skills. Place a check mark next to those skills you most want to work on.

_____ 1. In my informative speeches I follow the principles of informative speaking: I stress the information's usefulness, relate new information to information the audience already knows, present information through several senses, adjust the level of complexity, limit the amount of information I present, and recognize cultural variations.

_____ 2. For my informative speeches I select a variety of amplifying materials; examples, illustrations, and narratives; testimony; definitions; numerical data; and visual aids.

_____ 3. When developing a speech of information, I follow the suggestions for constructing speeches of description, definition, and demonstration.

Key Word Quiz

The Language of Informative Speaking

Match the terms about informative speaking with their definitions. Record the number of the definition next to the appropriate term.

_____ a. speech of description (280)

_____ b. guide phrases (269)

_____ c. operational definition (272)

_____ d. speech of demonstration (283)

_____ e. example (270)

_____ f. etymology (272)

_____ g. testimony (270)

_____ h. restatement (273)

_____ i. narrative (270)

_____ j. illustration (270)

1. An expert's opinion or a witness's account.
2. A relatively brief specific instance.
3. A means of defining a term by tracing its historical or linguistic development.
4. A speech in which you explain an object, person, event, or process.
5. Repetition in different words for emphasis and clarity.
6. A relatively long illustration presented as an anecdote or story.
7. Repeat of an idea in different words.
8. A speech in which you show listeners how to do something or how something works.
9. A longer and more detailed example.
10. A description of how something would be produced.

These ten terms and additional terms used in this chapter can be found in the glossary and on flashcards on MyCommunicationLab (**www.mycommunicationlab.com**).

Answers: a. 4 b. 10 c. 7 d. 8 e. 2 f. 3 g. 1 h. 5 i. 6 j. 9

MyCommunicationLab

PEARSON
mycommunicationlab

www.mycommunicationlab.com

Visit MyCommunicationLab (**www.mycommunicationlab.com**) for additional information on informative speech. Flash cards, videos, skill building exercises, sample text questions, and additional examples and discussions will help you continue your study of preparing information and presenting it to an audience.

14 The Persuasive Speech

Why read this chapter?

Because you will learn about:

- the process of persuasion and how attitudes, beliefs, values, and behaviors are influenced
- the techniques that persuaders use to influence others

Because you will learn to:

- use the techniques and strategies of persuasion in a wide variety of situations
- prepare persuasive speeches on questions of fact, value, and policy
- prevent yourself from being unfairly or unethically influenced

You'll no doubt find yourself in a wide variety of situations in which you'll have to persuade others—to urge others to accept or reject a union proposal, redesign a company's website, negotiate a business deal, or donate blood or money or time, to give only a few examples. As with having to provide information, the higher up you go in your organization's hierarchy, the more you'll find yourself having to persuade others.

Goals of Persuasion

Persuasion is the process of influencing another person's *attitudes, beliefs, values, and/or behaviors*. Here is a brief glossary of each of these terms:

- **Attitude:** The tendency to respond to something in a certain way. For example, if your audience has a positive attitude toward the current administration, then they're likely to favor the policies, proposals, and values of the administration. If they have a negative attitude, they're likely to oppose administration policies and the like.
- **Belief:** The conviction about the existence or reality of something or about the truth of some assertion. For example, if your audience believes that soft drugs lead to hard drugs, then they're likely to oppose legalizing marijuana and perhaps to favor harsher penalties for soft drug use.
- **Value:** An indicator of what a person thinks is good or bad, ethical or unethical, just or unjust. For example, if your audience positively values "free speech," then they'll probably oppose increased restrictions on what can and cannot be said publicly and will probably oppose increased surveillance of their e-mail or phone calls.
- **Behavior:** Overt, observable actions, such as voting for increased funding for education, voting for a particular person, contributing money to the Red Cross, or buying a Ford.

Your persuasive speeches may focus on influencing listeners' attitudes, beliefs, values, and/or behaviors. You may want to accomplish any one of the following three general goals of persuasive speaking:

- *To strengthen or weaken attitudes, beliefs, or values.* Persuasion often aims to strengthen audience views. For example, religious sermons and public service announcements usually seek to strengthen the existing beliefs of the listeners. At times, however, you may want to weaken the existing beliefs of the audience—to suggest that what they currently believe may not be entirely true.
- *To change attitudes, beliefs, or values.* Sometimes you'll want to change how your audience feels. You might want to change their attitudes toward the college's no-smoking rules, their beliefs about television's influence on viewer violence, or their values about the efficacy of war.
- *To motivate to action.* Ultimately, your goal is to get people to do something—for example, to vote for one person rather than another, to donate money to a fund for the homeless, or to take a course in personal finance.

It's useful to view the effects of persuasion as a continuum ranging from one extreme to another. Let's say, to take an example from the news, that you want to give a persuasive speech on same-sex marriage. You might visualize your audience as existing on a continuum ranging from strongly in favor to strongly opposed, as shown in Figure 14.1. Your task is to move your audience in the direction of your persuasive purpose, which you can do in any of three ways (corresponding to the goals of persuasion). You can design your persuasive speech to attempt to:

- strengthen or weaken your listeners' attitudes, beliefs, or values about same-sex marriage.
- change your listeners' attitudes, beliefs, or values about same-sex marriage.
- move your listeners to act—to protest, write letters, or sign a petition.

Strongly in favor of same-sex marriage : __ : __ : __ : __ : __ : __ Strongly opposed to same-sex marriage

FIGURE 14.1 **The Persuasion Continuum**

Any movement along the continuum would be considered a result of persuasion.

If your purpose is to persuade the audience to *oppose* same-sex marriage, then in Figure 14.1 any movement toward the right will be successful persuasion; if your purpose is to persuade listeners to *support* same-sex marriage, then any movement toward the left will be successful persuasion. Notice, however, that it's quite possible to give a speech in which you attempt to move your listeners in one direction but actually succeed in moving them in the other direction. This "negative persuasion" effect could occur, for example, if the audience perceives you as dishonest or self-promoting or feels that you presented biased evidence or faulty reasoning.

Guidelines for Persuasive Speaking

You can become more successful in strengthening or changing attitudes or beliefs and in moving your listeners to action by following these guidelines for persuasive speaking.

FOCUS ON YOUR AUDIENCE

Begin constructing your persuasive speech with a knowledge of your specific audience. What will work with one audience will not work with another; appeals to increase salaries for teaching will probably prove effective with teachers but may not do so well with homeowners who feel overtaxed.

If you show your audience that you and they share important attitudes, beliefs, and values, you'll clearly advance your persuasive goal. For example, if you know your listeners are concerned with helping the homeless, you might share your own experiences in working at a homeless shelter. Similarities of cultural, educational, or social background may also help you identify yourself with your audience. Beware, however: insincere or dishonest attempts at identification are likely to backfire and create problems, so avoid even implying similarities between yourself and your audience that don't exist.

"The audience is not the least important actor in the plot, and if it will not do its allotted share, the play falls to pieces."

—W. SOMERSET MAUGHAM

ASK FOR REASONABLE AMOUNTS OF CHANGE

Persuasion is most effective when it strives for small changes and works over a period of time. Put in terms of the continuum of persuasion shown in Figure 14.1, this guideline suggests that you'll be more successful if you ask for small (rather than large) movements. The greater and more important the change you want your audience to make, the more difficult your task will be. The reason is simple: Listeners demand a greater number of reasons and a lot more evidence before making big changes such as changing careers, moving to another state, or committing to an investment strategy.

When you're addressing an audience that is opposed to your position and your goal is to change their attitudes, beliefs, or values, it is especially important that you focus on small changes. Let's say, for example, that your ultimate goal is to get a pro-life group to favor abortion on demand. Obviously, this goal is too great to achieve in one speech. Therefore, you need to strive for small changes. Here, for example, is an excerpt in which the speaker tries to get a pro-life audience to agree that at least some abortions should be legal. Notice that the speaker does not state a pro-choice position but instead focuses on one situation involving abortion and attempts to get the audience to agree that in some cases abortion should be legal.

One of the great lessons I learned in college was that most extreme positions are wrong. Most of the important truths lie somewhere between the extreme opposites. And today I want to talk with you about one of these truths. I want to talk with you about rape and the problems faced by the mother carrying a child conceived in this most violent of all violent crimes.

ANTICIPATE SELECTIVE EXPOSURE

As discussed in Chapter 2, perception follows the principle of **selective exposure**. According to this principle (1) listeners actively seek out information that supports their opinions, beliefs, values, decisions, and behaviors; and (2) listeners actively avoid information that contradicts their existing opinions, beliefs, attitudes, values, decisions, and behaviors.

Let's say you're giving a speech on the need to reduce spending on college athletic programs. If your audience consists largely of people who agree with you, you can lead with your thesis and show them that you're on the same side. Your introduction might go something like this:

> Our college athletic program is absorbing money that we can more profitably use for the library and computer labs. Let me explain how the excessive money now going to athletic programs could be better spent in these other areas.

But if you want to persuade an audience that holds attitudes different from those you're advocating, you'll need to anticipate selective exposure and proceed inductively; that is, hold back on your thesis until you've given your evidence and argument, then relate this evidence and argument to your thesis. If you present your listeners with your thesis first, they may tune you out without giving your position a fair hearing.

Communication Choice Point

Changing Behavior

You're supervising a workforce of 20 people. Your problem is that computer parts are being stolen by one or more of the workers, and you've been assigned the task of stopping the theft. You decide to tackle this in your weekly meeting with the workers and to apply the principles of persuasion. *What are some of the things you might say?*

FOLLOW A MOTIVATING SEQUENCE

One time-honored principle of persuasion is the **motivated sequence**, introduced in Chapter 11 in the discussion of organization (pp. 233–234). The motivated sequence, especially relevant to persuasion, holds that as a persuasive speaker you need to do five things: gain attention, establish a need for a change, advance a proposal to satisfy the need, visualize for the audience what things would be like were they to do what you suggest, and last, move them to action.

Let's say you want to persuade your audience to boycott a local restaurant because of its discriminatory policy toward immigrants. You might develop a speech something like this:

- *[Attention:]* How would you like it if you earned only 50 percent of what other people earn for the exact same work? . . .
- *[Need:]* Discrimination infects the entire community; it needs to be stopped. . . .
- *[Satisfaction:]* We *can* force management to stop these policies. . . .
- *[Visualization:]* If this policy were ended we'd all experience a wealth of rewards. . . .
- *[Action:]* Boycott the XYZ Restaurant.

Table 14.1 (p. 294) provides a way of looking at the motivated sequence in terms of audience responses and some cautions to observe in using the motivated sequence.

Supporting Materials

In addition to the supporting materials described in Chapter 13—for example, materials such as examples or testimony or statistics—three forms of support are of special importance in persuasive speeches: logical, emotional, and credibility appeals.

LOGICAL APPEALS

When you use logical appeals—when you argue on the basis of **logic** supported by reliable facts and evidence—your listeners are more likely to remain persuaded

"In the interest of streamlining the judicial process, we'll skip the evidence and go directly to sentencing."

© J. B. Handelsman/Condé Nast Publications/www.cartoonbank.com.

TABLE 14.1 The Motivated Sequence as a Persuasive Strategy

This table summarizes persuasive strategies in terms of the motivated sequence.

Step	Purpose	Audience Question Speaker Should Answer	Ideal Audience Response	Cautions to Observe
Attention	Focus listeners' attention on you and your message.	Why should I listen? Is this worth my time?	This sounds interesting. Tell me more.	Make attention relevant to speech topic.
Need	Demonstrate that there is a problem that affects them.	Why do I need to know or do anything?	Ok, I understand; there's a problem.	Don't overdramatize the need.
Satisfaction	Show listeners how they can satisfy the need.	How can I do anything about this?	I can change things.	Answer any objections listeners might have to your plan.
Visualization	Show listeners what the situation will be like with the need satisfied.	How would anything be different or improved?	*Wow!* Things look a lot better this way.	Be realistic; don't portray the solution as perfect.
Action	Urge listeners to act.	What can I do to effect this change?	Let me sign up. Here's my contribution. I'll participate.	Be specific. Ask for small changes in behaviors.

over time and to resist counterarguments that may come up in the future (Petty & Wegener, 1998). There are three main ways of using logical appeals: specific instances, causes and effects, and sign.

Reasoning from Specific Instances and Generalizations In reasoning from **specific instances** (or examples), you examine several specific instances and then conclude something about the whole. This form of reasoning, known as induction, is useful when you want to develop a general principle or conclusion but cannot examine the whole. For example, you sample a few communication courses and conclude something about communication courses in general; you visit several Scandinavian cities and conclude something about the whole of Scandinavia.

In reasoning from specific instances, be sure to examine a sufficient number of instances. Three general guidelines will help you determine how much is enough.

- First, the larger the group you want your conclusion to cover, the greater the number of specific instances you should examine. If you wish to draw conclusions about members of an entire country or culture, you'll have to examine a considerable number of people before drawing even tentative conclusions. On the other hand, if you're attempting to draw a conclusion about a bushel of 130 apples, sampling a few is probably sufficient.

- Second, the greater the diversity of items in the class, the more specific instances you will have to examine. Pieces of pasta in boiling water are all about the same; thus, sampling one usually tells you something about all the others. On the other hand, college courses are probably very different from one another, so valid conclusions about the entire range of college courses will require a much larger sample.

- Third, beware of anecdotal evidence. Often you'll hear people use anecdotes to "prove" a point: "Women are like that; I have three sisters." "That's the way Japanese managers are; I've seen plenty of them." One reason this type of "evidence" is inadequate is that it overgeneralizes on the basis of too few observations. A second reason is that one person's observations may be unduly clouded by his or her own attitudes and beliefs.

Reasoning from Causes and Effects In reasoning from **causes and effects**, you may go in either of two directions: (1) You may reason from cause to effect—for example, *Smoking (the cause) contributes to lung cancer (the effect)*—or (2) you may reason from effect to cause: for example, *Low reading scores among elementary school children (the effect) are due to poverty (the cause)*. In order to establish a cause–effect connection, you need to prove that possible causes other than the one you're postulating are not producing the effect. And so you'd need to determine whether causes other than smoking may contribute to lung cancer, or whether factors other than poverty contribute to low reading scores. Usually you won't be able to rule out *all* other factors, but it's important to demonstrate that the factors you are identifying are the main contributors. For example, in this case you'd need to show that, although other factors also may contribute to lung cancer, smoking is a major (if not *the* major) culprit. Similarly, you'd need to demonstrate that poverty more than any other factor accounts for low reading scores. Scientific studies on the effects of smoking on cancer rates and the effects of poverty on reading scores would enable you to establish these cause–effect relationships.

You'd also want to demonstrate that the causation is in the direction you say it is. If two things occur together, it's often difficult to determine which is the cause and which is the effect. For example, a lack of interpersonal intimacy and a lack of self-confidence often occur in the same person. A person who lacks self-confidence seldom has successful intimate relationships with others. But which is the cause and which is the effect? Does the lack of intimacy "cause" low self-confidence, or does low self-confidence "cause" a lack of intimacy? Of course, it might also be that some other previously unexamined cause (a history of negative criticism, for example) might be contributing to both the lack of intimacy and the low self-confidence.

Reasoning from Sign **Reasoning from sign** involves drawing a conclusion on the basis of the presence of clues or symptoms that frequently occur together. Medical diagnosis is a good example of reasoning by sign. The general procedure is simple: If a sign and an object, event, or condition are frequently paired, the presence of the sign is taken as proof of the presence of the object, event, or condition. For example, fatigue, extreme thirst, and overeating serve as signs of hyperthyroidism, because they frequently accompany the condition.

You'd also want to show that other signs cannot logically point to the same conclusion. In the thyroid example, extreme thirst could be brought on by any number of factors. Similarly, the fatigue and the overeating could be attributed to other causes. Yet, taken together, the three signs seem to point to thyroid problems as a reasonable diagnosis. Generally, the more signs that point toward the conclusion, the more confidence you can have that it's valid.

AVOIDING THE FALLACIES OF LOGICAL ARGUMENT

At the same time that you'll want to reason logically from specific instances, causes and effects, and sign, you'll want to avoid the fallacies of argument: persuasive tactics that have the feel of real arguments and seem to involve logical reasoning but are actually logically unsound and misleading. These fallacies appear to address the issues but really don't. Here are a few such fallacies that you'll want to avoid as a speaker and recognize as a listener (Lee & Lee 1972, 1995; Pratkanis & Aronson, 1991; Herrick, 2004).

Attacking the Person Instead of the Issue Known in logic as the argument *ad hominem* (literally, against the man), this fallacy involves attacking a person's character instead of addressing the issue or the argument he or she is making.

A personal attack can take many forms: For example, you might use unflattering labels (which of course would vary with your audience) such as *racist, soft on terrorism*, or *sexist* (e.g., "They're anti-union, what do you expect?"). Another type of personal attack is to accuse someone of some wrongdoing or some character flaw, for example, having committed plagiarism while in college or having taken drugs (e.g., "How can we support a candidate who has been unfaithful and has lied?").

Appealing to Authority as Proof   This fallacy can take either of two forms. In the more common form, someone is passed off as an authority when the person actually has little authority, expertise, or knowledge in the subject under discussion. The commercials with Alex Trebek for life insurance or Robert Wagner for reverse mortgages are good examples. Sometimes this fallacy takes the form of "experts say . . . "—without telling you who the experts are—or "economists think . . ." or "psychologists say . . ."; one problem with this is that it implies the speaker is giving an accurate reading of all these experts' opinions.

In another form, this fallacy consists of using an authority's opinion instead of or as a substitute for facts and evidence. An opinion is an opinion, and unless it's backed up by evidence, it's still only an opinion. This doesn't mean that you need to disregard the opinions of relevant authorities; in fact, that would be illogical. Usually, an authority is an authority precisely because she or he has examined the facts and evidence, so a more logical reaction would be to seriously consider an authority's opinions but not to use them as proof positive. Again, there is nothing wrong with citing authorities; in fact, it's recommended. The fallacy is in the speaker's substituting appeals to authority for evidence or facts.

Appealing to Numbers as Truth   An appeal to numbers (from the Latin *ad numerum*—literally, *to the numbers*—also referred to as *ad populum, to the people*), known as the bandwagon fallacy, argues that truth is determined by an idea's popularity. This argument takes the form of the familiar expression "Fifty thousand French people can't be wrong." They certainly can be. The fact that a majority of people believes something does not make their belief correct or true.

The best example is what was a near-universal belief before Columbus and at the time of Galileo, that the world was flat and that the sun revolved around the earth. We know now that a majority does not make a belief true. People (even all people) can be and have been wrong.

Sliding Down the Slippery Slope   This fallacy involves the assumption that one event (i.e., the one the person is arguing against) will lead to another event that everyone agrees would be undesirable. In some cases, the connection between one event and another event is assumed to be direct (e.g., smoking pot will lead to smoking crack). In other cases, the connection between the original event and the unpleasant ultimate event is made through a series of linkages (e.g., smoking pot will lead to smoking crack, which will lead to more robberies, which will lead to general lawlessness).

Once you start on a course, the argument goes, you're on a slippery slope that will quickly lead to an extremely negative result. So, as it was argued not too long ago, prohibiting smoking in restaurants would lead to fewer customers, which would lead to restaurants and culinary schools closing, which would ultimately result in millions of people being out of work. Therefore, smoking should not be prohibited in restaurants, because this would cause an enormous increase in unemployment. Of course, that never happened. More recently you may have witnessed the fallacious argument that same-sex marriage will lead to the destruction of the U.S. family and possibly the breakdown of our entire society.

EMOTIONAL APPEALS

Emotional appeals, often called motivational appeals, are appeals to your listeners' feelings, needs, desires, and wants, and are extremely powerful in persuasion. When you use emotional appeals, you appeal to those forces that motivate people to develop, change, or strengthen attitudes or ways of behaving.

Developed more than 30 years ago, one of the most useful analyses of human motives remains Abraham Maslow's fivefold hierarchy of needs, reproduced in Figure 14.2 (p. 298) (Maslow, 1970; Benson & Dundis, 2003; Hanley & Abell, 2002; Kiel, 1999). One of the assumptions of Maslow's hierarchy is that people seek to fulfill the needs that are at the lowest

Guarding against being swayed by fallacious arguments requires special alertness when listening.

In listening to **personal attacks**, ask yourself:

- Is the speaker using personal attacks that have nothing to do with the issue at hand?
- Is the speaker substituting arguments against the person instead of addressing the issue?

In listening to **appeals to authority**, ask yourself:

- Does the authority offer proof or reliable evidence? If so, then this is not fallacious reasoning.
- Is this pure opinion? If so, then ask whether this person is a recognized authority in the pertinent field? If yes, then the argument is worth listening to. If not, then the argument may be logically suspect.
- Are appeals to authority used along with facts and evidence? If so, then this is a fine persuasive technique. If not, ask, Where's the proof?

In listening to **argument by the numbers**, ask yourself:

- Do these people have evidence for thinking as they do? If they have, then examine the evidence.

If they have good reasons instead, then examine the logic of their reasoning.

- Does it make sense?

In listening to arguments implying a **slippery slope**, ask yourself:

- What evidence is there for the influence of one event on another event?
- How likely is it that the original event will cause the disastrous final event? As the chain of events gets longer, the connection becomes more suspect.

How dangerous it always is to reason from insufficient data.

—SHERLOCK HOLMES, fictional detective created by Arthur Conan Doyle (1859–1930)

---

level first, and that only when those needs are satisfied do the needs at the next level begin to influence behavior. For example, people do not concern themselves with the need for security or freedom from fear if they are starving (i.e., if their need for food has not been met). As a speaker, therefore, you have to know what needs of your audience are unsatisfied. These are the needs you can appeal to in motivating your listeners.

Physiological Needs   In many parts of the world, and even parts of the United States, people's basic physiological needs are not fully met, and thus are powerful motivating forces. In such circumstances the speaker who promises to meet fundamental physiological needs is the one the people will follow.

Safety Needs   Those who do not have their basic safety and freedom-from-fear needs met will be motivated by appeals to security, protection, and freedom from physical and psychological harm. You see this need addressed in advertisements for burglar protection devices for home and car and in political speeches promising greater police protection in schools. Sometimes the safety motive is seen in individuals' desire for order, structure, and organization—motives clearly appealed to in advertisements for personal data assistants like the BlackBerry, cell phones, and information management software.

"He who gives food to the people will win."

—LECH WALESA

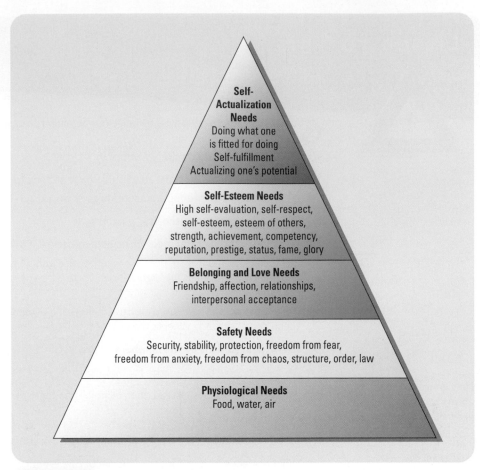

FIGURE 14.2 **Maslow's Hierarchy of Needs**

From which of these motives would your class members be convinced that campus violence is a real problem? Which might move them to donate their used books to students who can't afford them?

Source: From Abraham Maslow, *Motivation and Personality,* 3rd ed., edited by Robert D. Frager and James Fadiman. Copyright © 1987. Reprinted by permission of Pearson Education, Inc., Upper Saddle River, NJ.

Belonging and Love Needs   Belonging and love needs comprise a variety of specific motives. For most persons, love and its pursuit occupy a considerable amount of time and energy. If you can teach your audience how to be loved and how to love, your audience will be not only attentive but also grateful.

We also want affiliation—friendship and companionship. We want to be a part of a group, despite our equally strong desire for independence and individuality. Notice how advertisements for dating services, singles clubs, apartments with lounges and club rooms, and cruises appeal to this need for affiliation.

Self-Esteem Needs   We all want to see ourselves as self-confident, worthy, and contributing human beings. Inspirational speeches, speeches of the "you're the greatest" type, never seem to lack receptive and suggestible audiences. Self-esteem is raised by success and if your speech can tell people how to succeed in what they set out to do, you'll probably have an active and receptive audience.

Financial gain, in our culture and in many others, makes people feel good and raises their self-esteem. Concern for lower taxes, higher salaries, and fringe benefits is clearly related to the financial gain motive. Show the audience that what you're saying

Communication Choice Point

Fear Appeals

You're a parent of two young teenagers, and you want to dissuade them from engaging in sex. *Would it be ethical for you to use fear appeals to get them to avoid sexual relationships? Similarly, would it be ethical to use fear appeals in a public campaign to help prevent sexually transmitted diseases? Would it be ethical to use fear appeals if your motive was to sell SUVs? What are your choices for dealing with these situations persuasively and ethically?*

Emotional appeals are all around. People who want to censor the Internet may appeal to parents' fears about their children's accessing pornographic materials. Those who want to restrict media portrayals of violence may appeal to people's fear of increased violence in their own communities. Here are a few questions to consider as you develop your own ethical guidelines for the use of emotional appeals:

Where we have strong emotions, we're liable to fool ourselves.

—CARL SAGAN
(1934–1996), U.S. astronomer

- Is the real estate broker ethical in appealing to your desire for status?
- Is the friend who wants a favor and appeals to your desire for social approval acting ethically?
- Is the car salesperson's appeal to your desire for sexual rewards ethical?
- Is it ethical for parents to use fear appeals to exaggerate the dangers of sex or smoking pot to prevent their children from engaging in these behaviors?
- Is it ethical for parents to use fear appeals to prevent their children from interacting with people of different races or nationalities or affectional orientation?

or advocating will make them money, and they'll listen with considerable interest—much as they read the get-rich-quick books that constantly flood the bookstores and possibly your e-mail mailbox.

Self-Actualization Needs   At the top of Maslow's hierarchy is the **self-actualization** motive. Each of us has a desire to self-actualize, to become what we feel we're fit for. If you see ourself as a poet, you must write poetry. If you see yourself as a teacher, you must teach. Appeals to self-actualization needs—to people's yearning "to be the best they can be"—encourage listeners to strive for their highest ideals and are welcomed by many listeners.

CREDIBILITY APPEALS

Your **credibility** is the degree to which your audience regards you as a believable spokesperson. Your credibility is in the minds of your audience; if your listeners see you as competent and knowledgeable, of good character, and charismatic or dynamic, they'll find you credible (i.e., believable). As a result, you'll be more effective in changing their attitudes or in moving them to do something.

What makes a speaker credible will vary from one culture to another. In some cultures people see competence as the most important factor in, say, their choice of a teacher for their preschool children. In other cultures the most important factor might be the goodness or moral tone of the teacher or perhaps the reputation of the teacher's family. At the same time, each culture may define each of the factors of credibility differently. For example, "character" may mean following the rules of a specific religion in some cultures but following your individual conscience in others. The Quran, the Torah, and the New Testament will be ascribed very different levels of credibility depending on the religious beliefs of the audience. And this will be true even when all three books say essentially the same thing.

Before reading any farther about the ways to establish your credibility, you may wish to take the self-test "How credible are you?"

Communication Choice Point

Ignoring the Negative

You're giving a persuasive speech arguing for condom machines in rest rooms on campus. You know, however, that the money to install these machines will have to come from an increase in student fees. You wonder if you can ethically give the speech without mentioning that student fees will have to be increased. *How might you deal with this issue and be both persuasive and ethical?*

How Credible Are You?

Respond to each of the following phrases to indicate how you think members of your class see you when you deliver a public speech. Use the following scale:

5 = Definitely true; **4 =** probably true; **3** = neither true nor untrue; **2** = probably untrue; and **1** = definitely untrue

_____ ❶ Knowledgeable about the subject matter

_____ ❷ Experienced

_____ ❸ Informed about the subject matter

_____ ❹ Fair in the presentation of material (i.e., evidence and argument)

_____ ❺ Concerned with the audience's needs

_____ ❻ Consistent over time on the issues addressed in the speech

_____ ❼ Assertive in personal style

_____ ❽ Enthusiastic about the topic and in general

_____ ❾ Active rather than passive

HOW DID YOU DO? This test focuses on the three qualities of credibility—competence, character, and charisma—and is based on a large body of research (see McCroskey, 2007; Riggio, 1987). Items 1 to 3 refer to perceived competence: How capable do you seem to the audience? Items 4 to 6 refer to character: Does the audience see you as a good and moral person? Items 7 to 9 refer to charisma: Does the audience see you as dynamic and active? Total scores will range from a high of 45 to a low of 9. If you scored relatively high (around 32 or higher), then you feel your audience sees you as credible. If you scored relatively low (below 27), then you feel your audience sees you as lacking in credibility.

WHAT WILL YOU DO? Think about how you might go about increasing your credibility. What specific steps can you take to change undesirable audience perceptions of your credibility? As you read the following discussion, consider how you might strengthen your competence, character, and/or charisma.

"I've never actually stormed a castle, but I've taken a bunch of siege-management courses."

© Danny Shanahan/Condé Nast Publications/www.cartoonbank.com.

Competence To demonstrate your **competence**, show your listeners that you are knowledgeable and thoroughly familiar with your topic. The more knowledge and expertise the audience attributes to you, the more likely the audience will believe you, just as you are more likely to believe a teacher or doctor if you think he or she is knowledgeable about the subject at hand.

One way to demonstrate your competence is simply to tell listeners about it. Let the audience know of any special experience or training that qualifies you to speak on your topic. If you're speaking on communal living and you've lived on a commune yourself, then say so in your speech.

Another way to demonstrate competence is to cite a variety of research sources. Make it clear to your audience that you've thoroughly researched your topic. Do this by mentioning some of the books you've read, the people you've interviewed, and/or the articles you've consulted. At the same time, stress the competencies of your sources. Say something like, "Senator Cardova, who headed the finance committee for three years and was formerly a professor of economics at MIT, thinks . . ."

Character   An audience will see you as credible if they perceive you as someone of high moral **character**, someone who is honest and whom they can trust. One way to establish your moral character is to stress fairness. Stress, for example, that you've examined both sides of the issue (if indeed you have). Also, make it clear to the audience that you're interested in their welfare rather than seeking self-gain. If the audience feels that you're "out for yourself," they'll justifiably question your credibility. Tell your audience how the new legislation will reduce *their* taxes, how recycling will improve *their* community, how a knowledge of sexual harassment will make *their* workplace more comfortable and stress free.

Charisma   **Charisma** is a combination of your personality and dynamism as seen by the audience. An audience will perceive you as credible if they like you and see you as friendly and pleasant rather than aloof and reserved. Similarly, audiences favor the dynamic speaker over the hesitant, nonassertive speaker.

One way to stress charisma is to demonstrate a positive outlook. Show the audience that you have a positive orientation to the public speaking situation and to the entire speaker–audience encounter. Positive and forward-looking people are seen as more credible than negative and backward-looking people. Stress your pleasure at addressing the audience. Stress hope rather than despair, happiness rather than sadness. Demonstrate enthusiasm. The lethargic speaker, the speaker who somehow plods through the speech, is the very opposite of the charismatic speaker. Let the audience see your energy.

Be emphatic. Use language that's vivid and concrete rather than colorless and vague. Use gestures that are clear and decisive rather than random and hesitant. Demonstrate a firm commitment to the position you're advocating.

Communication Choice Point

Introducing Credibility

You are going to speak to an audience about Internet censorship, and you need to provide a brief introduction (about one minute in length or about 150 words) about yourself for someone else to use to introduce you. You want this introduction to establish your competence, character, and charisma. *What are some of the things you might want to include? What would you say?*

SUPPORTING MATERIALS IN CULTURAL PERSPECTIVE

The cultural distinctions discussed in earlier chapters become especially important in persuasion; the appeals you'd use to influence one cultural group would not be the same you'd use for a different group. You can appreciate the importance of this by reviewing five key dimensions of culture with persuasive strategies in mind—noting, for example, the types of appeals that will work and those that won't work in different cultures (Singh & Pereira, 2005):

- *Individualist and collectivist cultures.* In addressing members of a collectivist culture, you'll need to emphasize the importance of family, loyalty (to brand names or local organizations), and national identity and pride. On the other hand, if you were trying to appeal to members of individualistic cultures, you'd emphasize such themes as independence, nonconformity, and uniqueness. In collectivist cultures, to stress your own competence or that of your corporation may be taken as a suggestion that your audience members are inferior or that their corporations are not as good as yours. In individualist cultures, if you don't stress your competence, your listeners may assume it's because you don't have any.

- *High- and low-power-distance cultures.* With members of a high-power-distance culture, references to important and prominent people and to what they believe and advocate will prove effective. In contrast, in a low-power-distance culture these appeals will prove less effective than would, say, references to or testimonials from people much like the people you want to influence.

- *High- and low-uncertainty-avoidance cultures.* Audiences high in uncertainty avoidance want information from experts (or supported by experts); they want to know very clearly where they can go for information and guidance. These audiences also value tradition, so appeals to the past will prove effective with such groups. Audiences low in uncertainty avoidance can tolerate more ambiguity, and appeals to the new and different will be more effective.

- *Masculine and feminine cultures.* Audiences from cultures high in masculinity will be motivated by appeals to achievement, adventure, and enjoyment and will welcome the "hard sell"; listeners high in femininity will be motivated by "soft sell" appeals to harmony and aesthetic qualities.

- *High- and low-context cultures.* Listeners from high-context cultures will favor appeals that are indirect and implied; listeners from low-context cultures will want detail, directness, and explicitness.

Persuasive Speeches on Questions of Fact

Questions of fact concern what is or is not true, what does or does not exist, what did or did not happen. Some questions of fact are easily answered. These include many academic questions you're familiar with: Who was Aristotle? How many people use the Internet to get news? When was the first satellite launched? Questions of fact also include more mundane questions: What's on television? When is the meeting? What's Jenny's e-mail address? You can easily find answers to these questions by looking at some reference book, finding the relevant website, or asking someone who knows the answer.

The questions of fact that persuasive speeches deal with are a bit different. Although these questions also have answers, the answers are not that easy to find and in fact may never be found. The questions concern controversial issues for which different people have different answers. Daily newspapers abound in questions of fact. For example, on April 30, 2009, Google News (www.googlenews.com) dealt with questions of fact that included such issues as these: What did President Obama accomplish in his first 100 days? Does Alex Rodriguez deserve to be disciplined by the Yankees? Has same-sex marriage had any measurable positive or negative effects on society at large? Is the U.S. economic decline slowing? Does Kenneth Lewis deserve to be fired by Bank of America? Does profanity on television have negative effects on viewers?

THESIS AND MAIN POINTS

For a persuasive speech on a question of fact, you'll formulate a thesis on the basis of a factual statement such as "This company has . . . ," "The plaintiff was . . . ," or "The death was a case of . . . "

If you were preparing a persuasive speech, you might phrase your thesis as "This company discriminates against women." Whether or not the company does discriminate is a question of fact; clearly the company either does or does not discriminate. Whether you can prove it does or it doesn't, however, is another issue.

Once you've formulated your thesis, you can generate your main points by asking the simple question, *How do I know this?* or *Why would I believe this is true (factual)?* The answers to one of these questions will enable you to develop your main points. The bare bones of your speech might then look something like this:

General purpose: To persuade

Specific purpose: To persuade my listeners that this company discriminates against women.

Thesis: This company discriminates against women. (How can we tell that this company discriminates against women?)

I. Women earn less than men.

II. Women are hired less often than men.

III. Women occupy fewer managerial positions than men.

Make sure that you clearly connect your main points to your thesis in your introduction, when introducing each of the points, and again in your summary. Don't allow the audience to forget that the lower salaries that women earn directly support the thesis that this company discriminates against women.

Practicing the art of persuasion will prove useful in a wide variety of communication situations.

Select one of the following thesis statements and (1) identify the type of persuasive speech it is—fact, value, or policy; (2) from this thesis, generate two, three, or four main points for a persuasive speech; (3) identify a few forms of supporting material that might prove useful; and (4) select a suitable organizational pattern.

1. Condoms should be distributed to students in junior and senior high school.
2. Sports involving cruelty to animals, such as bullfighting, cockfighting, and foxhunting, should be universally condemned and declared illegal.
3. All states should recognize same-sex marriage.

SUPPORT

Having identified your main points, you would then begin searching for information to support them. Taking the first point, you might develop it something like this:

I. Women earn less than men.
  A. Over the past five years, the average salary for editorial assistants was $6,000 less for women than it was for men.
  B. Over the past five years, the entry-level salaries for women averaged $4,500 less than the entry-level salaries for men.
  C. Over the past five years, the bonuses earned by women were 20 percent below the bonuses earned by men.

This speech focuses entirely on a question of fact; the thesis itself is a question of fact. In other speeches, however, you may want only one of your main points to center on a question of fact, and then the speech as a whole may be one of policy or value.

In a speech on questions of fact, you'd want to emphasize logical proof. Facts are your best support. The more facts you have, the more persuasive you'll be in dealing with questions of fact. For example, the more evidence you can find that women earn less than men, the more convincing you will be in proving that women do in fact earn less and, ultimately, that women are discriminated against.

Use the most recent materials possible. The more recent your materials, the more relevant they will be to the present time and the more persuasive they're likely to be. Note that, in this example, if you were to say that in 1980 women earned on average $13,000 less than men, it would be meaningless in proving that the company discriminates against women *now*.

ORGANIZATION

Speeches on questions of fact probably fit most clearly into a topical organizational pattern, in which each reason for your thesis is given approximately equal weight. Notice, for example, that the outline for this "discrimination" example uses a topical order: All three facts pointing to discrimination are treated as equal main points.

Persuasive Speeches on Questions of Value

Questions of value concern what people consider good or bad, moral or immoral, just or unjust. The April 30, 2009, issue of Google News dealt with such questions of value as these: Is the new credit card bill helpful to consumers? Will Chrysler's deal with Fiat help the auto industry? What's the value in disciplining or not disciplining Alex Rodriguez?

"The object of oratory alone is not truth, but persuasion."

—THOMAS BABINGTON MACAULAY

Should same-sex marriage be made legal? Will Bank of America's firing of Kenneth Lewis help the financial industry? Should single utterance profanity on television be subject to government fines?

Speeches on questions of value will usually seek to strengthen audiences' existing attitudes, beliefs, or values. This is true of much religious and political speaking: For example, people who listen to religious speeches usually are already believers and are willing to listen; these speeches strive to strengthen the beliefs and values the people already hold. Speeches that seek to change audience values are much more difficult to construct, because most people resist change. When you try to get people to change their values or beliefs, you're fighting an uphill (though not necessarily impossible) battle.

Be sure that you define clearly the specific value on which you're focusing. For example, let's say that you're developing a speech to persuade high school students to attend college. You want to stress that college is of value, but what type of value do you focus on? The financial value (e.g., that college graduates earn more money than nongraduates)? The social value (e.g., that college is a lot of fun and a great place to make friends)? The intellectual value (e.g., that college will broaden your view of the world and make you a more critical and creative thinker)? Once you clarify the type of value on which you'll focus, you'll find it easier to develop the relevant points. You'll also find it easier to locate appropriate supporting materials.

THESIS AND MAIN POINTS

Theses devoted to questions of value might look something like: "The death penalty is unjustifiable," "Bullfighting is inhumane," or "Sexual discrimination is wrong."

As with speeches on questions of fact, you can generate the main points for a speech on a question of value by asking a strategic question of your thesis, such as *Why is this good?* or *Why is this immoral?* For example, you can take the first thesis and ask yourself, *Why is the death penalty unjustifiable?* The answers to this question will give you the speech's main points. The body of your speech might then look something like this:

General purpose: To persuade

Specific purpose: To persuade my listeners that the death penalty is unjustifiable

Thesis: The death penalty is unjustifiable. (Why is the death penalty unjustifiable?)

I. The criminal justice system can make mistakes.

II. The death penalty constitutes cruel and unusual punishment.

III. No one has the moral right to take another's life.

SUPPORT

To support your main points, search for relevant evidence. For example, to show that mistakes have been made, you might itemize three or four high-profile cases in which people were put to death and later, through DNA, found to have been innocent.

At times, and with certain topics, it may be useful to identify the standards you would use to judge something moral, justified, fair, or good. For example, in the "bullfighting is inhumane" speech, you might devote your first main point to defining when an action can be considered inhumane. In this case, the body of your speech might look like this:

I. An inhumane act has two qualities.
   A. It is cruel and painful.
   B. It serves no human necessity.
II. Bullfighting is inhumane.
   A. It is cruel and painful.
   B. It serves no necessary function.

Consult the online dictionary of topics on MyCommunicationLab (**www.mycommunicationlab.com**) for suggestions for persuasive speech topics. Select a topic and then create a rough outline in which you:

1. identify a specific purpose and thesis,
2. analyze your classroom audience and note adaptations you'd make,
3. generate at least two main points with persuasive supporting materials,
4. construct a conclusion and an introduction.

Notice that in the example of capital punishment the speaker aims to strengthen or change the listeners' beliefs about the death penalty. The speaker is not asking the audience to do anything about capital punishment, but merely to believe that it's not justified. However, you might also use a question of value as a first step toward persuading your audience to take some action. For example, once you got your listeners to see the death penalty as unjustified, you might then ask them to take certain actions—perhaps in your next speech—to support an anti-death-penalty politician, to vote for or against a particular proposition, or to join an organization fighting against the death penalty.

ORGANIZATION

Like speeches on questions of fact, speeches on questions of value often lend themselves to topical organization. For example, the speech on capital punishment outlined earlier uses a topical order. But within this topical order there is another level of organization, an organization that begins with those items on which there is least disagreement or opposition and moves on to the items that your listeners are likely to see very differently. It's likely that even those in favor of the death penalty would agree that mistakes can be made; in fact, they probably would be willing to accept evidence that mistakes have been made, especially if you cite reliable statistical evidence and expert testimony. By starting with this issue, you secure initial agreement and can use that as a basis for approaching aspects on which you and the audience are more likely to disagree.

> ### Communication Choice Point
> **Persuasive Strategy**
> You want to get listeners to contribute three hours per week to the college's program of helping at-risk high school students prepare for college. *What are some of the persuasive strategies you might use in this situation?*

Persuasive Speeches on Questions of Policy

When you move beyond focusing on values to urging your audience to do something about an issue, you've broached a **question of policy**. For example, in a speech designed to convince your listeners that bullfighting is inhumane, you'd be focusing on a question of value. But, if you were to urge that bullfighting should therefore be declared illegal, you'd be focusing on a question of policy. Items that focused on questions of policy in the April 30, 2009, issue of Google News included the following: What should U.S. policy be toward Pakistan's Taliban uprising? How should the United States respond to the swine flu epidemic? What disciplinary action should the Yankees take against Alex Rodriguez? How should Maine vote on same-sex marriage? How can colleges prevent violence on campus? Should Bank of America fire Kenneth Lewis? What should the policy be toward profanity on television?

Questions of policy concern what should be done, what procedures should be adopted, what laws should be changed—in short, what policy should be followed. In some speeches you may want to defend a specific policy; in others you may wish to argue that a current policy should be discontinued.

THESIS AND MAIN POINTS

Persuasive speeches frequently revolve around questions of policy and may use theses such as the following:

- Hate speech should be banned in colleges.
- Our community should adopt a zero-tolerance policy for guns in schools.
- Abortion should be available on demand.
- Music CDs should be rated for violence and profanity.
- Medical marijuana should be legalized.
- Smoking should be banned from all public buildings and parks.

As you can tell from these examples, questions of policy almost invariably involve questions of values. To argue, for example, that hate speech should be banned in colleges is based on the value judgment that hate speech is wrong. To argue for a zero-tolerance policy on guns in schools implies that you think it's wrong for students or faculty to carry guns to school.

You can develop your speech on a question of policy by asking a strategic question of your thesis. With policy issues the question will be, *Why should the policy be adopted? Why should this policy be discontinued?* or *Why is this policy better than what we have now?* Taking the first example thesis, you might ask, *Why should hate speech be banned on campus?* From the answers to this question, you would develop your main points, which might look something like this:

I. Hate speech teaches hate instead of tolerance.

II. Hate speech denigrates women and minorities.

III. Hate speech encourages violence against women and minorities.

SUPPORT

You would then support each main point with a variety of supporting materials that would convince your audience that hate speech should be banned from college campuses. For example, you might cite the websites put up by certain groups that advocate violence against women and minority members or quote from the lyrics of performers who came to campus. You might cite examples of actual violence that had been accompanied by hate speech or hate literature.

In some speeches on questions of policy, you might simply want your listeners to agree that the policy you're advocating is a good one. In other cases you might want them to do something about the policy—to vote for a particular candidate, to take vitamin C, to write to their elected officials, to participate in a walkathon, to wear an AIDS awareness ribbon, and so on.

ORGANIZATION

Speeches on questions of policy may be organized in a variety of ways. For example, if you're comparing two policies, consider the comparison-and-contrast method. If the existing policy is doing harm, consider using a cause-to-effect pattern. If your proposed policy is designed to solve a problem, consider the problem–solution pattern. For example, a speech advocating zero tolerance for guns in school could be divided into two basic parts:

I. Guns are destroying our high schools. *[problem]*

II. We must adopt a zero tolerance policy. *[solution]*

Communication Choice Point

Persuasive Appeals

You want to give a speech urging your listeners to vote in favor of establishing a hate speech code at the college. *What are some persuasive appeals you might use to get students to vote for a hate speech code?*

The Public Speaking Sample Assistant

AN EXCELLENT PERSUASIVE SPEECH

The title of the speech is intriguing and makes you wonder what exactly the speaker is going to talk about.

THE MERCHANTS OF DEATH

*Andrew Farmer**

Khaled Masri was detained in Germany, "beaten, stripped, shackled," then flown to Afghanistan to be interrogated for a crime he never committed. According to the *International Enforcement Law Reporter* of May 2005, Masri was mistaken for a known terrorist with a similar name and, despite this mistake, was detained for over five months. In February 2003 Abu Omar was grabbed off a sidewalk in Milan, maced, then kidnapped by assailants in an unmarked van. Also presumed innocent, with no evidence connecting Omar to terrorism, he remains missing to this day over three years later.

Using these two dramatic examples clearly gains attention. We've all heard about these kinds of injustices, so we feel we're on familiar ground. But then the topic turns to an issue that many people know little if anything about, the private military forces.

These acts resemble those of an American government willing to make any sacrifice to make gains in a war on terror. But they weren't committed by the U.S. Army, at least not technically. The PBS *Frontline* online of June 21, 2005, defines Private Military Forces, or PMFs, as civilian workers employed by private military companies to guard "supply lines, [run] U.S. military bases and [protect] U.S. diplomats and generals." However, PMFs are also committing torturous atrocities that undermine our relations with other countries and the safety of our soldiers abroad. A December 7, 2005, press release for the new documentary *Shadow Company* states that there are over 20,000 private soldiers currently operating in Iraq alone who cannot be constrained by executive or Congressional mandate. With numbers of these soldiers already in place in Afghanistan, Bosnia, and Colombia, as well as parts of Africa and other parts of South America, it is crucial that we, first, understand the problems associated with these types of soldiers; second, explore the causes of their increased usage; and finally, determine how we may better regulate companies that the *Ottawa Citizen* of November 16, 2005, states are "a way for mercenaries to gain legitimacy."

Notice how the speaker wisely gives an authoritative definition—the audience is likely to accept a definition by PBS *Frontline*. These definitions of key terms not only are helpful to those who don't know the topic, or don't know it well, but also help focus the discussion to follow.

The second point made in this introduction is designed to stress the importance of the topic: The topic is important because PMFs' actions undermine our relations with other countries and jeopardize the safety of soldiers.

The third part of this introduction is to orient the audience. Notice that the speaker very clearly indicates the three points he will cover: (1) the problems with PMFs, (2) the causes of their increase, and (3) ways in which they can be regulated.

The *Edmonton Journal* of November 13, 2005, estimates that the U.S. spends 100 billion dollars annually to employ nearly half a million PMFs in over 50 countries. Outsourcing our military to private soldiers is problematic given their

The speaker doesn't explicitly establish the credibility of the *Edmonton Journal* or other source material. The wealth of cited sources, however, makes you feel that the research was sound and extensive. If you feel your audience might not accept the authority of your sources, you might say something about their authoritativeness or perhaps give the qualifications of the writers of the articles.

*Andrew Farmer is a student at the University of Texas at Austin. The speech was delivered at the 2006 American Forensic Association National Individual Events Tournament in Gainesville, Florida, and was accompanied by a complete list of works cited. It is reprinted by permission of the speaker.

unreliability, the blatant human rights violations they commit, and the corrupting power of money.

The *Defense Daily International* of August 12, 2005, explains that the U.S. military cannot coordinate or control PMFs, "because private security contractors have no direct contractual relationship with the commander." For instance, the *New York Times* of September 10, 2005, states that Global Strategies, a private military company operating out of Iraq, closed and abandoned Baghdad Airport for 48 hours complaining they had not been paid. This reckless strike nearly allowed the airport to fall into the hands of insurgents.

To further complicate the situation, the *Charleston Gazette* of April 11, 2005, notes that PMFs are not accountable to any government oversight and thus do not follow normal rules of combat—which may lead to human rights violations that go unpunished. The *Raleigh News and Observer* of March 23, 2006, states that private military contractors in Iraq "regularly shoot into civilian cars with little accountability." The *Al-Ahram Weekly* of February 16, 2006, reports that military contractors have killed over 1,800 Iraqi civilians since 2003. And when Dyncorp, a private military firm, discovered that 13 of its employees had bought and sold Bosnian women as sex slaves, our government ruled it had no jurisdiction to punish the forces. In fact, the *Vancouver Sun* of November 12, 2005, reveals that the men didn't even receive so much as a slap on the wrist after destroying the lives of women they were supposedly sent to protect.

Additionally, as P. W. Singer writes in his 2005 book *Corporate Warriors*, PMFs have shown themselves to be corruptible. They are businesses for profit, and their loyalty is to the highest bidder—not national interests. The *L.A. Times* of March 4, 2006, explains that since private military companies are reimbursed all operating costs and their profit is a percentage of total money spent, contractors are driven to inflate costs of operation in order to receive greater profit. By hinging our security on those trying to make money off our country rather than defend it, we create an atmosphere of unreliablility and corruption.

While the American Revolution, the War of 1812, two world wars, and other conflicts have all been fought by the American military, PMFs are in charge of defending American democracy today for three reasons: an increased demand for soldiers, the economics of outsourcing, and the ability of PMFs to divert scrutiny placed on military actions.

As American military presence rises internationally, the United States looks to military contractors to compensate for understaffed or undertrained military personnel. An NPR broadcast on January 4, 2006, states that the army missed its recruitment goals by 20 percent in 2005, prompting an increased reliance on private military contractors to

---

The first major point is divided clearly into three parts. There are three reasons why PMFs present problems: (1) They are unreliable; (2) they commit violations; and (3) they are guided by money. Each of these is covered in a separate paragraph in the written speech.
Here the speaker establishes PMFs' unreliability.

Here the speaker identifies in a very dramatic way the violations these PMFs commit.

Here the speaker demonstrates PMFs' focus on money and how it leads to corruption.

Here the speaker leads into the second major point, the reasons why the use of these mercenaries is growing. Again, there are three clearly identified reasons: (1) increased demand, (2) economics, and (3) PMFs' ability to deflect scrutiny.

Here the speaker establishes why there's a growing demand for PMFs.

perform the duties that were once the responsibility of our men and women in uniform. In fact, as a Government Accountability Office report of July 28, 2005, reveals, the government is forced to subcontract with private security providers because U.S. armed forces lack training in occupation and rebuilding.

Governments that employ PMFs find outsourcing to contractors to be a sound economic practice. The *Liverpool Daily Echo* of June 1, 2005, notes that governments believe private soldiers are more cost effective in the long term because they are not eligible for government retirement or death benefits. Surprisingly, as the *Ottawa Citizen* explains on November 13, 2005, over half of the private military forces currently employed in Iraq are from developing nations because their labor is both cheap and readily available.

> Here the speaker illustrates the economic foundation for the practice.

PMFs are also useful in diverting attention away from the military. Private forces are being deployed without Congress or the media knowing where PMFs are located. The previously cited *Edmonton Journal* states that since Congress does not currently know the logistics of our use of private soldiers, the United States is open to deny involvement in operations abroad. This practice sounds alarmingly similar to those of countries who finance terrorists to do their will—the very countries we call the "axis of evil."

> Here the speaker demonstrates that PMFs divert attention from the regular military.

PMFs need to find ways to provide constructive rather than destructive roles in emergencies. Solutions must be explored to regulate PMFs by the government, encourage PMFs to play positive roles on the home front, and raise public awareness.

> Here the speaker introduces his most important point, and the one that is at the center of the speech: Changes are needed. The speaker's suggestions are three: (1) Enact legislation to regulate PMF; (2) encourage PMFs' playing a more positive role, and (3) increase public awareness. This section most clearly identifies the address as a speech on a question of policy.

This past October, legislators passed the Contractors on the Battlefield Regulatory Act in an attempt to limit the powers of private soldiers. However, an October 20, 2005, *Inside the Pentagon* article asserts the directive "still doesn't answer . . . the fundamental questions of legal status and accountability." Legislators must work to pass detailed legislation that clearly defines PMF accountability to the military chain of command and auditing procedures to safeguard against inflated reimbursements. The *Baltimore Sun* of October 6, 2005, contends that legislators must hold the executive branch accountable to provisions stipulated in the War Powers Act of 1973, which mandates that Congress be consulted before American forces are sent into combat, even if the forces are only paid for by America.

> Here the speaker calls for legislation to define PMF's accountability.

Next, an alternative use of PMFs is needed. The *Christian Science Monitor* of September 19, 2005, suggests that in light of Katrina, PMFs can find a productive role in domestic reconstruction, rather than in dangerous operations abroad. Domestic use of private security forces ensures greater scrutiny and accountability. Using PMFs at

> Here the speaker shows that there are more positive roles for PMFs to play.

home ensures that PMFs are closely monitored and play productive, rather than destructive, roles.

Finally, we have to change our attitudes about the way we allow our military to act on our behalf. Visit the websites of human rights and military watchdog organizations such as Amnesty International, the Human Rights and Displacement Consultancy, or the Humanitarian Law Center and educate yourself about ongoing human rights violations. Or better yet, join one of these groups. Military privatization is a public concern, and PMFs need to be held to the same standards as our men and women in uniform.

Machiavelli's *The Prince* warns that "mercenaries and auxiliaries are useless and dangerous, and if anyone supports his state by the arms of mercenaries, he will never stand firm or sure." Heeding his warning, we should act quickly to ensure that we do not let the power of our military fall into the hands of those with dollar signs on the brain. By analyzing atrocities commited by PMFs, and reasons for their widespread use, we can take steps to ensure that private military groups are used ethically. While no steps can be taken to give Khaled Masri five months of his life back, precautions can be made to ensure that no one else ever suffers such a fate.

Here the speaker argues that we have to change our attitudes about PMFs.

Notice that in the last part of this third point, the speaker asks the audience to do something—in this case, increase their awareness of the problem. And he's very helpful in directing this call for increased awareness by offering listeners different options; one simple suggestion is to visit a variety of websites, whereas a more extensive commitment would be to join organizations concerned with PMFs.

The quotation from Machiavelli is particularly apt, because most college students will have heard or read of Machiavelli in political science or history classes.

Here the speaker summarizes his speech, repeating the three major points raised in the speech. He then closes the speech by referring back to an example used in the introduction, thus effectively reestablishing the importance of this topic in human terms.

Summary of Concepts and Skills

This chapter looked at the persuasive speech, first covering guidelines and types of supporting materials for persuasion and then discussing three main types of persuasive speeches.

1. Persuasion has three main goals: (1) to strengthen or weaken attitudes, beliefs, or values, (2) to change attitudes, beliefs, or values, and (3) to motivate to action.
2. Among the important guidelines for persuasive speaking are (1) anticipate selective exposure, (2) ask for reasonable amounts of change, and (3) identify with your audience.
3. Three major types of support have special importance in speeches of persuasion: logical appeals, emotional appeals, and credibility appeals.
4. Persuasive speeches on questions of fact focus on what is or is not true.
5. Speeches on questions of value focus on issues of good and bad, justice and injustice.
6. Speeches on questions of policy focus on what should or should not be done, what procedures should or should not be adopted.

To be an effective public speaker, you need to master a variety of persuading skills. Place a check mark next to those skills you want to work on most.

_____ 1. In my persuasive speeches I apply (where relevant) the principles of persuasion: selective exposure, amounts of change, and identification.

_____ 2. In my persuasive speeches I critically analyze reasoning from specific instances to generalizations, causes and effects, and sign.

_____ 3. When listening to persuasive attempts, I detect fallacies such as personal attacks, appeals to authority, appeal to numbers, and the slippery slope.

_____ 4. To motivate my audience I use motivational appeals: for example, appeals to desires for power, control, and influence; self-esteem and approval; safety; achievement; and financial gain.

_____ 5. In my speeches I seek to establish my credibility by displaying competence, high moral character, and dynamism, or charisma.

Key Word Quiz

The Language of Persuasive Speaking

Match the terms about the persuasive speech with their definitions. Record the number of the definition next to the appropriate term.

_____ a. attitude (291)

_____ b. credibility (299)

_____ c. selective exposure (293)

_____ d. belief (291)

_____ e. questions of value (304)

_____ f. self-actualization (299)

_____ g. charisma (301)

_____ h. reasoning from sign (295)

_____ i. questions of policy (305)

_____ j. questions of fact (302)

1. Drawing conclusions from clues (or symptoms) that often occur together.
2. A motive that influences people only after all other needs are satisfied.
3. Issues that concern what should be done or what procedures should be followed.
4. The tendency to respond in a certain way.
5. Issues that concern what is or is not true or what does or doesn't exist.
6. The degree to which your audience regards you as believable.
7. Principle stating that listeners will actively seek out information that supports their beliefs and will actively avoid information that contradicts their existing beliefs.
8. Conviction of the existence or reality of something or of the truth of some assertion.
9. A quality of personal attractiveness, dynamism, and forcefulness that enhances credibility.
10. Issues that concern what people consider good or bad, just or unjust.

These ten terms and additional terms used in this chapter can be found in the glossary and on flashcards on MyCommunicationLab (www.mycommunicationlab.com).

Answers: a. 4 b. 6 c. 7 d. 8 e. 10 f. 2 g. 9 h. 1 i. 3 j. 5

MyCommunicationLab

mycommunicationlab

www.mycommunicationlab.com

Visit MyCommunicationLab (www.mycommunicationlab.com) for additional materials on persuasion. Flash cards, videos, skill building exercises, sample text questions, and additional examples and discussions will help you continue your study of persuasive speaking.

Glossary

Listed here are definitions of the technical terms of human communication—the words that are peculiar or unique to this discipline—along with relevant skills where applicable (in *italic*). These definitions and skill statements should make new or difficult terms a bit easier to understand and should serve as reminders of the skills discussed throughout this text. All boldface terms within the definitions appear as separate entries in the glossary.

ableism. Discrimination against people with disabilities. *Use person-first language; put the person first and the disability second, not "the blind boy" but "the boy who is blind . . ."*

abstraction. A general concept derived from a class of objects; a part representation of some whole. Also, the quality of being abstract. *Use both abstract and specific terms when describing or explaining.*

abstraction process. The process by which a general concept is derived from specifics; the process by which some (never all) characteristics of an object, person, or event are perceived by the senses or included in some term, phrase, or sentence.

accent. The stress or emphasis placed on a syllable when it is pronounced.

accommodation. The process of adjusting your communication patterns to those with whom you're interacting. *Accommodate to the speaking style of your listeners in moderation; too much mirroring of the other's style may appear manipulative.*

acculturation. The processes by which a person's culture is modified or changed through contact with or exposure to another culture.

active listening. A process of putting together into some meaningful whole an understanding of a speaker's total message—the verbal and the nonverbal, the content and the feelings. *If you wish to listen actively, paraphrase the speaker's meaning, express understanding of the speaker's feelings, and ask questions when you need something clarified.*

adaptors. Nonverbal behaviors that satisfy some personal need and usually occur without awareness, such as scratching to relieve an itch or moistening your lips to relieve dryness. Three types of adaptors are often distinguished: **self-adaptors, alter-adaptors,** and **object-adaptors.**

adjustment (principle of). The principle of verbal interaction that claims that communication takes place only to the extent that the parties communicating share the same system of signals.

advice. Messages that tell another person what he or she should do.

affect displays. Movements of the facial area that convey emotional meaning—for example, anger, fear, or surprise.

affinity-seeking strategies. Behaviors designed to increase interpersonal attractiveness. *Use in moderation.*

affirmation. The communication of support and approval.

agapic love. One of Lee's (1976) six types of love; compassionate and selfless love offered without concern for personal reward and without any expectation reciprocation.

ageism. Discrimination based on age. *Avoid it.*

agenda. A list of the items that a small group must deal with in the order in which they should be covered. *As a leader or member, keep focused on the agenda.*

aggressiveness. *See* **verbal aggressiveness.**

allness. The assumption that all can be known or is known about a given person, issue, object, or event. *Avoid allness statements (for example, statements containing such words as all, never, or always); they invariably misstate the reality and will often offend the other person.*

alter-adaptors. Body movements you make in response to your current interactions, such as crossing your arms over your chest when someone unpleasant approaches or moving closer to someone you like.

altercasting. Placing the listener in a specific role for a specific purpose and asking that the listener approach the question or problem from the perspective of this specific role.

ambiguity. The condition in which a message can be interpreted as having more than one meaning. *Recognize that all messages are potentially ambiguous, so clarify as necessary.*

amount of change principle. A principle of persuasion stating that the greater and more important the change desired by the speaker, the more difficult its achievement will be.

amplification. *See* **support.**

analogy (reasoning from). A type of reasoning in which you compare similar things and conclude that, because they are alike in so many respects, they also must be alike in some other respect.

anger management. The methods and techniques by which anger is controlled and managed. *Calm down as best you* *can; then consider your communication options and the relevant communication skills for expressing your feelings.*

apology. Expressions of regret or sorry for having done what you did or for what happened.

appeals to authority. A fallacy of reasoning in which someone is passed off as an authority when the person logically has little authority, expertise, or knowledge in the subject under discussion. *Ask for evidence.*

appeals to numbers. Appeals to numbers in which the speaker argues that truth is determined by popularity.

apprehension. *See* **communication apprehension.**

arbitrariness. A feature of human language; the absence of a real or inherent relationship between the form of a word and its meaning. If we do not know anything of a particular language, we cannot examine the form of a word and thereby discover its meaning.

argument. Evidence (for example, facts or statistics) and a conclusion drawn from the evidence.

argumentativeness. A willingness to speak your mind, to argue for a point of view. *In conflict, avoid attacking the other person's self-concept. Instead, focus logically on the issues, emphasize finding solutions, and work to ensure that what is said will result in positive self-feelings for both individuals.* Distinguished from **verbal aggressiveness.**

articulation. The physiological movements of the speech organs as they modify and interrupt the air stream emitted from the lungs.

artifactual messages. Messages conveyed through the wearing and arrangement of various artifacts—for example, clothing, jewelry, buttons, or the furniture in your house and its arrangement. *Use artifacts (e.g., color, clothing, body adornment, space decoration) to communicate your desired messages. But check to find out whether others are in fact receiving the messages you think you are communicating.*

assertiveness. A willingness to stand up for your rights while maintaining respect for the rights of others. *Increase your own assertiveness by analyzing the assertive messages of others, rehearsing assertive messages, and communicating assertively by describing the problem, saying how the problem affects you, proposing solutions, confirming your understanding, and reflecting on your own assertiveness.*

assimilation. A process of distortion in which we reconstruct messages to make them conform to our own attitudes, prejudices, needs, and values.

asynchronous. Communication in which sending and receiving of a message takes place at different times. *Contrast* **synchronous.**

attack. A persuasive technique that involves accusing another person (usually an opponent) of some serious wrongdoing so that the issue under discussion never gets examined. *Avoid this as a speaker and recognize it for what it is as a listener.*

attention. The process of responding to a stimulus or stimuli; usually involves some consciousness of responding.

attitude. A predisposition to respond for or against an object, person, or position.

attraction. The state or process by which one individual is drawn to another, forming a highly positive evaluation of that other person.

attraction theory. A theory holding that we form relationships on the basis of our attraction for another person.

attractiveness. The degree to which a person is perceived to be physically attractive and to possess a pleasing personality.

attribution. A process through which we attempt to understand the behaviors of others (as well as our own), particularly the reasons or motivations for these behaviors.

attribution theory. A theory concerned with the processes involved in attributing causation or motivation to a person's behavior.

audience analysis. The process of analyzing a speaker's intended listeners. *Analyze the audience in terms of its sociological and psychological characteristics and adapt your speech based on these findings.*

audience participation principle. A principle of persuasion stating that persuasion is achieved more effectively when the audience participates actively.

authoritarian leader. A group leader who determines the group policies or makes decisions without consulting or securing agreement from group members.

avoidance. An unproductive conflict strategy in which a person takes mental or physical flight from the actual conflict. *Do not practice avoidance; engaging in conflict actively is generally the more effective management strategy.*

backchanneling cues. Listener responses to a speaker that do not ask for the speaking role.

bandwagon. A persuasive technique in which the speaker tries to gain compliance by saying that "everyone is doing it" and urging audience members to jump on the bandwagon.

barriers to communication. Physical or psychological factors that prevent or hinder effective communication.

behavioral synchrony. The similarity in the behavior, usually nonverbal, of two persons; generally taken as an index of mutual liking.

belief. Confidence in the existence or truth of something; conviction.

beltlining. An unproductive conflict strategy in which one person hits at the emotional level at which the other person cannot withstand the blow. *Avoid it; beltlining is likely to cause resentment that may extend well beyond the argument itself.*

blame. An unproductive conflict strategy in which we attribute the cause of the conflict to the other person or devote our energies to discovering who is the cause and avoid talking about the issues causing the conflict. *Focus on resolving the conflict rather than affixing blame.*

boundary marker. A marker dividing one person's territory from another's—for example, a fence.

brainstorming. A technique for generating ideas either alone or, more usually, in a small group. *Follow these general rules: Avoid negative criticism, strive for quantity, combine and extend the contributions of others, and contribute as many wild ideas as possible. Appropriately restimulate a brainstorming group that has lost its steam by asking for additional contributions or for further extensions of previously contributed ideas.*

breadth. The number of topics about which individuals in a relationship communicate.

causes and effects (reasoning from). A form of reasoning in which you conclude that certain effects are due to specific causes or that specific causes produce certain effects. *Be careful that you don't fall into the trap of assuming that, because things occur in sequence, one necessarily causes the other.*

censorship. Legal restriction imposed on the right to produce, distribute, or receive various communications.

central marker. An item that is placed in a territory to reserve it for a specific person—for example, a sweater thrown over a library chair to signal that the chair is taken.

certainty. An attitude of closed-mindedness that creates a defensiveness among communication participants. *Contrast* **provisionalism.**

channel. The vehicle or medium through which signals are sent. *Assess your channel options (e.g., speaking face-to-face, sending e-mail, or leaving a voicemail message when you know the person won't be home) before communicating important messages.*

character. One of the qualities of **credibility;** the individual's honesty and basic nature; moral qualities.

charisma. One of the qualities of **credibility;** the individual's dynamism or forcefulness.

cherishing behaviors. Small behaviors we enjoy receiving from others, especially from our relational partner—for example, a kiss, a smile, or a gift of flowers. *Exchanging such behaviors is one way of increasing relationship satisfaction.*

chronemics. The study of the communicative nature of time—the way you treat time and use it to communicate. Two general areas of chronemics are **cultural time** and **psychological time.**

civil inattention. Polite ignoring of others so as not to invade their privacy.

cliché. An overused expression that has lost its novelty and part of its meaning and that calls attention to itself because of its overuse, such as "tall, dark, and handsome" as a description of a man.

closed-mindedness. An unwillingness to receive certain communication messages. *Listen openly even to messages that may contradict existing attitudes and beliefs.*

code. A set of symbols used to translate a message from one form to another.

coercive power. Power based on a person's ability to punish or to remove rewards from another person. *Exerting coercive power often creates resistance and defensiveness.*

cognitive restructuring. A process aimed at substituting logical and realistic beliefs for unrealistic ones; used in reducing communication apprehension and in raising self-esteem.

cohesiveness. A quality of togetherness; in group communication situations, the mutual attraction among members and the extent to which members work together as a group.

collective orientation. A cultural orientation that stresses the group's rather than the individual's goals and preferences. Contrast **individual orientation.**

collectivist culture. A culture that emphasizes the group's rather than the individual's goals; a culture that values, for example, benevolence, tradition, and conformity. Contrast **individualistic culture.**

color communication. The meanings that different cultures communicate via color. *Use color to reinforce your meanings and recognize the cultural differences in the way colors are given meaning.*

communication. (1) The process or act of communicating; (2) the actual message or messages sent and received; (3) the study of the processes involved in the sending and receiving of messages.

communication accommodation theory. Theory holding that speakers adjust their speaking style to their listeners to gain social approval and achieve greater communication effectiveness.

communication apprehension. Fear or anxiety over communicating; may be "trait apprehension" (i.e., fear of communication generally, regardless of the specific situation) or "state apprehension" (i.e., fear that is specific to a given communication situation). *Acquire communication skills and experiences, focus on your prior successes, reduce unpredictability, and put apprehension in perspective.*

communication competence. Knowledge of the rules and skills of communication; the qualities that make for effectiveness in communication.

communication network. The pathways of messages; the organizational structure through which messages are sent and received.

competence. One of the dimensions of **credibility;** consists of a person's perceived levels of ability and knowledge.

complementarity. A principle of **attraction** stating that we are attracted by qualities that we do not possess or that we wish to possess and to people who are opposite or different from ourselves. *Contrast* **similarity.**

complementary relationship. A relationship in which the behavior of one person serves as the stimulus for the complementary behavior of the other; in such relationships behavioral differences are maximized.

compliance-gaining strategies. Behaviors directed toward gaining the agreement of others; behaviors designed to persuade others to do as we wish.

compliance-resisting strategies. Behaviors directed at resisting the persuasive attempts of others.

compliment. A message of praise, flattery, or congratulations.

computer-mediated communication. A general term denoting all forms of communication between people that take place through some computer, electronic, or Internet connection.

confidence. A quality of interpersonal effectiveness; a comfortable, at-ease feeling in interpersonal communication situations.

confirmation. A communication pattern that acknowledges another person's presence and also indicates an acceptance of this person, this person's definition of self, and the relationship as defined or viewed by this other person. *When you wish to be confirming, acknowledge (verbally and/or nonverbally) others in your group and their contributions. Contrast* **disconfirmation.**

conflict. *See* **interpersonal conflict.**

congruence. A condition in which verbal and nonverbal behaviors reinforce each other.

connotation. The feeling or emotional aspect of meaning, generally viewed as consisting of evaluative (e.g., good/bad), potency (i.e., strong/weak), and activity (i.e., fast/slow) dimensions; the associations of a term. *As a speaker, clarify your connotative meanings if you have any doubts that your listeners might misunderstand you; as a listener, ask questions if you have doubts about the speaker's connotations. Contrast* **denotation.**

consensus. A process of reaching agreement (not necessarily unanimous) among group members.

consistency. A perceptual process that influences us to maintain balance among our perceptions; a process that makes us tend to see what we expect to see and to be uncomfortable when our perceptions run contrary to our expectations.

contact. The first stage of an interpersonal relationship, in which perceptual and interactional contact occurs.

contamination. A form of territorial encroachment that renders another's territory impure.

content and relationship dimensions. Two simultaneous aspects of any given communication: the aspect that pertains to the world external to both speaker and listener (i.e., content) and the aspect having to do with the relationship between the individuals (i.e., relationship). *Listen to both the content and the relationship aspects of messages, distinguish between them, and respond to both.*

context of communication. The physical, psychological, social, and temporal environment in which communication takes place.

contrast (principle of). Often-followed rule of perception: messages or people who are very different from each other probably don't belong together, and do not constitute a set or group.

controllability. One of the factors we consider in judging whether a person is responsible for his or her behavior.

If the person was in control, then we judge that he or she was responsible. *See also* **attribution theory.**

conversation. Two-person communication that usually includes an opening, feedforward, a business stage, feedback, and a closing.

conversational management. The ways in which a conversation is conducted.

conversational turns. The process of exchanging speaking and listening turns during a conversation.

conversational maxims. Principles that people follow in conversation to ensure that the goal of the conversation is achieved. *Follow (generally) the basic maxims of conversation, such as the maxims of quantity, quality, relations, manner, and politeness.*

conversational turns. The process of exchanging the speaker and listener roles during conversation. *Maintain relatively short conversational turns and then pass the speaker's turn to another person nonverbally or verbally.*

cooperation. An interpersonal process by which individuals work together for a common end; the pooling of efforts to produce a mutually desired outcome.

cooperation (principle of). Cultural principle stating that speaker and listener will cooperate in trying to communicate effectively and to understand each other.

credibility. The believability of a speaker; **competence, character,** and **charisma** (dynamism) are its major dimensions. *Seek to establish credibility by displaying competence, high moral character, and dynamism, or charisma.*

critical thinking. The process of logically evaluating reasons and evidence and reaching a judgment on the basis of this analysis.

critical-thinking-hats technique. A technique developed by Edward deBono in which a problem or issue is viewed from six distinct perspectives.

criticism. The reasoned judgment of some work; although often equated with fault finding, criticism can involve both positive or negative evaluations.

cultural display. Signs that communicate cultural identification; for example, group-specific clothing or religious jewelry.

cultural rules. Rules that are specific to a given cultural group. *Increase your sensitivity to these rules by learning about different cultures, recognizing and facing your own fears of intercultural interaction, recognizing differences between yourself and others, and becoming conscious of the cultural rules and customs of other cultures.*

cultural time. The meanings given to time communication by a particular culture.

culture. The relatively specialized lifestyle of a group of people—consisting of values, beliefs, artifacts, ways of behaving, and ways of communicating—that is passed on from one generation to the next.

culture shock. The psychological reaction we experience when we find ourselves in a culture very different from our own or from what we are used to.

date. An **extensional device** used to emphasize the notion of constant change and symbolized by a subscript; for example, John Smith$_{2008}$ is not John Smith$_{2011}$. *Use the date (verbally or mentally) to guard against static evaluation.*

deception cues. Verbal or nonverbal cues that reveal that a person is lying.

decoder. Something that takes a message in one form (e.g., sound waves) and translates it into another form (e.g., nerve impulses) from which meaning can be formulated (e.g., in vocal–auditory communication). In human communication the decoder is the auditory mechanism; in electronic communication the decoder is, for example, the telephone earpiece. *See also* **encoder.**

decoding. The process of extracting a message from a code—for example, translating speech sounds into nerve impulses. *See also* **encoding.**

defensiveness. The self-protective attitude of an individual or an atmosphere in a group characterized by threats, fear, and domination. Messages evidencing evaluation, control, strategy, neutrality, superiority, and certainty are assumed to lead to defensiveness. *Contrast* **supportiveness.**

delivery outline. The outline the speaker brings to the public speaking situation and refers to during the speech.

democratic leader. A group leader who stimulates self-direction and self-actualization of the group members.

denial. One of the obstacles to the expression of emotion; the process by which we deny our emotions to ourselves or to others. *Become mindful of the reasons for denial and the negative impact this generally has on communication.*

denotation. The objective or descriptive meaning of a word; its referential meaning. *Contrast* **connotation.**

depenetration. A reversal of penetration; a condition in which the **breadth** and **depth** of a relationship decrease. *See also* **social penetration theory.**

depth. The degree to which the inner personality—the inner core of an individual—is penetrated in interpersonal interaction.

deterioration. A stage in an interpersonal relationship in which the bonds holding the individuals together are weakened and the partners begin drifting apart.

determinism (principle of). The principle of verbal interaction that holds that all verbalizations are to some extent purposeful—that there is a reason for every verbalization.

dialogue. A form of **communication** in which each person is both speaker and listener; communication characterized by involvement, concern, and respect for the other person. *Treat conversation as a dialogue rather than a monologue; show concern for the other person, and for the relationship between you, with other-orientation. Contrast* **monologue.**

direct speech. Speech in which the speaker's intentions are stated clearly and directly.

disclaimer. Statement that asks the listener to receive what the speaker says as intended without its reflecting negatively on the image of the speaker. *Preface your comments with disclaimers if you feel you might be misunderstood. But avoid disclaimers when they aren't necessary; too many disclaimers can make you appear unprepared or unwilling to state an opinion.*

disclaiming. A form of feedforward in which you ask listeners to hear you favorably and without bias.

disconfirmation. Communication pattern in which someone ignores a person or that person's messages, even denying the right of the individual to define himself or herself. *Avoid sexist, heterosexist, racist, and ageist language; such language is disconfirming and insulting and invariably contributes to communication barriers. Contrast* **confirmation.**

dissolution. The breaking of the bonds holding an interpersonal relationship together.

dyadic communication. Two-person communication.

dyadic consciousness. An co-awareness of the interpersonal relationship between or pairing of two individuals; distinguished from situations in which two individuals are together but do not perceive themselves as being a unit or twosome.

dyadic effect. The process by which one person in a dyad, or two-person group, imitates the behavior of the other person. Usually refers to the tendency of one person's self-disclosures to prompt the other also to self-disclose. *Pay attention to the dyadic effect; it may indicate the other person's degree of involvement in the conversation.*

earmarker. A marker that identifies an item as belonging to a specific person—for example, a nameplate on a desk or initials on an attaché case. *Use earmarkers with a consideration for the rights of others as well as your own.*

effect. The outcome or consequence of an action or behavior; communication is assumed always to have some effect.

emblems. Nonverbal behaviors that directly translate words or phrases—for example, the signs for "OK" and "peace." *Use these with an awareness of the great cultural differences in the meanings given to various emblems.*

emergent leader. A leader who is not appointed but rather "emerges" during the group process.

emotions. The feelings you have—for example, feelings of joy, guilt, anger, or sorrow. *Express your emotions and interpret the emotions of others in light of the cultural rules dictating what is and what isn't appropriate emotional expression.*

empathy. The ability to feel what another person feels; feeling or perceiving something from another person's point of view. A key component of interpersonal effectiveness. *Communicate empathy when appropriate: resist evaluating the person's behaviors, focus concentration on the person, express active involvement through facial expressions and gestures, reflect back the feelings you think are being expressed, self-disclose, and address any mixed messages.*

encoder. Something that takes a message in one form (for example, nerve impulses) and translates it into another form (for example, sound waves). In human communication, the encoder is the speaking mechanism; in electronic communication, the encoder is, for example, the telephone mouthpiece. *See also* **decoder.**

encoding. The process of putting a message into a code—for example, translating nerve impulses into speech sounds. *See also* **decoding.**

enculturation. The process by which culture is transmitted from one generation to another.

e-prime. A form of the language that omits the verb "to be" except as an auxiliary or in statements of existence. E-prime is designed to eliminate the tendency toward **projection.** *When you feel that you may be overgeneralizing or making assumptions about all from only a few instances, try thinking in e-prime by eliminating the verb "to be."*

equality. An attitude that recognizes that each individual in a communication interaction is equal, that no one is superior to any other; encourages **supportiveness.**

equilibrium theory. A theory of **proxemics** holding that intimacy and physical closeness are positively related; as a relationship becomes more intimate, the distances between the individuals will diminish.

equity theory. A theory claiming that you experience relational satisfaction when there is an equal distribution of rewards and costs between the two persons in the relationship.

eros love. One of Lee's (1976) six types of love; seeks beauty and sensuality and focuses on physical attractiveness.

et cetera or **etc.** An **extensional device** used to emphasize the notion of infinite complexity; because one can never know all about anything, any statement about the world or an event must end with an explicit or implicit "etc." *Think with the etc., that is, be mindful that there is always more to say, see, hear, and so on.*

ethics. The branch of philosophy that deals with the rightness or wrongness of actions; the study of moral values.

ethnic identity. Commitment to the beliefs and customs of your culture.

ethnocentrism. The tendency to see others and their behaviors through our own cultural filters, often as distortions of our own behaviors; the tendency to evaluate the values and beliefs of our own culture more positively than those of another culture. *Recognizing our own ethnocentrism may help to prevent evaluating different cultural practices negatively.*

etymology. The historical or linguistic development of a word or phrase and often a useful way to help define a word.

euphemism. A polite word or phrase used to substitute for some **taboo** or otherwise offensive term.

example. A relatively brief specific instance.

excluding talk. Talk about a subject or in a vocabulary that only certain people understand, often in the presence of someone who does not belong to this group and therefore does not understand; use of terms unique to a specific culture as if they were universal.

excuse. An explanation designed to lessen the negative consequences of something done or said. *When using excuses, for example, to repair a conversation problem (1) demonstrate that you understand the problem, (2) acknowledge your responsibility, (3) acknowledge your regret for what you did, (4) request forgiveness, and (5) make it clear that this will never happen again.*

expectancy violations theory. A theory of **proxemics** holding that people have certain expectations for spatial relationships. If those expectations are violated (e.g., if a stranger stands too close to you or a romantic partner maintains an abnormally large distance from you), the relationship comes into clearer focus and you wonder why this "normal distance" is being violated.

experiential limitation. The limit of an individual's ability to communicate, as set by the nature and extent of that individual's experiences.

expert power. Personal power derived from expertise or knowledge.

expressiveness. Genuine involvement in speaking and listening, conveyed verbally and nonverbally; a component of interpersonal effectiveness. *Communicate active involvement in the interaction: Use active listening, address mixed messages, use I-messages, and use appropriate variations in paralanguage and gesture.*

extemporaneous speech. A speech that is thoroughly prepared and organized in detail and in which certain aspects of style are predetermined.

extensional devices. Linguistic devices proposed by Alfred Korzybski to keep language a more accurate means for talking about the world. The extensional devices include **et cetera, date,** and **index** (i.e., the working devices) and the **hyphen** and **quotes** (i.e., the safety devices). *Think mindfully with these devices in mind.*

extensional orientation. A tendency to give primary consideration to the world of experience and only secondary consideration to labels. *Look first to the event, the person, or the situation and only then to the way it's talked about. Contrast* **intensional orientation.**

face-attacking conflict strategies. Strategies that attack a person's positive face or self-esteem or a person's negative face or need for autonomy and independence. *Avoid these.*

face-enhancing conflict strategies. Strategies that support and confirm a person's positive face or self-esteem or a person's negative face or need for autonomy. *Use these when appropriate.*

face-saving. Maintaining a positive public self-image in the minds of others. *In conflict use face-saving strategies to allow your opponent to save face; avoid beltlining, or hitting your opponent with attacks that he or she will have difficulty absorbing and will resent.*

facial feedback hypothesis. The theory that a person's facial expressions can produce physiological and emotional effects in the person.

facial management techniques. Techniques used to mask certain emotions and to emphasize others: for example, intensifying your expression of happiness to make a friend feel good about a promotion. *Use these ethically as well as effectively. Use facial expressions to communicate that you're involved in the interaction. As a listener, look to the emotional facial expressions of others as additional cues to their meaning.*

fact–inference confusion. A misevaluation in which someone makes an inference, regards it as a fact, and acts on it as if it were a fact. *Distinguish facts (i.e., verifiably true past events) from inferences (i.e., guesses, hypotheses, hunches), and act on inferences with tentativeness and with mindfulness that they may turn out to be incorrect.*

factual statement. A statement made by the observer after observation and limited to what is observed. *Contrast* **inferential statement.**

family. A group of people who consider themselves related and connected to one another and among whom the actions of one person have consequences for others.

fear appeal. An effort to exploit or create fear in an individual or group of individuals in order to persuade them to believe or act in a certain way.

feedback. Information that is given back to the source. Feedback may come from the source's own messages (as when we hear what we are saying) or from the receiver(s)—in forms such as applause, yawning, puzzled looks, questions, letters to the editor of a newspaper, increased or decreased subscriptions to a magazine, and so forth. *Listen to both verbal and nonverbal feedback—from yourself and from others—and use these cues to help you adjust your messages for greatest effectiveness. See also* **negative feedback; positive feedback.**

feedforward. Information that is sent before a regular message telling the listener something about what is to follow. *Preface your messages with some kind of feedforward when you feel your listener needs some background or when you want to ease into a particular topic, such as bad news.*

flexibility. The ability to adjust communication strategies on the basis of the unique situation. *Because no two communication situations are identical, because everything is in a state of flux, and because everyone is different, cultivate flexibility and adjust your communication to the unique situation.*

flirting. A type of communication in which you signal romantic interest.

focus group. A group designed to explore the feelings and attitudes of its members; usually follows a question-and-answer format.

force. An unproductive conflict strategy in which someone attempts to win an argument by physical force, threats of force, or some type of psychological bullying.

forum. A small group format in which members of the group answer questions from the audience; often follows a **symposium.**

friendship. An interpersonal relationship between two persons that is mutually productive, established and maintained through perceived mutual free choice, and characterized by mutual positive regard. *Establish friendships to help serve such needs as utility, ego support, stimulation, and security. At the same time, seek to serve similar needs that your friends have.*

fundamental attribution error. The tendency to attribute a person's behavior to the kind of person he or she is (to internal factors such as the person's personality) and not to give sufficient importance to the situation the person is in. *Avoid the fundamental attribution error by mindfully focusing on the possible influence of situational forces.*

game. A simulation of some situation with rules governing the behaviors of the participants and with some payoff for winning. In transactional analysis, a "game" is a series of ulterior transactions that lead to a payoff; the term also refers to a basically dishonest kind of transaction in which participants hide their true feelings.

general semantics. The study of the relationships among language, thought, and behavior.

glittering generality. The opposite of **name calling;** a speaker's effort to gain your acceptance of an idea by associating it with things you value highly.

gobbledygook. Overly complex language that overwhelms the listener instead of communicating meaning. *Simplify your own language and ask for clarification when in doubt.*

gossip. Communication about someone who is not present, usually about matters that are private to this third party.

grapevine. Informal routes by which messages in an organization may travel; these informal lines resemble the physical grapevine, with its unpredictable pattern of branches.

group. A collection of individuals who are related to one another by some common purpose and in which some structure exists.

group norm. Rules or expectations for appropriate behavior for a member of a group. *Actively seek to discover the norms of a group, and take these norms into consideration when interacting in the group.*

groupthink. A tendency observed in some groups in which agreement among members becomes more important than the exploration of the issues at hand. *Recognize and actively counter any groupthink tendencies evidenced in a group.*

gunnysacking. An unproductive conflict strategy of storing up grievances—as if in a gunnysack—and holding them in readiness to dump on the other person in a conflict.

halo effect. The tendency to generalize an individual's virtue or expertise from one area to another.

haptics. The study of touch communication.

heterosexist language. Language that assumes all people are heterosexual and that thereby denigrates lesbians and gay men.

high-context culture. A culture in which much of the information in communication is in the context or in the person rather than explicitly coded in the verbal messages. **Collectivist cultures** are generally high context. *Adjust your messages and your listening in light of the differences between high- and low-context cultures.* Contrast **low-context** culture.

home field advantage. The increased power that comes from being in your own territory.

home territories. Territories about which individuals have a sense of intimacy and over which they exercise control—for example, a person's home.

hyphen. An **extensional device** used to illustrate that what may be separated verbally may not be separable on the event level or on the nonverbal level; for example, although body and mind are often discussed as if they were separable, in reality they are better referred to as body–mind.

idea-generation group. A group whose purpose is to generate ideas. *See also* **brainstorming.**

idioms. Expressions that are unique to a specific language and whose meaning cannot be deduced from the individual words used.

illustration. A relatively long and more detailed example.

illustrators. Nonverbal behaviors that accompany and literally illustrate verbal messages—for example, upward hand movements that accompany the verbalization "It's up there."

I-messages. Messages in which the speaker accepts responsibility for personal thoughts and behaviors; messages in which the speaker's point of view is stated explicitly. *Use I-messages when communicating your feelings; take responsibility for your own feelings (as in "I get angry when you . . .") rather than attributing them to others (as in "you make me angry").* Contrast **you-messages.**

immediacy. A sense of contact and togetherness; a feeling of interest in and liking for the other person in an interchange. A quality of interpersonal effectiveness. *Maintain nonverbal immediacy through close physical distances, eye contact, and smiling; maintain verbal immediacy by using the other person's name and focusing on the other's remarks.*

impression formation. The processes you go through in forming an impression of another person.

impression management. The processes you go through to create the impression you want the other person to have of you.

impromptu speech. A speech delivered off-the-cuff, without preparation.

inclusion principle. In verbal interaction, principle stating that all members should be a part of (i.e., included in) the interaction.

inclusive talk. Communication that includes all people; communication that does not exclude certain groups, such as women, lesbians and gays, or members of certain races or nationalities.

index. An **extensional device** used to emphasize the notion of nonidentity (i.e., that no two things are the same) and symbolized by a subscript—for example, $politician_1$ is not $politician_2$.

indirect speech. Speech that may hide the speaker's true intentions or that may be used to make requests and observations indirectly. *Make judicious use of indirect messages when a more direct style might prove insulting or offensive. But be aware that indirect messages can create communication problems, because they are easier to misunderstand than direct messages.*

indiscrimination. A misevaluation caused when we categorize people, events, or objects into a particular class and respond to them only as members of the class; a failure to recognize that each individual is unique; a failure to apply the **index**. *Avoid indiscrimination by treating each situation and each person as unique (when possible) even when they're covered by the same label or name. Index your key concepts.*

individualistic culture. A culture that emphasizes the individual's rather than the group's goals and preferences. *Contrast* **collectivist culture.**

individual orientation. A cultural orientation that stresses the individual's rather than the group's goals and preferences. *Adjust your messages and your listening on the basis of differences between individualistic and collectivist cultures. Contrast* **collective orientation.**

individual roles (in groups). Behavior in groups that is usually dysfunctional and works against a sense of groupness. *In a group avoid playing the popular but dysfunctional individual roles—those of the aggressor, blocker, recognition seeker, self-confessor, and dominator.*

inevitability. In communication, the fact that communication cannot be avoided—that all behavior in an interactional setting is communication.

inferential statement. A statement that can be made by anyone, is not limited to what is observed, and can be made at any time. *Contrast* **factual statement.**

informal time terms. Expressions that denote approximate rather than exact time intervals, for example, "soon," "early," and "in a while."

information. That which reduces uncertainty.

information overload. A condition in which the amount of information is too great to be dealt with effectively or the number or complexity of messages is so great that the individual or organization is not able to deal with them.

information power. Power derived from the possession of information and the ability to communicate logically and persuasively. Also called "persuasion power."

informative interview. A type of **interview** in which the interviewer asks the interviewee, usually a person of some reputation and accomplishment, questions designed to elicit his or her views, predictions, and perspectives on specific topics.

informative speech. A public speech in which you describe, demonstrate, or define something. *Follow the principles of informative speaking: Stress the information's usefulness, relate new information to information the audience already knows, present information through several senses, adjust the level of complexity, vary the levels of abstraction, avoid information overload, and recognize cultural variations.*

inoculation principle. A principle stating that persuasion will be more difficult to achieve when the would-be persuader attacks beliefs and attitudes that have already been challenged previously, because the listener has built up defenses (i.e., has been "inoculated") against such attacks.

insulation. A reaction to territorial encroachment in which you erect some sort of barrier between yourself and the invaders.

intensional orientation. A tendency to give primary consideration to the way things are labeled and only secondary consideration (if any) to the world of experience. *Contrast* **extensional orientation.** *Avoid intensional orientation by responding to things first and to labels second; the way a person is talked about is not the best measure of who that person really is.*

interaction management. The control of interpersonal interaction to the satisfaction of both parties; management of conversational turns, fluency, and message consistency. A component of interpersonal effectiveness. *Speak in relatively short conversational turns, avoid long and frequent pauses, and use verbal and nonverbal messages that are consistent.*

interaction process analysis. A content analysis method that classifies messages into four general categories: social emotional positive, social emotional negative, attempted answers, and questions.

intercultural communication. Communication that takes place between persons of different cultures or persons who have different cultural beliefs, values, or ways of behaving. *When communicating interculturally, become mindful of (1) the differences between yourself and culturally different individuals, (2) the differences within the other cultural group, (3) cultural differences in meanings for both verbal and nonverbal signals, and (4) different cultural rules and customs. Communicate interculturally with appropriate openness, empathy, positiveness, immediacy, interaction management, expressiveness, and other orientation.*

internal summary. A statement that summarizes what you have already discussed in the speech, usually some major subdivision of your speech. *Use these to help your audience follow your speech.*

interpersonal communication. Communication between two persons or among a small group of persons, as distinguished from public or mass communication; communication of a personal nature, as distinguished from impersonal communication; communication between or among intimates or those involved in a close relationship; often, intrapersonal, dyadic, and small group communication in general.

interpersonal conflict. A conflict or disagreement between two persons. *Prepare for a conflict by arranging to fight in private, knowing what you're fighting about, and fighting about problems that can be solved. After the conflict, profit from it by learning what worked and what didn't, by keeping the conflict in perspective, and by increasing the exchange of rewards. Avoid the common causes of online conflicts—such as sending out unsolicited commercial messages, spamming, and flaming.*

interpersonal perception. The perception of people; the processes through which we interpret and evaluate people and their behavior.

interviewing. A particular form of interpersonal communication in which two persons interact largely through questions and answers for the purpose of achieving specific goals.

intimacy. The closest interpersonal relationship; usually involves a close primary relationship such as the relationship between spouses or partners.

intimacy claims. Obligations that a person incurs by virtue of being in a close and intimate relationship.

intimate distance. The closest proxemic distance, ranging from touching to 18 inches away. *See also* **proxemics.**

intrapersonal communication. Communication with the self.

invasion. Unwarranted entrance into another's territory that changes the meaning of the territory; territorial encroachment.

involvement. The stage in an interpersonal relationship that normally follows contact, in which the individuals get to know each other better and explore the potential for greater intimacy.

irreversibility. The impossibility of reversing communication; principle stating that once something has been communicated it cannot be uncommunicated.

jargon. The technical language of any specialized group, often a professional class, that is unintelligible to individuals not belonging to the group; "shop talk."

Johari window. A diagram of the four selves (i.e., open, blind, hidden, and unknown) that illustrates the different kinds of information in each self.

kinesics. The study of the communicative dimensions of facial and bodily movements.

laissez-faire leader. A group leader who allows the group to develop and progress or make mistakes on its own.

lateral communication. Communication among equals—for example, manager to manager, worker to worker.

leadership. The quality by which one individual directs or influences the thoughts and/or the behaviors of others. *See also* **laissez-faire leader, democratic leader,** and **authoritarian leader.**

leave-taking cues. Verbal and nonverbal cues that indicate a desire to terminate a conversation.

legitimate power. Power derived from people's belief that a person has a right, by virtue of position, to influence or control others' behavior.

leveling. A process of message distortion in which a message is repeated but the number of details is reduced, some details are omitted entirely, and some details lose their complexity.

level of abstraction. The relative distance of a term or statement from an actual perception; a low-order abstraction would be a description of the perception, whereas a high-order abstraction would consist of inferences about descriptions of the perception.

listening. An active process of receiving messages sent orally; this process consists of five stages: receiving, understanding, remembering, evaluating, and responding.

logic. The science of reasoning; the principles governing the analysis of inference making.

looking-glass self. The self-concept that results from the image of yourself that others reveal to you.

loving. An interpersonal process in which one person feels a closeness, a caring, a warmth, and an excitement in relation to another person.

low-context culture. A culture in which most of the information in communication is explicitly stated in the verbal messages. **Individualistic cultures** are usually low-context cultures. *Contrast* **high-context culture.**

ludic love. One of Lee's (1976) six types of love; based on entertainment and excitement, it is love as a game, not to be taken too seriously and with emotions held in check.

lying. The act of sending messages with the intention of giving another person information you believe to be false.

maintenance. A stage of relationship stability at which the relationship does not progress or deteriorate significantly; a continuation as opposed to a dissolution of a relationship.

maintenance strategies. Specific behaviors designed to preserve an interpersonal relationship.

manic love. One of Lee's (1976) six types of love; obsessive love, it is marked by a need for constant attention and affection, which when withheld leads to depression, jealousy, and self-doubt.

manipulation. An unproductive conflict strategy in which a person avoids open conflict but attempts to divert the conflict by being especially charming and getting the other person into a noncombative frame of mind.

manuscript speech. A speech designed to be read verbatim from a script.

markers. Devices that signify that a certain territory belongs to a particular person. *Become sensitive to the (central, boundary, and ear) markers of others, and learn to use these markers to define your own territories and to communicate the desired impression. See also* **boundary marker, central marker,** and **earmarker.**

mass communication. Communication that is addressed to an extremely large audience, mediated by audio and/or visual transmitters, and processed by gatekeepers before transmission.

matching hypothesis. The theory that we tend to date and mate with people who are similar to us—who match us—in physical attractiveness.

meaningfulness. As a principle of perception, our assumption that people's behavior is sensible, stems from some logical antecedent, and is consequently meaningful rather than meaningless.

mentoring. Guidance and support given by an experienced individual to a less-experienced person.

mere exposure hypothesis. The theory that repeated or prolonged exposure to a stimulus may result in a change in attitude toward the stimulus object, generally in the direction of increased positiveness.

message. Any signal or combination of signals that serves as a stimulus for a receiver.

meta-advice. Advice about advice, such as, when asked for advice, suggesting that the asker seek more expert advice.

metacommunication. Communication about communication. *Metacommunicate when you want to clarify the way you're talking or what you're talking about; for example, give clear feedforward and paraphrase your own complex messages.*

metalanguage. Language used to talk about language.

metamessage. A message that makes reference to another message: for example, remarks such as "Did I make myself clear?" or "That's a lie."

metaskills. Skills for regulating more specific skills. For example, skills of interpersonal communication such as openness and empathy must be regulated by the metaskills of flexibility, mindfulness, and metacommunication.

mindfulness and **mindlessness.** States of relative awareness. In a mindful state, we are aware of the logic and rationality of our behaviors and the logical connections existing among elements. In a mindless state, we are unaware of this logic and rationality. *Increase your mindfulness by creating and recreating categories, being open to new information and points of view, and avoiding excessive reliance on first impressions.*

mixed message. A message that contradicts itself; a message that asks for two different (often incompatible) responses. *Avoid encoding mixed messages by focusing clearly on your purposes when communicating and by increasing conscious control over your verbal and nonverbal behaviors.*

model. A representation of an object or process.

monochronic time orientation. A view of time in which things are done sequentially; one thing is scheduled at a time. *Contrast* **polychronic time orientation.**

monologue. A form of communication in which one person speaks and the other listens; there is no real interaction among participants. *Contrast* **dialogue.**

motivated sequence. An organizational pattern in which a speaker arranges the information in a discourse to motivate an audience to respond positively to the speaker's purpose. *In using the motivated sequence, gain attention, establish a need, satisfying the need, visualize the need satisfied, and move to action.*

motivational appeal. Appeals to an audience's motives and emotions rather than to their logic. *Use motivational appeals (i.e., appeals to motives such as fear; power, control, and influence; safety; achievement; or financial gain) as appropriate to the speech and audience.*

name calling. A persuasive technique in which the speaker gives an idea or a person a derogatory name.

narrative. A long example presented in the form of an anecdote or short story, for example, Aesop's fables.

negative face. The need and desire to be autonomous, to have the right to do as one wishes.

negative feedback. Feedback that serves a corrective function by informing the source that his or her message is not being received in the way intended; serves to redirect the source's behavior. Examples include looks of boredom, shouts of disagreement, letters critical of newspaper policy, and a teacher's instructions on how better to approach a problem. Contrast **positive feedback.**

netiquette. The rules for polite communication over the Internet. *Learn what these are and follow them.*

networking. A broad process of enlisting the aid of other people to help you solve a problem or offer insight that bears on your problem. *Establish a network of relationships to provide insights into issues relevant to your personal and professional life, and be willing to lend your expertise to the networks of others.*

neutrality. A response pattern lacking in personal involvement; encourages defensiveness. *Contrast* **empathy.**

noise. Anything that interferes with a person's receiving a message as the source intended the message to be received. Noise is present in a communication system to the extent that the message received is not the message sent. *Reduce the influence of physical, physiological, psychological, and semantic noise to the extent that you can; use repetition and restatement and, when in doubt, ask if you're being clear.*

nominal group. A collection of individuals who record their thoughts and opinions, which are then distributed to others. Without direct interaction, the thoughts and opinions are gradually pared down until a manageable list of solutions or decisions is produced. When this occurs, the nominal group (a group in name only) may restructure itself into a problem-solving group that analyzes the final list. *Use the nominal group technique to solve problems when anonymity in suggesting ideas may be desirable.*

non-allness. An attitude or point of view that recognizes that we can never know all about anything; that what we know, say, or hear is only a part of what there is to know, say, or hear.

nondirective language. Language that does not direct or focus our attention on certain aspects of a topic; neutral language.

nonnegotiation. An unproductive conflict strategy in which an individual refuses to discuss the conflict or to listen to the other person in the encounter.

nonverbal communication. Communication without words; for example, communication by means of space, gestures, facial expressions, touching, vocal variation, or silence.

nonverbal dominance. Nonverbal behavior through which one person psychologically dominates another.

norm. *See* **group norm.**

object-adaptors. Movements that involve manipulation of some object, such as punching holes in or drawing on a Styrofoam coffee cup, clicking a ballpoint pen, or chewing on a pencil.

object language. Language used to communicate about objects, events, and relations in the world; the structure of the object language is described in a metalanguage; the display of physical objects—for example, flower arranging and the colors of the clothes we wear.

olfactics. The study of communication by smell.

openness. A quality of interpersonal effectiveness encompassing (1) a willingness to interact openly with others, to self-disclose as appropriate; (2) a willingness to react honestly to incoming stimuli; and (3) a willingness to own your feelings and thoughts.

operational definition. A type of definition in which the steps to construct the object are identified.

oral style. The style of spoken discourse that, when compared with written style, consists of shorter, simpler, and more familiar words; more qualification, self-reference terms, allness terms, verbs and adverbs; and more concrete terms and terms indicative of consciousness of projection, such as "as I see it."

other-orientation. A quality of interpersonal effectiveness involving attentiveness, interest, and concern for the other person. *Acknowledge the importance of the other person; use focused eye contact and appropriate facial expressions; smile, nod, and lean toward the other person; express agreement when appropriate.*

other talk. Talk about the listener or about some third party.

overattribution. The tendency to attribute a great deal of what a person does or believes to one or two obvious characteristics of the person. *Avoid overattribution; rarely is any one factor an accurate explanation of complex human behavior.*

panel. A small group format in which "experts" meet to discuss a topic or solve a problem; participants often speak without any set pattern.

paralanguage. The vocal but nonverbal aspect of speech. Paralanguage consists of voice qualities (e.g., pitch range, resonance, tempo), vocal characterizers (e.g., laughing or crying, yelling or whispering), vocal qualifiers (e.g., intensity, pitch height), and vocal segregates (e.g., "uh-uh" meaning "no" or "sh" meaning "silence"). *Vary paralinguistic features such as rate, pausing, pitch, and volume to communicate your meanings and to add interest and color to your messages.*

parasocial relationship. Relationship between a person and an imagined or fictional character; usually refers to a relationship between a viewer and a fictional character in a television show.

pauses. Silent periods in the normally fluent stream of speech. Pauses are of two major types: filled pauses (i.e., interruptions in speech that are filled with such vocalizations as "er" or "um") and unfilled pauses (i.e., silences of unusually long duration). *Use pauses to signal transitions to allow listeners time to think or respond, and to signal the approach of a significant idea.*

perception. The process of becoming aware of objects and events via the senses. *Increase accuracy in interpersonal perception by (1) identifying the influence of your physical and emotional state; (2) making sure that you're not drawing conclusions from too little information; and (3) identifying any perceptions that may be the result of mind reading. See also* **interpersonal perception.**

perception checking. The process of verifying your understanding of some message or situation or feeling to reduce uncertainty.

perceptual accentuation. A process that leads you to see what you expect to see and what you want to see—for example, seeing people you like as better looking and smarter than people you do not like.

personal attack. A fallacy of argument in which the speaker attacks the person instead of the person's arguments. *Avoid this in your own reasoning and reject these when used by others.*

personal distance. The second closest **proxemic distance,** ranging from 18 inches to four feet. *See also* **proxemics.**

personality theory. A theory or set of assumptions about personality, complete with rules or systems, that each individual maintains and through which the individual perceives others. *In order to subject your perceptions and conclusions about people to logical analysis, bring to your mindful state your personality theory.*

personal rejection. An unproductive conflict strategy in which one person withholds love and affection and seeks to win the argument by getting the other person to break down under this withdrawal.

persuasion. The process of influencing attitudes, beliefs, values, and/or behavior.

persuasive speech. In public speaking, a speech designed to change an audience's attitudes or behaviors. *Apply (where*

relevant) the principles of persuasion: selective exposure, audience participation, identification, and amounts of change.

phatic communication. Communication that is primarily social; "small talk" designed to open the channels of communication rather than to communicate something about the external world. "Hello" and "How are you?" in everyday interaction are examples.

pitch. The highness or lowness of the vocal tone.

plagiarism. The process of claiming authorship for the work of another and can apply to ideas as well as specific words. *Avoid even the suggestion of plagiarism.*

plain folks. A persuasive strategy that identifies the speaker and his or her proposal with the audience.

polarization. A form of fallacious reasoning by which only the two extremes are considered; also referred to as "black-and-white" or "either/or" thinking or as two-valued orientation. *Avoid thinking and talking in extremes by using middle terms and qualifiers. At the same time, remember that too many qualifiers may make you appear unsure of yourself.*

politeness. Civility, consideration, refinement, respect, and regard for others as expressed verbally and nonverbally; interaction that follows the socially accepted rules for interpersonal interaction.

politeness strategies. Strategies that support another's face needs and may be used as a strategy to appear likeable.

polychronic time orientation. A view of time in which several things may be scheduled or engaged in at the same time. *Contrast* **monochronic time orientation.**

positive face. The need and desire to be viewed positively by others, to be thought of favorably.

positive feedback. Feedback that supports or reinforces the continuation of behavior along the same lines in which it is already proceeding—for example, applause during a speech. *Contrast* **negative feedback.**

positiveness. A characteristic of effective communication involving positive attitudes toward the self and toward the interpersonal interaction. *Communicate positiveness by expressing your own satisfaction with the interaction, compliment others by expressing your positive thoughts and feelings about and to the other person, and express acceptance and approval.*

power. The ability to control the behaviors of others. *Communicate power by avoiding such powerless message forms as hesitations, too many intensifiers, disqualifiers, tag questions, one-word answers, self-critical statements, overly polite statements, and vulgar and slang expressions.*

power distance. A cultural dimension referring to the degree of distance between those with power and those without power. *Adjust your messages and listening based on the power distance orientation of the culture in which you find yourself.*

power play. A consistent pattern of behavior in which one person tries to control the behavior of another. *Use cooperative strategies to deal with power plays: (1) Express your* feelings, (2) describe the behavior to which you object, and (3) state a cooperative response.

pragma love. One of Lee's (1976) six types of love; traditional approach to love, valuing social qualifications and family background and emphasizing logic and practicality over feelings.

pragmatic implication. An assumption that seems logical but is not necessarily true.

premature self-disclosures. Disclosures that are made before a relationship has developed sufficiently.

primacy effect. The condition by which what comes first exerts greater influence than what comes later. *Contrast* **recency effect.**

primacy–recency. Principle of **perception** stating that we generally use early information to get a general impression of a person and use later information to add specificity to this impression.

primary relationship. The relationship between two people who both consider it to be their most (or one of their most) important relationship: for example, the relationship between spouses or domestic partners.

primary source. Original information about a topic or event, for example, the original research study. *See* **secondary source.**

primary territory. An area that you can consider your exclusive preserve—for example, your room or office.

problem-solving group. A group whose primary task is to solve a problem or, more often, to reach a decision.

problem-solving sequence. A logical step-by-step process for solving a problem that is frequently used by groups; consists of defining and analyzing the problem, establishing criteria for evaluating solutions, identifying possible solutions, evaluating solutions, selecting the best solution, and testing the selected solutions.

process. Ongoing activity; communication is referred to as a process to emphasize that it is always changing, always in motion.

projection. A psychological process whereby we attribute characteristics or feelings of our own to others; often refers to the process whereby we attribute our own faults to others.

pronunciation. The production of syllables or words according to some accepted standard, for example, as presented in a dictionary. Avoid the common pronunciation errors of omission, substitution, addition, and pronouncing sounds that should be silent.

protection theory. A theory of proxemics referring to the fact that people establish a body-buffer zone to protect themselves from unwanted closeness, touching, or attack.

provisionalism. An attitude of open-mindedness that leads to the creation of supportiveness. *Contrast* **certainty.**

proxemic distances. The spatial distances that people maintain in communication and social interaction. *Use spatial distance to signal the type of relationship you are in: intimate,* personal, social, or public. Let your spatial relationships reflect your interpersonal relationships. Maintain spatial distances that are comfortable (i.e., neither too close nor too far apart) and that are appropriate to the situation and to your relationship with the other person.

proxemics. The study of the communicative function of space and of how people unconsciously structure their space—the distances between people in their interactions, the organization of space in homes and offices, and even the design of cities.

proximity. As a principle of **perception,** the tendency to perceive people or events that are physically close as belonging together or representing some kind of a unit. Also, physical closeness; one of the factors influencing interpersonal attraction.

psychological time. The importance you place on past, present, or future time.

public communication. Communication in which the source is one person and the receiver is an audience of many persons.

public distance. The longest **proxemic distance,** ranging from 12 to more than 25 feet.

public territory. Area that is open to all people—for example, a restaurant or park.

punctuation of communication. The breaking up of continuous communication sequences into short sequences with identifiable beginnings and endings or stimuli and responses.

punishment. Noxious or aversive stimulation.

pupillometrics. The study of communication through changes in the size of the pupils of the eyes.

purr words. Highly positive words that express the speaker's feelings rather than any objective reality. *Contrast* **snarl words.**

Pygmalion effect. Condition in which we make a prediction of success, act as if it were true, and thereby make it come true; a type of **self-fulfilling prophecy.**

quality circles. Groups of workers (usually 6 to 12) whose task it is to investigate and make recommendations for improving the quality of some organizational function.

questions of fact. Questions concerned with what is or is not true, what does or does not exist, what did or did not happen.

questions of policy. Questions concerning what should be or should not be done (or what policy should be adopted).

quotes. An **extensional device** to emphasize that a word or phrase is being used in a special sense and should therefore be given special attention.

racist language. Language that denigrates or is derogatory toward members of a particular race.

rate. The speed with which you speak, generally measured in words per minute.

receiver. Any person or thing that takes in messages. Receivers may be individuals listening to or reading a message, a group of persons hearing a speech, a scattered television audience, or machines that store information.

recency effect. The condition in which what comes last (i.e., happened most recently) exerts greater influence than what comes first. *Contrast* **primacy effect.**

redundancy. The quality of a message that makes it totally predictable and therefore lacking in information. A message of zero redundancy would be completely unpredictable; a message of 100 percent redundancy would be completely predictable. All human languages contain some degree of built-in redundancy, generally estimated to be about 50 percent.

referent power. Personal power derived from others' desire to identify with or be like the individual.

reflexiveness. The feature of human language that makes it possible for that language to be used to refer to itself; that is, reflexiveness lets us talk about our talk and create a **meta-language**—a language for talking about language.

regulators. Nonverbal behaviors that regulate, monitor, or control the communications of another person.

rehearsal. The process of fixing in mind the delivery of your public speech. *Rehearse your speech often, perfect your delivery, rehearse the speech as a whole, time the speech at each rehearsal, approximate the specific speech situation as much as possible, see and think of yourself as a public speaker, and incorporate any delivery notes that may be of value during the actual speech presentation.*

rejection. A response to an individual that disagrees with or denies the validity of something the individual says or does.

relational communication. Communication between or among intimates or people in close relationships; used by some theorists as synonymous with **interpersonal communication.**

relationship deterioration. The process whereby the bonds holding an interpersonal relationship together lessen. *To cope with the ending of a relationship, break the loneliness–depression cycle, take time out, bolster your self-esteem, seek the support of nourishing others, and avoid repeating negative patterns.*

relationship development. The stages of relationships during which you move closer to intimacy; in the model of relationships presented here, relationship development includes the **contact** and **involvement** stages.

relationship dialectics theory. A theory that describes relationships as defined by competing, opposite desires or motivations, such as the desire for autonomy and the desire to belong to someone, desires for novelty and predictability, and desires for closedness and openness.

relationship maintenance. The processes by which you attempt to keep a relationship stable.

relationship messages. Messages that comment on the relationship between the speakers rather than on matters external to them. *Formulate messages that are appropriate to the stage of the relationship, and listen for messages from relationship partners that may reveal differences in perception about your relationship stage.*

relationship rules. Principles that relationship partners establish to help define their relationship. *Follow the rules for maintaining relationships when you do in fact wish to maintain and even strengthen them.*

repair. Attempts to reverse the process of relationship **deterioration.** *Recognize the problem, engage in productive conflict resolution, pose possible solutions, affirm each other, integrate solutions into normal behavior, and take risks as appropriate.*

response. Any overt or covert behavior.

restatement. A message that repeats an idea in different words, often used to achieve emphasis or clarity.

reward power. Power based on a person's ability to reward another person.

rigid complementarity. Inability to break away from a complementary type of relationship that was once appropriate but is no longer.

role. The part an individual plays in a group; an individual's function or expected behavior.

roundtable. A small group format in which group members arrange themselves in a circular or semicircular pattern; participants meet to share information or solve problems without any set pattern as to who speaks when.

rules theory. A theory that describes relationships as interactions governed by a series of rules that the members agree to follow. When the rules are followed, the relationship is maintained; when they are broken, the relationship experiences difficulty.

schemata. Mental templates or structures that help us organize items of sensory information and information in memory. (Singular: *schema*)

script. A template or organizational structure describing the sequence of events in a given action, procedure, or occurrence.

secondary source. A summary or interpretation of information, for example, a newspaper's summary of a research study. See **primary source.**

secondary territory. Area that does not belong to a particular person but that has been occupied by that person and is therefore associated with her or him—for example, the seat a person normally takes in class.

selective exposure. Tendency of listeners to actively seek out information that supports their existing opinions, beliefs, attitudes, and values and to actively avoid information that contradicts them.

self-acceptance. Satisfaction with ourselves, our virtues and vices, and our abilities and limitations.

self-actualization needs. A basic need to become and do what you feel you must do; a need that is only satisfied, in Maslow's theory, after all other needs are satisfied.

self-adaptors. Movements that satisfy a physical need, especially to make you more comfortable; for example, scratching your head to relieve an itch, moistening your lips because they feel dry, or pushing your hair out of your eyes.

self-attribution. A process through which we seek to account for and understand the reasons and motivations for our own behaviors.

self-awareness. The degree to which a person knows himself or herself. *Increase self-awareness by listening to others, increasing your open self as appropriate, and seeking out information (discreetly) to reduce any blind spots.*

self-concept. An individual's self-evaluation or self-appraisal. *Learn who you are: See yourself through the eyes of others; compare yourself to similar (and admired) others; examine the influences of culture; and observe, interpret, and evaluate your own message behaviors.*

self-disclosure. The process of revealing something about ourselves to another. Usually refers to information that would normally be kept hidden. *In considering self-disclosure, consider the legitimacy of your motives for disclosing, the appropriateness of the disclosure, the listener's responses (is the dyadic effect operating?), and the potential burdens self-disclosures might impose.*

self-esteem. The value you place on yourself; your self-evaluation. Usually refers to a positive self-evaluation. *Raise your self-esteem: Increase your communication effectiveness, challenge self-destructive beliefs, seek out nourishing people with whom to interact, work on projects that will result in success, and engage in self-affirmation.*

self-fulfilling prophecy. The situation in which we make a prediction or prophecy that comes true because we act on it as if it were true. *Take a second look at your perceptions when they correspond very closely to your initial expectations; the self-fulfilling prophecy may be at work.*

self-monitoring. The manipulation of the image we present to others in interpersonal interactions so as to create a favorable impression.

self-serving bias. A bias in the self-attribution process that leads us to take credit for positive consequences and to deny responsibility for negative outcomes of our behaviors. *Become mindful of any self-serving bias; that is, of giving too much weight to internal factors (when explaining your positives) and too little weight to external factors (when explaining your negatives).*

self-talk. Talk about the self.

semantics. The area of language study concerned with meaning.

sexist language. Language derogatory to one gender, usually women. *Avoid it.*

sexual harassment. Unsolicited and unwanted sexual messages.

shyness. The condition of discomfort and uneasiness in interpersonal situations.

sign (reasoning from). A form of reasoning in which the presence of certain signs (clues) is interpreted as leading to a particular conclusion.

signal reaction. A conditioned response to a signal; a response to some signal that is immediate rather than delayed.

signal-to-noise ratio. In verbal interaction, the relationship between what is signal (i.e., meaningful) and what is noise (i.e., interference). This ratio also is relative to the communication analyst, the participants, and the context.

silence. The absence of vocal communication; often misunderstood to refer to the absence of any and all communication. Silence often communicates feelings or prevents communication about certain topics. *Because silence can communicate lots of different meanings (e.g., your anger or your need for time to think), examine your use of silence just as you would eye movements or body gestures.*

similarity. As a principle of **perception,** the tendency to see things that are physically similar as belonging together and/or constituting a unit. As a principle of **attraction,** our tendency to be attracted to people with qualities similar to our own and to people who are similar to us. *Contrast* **complementarity.**

simile. A figure of speech in which two unlike objects are compared using the words *like* or *as.*

situational listening. A view of listening holding that effective listening needs to be adjusted to the specific situation; one style of listening does not fit all forms of communication.

slang. Language used by special groups that is not considered proper by the general society.

slippery slope. A reasoning fallacy involving the assumption that one event (the one the person is arguing against) will inevitably or most likely lead to another event that everyone agrees would be undesirable. *Seek proof of causality.*

small group. A collection of individuals who are connected to one another by some common purpose, are interdependent, have some degree of organization among them, and see themselves as a group.

small group communication. Communication among a collection of individuals small enough in number that all members may interact with relative ease as both senders and receivers, the members being related to one another by some common purpose and with some degree of organization or structure.

small talk. Noncontroversial talk that is usually short in duration and often serves as a polite way of introducing one's self or a topic.

snarl words. Highly negative words that express the feelings of the speaker rather than any objective reality. *Contrast* **purr words.**

social comparison. The processes by which you compare aspects of yourself (e.g., your abilities, opinions, and values) with those of others and then assess and evaluate yourself; one of the sources of **self-concept.**

social distance. The third **proxemic distance,** ranging from 4 to 12 feet; the distance at which business is usually conducted.

social exchange theory. A theory hypothesizing that people develop relationships in which their rewards, or profits, will be greater than their costs and that people avoid or terminate relationships in which the costs exceed the rewards.

social network. An organizational structure that allows people to communicate, popularly used to refer to the online sites such as Facebook and MySpace that enable people to communicate with others who share a common interest.

social penetration theory. A theory describing how relationships develop from the superficial to the intimate levels and from few to many areas of interpersonal interaction.

source. Any person or thing that creates messages. A source may be an individual speaking, writing, or gesturing or a computer sending an error message.

specific instances (reasoning from). A form of reasoning in which a speaker examines several specific instances and forms a conclusion about the whole on the basis of those instances.

specific purpose. The information you want to communicate (in an informative speech) or the attitude or behavior you want to change (in a persuasive speech).

speech. Messages utilizing a vocal–auditory channel.

speech of demonstration. A speech devoted to showing how to do something or how something operates.

speech of description. A speech devoted to describing an object or person.

spontaneity. The communication pattern in which a person verbalizes what he or she is thinking without attempting to develop strategies for control; encourages **supportiveness.**

stability. As a principle of perception, the idea that our perceptions of things and of people are relatively consistent with our previous perceptions.

static evaluation. An orientation that fails to recognize that the world is characterized by constant change; an attitude that sees people and events as fixed rather than as constantly changing. *Mentally date your statements to avoid thinking and communicating that the world is static and unchanging. In your messages, reflect the inevitability of change.*

status. The relative level a person occupies in a hierarchy; status always involves a comparison, and thus one person's status is only relative to the status of another.

stereotype. In communication, a fixed impression of a group of people through which we then perceive specific individuals; stereotypes are most often negative but may also be positive. *Be careful of thinking and talking in stereotypes; recognize that members of all groups are different, and focus on the individual rather than on the individual's membership in one group or another.*

stimulus. Any external or internal change that impinges on or arouses an organism.

storge love. One of Lee's (1976) six types of love; a gradually unfolding, peaceful and tranquil love marked by companionability and shared interests and activities, sometimes difficult to distinguish from friendship.

subjectivity. As a principle of perception, the idea that our perceptions are not objective but are influenced by our wants and needs and our expectations and predictions.

supporting materials. Usually used in reference to public speaking, enlarging a concept or principle through the use of examples, illustrations, and narratives; testimony; definitions; statistics; and visual aids. *Use supporting materials that will prove interesting to your audience, that are consistent in style with the rest of the speech, and that clearly relate to the concept and principle that they are designed to explain.*

supportiveness. An attitude of an individual or an atmosphere in a group that is characterized by openness, absence of fear, and a genuine feeling of equality. *Try to respond supportively by expressing your empathy, being open even to opposing viewpoints, and acting as an equal in the interaction.* Contrast **strategy.**

symmetrical relationship. A relation between two or more persons in which one person's behavior serves as a stimulus for the same type of behavior in the other person(s). Examples of such relationships include those in which anger in one person encourages or serves as a stimulus for anger in another person or in which a critical comment by the person leads the other person to respond in like manner.

symposium. A small group format in which each member of the group delivers a relatively prepared talk on some aspect of the topic. Often combined with a **forum.**

systematic desensitization. A theory and technique for dealing with a variety of fears (such as communication apprehension) in which you gradually expose yourself to an anxiety-producing stimulus so as to become hardened to it.

taboo. Forbidden; culturally censored. Taboo language is language that is frowned on by "polite society." Topics and specific words may be considered taboo—for example, death, sex, certain forms of illness, and various words denoting sexual activities and excretory functions. *Generally, avoid violating any cultural taboo; the more formal the situation, the more important it is to avoid such taboos.*

tag questions. Questions that ask for another's agreement and often signal weakness or uncertainty, for example, "That dinner was fine, don't you think?" *Avoid these when you want your speech to have power.*

team. A particular kind of small group that is constructed for a specific task, whose members have clearly defined roles, are committed to achieving the same goal, and content focused.

template outline. A type of outline that contains the essential categories of a speech to be filled in during speech preparation.

temporal communication. The messages communicated by a person's time orientation and treatment of time.

territoriality. A possessive or ownership reaction to an area of space or to particular objects.

testimonial. A persuasive technique in which the speaker uses the authority or image of some positively evaluated person to gain an audience's approval or of some negatively evaluated person to gain listeners' rejection.

testimony. A form of supporting material consisting of an experts' opinions or witnesses' accounts and may add an authoritative tone to your arguments.

theory. A general statement or principle applicable to related phenomena.

thesis. The main assertion of a message—for example, the theme of a public speech.

topical pattern. An organizational pattern for a public speech I which the topic is organized into its subtopics or component parts.

touch avoidance. The tendency to avoid touching and being touched by others. *Respect the touch-avoidance tendencies of others; pay special attention to cultural and gender differences in touch preferences and in touch avoidance.*

touch communication. Communication through tactile means.

transactional. Characterized by mutual influence and interdependence; communication is a transactional process because no element is independent of any other element.

transfer. A persuasive technique in which a speaker associates an idea with something the audience respects in order to gain approval or with something the audience dislikes in order to gain rejection.

transitions. Words or statements that connect what was said to what will be said. *Use transitions and internal summaries to connect the parts of a speech and to help listeners remember the speech.*

turn-denying cues. Verbal or nonverbal cues indicating that the listener does not want to assume the role of speaker.

turn-maintaining cues. Verbal or nonverbal cues that communicate your wish to maintain the role of speaker.

turn-taking cues. Speaker and listener verbal and nonverbal cues that comment on their roles in a conversation. *Respond to both the verbal and the nonverbal conversational turn-taking cues given you by others, and make your own cues clear to others.*

turn-yielding cues. Verbal or nonverbal cues indicating the speaker's desire to give up the speaker's role.

uncertainty reduction strategies. Passive, active, and interactive ways of increasing accuracy in interpersonal perception.

uncertainty reduction theory. Theory holding that as relationships develop, uncertainty is reduced; relationship development is seen as a process of reducing uncertainty about one another.

universal of interpersonal communication. A feature of communication common to all interpersonal communication acts.

unknown self. A part of the self that is unknown to us as well as to others, but that is inferred to exist on the basis of various projective tests, slips of the tongue, dream analyses, and the like.

upward communication. Communication in which the messages are sent from lower levels to upper levels of an organization or hierarchy—for example, from line worker to management.

value. Relative worth of an object; a quality that makes something desirable or undesirable; an ideal or custom about which we have emotional responses, whether positive or negative.

verbal aggressiveness. A method of winning an argument by attacking the other person's **self-concept.** *Contrast* **argumentativeness.**

violation. Unwarranted use of another's territory.

visual dominance. The use of your eyes to maintain a superior or dominant position; for example, when making an especially important point, you might look intently at the other person.

voice qualities. Aspects of **paralanguage**—specifically, pitch range, vocal lip control, glottis control, pitch control, articulation control, rhythm control, resonance, and tempo.

volume. The relative loudness of the voice. *Use volume to reinforce the meanings you want to communicate.*

weasel words. Words whose meanings are slippery and difficult to pin down. *Ask for specifics when confronted with weasel words.*

win–win solutions. Solutions that benefit both parties in a conflict. *Consider the possibility of solutions in which both parties gain from the conflict. Focus on these rather than solutions in which one person wins and the other loses.*

withdrawal. (1) A reaction to territorial encroachment in which we leave the territory. (2) A tendency to close yourself off from conflicts rather than confront the issues.

you-messages. Messages in which the speaker denies responsibility for his or her own thoughts and behaviors; messages that attribute the speaker's perception to another person; messages of blame. *Contrast* **I-messages.**

Bibliography

Abel, G. G., & Harlow, N. (2001). *The stop child molestation book.* Philadelphia: Xlibris.

Acor, A. A. (2001). Employers' perceptions of persons with body art and an experimental test regarding eyebrow piercing. *Dissertation Abstracts International: Section B. The Sciences and Engineering, 61,* 3885.

Adams-Price, C. E., Dalton, W. T., & Sumrall, R. (2004). Victim blaming in young, middle-aged, and older adults: Variations on the severity effect. *Journal of Adult Development, 11,* 289–295.

Adrianson, L. (2001). Gender and computer-mediated communication: Group processes in problem solving. *Computers in Human Behavior, 17,* 71–94.

Afifi, W. A. (2007). Nonverbal communication. In B. B. Whaley, & W. Samter (Eds.), *Explaining communication: Contemporary theories and exemplars* (pp. 39–60). Mahwah, NJ: Lawrence Erlbaum.

Afifi, W. A., & Johnson, M. L. (2005). The nature and function of tie-signs. In V. Manusov (Ed.), *The sourcebook of nonverbal measures: Going beyond words* (pp. 189–198). Mahwah, NJ: Lawrence Erlbaum.

Akinnaso, F. N. (1982). On the differences between spoken and written language. *Language and Speech, 25*(Part 2), 97–125.

Alessandra, T. (1986). How to listen effectively. *Speaking of success* [Videotape series]. San Diego, CA: Levitz Sommer Productions.

Altman, I. (1975). *The environment and social behavior.* Monterey, CA: Brooks/Cole.

Altman, I., & Taylor, D. (1973). *Social penetration: The development of interpersonal relationships.* New York: Holt, Rinehart & Winston.

Amato, P. R. (1994). The impact of divorce on men and women in India and the United States. *Journal of Comparative Family Studies, 25,* 207–221.

Andersen, J. F., Andersen, P. A., & Lustig, M. W. (1987). Opposite sex touch avoidance: A national replication and extension. *Journal of Nonverbal Behavior, 11,* 89–109.

Andersen, P. A. (1991). Explaining intercultural differences in nonverbal communication. In L. A. Samovar & R. E. Porter (Eds.), *Intercultural communication: A reader* (6th ed., pp. 286–296). Belmont, CA: Wadsworth.

Andersen, P. A. (2004). *The complete idiot's guide to body language.* New York: Penguin Group.

Andersen, P. A., & Leibowitz, K. (1978). The development and nature of the construct of touch avoidance. *Environmental Psychology and Nonverbal Behavior, 3,* 89–106.

Argyle, M. (1986). Rules for social relationships in four cultures. *Australian Journal of Psychology, 38,* 309–318.

Argyle, M. (1988). *Bodily communication* (2nd ed.). New York: Methuen.

Argyle, M., & Henderson, M. (1984). *The anatomy of relationships: And the rules and skills needed to manage them successfully.* London: Heinemann.

Argyle, M., & Ingham, R. (1972). Gaze, mutual gaze and distance. *Semiotica, 1,* 32–49.

Aronson, E., Wilson, T. D., & Akert, R. M. (2007). *Social psychology: The heart and the mind* (4th ed.). New York: Longman.

Aronson, J., Cohen, J., & Nail, P. (1998). Self-affirmation theory: An update and appraisal. In E. Harmon-Jones & J. S. Mills (Eds.), *Cognitive dissonance theory: Revival with revisions and controversies* (pp. 127–147). Washington, DC: American Psychological Association.

Asch, S. (1946). Forming impressions of personality. *Journal of Abnormal and Social Psychology, 41,* 258–290.

Ashcraft, M. H. (1998). *Fundamentals of cognition.* New York: Longman.

Axtell, R. E. (1990). *Do's and taboos of hosting international visitors.* New York: Wiley.

Axtell, R. E. (1993). *Do's and taboos around the world* (3rd ed.). New York: Wiley.

Axtell, R. E. (2007). *Essential do's and taboos: The complete guide to international business and leisure travel.* Hoboken, NJ: Wiley.

Ayres, J. (1986). Perceptions of speaking ability: An explanation for stage fright. *Communication Education, 35,* 275–287.

Bach, G. R., & Wyden, P. (1968). *The intimate enemy.* New York: Avon.

Balsam, K. F., Beauchaine, T. P., Rothblum, E. D., & Solomon, S. E. (2008). Three-year follow-up of same-sex couples who had civil unions in Vermont, same-sex couples not in civil unions, and heterosexual married couples. *Developmental Psychology, 44,* 102–116.

Barker, L. L. (1990). *Communication* (5th ed.). Englewood Cliffs, NJ: Prentice-Hall.

Barker, L., Edwards, R., Gaines, C., Gladney, K., & Holley, F. (1980). An investigation of proportional time spent in various communication activities by college students. *Journal of Applied Communication Research, 8,* 101–109.

Barnlund, D. C. (1970). A transactional model of communication. In J. Akin, A. Goldberg, G. Myers, & J. Stewart (Eds.), *Language behavior: A book of readings in communication.* The Hague: Mouton.

Barnlund, D. C. (1975). Communicative styles in two cultures: Japan and the United States. In A. Kendon, R. M. Harris, & M. R. Key (Eds.), *Organization of behavior in face-to-face interaction.* The Hague: Mouton.

Barnlund, D. C. (1989). *Communicative styles of Japanese and Americans: Images and realities*. Belmont, CA: Wadsworth.

Baron, R. A., & Byrne, D. (1984). *Social psychology: Understanding human interaction* (4th ed.). Boston: Allyn & Bacon.

Barrett, L., & Godfrey, T. (1988). Listening. *Person Centered Review, 3*, 410–425.

Barry, D. T. (2003). Cultural and demographic correlates of self-reported guardedness among East Asian immigrants in the U.S. *International Journal of Psychology, 38*, 150–159.

Basso, K. H. (1972). To give up on words: Silence in Apache culture. In P. P. Giglioli (Ed.), *Language and social context*. New York: Penguin.

Bavelas, J. B. (1990). Can one not communicate? Behaving and communicating: A reply to Motley. *Western Journal of Speech Communication, 54*, 593–602.

Baxter, L. A. (1983). Relationship disengagement: An examination of the reversal hypothesis. *Western Journal of Speech Communication, 47*, 85–98.

Baxter, L. A. (1984). An investigation of compliance-gaining as politeness. *Human Communication Research, 10*, 427–456.

Baxter, L. A. (1986). Gender differences in the heterosexual relationship rules embedded in break-up accounts. *Journal of Social and Personal Relationships, 3*, 289–306.

Beatty, M. J. (1988). Situational and predispositional correlates of public speaking anxiety. *Communication Education, 37*, 28–39.

Beatty, M. J., Rudd, J. E., & Valencic, K. M. (1999). A re-evaluation of the verbal aggressiveness scale: One factor or two? *Communication Research Reports, 16*, 10–17.

Bechler, C., & Johnson, S. D. (1995). Leadership and listening: A study of member perceptions. *Small Group Research, 26*, 77–85.

Beck, A. T. (1988). *Love is never enough*. New York: Harper & Row.

Bedford, V. H. (1996). Relationships between adult siblings. In A. E. Auhagen & M. von Salisch (Eds.), *The diversity of human relationships* (pp. 120–140). New York: Cambridge University Press.

Beebe, S. A., & Masterson, J. T. (2009). *Communicating in small groups: Principles and practices* (8th ed.). Glenview, IL: Scott, Foresman.

Bell, R. A., & Daly, J. A. (1984). The affinity-seeking function of communication. *Communication Monographs, 51*, 91–115.

Bellafiore, D. (2005). Interpersonal conflict and effective communication. Retrieved May 7, 2006, from www.drbalternatives.com/articles/cc2.html

Benne, K. D., & Sheats, P. (1948). Functional roles of group members. *Journal of Social Issues, 4*, 41–49.

Bennis, W., & Nanus, B. (1985). *Leaders: The strategies for taking charge*. New York: Harper & Row.

Benoit, W. L., & Benoit, P. J. (1990). Memory for conversational behavior, *Southern Communication Journal, 55*, 17–23.

Benson, S. G., & Dundis, S. P. (2003). Understanding and motivating health care employees: Integrating Maslow's hierarchy of needs, training and technology. *Journal of Nursing Management, 11*, 315–320.

Berg, J. H., & Archer, R. L. (1983). The disclosure–liking relationship. *Human Communication Research, 10*, 269–281.

Berger, C. R., & Bradac, J. J. (1982). *Language and social knowledge: Uncertainty in interpersonal relations*. London: Edward Arnold.

Bernstein, W. M., Stephan, W. G., & Davis, M. H. (1979). Explaining attributions for achievement: A path analytic approach. *Journal of Personality and Social Psychology, 37*, 1810–1821.

Berry, J. N. III (2004). Can I quote you on that? *Library Journal, 129*, 10.

Blake, R. R., & Mouton, J. S. (1984). *The managerial grid III* (3rd ed.). Houston, TX: Gulf.

Blieszner, R., & Adams, R. G. (1992). *Adult friendship*. Newbury Park, CA: Sage.

Bochner, S., & Hesketh, B. (1994). Power distance, individualism/collectivism, and job-related attitudes in a culturally diverse work group. *Journal of Cross-Cultural Psychology, 25*, 233–257.

Bok, S. (1978). *Lying: Moral choice in public and private life*. New York: Pantheon.

Bok, S. (1983). *Secrets*. New York: Vintage.

Borden, G. A. (1991). *Cultural orientation: An approach to understanding intercultural communication*. Englewood Cliffs, NJ: Prentice-Hall.

Bower, S. A., & Bower, G. A. (2005). *Asserting yourself: A practical guide for positive change*. Cambridge, MA: DaCapo Press.

Brashers, D. E. (2007). A theory of communication and uncertainty management. In B. B. Whaley & W. Samter (Eds.), *Explaining communication: Contemporary theories and exemplars* (pp. 201–218). Mahwah, NJ: Lawrence Erlbaum.

Bridges, C. R. (1996). The characteristics of career achievement perceived by African American college administrators. *Journal of Black Studies, 26*, 748–767.

Brilhart, J., & Galanes, G. (1992). *Effective group discussion* (7th ed.). Dubuque, IA: Brown & Benchmark.

Brown, P. (1980). How and why are women more polite: Some evidence from a Mayan community. In S. McConnell-Ginet, R. Borker, & M. Furman (Eds.), *Women and language in literature and society* (pp. 111–136). New York: Praeger.

Brownell, J. (1987). Listening: The toughest management skill. *Cornell Hotel and Restaurant Administration Quarterly, 27*, 64–71.

Brownell, J. (2006). *Listening: Attitudes, principles, and skills* (3rd ed.). Boston: Allyn & Bacon.

Brownell, J. (2008). Exploring the strategic ground for listening and organizational effectiveness. *Scandinavian Journal of Hospitality and Tourism, 8*, 211–229.

Bruneau, T. (1985). The time dimension in intercultural communication. In L. A. Samovar & R. E. Porter (Eds.), *Intercultural communication: A reader* (4th ed., pp. 280–289). Belmont, CA: Wadsworth.

Bruneau, T. (1990). Chronemics: The study of time in human interaction. In J. A. DeVito & M. L. Hecht (Eds.), *The nonverbal communication reader* (pp. 301–311). Prospect Heights, IL: Waveland Press.

Buber, M. (1958). *I and thou* (2nd ed.). New York: Scribner's.

Buller, D. B., LePoire, B. A., Aune, K., & Eloy, S. (1992). Social perceptions as mediators of the effect of speech rate similarity on compliance. *Human Communication Research, 19,* 286–311.

Burgoon, J. K., & Bacue, A. E. (2003). Nonverbal communication skills. In J. O. Greene & B. R. Burleson (Eds.), *Handbook of communication and social interaction skills* (pp. 179–220). Mahwah, NJ: Erlbaum.

Burgoon, J. K., & Hale, J. L. (1988). Nonverbal expectancy violations: Model elaboration and application to immediacy behaviors. *Communication Monographs, 55,* 58–79.

Burgoon, J. K., & Hoobler, G. D. (2002). Nonverbal signals. In M. L. Knapp & J. A. Daly (Eds.), *Handbook of interpersonal communication* (3rd ed., pp. 240–299). Thousand Oaks, CA: Sage.

Burgoon, J. K., Berger, C. R., & Waldron, V. R. (2000). Mindfulness and interpersonal communication. *Journal of Social Issues, 56,* 105–127.

Burgoon, J. K., Buller, D. B., & Woodall, W. G. (1996). *Nonverbal communication: The unspoken dialogue* (2nd ed.). New York: McGraw-Hill.

Burleson, B. R., Holmstrom, A. J., & Gilstrap, C. M. (2005). "Guys can't say *that* to guys": Four experiments assessing the normative motivation account for deficiencies in the emotional support provided by men. *Communication Monographs, 72,* 468–501.

Burleson, B. R., Kunkel, A. W., & Birch, J. D. (1994). Thoughts about talk in romantic relationships: Similarity makes for attraction (and happiness, too). *Communication Quarterly, 42,* 259–273.

Burleson, B. R., Samter, W., & Luccetti, A. E. (1992). Similarity in communication values as a predictor of friendship choices: Studies of friends and best friends. *Southern Communication Journal, 57,* 260–276.

Burnard, P. (2003). Ordinary chat and therapeutic conversation: Phatic communication and mental health nursing. *Journal of Psychiatric and Mental Health Nursing, 10,* 678–682.

Butler, J., Pryor, B., & Grieder, M. (1998). Impression formation as a function of male baldness. *Perceptual and Motor Skills, 86,* 347–350.

Butler, P. E. (1981). *Talking to yourself: Learning the language of self-support.* New York: Harper & Row.

Byers, E. S., & Demmons, S. (1999). Sexual satisfaction and sexual self-disclosure within dating relationships. *Journal of Sex Research, 36,* 180–189.

Cahn, D. D., & Abigail, R. A. (2007). *Managing conflict through communication* (3rd ed.). Boston: Allyn & Bacon.

Cai, D. A., & Fink, E. L. (2002). Conflict style differences between individualists and collectivists. *Communication Monographs, 69,* 67–87.

Canary, D. J. (2003). Managing interpersonal conflict: A model of events related to strategic choices. In J. O. Greene & B. R. Burleson (Eds.), *Handbook of communication and social interaction skills* (pp. 515–550). Mahwah, NJ: Erlbaum.

Canary, D. J., & Hause, K. (1993). Is there any reason to research sex differences in communication? *Communication Quarterly, 41,* 129–144.

Canary, D. J., Cupach, W. R., & Messman, S. J. (1995). *Relationship conflict: Conflict in parent-child, friendship, and romantic relationships.* Thousand Oaks, CA: Sage.

Cappella, J. N. (1993). The facial feedback hypothesis in human interaction: Review and speculation. *Journal of Language and Social Psychology, 12,* 13–29.

Carroll, D. W. (1994). *Psychology of language* (2nd ed.). Pacific Grove, CA: Brooks/Cole.

Cate, R. J., Henton, J., Koval, R., Christopher, F., & Lloyd, S. (1982). Premarital abuse: A social psychological perspective. *Journal of Family Issues, 3,* 79–90.

Cawthon, S. W. (2001). Teaching strategies in inclusive classrooms with deaf students. *Journal of Deaf Studies and Deaf Education, 6,* 212–225.

Chadwick-Jones, J. K. (1976). *Social exchange theory: Its structure and influence in social psychology.* New York: Academic Press.

Chang, H., & Holt, G. R. (1996). The changing Chinese interpersonal world: Popular themes in interpersonal communication books in modern Taiwan. *Communication Quarterly, 44,* 85–106.

Chanowitz, B., & Langer, E. (1981). Premature cognitive commitment. *Journal of Personality and Social Psychology, 41,* 1051–1063.

Cheney, G., & Tompkins, P. K. (1987). Coming to terms with organizational identification and commitment. *Central States Speech Journal, 38,* 1–15.

Childress, H. (2004). Teenagers, territory and the appropriation of space. *Childhood: A Global Journal of Child Research, 11,* 195–205.

Chung, L. C., & Ting-Toomey, S. (1999). Ethnic identity and relational expectations among Asian Americans. *Communication Research Reports, 16,* 157–166.

Clark, H. (1974). The power of positive speaking. *Psychology Today, 8,* 102, 108–111.

Cody, M. J., & Dunn, D. (2007). Accounts. In B. B. Whaley and W. Samter (Eds.), *Explaining communication: Contemporary theories and exemplars* (pp. 237–256). Mahwah, NJ: Lawrence Erlbaum.

Coleman, P. (2002). *How to say it for couples: Communicating with tenderness, openness, and honesty.* Paramus, NJ: Prentice-Hall.

Collins, J. E., & Clark, L. F. (1989). Responsibility and rumination: The trouble with understanding the dissolution of a relationship. *Social Cognition, 7,* 152–173.

Comer, L. B., & Drollinger, T. (1999). Active emphatic listening and selling success: A conceptual framework. *Journal of Personal Selling and Sales Management, 19,* 15–29.

Cooley, C. H. (1922). *Human nature and the social order* (Rev. ed.). New York: Scribner's.

Cooper, A., & Sportolari, L. (1997). Romance in cyberspace: Understanding online attraction. *Journal of Sex Education and Therapy, 22,* 7–14.

Cornwell, B., & Lundgren, D. C. (2001). Love on the Internet: Involvement and misrepresentation in romantic relationships in cyberspace vs. realspace. *Computers in Human Behavior, 17,* 197–211.

Crawford, M. (1994). Rethinking the romance: Teaching the content and function of gender stereotypes in the Psychology of Women course. *Teaching of Psychology, 21,* 151–153.

Crowley, A. (1999, August 30). Project leaders wanted. *PC Week,* 76.

Crown, C. L., & Cummins, D. A. (1998). Objective versus perceived vocal interruptions in the dialogues of unacquainted pairs, friends, and couples. *Journal of Language and Social Psychology, 17,* 372–389.

Davitz, J. R. (Ed.). (1964). *The communication of emotional meaning.* New York: McGraw-Hill.

Deal, J. E., & Wampler, K. S. (1986). Dating violence: The primacy of previous experience. *Journal of Social and Personal Relationships, 3,* 457–471.

deBono, E. (1976). *Teaching thinking.* New York: Penguin.

Dell, K. (2005, February 14). Just for dudes. *Time,* B22.

Derlega, V. J., Winstead, B. A., & Wong, P. T. P., & Greenspan, M. (1987). Self-disclosure and relationship development: An attributional analysis. In M. E. Roloff & G. R. Miller (Eds.), *Interpersonal processes: New directions in communication research* (pp. 172–187). Thousand Oaks, CA: Sage.

DeTurck, M. A. (1987). When communication fails: Physical aggression as a compliance-gaining strategy. *Communication Monographs, 54,* 106–112.

DeVito, J. A. (1965). Comprehension factors in oral and written discourse of skilled communicators. *Communication Monographs, 32,* 124–128.

DeVito, J. A. (1976). Relative ease in comprehending yes/no questions. In J. Blankenship & H. G. Stelzner (Eds.), *Rhetoric and communication* (pp. 143–154). Urbana: University of Illinois Press.

DeVito, J. A. (1981). *The psychology of speech and language: An introduction to psycholinguistics.* Washington, DC: University Press of America.

DeVito, J. A. (1996). *Brainstorms: How to think more creatively about communication (or about anything else).* New York: Longman.

DeVito, J. A. (2003). SCREAM before you scream. *ETC: A Review of General Semantics* 60 (Spring), 42–45.

Dillard, J. P., & Marshall, L. J. (2003). Persuasion as a social skill. In J. O. Greene & B. R. Burleson (Eds.), *Handbook of communication and social interaction skills* (pp. 479–514). Mahwah, NJ: Erlbaum.

Dindia, K., & Canary, D. J. (Eds). *Sex differences and similarities in communication* (2nd ed.). Mahwah, NJ: Lawrence Erlbaum.

Donahue, W. A., with Kolt, R. (1992). *Managing interpersonal conflict.* Thousand Oaks, CA: Sage.

Donaldson, S. (1992). Gender and discourse: The case of interruptions. *Carleton Papers in Applied Language Studies, 9,* 47–66.

Dovidio, J. F., Gaertner, S. E., Kawakami, K., & Hodson, G. (2002). Why can't we just get along? Interpersonal biases and interracial distrust. *Cultural Diversity and Ethnic Minority Psychology, 8,* 88–102.

Drass, K. A. (1986). The effect of gender identity on conversation. *Social Psychology Quarterly, 49,* 294–301.

Dresser, N. (1996). *Multicultural manners: New rules of etiquette for a changing society.* New York: Wiley.

Drews, D. R., Allison, C. K., & Probst, J. R. (2000). Behavioral and self-concept differences in tattooed and nontattooed college students. *Psychological Reports, 86,* 475–481.

Dreyfuss, H. (1971). *Symbol sourcebook.* New York: McGraw-Hill.

Drummond, K., & Hopper, R. (1993). Acknowledgment tokens in series. *Communication Reports, 6,* 47–53.

Dsilva, M., & Whyte, L. O. (1998). Cultural differences in conflict styles: Vietnamese refugees and established residents. *The Howard Journal of Communication, 9,* 57–68.

Dunbar, N. E., & Burgoon, J. K. (2005). Measuring nonverbal dominance. In V. Manusov (Ed.), *The sourcebook of nonverbal measures: Going beyond words* (pp. 361–374). Mahwah, NJ: Lawrence Erlbaum.

Dunbar, R. I. M. (2004). Gossip in evolutionary perspective. *Review of General Psychology 8,* 100–110.

Duncan, S. D., Jr. (1972). Some signals and rules for taking speaking turns in conversation. *Journal of Personality and Social Psychology, 23,* 283–292.

Dunn, D., & Cody, M. J. (2000). Account credibility and public image: Excuses, justifications, denials, and sexual harassment. *Communication Monographs, 67,* 372–391.

Duval, T. S., & Silva, P. J. (2002). Self-awareness, probability of improvement, and the self-serving bias. *Journal of Personality and Social Psychology, 82,* 49–61.

Eder, D., & Enke, J. L. (1991). The structure of gossip: Opportunities and constraints on collective expression among adolescents. *American Sociological Review, 56,* 494–508.

Ehrenhaus, P. (1988). Silence and symbolic expression. *Communication Monographs, 55,* 41–57.

Einhorn, L. (2006). Using e-prime and English minus absolutisms to provide self-empathy. *ETC: A Review of General Semantics, 63,* 180–186.

Ekman, P. (1985). *Telling lies: Clues to deceit in the marketplace, politics, and marriage.* New York: Norton.

Ekman, P. (2009). *Telling lies: Clues to deceit in the marketplace, politics, and marriage* (3rd ed.). New York: Norton.

Ekman, P., & Friesen, W. V. (1969). The repertoire of nonverbal behavior: Categories, origins, usage, and coding. *Semiotica, 1,* 49–98.

Ekman, P., Friesen, W. V., & Ellsworth, P. (1972). *Emotion in the human face: Guidelines for research and an integration of findings.* New York: Pergamon Press.

Elfenbein, H. A., & Ambady, N. (2002). Is there an in-group advantage in emotion recognition? *Psychological Bulletin, 128,* 243–249.

Ellis, A. (1988). *How to stubbornly refuse to make yourself miserable about anything, yes anything.* Secaucus, NJ: Lyle Stuart.

Ellis, A., & Dryden, W. (2007). *The practice of rational emotive therapy* (2nd ed.). New York: Springer.

Elmes, M. B., & Gemmill, G. (1990). The psychodynamics of mindlessness and dissent in small groups. *Small Group Research, 21,* 28–44.

Emmers-Sommer, T. M. (2004). The effect of communication quality and quantity indicators on intimacy and relational satisfaction. *Journal of Social and Personal Relationships, 21,* 99–411.

Exline, R. V., Ellyson, S. L., & Long, B. (1975). Visual behavior as an aspect of power role relationships. In P. Pliner, L. Krames, & T. Alloway (Eds.), *Nonverbal communication of aggression.* New York: Plenum Press.

Faigley, L. (2009). *The Penguin handbook* (3rd ed.). New York: Longman.

Fengler, A. P. (1974). Romantic love in courtship: Divergent paths of male and female students. *Journal of Comparative Family Studies,* 134–139.

Festinger, L. (1954). A theory of social comparison processes. *Human Relations, 7,* 117–140.

Fielder, F. E. (1967). *A theory of leadership effectiveness.* New York: McGraw-Hill.

Fitzpatrick, M. A. (1983). Predicting couples' communication from couples' self-reports. In R. N. Bostrom (Ed.), *Communication Yearbook 7* (pp. 49–82). Thousand Oaks, CA: Sage.

Fitzpatrick, M. A. (1988). *Between husbands and wives: Communication in marriage.* Thousand Oaks, CA: Sage.

Fitzpatrick, M. A. (1991). Sex differences in marital conflict: Social psychophysiological versus cognitive explanations. *Text, 11,* 341–364.

Fitzpatrick, M. A., Jandt, F. E., Myrick, F. L., & Edgar, T. (1994). Gay and lesbian couple relationships. In R. J. Ringer (Ed.), *Queer words, queer images: Communication and the construction of homosexuality* (pp. 265–285). New York: New York University Press.

Floyd, K., & Mikkelson, A. C. (2005). In V. Manusov (Ed.), *The sourcebook of nonverbal measures: Going beyond words* (pp. 47–56). Mahwah, NJ: Lawrence Erlbaum.

Folger, J. P., Poole, M. S., & Stutman, R. K. (1997). *Working through conflict: A communication perspective* (3rd ed.). New York: Longman.

Forbes, G. B. (2001). College students with tattoos and piercings: Motives, family experiences, personality factors, and perception by others. *Psychological Reports, 89,* 774–786.

French, J. R. P., Jr., & Raven, B. (1968). The bases of social power. In D. Cartwright & A. Zander (Eds.), *Group dynamics: Research and theory* (3rd ed., pp. 259–269). New York: Harper & Row.

Fridlund, A. J., & Russell, J. A. (2006). The functions of facial expressions. What's in a face? In V. Manusov & M. L. Patterson (Eds.), *Sage Handbook of Nonverbal Communication* (pp. 299–320). Newbury Park, CA: Sage.

Fukushima, S. (2000). *Requests and culture: Politeness in British English and Japanese.* New York: Peter Lang.

Fuller, D. (2004). Electronic manners and netiquette. *Athletic Therapy Today, 9,* 40–41.

Furlow, F. B. (1996). The smell of love. *Psychology Today,* 38–45.

Galvin, K., Bylund, C., & Brommel, B. J. (2007). *Family communication: Cohesion and change* (7th ed.). New York: Longman.

Gamble, T. K., & Gamble, M. W. (2003). *The gender communication connection.* Boston: Houghton Mifflin.

Gamson, J. (1998). Publicity traps: Television talk shows and lesbian, gay, bisexual, and transgender visibility. *Sexualities* 1 (February), 11–41.

Gao, G., & Gudykunst, W. B. (1995). Attributional confidence, perceived similarity, and network involvement in Chinese and American romantic relationships. *Communication Quarterly, 43,* 431–445.

Gelfand, M. J., Nishii, L. H., Holcombe, K. M., Dyer, N., Ohbuchi, K., & Fukuno, M. (2001). Cultural influences on cognitive representations of conflict: Interpretations of conflict episodes in the United States and Japan. *Journal of Applied Psychology, 86,* 1059–1074.

Georgas, J., et al. (2001). Functional relationships in the nuclear and extended family: A 16-culture study. *International Journal of Psychology, 36,* 289–300.

Gergen, K. J., Greenberg, M. S., & Willis, R. H. (1980). *Social exchange: Advances in theory and research.* New York: Plenum Press.

Gibb, J. (1961). Defensive communication. *Journal of Communication, 11,* 141–148.

Giles, H. (2008). Communication accommodation theory. In L. A. Baxter & D. O. Braithwaite (Eds.), *Engaging theories in interpersonal communication: Multiple perspectives* (pp. 161–173). Los Angeles, CA: Sage.

Giles, H., Mulac, A., Bradac, J. J., & Johnson, P. (1987). Speech accommodation theory: The first decade and beyond. In M. L. McLaughlin (Ed.), *Communication yearbook 10* (pp. 13–48). Thousand Oaks, CA: Sage.

Goffman, E. (1967). *Interaction ritual: Essays on face-to-face behavior.* New York: Pantheon.

Goffman, E. (1971). *Relations in public: Microstudies of the public order.* New York: HarperCollins.

Goldin-Meadow, S., Nusbaum, H., Kelly, S. D., & Wagner, S. (2001). Gesture—psychological aspects. *Psychological Science, 12,* 516–522.

Goldsmith, D. J. (2007). Brown and Levinson's politeness theory. In B. B. Whaley & W. Samter (Eds.), *Explaining communication: Contemporary theories and exemplars* (pp. 219–236). Mahwah, NJ: Lawrence Erlbaum.

Goldsmith, D. J., & Fulfs, P. A. (1999). "You just don't have the evidence": An analysis of claims and evidence. In M. E. Roloff (Ed.), *Communication yearbook 22* (pp. 1–49). Thousand Oaks, CA: Sage.

Goleman, D. (1995). *Emotional intelligence*. New York: Bantam.

Gonzalez, A., & Zimbardo, P. G. (1985). Time in perspective. *Psychology Today, 19,* 20–26.

Goodwin, R., & Lee, I. (1994). Taboo topics among Chinese and English friends: A cross-cultural comparison. *Journal of Cross-Cultural Psychology, 25,* 325–338.

Gorden, W. I., & Nevins, R. J. (1993). *We mean business: Building communication competence in business and professions*. New York: HarperCollins.

Gordon, T. (1975). *P.E.T.: Parent effectiveness training*. New York: New American Library.

Gottman, J. M., & Carrere, S. (1994). Why can't men and women get along? Developmental roots and marital inequities. In D. J. Canary and Laura Stafford (Eds.), *Communication and relational maintenance* (pp. 203–229). San Diego, CA: Academic Press.

Gottman, J. M., & Levenson, R. W. (1999). Dysfunctional marital conflict: Women are being unfairly blamed. *Journal of Divorce and Remarriage, 31,* 1–17.

Graham, J. A., & Argyle, M. (1975). The effects of different patterns of gaze combined with different facial expressions on impression formation. *Journal of Movement Studies, 1,* 178–182.

Graham, J. A., Bitti, P. R., & Argyle, M. (1975). A cross-cultural study of the communication of emotion by facial and gestural cues. *Journal of Human Movement Studies, 1,* 68–77.

Greengard, S. (2001). Gossip poisons business. HR can stop it. *Workforce, 80,* 24–28.

Greif, E. B. (1980). Sex differences in parent-child conversations. *Women's Studies International Quarterly, 3,* 253–258.

Gross, L. (1991). The contested closet: The ethics and politics of outing. *Critical Studies in Mass Communication, 8,* 352–388.

Gross, T., Turner, E., & Cederholm, L. (1987, June). Building teams for global operation. *Management Review,* 32–36.

Grossin, W. (1987). Monochronic time, polychronic time and policies for development. *Studi di Sociologia, 25,* 18–25.

Gu, Y. (1997). Polite phenomena in modern Chinese. *Journal of Pragmatics, 14,* 237–257.

Gudykunst, W. B. (1991). *Bridging differences: Effective intergroup communication*. Newbury Park, CA: Sage.

Gudykunst, W. B. (1994). *Bridging differences: Effective intergroup communication* (2nd ed.). Newbury Park, CA: Sage.

Gudykunst, W. B., & Kim, Y. Y. (Eds.). (1992). *Readings on communication with strangers: An approach to intercultural communication*. New York: McGraw-Hill.

Guerrero, L. K., & Andersen, P. A. (1991). The waxing and waning of relational intimacy: Touch as a function of relational stage, gender and touch avoidance. *Journal of Social and Personal Relationships, 8,* 147–165.

Guerrero, L. K., & Andersen, P. A. (1994). Patterns of matching and initiation: Touch behavior and touch avoidance across romantic relationship stages. *Journal of Nonverbal Behavior 18,* 137–153.

Guerrero, L. K., & Hecht, M. L. (Eds.). (2006). *The nonverbal communication reader: Class and contemporary readings* (3rd ed.). Prospect Heights, IL: Waveland Press.

Guerrero, L. K., Andersen, P. A., & Afifi, W. A. (2007). *Close encounters: Communication in relationships* (2nd ed.). Thousand Oaks, CA: Sage.

Haar, B. F., & Krabe, B. (1999). Strategies for resolving interpersonal conflicts in adolescence: A German–Indonesian comparison. *Journal of Cross-Cultural Psychology, 30,* 667–683.

Hackman, M. Z., & Johnson, C. E. (1991). *Leadership: A communication perspective*. Prospect Heights, IL: Waveland Press.

Hafen, S. (2004). Organizational gossip: A revolving door of regulation and resistance, *Southern Communication Journal, 69* (Spring), 223–240.

Haga, Y. (1988). Traits de langage et caractère Japonais. *Cahiers de Sociologie Economique et Culturelle, 9,* 105–109.

Hall, E. T. (1959). *The silent language*. Garden City, NY: Doubleday.

Hall, E. T. (1963). A system for the notation of proxemic behavior. *American Anthropologist, 65,* 1003–1026.

Hall, E. T. (1966). *The hidden dimension*. Garden City, NY: Doubleday.

Hall, E. T. (1976). *Beyond culture*. Garden City, NY: Doubleday.

Hall, E. T. (1983). *The dance of life: The other dimension of time*. New York: Anchor Books/Doubleday.

Hall, E. T., & Hall, M. R. (1987). *Hidden differences: Doing business with the Japanese*. Garden City, NY: Doubleday.

Hall, J. A. (1998). How big are nonverbal sex differences? The case of smiling and sensitivity to nonverbal cues. In D. J. Canary & K. Dindia (Eds.), *Sex differences and similarities in communication: Critical essays and empirical investigations of sex and gender in interaction* (pp. 155–178). Mahwah, NJ: Erlbaum.

Haney, W. (1973). *Communication and organizational behavior: Text and cases* (3rd ed.). Homewood, IL: Irwin.

Hanley, S. J., & Abell, S. C. (2002, Fall). Maslow and relatedness: Creating an interpersonal model of self-actualization. *Journal of Humanistic Psychology, 42,* 37–56.

Hart, F. (1990). The construction of masculinity in men's friendships: Misogyny, heterosexuality, and homophobia. *Resources for Feminist Research, 19,* 60–67.

Hastings, S. O. (2000). "Egocasting" in the avoidance of disclosure: An intercultural perspective. In S. Petronio (Ed.), *Balancing the secrets of private disclosures* (pp. 235–248). Mahwah, NJ: Erlbaum.

Hatfield, E., & Rapson, R. L. (1996). *Love and sex: Cross-cultural perspectives*. Boston: Allyn & Bacon.

Hayakawa, S. I., & Hayakawa, A. R. (1989). *Language in thought and action* (5th ed.). New York: Harcourt Brace Jovanovich.

Hays, R. B. (1989). The day-to-day functioning of close versus casual friendships. *Journal of Social and Personal Relationships, 6,* 21–37.

Heap, J. L. (1992). Seeing snubs: An introduction to sequential analysis of classroom interaction. *Journal of Classroom Interaction, 27,* 23–28.

Heasley, J. B., Babbitt, C. E., & Burbach, H. J. (1995). Gender differences in college students' perceptions of "fighting words." *Sociological Viewpoints,* 11 (Fall), 30–40.

Heath, W. P., Stone, J., Darley, J. M., & Grannemann, B. D. (2003). Yes, I did it, but don't blame me: Perceptions of excuse defenses. *Journal of Psychiatry and Law, 31,* 187–226.

Hecht, M. L. (1978). The conceptualization and measurement of interpersonal communication satisfaction. *Human Communication Research, 4,* 253–264.

Hecht, M. L., Jackson, R. L., & Ribeau, S. (2003). *African American communication: Exploing identify and culture* (2nd ed.). Mahwah, NJ: Erlbaum.

Helgeson, V. S. (2009). *Psychology of gender* (3rd ed.). Upper Saddle River, NJ: Prentice-Hall.

Hendrick, C., & Hendrick, S. (1990). A relationship-specific version of the love attitudes scale. In J. W. Heulip (Ed.), Handbook of replication research in the behavioral and social sciences [Special issue]. *Journal of Social Behavior and Personality, 5,* 239–254.

Hendrick, C., Hendrick, S., Foote, F. H., & Slapion-Foote, M. J. (1984). Do men and women love differently? *Journal of Social and Personal Relationships, 1,* 177–195.

Herrick, J. A. (2004). *Argumentation: Understanding and shaping arguments.* State College, PA: Strata.

Hersey, P., Blanchard, K. H., & Johnson, D. E. (2001). *Management of organizational behavior: Leading human resources* (8th ed.). Upper Saddle River, NJ: Prentice-Hall.

Hewitt, J., & Stokes, R. (1975). Disclaimers. *American Sociological Review, 40,* 1–11.

Himle, J. A., Abelson, J. L., & Haghightgou, H. (1999). Effect of alcohol on social phobic anxiety. *American Journal of Psychiatry, 156,* 1237–1243.

Hocker, J. L., & Wilmot, W. W. (1985). *Interpersonal conflict* (2nd ed.). Dubuque, IA: William C. Brown.

Hofstede, G. (1997). *Cultures and organizations: Software of the mind.* New York: McGraw-Hill.

Hoft, N. L. (1995). *International technical communication: How to export information about high technology.* New York: Wiley.

Holmes, J. (1995). *Women, men and politeness.* New York: Longman.

Hunt, M. O. (2000). Status, religion, and the "belief in a just world": Comparing African Americans, Latinos, and whites. *Social Science Quarterly, 81,* 325–343.

Iizuka, Y. (1993). Regulators in Japanese conversation. *Psychological Reports, 72,* 203–209.

Infante, D. A. (1988). *Arguing constructively.* Prospect Heights, IL: Waveland Press.

Infante, D. A., & Rancer, A. (1982). A conceptualization and measure of argumentativeness. *Journal of Personality Assessment, 46,* 72–80.

Infante, D. A., & Rancer, A. S. (1995). Argumentativeness and verbal aggressiveness: A review of recent theory and research. In B. R. Burleson (Ed.), *Communication yearbook, 19* (pp. 319–351). Thousand Oaks, CA: Sage.

Infante, D. A., & Wigley, C. J. (1986). Verbal aggressiveness: An interpersonal model and measure. *Communication Monographs, 53,* 61–69.

Infante, D. A., Rancer, A. S., & Womack, D. F. (2003). Building communication theory (4th ed.). Prospect Heights, IL: Waveland Press.

Jacobson, D. (1999). Impression formation in cyberspace: Online expectations and offline experiences in text-based virtual communities. *Journal of Computer Mediated Communication, 5.*

Jambor, E., & Elliott, M. (2005, Winter). Self-esteem and coping strategies among deaf students. *Journal of Deaf Studies and Deaf Education, 10,* 63–81.

Jandt, F. E. (2004). *Intercultural communication.* Thousand Oaks, CA: Sage.

Janis, I. (1983). *Victims of group thinking: A psychological study of foreign policy decisions and fiascoes* (2nd ed.). Boston: Houghton Mifflin.

Jaworski, A. (1993). *The power of silence: Social and pragmatic perspectives.* Newbury Park, CA: Sage.

Jecker, J., & Landy, D. (1969). Liking a person as a function of doing him a favor. *Human Relations, 22,* 371–378.

Johannesen, R. L. (2001). *Ethics in human communication* (6th ed.). Prospect Heights, IL: Waveland Press.

Johannesen, R. L., Valde, K. S., & Whedbee, K. E. (2007). *Ethics in human communication* (6th ed.). Prospect Heights, IL: Waveland.

Johansson, W., & Percy, W. A. (1994). *Outing: Shattering the conspiracy of silence.* New York: Harrington Park Press.

Johnson, C. E. (1987). An introduction to powerful and powerless talk in the classroom. *Communication Education, 36,* 167–172.

Johnson, S. D., & Bechler, C. (1998). Examining the relationship between listening effectiveness and leadership emergence: Perceptions, behaviors, and recall. *Small Group Research, 29,* 452–471.

Johnson, S. M., & O'Connor, E. (2002). *The gay baby boom: The psychology of gay parenthood.* New York: New York University Press.

Joinson, A. N. (2001). Self-disclosure in computer-mediated communication: The role of self-awareness and visual anonymity. *European Journal of Social Psychology, 31,* 177–192.

Jones, B. C., DeBruine, L. M., Little, A. C., Burriss, R. P., & Feinberg, D. R. (2007). Social transmission of face preferences among humans. *Proceedings of the Royal Society* 274 (March 22): 899–903.

Jones, C., Berry, L., & Stevens, C. (2007). Synthesized speech intelligibility and persuasion: Speech rate and non-native listeners. *Computer Speech and Language, 21,* 641–651.

Jones, S. (2005). The touch-log record: A behavioral communication measure. In V. Manusov (Ed.), *The sourcebook of nonverbal measures: Going beyond words* (pp. 67–81). Mahwah, NJ: Lawrence Erlbaum.

Jones, S., & Yarbrough, A. E. (1985). A naturalistic study of the meanings of touch. *Communication Monographs, 52,* 19–56.

Jourard, S. M. (1968). *Disclosing man to himself.* New York: Van Nostrand Reinhold.

Jourard, S. M. (1971a). *Self-disclosure.* New York: Wiley.

Jourard, S. M. (1971b). *The transparent self* (Rev. ed.). New York: Van Nostrand Reinhold.

Judge, T. A., & Cable, D. M. (2004). The effect of physical height on workplace success and income. *Journal of Applied Psychology, 89,* 428–441.

Kallos, J. (2005). *Because netiquette matters! Your comprehensive reference guide to e-mail etiquette and proper technology use.* Philadelphia: Xlibris.

Kanner, B. (1989, April 3). Color schemes. *New York Magazine,* pp. 22–23.

Kapoor, S., Hughes, P. C., Baldwin, J. R., & Blue, J. (2003). The relationship of kindividualism-collectivism and self-construals to communication styles in India and the United States. *International Journal of Intercultural Relations, 27,* 683–700.

Katz, S. (2003). *Down to earth sociology: Introductory readings* (12th ed., pp. 313–320). Henslin, J. W. (Ed.). New York: Free Press.

Kelley, H. H., & Thibaut, J. W. (1978). *Interpersonal relations: A theory of interdependence.* New York: Wiley/Interscience.

Kelly, P. K. (1994). *Team decision-making techniques.* Irvine, CA: Richard Chang Associates.

Kennedy, C. W., & Camden, C. T. (1988). A new look at interruptions. *Western Journal of Speech Communication, 47,* 45–58.

Ketcham, H. (1958). *Color planning for business and industry.* New York: Harper.

Keyes, R. (1980). *The height of your life.* New York: Warner.

Kiel, J. M. (1999). Reshaping Maslow's hierarchy of needs to reflect today's education and managerial philosophies. *Journal of Instructional Psychology, 26,* 167–168.

Kindred, J., & Roper, S. L. (2004). Making connections via instant messenger (IM): Student use of IM to maintain personal relationships. *Qualitative Research Reports in Communication, 5,* 48–54.

Kleinfeld, N. R. (1992, October 25). The smell of money. *The New York Times* (Section 9), pp. 1, 8.

Kleinke, C. L. (1986). *Meeting and understanding people.* New York: W. H. Freeman.

Knapp, M. L. (1984). *Interpersonal communication and human relationships.* Boston: Allyn & Bacon.

Knapp, M. L. (2007). *Lying and deception in human interaction.* Boston: Pearson.

Knapp, M. L., & Hall, J. (2005). *Nonverbal communication in human interaction* (6th ed.). Fort Worth, TX: Harcourt Brace Jovanovich.

Knapp, M. L., & Vangelisti, A. (2000). *Interpersonal communication and human relationships* (4th ed.). Boston: Allyn & Bacon.

Knapp, M. L., Hart, R. P., Friedrich, G. W., & Shulman, G. M. (1973). The rhetoric of goodbye: Verbal and nonverbal correlates of human leave-taking. *Communication Monographs, 40,* 182–198.

Knobloch, L. K., & Solomon, D. H. (1999). Measuring the sources and content of relational uncertainty. *Communication Studies, 50,* 261–278.

Knobloch, L. K., Haunani, D., & Theiss, J. A. (2006). The role of intimacy in the production and perception of relationship talk within courtship. *Communication Research, 33,* 211–241.

Komarovsky, M. (1964). *Blue collar marriage.* New York: Random House.

Koppelman, K. L., with Goodhart, R. L. (2005). *Understanding human differences: Multicultural education for a diverse America.* Boston: Allyn & Bacon.

Krebs, G. L. (1989). *Organizational communication* (2nd ed.). Boston: Allyn & Bacon.

Krivonos, P. D., & Knapp, M. L. (1975). Initiating communication: What do you say when you say hello? *Central States Speech Journal, 26,* 115–125.

Kurdek, L. A. (1994). Areas of conflict for gay, lesbian, and heterosexual couples: What couples argue about influences relationship satisfaction. *Journal of Marriage and the Family, 56,* 923–934.

Lakoff, R. (1975). *Language and women's place.* New York: Harper & Row.

Lamm, K., & Lamm, K. (1999). *10,000 ideas for term papers, projects, reports, and speeches* (5th ed.). New York: Arco.

Langer, E. J. (1989). *Mindfulness.* Reading, MA: Addison-Wesley.

Lanzetta, J. T., Cartwright-Smith, J., & Kleck, R. E. (1976). Effects of nonverbal dissimulations on emotional experience and autonomic arousal. *Journal of Personality and Social Psychology, 33,* 354–370.

Larsen, R. J., Kasimatis, M., & Frey, K. (1992). Facilitating the furrowed brow: An unobtrusive test of the facial feedback hypothesis applied to unpleasant affect. *Cognition and Emotion, 6,* 321–338.

Lauer, C. S. (2003, February 10). Listen to this. *Modern Healthcare, 33,* 34.

Leathers, D., & Eaves, M. H. (2008). *Successful nonverbal communication: Principles and applications* (4th ed.). Boston: Allyn & Bacon.

Lederer, W. J. (1984). *Creating a good relationship.* New York: Norton.

Lee, A. M., & Lee, E. B. (1972). *The fine art of propaganda.* San Francisco: International Society for General Semantics.

Lee, A. M., & Lee, E. B. (1995). The iconography of propaganda analysis. *ETC: A Review of General Semantics, 52,* 13–17.

Lee, C. M., & Gudykunst, W. B. (2001). Attraction in initial interethnic interactions. *Journal of Intercultural Relations, 25,* 373–387.

Lee, H. O., & Boster, F. J. (1992). Collectivism–individualism in perceptions of speech rate: A cross-cultural comparison. *Journal of Cross-Cultural Psychology, 23,* 377–388.

Lee, J. A. (1976). *The colors of love.* New York: Bantam.

Lee, R. L. M. (1984). Malaysian queue culture: An ethnography of urban public behavior. *Southeast Asian Journal of Social Science, 12,* 36–50.

Lenhart, A. (2009). Social networks grow: Friending Mom and Dad. Retrieved January 27, 2009, from http://www.Pewresearch.org/.../social-networks

Leung, K. (1988, March). Some determinants of conflict avoidance. *Journal of Cross-Cultural Psychology, 19,* 125–136.

Leung, S. A. (2001). Editor's introduction. *Asian Journal of Counseling, 8,* 107–109.

Lever, J. (1995). The 1995 Advocate survey of sexuality and relationships: The women, lesbian sex survey. *The Advocate, 687/688,* 22–30.

Levine, D. (2000). Virtual attraction: What rocks your boat. *Cyber Psychology and Behavior, 3,* 565–573.

Levine, M. (2004, June 1). Tell the doctor all your problems, but keep it to less than a minute. *The New York Times,* p. F6.

LeVine, R., & Bartlett, K. (1984). Pace of life, punctuality, and coronary heart disease in six countries. *Journal of Cross-Cultural Psychology, 15,* 233–255.

Lindeman, M., Harakka, T., & Keltikangas-Jarvinen, L. (1997). Age and gender differences in adolescents' reactions to conflict situations: Aggression, prosociality, and withdrawal. *Journal of Youth and Adolescence, 26,* 339–351.

Luft, J. (1984). *Group process: An introduction of group dynamics* (3rd ed.). Palo Alto, CA: Mayfield.

Lukens, J. (1978). Ethnocentric speech. *Ethnic Groups, 2,* 35–53.

Lustig, M. W., & Koester, J. (2006). *Intercultural competence: Interpersonal communication across cultures* (5th ed.). Boston: Allyn & Bacon.

Ma, K. (1996). *The modern Madame Butterfly: Fantasy and reality in Japanese cross-cultural relationships.* Rutland, VT: Charles E. Tuttle.

Mackey, R. A., Diemer, M. A., & O'Brien, B. A. (2000). Psychological intimacy in the lasting relationships of heterosexual and same-gender couples. *Sex Roles, 43,* 201–227.

MacLachlan, J. (1979). What people really think of fast talkers. *Psychology Today, 13,* 113–117.

Madon, S., Guyll, M., & Spoth, R. L. (2004). The Self-fulfilling prophecy as an intrafamily dynamic. *Journal of Family Psychology, 18,* 459–469.

Mahaffey, A. L., Bryan, A., & Hutchison, K. E. (2005, March). Using startle eye blink to measure the affective component of antigay bias. *Basic and Applied Social Psychology, 27,* 37–45.

Malandro, L. A., Barker, L., & Barker, D. A. (1989). *Nonverbal communication* (2nd ed.). New York: Random House.

Marano, H. E. (2003). Procrastination: Ten things to know. *Psychology Today.* Retrieved September 12, 2009, from http://www.psychologytoday.com/articles/200308/procrastination-ten-things-know

Marsh, P. (1988). *Eye to eye: How people interact.* Topside, MA: Salem House.

Marshall, L. L., & Rose, P. (1987). Gender, stress and violence in the adult relationships of a sample of college students. *Journal of Social and Personal Relationships, 4,* 299–316.

Martin, G. N. (1998). Human electroencephalographic (EEG) response to olfactory stimulation: Two experiments using the aroma of food. *International Journal of Psychophysiology, 30,* 287–302.

Martin, M. M., & Anderson, C. M. (1993). Psychological and biological differences in touch avoidance. *Communication Research Reports, 10,* 141–147.

Martin, M. M., & Anderson, C. M. (1995). Roommate similarity: Are roommates who are similar in their communication traits more satisfied? *Communication Research Reports, 12,* 46–52.

Maslow, A. (1970). *Motivation and personality.* New York: Harper-Collins.

Matsumoto, D. (1991). Cultural influences on facial expressions of emotion. *Southern Communication Journal, 56,* 128–137.

McBroom, W. H., & Reed, F. W. (1992). Toward a reconceptualization of attitude-behavior consistency. Special Issue. Theoretical advances in social psychology. *Social Psychology Quarterly, 55,* 205–216.

McCarthy, M. (2003, January). Talking back: "Small" interactional response tokens in everyday conversation. *Research on Language and Social Interaction, 36,* 33–63.

McCroskey, J. C. (1997). *An introduction to rhetorical communication* (7th ed.). Englewood Cliffs, NJ: Prentice-Hall.

McCroskey, J. C., & Wheeless, L. (1976). *Introduction to human communication.* Boston: Allyn & Bacon.

McDevitt, M., Kiousis, S., & Wahl-Jorgensen, K. (2003). Spiral of moderation: Opinion expression in computer-mediated discussion. *International Journal of Public Opinion Research, 15,* 454–470.

McDonald, E. J., McCabe, K., Yeh, M., Lau, A., Garland, A., & Hough, R. L. (2005). Cultural affiliation and self-esteem as predictors of internalizing symptoms among Mexican American adolescents. *Journal of Clinical Child and Adolescent Psychology, 34,* 163–171.

McGill, M. E. (1985). *The McGill report on male intimacy.* New York: Harper & Row.

McKerrow, R. E., Gronbeck, B. E., Ehninger, D., & Monroe, A. H. (2000). *Principles and types of speech communication* (14th ed.). Boston: Allyn & Bacon.

McNamee, S., & Gergen, K. J. (Eds.). (1999). *Relational responsibility: Resources for sustainable dialogue.* Thousand Oaks, CA: Sage.

Merton, R. K. (1957). *Social theory and social structure.* New York: Free Press.

Messick, R. M., & Cook, K. S. (Eds.). (1983). *Equity theory: Psychological and sociological perspectives*. New York: Praeger.

Metts, S., & Planalp, S. (2002). Emotional communication. In M. L. Knapp & J. A. Daly (Eds.), *Handbook of interpersonal communication* (3rd ed., pp. 339–373). Thousand Oaks, CA: Sage.

Midooka, K. (1990). Characteristics of Japanese style communication. *Media Culture and Society, 12,* 47–49.

Miller, G. R. (1978). The current state of theory and research in interpersonal communication. *Human Communication Research, 4,* 164–178.

Miller, G. R. (1990). Interpersonal communication. In G. L. Dahnke & G. W. Clatterbuck (Eds.), *Human communication: Theory and research* (pp. 91–122). Belmont, CA: Wadsworth.

Miller, G. R., & Parks, M. R. (1982). Communication in dissolving relationships. In S. Duck (Ed.), *Personal relationships: Vol. 4. Dissolving personal relationships.* New York: Academic Press.

Miller, L. R. (1997, December). Better ways to think and communicate. *Association Management, 49,* 71– 73.

Moghaddam, F. M., Taylor, D. M., & Wright, S. C. (1993). *Social psychology in cross-cultural perspective.* New York: W. H. Freeman.

Molloy, J. (1981). *Molloy's live for success.* New York: Bantam.

Montagu, A. (1971). *Touching: The human significance of the skin.* New York: Harper & Row.

Moon, D. G. (1966). Concepts of "culture": Implications for intercultural communication research. *Communication Quarterly, 44,* 70–84.

Morrill, C. (1992). Vengeance among executives. *Virginia Review of Sociology, 1,* 51–76.

Morris, D. (1977). *Manwatching: A field guide to human behavior.* New York: Abrams.

Motley, M. T. (1990a). On whether one can(not) not communicate: An examination via traditional communication postulates. *Western Journal of Speech Communication, 54,* 1– 20.

Motley, M. T. (1990b). Communication as interaction: A reply to Beach and Bavelas. *Western Journal of Speech Communication, 54,* 613–623.

Mottet, T., & Richmond, V. P. (1998). Verbal approach and avoidance items. *Communication Quarterly, 46,* 25–40.

Mullen, B., Salas, E., & Driskell, J. (1989). Salience, motivation, and artifact as contributions to the relation between participation rate and leadership. *Journal of Experimental Social Psychology, 25,* 545–559.

Mullen, B., Tara, A., Salas, E., & Driskell, J. E. (1994). Group cohesiveness and quality of decision making: An interaction of tests of the groupthink hypothesis. *Small Group Research, 25,* 189–204.

Myers, S. A., & Zhong, M. (2004). Perceived Chinese instructor use of affinity-seeking strategies and Chinese college student motivation. *Journal of Intercultural Communication Research 33* (September–December), 119–130.

Napier, R. W., & Gershenfeld, M. K. (1989). *Groups: Theory and experience* (4th ed.). Boston: Houghton Mifflin.

Neher, W. W., & Sandin, P. (2006). *Communicating ethically.* Boston: Allyn & Bacon.

Neugarten, B. (1979). Time, age, and the life cycle. *American Journal of Psychiatry, 136,* 887–894.

Neuliep, J. W., Chaudoir, M., & McCroskey, J. C. (2001). A cross-cultural comparison of ethnocentrism among Japanese and United States college students. *Communication Research Reports, 18,* 137–146.

Neuliep, J. W., & Grohskopf, E. L. (2000). Uncertainty reduction and communication satisfaction during initial interaction: An initial test and replication of a new axiom. *Communication Reports, 13,* 67–77.

Ng, S. H., Loong, C. S. F., He, A. P., Liu, J. H., & Weatherall, A. (2000). Communication correlates of individualism and collectivism: Talk directed at one or more addressees in family conversations. *Journal of Language and Social Psychology, 19,* 26–45.

Noelle-Neumann, E. (1973). Return to the concept of powerful mass media. In H. Eguchi & K. Sata (Eds.), *Studies in broadcasting: An international annual of broadcasting science* (pp. 67–112). Tokyo: Nippon Hoso Kyokai.

Noelle-Neumann, E. (1980). Mass media and social change in developed societies. In G. C. Wilhoit & H. de Bock (Eds.), *Mass communication review yearbook* (Vol. 1, pp. 657–678). Thousand Oaks, CA: Sage.

Noelle-Neumann, E. (1991). The theory of public opinion: The concept of the spiral of silence. In J. A. Anderson (Ed.), *Communication yearbook 14* (pp. 256–287). Thousand Oaks, CA: Sage.

Noller, P. (1993). Gender and emotional communication in marriage: Different cultures or differential social power? [Special issue: Emotional Communication, Culture, and Power.] *Journal of Language and Social Psychology, 12,* 132–152.

Noller, P., & Fitzpatrick, M. A. (1993). *Communication in family relationships.* Englewood Cliffs, NJ: Prentice-Hall.

Northouse, P. G. (1997). *Leadership: Theory and practice.* Thousand Oaks, CA: Sage.

O'Hair, D., Cody, M. J., & McLaughlin, M. L. (1981). Prepared lies, spontaneous lies, Machiavellianism, and nonverbal communication. *Human Communication Research, 7,* 325–339.

Osborn, A. (1957). *Applied imagination* (Rev. ed.). New York: Scribner's.

Park, H. S., Levine, T. R., McCornack, S. A., Morrison, K., & Ferrara, M. (2002). How people really detect lies. *Communication Monographs, 69,* 144–157.

Paul, A. M. (2001). Self-help: Shattering the myths. *Psychology Today, 34,* 60ff.

Pearson, J. C., & Spitzberg, B. H. (1990). *Interpersonal communication: Concepts, components, and contexts* (2nd ed.). Dubuque, IA: William C. Brown.

Pearson, J. C., West, R., & Turner, L. H. (1995). *Gender and communication* (3rd ed.). Dubuque, IA: William C. Brown.

Pei, M. (1978). *Weasel words: the art of saying what you don't mean.* New York: Harper & Row.

Pelham, A. M., & Kravitz, P. (2008). An exploratory study of the influence of sales training content and salesperson evaluation on salesperson adaptive selling, customer orientation, listening and consulting behaviors. *Journal of Strategic Marketing, 16,* 413–435.

Penfield, J. (Ed.). (1987). *Women and language in transition.* Albany, NY: State University of New York Press.

Peterson, C. C. (1996). The ticking of the social clock: Adults' beliefs about the timing of transition events. *International Journal of Aging and Human Development, 42,* 189–203.

Pittenger, R. E., Hockett, C. F., & Danehy, J. J. (1960). *The first five minutes.* Ithaca, NY: Paul Martineau.

Place, K. S., & Becker, J. A. (1991). The influence of pragmatic competence on the likeability of grade school children. *Discourse Processes, 14,* 227–241.

Placencia, M. E. (2004). The online disinhibition effect. *Journal of Sociolinguistics, 8,* 215–245.

Plaks, J. E., Grant, H., & Dweck, C. S. (2005). Violations of implicit theories and the sense of prediction and control: Implications for motivated person perception. *Journal of Personality and Social Psychology, 88,* 245–262.

Pornpitakpan, C. (2003). The effect of personality traits and perceived cultural similarity on attraction. *Journal of International Consumer Marketing, 15,* 5–30.

Porter, R. H., & Moore, J. D. (1981). Human kin recognition by olfactory cues. *Physiology and Behavior, 27,* 493–495.

Pratkanis, A., & Aronson, E. (1991). *Age of propaganda: The everyday use and abuse of persuasion.* New York: W. H. Freeman.

Rancer, A. S. (1998). Argumentativeness. In J. C. McCroskey, J. A. Daly, M. M. Martin, & M. J. Beatty (Eds.), *Communication and Personality: Trait Perspectives* (pp. 149–170). Cresskill, NJ: Hampton Press.

Rancer, A. S., & Avtgis, T. A. (2006). *Argumentative and aggressive communication: Theory, research, and application.* Thousand Oaks, CA: Sage.

Rapsa, R., & Cusack, J. (1990). Psychiatric implications of tattoos. *American Family Physician, 41,* 1481–1486.

Raven, R., Centers, C., & Rodrigues, A. (1975). The bases of conjugal power. In R. E. Cromwell & D. H. Olson (Eds.), *Power in families* (pp. 217–234). New York: Halsted Press.

Read, A. W. (2004). Language revision by deletion of absolutisms. *ETC: A Review of General Semantics, 61,* 456–462.

Reisman, J. M. (1979). *Anatomy of friendship.* Lexington, MA: Lewis.

Reisman, J. M. (1981). Adult friendships. In S. Duck & R. Gilmour (Eds.), *Personal relationships. 2: Developing personal relationships* (pp. 205–230). New York: Academic Press.

Rich, A. L. (1974). *Interracial communication.* New York: Harper & Row.

Richards, I. A. (1951). Communication between men: The meaning of language. In Heinz von Foerster (Ed.), *Cybernetics: Transactions of the Eighth Conference.*

Richmond, V. P., & McCroskey, J. C. (1998). *Communication: Apprehension, avoidance, and effectiveness* (5th ed.). Needham Heights, MA: Allyn & Bacon.

Richmond, V. P., Davis, L. M., Saylor, K., & McCroskey, J. C. (1984). Power strategies in organizations: Communication techniques and messages. *Human Communication Research, 11,* 85–108.

Richmond, V. P., McCroskey, J. C., & Hickson, M. L. (2008). *Nonverbal behavior in interpersonal relations* (6th ed.). Boston: Allyn & Bacon.

Richmond, V. P., McCroskey, J. C., & McCroskey, L. L. (2005). *Organizational communication for survival: Making work, work.* Boston: Allyn & Bacon.

Richmond, V. P., Smith, R., Heisel, A., & McCroseky, J. C. (2001). Nonverbal immediacy in the physician/patient relationship. *Communication Research Reports, 18,* 211–216.

Riggio, R. E. (1987). *The charisma quotient.* New York: Dodd, Mead.

Riggio, R. E., & Feldman, R. S., Eds. (2005). *Applications of nonverbal communication.* Mahwah, NJ: Lawrence Erlbaum.

Robbins, S. P., & Hunsaker, P. L. (2009). Training in interpersonal skills (5th ed.). Boston: Allyn & Bacon.

Rogers, C. (1970). *Carl Rogers on encounter groups.* New York: Harrow Books.

Rogers, C., & Farson, R. (1981). Active listening. In J. DeVito (Ed.), *Communication: Concepts and processes* (3rd ed., pp. 137–147). Upper Saddle River, NJ: Prentice-Hall.

Roisman, G. I., Clausell, E., Holland, A., Fortuna, K., & Elieff, C. (2008). Adult romantic relationships as contexts of human development: A multimethod comparison of same-sex couples with opposite-sex dating, engaged, and married dyads. *Developmental Psychology, 44,* 91–101.

Rose, A. J., & Asher, S. R. (1999, January). Children's goals and strategies in response to conflicts within a friendship. *Developmental Psychology, 35,* 69–79.

Rosenthal, R. (2002). Covert communication in classrooms, clinics, courtroom, and cubicles. *American Psychologist, 57,* 839–849.

Roth, P. L., Schleifer, L. L. F., & Switzer, F. S. (1995). Nominal group technique—An aid in implementing TQM. *The CPA Journal, 65,* 68–69.

Rubin, R. B., Fernandez-Collado, C., & Hernandez-Sampieri, R. (1992). A cross-cultural examination of interpersonal communication motives in Mexico and the United States. *International Journal of Intercultural Relations, 16,* 145–157.

Rubin, Z. (1973). *Liking and loving: An invitation to social psychology.* New York: Holt, Rinehart & Winston.

Sagrestano, L. M., Heavey, C. L., & Christensen, A. (2006). Individual differences versus social structural approaches to explaining demand-withdrawal and social influence behaviors. In K. Dindia & D. J. Canary (Eds.), *Sex differences and similarities in communication* (2nd ed., pp. 379–395). Mahwah, NJ: Lawrence Erlbaum.

Samovar, L. A., & Porter, R. E. (Eds.). (1991). *Communication between cultures.* Belmont, CA: Wadsworth.

Samter, W., & Cupach, W. R. (1998). Friendly fire: Topics variations in conflict among same- and cross-sex friends. *Communication Studies, 49,* 121–138.

Sanders, J. A., Wiseman, R. L., & Matz, S. I. (1991). Uncertainty reduction in acquaintance relationships in Ghana and the United States. In S. Ting-Toomey & F. Korzenny (Eds.), *Cross-cultural interpersonal communication* (pp. 79–98). Thousand Oaks, CA: Sage.

Satir, V. (1983). *Conjoint family therapy* (3rd ed.). Palo Alto, CA: Science and Behavior Books.

Scandura, T. (1992). Mentorship and career mobility: An empirical investigation. *Journal of Organizational Behavior, 13,* 169–174.

Schaap, C., Buunk, B., & Kerkstra, A. (1988). Marital conflict resolution. In P. Noller & M. A. Fitzpatrick (Eds.), *Perspectives on marital interaction* (pp. 203–244). Philadelphia: Multilingual Matters.

Schafer, M., & Crichlow, S. (1996). Antecedents of groupthink. *Journal of Conflict Resolution, 40,* 415–435.

Schegloff, E. (1982). Discourses as an interactional achievement: Some uses of "uh huh" and other things that come between sentences. In Deborah Tannen (Ed.), *Georgetown University roundtable on language and linguistics* (pp. 71–93). Washington, DC: Georgetown University Press.

Scherer, K. R. (1986). Vocal affect expression. *Psychological Bulletin, 99,* 143–165.

Scheufele, D. A., & Moy, P. (2000). Twenty-five years of the spiral of silence: A conceptual review and empirical outlook. *International Journal of Public Opinion Research, 12,* 3–28.

Schnoor, L. G. (Ed.). (1997). *Winning orations of the interstate oratorical association.* Mankato, MN: Interstate Oratorical Association.

Schnoor, L. G. (Ed.). (1999). *Winning orations of the interstate oratorical association.* Mankato, MN: Interstate Oratorical Association.

Schnoor, L. G. (Ed.). (2000). *Winning orations of the interstate oratorical association.* Mankato, MN: Interstate Oratorical Association.

Schultz, B. G. (1996). *Communicating in the small group: Theory and practice* (2nd ed.). New York: HarperCollins.

Schwartz, E. (2005). Watch what you say. *InfoWorld* 27 (February, 28), 8.

Schwartz, M., & Task Force on Bias-Free Language of the Association of American University Presses. (1995). *Guidelines for bias-free writing.* Bloomington: Indiana University Press.

Scott, M. L., & Lyman, S. M. (1968). Accounts. *American Sociological Review, 33,* 46–62.

Seiter, J. S., & Sandry, A. (2003). Pierced for success? The effects of ear and nose piercing on perceptions of job candidates' credibility, attractiveness, and hirability. *Communication Research Reports, 20,* 287–298.

Sethna, B., Barnes, C. C., Brust, M., & Kay, L. (1999). E-mail communications in colleges and universities: Are they private? *Journal of Education for Business, 74,* 347–350.

Severin, W. J. & Tankard, J. W., Jr. (2001). *Communication theories: Origins, methods, and uses in the mass media.* Boston: Allyn & Bacon.

Shaw, M. E., & Gouran, D. S. (1990). Group dynamics and communication. In G. Dahnke & G. W. Clatterbuck (Eds.), *Human communication: Theory and research.* Belmont, CA: Wadsworth.

Shechtman, Z., Hiradin, A., & Zina, S. (2003). The impact of culture on group behavior: A comparison of three ethnic groups. *Journal of Counseling and Development, 81,* 208–216.

Shimanoff, S. (1980). *Communication rules: Theory and research.* Thousand Oaks, CA: Sage.

Shuter, R. (1990). The centrality of culture. *Southern Communication Journal, 55,* 237–249.

Siavelis, R. L., & Lamke, L. K. (1992). Instrumentalness and expressiveness: Predictors of heterosexual relationship satisfaction. *Sex Roles, 26,* 149–159.

Sieter, J. S. (2007). Ingratiation and gratuity: The effect of complimenting customers on tipping behavior in restaurants. *Journal of Applied Social Psychology, 37,* 478–485.

Signorile, M. (1993). *Queer in America: Sex, the media, and the closets of power.* New York: Random House.

Singelis, T. M. (1994). The measurement of independent and interdependent self-construals. *Personality and Social Psychology Bulletin, 20,* 580–591.

Singh, N., & Pereira, A. (2005). *The culturally customized web site.* Oxford, UK: Elsevier Butterworth-Heinemann.

Slade, M. (1995, February 19). We forgot to write a headline. But it's not our fault. *The New York Times,* p. 5.

Smith, M. H. (2003). Body adornment: Know the limits. *Nursing Management, 34,* 22–23.

Smith-Lovin, L., & Brody, C. (1989). Interruptions in group discussions: The effects of gender and group composition. *American Sociological Review, 54,* 424–435.

Smoreda, Z., & Licoppe, C. (2000). Gender-specific use of the domestic telephone. *Social Psychology Quarterly, 63,* 238–252.

Snyder, C. R. (1984). Excuses, excuses. *Psychology Today, 18,* 50–55.

Snyder, C. R., Higgins, R. L., & Stucky, R. J. (1983). *Excuses: Masquerades in search of grace.* New York: Wiley.

Snyder, M. (1992). A gender-informed model of couple and family therapy: Relationship enhancement therapy. *Contemporary Family Therapy: An International Journal, 14,* 15–31.

Sorenson, P. S., Hawkins, K., & Sorenson, R. L. (1995). Gender, psychological type and conflict style preferences. *Management Communication Quarterly, 9,* 115–126.

Spitzberg, B. H., & Cupach, W. R. (1989). *Handbook of interpersonal competence research.* New York: Springer.

Spitzberg, B. H., & Cupach, W. R. (2002). Interpersonal skills. In M. L. Knapp & J. A. Daly (Eds.), *Handbook of interpersonal communication* (3rd ed., pp. 564–611). Thousand Oaks, CA: Sage.

Spitzberg, B. H., & Hecht, M. L. (1984). A component model of relational competence. *Human Communication Research, 10,* 575–599.

Sprecher, S. (1987). The effects of self-disclosure given and received on affection for an intimate partner and stability of the relationship. *Journal of Social and Personal Relationships, 4,* 115–127.

Sprecher, S., & Metts, S. (1989). Development of the "romantic beliefs scale" and examination of the effects of gender and gender-role orientation. *Journal of Social and Personal Relationships, 6,* 387–411.

Stafford, L. (2008). Social exchange theories. In L. A. Baxter & D. O. Braithwaite (Eds.), *Engaging theories in interpersonal communication: Multiple perspectives* (pp. 377–389). Los Angeles, CA: Sage.

Steil, L. K., Barker, L. L., & Watson, K. W. (1983). *Effective listening: Key to your success.* Reading, MA: Addison-Wesley.

Stern, L. (2007). *What every student should know about avoiding plagiarism.* Boston: Pearson Education.

Stewart, L. P., Cooper, P. J., & Stewart, A. D., with Friedley, S. A. (2003). *Communication and gender* (4th ed.). Boston: Allyn & Bacon.

Stratford, J. (1998). Women and men in conversation: A consideration of therapists' interruptions in therapeutic discourse. *Journal of Family Therapy, 20,* 383–394.

Stratford, J. (1998). Women and men in conversation: A consideration of therapists' interruptions in therapeutic discourse. *Journal of Family Therapy, 20,* 383–394.

Strom, D. (2006, April 5). I.M. generation is changing the way business talks. *The New York Times,* p. D4.

Suler, J. (2004). The online disinhibition effect. *CyberPsychology and Behavior, 7,* 321–326.

Sunnafrank, M., & Ramirez, A. (2004). At first sight: Persistent relational effects of get-acquainted conversations. *Journal of Social and Personal Relationships, 21,* 361–379.

Tang, T. L., & Butler, E. A. (1997). Attributions of quality circles' problem-solving failure: Differences among management, supporting staff, and quality circle members. *Public Personnel Management, 26,* 203–225.

Tannen, D. (1990). *You just don't understand: Women and men in conversation.* New York: Morrow.

Tannen, D. (1994a). *Gender and discourse.* New York: Oxford University Press.

Tannen, D. (1994b). *Talking from 9 to 5: How women's and men's conversational styles affect who gets heard, who gets credit, and what gets done at work.* New York: Morrow.

Tannen, D. (2006). *You're wearing that? Understanding mothers and daughters in conversation.* New York: Random House.

Tardiff, T. (2001). Learning to say "no" in Chinese. *Early Education and Development, 12,* 303–323.

Tata, J. (2000). Toward a theoretical framework of intercultural account-giving and account evaluation. *International Journal of Organizational Analysis, 8,* 155–178.

Thibaut, J. W., & Kelley, H. H. (1959). *The social psychology of groups.* New York: Wiley. Reissued (1986). New Brunswick, NJ: Transaction Books.

Thompson, C. A., & Klopf, D. W. (1991). An analysis of social style among disparate cultures. *Communication Research Reports, 8,* 65–72.

Thompson, C. A., Klopf, D. W., & Ishii, S. (1991). A comparison of social style between Japanese and Americans. *Communication Research Reports, 8,* 165–172.

Tierney, P., & Farmer, S. M. (2004). The Pygmalion process and employee creativity. *Journal of Management, 30,* 413–432.

Timmerman, L. J. (2002). Comparing the production of power in language on the basis of sex. In M. Allen & R. W. Preiss (Eds.), *Interpersonal communication research: Advances through meta-analysis* (pp. 73–88). Mahwah, NJ: Erlbaum.

Ting-Toomey, S. (1981). Ethnic identity and close friendship in Chinese-American college students. *International Journal of Intercultural Relations, 5,* 383–406.

Ting-Toomey, S. (1985). Toward a theory of conflict and culture. *International and Intercultural Communication Annual, 9,* 71–86.

Tolhuizen, J. H. (1989). Communication strategies for intensifying dating relationships: Identification, use, and structure. *Journal of Social and Personal Relationships, 6,* 413–434.

Trager, G. L. (1958). Paralanguage: A first approximation. *Studies in Linguistics, 13,* 1–12.

Trager, G. L. (1961). The typology of paralanguage. *Anthropological Linguistics, 3,* 17–21.

Trower, P. (1981). Social skill disorder. In S. Duck & R. Gilmour (Eds.), *Personal relationships* 3 (pp. 97–110). New York: Academic Press.

Vainiomaki, T. (2004). Silence as a cultural sign. *Semiotica, 150,* 347–361.

Varma, A., Toh, S. M, Pichler, S. (2006). Ingratiation in job applications: Impact on selection decisions. *Journal of Managerial Psychology, 21,* 200–210.

Veenendall, T. L., & Feinstein, M. C. (1995). *Let's talk about relationships: Cases in study* (2nd ed.). Prospect Heights, IL: Waveland Press.

Velting, D. M. (1999). Personality and negative expectations: Trait structure of the Beck Hopelessness Scale. *Personality and Individual Differences, 26,* 913–921.

Victor, D. (1992). *International business communication.* New York: HarperCollins.

Vonk, R. (2002). Self-serving interpretations of flattery: Why ingratiation works. *Journal of Personality and Social Psychology, 82,* 515–526.

Wallace, K. (1955). An ethical basis of communication. *Communication Education, 4,* 1–9.

Walster, E., Walster, G. W., & Berscheid, E. (1978). *Equity: Theory and research.* Boston: Allyn & Bacon.

Watkins, K. (2007). How much time do you spend listening? Retrieved August 9, 2009, from http://articles/webraydian.com/article4793-How_much_time_do_you_spend_listening.html

Watzlawick, P. (1977). *How real is real? Confusion, disinformation, communication: An anecdotal introduction to communications theory.* New York: Vintage.

Watzlawick, P. (1978). *The language of change: Elements of therapeutic communication.* New York: Basic Books.

Watzlawick, P., Beavin, J., & Jackson, D. D. (1967). *Pragmatics of human communication: A study of interactional patterns, pathologies, and paradoxes.* New York: Norton.

Weathers, M. D., Frank, E. M., & Spell, L. A. (2002). Differences in the communication of affect: Members of the same race versus members of a different race. *Journal of Black Psychology, 28,* 66–77.

Weinberg, H. L. (1959). *Levels of knowing and existence.* New York: Harper & Row.

Wennerstrom, A., & Siegel, A. F. (2003). Keeping the floor in multiparty conversation: Intonation, syntax, and pause. *Discourse Processes, 36,* 77–107.

Wert, S. R., & Salovey, P. (2004). Introduction to the special issue on gossip. *Review of General Psychology, 8,* 76–77.

Westwood, R. I., Tang, F. F., & Kirkbride, P. S. (1992). Chinese conflict behavior: Cultural antecedents and behavioral consequences. *Organizational Development Journal, 10,* 13–19.

Wetzel, P. J. (1988). Are "powerless" communication strategies the Japanese norm? *Language in Society, 17,* 555–564.

Wheeless, L. R., & Grotz, J. (1977). The measurement of trust and its relationship to self-disclosure. *Human Communication Research, 3,* 250–257.

Whitty, M., & Gavin, J. (2001). Age/sex/location: Uncovering the social cues in the development of online relationships. *Cyber-Psychology and Behavior, 4,* 623–630.

Wigley, C. J., III. (1998). Verbal aggressiveness. In J. C. McCroskey, J. A. Daly, M. M. Martin, & M. J. Beatty (Eds.), *Communication and personality: Trait perspectives* (pp. 191–214). Cresskill, NJ: Hampton Press.

Wilkins, B. M., & Andersen, P. A. (1991). Gender differences and similarities in management communication: A meta-analysis. *Management Communication Quarterly, 5,* 6–35.

Willis, J., & Todorov, A. (2006). First impressions: Making up your mind after a 100-Ms Exposure to a Face. *Psychological Science, 17,* 592–598.

Windy, D., & Constantinou, D. (2005). *Assertiveness step by step.* London: Sheldon Press.

Witcher, S. K. (1999, August 9–15). Chief executives in Asia find listening difficult. *Asian Wall Street Journal Weekly,* p. 11.

Won-Doornink, M. (1985). Self-disclosure and reciprocity in conversation: A cross-national study. *Social Psychology Quarterly, 48,* 97–107.

Won-Doornink, M. (1991). Self-disclosure and reciprocity in South Korean and U.S. male dyads. In S. Ting-Toomey & F. Korzenny (Eds.), *Cross-cultural interpersonal communication* (pp. 116–131). Newbury Park, CA: Sage.

Wood, J. T. (1994). *Gendered lives: Communication, gender, and culture.* Belmont, CA: Wadsworth.

Wrench, J. S., & McCroskey, J. C. (2003). A communibiological examination of ethnocentrism and homophobia. *Communication Research Reports, 20,* 24–33.

Wrench, J. S., McCroskey, J. C., & Richmond, V. P. (2008). *Human communication in everyday life: Explanations and applications.* Boston: Allyn & Bacon.

Yau-fair Ho, D., Chan, S. F., Peng, S., & Ng, A. K. (2001). The dialogical self: Converging East–West constructions. *Culture and Psychology, 7,* 393–408.

Zaleski, Z., Cycon, A., & Kurc, A. (2001). Future time perspective and subjective well-being in adolescent samples. In P. Schmuck & K. M. Sheldon (Eds.), *Life goals and wellbeing: Towards a positive psychology of human striving* (pp. 58–67). Cambridge, MA: Hogrefe & Huber.

Zuckerman, M., Klorman, R., Larrance, D. T., & Spiegel, N. H. (1981). Facial, autonomic, and subjective components of emotion: The facial feedback hypothesis versus the externalizer–internalizer distinction. *Journal of Personality and Social Psychology, 41,* 929–944.

Zunin, L. M., & Zunin, N. B. (1972). *Contact: The first four minutes.* Los Angeles, CA: Nash.

Index

Note: Italicized letters *f* and *t* following page numbers indicate figures and tables, respectively.

Visualization, 234
   and persuasive speech, 294*t*
Vividness, 241–242, 241*t*
Voice, in speeches, 254–256
Volume, in speech delivery, 254

Weasel words, 63*t*
Win-lose situations, 164
Win-win situations, 165, 166

Withdrawal from relationships,
   143
Word charts in informative speech,
   274, 275*f*
Word choice
   in cultural identification, 83–84
   racist, 79–80
   sexist, 82
   in speeches, 240–243, 241*t*

Workplace
   problem-solving in, 188–190
   relationships in, 156
   risks of self-disclosure and, 34
   rules of, 151–152
   spatial distance in, 102
Written-style expressions, 242

You-messages, 167

Credits

Text Credits

Page 21: The Human Relations Attitude Inventory, from the companion website to *Understanding Human Differences*, Second Edition by Kent Koppelman and Lee Goodheart. Copyright © 2008 Allyn & Bacon. Reprinted by permission of Pearson Education, Inc.

Pages 21–22: This test is taken from James W. Neuliep, Michelle Chadoir, and James McCroskey (2001). A cross-cultural comparison of ethnocentrism among Japanese and United States college students. *Communication Research Reports 18* (Spring): 137–146. Reprinted by permission of the Taylor & Francis Group.

Page 27: From Joseph Luft, *Group Processes: An Introduction to Group Dynamics*, 3/e. Copyright © 1984 by The McGraw Hill Companies, Inc. Reprinted with permission of the publisher.

Page 109–110: What Time Do You Have? Adapted from "Time in Perspective" by Alexander Gonzalez and Philip G. Zimbardo, *Psychology Today*, Copyright © 1985 Sussex Publishers, Inc. Reprinted by permission.

Pages 146–147: From "A Relationship-Specific Version of the Love Attitudes Scale" by C. Hendrick and S. Hendrick. Copyright © 1990 Select Press, *Journal of Social Behavior and Personality 5*, 1990. Reprinted by permission.

Pages 171–172: From "How Verbally Aggressive Are You?" by Dominic Infante & C. J. Wigley, *Communication Monographs*, 53 (1986). Reprinted by permission of the Taylor & Francis Group.

Pages 172–173: This scale was developed by Dominic Infante and Andrew Rancer and appears in Dominic Infante and Andrew Rancer, "A Conceptualization and Measure of Argumentativeness" in *Journal of Personality Assessment 46* (1982), pp. 72–80. Reprinted with permission of the Taylor & Francis Group.

Pages 181–182: From *An Introduction to Rhetorical Communication*, 7th ed., by James C. McCroskey. Copyright © 1997 by Allyn & Bacon. Reprinted by permission.

Page 199: The Situational Leadership® model, Addendum A. Copyright © 2006. Reprinted with permission of the Center for Leadership Studies, Escondido, CA 92025. www.situational.com. All rights reserved.

Page 211: Adapted from *An Introduction to Rhetorical Communication*, 7th ed., by James McCroskey. Copyright © 1997 by Allyn & Bacon. Reprinted by permission.

Page 267: This test was adapted for public speaking on the basis of the conversational satisfaction test developed by Michael Hecht, "The Conceptualization and Measurement of Interpersonal Communication Satisfaction," *Human Communication Research 4* (1978): 253–264 and is used by permission of the author and International Communication Association.

Pages 285–288: "Controlling the Weather: Moshe Alamaro's Plan for Hurricane Mitigation" by Jillian Collum. Reprinted by permission.

Page 298: From Abraham Maslow, *Motivation and Personality*, 3rd ed., edited by Robert D. Frager and James Fadiman. Copyright © 1987. Reprinted by permission of Pearson Education, Inc., Upper Saddle River, NJ.

Pages 307–310: "The Merchants of Death" by Andrew Farmer. Andrew Farmer is a student at the University of Texas at Austin. The speech was delivered at the 2006 American Forensic Association National Individual Events Tournament in Gainesville, Florida, and was accompanied by a complete list of works cited. It is reprinted by permission of the speaker.

Photo Credits

page 1: Image State/Alamy Images; 8, (Table 1.1): left to right: ©New York Daily News, L. P. Reprinted with permission; PA Photos/Landov; © STAN HONDA/AFP/Getty Images; Getty Images; 10, Andersen Ross/Corbis RF; 19, © Craig Lovell/CORBIS; 20, © David Turnley/CORBIS. All Rights Reserved; 25, David Young-Wolff/PhotoEdit Inc.; 29, © Gary Conner/PhotoEdit; 34, Queerstock, Inc./Alamy Images; 38, © Bob Daemmrich/The Image Works; 53, © DreamPictures/Stone/Getty Images; 54, © Jose Luis Pelaez; Inc./CORBIS. All Rights Reserved; 56, (Table 3.1) left to right: Ludwig van Beethoven (1770–1827) Composing his "Missa Solemnis," 1819 (oil on canvas), Stieler, Joseph Carl (1781–1858)/Beethoven Haus, Bonn, Germany/The Bridgeman Art Library; The Granger Collection, New York; AP Images/Robert E. Klein; Kelsey McNeal/© ABC/Everett Collection; 62, © Paul Barton/CORBIS; 65, © Esbin-Anderson/The Image Works; 71, BMI/Alamy Images; 74, © Ajax/CORBIS All Rights Reserved; 80, © Lara Jo Regan/Getty Images; 89, Blend Images/Alamy Images; 92, Masterfile Royalty Free Division; 94, © Kevin Radford/Superstock; 98, © Royalty-Free/CORBIS; 100, © Tom Stewart/CORBIS; 113, Jeff Greenberg/PhotoEdit Inc.; 119, © Esbin-Anderson/The Image Works; 122, (Table 6.1) left to right: The Granger Collection, New York; Al Francekevich/Photographer's Choice/Getty Images; Bettmann/Corbis; AP Images/Jeff Adkins; 125, © Artiga Photo/CORBIS; 127, © Christopher Bissel/Getty Images; 133, Jeff Greenberg/PhotoEdit Inc.; 140, Masterfile Royalty Free Division; 145, Bruce Ayers/Getty Images; 147, © Najlah Feanny-Hicks/CORBIS. All Rights Reserved; 154, MBI/Alamy Images; 159, © Meeke/CORBIS. All Rights Reserved; 161, © Gabriela Medina/Blend Images/CORBIS. All Rights Reserved; 168, AP/Wide World Photos; 171, Image Source/AGE Fotostock America, Inc.; 172, © Richard Lord/The Image Works; 176, Mark Richards/PhotoEdit Inc.; 177, © Heinz-Peter Bader/Reuters/CORBIS; 182, © Spencer Grant/PhotoEdit; 184, Ronnie Kaufman/CORBIS–NY; 188, © Charles Gupton/Getty Images; 192, Getty Images; 195, arabianEye FZ LLC/Alamy Images; 198, Marilyn "Angle" Wynn/Nativestock.com; 202, Chuck Nacke/Alamy Images; 205, © Mark Richards/PhotoEdit; 209, Rachel Epstein/PhotoEdit Inc.; 221, © Image Source/SuperStock; 223, © Bob Daemmrich/The Image Works; 233, Alamy Images; 239, Alamy Images Royalty Free; 243, David Young-Wolff/PhotoEdit Inc.; 256, Blend Images/Alamy Images; 259, Jon Feingersh/Getty Images–Blend Images; 266, Rachel Epstein/PhotoEdit Inc.; 270, © Joseph Nettis/Stock Boston; 271, Getty Images, Inc.—Comstock Images RF; 283, © Royalty-Free/CORBIS; 290, Photofusion Picture Library/Alamy Images; 292, © Jose Luis Pelaez, Inc./CORBIS; 297, © Alison Wright/CORBIS. All Rights Reserved; 304, Paula Soloway/Alamy Images